Figures available in three downloadable sizes (resolutions)

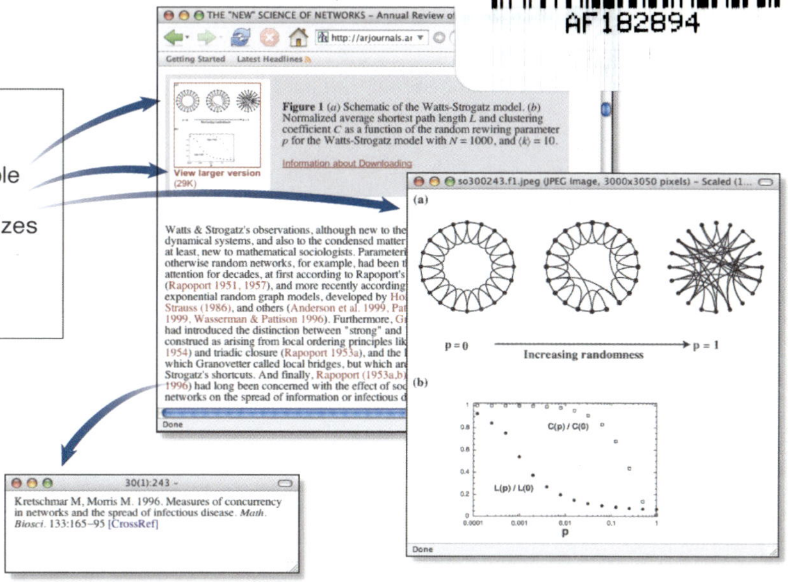

Citations in text link to references in bibliography

References in Annual Reviews chapter bibliography link out to sources of cited articles online

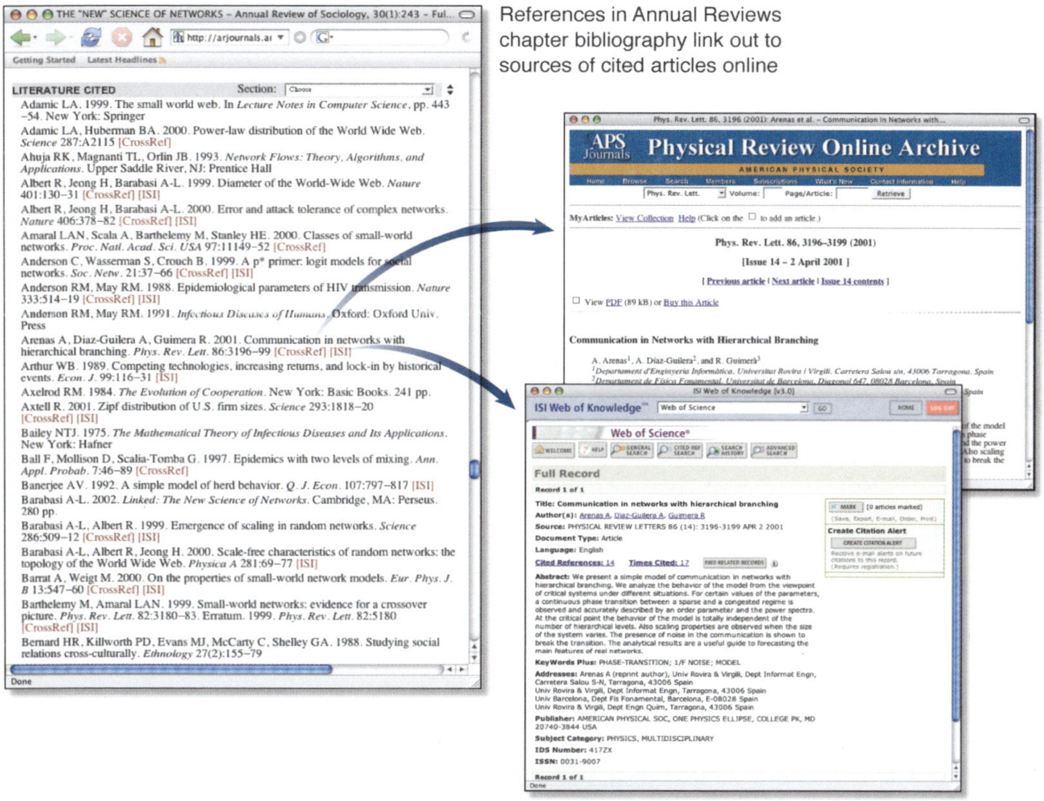

Annual Review of Law and Social Science

ANNUAL REVIEW OF LAW AND SOCIAL SCIENCE

VOLUME 2, 2006

JOHN HAGAN, *Editor*
Northwestern University

KIM LANE SCHEPPELE, *Associate Editor*
Princeton University

TOM R. TYLER, *Associate Editor*
New York University

www.annualreviews.org science@annualreviews.org 650-493-4400

ANNUAL REVIEWS
4139 El Camino Way • P.O. Box 10139 • Palo Alto, California 94303-0139

ANNUAL REVIEWS
Palo Alto, California, USA

International Standard Serial Number: 1550-3585
International Standard Book Number: 0-8243-4102-3

TYPESET BY TECHBOOKS, FALLS CHURCH, VIRGINIA
PRINTED AND BOUND BY MALLOY INCORPORATED, ANN ARBOR, MICHIGAN

Annual Review of Law and Social Science
Volume 2, 2006

CONTENTS

ERRATA

An online log of corrections to *Annual Review of Law and Social Science* chapters (if any) may be found at http://lawsocsci.annualreviews.org

ANNUAL REVIEWS is a nonprofit scientific publisher established to promote the advancement of the sciences. Beginning in 1932 with the *Annual Review of Biochemistry*, the Company has pursued as its principal function the publication of high-quality, reasonably priced *Annual Review* volumes. The volumes are organized by Editors and Editorial Committees who invite qualified authors to contribute critical articles reviewing significant developments within each major discipline. The Editor-in-Chief invites those interested in serving as future Editorial Committee members to communicate directly with him. Annual Reviews is administered by a Board of Directors, whose members serve without compensation.

Annual Reviews of

Anthropology
Astronomy and Astrophysics
Biochemistry
Biomedical Engineering
Biophysics and Biomolecular Structure
Cell and Developmental Biology
Clinical Psychology
Earth and Planetary Sciences
Ecology, Evolution, and Systematics
Entomology
Environment and Resources
Fluid Mechanics
Genetics
Genomics and Human Genetics
Immunology
Law and Social Science
Materials Research
Medicine
Microbiology
Neuroscience
Nuclear and Particle Science
Nutrition
Pathology: Mechanisms of Disease
Pharmacology and Toxicology
Physical Chemistry
Physiology
Phytopathology
Plant Biology
Political Science
Psychology
Public Health
Sociology

SPECIAL PUBLICATIONS
Excitement and Fascination of Science, Vols. 1, 2, 3, and 4

Marc Galanter

Annu. Rev. Law Soc. Sci. 2006. 2:1–16
doi: 10.1146/annurev.lawsocsci.2.081805.105946

First published online as a Review in Advance on August 1, 2006

IN THE WINTER OF OUR DISCONTENT: Law, Anti-Law, and Social Science

Marc Galanter
University of Wisconsin School of Law, Madison, Wisconsin 53706-1399; email: msgalant@wisc.edu

Key Words legalization, expansion of remedies, lawyers, legal knowledge, law schools

■ **Abstract** Law and social science took shape as a field of inquiry in the third quarter of the past century, an era of expanding rights and remedies and optimism about the capacity of law, government, and social science to address intractable social problems. It put down vigorous institutional roots in organizations, publications, teaching, and research that enabled it to survive the erosion of the reformist soil that nurtured it and to adapt to a new era in which the prevailing common sense is a jaundiced view that emphasizes the weaknesses, costs, and dangers of law. A significant body of research has rebutted many of the components of the jaundiced view, but with little effect on the prevailing folklore. The legal system's distinctive susceptibility to such misreadings and misrepresentations is aggravated by a late and weak development of empirical knowledge and a lack of credible guardians of its knowledge base.

INTRODUCTION

Law and social science (LSS) (also known as socio-legal studies, law and society, empirical legal studies, and somewhat misleadingly sociology of law) is only one of several intersecting knowledges about law and its relation to society. By law I refer not to a discipline of inquiry, but to a set of practices, roles, and ideas embodied in distinctive institutions and reflected in general culture. The most prominent knowledge about law is the internal legal learning located among the professional groups that occupy and operate legal institutions (judges, lawyers, legislators, administrators, and their academic and journalistic auxiliaries). These actors carry, expound, produce, and remake a body of authoritative normative learning that regulates and instructs officials and citizens. Entwined with this internal legal learning is an emergent external learning about law and legal institutions found mainly in academic and research settings (Edelman & Galanter 2001). LSS is a prominent part of this external learning about law. It seeks explanation rather than justification. It emphasizes social structures and processes rather than rules. It rejects the notion of law as an autonomous self-contained realm; it appreciates the dynamics of law as part of more inclusive patterns of social life. Another prominent (and sometimes overlapping) sort of external learning about law is law and economics. Other lines of scholarly work (e.g., critical race theory, feminist legal studies) lie athwart the internal/external line. All these organized and cultivated knowledges are submerged in a sea of legal culture and consciousness (Ewick & Silbey 1998), fed by streams flowing from popular culture (Mezey & Niles 2005, Jarvis & Joseph 1998), folklore (Galanter 1998, 2005a), the news and entertainment industries (Haltom & McCann 2004), and political discourse. Although one or the other of these knowledges of law may be dominant in a particular setting, they influence and interpenetrate one another (Sherwin 2000). The career of LSS is connected indirectly but importantly to the careers of these other discourses and institutions.

Although LSS can boast of distinguished ancestors and precursors, systematic social inquiry about law was envisioned only in the early years of the twentieth century, and the emergence of a community of scholars continuously and cumulatively pursuing such inquiry dates from the middle of the century. The immediate forebear of LSS was American Legal Realism, which roiled the legal academy from the late 1920s (Schlegel 1995). The realists aspired to use law to reform society by transforming professional legal knowledge, incorporating empirical inquiry, and dismantling formalism that they regarded as intellectually mistaken and inimical to the fulfillment of law's moral promise.

If the realists supplied or carried the intellectual seed, the fertile soil on which it alighted was the New Deal's expansive improvisation of legal regulation to stimulate the economy and weave a net of protections for ordinary citizens, a process that gave social science an enlarged role in the functioning of government (Simon 1999). The years after World War II saw an elaboration of legal remedies and protections that one historian has called a "legalist reformation" (Nelson 2001). Courts lowered barriers to litigation, removing procedural obstacles and projecting due process into many settings. They widened standing, dismantled immunities, and enlarged remedies (Friedman 1985). Accountability in tort was expanded by the shift to comparative negligence and the rise of new theories of liability; contract law was shorn of much of its formalism; and above all civil rights for blacks were disinterred and new rights extended to many sorts of subordinates and outsiders, from students to consumers to women to prisoners. The proliferation of new rights was accompanied by the arrival of new players on the legal stage (as in the consumer, environmental, and women's movements) and the appearance of new formats for legal services (as in legal services for the poor and public interest law firms). Dynamic minority, consumer, environmental, and women's movements institutionalized the claims of these constituencies and made them a presence on the legal scene (Epp 1998). By the mid-1960s, courts, legislatures, lawyers, and activist groups had transformed the legal landscape, enlarging opportunities for successful assertion of rights by outsiders, dependents, and subordinates against society's managers and authorities. One example of the new dispensation was school litigation. "In the first half of the twentieth century," Tyack & Benavot (1985) report, "judges largely upheld school officials in situations of conflict." It was, they conclude, "a comfortable world for those who held power and wanted to preserve the status quo, but it left untouched some of the most pressing questions of social justice in public education" (pp. 364, 373–74). From the 1950s, there was a change in the amount and thrust of school litigation, holding those who ran schools to a new accountability to minorities, students, the disabled, and others who had been excluded from a voice in educational policy.

Civil rights, enlarged tort liability, the emergence of poverty law, consumerism, and environmentalism all reflected higher expectations of institutional performance by manufacturers, doctors, school authorities, and government agencies. Government responded to and promoted rising public expectations by enacting a wave of civil rights, consumer, and environmental legislation, by establishing new entitlements like Medicare, and by launching a "War on Poverty."

These developments expressed and elevated a high optimism that law could be used not merely to protect interests and preserve rights, but to address intractable social problems. The base metal of law, it seemed to many, could be transmuted into a shining sword, an instrument that could be used by dedicated judges and officials, prodded by energetic and imaginative lawyers, to dismantle oppressive structures and find new paths to substantive justice (*Yale Law J.* 1970, Schrag 1972). The exuberant estimation of legal possibilities was matched by confidence in the capacity of the burgeoning social sciences to identify constraints and to design more efficacious interventions. Within the academy, undergoing rapid expansion to accommodate the baby boom cohorts and rising commitments to higher education, there were high hopes for transcending disciplinary compartments to achieve new synergies.

LSS flourished at the intersection of legal optimism, academic expansion, and interdisciplinary enterprise. The Law and Society Association was founded in 1964, the year that the federal government launched the War on Poverty and embarked on an ambitious program of employing legal services strategically to improve the condition of the poor (Johnson 1974). A combination of lawyers and social scientists, mainly sociologists and political scientists, the association embraced high expectations about expanding legal rights at the same time that it provided a base for critical assessment of the failure of law to fulfill its promises of equality, fairness, access, and remedy. When the association in 1966 commenced publication of the *Law & Society Review*, the first distinctively LSS journal, the lead article in the first issue was an extended assessment of "Civil Justice and the Poor" in which the authors, after cataloging the many things the law could do, reflected that

> a basic limitation of the law is its inability to treat the problems of the poor as essentially collective or class phenomena. The law has been slow to recognize and remedy the collective problems of slum tenants, low-income buyers and public assistance recipients. And it has been slow to respond to the collective problems of Negroes in gaining full citizenship (Carlin et al. 1966, p. 27).

A similar combination of celebration of enlarged legal rights with critical assessment of legal practice informed the lead article in the second issue, Blumberg's (1967) "The Practice of Law as a Confidence Game." This much-reprinted article, which has attained canonical status (Cotterrell 1994, Seron 2006), found it ironic that enlargement of defendants' rights was transformed into a more sophisticated apparatus for manipulating defendants into guilty pleas, a failing attributed to the Supreme Court's sociological naiveté. Carlin et al. (1966) and Blumberg (1967) expressed a central tenet of LSS in that formative time that understanding of the social was a crucial missing ingredient necessary to make law effective in realizing shared aspirations for justice and equality.

Rejecting the legalist premise that promulgating good rules would automatically produce desired social change, LSS affirmed that law is inseparably embedded in the social and political. The conviction that the connection between rules and outcomes is mediated by complex and contingent social and political processes was expressed in a critique of legalist models of reform (Scheingold 1974, Galanter 1974, Trubek & Galanter 1974, Macaulay 1979) that has remained central to LSS, inoculating it against the wrenching disillusionment that accompanied the collapse of elevated expectations of legal felicity.

INSTITUTIONALIZATION OF LSS

Since those early days, LSS has been institutionalized in organizations (e.g., the Law and Society Association and law sections in several social science associations), a National Science Foundation program, a scattering of academic programs and research institutions, more than a dozen journals, and most recently this *Annual Review* (Friedman 2005). The success of LSS in creating a cross-disciplinary research community involving exchange and collaboration among scholars in anthropology, criminology, economics, history, law, political science, psychology, and sociology (Galanter & Edwards 1997, Silbey 2000) may owe something to the timing of its development. Looking back, I realize that I was the first editor (1972–1976) of the *Law & Society Review* to hold a law degree rather than a PhD. In those early days of LSS, a time when the prestige of social science was at its height, the social scientists occupied the high ground; we lawyers were representatives of a discipline that was deficient, and they had what was missing and admired. So even though law professors as a group enjoyed somewhat higher status, the fellowship of deviant law professors and mainstream social scientists formed an amalgam that has proved remarkably resistant to the assertion of divisive disciplinary identities. (The commendable effacement of disciplinary lines frustrated my efforts to capture recent trends in the makeup of LSS: I learned that the Law and Society Association discontinued maintaining records of members' disciplinary affiliation sometime in the late 1980s.)

LEGALIZATION AND RECOIL

The expansion of rights and remedies that encompassed LSS at its emergence was part of a great burst of legalization of American society. Regulation proliferated, extending to aspects of life previously unsupervised by the state. And whole areas of governmental activity that were not previously thought needful of close articulation with legal principles were now subjected to judicial oversight. There was, by any measure, a great deal more law (Galanter 1992). The volume of authoritative legal material mounted steadily. The legal profession grew from some 385,933 lawyers in 1960 to over one million in 2000 (Carson 2004, p. 1). There was one lawyer for every 627 Americans in 1960; at the end of the century there was one lawyer for every 264. Spending on law increased dramatically, not only absolutely but relatively. In 1978, the receipts of law firms were something like $0.40 of every $100 of the gross domestic product. By 2002 they were more than $1.60 (Galanter 2005b, pp. 1378–79). So for the last third of the twentieth century, the law business grew several times as fast as the overall economy. These figures are only for law firms. If we add in the work of government lawyers and in-house lawyers, we can estimate that law represents about 2% of the nation's product. Amid all this growth, the place of law, lawyers, and courts in public consciousness continued to expand. Popular culture was ever more saturated with law. Mezey & Niles (2005, p. 93) report that, "of the thirty-seven original dramatic shows aired by the four major [television] networks in the 2003 Fall season, thirty-one . . . had elected officials, lawyers, police officers, former police officers who are now vigilantes, or forensic officials as main characters."

Burgeoning legalization was not confined to the United States (Galanter 1992): Increasing lawyer populations, multiplication of regulation, proliferation of rights-talk, and enhanced judicial authority are widespread throughout the rich democracies and beyond. But the legalization of the United States is particularly intense. Law has become the site and idiom of debate about policy to an extent unknown elsewhere. Lawyers became "the dominant profession in American society" (Gawalt 1984, p. vii). American political institutions, Miller (1995, p. 162) observes, "have adopted lawyers' ways, lawyers' language, as well as lawyers' approaches to problem solving." They emphasize procedure and process, rules and precedents; they take a rights-focused, case-by-case incremental approach to substantive social problems. Kagan (2001) traces this reliance on law, lawyers, and courts to the decentralized American political system and the fragmentation and indeterminacy of the American legal regime.

The expansion of regulation and remedy and the ascendancy of lawyers were not universally cheered. Earlier, various initiatives of the New Deal and of the Warren Court had encountered pointed resistance, but the overall climate remained favorable to the continued enlargement of remedies and protections for the less advantaged. But beginning in the mid-1970s (just as LSS was becoming embedded in the academy), there was a reversal of fortunes. The prevailing critique of the legal system, that it failed to provide justice to the weak, began to give way to a sense that the nation was afflicted by "too much law" (Galanter 1994). A medical malpractice insurance crisis in 1972–1974, followed by a crisis in product liability insurance in 1974–1976, led to modest curtailment of remedies and widespread alarm. The term "tort reform" became current in 1976 amid warnings about the infirmities and the dangers of the law.

The expansion of law was identified as an ominous threat. "[C]onsumerism, environmentalism, and other forms of Naderism" and the increasing litigiousness of Americans were seen to portend "a society in which business is endlessly besieged by legal problems" (Carruth 1973, p. 157). Critics accused the courts of overreaching and constituting an "imperial judiciary" (Glazer 1975, van den Haag 1978). The recoil came from within as well as from outside the legal establishment. Chief Justice Warren Burger decried a "litigation explosion" and denounced "legal activism" by judges and lawyers. In 1976, Burger organized a conference on "The Causes of Popular Dissatisfaction with the Administration of Justice" (Pound Conf. 1976), held on the 70th anniversary of Roscoe Pound's celebrated address on that topic. Attended by the attorney general and solicitor general, prominent judges, distinguished practitioners, and influential legal academics, the Pound Conference, as it has come to be known, was the emblematic pivot of the turn against the enlargement of remedies. Speakers emphasized the burden placed on the courts, especially federal courts, by increased caseload and ever-expanding demands for intervention to address social problems. There was a general consensus that the courts should scale back their excursions into problem solving, and that their quantitative burdens should be addressed by eliminating the diversity jurisdiction of the federal courts, by abandoning the use of the jury in civil cases, and by promoting the use of alternative dispute resolution (ADR).

By the late 1970s, expansive legal remedies were seen by a significant section of legal, political, and business elites as a systemic social problem. Laurence H. Silberman (1978), later a federal judge, asked "Will Lawyering Strangle Democratic Capitalism?" He traced how "the legal process, because of its unbridled growth, has become a cancer which threatens the vitality of our forms of capitalism and democracy" (p. 15) and detailed "the harmful impact of an ever expanding legal process on our society" (p. 44). The profligate creation of new individual rights was weakening the "intermediate institutions [families, churches, schools, corporations, labor unions, and political parties] . . . that are indispensable pillars of a pluralistic democracy" (p. 18). In addition, "litigation of all kinds [was] becoming a major structural impediment to our economy" (p. 21). Our bloated lawyer population, Silberman declared, "may confer a competitive advantage on our economic rivals in Japan and Europe" (p. 21). In this vision, rising litigation is not a parochial concern of certain industries or institutions, but a menace to public well-being. And lawyers are dangerous parasites in the national bloodstream.

THE TRIUMPH OF THE JAUNDICED VIEW

These notions became part of a familiar complex of beliefs about law, lawyers, and lawsuits that I have called the "jaundiced view," which holds that the United States is overflowing with frivolous lawsuits by self-styled victims, inspired by greedy lawyers and encouraged by irresponsible juries and activist judges (Galanter 1998). In this litigation lottery, claimants walk away with immense and undeserved sums.

Useful business and civic activities are inhibited. The legal system has spun out of control and causes immense damage, undermining the country's economic strength and unraveling the fabric of trust that underlies civic life. Among the abundance of examples of this mindset, I choose one whose authorship (by a lawyer who a few years later was elevated to solicitor general of the United States) testifies to the respectability as well as the audacity of such fulminations.

> Our mechanism for the peaceable resolution of civil disputes has transmogrified into an insatiable organism that is devouring a segment of our society and culture from the inside-out. Like the giant underground fungus discovered several years ago in Michigan, which manifests itself above the ground only in the form of an occasional mushroom, our civil justice system parasite is barely perceptible to the average person on a day-to-day basis, except for the occasional but increasingly frequent news reports of a freakish lawsuit or outlandish jury verdict. But the destructive process is nevertheless continuously at work, growing and relentlessly consuming vital resources and disabling our productive capacity (Olson 1994, p. 359).

The jaundiced view flourishes most luxuriantly among corporate and governmental elites, but many elements of it have been embraced by wider publics. It has become the reigning common sense about law in America (Haltom & McCann 2004, p. 22). It is supported by a web of stories about abusive lawsuits, frivolous claims, and outrageous awards. One of the salient features of this discourse is that it is a victimization tale that depicts upstanding, beneficent corporations and governments being exploited by unscrupulous individuals and their rapacious lawyers. The master narrative is that irresponsible and opportunistic claimants, who attempt to fasten responsibility on productive organizations and secure undeserved compensation, are "the source and carriers of [a] devastating social disease" (Haltom & McCann 2004, p. 59). These stories and the discourse in which they are embedded are disseminated by a massive "campaign to impugn the legal system" (Haltom & McCann 2004, p. 223) and to delegitimize claimants and their lawyers who invoke it. This propaganda campaign is promoted by corporations and their political allies, supported by right-wing foundations and think tanks, and has enjoyed great success in resisting debunking.

In recent years, there has been a significant body of careful LSS research that has joined battle with the assertions about litigation, lawyers, and juries that festoon the jaundiced view. For example, a long tradition of research has established the conscientiousness and responsibility of juries and the modesty of their awards (Hans 2000, Vidmar 1995). But the findings of well-researched empirical studies have not put much of a dent in the folklore about juries' anticorporate bias and excessive awards. What makes the jaundiced view so resilient? Why in the area of civil justice has folklore dominated public discourse and marginalized systematic social inquiry? What confounds the reading of the legal landscape? Why does systematic empirical knowledge about law fare so poorly in public discourse? Haltom & McCann (2004) argue that the jaundiced view triumphs over its empirical critics because, first, it resonates with enduring themes of individual responsibility and disparagement of law; and second, because its stories fit the templates and conventions of news and entertainment. Haltom & McCann fault the empirical antagonists of the jaundiced view for failing to present their findings in a compelling moral vision.

THE PREDICAMENT OF LAW

The discourse about other social institutions such as education, banking, or health care are undoubtedly infected with misinformation, but there seems to be a bedrock of facts that can be ignored only at the risk of losing credibility. Or so we would like to believe. In any event, the requirement of a modicum of deference to fact seems less rigorous in law, where endorsing and promoting fantastical views does not disqualify their proponents. What accounts for the marginalization of empirical studies in the civil justice wars? Is LSS peopled by scholars with substandard rhetorical skills or a less moral vision than empiricists who study other social institutions? Is there something about law, lawyers, and legal scholarship that makes it so susceptible to misrepresentation and misreading?

One factor that separates law from many social institutions is its derelict knowledge base. Until quite recently, what courts and litigants and lawyers were actually doing was only dimly known. In this low-information environment, misinformation flourished. For example, from the late 1960s when concern about growing product liability exposure agitated defendants and insurers, people started estimating the total number of product liability cases being filed annually. The numbers kept escalating, so that by the time of the product liability insurance crisis of the mid-1970s it was believed that the number of product liability cases had risen from 50,000 in 1963 to one million in 1975 (*Forbes* 1976, p. 57). In fact there were not one million product liability suits in the entire history of the United States to 1975 and probably fewer than 20,000 filed in that year.

It was only in the early 1980s that sizable bodies of reliable information about litigation patterns became available. The first of the Rand Institute for Civil Justice studies of jury verdicts was published in 1982 (Peterson & Priest 1982); findings from the University of Wisconsin Civil Litigation Research Project became available shortly after (Trubek et al. 1987). The National Center for State Courts (founded in 1971) published its first reliable figures on litigation in the state courts in 1986.

This flow of quantitative information was part of a wider opening of information about the legal world. The demise in 1977 of the norms forbidding lawyers to talk to reporters led to the rapid growth of a new kind of legal journalism, embodied in a new generation of trade journals (*The National Law Journal*, *The American Lawyer*, and various local counterparts) and more constant and intrusive attention from *The New York Times*, *The Wall Street Journal,* and other newspapers (Galanter & Palay 1991, pp. 68–73). Old norms of reticence fell by the wayside. Soon we knew much more about lawyers and their clients, their strategies, and their incomes.

Even though we have accumulated a great deal of data and insight during the past 40 years, the fund of systematic social knowledge about the working of the civil justice system is still rather scanty. Court statistics are rudimentary. For example, they do not record the detailed subject matter of cases, the characteristics of the parties, or the events in the case; information about settlements is not systematically collected; indeed, it is often shrouded in secrecy, with the support of courts. No one has seen fit to invest in the continuous collection of basic information.

The paucity of reliable systematic information about the law provides fertile soil for the kinds of flawed intuitive judgment described in the literature of cognitive psychology, which catalogs a number of factors that lead to biased inferences and judgments about uncertain events (Nisbet & Ross 1980, Loftus & Beech 1982). For example, decision makers often ignore relevant information about baseline frequencies, misattributing representativeness to data. The frequency of easily remembered events is exaggerated, leading to overestimation of risk from publicized hazards relative to less visible ones. "Vivid information, that is, concrete, sensory and personally relevant information, may have disproportionate impact on beliefs and inferences" (Nisbet & Ross 1980, p. 190). Furthermore, biased receptiveness to confirming evidence makes people excessively confident in the accuracy of their knowledge. In other words, the way our minds are built inclines us to think we know more than we do. But these cognitive imperfections, like germs, are everywhere. Why do they find such a nutritive environment in discourse about the law?

Most people, including lawyers, politicians, and corporate executives, derive much or most of their picture of the legal system from the media. But there is a pronounced tilt in media coverage of civil justice. The news media portray a world of ubiquitous litigation, outlandish claims, and successful plaintiffs winning excessive awards from beleaguered corporate defendants. For example, Garber (1998) studied newspaper coverage of verdicts in product liability cases against automobile manufacturers decided from 1985 to 1996. He found that almost three-quarters of those verdicts were in favor of the defendant, but newspapers reported just 3% of the defense verdicts and 41% of verdicts for plaintiffs. In other words, a verdict for the plaintiff is 12 times more likely to be reported than is a defense verdict. Consequently, in the reports that a conscientious and omnivorous newspaper reader would encounter, some four-fifths would have been verdicts for the plaintiff—roughly the opposite of the true percentage. Other studies have shown that the amounts won by plaintiffs in newspaper and magazine reports are 10 to 20 times as large as the run of awards (Bailis & MacCoun 1996, Chase 1995, Garber & Bower 1999). A comparable misrepresentation of litigation outcomes occurs in employment discrimination claims (Nielsen & Beim 2004). Notwithstanding occasional media efforts to debunk some of the litigation explosion legends, the regular consumer of media reports would be badly misinformed about the number of product liability and medical malpractice cases, the size of jury awards, the incidence of punitive damages, and the regularity with which corporate defendants succeed in defeating individual claimants.

If the distortions of the media are inadvertent, there are a host of professionals, consultants, and publicists who thrive by magnifying the sense of crisis and touting their ability to exorcize the menace of enhanced liability (Edelman et al. 1992). Their messages are amplified by a small industry of corporately supported think tanks, lobbyists, consultants, and grassroots groups that attempt to generate political support for reforms of the civil justice system (Deal & Doroshow 2000). Politicians and organizational entrepreneurs, in turn, echo the jaundiced view in order to cultivate financial support and garner votes. As one political operative advised his charges (Luntz 1997, p. 128):

> Unlike most complex issues, the problems in our civil justice system come with a ready made villain: the lawyer.... It's almost impossible to go too far when it comes to demonizing lawyers.... Talk about the hidden costs of our out-of-control civil justice system. Do not get bogged down with a numbers-laden economic argument; rather, put the impact of lawsuits on the economy in human terms by telling stories about how individual consumers end up paying far too much for everyday household products, medicines, car insurance... all because of unreasonable lawsuits.

This kind of entrepreneurship can flourish because, unlike scientific and technical fields, the law does not have a creditable set of custodians of its knowledge base. The world of law practice is agonistic and the lawyer's relation to truth is instrumental. As Campos (1998) puts it, "Lawyers make claims not because they believe them to be true, but because they believe them to be legally efficacious. If they happen to be true, then all the better." For centuries, the popular imagination has associated lawyers with operating in a theater of deceit, sharp practice, and gamesmanship, where the imperatives of truthfulness and personal morality are suspended or diluted (Galanter 2005a). It is difficult, if not impossible in the present climate of antilawyerism, for lawyers to avoid being discounted as partisans and hired guns who are in the advocacy business rather than the truth business.

Judges are credited with the requisite detachment, impartiality, and devotion to the public interest. But for many reasons, we cannot imagine them serving as effective guardians of empirical knowledge about the legal system. Their role commits them to be reactive, to respond only to individual cases, and to privilege text over context.

LSS IN THE LAW SCHOOLS

To nourish and project a body of empirically based knowledge of the law has been an aspiration of some legal academics since the days of the early legal realists (Schlegel 1995). But that ambition has not been taken to the bosom of the legal academy, whose ambivalence to empirical inquiry recalls an exchange recounted by Phillipa Strum in her biography of Louis Brandeis:

> Brandeis recalled having told [Justice Oliver Wendell] Holmes "that if he really wants to 'improve his mind' (as he always speaks of it), the way to do it is not to read more philosophic books . . . but to get some sense of the world of fact. And he asked me to map out some reading—he became much interested—and I told him that I'd . . . get some books, that books could carry him only so far, and that he should get some exhibits from life. I suggested the textile industry, and told him in vacation time he is near Lawrence and Lowell and he should go there and look about . . . " (Strum 1984, pp. 309–10).

Holmes reported this to his correspondent, Sir Frederick Pollack, and confided:

> "I hate facts. I always say the chief end of man is to form general propositions—adding that no general propositions is worth a damn . . . . I have little doubt that it would be good for my immortal soul to plunge into them [facts] . . . but I shrink from the bore" (Strum 1984, p. 310).

Like Holmes, the legal academy has followed the enchantments of text rather than the Brandeisian imperative of disciplined examination of context. Although legal academics have established their independence of the profession, taken in the aggregate they continue to mirror the intellectual styles of both judges and lawyers. Like judges, they privilege legal doctrine and justification. Like lawyers, they place "more value on the inventive, the new, the clever, the winning argument," and critical deconstruction of opposing arguments than on the collaborative process of "describing, explaining and exploring" the legal world (Carrillo 2005, p. 5). The reluctance of the law schools to be the seat of systematic cultivation of this contextual knowledge is indicated by the regular recurrence of calls for them to do so.

For all the hesitation, empirical research remains an aspiration, if not a high priority, of many law schools. Several changes in the law school world have encouraged LSS. The contraction of the required curriculum has opened pedagogic space; interdisciplinary courses in 30 leading law schools increased from 56 in 1960 to 812 in 2000 (Witte 2005, p. 444). The ascendancy of instrumentalism in legal discourse (Tamanaha 2006) has made LSS more salient. As legal scholarship has become more open to consequentialist and contextual arguments, the legal mainstream has been redefined to include much discourse and scholarship that would once have been regarded as nonlegal. There has been a palpable infiltration of empirical perspectives. LSS work is published in law reviews as mainstream legal scholarship. Significant numbers of law teachers hold degrees in one of the social sciences, and they are particularly numerous in high-prestige schools (George 2006); ambitious centers of interdisciplinary study sprout in many locations. That LSS is attractive to, if not exactly part of, the legal academic mainstream was marked by the adoption of empirical research as the theme of the 2006 Annual Meeting of the Association of American Law Schools.

LSS AFTER THE TURN

LSS faces a setting very different from that of its formative years. The era when high expectations of legal problem solving met soaring optimism about social science expired by the mid-1970s, under the weight of Vietnam, Watergate, and a general collapse of confidence in government (Lipset & Schneider 1987). The thrust for access to justice was replaced by worry about too much law, and expansion of remedies gave way to contraction via tort reform, mandated diversion to ADR, and deregulation. Boundless confidence in law was replaced by relentless recitation of its weaknesses and costs. Although legalization continues apace (Crews 2005), law, lawyers, and regulation are out of favor; privatization and reliance on markets are preferred.

Important streams of LSS research resist the contracting of legal remedies, the hollowing out of law by privatization and ADR, the restriction of access by mandatory arbitration, and the shift from adjudicative to managerial modes of governance. Although such generalizations are rightfully suspect, it is my impression that, in this antinomian era, the tenor of much LSS work has shifted counter-cyclically from skeptical assessment of law's limited efficacy to appreciation of its uneven accomplishments. Or perhaps the detached skepticism that stood in sharp contrast to the enthusiasm of an earlier day now, in a setting of passionate attacks on law and lawyers, appears supportive.

LSS has put down institutional roots that have enabled it to survive the erosion of the reformist soil that nurtured it. It has become less programmatic and more diverse; it has enlarged its intellectual repertoire, for example to include both rational actor and cultural studies approaches, and it has expanded its perspective from national to global.

The legal world that LSS addresses is increasingly populated by large corporate organizations rather than by natural persons (Galanter 2005b). Organizations purchase an increasing portion of legal services. They are more proficient players of the legal game. Enjoying the advantages of repeat players, they win more and lose less in courts and other forums. Nevertheless, they often consider themselves victims (Lande 1998) and campaign to diminish public controls.

LSS is a point of resistance not only to the corporately sponsored common sense about the legal system but also to the growing dominance of corporations in the legal arena. LSS encounters corporate actors in the university setting as well. As the sweep of LSS broadens and the tactical potential of empirical data rises, the incentive and opportunity to produce knowledge to support corporate positions are enlarged. Warren (2002) describes how a credit industry–supported, university-based research center, enjoying the imprimatur of a major university, promoted the Bankruptcy Reform Act of 2005 by producing legendary claims based on proprietary data that could not be examined by independent researchers. Warren describes how the presence of these compromised data led to an antimarket in data in which the presence of bad data leads to dismissal of good data as mutually canceling. A more subtle infiltration of research is the Exxon Corporation's seeding of the research of independent scholars in the hope of producing literature that would be useful ammunition for advocacy. Exxon promoted and supported extensive research on punitive damages by prominent scholars who were encouraged to place their results in refereed publications (Zarembo 2003, Freudenburg 2005). The findings of this research were later deployed in advocacy aimed at curtailing punitive damage awards (Brief as *Amici Curiae* 2001, Brief as *Amici Curiae* 2002), like the one facing the corporate sponsor in the Exxon Valdez oil spill case. The amicus briefs submitted on behalf of "certain leading business corporations" did not mention that Exxon had funded the research but simply drew attention to "recent social science research demonstrating that jurors are generally incapable of performing the tasks the law assigns to them in punitive damage cases" (Zarembo 2003, p. A20). Thus, we get a kind of counter-Brandeis brief in which an abundance of evidence about real juries in their real-world institutional setting is ignored in favor of laboratory simulations of questionable applicability (Vidmar 2004, Sharkey 2003).

Half a century on, LSS faces perils that its founders could hardly have anticipated because they are the perils of success in a setting very different from the one in which LSS arose. Can the diversity and detachment of the remarkable LSS research community survive the embrace of the law schools? Will the clusters and networks of social scientists outside the law schools—on whom falls the task of producing the next generation of researchers—remain robust in the face of the funding advantage of law schools? Will the competitive norms of legal discourse corrode the ethos of disinterested explanation that has been the hallmark of LSS?

Interest in empirical study of law is rising at the same time that universities are increasingly penetrated by corporations. We have seen the first traces of production of LSS knowledge as part of corporate campaigns in the legal arena. With the decline of public support for appointments and research, will a critical and independent LSS be able to resist the blandishments of corporate sponsorship and the inevitable deformation of the research agenda?

The *Annual Review of Law and Social Science* is online at http://lawsocsci.annualreviews.org

LITERATURE CITED

Bailis DS, MacCoun RJ. 1996. Estimating liability risks with the media as your guide: a content analysis of media coverage of tort litigation. *Law Hum. Behav.* 20:419–29

Blumberg AS. 1967. The practice of law as a confidence game. *Law Soc. Rev.* 1(2):15–39

Brief as *Amici Curiae* of Certain Leading Business Corporations in Support of Petitioner. 2001. *Cooper Industries, Inc. v. Leatherman Tool Group, Inc.*, 532 U.S. 424 (No. 99–2035)

Brief as *Amici Curiae* of Certain Leading Business Corporations in Support of Petitioner. 2002. *State Farm Mutual Automobile Insurance Company v. Curtis B. Campbell and Inez Preece Campbell*, 537 U.S. 1042 (No. 01–1289)

Campos PF. 1998. *Jurismania: The Madness of American Law*. New York: Oxford Univ. Press. 198 pp.

Carlin JE, Howard J, Messinger SL. 1966. Civil justice and the poor: issues for sociological research. *Law Soc. Rev*. 1(1):9–89

Carrillo J. 2005. *Links and choices: the idea of popular legal culture in the work of Lawrence M. Friedman*. Presented at conference in honor of Lawrence M. Friedman, Stanford Law Sch., Oct. 1

Carruth E. 1973. The "legal explosion" has left business shell-shocked. *Fortune*, April, pp. 65–69

Carson CN. 2004. *The Lawyer Statistical Report: The U.S. Legal Profession in 2000*. Chicago: Am. Bar Found. 250 pp.

Chase OG. 1995. Helping jurors determine pain and suffering awards. *Hofstra Law Rev.* 23:763–90

Cotterrell R. 1994. *Law and Society*. Aldershot: Dartmouth

Crews CWJ. 2005. *Ten Thousand Commandments: An Annual Snapshot of the Federal Regulatory State*. Washington, DC: Cato Inst.

Deal C, Doroshow J. 2000. *The Cala Files: The Secret Campaign by Big Tobacco and Other Major Industries to Take Away Your Rights*. New York/Washington, DC: Cent. Justice Democr./Public Citizen. 67 pp.

Edelman LB, Abraham SE, Erlanger HS. 1992. Professional construction of law: the inflated threat of wrongful discharge. *Law Soc. Rev.* 26:47–83

Edelman LB, Galanter M. 2001. Law: overview. *Int. Encycl. Soc. Behav. Sci.* 12:8538–44

Epp CR. 1998. *The Rights Revolution: Lawyers, Activists, and Supreme Courts in Comparative Perspective*. Chicago: Univ. Chicago Press. 326 pp.

Ewick P, Silbey S. 1998. *The Common Place of Law: Stories from Everyday Life*. Chicago: Univ. Chicago Press. 318 pp.

Forbes. 1976. Who Pays. Aug. 1, p. 57

Freudenburg WR. 2005. Seeding science, courting conclusions: reexamining the intersection of science, corporate cash, and the law. *Sociol. Forum* 20:3–33

Friedman LM. 1985. *Total Justice*. New York: Russell Sage. 166 pp.

Friedman LM. 2005. Coming of age: law and society enters an exclusive club. *Annu. Rev. Law Soc.* 1:1–15

Galanter M. 1974. Why the 'haves' come out ahead: speculations on the limits of legal change. *Law Soc. Rev.* 9:95–160

Galanter M. 1992. Law abounding: legalisation around the North Atlantic. *Mod. Law Rev.* 55:1–24

Galanter M. 1994. Predators and parasites: lawyer-bashing and civil justice. *Ga. Law Rev.* 28:633–81

Galanter M. 1998. An oil strike in hell. *Ariz. Law Rev.* 40:717–52

Galanter M. 2005a. *Lowering the Bar: Lawyer Jokes and Legal Culture*. Madison: Univ. Wis. Press. 429 pp.

Galanter M. 2005b. Planet of the APs: reflections on the scale of law and its users. *Buffalo Law Rev.* 53:1369–417

Galanter M, Edwards MA. 1997. Introduction: the path of the law ands. *Wis. Law Rev.* 1997:375–87

Galanter M, Palay TM. 1991. *Tournament of Lawyers: The Transformation of the Big Law Firm*. Chicago: Univ. Chicago Press. 197 pp.

Garber S. 1998. Product liability, punitive damages, business decisions and economic outcomes. *Wis. Law Rev.* 1998:237–95

Garber S, Bower AG. 1999. Newspaper coverage of automotive product liability verdicts. *Law Soc. Rev.* 33:95–122

Gawalt GW. 1984. *The New High Priests: Lawyers in Post–Civil War America*. Westport, CT: Greenwood. 214 pp.

George TE. 2006. An empirical study of empirical legal scholarship: the top law schools. *Indiana Law J.* 81:141–61

Glazer N. 1975. Towards an imperial judiciary. *Public Interest* 41:104–23

Haltom W, McCann M. 2004. *Distorting the Law: Politics, Media, and the Litigation Crisis*. Chicago: Univ. Chicago Press. 347 pp.

Hans VP. 2000. *Business on Trial: The Civil Jury and Corporate Responsibility*. New Haven, CT: Yale Univ. Press. 269 pp.

Jarvis RM, Joseph PR. 1998. *Prime Time Law: Fictional Television as Legal Narrative*. Durham, NC: Carolina Acad. Press. 323 pp.

Johnson EJ. 1974. *Justice and Reform: The Formative Years of the OEO Legal Services Program*. New York: Russell Sage. 416 pp.

Kagan RA. 2001. *Adversarial Legalism: The American Way of Law*. Cambridge, MA: Harvard Univ. Press. 339 pp.

Lande J. 1998. Failing faith in litigation? A survey of business lawyers' and executives' opinions. *Harvard Negot. Law Rev.* 3:1–70

Lipset SM, Schneider W. 1987. *The Confidence Gap: Business, Labor, and Government in the Public Mind*. Baltimore, MD: Johns Hopkins Univ. Press. 460 pp. Rev. ed.

Loftus E, Beech LR. 1982. Human inference and judgment: Is the glass half empty or half full? *Stanford Law Rev.* 34:938–56

Luntz F. 1997. *The Language of the 21st Century*. Alexandria, VA: Luntz Res. 222 pp.

Macaulay S. 1979. Lawyers and consumer protection laws. *Law Soc. Rev.* 14:115–71

Mezey N, Niles MC. 2005. Screening the law: ideology and law in American popular culture. *Columbia J. Law Arts* 28:91–185

Miller MC. 1995. *The High Priests of American Politics: The Role of Lawyers in American Political Institutions*. Knoxville: Univ. Tenn. Press. 228 pp.

Nelson WE. 2001. *The Legalist Reformation: Law, Politics and Ideology in New York 1920–1980*. Chapel Hill: Univ. N. C. Press. 457 pp.

Nielsen LB, Beim A. 2004. Media misrepresentation: Title VII, print media, and public perceptions of discrimination litigation. *Stanford Law Policy Rev.* 15:237–365

Nisbet RE, Ross L. 1980. *Human Inference: Strategies and Shortcomings of Social Judgment*. Englewood Cliffs, NJ: Prentice-Hall

Olson TB. 1994. The parasitic destruction of America's civil justice system. *SMU Law Rev.* 47:359–68

Peterson MA, Priest GL. 1982. *The Civil Jury: Trends in Trials and Verdicts, Cook County, Illinois, 1960–1979*. Santa Monica: RAND Inst. Civ. Justice. 73 pp.

Pound Conf. 1976. Addresses delivered at the National Conference on the Causes of Popular Dissatisfaction with the Administration of Justice. 70 *F.R.D.* 79–246

Scheingold SA. 1974. *The Politics of Rights: Lawyers, Public Policy and Political Change*. New Haven, CT: Yale Univ. Press. 224 pp.

Schlegel JH. 1995. *American Legal Realism and Empirical Social Science*. Chapel Hill: Univ. N. C. Press. 418 pp.

Schrag P. 1972. *Counsel for the Deceived: Case Studies in Consumer Fraud*. New York: Pantheon. 200 pp.

Seron C. 2006. *The Law and Society Canon*. Aldershot: Ashgate. 604 pp.

Sharkey CM. 2003. Punitive damages: should juries decide? *Tex. Law Rev.* 82:381–411

Sherwin R. 2000. *When Law Goes Pop: The Vanishing Line Between Law and Popular Culture*. Chicago: Univ. Chicago Press. 325 pp.

Silberman LH. 1978. Will lawyering strangle democratic capitalism? *Regulation* March/April 1978:15–44

Silbey SS. 2000. From the editor. *Law Soc. Rev.* 34:859–72

Simon J. 1999. Law after society. *Law Soc. Inq.* 24:143–94

Strum P. 1984. *Louis D. Brandeis: Justice for the People*. Cambridge, MA: Harvard Univ. Press. 508 pp.

Tamanaha BZ. 2006. *The perils of pervasive legal instrumentalism*. Montesquieu Lect. Ser., Tilburg Univ., Vol. 1, 2005. http://ssrn.com/abstract = 725582

Trubek DM, Galanter M. 1974. Scholars in self-estrangement: some reflections on the crisis of law and development studies in the United States. *Wis. Law Rev.* 1974:1062–102

Trubek DM, Grossman JB, Felstiner WLF, Kritzer HM, Sarat A. 1987. *Civil Litigation Research Project Final Report,* 3 Vols. Madison: Univ. Wis. Sch. Law

Tyack D, Benavot A. 1985. Courts and public schools: educational litigation in historical perspective. *Law Soc. Rev.* 19:339–80

van den Haag E. 1978. The growth of the imperial judiciary. *Policy Rev.* 4:57–67

Vidmar NJ. 1995. *Medical Malpractice and the American Jury: Confronting the Myths about Jury Incompetence, Deep Pockets, and Outrageous Damage Awards.* Ann Arbor: Univ. Mich. Press. 318 pp.

Vidmar NJ. 2004. Experimental simulations and tort reform: avoidance, error and overreaching in Sunstein et al.'s *Punitive Damages. Emory Law J.* 53:1359–403

Warren E. 2002. The market for data: the changing role of social sciences in shaping the law. *Wis. Law Rev.* 2002:1–43

Witte J. 2005. Law and religion: the challenges of Christian jurisprudence. *Univ. St. Thomas Law J.* 2:439–52

Yale Law J. 1970. 79(6):1005–197 (May)

Zarembo A. 2003. Column one: funding studies to suit need. *Los Angeles Times*, Dec. 3, p. 1A

Annu. Rev. Law Soc. Sci. 2006. 2:17–38
doi: 10.1146/annurev.lawsocsci.2.081805.105917

First published online as a Review in Advance on June 5, 2006

LAW AND SOCIAL MOVEMENTS: Contemporary Perspectives

Michael McCann
Department of Political Science, University of Washington, Seattle, Washington 98195; email: mwmccann@u.washington.edu

Key Words legal mobilization, social justice

■ **Abstract** Social movement scholars have long seemed little interested in law, and traditional legal scholars were little interested in social movement analysis by social scientists. However, recent years have seen growth of interest in the topic of law and social movements, with inquiry led by political scientists and law and society scholars. This review surveys that diverse literature, beginning with general theory regarding core concepts and then moving to a review of empirical studies organized around the multi-stage model derived from political process approaches and legal mobilization frameworks. The primary argument of the review is that law is contingent, and how it matters for social movements varies with the context and character of struggle. Most analysts agree that law generally works to support status quo conventions and hierarchical relationships, but sometimes law can be mobilized to challenge and even reconstitute the terms of institutional order.

INTRODUCTION

Rigorous study of law and social movements has been a surprisingly limited and marginal intellectual endeavor in the modern American academy.[1] Social science scholarship on social movements has documented many case studies in which legal claims, tactics, and actors figured or failed prominently, but these studies have rarely provided direct conceptual analysis about how law does or does not matter for the struggles at stake, and generally they have remained quite uninformed by sophisticated socio-legal analysis. In short, social movement scholars do not seem much interested in law. Traditional legal scholars in law schools, by contrast, have written at length about litigation campaigns, judicial actions, and normative aspirations for rights-based social justice connected to social movements. But most of this scholarship has remained court-centered, sticking close to official case law and actions of legal elites while remaining distant from grassroots movement activity. Most such study is neither empirically rigorous about identifying the key

[1]This review is a significantly revised and updated version of several essays that I have previously published in other volumes, including but not limited to McCann (1998, 2004).

elements of social movement organization, activity, and context nor theoretically informed by social movement theory.

Socio-legal scholars have drawn on social science traditions to provide manifold insights about both the ways that prevailing legal norms tend to legitimate social hierarchy and the complex manifestations of legal claims and tactics by groups aiming to challenge those hierarchies and injustices. Indeed, socio-legal scholars have contributed many types of studies—of judicial impact, interest group litigation, cause lawyering, the politics of rights, civil disputing, and everyday resistance, to name just a few—that are highly relevant to understanding the relationships of law and social movements. Again, however, most of this scholarship has granted at best passing notice to social movement theory.[2]

There are some signs that these tendencies have begun to change in the last decade, however, and that a productive dialogue is developing that connects previously separate modes of analysis regarding law and social movements. A lively debate developed in the mid-1990s between representatives of court-centered, top-down approaches to studying reform litigation and advocates of more legally decentered, movement-oriented studies of law. From initial debates spurred by several influential books (see Rosenberg 1991, 1992, 1996; McCann 1992, 1994, 1996, 2004) arose debates enlisting other scholars (Gottlieb & Schultz 1998) and many new studies of law, social movements, and judicial impact (Silverstein 1996, Canon & Johnson 1998, Polletta 2000, Marshall 2003, Pedriana 2004, Anderson 2005; M. Paris, unpublished manuscript). Whatever their differences, both camps adopted a generally sober view toward legal action as a resource for egalitarian social change and emphasized the study of contextual factors for understanding variable outcomes of litigation and other legal campaigns. A few years later a much cited volume of essays in the *University of Pennsylvania Law Review* (see especially Rubin 2001, Eskridge 2001, Siegel 2001) was dedicated to a separate analysis of law and social movements. Moreover, the most recent volume of the ongoing cause lawyering project by leading socio-legal scholars has focused specifically on the role of activist attorneys in social movements (Sarat & Scheingold 2006). Finally, scholars interested in social movement activity beyond the United States, in both national and transnational contexts, increasingly have focused on law and rights as important dimensions of struggles for justice.

Overall, these latter trends are welcome and signal promising lines of inquiry. However, there remain some problematic tendencies that limit even these recent scholarly efforts to connect law and social movements. For one thing, much of the new literature echoes old position-taking between those scholars who insist on complementary relationships between legal tactics and social movements and those who see mostly counterproductive tensions. This normative position-taking on the instrumental value of legal tactics is especially evident among law school scholars.

[2]Handler's (1978) classic drew heavily on resource mobilization models that were popular in the 1970s, and McCann (1986) integrated a mix of different theoretical elements into the study of law and social elements. But these are rare exceptions among scholarship prior to the 1990s.

For example, Eskridge (2001) has written an influential set of articles aiming to correct the failure of social scientists who study social movements to appreciate law and legal actors. In making his case, he generalizes repeatedly that "law and legal actors are critical to the instigation and dynamics, as well as the goals" of identity politics by social movements (Eskridge 2001, pp. 421–22). By contrast, Brown-Nagin (2005) challenges such a view in a study of recent affirmative action cases, contending that "social movements and juridical law are fundamentally in tension.... Social movements are more likely to achieve their goals when they are free from the constraints imposed by law and lawyers—even the politically astute ones" (p. 1502). Such entrenched normative commitments often overdetermine empirical accounts and discourage attention to the complexities, contingencies, and ironies at stake in legal mobilization. This contrasts with most social scientists who, while varying in the degrees of inherent skepticism about the proclivities of lawyers, litigation, and courts for promoting egalitarian social change, tend to view the relationships of social movement mobilization as highly variable and contingent on a mix of legal and extralegal social factors that should be the subject of empirical inquiry. "How law does and does not matter" is the key question, not taking sides in debates over instrumental effectiveness. As McCann (2004) has put it,

> Legal mobilization does not inherently disempower or empower citizens. How law matters depends on the complex, often changing dynamics of the context in which struggles occur. Legal relations, institutions, and norms tend to be double-edged, at once upholding the larger infrastructure of the status quo while providing limited opportunities for episodic challenges and transformations in that ruling order.[3]

Such study of how law matters for social movements is infinitely more complex, mixed, variable, and contingent than can be captured in simple position statements.[4]

Moreover, little effort to develop generalizable theoretical frameworks for understanding social movement engagements with law in comparative perspective has informed much of the recent study. Both the legal mobilization approach grounded in political process models of social movements and judicial impact studies historically have emphasized the systematic study of sociopolitical context as essential. Theorizing by social movement scholars—from resource mobilization and

[3]See also Scheingold (1974), Rosenberg (1991), McCann (1998), and Lovell & McCann (2004).

[4]"Hence although law in the aggregate surely tends to support hierarchical power relations, analysis should be attentive to the variability of legal conventions and practices within different contexts. In particular, we should be sensitive to how different legal norms and institutional arenas over time offer varying degrees of opportunity or space for creative challenge.... This is the primary thrust of the decentered view of law advanced here: not only that law is pluralistic and relatively independent of the state, but that its role in sustaining traditional hierarchies, and hence in structuring potential strategies of resistance, varies significantly among different terrains of social struggle" (McCann 1994, pp. 9–10).

political process models to theorizing about new social movements, framing theory, and concepts of contentious politics—has provided catalysts to continued development of socio-legal theory. However, although some legal scholars borrow from and dabble in social movement theory, few are concerned about theoretical development. The general debate between legal optimists and pessimists has hardly encouraged development of comparative analytical theory. Scholars focusing on cause lawyering have provided many interesting new case studies and insights, but they too generally have contributed little to theory building about movement dynamics.

Finally, many of the more recent studies build on relatively narrow but unarticulated conceptions of law, mostly focusing on litigation outcomes and the roles of lawyers. Old debates about whether lawyers are privileged elites or effective grassroots allies, whether courts can be relied on to respond to marginal voices, and the like continue to thrive. Again, position-taking tends to occlude attention to variation and contingency, and analyses cabining law to litigation, lawyers, and case law talk past and mischaracterize other more expansive understandings of law as cultural norms that have a life in resistances to and transformative mobilization apart from, and often at odds with, mainstream elite constructions of law. The point is not that there is a single correct or best framework for understanding law, but rather that much scholarship is committed to making claims about law without clearly thinking through the complex, multiple dimensions of what often are recognized as law and legality. The result is more heat than light, in this author's view.

These deficiencies and differences in the literature pose a daunting challenge for a review essay on scholarship about law and social movements. My solution is to draw on one approach to organize my review of the disparate arguments and insights advanced by other scholars. The general legal mobilization approach best serves the purpose for at least four reasons. It is (*a*) the most expansive and synthetic approach, thus facilitating organized integration of different contributions; (*b*) the most extensively grounded in social movement theory, building on political process models but adding other elements from other theories; (*c*) least committed to a simple view about the role of law in social movements, adopting instead a tragic view about law's considerable constraints and limited opportunities that vary with context; and (*d*) most adaptable by scholars outside the United States working in comparative and transnational studies (see O'Brien 1996, Keck & Sikkink 1998, Rajagopal 2003, Diamant et al. 2005, Santos & Rodriguez 2005, Shin 2006). Astute readers might also recognize that this general approach shamelessly draws most on my own scholarship, which means I am also least likely to misrepresent its aims and logic.

LAW AND SOCIAL MOVEMENTS: DEFINING CONCEPTS

Conceptualizing Law

Much of the diversity in assessing how law matters for social movements derives from quite divergent ways of understanding and studying law itself. Most generally, we use the term law to signify different types of phenomena. We refer sometimes to official legal institutions, like courts or administrative bureaucracies; sometimes to legal officials or elites, such as judges, bureaucrats, or lawyers; and sometimes to legal norms, rules, or discourses that structure practices in and beyond official legal institutions (Thompson 1975). Most recent studies grant attention to all three usages, although in somewhat unclear or unsystematic ways. Legal realists and behavioralists, for example, tend to identify law primarily in instrumental, determinate, positivist terms. Law, in this account, matters to the degree that official institutional actions cause direct, immediate, tangible effects on targeted behaviors (Rosenberg 1991, Bogart 2002). Measured by such a standard, legal institutions and officials often appear to provide powerful support for the status quo but feeble sources for challenging the prevailing order. Legal scholars who focus on lawyers, litigation, and judicial impact tend toward this approach, even when addressing how legal action does or does not inspire movements. This instrumentalist/realist perspective tends to privilege judgments and debates about whether law is or is not useful for movements.

By contrast, interpretive, process-oriented legal mobilization approaches are typically much more expansive in conceptualizing law, especially regarding the legal norms and discursive logics at stake in many social struggles. The interpretive perspective begins by rejecting conventional positivist understandings of law largely limited to discrete, determinate rules or policy actions and policy actors. Rather, law is understood as particular traditions of knowledge and communicative practice. The focus is not simply on behavior but on the intersubjective power of law in constructing meaning. As such, attention is directed to how legal discourses and symbols intersect with and are expressive of broader ideological formations within societies (Hunt 1990, McCann 1994, McCann & March 1996). Attention to legal meanings does not necessarily preclude instrumental considerations about effects or impacts of litigation, lawyers, and courts, but the latter are not the exclusive or even primary focus of inquiry. Indeed, most legal mobilization studies focus on the legal naming, blaming, and claiming by social movement activists in spaces where the shadows of official law and actors are often quite dim.

Such an understanding of law as knowledge and linguistic practice calls attention to law's power as a constitutive convention of social life (Brigham 1996). This constitutive power is ambiguous. On the one hand, legal knowledges to some degree shape, or prefigure, the identities and practical activities of subjects in society. Learned legal conventions mold the very terms of citizen understanding, expectation, and interaction with others. Law thus is a significant part of how we learn to live and act as citizens in society. Legal constructs shape our very capacities to imagine social or political possibilities. Among the most important of liberal legal conventions constituting both national and transnational relations are what we call rights—those legal forms that designate the distribution of legitimate social entitlements and burdens among citizens.

On the other hand, law is also understood to be a resource that citizens utilize to structure relations with others, to advance goals in social life, to formulate rightful claims, and to negotiate disputes where interests, wants, or principles collide. Legal knowledges thus can matter as both ends and means of action; law provides both normative principles and strategic resources for the conduct of social struggle. Indeed, this is the core meaning of what many scholars label legal mobilization: "Law is mobilized when a desire or want is translated into an assertion of right or lawful claim" (Zemans 1983). Most such specific legal claims refer, of course, to settled, relatively uncontested entitlements. But at other times citizens interpret laws in different ways, reconstructing law in the process to fit shifting visions of need and circumstance; we reconstitute to some degree the law that constitutes us. In this sense, legal conventions are understood as a quite plastic and malleable medium, routinely employed to reconfigure relations, redefine entitlements, and formulate aspirations for collective living. The concept of rights consciousness—as a developing understanding of social relations in terms of rights—has been particularly important for analysis of law and social movements throughout the world (McCann 1994, Marshall 2003).

This indeterminacy or plasticity of legal conventions is limited, of course. Legal practices carry with them their own inherent constraints on what is accepted as legally sensible or compelling, whereas governing authorities often impose even tighter constraints on accepted meaning through organized force. Official institutions function to police the range of law's legitimate meanings, to enforce boundaries on those meanings, and to use selectively organized violence against those who violate official readings of law or who are outside law's inherent protections. But law also thrives outside of such direct police power intervention, and outside of courtrooms in particular, where official legal meanings rule only indirectly as a possibility of intervening force to settle disputes or enforce particular legal practices. Indeed, this possibility, either implicit or explicitly threatened, that official third parties (such as judges or police) might intervene tends to shape social interaction and bargaining relations far more than actual direct official interventions (Galanter 1983).

It is law's complex life throughout society—within workplaces, corporate boardrooms, neighborhoods, and communities and throughout institutionalized public spaces of national and transnational politics—under the shadow of official rule on which most conflict-based, process-oriented studies of law and social movements focus attention. Indeed, the primary project of legal mobilization analysis is aimed at the constitutive role of legal rights both as a strategic resource and as a constraint, as a source of empowerment and disempowerment, for struggles to transform, or to reconstitute, the terms of social relations and power (see Scheingold 1989, Silverstein 1996). This understanding is especially important for appreciating the increasing power of human rights norms around the world, within polities and transnational or international arenas where authoritative legal institutions are often underdeveloped or contested.

One more aspect of law fills out the picture. In short, most scholars in the process-oriented, constitutive approach presume that law is a partial and contingent force in society. This calls attention, on the one hand, to the fact that legal tactics of social movements are usually coordinated with other political tactics such as legislative lobbying, partisan electoral advocacy, media campaigns, information disclosure, or public protest. Indeed, much study emphasizes that litigation and other official legal actions are most commonly and effectively utilized as a secondary or supplementary political strategy in social movement struggles. Similarly, this literature emphasizes that lawyers often are not only, or even primarily, litigators; they negotiate, counsel, coordinate, and even sometimes work to educate and mobilize movement constituents and resources (McCann & Silverstein 1998). The legalistic, litigation-obsessed propensities of some lawyers thus can divert or drain movement energies, but this is hardly always the case. On the other hand, the legal mobilization approach recognizes as well that legal conventions constitute just one of the many variable types of norms that govern and give meaning to social life. This suggests that any assessment of specific legal mobilization practices by social movements must be undertaken with reference to the larger context of multiple legal and extralegal norms or discourses that structure social relations.

Social Movements

The core term "social movements" is defined in quite variable ways by scholars, including by specialists on the topic. Tilly's (1984, p. 306) definition is as useful as any. A social movement is

> a sustained series of interactions between powerholders and persons successfully claiming to speak on behalf of a constituency lacking formal representation, in the course of which those persons make publicly visible demands for changes in the distribution or exercise of power, and back those demands with public demonstrations of support.

The problem with this definition is that it does not clearly distinguish social movements from interest groups, minority political parties, protesting mobs, civil disobedience, terrorist violence, and other forms of collective action. Scholarly efforts have been made to differentiate social movements by what they want, whom they represent, and what tactics they use—but few such efforts are entirely successful at an abstract level. The dilemma is exacerbated, further, by the fact that the organization and activities of what we call social movements often overlap with, grow out of, or transform into other forms of organization over time in complex, elusive ways. Indeed, frustrations over defining the boundaries of the term social movements have led several leading scholars to abandon the concept for the broader, more inclusive label of contentious politics (McAdam et al. 2001).

Despite these caveats, however, I limit the range of activity referred to as social movements for the purposes of this review. Social movement activity here is identified broadly with social struggles of a particular type. First, social movements aim for a broader scope of social and political transformation than do other more conventional political activities. Although social movements may press for tangible short-term goals within the existing structure of relations, they are animated by more radical aspirational visions of a different, better society. Second, social movements often employ a wide range of tactics, as do parties and interest groups, but they are far more prone to rely on communicative strategies of information disclosure and media campaigns as well as disruptive symbolic tactics such as protests, marches, strikes, and the like that halt or upset ongoing social practices. One of the surprising findings of much research is that litigation and other seemingly conventional legal tactics sometimes can be fused with such disruptive forms of political expression. Law sometimes serves disorder as well as order (Lowi 1971). Litigation can provide a form of, or forum for, rebellion (Meranto 1998) as well as a lethal weapon in social conflict (Turk 1976).

Third, social movements tend to develop from core constituencies of nonelites whose social position reflects relatively low degrees of wealth, prestige, or political clout. Although movements may find leadership or alliance among elites and powerful organizations, the core indigenous population of social movements tends to be "the nonpowerful, the nonwealthy and the nonfamous" (Zirakzadeh 1997). It is worth noting that this definition can include reactionary or highly conservative as well as progressive or left-leaning movements, although the overwhelming amount of academic study concerns the latter groups. Fourth, the discussion below includes traditional modernist social movements focusing on class relations and material politics as well as new (or postmodern) social movements that emphasize a broad range of principled social justice commitments, including especially human rights (Beuchler & Cylke 1997). Lastly, this review addresses social movements that develop within particular nations, generally focused on states as targets or means of transforming societies, as well as transnational movements for human rights, environmental change, peace, and the like. Studies of transnational activism have developed rapidly in recent years and tend to rely on dynamic process-based approaches similar to those emphasized here (Keck & Sikkink 1998, Santos & Rodriguez-Garavito 2005). Indeed, cooperation among transnational and domestic national social movements on human rights issues is one of the most important manifestations of contemporary legal mobilization politics (Sarat & Scheingold 2001).

LEGAL PRACTICES OF SOCIAL MOVEMENTS: A BROADLY PROCESS-BASED OVERVIEW

With these general understandings in mind, we can now review some of the insights generated by scholars about law and social movements. The legal mobilization approach in particular envisions social disputing or struggles as processes that involve different moments or stages of development and conflict. This discussion of law's workings in various social movements proceeds by focusing on potential stages of conflict. At each stage, I attempt to give examples of instances in which legal tactics and practices have proved empowering as well as disempowering for various movements.

I must emphasize at the outset, however, that legal practices or mobilization activities rarely are imposed as exogenous or alien forces on social relations. Social terrains of struggle themselves are always constituted by a complex array of institutional norms, relations, and structures of power, including in most cases legally authorized norms backed up by the violence of individual states, coalitions of states, or transnational institutions like the United Nations. Hence, legal mobilization politics typically involves reconstructing legal dimensions of inherited social relations, either by turning official but ignored legal norms against existing practices, by reimagining shared norms in new, transformative ways, or by importing legal norms from some other authoritative source into the context of the dispute. Again, law often significantly supports prevailing social relations as well as provides limited resources for challenging those relationships. This is one point on which virtually all scholars agree. Social movement struggles often entail struggles over the very meaning of indeterminate, contradictory legal principles.

Finally, law's meanings and constitutive force vary dramatically with different contexts. One major preoccupation of scholars is in identifying those factors internal and external to law that shape its relative significance. Scholars who focus on top-down approaches to judicial impact outline the variables that most influence the force of court decisions (Rosenberg 1991, Canon & Johnson 1998). Similarly, scholars who focus on process-based approaches to studying law in social movements emphasize various contextual factors. Opportunity structures, movement resources, and discursive terrains or legal consciousness are familiar organizing categories for such analyses. Some of the most interesting and important contributions of scholarship on social movements derive from this attention. Unfortunately, however, limited space does not permit discussion of these issues in the remaining pages of this essay. The best remedy for these important omissions is to read the leading original studies themselves.

Law and the Genesis of Social Movements

Perhaps the most significant point at which law matters for many social movements is during the earliest phases of organizational and agenda formation. The core insight has been expressed by Scheingold's (1974) well-known argument regarding the "politics of rights" (p. 131). As he put it, it is possible for marginalized groups "to capitalize on the perceptions of entitlement associated with (legal) rights to initiate and to nurture political mobilization." This process of what is conventionally labeled "rights consciousness raising" can be understood to involve two separate, if often intimately related, processes of cognitive transformation in movement constituents.

The first of these cognitive transformations entails the process of agenda setting by which movement actors draw on legal discourses to name and to challenge existing social wrongs or injustices. As such, legal norms and traditions can become important elements in the process of explaining how existing relationships are unjust, in defining collective group goals, and in constructing a common identity among diversely situated citizens (Schneider 1986, McCann 1994). "One of the main tasks that social movements undertake . . . is to make possible the previously unimaginable, by framing problems in such a way that their solution comes to appear inevitable," note Keck & Sikkink (1998, pp. 40–41). Some scholars emphasize ways in which sense of injury and political challenge are formulated in legal terms from the outset, while yet others emphasize the process of translation from nonlegal grievances to legal claims (M. Paris, unpublished manuscript). In either case, scholars emphasize how the very identities, interests, and ideals of movement activists can be constituted by, or even against, law (Brigham 1996).

A second related way in which legal practices can contribute to movement building is by reconstructing the overall opportunity structure within which movements develop (Anderson 2005). This insight draws on the common scholarly premise that movement formation and action are more likely in periods when dominant groups and state-authorized relationships are perceived as vulnerable to challenge (Piven & Cloward 1979, McAdam 1982). Advances through formal legal advocacy—and especially through high-profile litigation—many times have contributed to this sense of vulnerability among both state and nonstate authorities. In particular, judicial victories can impart salience or legitimacy to general categories of claims, such as equal rights, as well as to specific formulations of challenges within these broad legal traditions (Scheingold 1974, Burstein & Monaghan 1986, Burstein 1991a,b, Silverstein 1996). Indeed, many scholars have noted a sort of contagion effect generated by rights litigation over the past 40 years in the United States (Tarrow 1983, Epp 1998), by legal rights mobilization increasingly in other regions such as the European Union (Cichowski 2002), and by human rights advocacy around the world (Keck & Sikkink 1998). There is some evidence that legal mobilization often succeeds in movement building because the mass media tend to be particularly responsive to rights claims and litigation campaigns for social justice, although this evidence is primarily limited to the U.S. experience (McCann 1994, Haltom 1998) and is contested even there (Rosenberg 1991). It is also worth noting that such opportunities for mobilization typically define just one of several potential venues for activity, each of which may vary widely in its promise. Moreover, opportunities often carry with them significant constraining or disciplining logics whereby legal action requires moderation of claims, narrowing of demands, or forfeiting of other tactics. The history of U.S. labor activism exemplifies this point well (Forbath 1991), as do the legacies of labor struggle, gay and lesbian rights advocacy (Cain 1993, Anderson 2005), and other modes of human rights advocacy (Dezalay & Garth 2001) in various regions of the world.

These two dimensions of legal activism typically are interrelated in social movement development. For example, formal legal actions like litigation can work initially to expose systemic vulnerabilities and to render legal claims sensible or salient to aggrieved citizens. As marginalized groups act on these opportunities, they often gain sophistication and confidence in their capacity to mobilize legal conventions to name wrongs, to direct blame, to frame demands, and to advance their cause. When citizens "begin to assert their 'rights' that imply demands for change," Piven & Cloward (1979) noted long ago, there often develops "a new sense of efficacy; people who ordinarily consider themselves helpless come to believe that they have some capacity to alter their lot" (p. 4).

This complex process of legal catalysis was illustrated by the U.S. civil rights movement in the 1950s. A program of litigation leading up to the famous 1954 *Brown v. Board of Edu*cation decision was vital to the evolving civil rights movement in two ways. First, it sparked southern blacks' hopes by demonstrating that the southern white power structure was vulnerable at some points and by providing scarce practical resources for defiant action (Glennon 1991). Second, the increasing pressure on the southern white power structure to abolish racial domination led to a massive, highly visible attack—including legal assaults as well as physical violence—on the formal black leadership group, the National Association for the Advancement of Colored People (NAACP). These reactions in turn forced a split between local NAACP leaders urging more radical forms of protest action and the more bureaucratic, legally oriented leaders of the national organization. The result was a burst in both the momentum of the grassroots protest campaign among southern blacks generally and their frustration about the effectiveness of legal tactics alone. "The two approaches—legal action and mass protest—entered into a turbulent but workable marriage" (Morris 1984, p. 39; see also Polletta 1994). Moreover, the resulting escalation of conflicts between whites and blacks on both fronts expanded the scope of the dispute to include Washington officials, federal courts, the northern media, and national public opinion. Court decisions alone thus did not cause, by moral inspiration, defiant black grassroots action or, by coercion, federal support for the civil rights agenda. Critics like Rosenberg (1991) are correct in making this narrow claim. But legal tactics pioneered by the NAACP figured very prominently in the ongoing process of elevating civil rights claims and intensifying the initial terms of racial struggle in the South.

Similar dynamics have been evident in the movements for the rights of the disabled, gay rights, animal rights, and women's rights in the United States. These examples are especially interesting because they demonstrate that conclusive, far-reaching victories in courts or other official forums are not necessary to achieve this legal catalyzing effect. The wage equity issue in the United States, for example, largely developed in response to the limitations of traditional court-approved affirmative action policies for remedying discrimination against women workers locked into segregated jobs. After a string of defeats in the 1970s, the wage equity movement won a small victory in wage discrimination law at the Supreme Court level and one pathbreaking lower court ruling, which later was overturned on appeal. But in the five-year interim between the first and the last of these three rulings, movement leaders effectively used legal actions—despite doctrinal case law limitations—to organize women workers in hundreds of workplaces around the nation. A massive publicity campaign focusing on court victories initially put the issue on the national agenda and alerted leaders that wage equity was the working women's issue of the 1980s. Lawsuits were then filed on behalf of working women as the centerpiece of a successful union and movement organizing strategy in scores of local venues around the nation. Again, the evidence suggests not that court decisions worked to enlighten working women about their subordination, as sometimes is claimed. Rather, sustained legal action over time worked to render employers vulnerable to challenge, to expand the resources available to working women, to provide them a unifying claim of egalitarian rights, and to increase both their confidence and sophistication in advancing those claims (McCann 1994). Other scholars more recently have expanded on such insights in important ways by drawing on concepts of movement legal "framing" developed by social scientists (Marshall 2003, Pedriana 2004).

These latter insights are particularly relevant to appreciating the considerable power of human rights advocacy in defining challenges to authoritarian regimes. Indeed, framing social issues as human rights issues has often been quite effective and empowering for movement mobilization. Abel (1995) has shown how "speaking law to power" provided a potent orienting frame for mobilizing challenges to apartheid in South Africa. The enterprise of renaming women's rights as human rights, and specifically of challenging female circumcision as violence against women, has redefined the symbolic terrain of struggle and mobilized support by nongovernmental organizations (NGOs) for women's issues around the globe in recent decades (Keck & Sikkink 1998). There is also evidence that rights advocacy, often supplemented by litigation or other legal tactics, has generated considerable movement-building impetus in the European Union (Cichowski 2002), various parts of Latin America (Santos 1995, Cleary 1997, Meili 2001), and East Asia (O'Brien 1996, Diamant et al. 2005, Shin 2006).

Legal action often fails as a resource for expanding social movement activism, of course, largely owing to the absence of favorable social conditions. Extra-legal social factors undermined to some degree various environmental justice campaigns and actions for the poor or homeless (Harris 2004) in the United States. Many labor rights campaigns against the sweatshop conditions of U.S.-owned factories in developing countries and human rights campaigns against authoritarian violence, such as the massacre of protesting students in Mexico City's Tlatelolco Plaza and in Central Europe (Keck & Sikkink 1998), have proved similarly limited in capacity to mobilize strong movement support and public attention. Feminists in Israel likewise were unable to use notable victories in the Israeli High Court of Justice as effective grassroots mobilizing resources (Woods 2001).

Moreover, legal tactics have arguably worked sometimes to discourage, thwart, or contain social movement development. For example, the successful litigation represented by *Brown* clearly anchored the civil rights movement on a narrow desegregationist track, marginalizing black leaders with quite different visions of justice and transformation (Anderson 2003) and arguably containing or co-opting the possibilities of movement development. One common critique is that legal tactics divert resources to lawyers who focus on litigation rather than on grassroots mobilization and other forms of potentially more effective political organizing (Scheingold 1974, McCann & Silverstein 1998). There is some limited evidence for this tendency for particular struggles in many countries (McCann 1986,

Rosenberg 1992, Morag-Levine 2001, Brown-Nagin 2005) as well as for the thesis that lawyers are often co-opted or constrained by the elite institutional relations in which they are enmeshed (Handler 1978). Dezalay & Garth's (2001) argument about the containment of human rights lawyers' agendas in Latin America resulting from their dependence on U.S. foundations and target states identifies an especially sobering pattern of constraints in this regard.

Legal Mobilization as Political Pressure

Other dimensions of social movement activity involve a common legal dynamic. In particular, legal advocacy often provides movement activists a source of institutional and symbolic leverage against opponents. This coercive, adversarial dimension of legal mobilization in many ways is the flip side of its generative or consensus-building capacities. As in movement-building efforts, this second dimension of legal mobilization often but not always entails some measure of litigation or other formal legal action. In fact, we shall see that triumph in the courts is not always necessary to either short- or long-term successful legal leveraging. This is hardly a pathbreaking insight, of course, for it has been the primary focus of related studies on judicial impact (Rosenberg 1991, Canon & Johnson 1998, Bogart 2002). The uses of legal tactics and threats to compel informal resolution of everyday private disputes regarding divorce settlement, contractual obligations, liability for property damages, and the like are familiar to legal scholars (Galanter 1983). However, the complex dialectical relationship between formal and informal legal action in social movement politics has generally received less scholarly attention (but see Handler 1978, Olson 1984, Silverstein 1996).

There are several ways in which litigation offers formidable tactical leverage for social policy advocates. For one thing, institutions and groups targeted by reformers often are well aware that litigation can impose substantial costs in terms of both direct expenditures and long-term financial burdens. Indeed, court costs in major public disputes—over race and gender discrimination, unsafe workplaces, or environmental damage, for example—may run in the millions of dollars and can tie up economically vital operations for years. More important, powerful public and private interests typically fear losing control of decision-making autonomy—whether concerning capital investment, wage policy, externalized costs, or the like—to outside parties such as judges. Hence, they have a stake in cutting potential losses by negotiated settlements of conflicts directly with reform activists. Finally, one should not discount the symbolic normative power of rights claims themselves. Because populations around the world increasingly are responsive to rights claims, defiant groups often can mobilize legal norms, conventions, and demands to compel concessions even in the absence of clear judicial or other official support (Scheingold 1974, 1989; Handler 1978). Again, media propensities to publicize legal rights claims, especially when taken to official tribunes and linked to dramatic information disclosure, can magnify the public power of legal mobilization pressure tactics in many settings (McCann 1994, Keck & Sikkink 1998).

The implicit promise at stake here is that political struggles may advance more quickly, cheaply, and effectively when conducted in the shadow of favorable legal norms and threats of judicial intervention. Such legal gambits are hardly costless guarantees of success for social reformers, of course. Initiating legal action often does not generate concessions from powerful opponents, and thus may commit movement supporters to long, costly, high-risk legal proceedings that they can afford far less than their institutional foes. Even more important, eventual defeat in official forums can sap movement morale, undercut movement bargaining power, and exhaust movement resources. Consequently, legal leveraging is most successful when it works as an unfulfilled threat, but activists must be willing to follow through occasionally with action or lose considerable clout. In any case, the symbolic manifestations of law, as both a source of moral right and threat of potential outside intervention, invest rights discourse with its most fundamental social power.

It stands to reason that legal leveraging practices tend to depend on the existence of independent judiciaries or other official legal institutions, rules granting standing for legal action by relevant social movement groups, and a well-developed support structure of lawyers, organizations, and financial resources for legal advocacy (McCann 1994, Epp 1998). These conditions have long existed to some degree in the United States, especially with the proliferation of public interest law firms and cause lawyers in the post–World War II era. Many other nations have traditionally possessed some but not all of these elements. For example, many nations have national courts and constitutions, but those judiciaries often lack independence and, partially as a result, strong networks of legal advocates for opposition movements (Epp 1998). However, formal institutional structures, access to rights advocates, and networks of support for legal mobilization have proliferated across the globe at both national and transnational levels. The explosion of human rights, environmental, peace, and indigenous people's NGOs and cause lawyers along with the growth of regional (European Court of Justice) and international (World Court, United Nations) adjudicatory institutions has facilitated the rise of legal leveraging as a key tactic of social movement politics around the globe (Sarat & Scheingold 2001). Most notably, as Keck & Sikkink (1998) demonstrate, transnational human rights organizations often ally with domestic groups to produce boomerang pressures for change that effectively bypass traditional forms of state resistance.

As noted above, the deployment of legal resources to pressure dominant groups takes place at different points of movement struggles. I address two types of instrumental leverage here.

Generating Responsive Action

One phase of many struggles entails using legal tactics in an effort to generate responsiveness to basic policy demands, or at least some partial concessions, by the state or other authority. Silverstein (1996) has demonstrated how this tactic has generated some relatively important effects by the U.S. animal rights movement in recent years. In a variety of instances, she illustrates, litigation has been used to dramatize abuses of animals, to embarrass particular institutional actors, and to win favorable media attention. When carefully coordinated with demonstrations and other media events, high-profile litigation worked as a double-barreled threat, at once mobilizing public opinion against targeted abusers and threatening costly legal proceedings and possible defeats in court. Overall, such legal tactics have proved to be one of the movement's most effective modes of forcing change by state and nonstate authorities alike. Paris (unpublished manuscript) and Reed (2001) have separately demonstrated a similar dynamic in the very different state-level campaign for egalitarian school finance reform in the United States.

Such examples confirm again some often overlooked aspects of legal leveraging tactics. For one thing, these cases illustrate that repeated clear victories in courts or other official institutions are not necessary to effective legal mobilization. In some successful struggles, lawsuits have failed to generate appellate decisions directly authorizing many of the new rights and remedies that activists sought. The ability to win at least some small advances on related issues and to win a hearing in court for major claims often poses enough actual costs (bad publicity, legal fees) and potential risks (of judicially imposed policies) to pressure opponents into making significant concessions (Frymer 2003). Moreover, the very framing of issues in terms of rights can transform debates and add weight to claims. It is important to underline again, however, that legal tactics tend to be most useful in concert with other tactics, such as public demonstrations, legislative lobbying, collective bargaining, electoral mobilization, and media publicity. The fact that legal norms and institutional maneuvers constitute only one dimension of movement strategy complicates evaluation of their discrete contributions, to be sure. But, in each movement noted above, both activists and specific case histories confirm the importance of such contingent, secondary legal actions. Other notable examples of such legal leveraging dynamics could be cited from the environmentalist, consumer, women's rights, wage equity rights, civil rights, and disability rights movements in the United States.

Legal leveraging is often different and difficult in nations with less independent and powerful courts than in the United States. However, such tactics have generated influence for women's rights movements in specific European nations (Epp 1998), in the European Union (Cichowski 2002), in Latin America (Keck & Sikkink 1998, Santos & Rodriguez 2005), in East Asia (Diamant et al. 2005, Shin 2006), and in Israel (Woods 2001), Egypt (Moustafa 2003), Iran (Osanloo 2002), and other Middle Eastern nations. Human rights activity and litigation have provided a notable force for challenging authoritarian rule in Latin America, South Africa, Egypt, and other nations as well. Indeed, groups like Amnesty International and broader networks of rights activists have changed the whole calculus of politics within and between nations. Feldman (2000) has demonstrated in similar fashion how both rights and legal mobilization efforts have had great impact even in Japan, a nation where independent courts and cause lawyers traditionally have not played a major role in public policy.

Important examples of when legal tactics either have failed to generate or even have impeded progressive change are notable as well, however. The abortion case arguably offers a revealing legacy. Although U.S. feminists won support for women's right to choose in *Roe v. Wade*, the provision of both medical services and financial aid to pay for exercising those rights did not materialize to any great degree. What is more, *Roe* became the focus of a significant conservative countermovement bent on denying, or at least substantially restricting, the capacity of women to choose the abortion option (Rosenberg 1991). In short, legal tactics not only failed to leverage real change; they arguably undermined the potential for change that alternative tactics might have produced (but see Lemieux 2004). Similar patterns of failed campaigns can be seen in response to legal mobilization efforts around the globe, especially in places lacking strong legal traditions, institutions, and support structures of organized activists. Coglianese (2001) argues that the environmental movement was co-opted by bureaucratic processes and lost its critical, transformative vision in large part owing to its legalistic strategies. Morag-Levine (2001) has shown how litigation-focused, rights-oriented approaches imported from the United States fail, and actually divert effective politics, in more corporatist political contexts such as in Israel. Finally, rights-based legal mobilization efforts have generated backlashes in virtually every part of the world, including the United States, where social movements have attempted to challenge hierarchical social power and authoritarian state rule.

Policy Implementation and Enforcement

Legal leveraging often figures prominently at the policy implementation stage of political struggles as well. This is important, for gaining acceptance of new laws or policies on the books without effective policy implementation accomplishes little. And it is at this stage that many scholars, with some justification, have contended that legal tactics are most limited in significance. The most common explanation for these constraints is that both national and transnational courts generally lack the independence and resources to enforce their decisions against recalcitrant groups in government and society (Scheingold 1974, Handler 1978, McCann 1986, Rosenberg 1991).

Nevertheless, legal mobilization studies have provided some useful insights into how law can and sometimes does matter for struggles over policy implementation. In particular, a host of empirical inquiries have documented how legal tactics—and especially actual or threatened litigation—can help movement activists to win voice, position, and influence in the process of reform policy implementation, whether sanctioned by state or nonstate authorities. These include policy areas regarding the environment, gender and race discrimination, and the rights of the disabled, among others in the United States. There is evidence for similar dynamics in the European Union and in various nations around the world, but the politics of legal leveraging at implementation has been studied rather less than other stages of social movement activity.

Law is often especially important to one specific aim of many outsider groups—that of formalizing policy formulation and implementation processes. Formality, as understood here, refers to the degree to which relations are conducted according to procedures and standards that are public, general, explicit, and uniform (Lowi 1971). The core premise at stake here is that dominant groups tend to prefer relatively insular (autonomous or hidden) modes of discretionary policy implementation unhampered by standardized procedures, substantive guidelines, transparency, and outside supervision. In such informal settings, established prerogatives of powerful elites can more easily prevail to minimize costs, maintain control, and protect their own privileges while granting empty symbolic gestures to challengers. By contrast, marginalized groups often can benefit from more formalized processes in which specified procedural rights and substantive standards can be employed to render accountable dominant interests who control the bulk of material and organizational resources (Delgado et al. 1985).

Social movement groups often use litigation specifically to create such formal institutional access to state power or other institutions as well as to apply pressure to make that access consequential. In this way, legal resources may provide a series of more refined tools—basic procedures, standards, and practices—along with blunt leveraging tactics for shaping the structure of ongoing administrative relations at the remedial stage of struggles over policy (Galanter 1983). For example, Edelman (1990) has demonstrated how employers routinely established in-house offices to avoid litigation and maintain an appearance of good faith compliance with race-based affirmative action principles in the United States during the 1970s. Although initially established for largely deceptive or defensive purposes, such offices occasionally mobilized antidiscrimination norms and the specter of litigation to force real changes from within many corporate and state institutions. In many nations, this concern for formality likewise has led human rights and other activists to work for increased independence of courts, of judicial appointments, of the legal profession, and of procedures identified with the rule of law in an effort to provide leverage against recalcitrant state and social interests. Indeed, transnational NGOs, local opposition groups, and judges often form alliances that strengthen courts and groups alike against authoritarian or undemocratic rule. This process can be seen in Egypt, Israel, various Latin American nations, and the European Union since the 1980s, and even to some degree in various historical moments of American politics.

Of course, as judicial impact studies suggest, legal leveraging may offer as little to reformers in policy implementation battles as at other stages of struggle (Handler 1978, Rosenberg 1991). The fact that judges and other legal officials shrink from cases requiring great technical knowledge and experience may make leveraging tactics less effective generally at the policy implementation stage. Moreover, openly hostile courts can greatly undercut opportunities and deny resources in ways that actually disempower movement actors in the policy process. And even when courts act favorably for disadvantaged groups, injustice in most institutional settings will go unchallenged in the absence of well-organized constituencies willing to mobilize legal resources for change. Indeed, apparent advances in official law may add insult to injury for marginalized citizens lacking organizational resources. In short, law's relative formality does not always help reformers and may constitute a considerable constraint on action. Again, understanding these variations requires analysis of law's workings within the larger web of social relations where struggle occurs.

THE LEGACY OF LAW IN/FOR STRUGGLE

A final dimension of movement activity requires the most complex, subtle, and unique reflections both about law and about social change. This can be labeled the legacy phase. It concerns the aftermath of movement struggles for people, relationships, and institutions throughout society. Legacies surely include movement agents and targets of specified policy reform actions, but they can include far more general or unintended implications as well. These latter sorts of implications are the least studied aspect of law and change, so I rely heavily on my own research to illustrate very briefly my point.

In my own studies of wage equity in over a dozen organizational settings in the United States, I found that the direct and tangible policy accomplishments were modest but important (McCann 1994). While women's jobs were accorded rather less than full equity, women often received increases of 10% to 25% in their wages. But interviews with women revealed that the increases were not the only, or even the most important, gain. Rather, women workers repeatedly reported matters of what we might call workplace empowerment. They testified that their individual sense of efficacy as citizens was greatly enhanced and that their identification with other women workers had been increased markedly. The latter was related to a growth in the organizational power of women within their unions and of their unions relative to their employers. Many women specifically talked about the significance of increased rights consciousness that resulted from the legal mobilization efforts around wage equity. The result is that, in most workplaces, the pay equity struggle quickly gave rise to new issue demands for maternity leave, fringe benefits, job mobility opportunities, better work conditions, and the like. In short, the very context of discursive possibility and relational power often was transformed to some degree.

Such evidence makes it hard to deny that law and legal mobilization activity made a difference in many people's lives and institutional situations. At the same time, my study did not find this same outcome everywhere. In some venues, there was little clear trace of positive change; in some workplaces, conditions had even deteriorated and women involved in the earlier struggle had largely given up or left. Similarly mixed legacies can be traced in the aftermath of the black civil rights movement, the second wave of women's rights activism, environmental legal advocacy, prisoner rights advocacy, animal rights, and other movements in the United States. Yet other movements—including advocacy for gay and lesbian rights, welfare rights, and rights of the homeless—have found very little at all to cheer about in the records of legal action. Indeed, legal rights claiming and appeals to official legal institutions in many cases have generated far more backlash or countermobilization from reactionary political forces in the United States (Rosenberg 1991, Goldberg-Hiller 2002, Haltom & McCann 2004, Dudas 2003, but also see Lemieux 2004).

It is quite early to assess the legacies of rights-based legal mobilization by social movements in other parts of the world, but evidence likewise suggests a wide range of implications. Specific human rights struggles have often generated considerable drama and transformed the terms of political struggles, but patterns of significant change in social relations, state power, and material welfare have been more variable. As noted above, legal mobilization efforts have generated the full gambit of short-term impacts on social relations, and variability in the longer-term implications—from transformative legacies to backlash—are only to be expected. Attention to the backlashes and retrenchment following rights-based movement struggles defines one of the most important and interesting areas of future inquiry for socio-legal scholars.

That brings us back to the starting point on which most analysts agree: Legal mobilization tactics do not inherently empower or disempower citizens. Legal institutions and norms tend to be Janus-faced, at once securing the status quo of hierarchical power while sometimes providing limited opportunities for episodic challenges to and transformations in that reigning order (Scheingold 1974). How law matters depends on the complex, often changing dynamics of the context in which struggles occur.

The *Annual Review of Law and Social Science* is online at http://lawsocsci.annualreviews.org

LITERATURE CITED

Abel R. 1995. *Politics by Other Means: Law in the Struggle Against Apartheid, 1980–1994*. New York: Routledge

Anderson C. 2003. *Eyes Off the Prize: The United Nations and the African American Struggle for Human Rights, 1944–1955*. Cambridge, UK: Cambridge Univ. Press

Anderson EA. 2005. *Out of the Closets and into the Courts*. Ann Arbor: Univ. Mich. Press

Beuchler SM, Cylke FKJ, eds. 1997. *Social Movements: Perspectives and Issues*. Mountain View, CA: Mayfield

Bogart WA. 2002. *Consequences: The Impact of Law and Its Complexity*. Toronto: Univ. Toronto Press

Brigham J. 1996. *The Constitution of Interests: Beyond the Politics of Rights*. New York: NY Univ. Press

Brown-Nagin T. 2005. Elites, social movements, and the law: the case of affirmative action. *Columbia Law Rev*. 105:1436–528

Burstein P. 1991a. Legal mobilization as a social movement tactic: the struggle for equal employment opportunity. *Am. J. Sociol.* 96:1201–25

Burstein P. 1991b. Reverse discrimination cases in the federal courts: legal mobilization by a countermovement. *Sociol. Q.* 32(4):511

Burstein P, Monaghan K. 1986. Equal

employment opportunity and the mobilization of the law. *Law Soc. Rev.* 20:355–88

Cain P. 1993. Litigating for lesbians and gay rights: a legal history. *Va. Law Rev.* 79:1551–642

Canon BC, Johnson CA. 1998. *Judicial Policies: Implementation and Impact*. Washington, DC: Congr. Q. Press. 2nd ed.

Cichowski R. 2002. 'No discrimination whatsoever:' women's transnational activism and the evolution of European sex equality policy. In *Women's Community Activism and Globalization*, ed. N Naples, A Desai, pp. 220–38. New York: Routledge

Cleary EL. 1997. *The Struggle for Human Rights in Latin America*. Westport, CT: Praeger

Coglianese C. 2001. Social movements, law and society: the institutionalization of the environmental law movement. *Univ. Pa. Law Rev.* 150:85

Delgado R, Dunn C, Brown P, Lee H, Hubbert D. 1985. Fairness and formality: minimizing the risk of prejudice in alternative dispute resolution. *Wis. Law Rev.* 85:1359

Dezalay Y, Garth BG. 2001. Constructing law out of power: investing in human rights as an alternative political strategy. See Sarat & Scheingold 2001, pp. 354–81

Diamant N, Lubman SB, O'Brien KJ, eds. 2005. *Engaging Law in China: State, Society, and Possibilities for Justices*. Stanford, CA: Stanford Univ. Press

Dudas J. 2003. *Rights, resentment, and social change: treaty rights in contemporary America*. PhD thesis. Univ. Wash.

Edelman LB. 1990. Legal environments and organizational governance: the expansion of due process in the American workplace. *Am. J. Sociol.* 97:1401–40

Epp C. 1998. *The Rights Revolution: Lawyers, Activists, and Supreme Courts in Comparative Perspective*. Chicago: Univ. Chicago Press

Eskridge WNJ. 2001. Channeling: identity-based social movements and public law. *Univ. Pa. Law Rev.* 150:419

Feldman EA. 2000. *The Ritual of Rights in Japan: Law, Society, and Health Policy*. Cambridge, UK: Cambridge Univ. Press

Forbath WE. 1991. *Law and the Shaping of the American Labor Movement*. Cambridge, MA: Harvard Univ. Press

Frymer P. 2003. Acting when elected officials won't: federal courts and civil rights enforcement in U.S. labor unions 1935–85. *Am. Polit. Sci. Rev.* 3:483–99

Galanter M. 1983. The radiating effects of courts. In *Empirical Theories of Courts*, ed. KD Boyum, L Mather, pp. 117–42. New York: Longman

Glennon RJ. 1991. The role of law in the Civil Rights movement: the Montgomery bus boycott, 1955–1957. *Law Hist. Rev.* 9:59–112

Goldberg-Hiller J. 2002. *The Limits to Union: Same-Sex Marriage and the Politics of Civil Rights*. Ann Arbor: Univ. Mich. Press

Gottlieb SE, Schultz D, eds. 1998. *Leveraging the Law: Using Courts to Achieve Social Change*. New York: Lang

Haltom W. 1998. *Reporting on the Courts: How the Mass Media Cover Judicial Actions*. Chicago: Nelson-Hall

Haltom W, McCann M. 2004. *Distorting the Law: Politics, Media, and the Litigation Crisis*. Chicago: Univ. Chicago Press

Handler JF. 1978. *Social Movements and the Legal System: A Theory of Law Reform and Social Change*. New York: Academic

Harris B. 2004. *Defending the Right to a Home: The Power of Anti-Poverty Lawyers*. Hampshire, UK: Ashgate

Hunt A. 1990. Rights and social movements: counter-hegemonic strategies. *J. Law Soc.* 17:309–28

Keck ME, Sikkink K. 1998. *Activists Beyond Borders: Advocacy Networks in International Politics*. Ithaca, NY: Cornell Univ. Press

Lemieux S. 2004. *Constitutional politics and the political impact of abortion litigation: judicial power and judicial independence in comparative perspective*. PhD thesis. Univ. Wash.

Lovell G, McCann M. 2004. A tangled legacy: federal courts and the politics of democratic inclusion. In *The Politics of Democratic Inclusion*, ed. C Wolbrecht, RE Hero, pp. 257–80. Philadelphia, PA: Temple Univ. Press

Lowi TJ. 1971. *The Politics of Disorder*. New York: Basic Books

Marshall AM. 2003. Injustice frames, legality, and the everyday construction of sexual harassment. *Law Soc. Inq.* 28(3):659–90

McAdam D. 1982. *Political Process and the Development of Black Insurgency, 1930–1970*. Chicago: Univ. Chicago Press

McAdam D, Tarrow S, Tilly C. 2001. *Dynamics of Contention*. Cambridge, UK: Cambridge Univ. Press

McCann MW. 1986. *Taking Reform Seriously: Perspectives on Public Interest Liberalism*. Ithaca, NY: Cornell Univ. Press

McCann MW. 1992. Reform litigation on trial. *Law Soc. Inq.* 17(4):715–43

McCann MW. 1994. *Rights at Work: Pay Equity Reform and the Politics of Legal Mobilization*. Chicago: Univ. Chicago Press

McCann MW. 1996. Causal versus constitutive explanations (or, on the difficulty of being so positive. . .). *Law Soc. Inq.* 21(2):457–82

McCann MW. 1998. How does law matter for social movements? In *How Does Law Matter?* ed. B Garth, F Levine, A Sarat, pp. 76–108. Evanston, IL: Northwest. Univ. Press

McCann MW. 2004. Law and social movements. In *The Blackwell Companion to Law and Society*, ed. A Sarat, pp. 506–22. London: Blackwell/Dartmouth

McCann MW, March T. 1996. Law and everyday forms of resistance: a socio-political assessment. *Stud. Law Polit. Soc.* 15:207–36

McCann MW, Silverstein H. 1998. The 'lure of litigation' and other myths about cause lawyers. In *The Politics and Practice of Cause Lawyering*, ed. A Sarat, S Scheingold, pp. 261–92. New York: Oxford Univ. Press

Meili S. 2001. Latin American cause-lawyering networks. See Sarat & Scheingold 2001, pp. 307–33

Meranto O. 1998. Litigation as rebellion. In *Social Movements and American Political Institutions*, ed. A Costain, A McFarland, pp. 216–32. Lanham, MD: Rowman & Littlefield

Morag-Levine N. 2001. The politics of imported rights: transplantation and transformation in an Israeli environmental cause-lawyering organization. See Sarat & Scheingold 2001, pp. 334–53

Morris A. 1984. *The Origins of the Civil Rights Movement*. New York: Free Press

Moustafa T. 2003. *Law versus the state: the expansion of constitutional power in Egypt, 1980–2001*. PhD thesis. Univ. Wash.

O'Brien K. 1996. Rightful resistance. *World Polit.* 49(1):31–55

Olson SM. 1984. *Clients and Lawyers: Securing the Rights of Disabled Persons*. Westport, CT: Greenwood

Osanloo A. 2002. *At the juncture of Islam and republic: socio-legal constructions of women's rights in Iran*. PhD thesis. Dep. Cult. Soc. Anthropol., Stanford Univ.

Pedriana N. 2004. Help wanted NOW: legal resources, the women's movement, and the battle over sex-segregated job advertisements. *Soc. Probl.* 51(2):182–201

Piven FF, Cloward RA. 1979. *Poor People's Movements: Why They Succeed, How They Fail*. New York: Vintage

Polletta F. 1994. Strategy and identity in 1960s black protest. *Res. Soc. Mov. Confl. Chang.* 17:85–114

Polletta F. 2000. The structural context of novel rights claims: rights innovation in the southern Civil Rights movement, 1961–1966. *Law Soc. Rev.* 34:367–406

Rajagopal B. 2003. International law and social movements: challenges of theorizing resistance. *Columbia J. Transnatl. Law* 41:397

Reed D. 2001. *On Equal Terms: The Constitutional Politics of Educational Opportunity*. Princeton, NJ: Princeton Univ. Press

Rosenberg G. 1991. *The Hollow Hope: Can Courts Bring About Social Change?* Chicago: Univ. Chicago Press

Rosenberg G. 1992. Hollow hopes and other aspirations: a reply to Feeley and McCann. *Law Soc. Inq.* 17:761–78

Rosenberg G. 1996. Positivism, interpretivism, and the study of law: McCann's *Rights at Work*. *Law Soc. Inq.* 21:435–56

Rubin EL. 2001. Passing through the door: social movement literature and legal scholarship. *Univ. Pa. Law Rev.* 150:1–84

Santos BS. 1995. *Toward a New Common Sense: Law, Science, and Politics in the Paradigmatic Transition*. New York: Routledge

Santos BS, Rodríguez-Garavito CA, eds. 2005. *Law and Globalization from Below: Towards a Cosmopolitan Legality*. Cambridge, UK: Cambridge Univ. Press

Sarat A, Scheingold S, eds. 2001. *Cause Lawyering and the State in the Global Era*. Oxford: Oxford Univ. Press

Sarat A, Scheingold S. 2006. *Cause Lawyering and Social Movements*. Stanford, CA: Stanford Univ. Press. In press

Scheingold SA. 1974. *The Politics of Rights: Lawyers, Public Policy, and Political Change*. New Haven, CT: Yale Univ. Press

Scheingold SA. 1989. Constitutional rights and social change. In *Judging the Constitution*, ed. MW McCann, GL Houseman, pp. 73–91. Glenview, IL: Scott, Foresman/Little, Brown

Schneider EM. 1986. The dialectic of rights and politics: perspectives from the women's movement. *NY Univ. Law Rev.* 61:589–652

Shin K. 2006. *Women's legal mobilization in strong states*. PhD thesis. Dep. Polit. Sci., Univ. Wash.

Siegel RB. 2001. Text in context: gender and the Constitution from a social movement perspective. *Univ. Pa. Law Rev.* 150:297

Silverstein H. 1996. *Unleashing Rights: Law, Meaning, and the Animal Rights Movement*. Ann Arbor: Univ. Mich. Press

Tarrow S. 1983. *Struggling to reform: social movements and policy change during cycles of protest*. Cent. Int. Stud., West. Soc. Occas. Pap. No. 15, Cornell Univ., Ithaca, NY

Thompson EP. 1975. *Whigs and Hunters: The Origins of the Black Act*. New York: Pantheon

Tilly C. 1984. Social movements and national politics. In *Statemaking and Social Movements*, ed. C Bright, S Harding, pp. 297–317. Ann Arbor: Univ. Mich. Press

Turk A. 1976. Law as a weapon in social conflict. *Soc. Probl.* 23:276–91

Woods P. 2001. *Courting the court: social visions, state authority, and the religious law conflict in Israel*. PhD thesis. Dep. Polit. Sci., Univ. Wash.

Zemans FK. 1983. Legal mobilization: the neglected role of law in the political system. *Am. Polit. Sci. Rev.* 77:690–703

Zirakzadeh CE. 1997. *Social Movements in Politics: A Comparative Study*. London: Longman

Annu. Rev. Law Soc. Sci. 2006. 2:39–60
doi: 10.1146/annurev.lawsocsci.2.081805.110001

First published online as a Review in Advance on June 13, 2006

The Social and Legal Construction of Suspects

Simon A. Cole[1] and Michael Lynch[2]
[1]*Department of Criminology, Law & Society, University of California, Irvine, California 92697; email: scole@uci.edu*
[2]*Department of Science & Technology Studies, Cornell University, Ithaca, New York 14853; email: mel27@cornell.edu*

Key Words DNA evidence, criminal databases, suspect populations, forensic science

■ **Abstract** DNA profiling and searchable databases enhance the ability of policing organizations to search for criminal suspects. In many respects, these technologies are incorporated within traditions of police work, supplementing familiar "subjective" methods of constructing suspects. In other ways, however, the construction of DNA databases in Britain, the United States, and elsewhere shifts criminal investigation toward suspect populations and statistical suspects. Not only is DNA evidence used to confirm that a criminal suspect is the source of crime scene evidence, it can be used to search freely through a suspect population for a possible source of such evidence. This method, commonly known as database trawling, comprises a new way of constructing suspects, one that bears close connections with new data mining technologies for prospectively identifying terrorist suspects.

INTRODUCTION

What is a suspect? In common language, a suspect is a particular person who is an object of suspicion. Suspicion is the opposite of trust and thus represents a rupture in the taken-for-granted fabric of social life. In legal discourse, a suspect is circumscribed by a bundle of definitions, procedures, and rights, but, consistent with the broader opposition between trust and distrust, the suspect represents a potential threat to a taken-for-granted order. In this review, we discuss two categories of suspect: criminal suspects and suspect populations. We also discuss trace evidence and probability statistics, which often mediate between the two categories. We focus on novel features of suspects and suspect populations that have become increasingly prominent, and sometimes controversial, in recent years. Drawing on research in science and technology studies and law and criminology, this review critically examines a much-heralded transformation of criminal suspects through the use of novel forensic technologies and searchable databases.

THE CONSTRUCTION OF SUSPECTS

Criminal suspects—individuals suspected of having committed a particular crime—are the most familiar kind of suspect. However, there is another broad category of suspect: a suspect group, pool, or population. Technically, a suspect population includes anyone in the world who has not yet been excluded by the criminal evidence (Donnelly & Friedman 1999), but usually such populations are limited to groups convicted of past offenses or deemed likely to include possible offenders. Individuals who constitute suspect populations also may be suspected of posing a possible future threat. In the post-9/11 "War on Terror" by the U.S. government, suspect populations have taken on increased importance, and suspect and convict populations have converged in the novel category of enemy combatant (Cole 2003). However, criminal suspects and suspect populations have never been completely distinct, as societies tend to draw criminal suspects from suspect populations at a higher rate than from non-suspect or trusted populations, and the converse is probably true as well (Cole 2001, Knechtel 2005, Valier 1998).

How might a suspect be socially constructed? When social scientists call something constructed, they often draw a contrast to a conventional objectivist view, which holds that the object (entity, concept, idea) in question exists in the world, independent of the social processes that configure and apprehend it (Hacking 1999): In this case, an objectivist view holds that suspects are in the world and are identified by specific characteristics. Such a view can be attributed to many agents in the criminal justice system (especially police, prosecutors, and judges) who treat crimes as objective acts and criminals as individuals with specific character traits and behavioral tendencies. And, of course, the objectivist view has been supported by traditions of criminological research that have sought to define criminal types (Horn 2003, Pasquino 1991, Rafter 2004). In contrast, constructionists hold that suspects are constituted through social interaction with criminal justice agents, agencies, and processes. The agents deploy informal and formal typologies, which indiscriminately mix legal, scientific, and prejudicial categories. So, for example, in criminal investigations police often start with a pool of potentially suspicious persons based on evidence in the particular case, but as many studies have shown, membership in this pool is skewed by race, class, gender, and geographic characteristics. The pool of presuspects is progressively narrowed during criminal investigations, as police and prosecutors gather evidence that allows them to exclude individuals from further suspicion. As the pool narrows, the remaining individuals become increasingly suspect, until, in some cases, a single individual is identified: the prime suspect (Innes 2003, p. 233). In addition to narrowing the pool of suspects, the discretionary processes at each stage also differentially concentrate the demographic, socioeconomic, and cultural stigma that criminal justice agents associate with suspect status (Duster 2004).

Sociologists and criminologists have documented the construction of suspects with detailed studies of discretionary processes at every stage of criminal investigation. Ericson's (1981) work was groundbreaking by showing how detectives produce, rather than merely detect, suspects and crimes, and this vein has been further mined by Innes (2003) and, from a less constructionist perspective, Jackall (2005). Such studies portray detective work as a kind of pragmatic semiotics in which the detective uses experience and common sense to interpret clues, acting as a practical historian, semiotician, physician, or scientist (Eco & Sebeok 1983, Frank 2003, Sacks 1972, Thomas 1999).

Innes (2003) divides investigative processes into "focused" and "unfocused." Focused processes are directed by information about particular persons, whereas unfocused processes reflect broader trawls for information, such as house-to-house searches or media appeals. Detectives characterize murders, for example, either as "self-solvers," in which the perpetrator is obvious, or as "whodunits" that require lengthy investigation or trawling through suspect pools. For obvious reasons, police prefer focused investigation to trawling. In this review, however, we draw attention to an emerging shift toward trawling fueled by technology, especially DNA profiling and databases. Currently, this technology is heralded as an objective solution to the subjective and prejudicial discrimination associated with investigative practices such as racial profiling. However, as we argue in this review, such objective modes of profiling also construct suspects, sometimes in ways that enhance police powers with scientific authority.

DNA TYPING AND SEARCHABLE DATABASES

In recent years, policing organizations and the mass media have publicized a significant shift in the methods of criminal investigation. This shift involves two related technological developments: first, novel forensic techniques, particularly but not exclusively related to forensic DNA profiling; and second, the development of large databases for identifying and tracking suspects. Both developments come together in databases of genetic biometric information. Although police culture traditionally resists technological change, it is widely believed that these developments will engender dramatic changes in practices for identifying suspects. The image of detective work found in the existing sociological literature is a familiar one: The detective combines common sense, street smarts, inductive (or abductive) reasoning, intelligence, physical evidence, intuition, and experience to piece together the puzzle of the crime. Forensics plays an increasing, though not dispositive, role (Innes 2003, p. 118; Jackall 2005, p. 257). Detectives proceed methodically, in most murder cases working outward from the acquaintances of the deceased. In contrast to this picture, forensic science has long enjoyed a mythic status, especially in popular culture but in law as well, as an almost magical means for solving crimes. Forensics is the "silent witness," it "never lies," and it cannot misremember or be biased or bribed. Historically, however, scientific evidence has never quite lived up to law's expectations (Mnookin 1999). Forensic evidence was simply not always available and, even when available, did not always provide probative (case-cracking) information; it often yielded ambiguous, or simply uninformative, results. Today, we are told, once again, that the limitations of the past are being overcome through the increasing sophistication and sensitivity of new forensic techniques. In no area is this more apparent than with genetic profiling technology.

DNA Typing

In the mid-1980s, Alec Jeffreys and a number of associates at the University of Leicester developed a method they called "DNA fingerprinting." This method involved the use of radioactive probes to develop a bar code–like pattern of bands on a graphic display. Bands represented selected sequences of DNA, which were known to be highly variable in the human population. Initially, DNA "fingerprints" were used for testing paternity claims in connection with British immigration cases, but they quickly were adapted for criminal investigations. By visually comparing the pattern of bands developed from a crime stain (blood or semen sample recovered from a crime scene or rape victim) with that of a suspect sample (initially a particular suspect's blood sample), it was possible to determine if the bands lined up or matched.

Unlike the details of a fingerprint, a "DNA fingerprint" is made up of hereditable elements, and so it was deemed necessary to develop population frequency data on how often a specific combination of alleles in a given profile would occur at random in the relevant population (this probability figure is sometimes called the random match probability, or RMP). Initially, such data were not available, and forensic organizations made efforts to develop allele frequency tables for samples drawn from blood banks, volunteers (often from police forces), and other sources. Heated debates in the courts and science press arose about the fact that reference frequencies assigned to particular alleles and profiles varied depending on the amount of inbreeding in the relevant population group or subgroup. For example, a suspect for a rape occurring in an isolated village or segregated urban neighborhood is likely to be more closely related to other local men than to members of a more broadly defined reference population (Lewontin & Hartl 1991). Moreover, the singular circumstances of the crime may raise the possibility that a suspect's brother or father also could be suspect. Worse, patterns of consanguinity may only be partially known to investigators (this is sometimes called the "hidden half-brother" problem). Consequently, the inherited alleles found in the crime stain are likely to be more frequent in the singular suspect pool than in a broad reference population. The exact composition of the suspect pool is a product of conventional police investigation and of common assumptions about patterns of criminality in neighborhoods. As a way to handle this problem, forensic organizations used rough racial or ethnic classifications and developed separate allele frequency tables in the United States for African American, Hispanic, and Caucasian subpopulations. More refined population frequencies, and tests of close family members, could be commissioned when the evidence in a case seemed to require them, but rarely were allele frequencies refined for the specific suspect pool in a given case. Instead, forensic services used "conservative" correction factors to standard allele frequencies to account for genetic inbreeding factors (Natl. Res. Counc. 1992, 1996). As for the possibility that a closely related person (a brother, etc.) could be a suspect, the burden shifts to the defense to nominate such suspects so that they, too, may be tested (Redmayne 1995).

Although standard population-genetic frequencies are used as proxies for allele frequencies in the pool of possible suspects, the value of DNA evidence for identifying a perpetrator depends on other evidence. Although it has become increasingly common to read that DNA evidence proves guilt or innocence, it can only do so when framed by a story about the specific case. So, for example, before any bodily material recovered at the scene of a burglary can become meaningful criminal evidence, investigators must exclude possible sources who had legitimate access to the scene (residents, police investigators, etc.). "Normal" features of the crime (Sudnow 1965), such as fresh bloodstains found near a broken window used as an apparent point of entry for a burglary, define the significance of bodily evidence. The story of the evidence also includes the story of a police investigation—as it did, famously, in the 1994–1995 O.J. Simpson double-murder case (Jasanoff 1998, Lynch 1998)—and a juror's evaluation of what matching DNA evidence proves, or does not prove, can be heavily influenced by testimony about police motives, competency, and the like.

When first developed for criminal investigations in the mid-1980s, forensic DNA profiling required substantial amounts of bodily fluid and thus was useful mainly for sexual assault cases and murders. Today, with the STR (short tandem repeat) system, it is possible to use very small amounts of DNA-containing material. The STR system uses the polymerase chain reaction (PCR) technique to greatly increase the quantity and analyzability of DNA sequence information in a sample. In principle, one could now analyze DNA from hair, sweat, saliva, skin cells, and even, in the laboratory, fingerprints. Combined with technology that enables more exact visualization of profile elements, the STR system has been cited as a basis for some profound developments. First, because STR can be used to analyze old, and even degraded, evidence, it challenges assumptions behind statutes of limitations and the legal principle of finality (Berger 2004). Second, because it does not require much sample, less invasive methods can be used for collecting individual samples such as hairs and cheek swabs. Third, the graphic measures are more readily represented in digital, automatically searchable form than are older forms of profile evidence.

The universe of crimes solvable by DNA has expanded commensurately and now includes routine robberies, burglaries, and vehicle thefts. Senders have been linked to letters by saliva left when licking the envelope, thus potentially bringing not only such crimes as extortion and kidnapping into play, but also the entire universe of white-collar crimes. In the relatively near future, many commentators expect usable, "low copy number" DNA samples to be recoverable from ever more minute biological traces, down to the level of a single cell containing DNA (Raymond et al. 2004). However, as the amount of DNA in a sample decreases, successfully developing profiles becomes more difficult, and the significance of contamination by extraneous sources of DNA increases. Despite such difficulties, commentators imagine that the analysis of such samples will become increasingly automated, faster, cheaper, and more mobile, with, for example, "DNA on a chip," a small, handheld device through which nonexpert police investigators could analyze DNA samples at the scene of a crime (Stevens 2002). All told, "DNA" (a commonly used shorthand expression for a growing family of DNA testing, typing, and profiling systems) is said to be well on the way to remaking the technology of justice (Lazer 2004). Crime laboratories, with their white-coated staff, increasingly are involved in the work of identifying suspects. Forensic investigation is positioned to displace much of the "good, old-fashioned detective work" of canvasing neighborhoods, questioning witnesses, interrogating suspects, and cultivating informants (Fuhrman 2003, p. 222).

Searchable Databases

It is not always appreciated that the new sciences of forensic investigation are based on a less glamorous "technological platform" (Keating & Cambrosio 2003): the criminal information database. Without a database, forensic information can be used for linking a known suspect to the crime and for eliminating a suspect from a pool of possible suspects. But when no suspect has been identified by conventional means, forensic evidence by itself is of limited use. In such cases, a database is indispensable.

A database opens a whole new realm of suspect identification, however. With a database, forensic evidence can help resolve suspectless crimes (Walsh & Buckleton 2005). The population of the database becomes, in effect, a pool of suspects or presuspects [to draw an analogy with Goffman's (1961) "prepatient" stage of the moral career of a mental patient]. Databases date back to the "rogues galleries" of photographs used in the nineteenth century, the "signaletic" cards developed by Alphonse Bertillon in Paris, and the fingerprint classification systems developed in India and Argentina (Cole 2001, Ginzburg 1983, Sekula 1986, Sengoopta 2002). However, before the development of automated database searching, such filing systems were of limited utility for investigating crimes. Fingerprint files were indexed according to the pattern type on all ten fingers and were extremely useful for determining whether a person in custody had a prior criminal record under an alias. A single latent fingerprint (or mark) recovered from a crime scene, however, posed a different problem. When a suspect was in hand, so to speak, the mark of unknown origin could be compared to the suspect's inked prints. But if no suspects were identified, the fingerprint files were less useful. A mark recovered from a crime scene would not necessarily contain sufficient information to tell an investigator where to look in the files for a matching card. If the investigator were truly determined to search the files for a match to an unidentified mark—for example, in an extremely high-profile case—it might be necessary to search the entire database. Such an undertaking was called a cold search.

Although automated searching of fingerprint files and other criminal identification databases dates back to the 1930s, when IBM punch card systems were first used, such systems were cumbersome and of limited utility. Not until the end of the twentieth century was it possible for criminal justice organizations easily to conduct large-scale searches on databases indexed according to biometric information (fingerprints and DNA profiles) (Cole 2004). The development of such automatically searchable databases generated a significant but little-noticed change in the relationship between criminal investigation and suspect evidence. No longer a repository of information to be consulted only in rare cases, when all traditional investigative avenues had failed, the database became an active agent of criminal investigation. Trace evidence recovered from crime scenes could be routinely searched against criminal identification databases as a first, rather than last, resort.

When DNA profiling was first used in criminal investigations, no databases were available. To conduct a population search, police would sometimes use a controversial practice called mass screening. For example, during the first criminal investigation using DNA profiling in 1986 and 1987, Alec Jeffreys assisted a police investigation of two rape-murder cases in nearby Leicestershire villages. The investigation was chronicled by crime writer Joseph Wambaugh (1989) in his book *The Blooding*, the title of which refers to the mass screening of blood samples from more than 2000 local men. A mentally imbalanced kitchen porter was initially suspected of the murders, and he even gave an ambiguous confession, but he was excluded when his DNA evidence did not match the crime samples (this was the first case of what later became known as a DNA exoneration). A key part of the story was that Colin Pitchfork, who eventually was convicted of the crime, initially evaded detection by submitting a blood sample given to him by a friend (US Congr. Off. Technol. Assess. 1990, p. 8).

Mass screening employs an ad hoc population of presuspects—persons who are invited to give evidence on the basis of general characteristics (sex, age range, and local residence, in this case). The aggregate pool of presuspects is designed to include the perpetrator. Individual presuspects are quickly eliminated from the suspect pool when their profiles do not match the criminal evidence. Interestingly, persons who refuse to give "voluntary" samples (which is their legal right) attract police attention and become more suspicious as a result (Walsh & Buckleton 2005, p. 459). The practice of mass screening has been criticized as an infringement upon civil liberties, and, although it continues to be employed in the United Kingdom and is sometimes used in the United States, it has limited utility. It is expensive, requiring concentrated police and forensic effort, and tends to be used only for major crime investigations, such as rape-murder cases in which there is no obvious suspect. It also is most effective when the pool of possible suspects is relatively bounded and small, such as in a geographically isolated village area. For most forensic DNA investigations, population databases with more abstract, but stable, composition are used.

Small databases were developed starting in the late 1980s, but not until 1995 in the United Kingdom was development started on the first national criminal database [the National DNA Database (NDNAD)]. It included STR profiles of suspects and persons convicted of recordable offenses (roughly, any offense more serious than a traffic violation). Suspects were supposed to be removed from the searchable database when charges were dropped, although in a few widely publicized cases this did not happen, and laws were later changed to allow data to be left in the database even after a suspect is cleared (Williams et al. 2004). A separate database included crime scene evidence collected during investigations of unsolved crimes. A 1994 revision of the Criminal Justice and Public Order Act in the United Kingdom facilitated the collection of cheek swab evidence by downgrading the moral status of the mouth from being an "intimate" to a "nonintimate" territory of the body. Consequently, police required less paperwork to pry into a suspect's mouth (Dovaston 1994).

In the United Kingdom, the Home Office planned the NDNAD to encompass a sufficient proportion of the (mostly male) population of habitual criminals in order to track individuals as they worked their way up from petty to serious crimes. The idea was to catch them early in their criminal careers and place their data on record. In theory, those who failed to be deterred would be caught repeatedly and presumably incarcerated for longer periods. By 2005, the national criminal database included almost three million people, including almost 9% of the male population (not many women are in the database) (Forensic Sci. Serv. 2005). Donnelly & Friedman (1999, p. 940) mention that the manager of the database expected that it would eventually include one third of all English men between the ages of 16 and 30. Currently, 250,000 crime scene profiles are in the database. In the United States, the FBI and many states and localities are developing DNA databases, although the U.K.'s efforts are more advanced at present. All the larger databases have suffered from backlog problems, in some cases running to hundreds of thousands of cases waiting for analysis, necessitating selective attention to the most important cases (Gaughan 1996, Pratt et al. 2006). In the remainder of this review, we discuss some of the ways the use of such databases has reconfigured suspects—sometimes making suspects in distinctive ways, and sometimes unmaking suspects (and even convicts) who had been made by other means.

MAKING AND UNMAKING SUSPECTS

Unmaking Suspects: The Innocence Project

Perhaps the best known—although, we suggest, less significant—use of DNA technology is the use of postconviction DNA testing [in this case, as Johnson & Williams (2004) note, mainly in the United States] to exonerate individuals previously convicted of crimes. Exploiting the long shelf life of DNA, the Innocence Project (Scheck et al. 2003) was able to test for the first time (or, in some cases, retest) bodily evidence from criminal investigations that had resulted in convictions some years, or even decades, before. In most of these exonerations, a DNA exclusion (mismatch between suspect and criminal evidence) was sufficient to demonstrate "actual innocence." Such exonerations often were obtained only after strenuous efforts to reopen the cases in the face of formidable procedural hurdles. District attorneys sometimes resisted such efforts, while expressing strong confidence in the eyewitness testimony, confessions, and other forms of ordinary and forensic evidence that led to the original convictions. To overcome such resistance, the Innocence Project successfully drew on the epistemic authority of science, and all other forms of evidence gave way to "DNA."

The phenomenon of postconviction exoneration thus set the stage for a shift in the production of suspects. The Innocence Project produced the most concentrated cohort of what we might call false suspects, related to the "falsely accused" category in Becker's (1963) classic typology in the sociology of deviance. As Pollner (1974) and Woolgar & Pawluch (1985) have noted, to say that the accusation was false presupposes the truth about the case. Proponents of postconviction DNA testing often explicitly equate "DNA" with an inherent scientific truth that undermines the legitimacy of conventional criminal investigation. (They tend to ignore the fact that three of the convictions that were overturned had originally involved DNA evidence—a potential regress that is halted by assuming that the later results are based on more discriminating and reliable techniques or analyses than the DNA tests used in the original conviction.) Objectivity also is mentioned in this connection, recalling the category of "mechanical objectivity" (Daston & Galison 1992, Porter 1995) commonly associated with science and statistics, and was assumed to be free from the biasing subjectivity that plagues conventional criminal investigation, including older forms of forensic science (Saks & Koehler 2005).

Making Suspects: Cold Hits and Cold Cases

DNA exonerations are dramatic and heartening, but they have given many commentators the impression that DNA is largely a tool of exoneration. In fact, the use of DNA analysis for exoneration may be less significant than its use for producing suspects and convicts. In many cases, DNA testing is used alongside conventional criminal identification methods. However, searchable databases of DNA profiles set the stage for an entirely new category of suspect, what we call the cold hit suspect. Cold hit suspects are individuals for whom—either at one stage of the investigation or throughout—there is no basis for suspicion other than a database hit (or match). Although cold hit suspects certainly existed before the development of easily searchable databases, they were extremely rare when compared with the hundreds of thousands of cold hits that have been made in the past decade with DNA databases. In the vast majority of cases, a person–crime stain match is corroborated by other evidence—contextual information that connects the suspect to the crime—but in some very interesting cases, the DNA evidence was not corroborated and was even contradicted by other evidence. Such cases create an interesting type of "reality disjuncture" (Pollner 1975), in which the criminal justice system is forced to choose between the "genetic witness" and other, sometimes highly plausible, evidence (Lynch & McNally 2003).

Perhaps the paradigmatic case of such a disjuncture occurred during a 1999 investigation of a house burglary in Bolton, England, in which the police recovered blood evidence that they assumed had come from the burglar when he broke and entered through a kitchen window. A search of the NDNAD revealed a match (a cold hit) between the blood sample and Raymond Easton, whose DNA profile had been placed in the database following a police caution in connection with a domestic dispute. The forensic analysis identified six matching STR loci and declared an RMP of 1 in 37 million. The police charged Easton with burglary, despite some striking anomalies: Easton lived in Swindon, almost 200 miles from the scene of the burglary; he suffered from severe Parkinson tremors and so could not drive, dress himself, or walk for more than a short distance; and he had an alibi that other family members could corroborate. Nevertheless, he was arrested and held in a police cell for several hours before being granted bail. Although, according to his solicitor, he had never traveled north of Birmingham, the police tried to discount his evidence and to imagine unlikely scenarios in which he secretly traveled to Bolton and, perhaps with the help of an accomplice, managed to hoist himself through the kitchen window. The case went on for months until he was exonerated after the prosecution retested the samples with a technique using ten STR loci (BBC 2000; Mnookin 2001, pp. 49–50). This case illustrates that the genetic witness was not questioned until contradicted by an even more powerful genetic witness, and the disjunctive "common sense" evidence was countered with some highly uncommon scenarios that preserved the testimony of the DNA evidence. There have been several other such cases as well (Thompson 2006).

More complicated issues arose in a recent reinvestigation of the 1969 murder of a University of Michigan law student named Jane Mixer. In the Mixer investigation, detectives discovered stains on the victim's clothing that yielded DNA suitable for testing. Profiles were generated, and these profiles were searched against the Michigan database. Two different stains yielded two different hits. One matched Gary Leiterman, a 60-year-old registered nurse who was in the database because he had been convicted of forging narcotics prescriptions. The other matched John Ruelas, a 40-year-old man who had been convicted of murdering his mother. Ruelas was four years old at the time of Jane Mixer's murder. Prosecutors were not able to forge any other link between Leiterman, Ruelas, or Mixer. At one point during Leiterman's trial, the prosecutor surmised that the four-year-old Ruelas was a "chronic nose-bleeder" and that he had bled at the scene of the crime. For the most part, however, he simply left the match to Ruelas unexplained. However, laboratory contamination posed a potential explanation: Leiterman's and Ruelas's samples were processed in the same laboratory on the same day as the evidence from the Mixer case (Thompson 2006).

In this case, DNA database searching yielded two cold hit suspects: one plausible and one implausible. The implausibility of the second suspect did not ultimately undermine the jury's confidence in DNA typing as a suspect-generating technology; Leiterman was convicted of murder and sentenced to life in prison. Other cold hit suspects have turned out to be implausible, but, as we have seen, judgments about plausibility are quite malleable, and in the face of a disjuncture with a DNA match there is a tendency to stretch plausibility to extremes in order to confirm the match with the other evidence.

Cold hits also can occur with fingerprint databases (Winton & Landsberg 2003). Perhaps the most notorious fingerprint cold hit case emanated from terrorist bombings of Madrid train stations on March 11, 2004, that killed 191 people and were attributed to al Qaeda operatives. On May 6, an affidavit was filed in federal district court in Oregon to hold a Portland-area attorney named Brandon Mayfield as a material witness in the bombings. The principal basis for the government's request was an FBI report attributing a latent fingerprint recovered from a plastic bag containing detonators that had been recovered from the parking lot of the Alcala de Henares train station in Madrid. All the bombed trains had passed through that station. Unable to identify the source of the latent print, the Spanish National Police (SNP) had circulated a digital image of it to police agencies worldwide, where it was searched in various national databases. The FBI search yielded a potential match to Mayfield (Thompson & Cole 2005, Wax & Schatz 2004).

An FBI examiner reviewed the candidates produced by the search of the Madrid print and concluded that Mayfield was the source. Two additional FBI examiners (one retired) corroborated this conclusion, but the SNP remained unconvinced. Mayfield was a pure cold hit suspect, and there was no initial reason to suspect him. He did not possess a passport and claimed not to have left the United States in ten years. Further investigation yielded no direct links between him and the bombing. Having identified him, however, the FBI amassed further reasons to construe him as a plausible suspect. Mayfield, a white man from Kansas, was a Muslim convert, and his wife was Egyptian. He had served in the U.S. Army (with the implied possibility of demolitions training). In a child custody case, he had represented a member of the Portland Seven, a group of Muslims who had been convicted of conspiracy to wage war against the United States. A telephone call from Mayfield's home had been logged to the director of an organization that had been designated a terrorist agency by the U.S. Treasury Department. And Mayfield had advertised legal services in a business directory that could be linked through three degrees of separation to Osama bin Laden himself.

These "suspicious facts" made Mayfield a plausible cold hit suspect, though once again one can appreciate how the unquestioned credibility assigned to the cold hit was the foundation of a strenuous effort to develop a corroborating narrative. However, in this case, the narrative fell apart, as the fingerprint evidence collapsed and Mayfield was consigned to the category of "false suspect." The SNP, long skeptical of the Mayfield match, eventually attributed the latent print to an Algerian living in Spain, Ouhnane Daoud. Upon viewing Daoud's print, the FBI recanted its identification of Mayfield, resulting in major challenges to the credibility of fingerprint evidence in the United States and a public apology to Mayfield. The case suggests how forensic database searching can suddenly switch the valence of an individual's suspiciousness. As Edmond (2002) observes, this process is symmetrical: Evidence in disputed cases is constructed in light of the overall theory of ground truth, whether it be guilt or innocence. Without the fingerprint match, Mayfield was hardly a suspect at all; with it, suspicious aspects of his history and identity began to fill out the picture of a suspect. Indeed, with the fingerprint match, even those facts that would seem to detract from Mayfield's suspiciousness were deemed suspect. For example, in the FBI affidavit, the fact that there were no records that Mayfield had traveled outside the United States itself was treated as evidence of effective concealment, rather than as disconfirming evidence (Cole 2005).

Statistical Suspects

We view the above cold hit cases as harbingers of the future; indeed, in many respects, the future is now. Criminal databases are growing ever larger. Many states and nations are already entering into DNA databases individuals who are arrested and not convicted. The United Kingdom does so, as do the states of Virginia and Louisiana. California voters recently passed a proposition authorizing creation of an arrestee database, and the U.S. Congress is considering a similar proposal for federal jurisdictions. In light of databases' success at generating suspects, as policing resources are shifted from conventional investigative methods to the collection of forensic material that can be searched in these databases, we can expect an increasing proportion of suspects to be generated through database trawling rather than through conventional investigative methods (Donnelly & Friedman 1999). As an indication of how the situation has changed, Ericson (1981, pp. 135–36) did not even list database searches in his categorization of how detectives identified suspects in 96 cases.

Data trawling requires a profound change in a police culture that prefers conventional methods of constructing suspect pools. A recent study suggests that a surprising number of U.S. law enforcement agencies still do not conceive of DNA testing as an investigatory tool and are reluctant to submit DNA evidence for testing in "suspectless" cases (Pratt et al. 2006). As the authors note, "this is exactly the kind of situation where the existing offender DNA database is most useful." Consequently, agencies are being pressed to exploit DNA databases as autonomous generators of leads, suspects, and even crimes (Walsh & Buckleton 2005, p. 457). One way to do this is by making links between cases, even without individual suspects, for example, transforming a string of unsolved rapes into a case of a serial rapist. In the first ten years of operation, the British NDNAD generated 40,000 such crime scene–to–crime scene hits.

We might call database-generated suspects statistical suspects, echoing Jasanoff's (2002) notion of "the statistical victim," an individual whose actual harm from a toxic substance is perhaps unknowable but in whose case the legal system decides that a statistical likelihood is sufficient to demonstrate cause. Similarly, a statistical suspect's actual guilt may be unknown but may be estimated on the basis of probability calculations. Legal scholars have long wrestled with such conundrums in both criminal and civil law, with Tribe (1971, pp. 1350, 1372) famously saying that a system that finds individuals guilty (or civilly culpable) based solely on probabilistic evidence is "as inefficient as it is unfair" and perhaps "intrinsically immoral." It will be interesting to see whether such legal theories will be challenged by the sheer statistical power of the probabilities generated by forensic DNA matches, which, some might say, make the DNA database "a system not of evidence but of proof" (Gerlach 2004, p. 192).

Statistical suspects pose more difficulties for legal fact finders, whose task is to consummate a detective's suspicion. It is a cornerstone of the jury system that lay jurors possess sufficient commonsense wisdom and communal knowledge to assess the plausibility of the stories in which a suspect is featured. Statistical suspects, however, require fact finders to make statistical inferences, a task that laypersons are notoriously poor at doing. Database trawls raise particularly thorny issues in this regard. Already such cases have generated a lively debate among statisticians as to how cold database hits should be reported in trials. Initially, statisticians argued that, as a database grows larger, the probative value of a match increases. This occurs because, with a larger database, if no other match turns up, a greater number of cases is excluded. But then some statisticians argued precisely the opposite. Citing the famous "birthday problem"—a counterintuitive probability exercise, often performed in university classrooms, that demonstrates that the odds of finding two or more students with the same birthday are around 50:50 for a class of 22 students—these statisticians argued that the larger the database, the greater the likelihood that the crime scene profile would adventitiously match someone in it (for example, someone like Ray Easton in the case described above). Therefore, absent any corroborating information, a cold database hit should be treated as less probative as the database grows larger. In response to this problem, the National Research Council (1996) advised that the random match probability should be multiplied by the size of the database, but far from settling the problem, this solution gave rise to a lively debate among statisticians known as "the DNA database search controversy" (Balding 2002). It is as much a conceptual debate as a mathematical one. Frequentists, as represented in the National Research Council report, frame the problem as one of determining the probability that a trawl with the crime sample will match someone in the database. Bayesians, such as Donnelly & Friedman (1999), frame the problem as a matter of determining the probability that the defendant who matched the crime sample actually was the source of that evidence. Although this may seem to be a restatement of the same problem, it raises the question of the size of the database relative to the suspect population. If all possible suspects are included in the database, and only one of them matches the crime sample, then, leaving aside the possibility of error, that person is the source. In theory, a larger database (relative to the suspect population) should raise the probative value of the evidence.

The dispute was featured in a recent murder case, *United States v. Jenkins* (2005), in which the D.C. Court of Appeals overruled a defendant's successful challenge to the FBI's testimony about the results of a DNA inclusion generated by a database trawl. The case was then tried, resulting in a hung jury and mistrial in April 2006 (Cauvin 2006). Significantly, this murder case began with a plausible, conventionally generated suspect, Stephen Watson, who possessed the victim's credit cards and items taken from the victim's home. After DNA testing excluded

Watson, Raymond Jenkins was linked to the crime through a cold hit on the Virginia state database. Jenkins's defense referred to the DNA database search controversy, arguing that the scientific community had not reached consensus on how to treat database trawl results. The court agreed, but argued that the dispute was not about science: "These competing schools of thought do not question or challenge the validity of the computation and mathematics relied upon by others." Rather, they were disagreeing about how the probative value of the evidence should be conveyed, which, the court felt, fell into the legal, not the scientific, domain, and therefore the court did not need to defer to the consensus of the scientific community: "What is and is not relevant is not appropriately decided by scientists and statisticians." In other words, the court's boundary work (Gieryn 1983) separated an expert (scientific, statistical) aspect of the problem from the legal relevance of how the problem was framed. This was an interesting resolution, given the importance of the conceptual issues in the statistical debate.

Universal Databases

One solution to controversies about statistical representation that has been proposed is to construct universal DNA databases—databases that include profiles from every citizen (and that presumably could be extended to include resident aliens and even temporary visitors to a nation). Consequently, if one and only one person's profile in the database matched a crime stain, that individual would be identified as the "donor" (a term from diagnostics used, with disconcerting effect in this context, for the source of the crime stain). Such a universal database has been advocated on egalitarian grounds. Existing criminal databases, like existing criminal populations, are highly skewed in terms of sex, ethnicity, and class, among other demographic features. For example, in the United Kingdom 37% of black men are included in the NDNAD, but only 9% of white men. Whether these figures reflect actual crime rates or differential arrest practices is, predictably, a matter of intense debate (Randerson 2006). To be in a database is to be a suspect in every search, a technical form of racial profiling (Duster 2004). To avoid resentment by overrepresented ethnic groups, Alec Jeffreys, inventor of "DNA fingerprinting," and others have recommended that databases either be restricted to convicted persons or be extended to everyone (Jha 2004, Kaye & Smith 2004). Advocates of universal databases argue that only the guilty have to fear being in the database, but this presumes that the system is infallible. Currently, the balance of civil libertarian opinion is strongly opposed to such a design (Steinhardt 2004).

NOVEL AND NOT-SO-NOVEL SUSPECTS

Familial Searching

The construction of statistical suspects will be made even more complicated as new methods of database searching, particularly familial or low-stringency searching, are developed (Bieber & Lazer 2004, Bieber et al. 2006, Greely et al. 2006). When a database search does not yield a true hit, operators can now conduct low-stringency searches that will yield approximate rather than exact matches. The purposes of such searches is to construct a pool not only of suspects whose database profiles were marred by minor artifacts, but also of blood relatives of actual suspects. The rationale is that conventional police investigation of these close relatives may lead to a prime suspect whose DNA profile is not (yet) in the database.

Familial searching was first used in a long-unsolved homicide case in Wales. A low-stringency search yielded a close match with a juvenile delinquent who had not been born at the time of the murder. Upon questioning, family members identified his uncle, Jeffrey Gafoor, as a likely perpetrator, and he confessed. As this case illustrates, familial searching necessarily combines statistical and contextual information. To date, the United Kingdom has used familial searching with apparent success in at least nine cases. The technique has also been used at least once in the United States. In a postconviction DNA exoneration rape-murder case, a database search for the true perpetrator produced a close match. The investigation focused on that individual's brother, Willard Brown, who pleaded guilty (Willing 2005b).

Perhaps the ultimate familial database conundrum thus far was posed in the investigation of a 1999 rape in Grand Rapids, Michigan. In 2004, a sample from a rape kit was searched against the local DNA database and produced a hit: Jerome Cooper, who was already serving time for home invasion. But Jerome's identical twin brother, Tyrone, was by definition also consistent with the sample and was serving time for a sex offense. Both brothers were plausible suspects, and thus far they have both refused to implicate themselves or one another (Willing 2004). The remaining hope of solving the mystery is to find a mutation that distinguishes one twin from the other (Kolker 2004).

DNA Photofits

Not long after the development of forensic DNA profiling, geneticists suggested that DNA photofitting might someday be possible (Jeffreys 1993). Because genetic patterns are associated with phenotypic traits, investigators might be able to reverse engineer the perpetrator's appearance from a crime scene sample. The reality, thus far, has been more mundane, dealing with gross phenotypic characteristics such as hair color, race, and ethnicity (Lowe et al. 2001). In 2003, DNAPrint Genomics, a company whose primary business involved determining individuals' exact geographic and ethnic ancestry for genealogical purposes (Nelson 2006), began marketing its ability to make probabilistic estimations of ancestry from crime scene samples. Its services were used for the first time in a criminal investigation by police near Baton Rouge, Louisiana, investigating seven rape-murders. Eyewitnesses reported seeing a white man in a white truck near two of the crime scenes. Police had already conducted a mass screening of 1200 white men. According to DNAPrint Genomics, however, the perpetrator was likely to be a man with 85%

sub-Saharan African and 15% Native American ancestry. Police shifted their investigation to African Americans and eventually focused on Derrick Todd Lee. With Lee in custody, a known DNA sample could be drawn, and it matched the crime scene samples. In this case, DNA reversed the expectations generated by the conventional investigation (Willing 2005a). Ancestry tests do not substitute for conventional investigations, but they do shape and direct them. Interestingly, the seeming precision of DNA testing can feed into cruder contextual judgments in a technology-led variant of racial profiling (Duster 2004).

John Doe Warrants and Statutes of Limitations

Statistical suspects have been concretized and individuated in a further technological development. A trend in many U.S. states has been to indict DNA profiles under John Doe warrants, when statutes of limitations are about to run out. In such warrants, a DNA profile stands proxy for the anonymous person (John Doe) who presumably "donated" the evidence to the crime scene. Courts in California and many other U.S. states have upheld the legality of such warrants and of any arrests based on them (Imwinkelried 2004, p. 95). Such warrants typically list a technical description of John Doe's features: the type of profile (STR, the current technique used by most forensic organizations); the name of the particular technique; a list of chromosomal loci and alleles found at those loci; and probability figures for three broadly defined racial or ethnic populations (Caucasian, African American, and Hispanic). Notably, the warrants describe the particular profile as unique, as the probability figures imply that the profile is so rare that it would be virtually impossible to be found for any person other than the perpetrator who now lives on earth, or who ever lived, or will ever live in the future.

In such cases, the suspect is both statistical and individual—the figures are calculated, but they point to the virtual impossibility that the evidence could match anyone other than the perpetrator. The probability figures, of course, do not take into account the possibility that the perpetrator has an identical twin (as we saw above in the case of the Cooper twins). Nor do they take into account the many possibilities for generating false-positive results that reside in the practices of collecting and analyzing evidence.

There is also a conceptual problem that is glossed over when "DNA" is treated as evidence of guilt and innocence. To identify a person as a suspect implies that he or she was capable of, and in a position to, commit the crime in question. As noted above, a four-year-old child cannot be a suspect in a rape case. Circumstantial evidence is often crucial for including or excluding possible suspects during the investigation of a crime. A man whose DNA profile matches the profile from the semen recovered from examination of a rape victim may also be excluded from being a suspect when his and/or the victim's testimony satisfies investigators that the two had consensual intercourse. A similar logic holds for DNA evidence. To stand proxy for a unique suspect, a DNA sample must somehow be deemed uniquely suspicious. Much like a fingerprint recovered from a burglary scene, the evidence must have a material relation to the crime that renders it suspicious—that is, it should not match the prints of persons who had legitimate access to the scene, it should be found on an apparent entry point such as a window or at the surface of the safe or jewelry box from which items were pilfered. In other words, the suspect character of the material evidence depends on how it fits into the story of the crime and of the circumstances of that crime.

Suspects Who are Not Suspected

The category of criminal suspect presupposes a crime located in the past; another category encompasses those who are suspected of being inclined or prone to commit a crime at some time in the future. Today, the quintessential future suspect is the terrorist (Cole 2003). As in the case of criminal suspects, rapid developments in forensic and information technology are being touted as promising fundamental advances in the detection of such potential suspects.

The scale of damage unleashed by the 9/11 attacks on the world's greatest military power, coupled with rapid, worldwide ascendance of suicide attacks as a terrorist tactic, have generated an urgent demand for the predictive identification of suspects. The generation of suspects for past crimes is of little comfort when faced with terrorist attacks. Governments have, therefore, sought to harness a predictive power out of large information databases. These efforts at predictive surveillance (Lyon 2001, p. 60) fall under the general rubric of data mining, and many such efforts are familiar to us (Gandy 2006, Haggerty & Ericson 2006). The Computer Assisted Passenger Prescreening System (CAPPS) I and II are airline passenger screening systems used by the U.S. government. The much-maligned Total Information Awareness (TIA) program sought to find terrorist patterns in routine business transactions—credit card purchases, airline reservations, and so on. After a series of public relations blunders—including naming Iran-Contra figure Admiral John Poindexter as director and adopting a blatantly Orwellian logo—the program was quietly renamed Terrorism Information Awareness, but it still exists. Poindexter also launched another ill-fated proposal to create a futures market in terrorist acts, thus supposedly harnessing the invisible information contained in the market. Even DNA databases, reconceived as DNA intelligence databases, are now being viewed as offering prospective, as much as retrospective, information (Raymond et al. 2004, p. 675).

In one sense, such efforts are nothing new. Migrant-receiving nations have long used crude racial, ethnic, and class markers to exclude suspect individuals from the immigrant pool (Torpey & Caplan 2001). The current suspicion that Middle Easterners might be terrorists is little different from the suspicion a century ago that Eastern and Southern Europeans might be anarchists. Today, governments seek to use databases to hone their profiles of suspects, but in some sense high-tech profiles are little more than a return to old-fashioned ethnic- and class-based profiling.

The success of such efforts is highly uncertain. Data mining efforts hinge upon the as yet unproven claim that there is such a thing as a terrorist profile that can be culled from enormous masses of information without suffering from information overload and that can be distinguished from innocent behavior with some reasonable degree of accuracy. The use of such tools as watch lists and facial recognition, meanwhile, depend heavily on inputs—simply put, the suspect must be identified as such in order to be blocked. Presumably, the aim of terrorist organizations is to recruit as operatives precisely those individuals who had avoided being preemptively identified as suspect.

Such precautions stand in marked contrast to the 9/11 operatives themselves, some of whom were identified as suspects and yet were neither barred from entry to the United States nor pursued once they had entered (Natl. Comm. Terror. Attacks 2004). The recent report that a secret Pentagon data mining project called Able Danger actually identified 9/11 ringleader Mohammed Atta as a threat in 2000 and repeatedly sought to convey this information to the FBI only to be thwarted by the military's own lawyers (Jehl et al. 2005) raises the specter of the suspect who is not treated as suspect.

CONCLUSION

The convergence between terrorist profiling and the reconception of criminal identification databases as intelligence databases accompanies the convergence between criminal suspects and suspect populations. In particular, the boundary between retrospective and prospective consultation of databases—with their concomitant legal and statistical issues—is becoming increasingly fuzzy.

To be sure, new technologies promise to wreak great changes in the making of suspects through police investigation, changes that are both welcomed and feared. But new data mining technologies do not simply create new kinds of suspects; they do so in conjunction with conventional forms of criminal investigation. Moreover, they reproduce many of the racial and other forms of discrimination that characterize discretionary criminal justice practices. Although identified in novel ways, the suspect of the future may end up looking very much like the suspect of the past.

ACKNOWLEDGMENTS

This material is based partially on work supported by the National Science Foundation under Grant No. 0115305. Any opinions, findings, and conclusions or recommendations expressed in this material are those of the authors and do not necessarily reflect the views of the National Science Foundation. We are grateful to Dr. Ruth McNally, ESRC Center for Economic and Social Aspects of Genomics, Cardiff University, for supplying information on the National DNA Database in the United Kingdom.

The *Annual Review of Law and Social Science* is online at http://lawsocsci.annualreviews.org

LITERATURE CITED

Balding DJ. 2002. The DNA database search controversy. *Biometrics* 58:241–44

BBC. 2000. File on 4. *BBC Radio 4*. July 4

Becker H. 1963. *Outsiders: Studies in the Sociology of Deviance*. New York: Free Press

Berger MA. 2004. Lessons from DNA: restriking the balance between finality and justice. See Lazer 2004, pp. 109–31

Bieber FR, Brenner CH, Lazer D. 2006. Finding criminals through DNA of their relatives. *Science* 312:1315–16

Bieber F, Lazer D. 2004. Guilt by association. *New Scientist,* Oct. 23, p. 20

Cauvin HE. 2006. Jury deadlocks in case that relied on DNA. *Washington Post,* Apr. 15, p. B10

Cole D. 2003. *Enemy Aliens: Double Standards and Constitutional Freedoms in the War on Terrorism*. New York: New Press

Cole SA. 2001. *Suspect Identities: A History of Fingerprinting and Criminal Identification*. Cambridge, MA: Harvard Univ. Press

Cole SA. 2004. History of fingerprint pattern recognition. In *Automatic Fingerprint Recognition Systems*, ed. NK Ratha, R Bolle, pp. 1–25. New York: Springer-Verlag

Cole SA. 2005. Brandon Mayfield, suspect. See Knechtel 2005, pp. 172–85

Daston L, Galison P. 1992. The image of objectivity. *Representations* 40:81–128

Donnelly P, Friedman RD. 1999. DNA database searches and the legal consumption of scientific evidence. *Mich. Law Rev*. 97:931–84

Dovaston DF. 1994. *A DNA database (1) report for consideration by ACPO Crime Committee*. Assoc. Chief Police Off., London, Sept. 28/29

Duster T. 2004. Selective arrests, an ever-expanding DNA forensic database, and the specter of an early-twenty-first-century equivalent of phrenology. See Lazer 2004, pp. 315–34

Eco U, Sebeok TA, eds. 1983. *The Sign of Three: Dupin, Holmes, Peirce*. Bloomington: Indiana Univ. Press

Edmond G. 2002. Constructing miscarriages of justice: misunderstanding scientific evidence in high profile criminal appeals. *Oxford J. Leg. Stud.* 22:53–89

Ericson RV. 1981. *Making Crime: A Study of Detective Work*. Toronto: Butterworths

Forensic Sci. Serv. 2005. *The National DNA Database (NDNAD) fact sheet (3)*. Forensic Sci. Serv., Birmingham, UK, Dec. 5

Frank L. 2003. *Victorian Detective Fiction and the Nature of Evidence: The Scientific Investigations of Poe, Dickens, and Doyle*. New York: Palgrave

Fuhrman M. 2003. *Death and Justice: An Exposé of Oklahoma's Death Row Machine*. New York: Morrow

Gandy OH Jr. 2006. Data mining, surveillance and discrimination in the post-9.11 environment. See Haggerty & Ericson 2006, pp. 363–84

Gaughan PA. 1996. *Delivery of DNA evidence in the criminal justice system.* MSc thesis. Study Secur. Manag., Univ. Leicester, UK

Gerlach N. 2004. *The Genetic Imaginary: DNA in the Canadian Criminal Justice System*. Toronto: Univ. Toronto Press

Gieryn T. 1983. Boundary-work and the demarcation of science from non-science. *Am. Sociol. Rev*. 48:781–95

Ginzburg C. 1983. Morelli, Freud, and Sherlock Holmes: clues and scientific method. See Eco & Sebeok 1983, pp. 81–118

Goffman E. 1961. *Asylums: Essays on the Social Situation of Mental Patients and Other Inmates*. Garden City, NY: Doubleday-Anchor

Greely HT, Riordan DP, Garrison NA, Mountain JL. 2006. Family ties: the use of DNA offender databases to catch offenders' kin. *J. Law Med. Ethics* 34:248–62

Hacking I. 1999. *The Social Construction of What?* Cambridge, MA: Harvard Univ. Press

Haggerty KD, Ericson RV, eds. 2006. *The New Politics of Surveillance and Visibility*. Toronto: Univ. Toronto Press

Horn DG. 2003. *The Criminal Body: Lombroso and the Anatomy of Deviance*. New York: Routledge

Imwinkelried EJ. 2004. The relative priority that should be assigned to trial stage DNA issues. See Lazer 2004, pp. 91–107

Innes M. 2003. *Investigating Murder: Detective Work and the Police Response to Criminal Homicide*. Oxford: Oxford Univ. Press

Jackall R. 2005. *Street Stories: The World of Police Detectives*. Cambridge, MA: Harvard Univ. Press

Jasanoff S. 1998. The eye of everyman: witnessing DNA in the Simpson trial. *Soc. Stud. Sci.* 28:713–40

Jasanoff S. 2002. Science and the statistical victim: modernizing knowledge in breast implant litigation. *Soc. Stud. Sci.* 32:37–70

Jeffreys AJ. 1993. DNA typing: approaches and applications. *J. Forensic Sci. Soc.* 33:204–11

Jehl D, Shenon P, Schmitt E. 2005. 4 in 9/11 plot are called tied to Qaeda in '00. *New York Times,* Aug. 9, p. A1

Jha A. 2004. DNA fingerprinting "no longer foolproof": pioneer calls for upgrade. *Guardian* (London), Sept. 9

Johnson P, Williams R. 2004. Post-conviction DNA testing: the UK's first "exoneration" case. *Sci. Justice* 44:77–82

Kaye DH, Smith ME. 2004. DNA databases for law enforcement: the coverage question and the case for a population-wide database. See Lazer 2004, pp. 247–84

Keating P, Cambrosio A. 2003. *Biomedical Platforms: Realigning the Normal and the Pathological in Late-Twentieth-Century Medicine*. Cambridge, MA: MIT Press

Knechtel J, ed. 2005. *Suspect, Alphabet City 10.* Cambridge, MA: MIT Press

Kolker K. 2004. Lab offers free DNA test of twins in rape case. *Grand Rapids Press*, Aug. 10, p. A.1

Lazer D, ed. 2004. *DNA and the Criminal Justice System: The Technology of Justice.* Cambridge, MA: MIT Press

Lewontin RC, Hartl DJ. 1991. Population genetics in forensic DNA typing. *Science* 254:1745–50

Lowe AL, Urquhart A, Foreman LA, Evett IW. 2001. Inferring ethnic origin by means of an STR profile. *Forensic Sci. Int.* 119:17–22

Lynch M. 1998. The discursive production of uncertainty: the OJ Simpson 'dream team' and the sociology of knowledge machine. *Soc. Stud. Sci.* 28:829–68

Lynch M, McNally R. 2003. "Science," "common sense," and DNA evidence: a legal controversy about the public understanding of science. *Public Underst. Sci.* 12:83–105

Lyon D. 2001. *Surveillance Society: Monitoring Everyday Life*. Buckingham, UK: Open Univ. Press

Mnookin JL. 1999. *Images of truth: evidence, expertise, and technologies of knowledge in the American courtroom*. PhD thesis. MIT, Cambridge, MA. 441 pp.

Mnookin JL. 2001. Fingerprint evidence in the age of DNA profiling. *Brooklyn Law Rev.* 67(Fall):13–70

Natl. Comm. Terror. Attacks. 2004. *The 9/11 Commission Report: Final Report of the National Commission on Terrorist Attacks Upon the United States*. New York: Norton

Natl. Res. Counc. 1992. *DNA Technology in Forensic Science*. Washington, DC: Natl. Acad. Press

Natl. Res. Counc. 1996. *The Evaluation of Forensic DNA Evidence*. Washington, DC: Natl. Acad. Press

Nelson A. 2006. Genealogical branches, genetic roots, and the pursuit of African ancestry. In *Revisiting Race in a Genomic Age*, ed. B Koenig, SS-J Lee. New Brunswick, NJ: Rutgers Univ. Press. Under review

Pasquino P. 1991. Criminology: the birth of a special knowledge. In *The Foucault Effect: Studies in Governmentality*, ed. G Burchell, C Gordon, P Miller, pp. 235–50. London: Havester Wheatsheaf

Pollner M. 1974. Sociological and commonsense models of the labeling process. In *Ethnomethodology*, ed. R Turner, pp. 27–40. Harmondsworth, UK: Penguin

Pollner M. 1975. The very coinage of your brain: the anatomy of reality disjunctures. *Philos. Soc. Sci.* 5:411–30

Porter T. 1995. *Trust in Numbers: The Pursuit of Objectivity in Science and Public Life*. Princeton, NJ: Princeton Univ. Press

Pratt TC, Gaffney MJ, Lovrich NP, Johnson CL. 2006. This isn't 'CSI': estimating the national backlog of forensic DNA cases and the barriers associated with case processing. *Crim. Justice Policy Rev.* 17(1):32–47

Rafter N. 2004. Earnest A. Hooton and the biological tradition in American criminology. *Criminology* 42:735–71

Randerson J. 2006. DNA of 37% of black men held by police. *Guardian* (London), Jan. 5

Raymond JJ, Walsh SJ, Van Oorchot RA, Gunn PR, Roux C. 2004. Trace DNA: an underutilized resource or Pandora's box? A review of the use of trace DNA analysis in the investigation of volume crime. *J. Forensic Identif.* 54:668–86

Redmayne M. 1995. Doubts and burdens: DNA evidence, probability and the courts. *Crim. Law Rev.* 1995:464–82

Sacks H. 1972. Notes on police assessment of moral character. In *Studies in Social Interaction*, ed. D Sudnow, pp. 280–93. New York: Free Press

Saks MJ, Koehler JJ. 2005. The coming paradigm shift in forensic identification science. *Science* 309:892–95

Scheck B, Neufeld P, Dwyer J. 2003. *Actual Innocence: When Justice Goes Wrong and How to Make It Right*. New York: New Am. Libr.

Sekula A. 1986. The body and the archive. *October* 39:3–64

Sengoopta C. 2002. *Imprint of the Raj: The Emergence of Fingerprinting in India and its Voyage to Britain*. London: Macmillan

Steinhardt B. 2004. Privacy and forensic DNA data banks. See Lazer 2004, pp. 173–96

Stevens L. 2002. Science on the case. *Popul. Sci.* 261(Oct.):68–69

Sudnow D. 1965. Normal crimes: sociological features of the penal code in a public defender's office. *Soc. Probl.* 12:255–76

Thomas RR. 1999. *Detective Fiction and the Rise of Forensic Science*. Cambridge, UK: Cambridge Univ. Press

Thompson WC. 2006. Tarnish on the 'gold standard:' Understanding recent problems in forensic DNA testing. *Champion* 30(1):10–16

Thompson WC, Cole SA. 2005. Lessons from the Brandon Mayfield case. *Champion* 29(3):42–44

Torpey J, Caplan J, eds. 2001. *Documenting Individual Identity: The Development of State Practices Since the French Revolution*. Princeton, NJ: Princeton Univ. Press

Tribe LH. 1971. Trial by mathematics: precision and ritual in the legal process. *Harvard Law Rev.* 84:1329–93

United States v. Jenkins, No. 05-CO-333 (D.C. Cir. 2005)

US Congr. Off. Technol. Assess. 1990. *Genetic Witness: Forensic Uses of DNA Tests, OTA-BA-438*. Washington, DC: US GPO

Valier C. 1998. True crime stories: scientific methods of criminal investigation, criminology and historiography. *Br. J. Criminol.* 38:88–105

Walsh S, Buckleton J. 2005. DNA intelligence databases. In *Forensic DNA Evidence Interpretation*, ed. J Buckleton, CM Triggs, SJ Walsh, pp. 439–69. Boca Raton, FL: CRC Press

Wambaugh J. 1989. *The Blooding*. New York: Morrow

Wax ST, Schatz CJ. 2004. A multitude of errors: the Brandon Mayfield case. *Champion* 28(8):6

Williams R, Johnson P, Martin P. 2004. *Genetic Information and Crime Investigation: Social, Ethical and Public Policy Aspects of the Establishment, Expansion, and Police Use of the National DNA*

Database. Funded by the Wellcome Trust. Sch. Appl. Soc. Sci., Univ. Durham, UK. http://www.dur.ac.uk/p.j.johnson/

Willing R. 2004. Identical twins complicate use of DNA testing. *USA Today,* June 3, p. A. 03

Willing R. 2005a. DNA tests offer clues to suspect's race. *USA Today,* Aug. 16, p. A.1

Willing R. 2005b. Suspects get snared by a relative's DNA. *USA Today,* June 7, p. A.1

Winton R, Landsberg M. 2003. 45 years later, fingerprint points to a suspect in case that shocked a city. *Los Angeles Times,* Jan. 30, pp. A1–16

Woolgar S, Pawluch D. 1985. Ontological gerrymandering: the anatomy of social problems explanations. *Soc. Probl.* 32:214–27

Annu. Rev. Law Soc. Sci. 2006. 2:61–81
doi: 10.1146/annurev.lawsocsci.2.081805.105800

First published online as a Review in Advance on June 5, 2006

MAX WEBER'S CONTRIBUTION TO THE ECONOMIC SOCIOLOGY OF LAW

Richard Swedberg
Department of Sociology, Cornell University, Ithaca, New York 14853; email: rs328@cornell.edu

Key Words law and economics, law and economy, capitalism

■ **Abstract** During recent years, a few scholars have advocated that more attention be paid to the intersection of law, economics, and sociology—what may be called the economic sociology of law. This review suggests that a theoretical foundation for such a field of study, or parts of such a foundation, may be found in the work of Max Weber. It also provides an introduction to those parts of Weber's work that are relevant in this context. Weber especially emphasizes the role that law plays in raising the probability that actions will take place, in the economy and elsewhere, and that this probability has to be established while taking the motives of the actors into account. The main contribution of the legal system to modern capitalism, Weber also argues, is to make economic life more calculable. This review also discusses which factors account for the increasing rationalization of law, including economic factors.

INTRODUCTION

Recently, scholars have suggested that we need more studies at the intersection of economics, law, and sociology—what has been called the economic sociology of law (Swedberg 2003; for similar arguments, see Stryker 2003, Edelman & Stryker 2005). Its main focus would be sociological studies of the role of law in economic life. These studies would fill a void that exists in economic sociology, a new and burgeoning field that defines itself as the study of economic life from a sociological perspective (e.g., Smelser & Swedberg 2005). The economic sociology of law would also add to the repertoire of the sociology of law, which is an older and more established field. Finally, but of much importance, the economic sociology of law would clearly overlap with the area claimed by law and economics. Indeed, one of the main tasks today of the economic sociology of law, I argue, is precisely to challenge law and economics on several points, since this perspective is woefully underdeveloped when it comes to the sociological dimension of law and economy.

The main purpose of this review is to provide an introduction to the contribution of Max Weber to the economic sociology of law. There are several reasons for singling out Max Weber in this respect. The most important of these is that Weber himself was involved in a project very similar to that of the economic sociology of law. As a formidable theoretician with an encyclopedic knowledge of a number of social science disciplines, Weber clearly has much to say on economy and law that is of great interest to the economic sociology of law.

Although this review aims to provide a short introduction to Weber's economic sociology of law, it is exploratory in nature in the sense that most studies of Weber's work are exploratory. There exist few studies of Weber that in any sense can be called definitive for the simple reasons that his ideas are exceedingly complex and that the secondary literature on Weber's work is enormous. What is needed to make real progress on a topic such as Weber's economic sociology of law is attention from a number of scholars over a period of time.

LAW, ECONOMICS, AND SOCIOLOGY IN WEBER'S LIFE

One can argue that to work in a field such as the economic sociology of law, one ideally needs to be an expert in three areas: law, economics, and sociology. If that is true, Weber had indeed the perfect qualifications; he not only was a master sociologist but also had important careers in law as well as in economics. Although some knowledge of Weber's work in each of these three disciplines is indispensable for understanding how he attempts to position his sociological analysis of law and the economy, I have not included a detailed discussion of these issues in the main section of this review, in part because some readers are likely to view this type of information as irrelevant and to be eager to get to Weber's analysis of law and economy. I have therefore put this information in an Appendix at the end of the review, to which the reader is referred.

A few points must nonetheless be made already here, when it comes both to Weber's education and to the status of *Economy and Society*, the work in which one can find most of Weber's sociology of law. First, Weber had a very thorough education in law, especially in the history of law. He also very early became fascinated with the economic dimension of legal phenomena and spent much time educating himself in this area.

Second, the fact that Weber later switched from the discipline of law to that of economics, and taught classes in economics for several years, means that he was uniquely qualified to take on a topic such as the economic sociology of law. He intimately knew the way of thinking and reasoning in legal science as well as in economics. The reader should also be aware that Weber was competent in two different types of economic science, both of which were important in Weber's time. These were the analytical type of economics (usually associated with English nineteenth century economics and the one that today dominates mainstream economics) and the historical type of economics (usually associated with Germany and some scholars whom Weber knew personally and/or had taken courses with).

To this must also be added that the separation between Weber's so-called legal period, on the one hand, and his so-called economic period, on the other, has often been exaggerated. During both of these periods, Weber was deeply interested in the interaction between legal and economic phenomena. This interest also continued during the last ten or so years of Weber's life when he started to view himself primarily as a sociologist.

Weber's main attempt to deal with law from a sociological perspective can be found in *Economy and Society*. Recent scholarship on Weber has shown that this work consists of manuscripts from several different periods that were put together after Weber's death by various editors who proceeded according to their own ideas. It is not known how Weber himself wanted the final version of this work to look, nor if *Economy and Society* is the title that Weber wanted.

The confusion surrounding *Economy and Society* also extends to the general character of this work. Did Weber want to create a work in general sociology (including its major subfields), or did he want to produce a work that primarily deals with economy and society, as indicated by the title as well as by the fact that this work was part of a giant handbook in social economics (*Grundriss der Sozialökonomik*) that Weber was in charge of? From the perspective of the analysis of law that can be found in *Economy and Society*, one cannot clearly see if this analysis was primarily intended as an exercise in sociology of law in general or as an attempt to analyze the relationship of law to the economy, from a sociological perspective. Two logics, in brief, seem to be present in the same work: the logic of general sociology and the logic of a sociological analysis of economy and society.

And finally, there is the problem of interpreting the fact that Weber assigned the topic of "modern private law and capitalism" to jurist Alexander Leist in the handbook of social economics. I argue that this means that Weber did not feel that he had to cover this topic himself in *Economy and Society.* One can also argue, however, that because Weber wanted the analysis in *Economy and Society* to be sociological, he had to cover the same area as Leist, but from a sociological as opposed to a legal perspective. Again, in brief, the ambiguity that surrounds *Economy and Society* enters into our understanding of Weber's economic sociology of law.

WEBER'S ANALYSIS OF ECONOMY AND LAW

With this brief comment on the role of law, economics, and sociology in the life of Weber, I turn to his contribution to the analysis that is here termed the economic sociology of law. To do this in a satisfactory manner, however, is also difficult for a few reasons other than those just mentioned. First, Weber's work has a fragmentary nature. He never produced the final, rewritten version of the section in *Economy and Society* that he refers to as his "sociology of law," and the status of the various manuscripts on law in *Economy and Society* is somewhat unclear, at least until the volume on "Law" has appeared in Weber's *Collected Works*, which are currently being published in Germany (*MWG/22–4*, edited by Werner Gephart).

Second, what Weber wrote on the theme of economy and law is scattered throughout his life work, which is voluminous and hard to penetrate. One must consider not only Weber's sociological work, roughly from 1905 to 1920, especially the essays in *The Economic Ethics of the World Religions* and the bulk of *Economy and Society*, including the crucial Chapter 2 on economic sociology and the sections on the state (Weber [1920] 1951, [1921] 1952, [1921] 1958; see also, e.g., Weber 1988, pp. 71–76). One must also consider his presociological work, which includes his two dissertations, his study of antiquity, and the inaugural lecture at Freiburg, with its bold pronouncement that economic thought is about to replace law as the leading discourse in society and that one therefore has to be aware of its normative implications (Weber [1909] 1976, [1895] 1989).

In trying to extract Weber's contribution to the economic sociology of law, one may naturally turn to the secondary literature on his work, especially his sociology of law, because economic sociologists have paid little attention to what Weber has to say on law (but see Swedberg 1998, pp. 82–107). My estimate, based primarily on existing bibliographies, is that approximately 50 articles and a few monographs in English have been devoted to Weber's sociology of law, and that the number for the non-English languages may well be roughly the same (for the literature in English, see Sica 2004, and for especially important contributions, see, e.g., Rheinstein 1954, Winckelmann 1967, Kronman 1983, Breuer & Treiber 1984, Rehbinder & Tieck 1987, Gephart 1993, Turner & Factor 1994, Lascoumes 1995, Schluchter 2002).

Most of this literature sets as its task to lay bare and/or discuss Weber's sociology of law but ignores that Weber produced his sociology of law as part of a commitment to a handbook in economics. They only look, so to speak, at one of the two logics of *Economy and Society*. Another weakness with much of this literature is that it has been produced by scholars who are primarily interested in what Weber has to say on law but not on other topics. That Weber's sociology of law is closely related to his other types of sociology (say, his sociology of the state and economic sociology) and to his project of an interpretive sociology more generally is usually ignored (for exceptions, see, e.g., Winckelmann 1967, Schluchter 2002).

This last point is also relevant to a discussion of the relationship between economy and law in Weber's work. This theme is unfortunately often discussed without much reference to Weber's voluminous writings on the economy. Although useful studies do exist concerning what Weber has to say on economy and law—especially when it comes to the contract and the general role of law in modern capitalism—there is also the misplaced energy that has been devoted to the discussion of the so-called England Problem. While an early and highly competent commentator such as Max Rheinstein (1954, p. 1) simply noted in passing that modern capitalism, according to Weber, was usually accompanied by a formal type of law, David Trubek (1972) some years later announced that there exists a fatal contradiction in Weber's argument about the link between law and modern capitalism. The contradiction consists of the fact that although Weber says that modern capitalism has to be accompanied by formal law, this did not happen in the case of England. For rebuttals of Trubek's argument, the reader is referred to the secondary literature on the England Problem, as well as to relevant passages in the work of Weber himself (see especially Ewing 1987, and more generally Weber [1922] 1978, pp. 814, 855, 890; [1920] 1951, pp. 102, 149–50).

My suggestion for an easier understanding of Weber's contribution to the sociological analysis of economy and law is as follows. The most important material on this topic was written while Weber worked on the early versions of *Economy and Society*; and if one goes to the two existing plans for this work (see the Appendix), one finds that Weber divided up the topic of economy and law into three parts: the two parts that he assigned to himself and the part he assigned to Alexander Leist. Weber, in short, appears to have felt that the theme of economy and law could be adequately covered by looking at the following three topics (and I use his terminology from the 1914 plan): Economy and Law and the Principles of Their Relationship, Developmental Conditions of Law, and Modern Private Law and Capitalism.

I suggest presenting Weber's work on the economic sociology of law under these three headings, as follows. Throughout his writings Weber often addressed issues relating to economy and law that are of a very general nature (Topic 1: Economy and Law and the Principles of Their Relationship). Weber was also fascinated by the various forces that drove the development of law, especially the ones that transformed it in a formal, rationalistic direction (Topic 2: Developmental Conditions of Law). And even though Weber basically handed over the topic of the relationship between economy and law in contemporary capitalism to Alexander Leist, he nonetheless touched on it now and then (Topic 3: Modern Private Law and Capitalism).

Topic 1: Economy and Law and the Principles of Their Relationship

The primary text that addresses Topic 1 is the short section entitled "The Economy and Social Norms" in *Economy and Society* (Weber [1922] 1978, pp. 311–38).[1] Weber here discusses some very general questions about the nature of law from a sociological perspective, what distinguishes the approach of the sociology of law from those of jurisprudence and economic theory, and some questions about the general relationship between economic phenomena and legal phenomena. There is a mixture in this text, in other words, of what I referred to above as the two different logics of *Economy and Society*—sociology of law and the relationship of law to the economy, from a sociological perspective.

According to Weber, jurisprudence and the sociology of law look at law very differently. Although jurisprudence sees law as a set of rules that should be followed, the sociology of law views law as "a complex of actual determinants of human conduct" (Weber [1922] 1978, p. 312; cf. Weber [1922] 1978, p. 33; [1907] 1977, pp. 115–26, 131). From a sociological perspective, Weber specifies, you may speak of a legal order, and the impact of the legal order on the behavior of actors

[1]Mommsen dates this manuscript to 1913 or 1914, whereas according to Schluchter there exist two versions of this text—one presumably from before 1910 and one from not later than 1913 (Mommsen 2000, p. 176; Schluchter 2002, p. 269).

comes from the fact that these latter orient their actions to it (Weber [1922] 1978, p. 312). Other factors than the legal order, in short, may drive their actions and typically do so.

Also in "The Economy and Social Norms," Weber provides an early version of his sociological definition of law that would be given its final, famous formulation some years later in Chapter 1 in *Economy and Society*: "An order will be called. . .*law* if it is guaranteed by the probability that physical or psychological coercion will be applied by a *staff* of people in order to bring about compliance or avenge violation" (Weber [1922] 1978, pp. 34; cf. pp. 313, 336).

Two elements in this definition of law are essential to Weber's sociology of law. The first is easy to spot because Weber has put it in italics, and this is the *staff*. What is characteristic of law as a sociological phenomenon, and also sets it apart from norms (conventions), is that there has to be a special group of people who have as their task to enforce these norms. Although it is easy enough to identify members of such a staff in modern society—Weber mentions "judges, prosecuting attorneys, administrative officials, or sheriffs"—this becomes more difficult, he says, in premodern times (Weber [1922] 1978, pp. 34–35). Nonetheless, even a clan can operate as an enforcing agency, as long as there are rules for the enforcement.

The second word that should be highlighted in Weber's definition of law is *probability*; here the key idea is that the main effect of a law, from a sociological perspective, is to increase the probability that a certain type of behavior will take place. Law is ultimately no different, to Weber's mind, from other social phenomena that also increase the probability that some action will take place, say material interests and tradition. That someone has a legal right, Weber explains, similarly means that the probability is now quite large, thanks to the law, that the actor will not be disappointed.

According to Weber, important differences also exist between the way that law is conceptualized in sociology and in economic theory. First, in economic theory the assumption is made that the actor will obey the law and that the role of norms can be disregarded. From a sociological perspective, in contrast, one always has to determine empirically if and to what extent the actor is influenced by the law in his or her behavior (Weber [1922] 1978, p. 327). Weber notes, for example, in this context that businessmen typically prefer not to go to court to settle their differences (Weber [1922] 1978, p. 328). This observation is usually associated with the work of Macaulay in the sociology of law, but it can already be found in Weber (although Weber, in contrast to Macaulay, does not explain why this is the case; cf. Macaulay 1963). Second, Weber argues that a crucial difference between viewing an economic action from the perspective of economic theory versus sociological theory is that the latter always has to take economic power into account ("power of control and disposal [*Verfügungsgewalt*]"; Weber [1922] 1978, p. 67). Economics, in contrast, ignores power.

Weber ends his 30-page text "The Economy and Social Norms" with an enumeration of six very general statements about law and the economy that are presumably applicable to most or perhaps all societies (Weber [1922] 1978, pp. 333–37). He here writes that (1) the law defends many types of interests in society, not only economic ones; (2) a legal order can remain unchanged while economic relations have changed; (3) the economic consequences of two different legal provisions can be the same; and (4) law guarantees economic interests, and "economic interests are among the strongest factors influencing the creation of law" (Weber [1922] 1978, p. 334). There exist, on the other hand, (5) limits to the extent to which one can use law to make people engage in some specific form of economic behavior. And finally, (6) law, including economic legislation, does not necessarily have to be enforced by a state; other social groups may also perform the disciplinary function.

All these relationships can be further explicated, and I thus briefly address each of them here.

1. The notion that the law does not only defend economic interests but also other types of interests should probably be seen within the context of Weber's relationship to Marxism, including the Marxist analysis of law. In Weber's view, Marx was wrong in only seeing economic interests as important driving forces for human beings. According to a famous formulation by Weber, "material and ideal interests directly govern men's conduct"—by which is meant that also such interests as religious and political interests may importantly affect the behavior of human beings (Weber 1946, p. 280).
2. Weber's second example of a general relationship between law and the economy is also close to Marxism, namely that the law does not by necessity have to change in situations in which economic relations are changing (compare, e.g., Renner 1949). While a Marxist would argue that the reason for this is that the base (the economy) is what really matters, and not the superstructure (the law), Weber notes that even in situations in which the law does not change so as to match new economic conditions, it still maintains its capacity to unleash coercive powers when called upon.
3. Relatedly, Weber also argues that although it is true that the same economic phenomenon may be handled differently, in different legal texts, the practical economic consequences of doing this may nonetheless be the same.
4. Weber's fourth statement about a general relationship between law and the economy relates to his thesis that economic interests are among the strongest factors that influence the creation of law. According to Weber, this is so "even where this does not seem to be [the case]." The reason for this is that law is usually backed by the major social groups, and all these groups have strong economic interests to defend. "Any authority guaranteeing a legal order depends, in some way, upon the consensual action of the constitutive social groups, and the formation of social groups depends, to a large extent, upon constellations of material interests" (Weber [1922] 1978, p. 334).
5. While economic interests may influence the law in a powerful way, Weber continues, the law, in contrast, can only direct the behavior of economic actors

in a limited way. According to Weber, there are two factors in a modern capitalist economy that especially limit the impact of the law: Economic interests may go counter to the intentions of the law, and the disposition (*habitus*) of the economic actor is hard to change. This means that predicting the general impact of a law on economic life is difficult. Or in Weber's formulation: "The extent of factual impact of the law on economic conduct cannot be determined generally, but must be calculated for each particular case" (Weber [1922] 1978, p. 336).

6. The final general relationship between law and the economy that Weber discusses has to do with the role of the state. The first point that he makes is that law, including economically relevant law, does not have to be enforced by a state; other social groups may also perform the disciplinary function. Weber, however, also adds a very important qualification to this statement, namely that in the modern capitalist world only the state can be in charge of the legal system. The rational capitalist economy demands "a promptly and predictably functioning legal system," something that only the modern state can guarantee.

Topic 2: Developmental Conditions of Law

I now proceed to the second major theme in Weber's work, namely Developmental Conditions of Law. The main text here is the famous Chapter 8 in *Economy and Society*, which is what most commentators have in mind when they refer to Weber's sociology of law.[2] Its current title is "Economy and Law (Sociology of Law)," and it is probably a text of this scope that Weber had in mind when he referred to "Economy and Law (. . . 2. Periods of Development until the Present)" in his plan from 1910, and later as "Developmental Conditions of Law" in his plan from 1914 (see the Appendix at the end of this review). Although the formulations used in the title of these two plans vary slightly, I suggest that the main difference between them is to be found elsewhere. In the 1914 plan, Weber had removed the section on law and its development from its placement next to "Economy and Law (1. Principal Relations)" and instead placed it in a section that deals with such topics as political organizations and the nation. This placement indicates a shift toward an analysis in which Weber wanted not only to discuss which economic factors drive the development of the law, but also to pay attention to political and other noneconomic factors. This is also what he does in Chapter 8 in *Economy and Society*.

The bulk of Chapter 8 is otherwise taken up by a discussion of how the following factors affect private law (public law is discussed in the chapter on domination): economic factors, political factors, religious factors, the legal profession, and administrators (Weber [1922] 1978, pp. 641, 653). In discussing the impact of these

[2]According to Mommsen, this manuscript was presumably written in 1913 or 1914 and approved by Weber for publication in 1920 (Mommsen 2000, pp. 377, 381).

noneconomic factors, Weber also raises the question of the extent to which they, in their turn, are related to economic factors.

He similarly inquires about the role of the economic factors in what he views as the general thrust of the overall development in Western legal doctrine, namely its move in the direction of an increasing rationalization (Weber [1922] 1978, p. 882). This process has a distinctly formal dimension (related to procedure, logic, and generality) as well as a distinctly substantive dimension (related to values, a sense of justice, and individual cases); and the former has clearly overtaken the latter in the West (Weber [1922] 1978, p. 893). According to Weber, economic forces have only played an indirect role in this whole process (Weber [1922] 1978, p. 776; cf. p. 883). "We may thus conclude that capitalism has not been a decisive factor in the promotion of that form of rationalization of the law that has been peculiar to the continental West ever since the Romanist studies in the medieval universities" (Weber [1922] 1978, p. 892).

Political actors have sometimes introduced a formal-rational dimension to law, as exemplified by their attempts to create uniform laws for their empires. Authoritarian rulers, however, have typically preferred less formal systems of law to keep control over their subjects, and the main advocates of the formal dimension of law have been the administrators of the princes rather than the princes themselves. Princes in Europe have, however, often been interested in eliminating the power of the estates and more generally in introducing enough logic and clarity in the law to ensure their fiscal interests. The European bourgeoisies have been similarly positive to the attempt to eliminate the power of the estates; they have also tried to limit the influence of religion on law and of tradition more generally.

Weber is also famous for his discussion of how legal education has influenced the development of law and of how its impact differs depending on whether law is taught as a craft (from practitioners) or as a science (in special schools). Although the legal profession in England, Scandinavia, and some other countries blocked the introduction of Roman law, this did not mean, according to Weber, that it was not positive to powerful economic interests or did not get along with these. Capitalism can live with different legal systems, Weber argues, as long as there is a certain degree of calculability involved (e.g., Weber [1922] 1978, pp. 847, 855, 1394; [1920] 1951, p. 103).

Because Weber's emphasis on calculability is at the heart of how he viewed the role of law in modern rational capitalism, it is important to try to specify what Weber meant by this term. First of all, modern rational capitalism has to fulfill a number of requirements to qualify as such, according to Weber, and one of these is what he terms calculable law (Weber [1922] 1978, pp. 161–62; cf. e.g., Weber 1982, pp. 277, 313). Weber seems to have had especially three items in mind when he referred to calculability in this context: (*a*) that the legal text lends itself to prediction; (*b*) that the administration of the law is not arbitrary; and (*c*) that contracts are legally enforced (see, especially, Weber [1922] 1978, p. 847). That the text is predictable typically (but not necessarily) means that it is of high formal quality. That the administration of the law is not arbitrary means that it is independent or free from undue political and religious pressure. And that contracts can be legally enforced is important because a capitalist economy is primarily an exchange economy.

Two more points need to be made about what calculable law meant to Weber. First, this type of law means a predominance of the formal qualities of law over its substantive qualities, or that form is predominant over justice. The reason for this is that generality is related to form for Weber, whereas justice resides in the unique qualities of the single case. Second, a calculable legal order tends to favor those with economic power, whereas it does little for those without economic resources (Weber [1922] 1978, p. 813).

In Chapter 8 in *Economy and Society*, Weber also states that "the development of those legal institutions, indispensable for a modern capitalist society, will be discussed elsewhere," and with "elsewhere" he meant the section assigned to Alexander Leist (Weber [1922] 1978, p. 682). As a result of this decision by Weber, one will only find in Chapter 8 and in Weber's other texts on law in *Economy and Society* a discussion of the legal institutions that existed *before* modern capitalism. This roughly means that Weber discusses legal-economic institutions up to and including the Middle Ages. However, to make this difficult part of Weber's analysis easier to follow, I save the discussion of Weber's comments on early capitalism and law for the section on Modern Private Law and Capitalism, below.

Leist died in 1918 and left behind an unfinished manuscript of some 20 pages that was published in 1925, five years after Weber's death.[3] We do not know if Weber ever read Leist's manuscript or, if he did, what he thought of it. In any case, the fact that Leist had been assigned the task of discussing law and capitalism in the handbook of social economics means that Weber stayed away from the topic. If we want to know Weber's position on this topic, we are in the difficult and unfortunate position of having to pull together all the brief statements that can be found in Weber's work on modern capitalism and its relationship to law. This difficult task of reconstruction merits its own separate study, and in this short review I limit myself to a discussion of a few of Weber's well-known statements on modern capitalism and its legal institutions.

Before this discussion, however, I must emphasize that from Weber's perspective the roots of modern rational capitalism stretch far back in time, and what he writes on capitalism and its relationship to law *before* modern times is sometimes also relevant to his portrait of modern rational capitalism. In Chapter 8, for example, Weber makes an important addition to his general statement of what law is

[3]Little is known about the relationship of Weber to Alexander Leist (1862–1918). It appears that Weber had read Leist's study of private law and capitalism, *Privatrecht und Kapitalismus im 19. Jh. Eine rechtsgeschichtliche Voruntersuchung* from 1911 (e.g., Weber 1994, pp. 195, 414, 419, 768, 800). In his contribution to Weber's handbook, "Die moderne Privatrechtsordnung und der Kapitalismus," Leist primarily focuses on the law about corporations and their financing, emphasizing the importance of looking at law in action as opposed to law on the books. His approach can be characterized as legal and broadly social.

when he states that law does not only mean constraint on action (as his famous definition of law may lead one to believe), but also can help to create new social relationships, not least in the economic sphere. This is especially the case with the contract, which is a very old legal institution (what Weber calls "the purposive contract" would eventually replace the original "status contract"). According to Weber, the contract belongs to the type of law that entails "*autonomy* to *regulate* [one's] *relations with others*" or what he refers to as "enabling law" and "legal empowerment law" (Weber [1922] 1978, pp. 668, 730).

This is also the point in Chapter 8 at which Weber discusses another crucial legal institution, the firm, which from a legal standpoint constitutes an associational contract and has its roots in premodern times. Weber draws particular attention to the historical importance of the emergence of the notion of legal personality or, in sociological terms, to the idea that people can create an actor or organization that is separate from their own individual being. This topic had also been at the center of Weber's first dissertation on medieval trading corporations (see the Appendix).

Weber carefully tries to follow how the idea of the modern firm has emerged in the West and what role economic factors have played in this development. He also carefully tracks the evolution of the firm in cultural contexts other than that of the West, in Chapter 8 as well as elsewhere in his work. One can also find an important attempt in Weber's later work to investigate the type of commercial law that has existed in several non-Western cultures, including India and China (cf. Swedberg 1998, pp. 91–99).

Topic 3: Modern Private Law and Capitalism

This brings us to modern rational capitalism, as Weber called it, and its relationship to the legal order. Some clues for how Weber might have handled this topic, if he had not assigned it to Leist, can for example be had from various statements scattered throughout his work. In one of these, he refers to "all characteristic legal institutes of modern capitalism," by which he meant institutions "from the share, the bond, the modern mortgage, the bill of exchange and all kinds of transaction forms to the capitalist forms of association in industry, mining and commerce" (Weber [1922] 1978, p. 1464, n. 14; cf. e.g., Weber 1982, p. 341). A close look at what Weber wrote about the legal dimension of commodity and stock exchanges in the 1890s also gives some indication of how he might have gone about the task of addressing the role of law in a modern economic institution (Weber 1999; for Weber's view of modern mortgage law, see also Weber [1895] 1985).

One can also find some other general statements in Weber's work about modern rational capitalism and its relationship to law. He points out, for example, that with huge investments in industry and the need to have complex economic organizations more generally, it becomes absolutely imperative to be able to calculate, as correctly as possible, the impact of various factors on economic matters, including the law. Although Weber's statements about formal law as a logical system without gaps and about how judges should operate as legal machines have often been commented on, the qualifications that he added about the economic usefulness of legal formalism have attracted less attention. Weber emphasizes, for example, that what is needed for economic operations to be calculable are not primarily formal elegance and coherence but predictability. One can also find a resistance among judges to act like legal machines, Weber says, because this type of behavior goes against their sense of status. Historically, as in the case of good faith, business may also benefit from irrationalities; indeed, many formal legal rules have their origin precisely in irrational behavior. Again, the kind of legal predictability and calculability that modern rational capitalism needs to function properly is considerably more complex than what one may at first think.

CONCLUDING REMARKS ON THE ECONOMIC SOCIOLOGY OF LAW VERSUS LAW AND ECONOMICS

One way of summarizing the argument in this review is to say that Weber's work at the intersection of law, economics, and sociology is complex and in need of further exploration and discussion. Several qualities of Weber's work are particularly useful. First, Weber supplies us with clear and useful definitions of several basic concepts in this enterprise (most famously law). Second, he outlines in an exemplary manner the differences between jurisprudence and a sociological approach to law and between a sociological approach to law and that of economic theory. Third, one can find useful statements in his work about the general relationship between legal and economic phenomena as well as suggestive analyses of the historical interaction between economic forces, on the one hand, and, say, law and politics or law and religion, on the other.

Before concluding this review, I raise a topic that I alluded to in the opening lines about the differences between the economic sociology of law and law and economics. The main similarity between these two approaches is their subject matter; they both focus on the intersection and interaction between law and the economy. The main difference is how this is done. While law and economics is deeply influenced by the method of economics, the economic sociology of law draws on the sociological method. The two methods also differ in the following ways: Whereas economics is normative, sociology is not; and whereas sociology is typically empirical, law and economics is typically not.

Being a sociologist, I find the approach of sociology preferable to that of economics, even if I realize that what makes economic logic so useful to the legal profession is that it can offer something that sociology is not able to provide, namely a normative logic or a type of reasoning that at one point says: This is how things should be done. Sociology is more skeptical, saving itself the errors that come with an explicit normative position, but also unable to become a useful and powerful everyday tool in the life of the law. This, of course, is the price that has to be paid by any social science that wants to adhere to Hume's dictum that you must keep "is" and "ought" separate (for Weber's advocacy of this position, see, e.g., Weber [1922] 1978, p. 312).

Nonetheless, the sociological approach is a powerful intellectual tool for analyzing empirical reality, including the places where law and economy meet, despite the fact that it does not easily lend itself to policy recommendations. This is especially the case with Max Weber, and because his work has been severely attacked by Richard Posner, the most important advocate of law and economics, a few words need to be said about this criticism.

While Posner refers approvingly to Weber's "enormous erudition" and even suggests that he has played "a founding role" in the law and economics movement (without specifying what he means by this statement), he also and more importantly argues that "Weber's methodology is not scientific" and that Weber has "a useless methodology" (Posner 1995, p. 268; 1998, pp. 684–85; 1999). Weber's methodology, according to Posner's reading, leads Weber mostly to observations about "vast world-historical movements" (Posner 1998, p. 685). "He is not a reformer, but a historian and a prophet." The main problem with Weber's methodology, Posner continues, is that it does not aim at "conditional predictions," which is what a scientific methodology should do. Proponents of law and economics, in contrast, have the right type of scientific methodology, and Posner gives the following example of a conditional prediction: "If you raise the cigarette tax, the output of cigarettes will fall; not, the output of cigarettes is going to continue on its downward path" (Posner 1995, p. 267; 1998, p. 685).

Despite what Posner says about Weber's methodology, one can find a few predictions of the type that Posner likes in the work of Weber (if you do this, this will happen), but this is not where the main difference between their methodologies exist. Theoretical economics, of the type that inspires Posner, starts from the notion of actors with assigned preferences that they also know how to realize. Weber's type of sociology, in contrast, starts from a very different position, namely that the actors themselves assign a meaning to their behavior, and that this meaning has to be empirically established because it has crucial consequences for the behavior of the actors. This last qualification, when it is worked out in a coherent and systematic manner—which is what Weber does in his interpretive sociology in *Economy and Society*—makes all the difference in the world. It assigns to the researcher the task of trying first of all to establish how the actors themselves view things, and, secondly, once this has been done, to determine what the consequences of their actions are, first for the actors and later also for other actors.

One may also phrase the difference between law and economics and the economic sociology of law as follows. Whereas law and economics has a traditional view of law as a few key actors getting together and dictating to others what they should do, the economic sociology of law has a much broader scope: Law and justice are what people make them into as well as how they perceive them, and this is something that must be studied empirically. Weber's type of work, in brief, leads in a very different direction from that of law and economics, both when it comes to the analysis and to its implications for political and legal action.

APPENDIX: LAW, ECONOMICS, AND SOCIOLOGY IN WEBER'S LIFE

Weber (1864–1920) had an expertise in each of the three areas that figure prominently in the economic sociology of law: law, economics, and sociology. His legal period began in 1882 when he enrolled at the University of Heidelberg, where he primarily studied law. It ended in 1894 when Weber moved to Freiburg and an appointment as professor in economics. Weber resigned his professorship in economics in 1903 (because of an illness that had started in 1897), and a few years later he began to devote himself primarily to sociology and especially to the enterprise of developing an interpretive sociology.

This gives us three periods in Weber's life: one in which the primary focus was on law (1882–1894), one in which it was on economics (1894–circa 1903), and one in which it was on sociology (circa 1905/1910–1920). In the secondary literature on Weber, scholars sometimes write that Weber first gave up law for economics, and later economics for sociology; one can also find a tendency to draw sharp boundaries between these three periods. Some modification, however, is probably needed on both accounts. It is known today, for example, that Weber's activities in law did not end with his acceptance of the professorship in Freiburg. He did important work on law while he worked as a professor of economics in the 1890s, and he was also interested in constitutional law throughout his life. A few years before his death, for example, he contributed importantly to the Weimar Constitution (e.g., Mommsen 1984, pp. 332–89; see also Weber's writings on Russia in Weber 1995). Scholars have also established that Weber's main work in sociology, *Economy and Society*, grew out of a task that he had accepted in his capacity as an economist, namely to edit a giant handbook in social economics. In his personal life, Weber was involved in a number of lawsuits and gave legal counseling to his friends—all fuelled by his intense and inflammatory sense of justice (e.g., Marianne Weber [1926] 1975, pp. 429–48). A few times he challenged people to duels, although he never fought one.

Weber's legal period began in 1882 when he enrolled at the University of Heidelberg. Among his teachers were experts on commercial law, such as Richard Schröder and Heinrich Brunner, and on mortgage law, such as Karl Ludwig von Bar and Ferdinand Regelsberger. The emphasis in Weber's legal education was on the historical dimension of law, and he was especially interested in commercial law and penal law (Schiera 1987, p. 162).

Weber passed his law exams in 1886, when he also started to work at the Royal District Court in Charlottenburg (Berlin). From 1886 to 1893 he worked in different capacities in the German court system (*Referendar*, *Assessor*). During the first part of this period, he was also a doctoral student and had as his thesis adviser

Levin Goldschmidt, who was an important pioneer in the history of commercial law (for Goldschmidt, see Weyhe 1996). Weber presented his dissertation in 1889 and received his doctorate in May the same year. The topic he had chosen for his thesis was medieval merchant companies, and he was clearly very attracted to topics at the intersection of legal history and economics.

Weber's thesis had a long and awkward title—"Development of the Principle of Joint Liability and the Separate Fund in the Public Trading Company from the Household and Trade Communities in Italian Cities"—and it was part of a larger study that appeared as a book [which today exists in English translation as *The History of Commercial Partnerships in the Middle Ages* (Weber [1889] 2003)]. Weber's second dissertation (*Habilitation*) was presented in 1891 and was also devoted to a topic that dealt with legal history and economics: the emerging market in land in Rome and its legal dimension. The thesis was entitled "Roman Agrarian History and Its Importance for State and Civil Law," and Weber's thesis adviser, August Meitzen, was an expert on agrarian history (Weber [1891] 1986).

When he approached the end of his legal education, Weber had still not decided on what type of career to pursue. He was also somewhat bored by legal studies and longed for a bit of action. In 1892, he was asked to substitute for Goldschmidt, who had fallen ill, and in this capacity he taught Roman legal history and commercial law at the University of Berlin. The next year he was appointed assistant professor in commercial law and German law, and the university authorities clearly regarded him as a rising young star and as Goldschmidt's replacement.

In 1894, Weber left Berlin and moved to Freiberg as professor in economics and public finance. The break between law and economics was, however, considerably less sharp than is often believed. Weber had began to study economics on his own already as a young student, and by 1891 he considered himself to have "become approximately one-third political economist" (Weber 1936, p. 327). An important reason for this development was Weber's sense that economics was a better tool than legal science for understanding and changing social reality. During his time as a law student, Weber had also become an active member in the main association for social reform in Germany, *Verein für Sozialpolitik*, to which most of the country's leading economists belonged.

Weber did not totally give up law when he moved to Freiburg and his professorship in economics. During the Freiburg period (1894–1897), he took a very active part in the attempt at the time to regulate the stock and commodity exchanges in Germany, and he published a number of articles in legal periodicals as part of this effort. According to the leading expert on this aspect of Weber's work, these writings constitute "the principal literary output [of Weber] during his years as Professor of Economics and Public Finance [at Freiburg]" (Borchardt 2002, p. 140). Weber also gave courses on commercial law, the history of German law, and the stock exchange and its law. He was further an active member in the newly created *Association for Comparative Studies in Legal Science and Economics* (Weber 1993, pp. 799–802). In brief, Weber tried during his Freiburg years to be active not only in economics but also in law.

At the University of Heidelberg, where Weber moved in 1897 (still as a professor in economics and public finance), he gave no courses in law but concentrated exclusively on economics. It is clear, however, from his lecture notes and from a proposal for a textbook in economics that he worked on during these years that he paid attention to law as part of what a student in economics should think about. In his general course on economics, for example, Weber touched on property, commercial legislation, and the relationship of law to economic power (e.g., Weber 1990, pp. 8–9, 24, 27, 58–59).

When he lectured on law in Heidelberg, however, he mainly did so from the perspective of economics. I now turn, therefore, to Weber's engagement with economics at Freiburg and Heidelberg, including the courses he taught in this subject (e.g., Tribe 1995). Because Weber had only taken one course in economics as a student, he had to read up quickly on the topic when he became professor at Freiburg. He had, however, already done some reading on his own, and he had also produced a very impressive study for the *Verein für Sozialpolitik* that counted as economics among its historically oriented members (see Weber [1892] 1984). Nonetheless, Weber had quite a bit of literature to catch up on to teach the type of courses that he would be giving during his years as a professor of economics: General Theoretical Economics; Practical Economics; Money, Banking, and the Stock Market; Finance; and quite a bit more.

When Weber worked as a professor of economics, the science of economics in Germany was divided into two camps that fought each other with all the energy they could muster. There were, on the one hand, those who advocated a type of analytical economics (along the lines of Ricardo and Menger) and, on the other, those who advocated what is today known as German historical economics (such as Schmoller and Karl Knies, Weber's one-time teacher in economics). Whereas the former approach largely excluded social (including legal) factors, the latter cast its net much wider. Weber took a stance somewhere between the two, knowing both types of economics and also drawing on both of them in his own work and thinking.

From his time in Freiburg until his death in 1920, Weber always presented himself publicly as an economist; in addition, his appointments after his resignation in 1903 from Heidelberg were broadly in economics (at the universities of Vienna and Munich, in 1918–1920). It is nonetheless clear that a distinct shift in Weber's primary interest took place sometime between 1905 and 1910 in the direction of sociology.[4] Exactly when the transition took place and how it developed over the years, after Weber had left his position at Heidelberg in 1903, is not known.

Weber's interest in history had always lent a certain social dimension to his writings, and one may read some of his writings from the 1890s as an early version of his sociology. But during approximately the last 15 years of his life, Weber embarked explicitly on a different enterprise, to try to lay the foundation

[4]Dirk Käsler sets the date at around 1908–1909, whereas Guenther Roth states that by 1910 Weber regarded his social and comparative type of work as sociology (Käsler 1988, p. 15; Bendix & Roth 1971, p. 37).

for the very special type of sociology that he termed interpretive sociology. The main place where he presented this *verstehende Soziologie* was in *Economy and Society*, even if some other works from this period are relevant as well.

The history of *Economy and Society* is special and centrally important to understanding Weber's sociology of law and its relationship to economics (e.g., Baier et al. 2000; cf. Schluchter 1989, Mommsen 2000). The most important fact for the purposes of this review is that *Economy and Society* was part of a giant handbook of social economics (*Grundriss der Sozialökonomik*) that Weber accepted to edit in 1909 and that eventually resulted in the production of about a dozen huge volumes. Just as Weber decided that the handbook should have sections on topics such as economy and nature, economy and technology, and economy and population, there was also to be a section—which Weber had reserved for himself!—on economy and society. The work that we today know as *Economy and Society* was not, in other words, originally conceived as a general work in sociology but as a sociological work about the relationship between the noneconomic and the economic parts of society. This fact is also relevant to our understanding of the analysis of law that this work contains.

In the end, the handbook of social economics turned out quite differently from Weber's original conception. According to the first plan from 1910, Weber was to write a large number of sections, including three that were labeled *Economy and Society* (for the full plan, see Weber 1994, pp. 766–74). These were described as follows (with the material on law in bold type) (Baier et al. 2000, p. 105):

A. **Economy and Law (1. Principal Relations, 2. Periods of Development until the Present).**
B. Economy and Social Groups (Family and Community [*Gemeinschaftsverband*], Status Groups [*Stände*], Classes, the State).
C. Economy and Culture (Critique of Historical Materialism).

Weber had also committed himself to write one of the two sections on The Legal Foundations of Modern Capitalism. Weber's section was called The Modern State and Capitalism, and its companion piece (to be written by jurist Alexander Leist) was called Modern Private Law and Capitalism. Weber, in brief, had from the very beginning of the project with the handbook decided *not* to write himself on the role of private law in modern capitalism.

By 1914, Weber had changed his mind about the handbook's structure on a number of points, including *Economy and Society* (for the new plan, see, e.g., Bücher et al. 1914). *Economy and Society* was to cover much more material in its new version. The idea of having a separate section in the handbook on the role of law in modern capitalism (*Modern Private Law and Capitalism*) had not changed, however. The structure of *Economy and Society* now looked as follows (Baier et al. 2000, p. 106):

1. Categories of Social Orders. **Economy and Law and the Principles of Their Relationship.** Economic Relationships of Associations in General.

2. Household, *Oikos*, and Enterprise.
3. Neighbourhood, Sib, Community.
4. Ethnic Communities.
5. Religious Communities. Class Conditioning of Religions; Cultural Religions and Economic Mentality.
6. Formation of Community through the Market [*Marktvergemeinschaftung*].
7. The Political Association. **Developmental Conditions of Law.** Status Groups, Classes, Parties. The Nation.
8. Domination: (*a*) The Three Types of Legitimate Domination, (*b*) Political and Hierocratic Domination, (*c*) Non-Legitimate Domination. Typology of Cities, (*d*) Development of the Modern State, (*e*) Modern Political Parties.

The two contributions to what Weber in the 1910 plan had called *The Legal Foundations of Modern Capitalism* were still part of the 1914 plan, but Weber had now dropped their common title. Their individual titles, however, remained the same: *The Modern State and Capitalism* and *Modern Private Law and Capitalism*.

Between the plan of 1914 and his death in 1920, Weber again changed his opinion about how his contribution to the handbook of social economics should be structured. He did not, however, write down or in some other way indicate what he wanted the new (and final) structure of *Economy and Society* to be like. All that we know about this final version—except that it was to be "*shorter*" and "more *textbook*-like"—comes from the fact that Weber finished the first four chapters (Winckelmann 1986, p. 46; Chapters 1–4; Weber [1922] 1978, pp. 1–307). More precisely, he produced a final version of the first four chapters, sent them off to the printer, and corrected the proofs just before he died. He also made references in these four chapters to three more chapters: one on sociology of law, one on sociology of the state, and one on sociology of religion.

All that we know about the final structure of *Economy and Society* can be summarized as follows:

Chapter 1. Basic Sociological Terms.

Chapter 2. Sociological Categories of Economic Action.

Chapter 3. The Types of Legitimate Domination.

Chapter 4. Status Groups and Classes.

Chapter X. [**Sociology of Law**].

Chapter X [Sociology of the State].

Chapter X [Sociology of Religion].

Chapter X - ???

The sections on law in the first edition of *Economy and Society,* published in 1921–1922, after Weber's death, are manuscripts that Weber had written before his decision to restructure this work one last time. In English these manuscripts are known as "The Economy and Social Norms" and "Economy and Law (Sociology of Law)" (Weber 1978, pp. 311–38, 641–900).

ACKNOWLEDGMENTS

For helpful comments I thank Mabel Berezin, Nicolas Eilbaum, Keith Tribe, and an anonymous reviewer.

LITERATURE CITED

Baier HM, Lepsius R, Mommsen W, Schluchter W. 2000. Overview of the text of *Economy and Society* by the editors of the Max Weber *Gesamtausgabe*. *Max Weber Stud.* 1:104–14

Bendix R, Roth G. 1971. *Scholarship and Partisanship: Essays on Max Weber.* Berkeley: Univ. Calif. Press

Borchardt K. 2002. Max Weber's writings on the bourse: puzzling out a forgotten corpus. *Max Weber Stud.* 2(2):139–62

Breuer S, Treiber H, eds. 1984. *Zur Rechtssoziologie Max Webers: Interpretation, Kritik, Weiterentwicklung*. Opladen: Westdeutscher Verlag

Bücher K, Schumpeter J, Heimann E. 1914. Grundriss der Sozialökonomik. In *Grundriss der Sozialökonomik I,* pp. x–xiii. Tübingen: Mohr

Edelman L, Stryker R. 2005. A sociological approach to law and the economy. See Smelser & Swedberg 2005, pp. 527–51

Ewing S. 1987. Formal justice and the spirit of capitalism: Max Weber's *Sociology of Law*. *Law Soc. Rev.* 21:487–512

Gephart W. 1993. *Gesellschaftstheorie und Recht. Das Recht im soziologischen Diskurs der Moderne*. Frankfurt am Main: Suhrkamp

Käsler D. 1988. *Max Weber: An Introduction to His Life and Work.* Cambridge, UK: Polity Press

Kronman A. 1983. *Max Weber*. Stanford, CA: Stanford Univ. Press

Lascoumes P, ed. 1995. *L'Actualité de Max Weber pour la Sociologie du Droit*. Paris: Libr. Gén. Droit Jurisprud.

Leist A. 1925. Die moderne Privatrechtordnung und der Kapitalismus. In *Grundriss der Sozialökonomik. Zweites Buch. Spezifiche Elemente der modernen kapitalitischen Wirtsch. IV, Abt. I Teil*, ed. H Nipperdey, pp. 27–48. Tübingen: Mohr

Macaulay S. 1963. Non-contractual relations in business: a preliminary study. *Am. Sociol. Rev.* 28:55–67

Mommsen W. 1984. *Max Weber and German Politics 1890–1920*. Chicago: Univ. Chicago Press

Mommsen W. 2000. Max Weber's 'grand sociology': the origins and composition of *Wirtschaft und Gesellschaft*. *Soziologie. Hist. Theory* 39:364–83

Posner R. 1995. The sociology of sociology of law: a view from economics. *Eur. J. Law Econ.* 2:265–84

Posner R. 1998. Weber, Max (1864–1920). In *The New Palgrave Dictionary of Economics and the Law*, ed. P Newman, 3:684–86. London: Macmillan Ref.

Posner R. 1999. Introduction. In *Encyclopaedia of Law and Economics*, pp. 1–2. http://allserv.rug.ac.be-gdegeest/foreward.htm

Rehbinder M, Tieck KP, eds. 1987. *Max Weber als Rechtssoziologe*. Berlin: Duncker & Humblot

Renner K. 1949. *The Institutions of Private Law and Their Social Functions*. London: Routledge & Kegan Paul

Rheinstein M. 1954. Introduction. In *Max Weber on Law in Economy and Society*, ed. M Rheinstein, pp. xvii–lxix. Cambridge, MA: Harvard Univ. Press

Schiera P. 1987. Max Weber und die Deutsche Rechtswissenschaft des 19. Jahrhunderts. See Rehbinder & Tieck 1987, pp. 151–68

Schluchter W. 1989. Economy and society: the end of a myth (including Appendix I and II). In *Rationalism, Religion, and Domination: A Weberian Perspective,* pp. 433–68. Berkeley: Univ. Calif. Press

Schluchter W. 2002. The sociology of law as an empirical theory of validity. *J. Class. Sociol.* 2(3):257–80

Sica A. 2004. *Max Weber: A Comprehensive Bibliography*. New Brunswick, NJ: Transaction Books

Smelser N, Swedberg R, eds. 2005. *The Handbook of Economic Sociology*. Princeton, NJ/New York: Princeton Univ. Press/Russell Sage Found. 2nd rev. ed.

Stryker R. 2003. Mind the gap: law, institutional analysis and socio-economics. *Socio-Econ. Rev.* 1:335–67

Swedberg R. 1998. *Max Weber and the Idea of Economic Sociology*. Princeton, NJ: Princeton Univ. Press

Swedberg R. 2003. The case for an economic sociology of law. *Theory Soc.* 32:1–37

Tribe K. 1995. Historical economics, the *Methodenstreit*, and the economics of Max Weber. In *Strategies of Economic Order*, pp. 66–94. Cambridge, UK: Cambridge Univ. Press

Trubek D. 1972. Max Weber on law and the rise of capitalism. *Wis. Law Rev.* 1972:720–53

Turner S, Factor R. 1994. *Max Weber: The Lawyer as Social Thinker*. London: Routledge

Weber M. [1889] 2003. *The History of Commercial Partnerships in the Middle Ages*. New York: Rowman & Littlefield

Weber M. [1891] 1986. *Die römische Agrargeschichte in ihrer Bedeutung für das Staatsrecht- und Privatrecht. Max Weber Gesamtausgabe I/2*. Tübingen: Mohr

Weber M. [1892] 1984. *Die Lage der Landarbeiter im ostelbischen Deutschland. 1892. Max Weber Gesamtausgabe I/3.* 2 Vols. Tübingen: Mohr

Weber M. [1895] 1985. 'Roman' and 'Germanic' law. *Int. J. Sociol. Law* 13:237–46

Weber M. [1895] 1989. The national state and economic policy (Freiburg address). In *Reading Weber,* ed. K Tribe, pp. 120–31. London: Routledge

Weber M. [1907] 1977. *Critique of Stammler*. New York: Free Press

Weber M. [1909] 1976. *The Agrarian Sociology of Ancient Civilizations*. London: New Left Books

Weber M. [1920] 1951. *The Religion of China: Confucianism and Taoism*. New York: Free Press

Weber M. [1921] 1952. *Ancient Judaism*. New York: Free Press

Weber M. [1921] 1958. *The Religion of India*. New York: Free Press

Weber M. [1922] 1978. *Economy and Society: An Outline of Interpretive Sociology*. 2 Vols. Berkeley: Univ. Calif. Press

Weber M. [1926] 1975. *Max Weber: A Biography*. New York: Wiley

Weber M. 1936. *Jugendbriefe*. Tübingen: Mohr

Weber M. 1946. *From Max Weber.* Transl. ed. H Gerth, CW Mills. New York: Oxford Univ. Press

Weber M. 1954. *On Law in Economy and Society*, ed. M Rheinstein. Cambridge, MA: Harvard Univ. Press

Weber M. 1960. *Rechtssoziologie*, ed. J Winckelmann. Neuwied: Luchterhand

Weber M. 1982. *General Economic History*. New Brunswick, NJ: Transaction Books

Weber M. 1988. *Gesammelte Aufsätze zur Soziologie und Sozialpolitik*. Tübingen: Mohr

Weber M. 1990. *Grundriss zu den Vorlesungen über Allgemeine ("theoretische") Nationalökonomie (1898)*. Tübingen: Mohr

Weber M. 1993. *Landarbeiterfrage, Nationalstaat und Volkswirtschaftspolitik Max Weber Gesamtausgabe I/4*. Tübingen: Mohr

Weber M. 1994. *Briefe 1909–1910. Max Weber Gesamtausgabe I/5*. Tübingen: Mohr

Weber M. 1995. *The Russian Revolutions*. Oxford: Polity Press

Weber M. 1999. *Börsenwesen. Schriften und Reden 1893–1898. Max Weber Gesamtausgabe I/5.* 2 Vols. Tübingen: Mohr

Weyhe L. 1996. *Levin Goldschmidt: Ein Gelehrtenleben in Deutschland. Grundfragen des Handelsrechts und der Zivilrechtswissenschaft in der zweiten Hälfte des 19, Jahrhunderts.* Berlin: Duncker & Humblot

Winckelmann J. 1963. Max Weber's dissertation. In *Max Weber zum Gedächtnis*, ed. R König, J Winckelmann, pp. 10–12. Cologne: Westdeutscher

Winckelmann J. 1967. Vorbericht. In *Rechtssoziologie*, ed. M Weber, pp. 15–65. Neuwied: Luchterhand. 2nd ed.

Winckelmann J. 1986. *Max Weber's hinterlassenes Hauptwerk*. Tübingen: Mohr

Annu. Rev. Law Soc. Sci. 2006. 2:83–104
doi: 10.1146/annurev.lawsocsci.2.081805.105900

First published online as a Review in Advance on June 5, 2006

GOVERNMENTALITY

Nikolas Rose,[1] Pat O'Malley,[2] and Mariana Valverde[3]

[1]*Department of Sociology, London School of Economics and Political Science, London WC2A 2AE, United Kingdom; email: n.rose@lse.ac.uk*

[2]*Department of Sociology and Anthropology and Faculty of Law, Carleton University, Ottawa, Ontario K1S 5B6, Canada; email: pat_omalley@carleton.ca*

[3]*Centre of Criminology, University of Toronto, Toronto, Ontario M5S 3H1, Canada; email: m.valverde@utoronto.ca*

Key Words Foucault, power, subjectivity, state, politics

■ **Abstract** This review surveys the development of Michel Foucault's analysis of political power in terms of governmentality and outlines its key characteristics. It examines the spread of this perspective, focusing in particular on how this genealogical approach to the analysis of the conduct of each and of all has been taken up and developed in the English-speaking world. It evaluates some of the key criticisms that have been made of the analytics of governmentality and argues for the continuing productivity and creativity of these ways of analyzing the emergence, nature, and consequences of the arts of government.

INTRODUCTION

Michel Foucault introduced the term governmentality in the 1970s in the course of his investigations of political power. Government, as he put it in the summary of his 1977–1978 course entitled "Security, Territory and Population," was "an activity that undertakes to conduct individuals throughout their lives by placing them under the authority of a guide responsible for what they do and for what happens to them" (Foucault 1997, p. 68). Or, as he put it a couple of years later summarizing the 1979–1980 course "On the Government of the Living," governmentality was "understood in the broad sense of techniques and procedures for directing human behavior. Government of children, government of souls and consciences, government of a household, of a state, or of oneself" (Foucault 1997, p. 82). In these lectures, together with those of 1978–1979 on "The Birth of Biopolitics" (see Foucault 1997, p. 73ff), his work with fellow researchers at the Collège de France such as François Delaporte, François Ewald, Alessandre Fontana, Pasquale Pasquino, and his seminars and lectures in the United States, he proposed a particular approach to the analysis of successive formulations of these arts of governing.

One of the first illustrations of this approach was his analysis, in the lectures of 1977–1978, of the emergence in the first half of the eighteenth century of the idea of reason of state (in Foucault 1997, p. 67ff). Reason of state, he suggested, displaces an earlier art of governing whose principles were borrowed from traditional virtues, "wisdom, justice, liberality, respect for divine laws and human customs," or from common abilities, such as "prudence, thoughtful decisions, taking care to surround oneself with the best adviser." This gives way to an art of governing that assigned priority to all that could strengthen that state and its power and that sought to intervene into and manage the habits and activities of subjects to achieve that end. In these lectures and seminars, Foucault traced a movement from such doctrines of reason of state, through those of *Polizeiwissenshaft*, or police science, through to a form of reason that took as its particular object the political problem of population. In the mid-eighteenth century, he suggests, one sees the emergence of a novel idea, that of humans as forming a kind of natural collectivity of living beings. This population has its own characteristics that are not the same as those that shape individual wills. Thus, populations had to be understood by means of specific knowledges and to be governed through techniques that are attuned to these emergent understandings.

THE ART OF GOVERNMENT

In part at least, Foucault's concern was to understand the birth of liberalism. This he understood not as a theory or ideology but as a political rationality, a way of doing things that was oriented to specific objectives and that reflected on itself in characteristic ways. Liberalism differs from reason of state in that it starts from the assumption that human behavior should be governed, not solely in the interests of strengthening the state, but in the interests of society understood as a realm external to the state. In liberalism, he suggests, one can observe the emergence of the distinction between state and society (Foucault 1997, pp. 74–75). In the course of an analysis that moves from the classical liberalism of the nineteenth century to German liberalism in the decades after World War II and the Chicago School liberalism of the 1970s, Foucault suggests that liberalism is not so much a substantive doctrine of how to govern. Rather, it is an art of governing that arises as a critique of excessive government—a search for a technology of government that can address the recurrent complaint that authorities are governing too much.

We return to liberalism later. For the present, however, we use these short examples to emphasize the novelty of this perspective on political power. This perspective views such power as always operating in terms of specific rationalizations and directed toward certain ends that arise within them. An analysis of governmentalities then, is one that seeks to identify these different styles of thought, their conditions of formation, the principles and knowledges that they borrow from and generate, the practices that they consist of, how they are carried out, their contestations and alliances with other arts of governing. From such a perspective, it becomes apparent that each formulation of an art of governing embodies, explicitly or implicitly, an answer to the following questions: Who or what is to be governed? Why should they be governed? How should they be governed? To what ends should they be governed? Thus, the governed are, variously, members of a flock to be nurtured or culled, juridical subjects whose conduct is to be limited by law, individuals to be disciplined, or, indeed, people to be freed.

Further, instead of seeing any single body—such as the state—as responsible for managing the conduct of citizens, this perspective recognizes that a whole variety of authorities govern in different sites, in relation to different objectives. Hence, a second set of questions emerges: Who governs what? According to what logics? With what techniques? Toward what ends? As an analytical perspective, then, governmentality is far from a theory of power, authority, or even of governance. Rather, it asks particular questions of the phenomena that it seeks to understand, questions amenable to precise answers through empirical inquiry.

In this review, we do not intend to provide an account of the development of governmentality in Foucault's own thought. Instead, we focus on the reception of this approach in the English-speaking world. In retrospect, it is possible to identify a number of factors that contributed to the spread of this style of analysis.

GOVERNMENTALITY: STRATEGIES, TECHNOLOGIES, PROGRAMS

At the start of the 1980s, Foucault's work was being taken up in different ways in various national and disciplinary contexts. In the United Kingdom, the context was undoubtedly political. In the late 1970s, many radical intellectuals of the left were seeking ways to extend and develop Marxist critical analysis to social, cultural, political, and legal practices. They wanted to find a way of analyzing these that did not simply regard them as expressions of, or as determined by, economic relations or the mode of production. Some had turned to Antonio Gramsci and especially his proposition that the exercise of rule involved hegemony or domination at the level of ideas (Gramsci 1971). However, Gramsci's ideas gave few clues as to how one might actually undertake empirical investigation of particular practices. Others had turned to the work of Louis Althusser and to his suggestion that capitalism reproduced itself through reproducing the relations of production, inducing the ideological conditions necessary for its survival through "ideological state apparatuses" (Althusser 1977). However, Althusser's approach also turned out to be functionalist and reductionist, presupposing that every aspect of the school system, religion, and cultural artifacts operated to maintain the existing social order.

Foucault's work had already begun to reorient these ways of thinking. *Madness and Civilization*, a truncated translation of Foucault's *Histoire de la Folie*, had been taken up in the broad cultural movement of antipsychiatry, and books such as *The Order of Things* and *The Archaeology of Knowledge* had been largely received as philosophical and epistemological interventions, not as historical works—although they were seen as containing implicit critiques of the realism of Marxist sociology (Foucault 1967, 1970, 1972). However, Foucault's approach to power had a more immediate effect. *Discipline and Punish* came into English in 1977

(Foucault 1977), and a number of Foucault's lectures and interviews on power dating from 1972–1977 were translated and published in English in 1980 with an extensive Afterword by Colin Gordon (Foucault & Gordon 1980). Many of those analyzing these issues had already recognized that these studies undermined the conventional view of the state as the origin, animator, beneficiary, or terminal point of power. They rendered power visible, in everyday life as well as in institutions, in a more tangible and material manner than Marxism. Even before the publication of the governmentality essay in English, this approach was generating empirical analyses of a number of sites for the creation and management of individuality. These included studies of asylum architecture, the development of the schoolroom (Jones & Williamson 1979), the regulatory role of psy-sciences such as psychology and psychiatry (Rose 1979; Miller 1980, 1981), the administration of the colonies, and much more.

Gordon's Afterword to *Power/Knowledge* identified the characteristics of Foucault's approach to power/knowledge in terms of the concepts of strategies, technologies, and programs (Foucault & Gordon 1980). He argued that each of these axes required an analysis that respected their distinctiveness. We live in a world of often rivalrous programs but not in a programmed world, and programs could not simply be implemented, as technologies have their own characteristics and requirements. Gordon also played a key role in arranging for the first translations of work on governmentality into English. The English translation of Foucault's February 1978 lecture on governmentality was published in 1979 in the short-lived but influential independent journal *Ideology and Consciousness* (I&C) (Foucault 1979). It had been preceded, in 1978, by the publication in the same journal of pieces by two of those in Foucault's seminar, Pasquino (1978) and Procacci (1978), that had demonstrated the fertility of this approach when applied to the political rationalities of police science and social economy, respectively. Each illustrated, through detailed investigation of original archival material, the new insights on political power that could be generated by a focus not on grand texts of political philosophy but on the more minor texts of political thinkers, polemicists, programmers, and administrators. Whether the concern was the economy or the moral order, each was made thinkable and practicable by these governors as a knowable and administrable domain. These analyses also showed how each art of government entailed certain conceptions of the nature and obligations of those who were its subjects, those who were to be governed.

Foucault's essay on governmentality argued that a certain mentality, that he termed governmentality, had become the common ground of all modern forms of political thought and action. Governmentality, he argued, was an "ensemble formed by the institutions, procedures, analyses and reflections, the calculations and tactics, that allow the exercise of this very specific albeit complex form of power..." (Foucault 1979, p. 20). He counterposed the arts of government that were taking shape in Europe in the eighteenth century to two other poles, those of sovereignty and of the family. Ways of thinking about power in terms of sovereignty were "too large, too abstract and too rigid," and the model of the family was "too thin, weak and insubstantial." Although the former was concerned with how a prince might best maintain his power over a territory, the model of the family was merely concerned with the enrichment of this small unit. Government, in distinction, was concerned with population that could not simply be controlled by laws or administrative fiat or conceived of as a kind of extended family.

This emphasis on population was grounded in the specific analyses that Foucault had presented in the earlier lectures in this series. For example, in relation to the politics of epidemics in the eighteenth century, he explored the processes through which authorities had come to realize that the population had a reality of its own, with its own regularities of birth, illness, and death, and its own internal processes that were independent of government and yet required the intervention of government. From this moment on, those who inhabited a territory were no longer understood merely as juridical subjects who must obey the laws issued by a sovereign authority nor as isolated individuals whose conduct was to be shaped and disciplined, but as existing within a dense field of relations between people and people, people and things, people and events. Government had to act upon these relations that were subject to natural processes and external pressures, and these had to be understood and administered using a whole range of strategies and tactics to secure the well-being of each and of all. Authorities now addressed themselves to knowing and regulating the processes proper to the population, the laws that modulate its wealth, health, and longevity, its capacity to wage war and engage in labor, and so forth. To govern, therefore, whether to govern a household, a ship, or a population, it was necessary to know that which was to be governed, and to govern in the light of that knowledge.

Clearly, then, rather than conceiving of the state as the origin of government, one had to ask a different question: How could one account for the governmentalization of the state? That is, how, at a certain historical moment, had the formal apparatus of the state come to embroil itself with the business of knowing and administering the lives and activities of the persons and things across a territory? Although traditional conceptions of power had seen the imperative to govern as the essence of the state, it was now clear that states did not always govern in this sense. And the increasing centrality of a political apparatus to government, beginning in the eighteenth century in the West, was not a matter of a central power extending its sway throughout society through the expansion of the State machinery of control. It was more useful to start from the reverse hypothesis—that at a particular historical moment, states had managed to connect themselves to a diversity of forces and groups that in different ways had long tried to shape and administer the lives of individuals in pursuit of various goals.

The issue of I&C that preceded the translation of Foucault's lecture published a translation of a piece by Jacques Donzelot (1979b) that began to consider the political implications of this approach. The piece was originally published as "Pour une nouvelle culture politique" in 1978, the same year as Foucault's governmentality lecture, and in it Donzelot was particularly concerned to stress the need to move the state from its central role in political analysis. In the politics that had taken shape in France following the student uprisings of 1968, the power of the state had taken over from capital as the target of political protest. For Donzelot, the danger was that power itself would become regarded as the new motor of history. He suggested that the term as currently conceived should be abandoned altogether.

> We would have then not a power and those who undergo it, but, as Foucault shows, *technologies*, that is to say always local and multiple, intertwining coherent or contradictory forms of activating and managing a population, and *strategies,* the formulae of government. . .theories which explain reality only to the extent that they enable the implementation of a program, the generation of actions; they provide through their coherence a 'practical object' (*practicable)* for corrective intervention of government programmes of redirection (Donzelot 1979b, p. 77, emphasis in original).

One effect of this analytical maneuver was that the state would not be seen as a subject of history, but instead only as "a support for technologies" or only as "an effect of governmental strategies" (Donzelot 1979b, p. 78). Donzelot illustrated his analytic with reference to the development of insurance and its nexus with the emergence of "the social." Insurance is depicted as a "very general technology" and a "mathematical solution" characterized by spreading the cost of compensating certain categories of injury or incapacity across "all social partners through a calculated distribution." In turn, it provided a condition of existence for a changing political imaginary oriented not so much around production, as in the nineteenth-century approaches to assistance, but around the provision of security. In this new governmental strategy of social security, new practices and agencies of governance emerge, such as social work, and new instruments of government are invented, such as family allowances. Technologies and strategies are thus seen us mutually formative and thus more or less consistently articulated.

Although these ideas were worked on in his *The Policing of Families* (Donzelot 1979a, originally published in French in 1977), and by the insurantial investigations of his colleagues, Ewald and Defert, not published in English until some years later (Ewald 1986, Defert 1991), this basic outline provided the foundation for later elaborations. During the 1980s, key elements were developed and made more explicit by a small group of British social theorists focusing particularly on the psy-sciences and on economic life (Miller 1986; Miller & O'Leary 1987, 1989; Miller & Rose 1988, 1990; Rose 1988, 1989; Burchell et al. 1991; Gordon 1991; Rose & Miller 1992). These studies also demonstrated that at particular historical moments, programs often had a family resemblance in that they operated to a greater or lesser extent within shared problematizations, or modes of problem formation, and were formulated within shared rationalities or styles of thinking.

This body of work exemplified a style of analysis that would prove very attractive to many others because of its apparent ability to generate detailed empirical studies, both historical and contemporary, of practices of government. One significant contribution was the insistence that the language of programs was not merely to be regarded as an epiphenomenon, a gloss on the practices of rule. Rather, it was an intellectual technology, "a mechanism for rendering reality amenable to certain kinds of action" (Miller & Rose 1990, p. 7).[1] The approach to language developed here was in stark contrast to the Marxist "critique of ideology" approach; but it also diverged, in the opposite direction, from the other main critical perspective current around 1990, namely, discourse analysis. In the United States, many readers of Foucault, familiar only with his early works, identified Foucault's work with discourse analysis, often taken as meaning that the internal organization of discourses directly forms and shapes realities and subjectivities. For example, in American debates on the history of sexuality, Foucault's name became almost synonymous with such an approach. Governmentality studies, however, rejected the notion, popular in some versions of cultural studies, that discourses themselves create realities and identities. Language and other signifying systems were instead regarded as one element among many for rendering reality governable.

Adopting and reworking the idea of translation from Callon & Latour, Miller & Rose argued that language should be analyzed as a key element in the process of forming networks through persuasion, rhetoric, and intrigue. In the assemblage of networks, authorities, groups, individuals, and institutions were enlisted, brought to identify their own desires and aspirations with those of others, so that they were or could become allies in governing. In particular, such networks made possible what Miller & Rose termed governing at a distance—that is to say, acting from a center of calculation such as a government office or the headquarters of a nongovernmental organization, on the desires and activities of others who were spatially and organizationally distinct.[2]

The English governmentality approach also drew upon Foucault's observation that technologies of the self were formed alongside the technologies of domination such as discipline. The subjects so created would produce the ends of government by fulfilling themselves rather than being merely obedient, and in Rose's phrase (Rose 1989) would be obliged to be free in specific ways. Central to this approach was that attention would not only focus on the great technologies such as the Panopticon but would turn to the mundane, little governmental techniques and tools, such as interviews, case records, diaries, brochures, and manuals, that were key to this creative process. By the early 1990s, as a result of this work, the analytical framework of governmentality had assumed the form that, more or less, it takes today.

---

[1]Miller & Rose here were drawing in particular on the work of Jack Goody, as, for example, in his classic paper "What's in a List?" (see Goody 1977).

[2]This idea of "governing at a distance" drew on Latour's play on the idea of "action at a distance"—the possibility of which had been a subject of dispute within the sciences, for example in early debates over the existence of such invisible forces as gravity that appeared to act on spatially distinct entities without any direct or immediate line of contact. Latour and others in the approach that became known as Actor Network Theory (ANT) undertook a number of illuminating studies of these processes (Callon & Latour 1981, Latour 1986, Law 1986; see also Latour 2005).

GOVERNING SUBJECTS

Although Foucault elaborated on his ideas about governmentality in a number of interviews conducted in the early 1980s, his own work began to focus more directly on the government of the self, in particular through developing a novel approach to ethics (Foucault 1982). The intrinsic relation between government and ethics linked Foucault's arguments into the lively debates at that time concerning the question of the subject. During the 1970s, many had argued that the constitution of subjectivity was a key political issue; that capitalism required the production of subjects who imagined themselves to be autonomous, self-possessed, bounded agentive individuals; and that radical thought needed to question this imaginary relation through semiotics or through a certain version of (French) psychoanalysis. The constitution of subjectivity had been a central theme in Marxist analyses of bourgeois ideology, notably in relation to the fiction of the isolated juridical subject of law, and this theme was given a renewed emphasis in Althusser's argument that the key work of ideology was to constitute individuals who took themselves to be autonomous subjects and who enacted their subjection as if it were a matter of their free will. Foucault's earlier work, in taking its distance from what he took to be the unproductive humanisms of phenomenology and existentialism, had, characteristically, addressed this issue genealogically, seeing the emergence of the centrality of the subject as a historical phenomenon, proposing an analysis of discourse that did not give priority to the subject that speaks, and, famously, remarking that this central image of humanism would soon be erased like a figure drawn in sand at the edge of the sea (Foucault 1970, p. 387).

Following his work on governmentality, Foucault began to mark out a new way of thinking about these issues in terms of ethics. Ethics, here, was understood in terms of technologies of the self—ways in which human beings come to understand and act upon themselves within certain regimes of authority and knowledge, and by means of certain techniques directed to self-improvement. Along these lines, Gordon (1987) considered some of Foucault's lectures on neo-liberalism and noted its proponents' ambition that individuals should conduct their lives as an enterprise, should become entrepreneurs of themselves. These arguments were developed in an empirical way in a number of papers by Nikolas Rose, notably in his 1989 book *Governing the Soul*, which focused in particular on the role of the knowledge and expertise of the social and human sciences in the rationales, practices, and technologies of contemporary government (Rose 1989). Although Rose's analysis shared much of its approach with that of earlier authors, it differed in one significant and provocative way in that it kept its distance from the rhetorics of social critique. Earlier authors had tended to link the ethical and the governmental in a diagram of control, allowing a positive space for freedom and self-expression as a site of resistance to government. However, Rose (1992) argued that central to contemporary strategies for governing the soul was the creation of freedom. Subjects were obliged to be free and were required to conduct themselves responsibly, to account for their own lives and their vicissitudes in terms of their freedom. Freedom was not opposed to government. On the contrary, freedom, as choice, autonomy, self-responsibility, and the obligation to maximize one's life as a kind of enterprise, was one of the principal strategies of what Rose termed advanced liberal government. Freedom could no longer be taken so easily as the ground of critique of social control—as in such precursors as Cohen's (1985) *Visions of Social Control*—because the very ethic of freedom was itself part of a particular formula for governing free societies.

LIBERALISM, WELFARISM, AND ADVANCED LIBERALISM

Although at one level this analytical framework was not tied to a specific set of problems, it should be regarded partly as a response to a particular challenge—how to make sense of the transformations in the arts of government that were under way in Britain, the United States, and, to a lesser extent, other Western countries. These took the form of a sustained critique of the welfare state, social security mechanisms, state planning, and state ownership of enterprises, indeed of the whole apparatus of the social state as it had taken shape across the twentieth century. Although many on the left had been critical of the practices of the welfare state, arguing that they were paternalistic, embedded discretionary professional power, extended social control, and actually sustained inequality, few found anything positive in the rise of what was often termed neo-liberalism. But it was in this context that a novel periodization of governmentalities began to take shape.

Liberal governmentalities stressed the limits of the political and stressed the role of a whole array of nonpolitical actors and forms of authority—medics, religious organizations, philanthropists, and social reformers—in governing the habits of the people. Strategies of social government had begun from the argument that such techniques were insufficient to ward off the twin perils of unbridled market individualism and the anomie it carried in its wake, or socialist revolution with all the dangers that it entailed. Government, from this point onward, would have to be conducted from the social point of view, and these obligations had to be accepted by the political apparatus itself—a point of view embodied in the doctrines of social right in France, the ethical principles of social solidarity and social citizenship, and the technologies of social welfare and social insurance. This approach, with its requirement that the state was both orchestrator and guarantor of the well-being of society and those who inhabited it, was problematized by neo-liberal critics in Europe, by Thatcherites in Britain, and by Reaganites in the United States. Like critics from the radical left, they regarded social government as generating government overload, fiscal crisis, dependency, and rigidity. Yet unlike those critics, they created another rationality for government in the name of freedom, and invented or utilized a range of techniques that would enable the state to divest itself of many of its obligations, devolving those to quasi-autonomous entities that would be governed at a distance by means of budgets, audits, standards, benchmarks, and other technologies that were both autonomizing and responsibilizing. Many of these technologies were adopted and retained by social democratic strategies, notably in the programs that came to be termed the Third Way. These new ways of thinking about and seeking to enact the government of freedom characterized the problem space of advanced liberalism.

This tripartite division of liberalism, welfarism, and advanced liberalism was initially a heuristic device to mark the differences among these new arts of government. Later, at least to some extent, it became formalized into a typology and chronology in which explanation consisted of trying to place each and every program, strategy, or technology analyzed under this general covering law. Nonetheless, this mode of analysis also proved its versatility and its productivity. It rendered visible and intelligible the new forms of power embodied in advanced liberal arts of government, and it demonstrated the complex costs and benefits of those rationalities and technologies that sought to govern through freedom.

LOCATING GOVERNMENTALITY

Intellectual innovations do not fall out of a clear blue sky. The concepts and methodological choices utilized in governmentality studies spread so successfully because they resonated with concurrent intellectual trends in a number of relatively independent fields. These helped to give the notion of governmentality and the research questions and perspectives associated with it traction across numerous disciplines, institutions, and geographical locations. Without attempting to be exhaustive, mentioning a few of these concurrent developments can help to illuminate some of the often serendipitous processes through which approaches associated with governmentality were disseminated (though by no means uncritically) across a variety of locations.

Within critical sociology and criminology, the social control analyses popularized in the 1970s and early 1980s were already being criticized as overly functionalist and simplistic by critical theorists before governmentality became a popular word. Corrigan & Sayer's (1985) *The Great Arch: English State Formation as Cultural Revolution* began to build links between Foucault's approach and a kind of neo-Marxism, using intellectual resources from both approaches to dislodge social control models for the study of what they called (following Durkheim) moral regulation. Not by chance, some of Philip Corrigan's Toronto friends and graduate students went on, in the early 1990s, to become part of the Toronto History of the Present group, which encouraged governmentality studies in a number of Toronto-area universities for about ten years. Subsequently, international scholarship in the area of moral regulation (including studies of sexuality and vice) became fertile ground for studies developing governmentality concepts and methods. Alan Hunt, through his studies of sumptuary laws (Hunt 1996) and his more general overview of moral regulation (Hunt 1999), was one of those who developed the conversation between the neo-Marxist approach to moral regulation and the perspective of governmentality. Mariana Valverde's (1998) study of the ways in which drinking and alcoholism have been important sites, in Anglo-Saxon countries, for the formation of liberal subjectivities came out of the same intellectual space but pointed in a more strictly Foucauldian direction (and hence avoided the term "moral regulation," with its Durkheimian connotations). Other work, much of it by feminist and postcolonial writers, explored issues of sexuality, race, and empire and used governmentality perspectives as useful resources to go beyond the denunciation of top-down control that had been popular in the 1970s (e.g., Stoler 1995).

On another front, scholars in Paris and elsewhere working in science and technology studies (STS), honing analytic tools that would later be called Actor Network Theory (ANT), were taking their work in a direction that converged with governmentality methods at three principal points of convergence. First was a radical rejection of structuralist habits of thought in favor of studies showing in detail how knowledge and other resources flow and get recycled in particular networks. Second was a common agnosticism about "why" and "in whose interests" questions, accompanied by a commitment to studying how things get done. Third was an antihumanist stance that refuses to privilege not only Great Men but even Great Movements, considering instead the possibility that material things and processes might play an active role in many important processes. Governmentality studies do not explicitly take up Latour's and Callon's call to consider the agency of things. But there is an affinity between the antisociology developed, for example, in Latour's (1993) *We Have Never Been Modern* and Foucault's interest in examining how material structures (for example prison cells constructed to a certain design) have specific political effects, quite apart from the class or other interests of the people controlling them.

Influential well beyond STS, the work of Hacking and other scholars interested in documenting changes in knowledge practices, codes, and formats (Hacking 1990, Porter 1995) also converged with governmentality studies. Hacking was probably the first major English-language philosopher to take Foucault seriously, and intellectuals who had been alerted by Hacking and others (e.g., Daston 1996) to the theoretical fruitfulness of studying such phenomena as the rise of statistics were predisposed to regard the study of knowledge practices as important for social theory, not only for intellectual history. Poovey's (1995, 1998) influential work, while not itself part of governmentality studies, could be seen as part of the bridge linking the field of the history and philosophy of science to governmentality studies. Finally, within political philosophy, a shift toward studying ideas in context had enabled at least some political theorists to take an interest in problems and topics previously consigned to historians. Tully, one of the few internationally known political philosophers to take an interest in governmentality work, played a particularly important role in this regard (Tully 1993).

The publication of *The Foucault Effect* (Burchell et al. 1991) further consolidated the belief that the analytics of governmentality integrated and extended the insights that were contained within many of these areas. Many of the pieces had been separately available for some time. Yet when the pieces were consolidated in this way and framed with a substantive introduction to governmental rationalities that summarized many of Foucault's unpublished lectures on these topics, something like a school of thought appeared to be taking shape. In fact, this was always something of an illusion because many of the pieces translated from the French had been written a decade earlier, and many of the authors had long since moved on to other work. Further, these papers did not partake in a coherent methodology, and many shared little with the version of governmentality that was being developed in the English-speaking world. Even in that world, in Great Britain and its former colonies, there were many differences of emphasis and different styles of criticism, with some regarding governmentality analyses as descriptive, and others seeking to utilize them within a politics of critique.

DISPERSING GOVERNMENTALITY

By the early 1990s, the fertility of this approach seemed to be demonstrated, in particular its capacity to render intelligible ways of thinking, acting, and governing in a multitude of different practical sites, distant from the lofty concerns of political philosophy and analyses of machinations in high places given by political scientists and others. Although this work was largely ignored in the mainstream of sociology and cognate disciplines, it was taken up in a number of areas. Notable here were low-status regions of applied knowledge such as social work and nursing. It was taken up here not only by theoreticians but also by practitioners. The latter recognized intellectual equipment that would enable them to make sense of the situations in which they found themselves: the ways of thinking and acting that they were obliged to enact and the cramped spaces and conflicting practices that they inhabited.

One key area explored concerned the economy and the government of economic life. This had been a central concern of Miller & Rose's influential paper of 1990 and had been the focus of a number of early papers published in I&C (Donzelot 1981, Meuret 1981). The capacity of this perspective to engage with economic issues was particularly welcome at a time when, with the degeneration of Marxism as a viable research program, many social scientists were abandoning the analysis of economic life in favor of apparently more fertile fields. From the perspective of governmentality, however, one could analyze the economy—from macro spaces of national economies to confined locales of factories or workplaces—in exactly the same way as one might analyze other domains (Miller 1986, 1990; Miller & O'Leary 1987, 1993, 1994; Miller & Rose 1988, 1995; Miller et al. 1991). One could chart the problem spaces within which these zones had been delineated and brought into existence as calculable and manageable spaces—the national economy, the industry, the factory. One could examine the emergence of the forms of knowledge and expertise such as that of management, human resources, or accountancy, which tried to render these spaces thinkable and develop tactics to govern them, often according to indices such as the national debt, the balance of payments, and the rate of profit, and one could examine, in particular, the role of work and the workplace as a crucial site for the formation and administration of individual and group identities.

It became clear that, from the perspective of government, work was as significant as a site of subjectification as it was as a site of economic exploitation, and economic life, from the workplace to the national economy, was crucial in programs for social government. And those gray and tedious sciences of economics, management, and accounting could be seen once again—as they had been by Marx, Weber, Sombart, and many other theorists of capitalism—as crucial for making up and governing a capitalist economy. Indeed, as Power (1995, 1997a,b, 2000) showed so clearly, the technologies of budgets, audits, standards, and benchmarks, apparently so mundane, were crucial for the operationalization of programs of governing at a distance that characterized the forms of new public management taking shape under rationalities of advanced liberalism.

Another central focus for the analytic of government was technologies of risk. Foucault, but more centrally his colleagues in Paris—Ewald, Donzelot, and Defert, among others—had advanced this project during the early 1980s. Ewald's (1986) *L'Ètat Providence*, focusing on risk as a central technology in the welfare state, was never translated. However, the papers by Ewald, Defert, and Castel that were translated in *The Foucault Effect* explored risk technologies, the first two dealing with insurance, the latter with psychiatry (Castel 1991, Defert 1991, Ewald 1991). For all three of these writers, risk is not regarded as intrinsically real, but as a particular way in which problems are viewed or imagined and dealt with. What is specific to risk, in their view, is that it is a probabilistic technique, whereby large numbers of events are sorted into a distribution, and the distribution in turn is used as a means of making predictions to reduce harm. As such it is highly abstract, giving rise to a very wide array of specific forms and ensembles of government. In such work, the interest not only is in the diversity of forms taken by risk, but also with their political and moral implications. Thus, in another foundational paper, Defert tracks the emergence of national workers' compensation insurance (Defert 1991). Although the actuarial nature of these national schemes meant that they were financially much more robust than the existing workers' mutual schemes, the new form of insurance meant that the insured no longer constituted a social community, but were the impersonal subjects of a probabilistic regime. In such analysis, governmentality was intended to describe not merely how government worked and what it sought to make of its subjects, but also what the implications would be for how life is to be led. This aspect was developed in particular by O'Malley (1996b) in his influential analysis of prudentialism, which showed how a central characteristic of regimes of insurance has been the inculcation of a prudent and calculative relation to the future in those who are its subjects.

The 1991 publication in English of these essays on risk and governmentality was closely followed by the English translation of Beck's *Risk Society,* which was immediately adopted by many mainstream sociologists such as Anthony Giddens (Beck 1992, Beck et al. 1994). Despite the shared focus on risk, there was an almost polar opposition between Beck's grand theoretical work, resonating with the grand ruptural sociologies of Marx, Durkheim, and Weber, and the kinds of analysis generated by the governmentality literature. Whereas governmentality eschews the reduction of complex social and governmental phenomena to sociological causes, for Beck the rise of risk society was the effect of scientific and technological development fueled by capitalist growth. By accelerating the rate of technological change, massively expanding its scale, and globally collapsing time-space distantiation, this unholy couple is seen as having created a new species of modernization risks. Exemplified by holes in the ozone layer, nuclear contamination, and global warming, these risks are viewed not only as global in their reach but also as unpredictable using risk technologies. Ironically, in the risk society, risk is seen as merely an ideology concealing the current ungovernability of modernization risks. Consequently, unlike studies conducted under the auspices of governmentality, Beck gives little or no attention to the diversity in form and implications of risk techniques; his theory deploys the vision of a thoroughgoing epochal rupture into the risk society driven by a single motor of history; his account creates a privileged access to reality behind the false surface of risk technology, and on its foundation he mounts a programmatic cosmopolitan politics (Beck 1996, 2000, 2002). In practice, therefore, although some have attempted to overcome this divide, for example Richard Ericson's work on policing and insurance (Ericson & Haggerty 1997, Ericson et al. 2000, Ericson & Doyle 2004) or Nigel Parton's work on risk and child protection (Parton 1991, 1997), governmentality and the theory of the risk society have tended to follow different courses (O'Malley 2004).

In another key area, the large number of scholars pursuing work in postcolonial studies in the 1990s drew on a host of traditions and methods, from psychoanalysis (Bhabha 1990, 1994) to Marxism (Arnold & Hardiman 1984, Spivak et al. 1996, Guha 1997). No generalization about this expanding field would do justice to it, but it is worth briefly noting here that some work in the postcolonial modality by scholars who, like the English Foucauldians discussed earlier, became disenchanted with Marxist theory, began to draw on Foucault's work for its own purposes. Foucault's histories of sexuality were probably of more significance for postcolonial work than the governmentality lecture and the subsequent English-speaking literature, but nevertheless, affinities developed and connections were made. Important here is the fact that Cohn, an older historian of British India, had already alerted scholars in and of the subcontinent to the importance of studying knowledge forms, numeration in particular, in articles collected in *Colonialism and Its Forms of Knowledge* (Cohn 1996). More recently, the influential historian and philosopher Chakrabarty (2000, especially Chapter 3) has used Foucault's governmentality essay (as well as the historiographic ideas of Foucault's colleague Paul Veyne) to help launch a wholesale attack on the static abstractions of conventional sociology, especially the questionable notion of power in general, that resonates at a number of levels with the concerns guiding the present review.

Finally, in this overview of the impact of governmentality approaches on various subfields, we should mention culture. Initially there had been some conflict between those who took up governmentality and those working in cultural studies. Hunter (1988, 1991, 1993, 1994) was one of the first to address culture from the perspective of government, arguing that early programs to extend schooling to the laboring classes, and in particular to inculcate the skills of literacy and artistic sensibility, had, as one of their central concerns, the shaping of citizens with a certain mode of self-reflection and certain civilized techniques of self-government. During the 1990s, many of those researching in the field of culture began to recognize that culture, too, could be analyzed from the perspective of government. A key contribution came from Bennett (1997, 2004), who argued that one could see cultural institutions, museums, exhibitions, and the like as explicitly partaking in certain governmental rationalities. Analyses by Bennett and others showed how these governmental aspirations were embodied in the aspirations of those who planned these developments, in how they situated bodies in space and time, and in their explicit wish to make possible a certain relation of subjects to others and to themselves (Bennett 2004). Culture itself, then, could be analyzed as a set of technologies for governing habits, morals, and ethics—for governing subjects.

CRITICISM AND RESPONSE

If one of the attractions of governmentality has been its capacity to render neo-liberalism visible in new ways, to understand its problematics and how these were linked to its innovative reshaping of liberal technologies, ironically in certain respects this also has become a handicap. Although some writers have made it clear that neo-liberalism is a highly specific rationality (Rose 1996a), a marked tendency has been to regard it as a more or less constant master category that can be used both to understand and to explain all manner of political programs across a wide variety of settings (e.g., O'Malley 1996a, Ruhl 1999). We argue rather that although elements of neo-liberal ways of thinking and acting can be found in most governing regimes and programs today—such as an emphasis on the market as a technology for optimizing efficiency—it is misleading to suggest that such contemporary arts of government are simply implementations of neo-liberal philosophies. To describe both the Blair and the Bush regimes of the early twenty-first century as neo-liberal ignores the fact that, for example, the architects of Blair's Third Way explicitly reject such a description and self-consciously incorporate elements—such as those derived from communitarianism—from elsewhere. Or, again, Bush's regime incorporates ways of thinking from self-styled neo-conservatives into its rationalities and strategies and grafts into the core of many programs and policies a religious moral agenda that has little or nothing in common with neo-liberal formulae.

To describe certain techniques or even programs as neo-liberal indicates their lineage and provides a point of family resemblance with other postsocial governance. This may be useful at a certain level of generality, but it is not the same as describing diverse contemporary regimes or rationalities as neo-liberal. On the one side, this latter move tends to blunt one of the cutting edges of governmentality—its specificity in identifying how government is formulated, how it problematizes, what techniques it uses, and so on. On the other side, it readily lends itself to a kind of cookie-cutter typification or explanation, a tendency to identify any program with neo-liberal elements as essentially neo-liberal, and to proceed as if this subsumption of the particular under a more general category provides a sufficient account of its nature or explanation of its existence. This practice, perhaps, has led to certain accusations that governmentality is guilty of homeostasis—that it provides rigid models of government that are so systematically integrated that change must be accounted for from elsewhere. In our view, to the contrary, the assembled nature of government always suggests that rationalization—the process of rendering the various elements internally consistent—is never a finished process. Rationalities are constantly undergoing modification in the face of some newly identified problem or solution, while retaining certain styles of thought and technological preferences. This is why it is useful to speak about social rationalities of government, without implying that these are all identical in origin or in detail: They form a broad family of ways of thinking about and seeking to enact government, conceiving of that which is to be governed as a society of interdependent citizens and interlinked social and economic processes that are amenable to knowledge and planning. Hence, they can be contrasted to postsocial or advanced liberal rationalities that reject some or all of these presuppositions. In light of this discussion, we can see why some might see analyses of governmentality as sharing with mainstream sociology the tendency to divide history into eras embodying a single principle and to treat these characterizations of the arts of government as conceptually equivalent to such mainstream sociological categories of the risk society or postmodernity. However, if there are foundational principles to governmentality, one of these is a rejection of such totalizing tendencies, replete with the overtones of grand theorization that explains the transformation of society into something substantially novel. To describe a family of programs, strategies, or technologies as postsocial or advanced liberal should not be taken to imply a necessary or linear transformation of government nor (even more problematically) a change at the level of whole societies. The emergence of postsocial governance involves the rather contingent coalescence of a wide array of criticisms of social forms of governance. These included the visions of those strains of laissez-faire liberalism that had from the start been resistant to what were perceived as the accompanying state intervention, diminution of individual responsibility, and constraint of market freedom. They also included critiques from the political left concerned with technocratic domination by welfare expertise, the implied centralization of state power, and even theorizations about the impending crisis of capital brought on by the fiscal crisis of the welfare state. The convergence of these critiques, their rationalization into a coherent political vision, their linking to innovative ways of rethinking markets and individuals, their capacity to utilize or invent mechanisms to translate these into techniques for governing, and their ascendancy into governmental prominence and even dominance came as a complete surprise. In the analytics of governmentality, in contrast to epochal sociologies, transformation was not preordained by the working out of some logic of productive forces, of the contradictions of modernist technology, or whatever. Neither was its success complete or total—in the words of Miller & Rose (1990), governmentality may be eternally optimistic, but government is a congenitally failing operation.

Some have suggested that these analyses focus only upon the mind of the programmer and ignore the messy world of realpolitik, of implementation and nonimplementation—a world far from the serene world pictured in the texts studied by the governmentalists. Analyses of governmentality are portrayed as merely creating abstract ideal types whose explanatory power is doubtful despite their attractiveness as generalized descriptions. Along the same lines, such critics argue that these analyses ignore the role of agency, experience, and resistance, thereby producing an image of government as a juggernaut that is somehow willing itself into existence, implementing itself into reality by mysterious means (Frankel 1997, O'Malley et al. 1997). Although these various criticisms appear closely interlinked, they need to be considered separately. We do not accept that the blueprints or programs of government that are analyzed in these studies of governmentality are ideal types. On the one hand, this image assumes that the blueprints are the second order constructs of analysis, produced by one-sided accentuation, and on the other it assumes that these are intended only as heuristic devices against which reality is to be contrasted. However, such blueprints are, rather, the empirically real plans and diagrams generated by programmers of various kinds. Certainly in some cases, such as the grouping of programs into families such as advanced liberalism, insurance, or the social, some analytical work is involved. But these do not aspire to identify some pure type. Thus, although Ewald focuses on the abstract risk technology as insurance's core characteristic, he is at some pains to stress that there is no one, right, or best application of this technology. It is merely an existing formula of government, common to insurance, that in practice is applied in diverse ways, according to the identification of new opportunities by the insurance imaginary. Indeed, subsequent governmentality research suggests that even this formula is not common to all insurance practice, especially in the era post-9/11 when many assumptions of insurance have been challenged and new innovations made to render insurance viable in this new environment (Ericson & Doyle 2003).

The orientation of governmentality work, then, is not ideal typification, but an empirical mapping of governmental rationalities and techniques. Further, there is no assumption that the mere existence of a diagram of government implies either its generalized acceptance or implementation. Associated accusations of hypostasis, while possibly applying to the work of some who deploy a governmental analytic, ignore governmentality's genealogical foundations and thus its emphasis on the contingent and invented (and thus always mutable) nature of governmental thought and technique. Indeed, once this focus on inventiveness is recognized, most of the force of critiques about the denial of agency also evaporates. Government is not assumed to be a by-product or necessary effect of immanent social or economic forces or structures. Rather, it is seen as an attempt by those confronting certain social conditions to make sense of their environment, to imagine ways of improving the state of affairs, and to devise ways of achieving these ends. Human powers of creativity are centered rather than marginalized, even though such creation takes place within certain styles of thought and must perforce make use of available resources, techniques, and so on.

Some suggest that these analyses are flawed on account of their neglect of resistance. This seems a misconceived criticism. Empirical studies and genealogies of government are full of accounts of conflicts and struggles, although resistance seldom takes the form of a heroic meta-subject. Thus, Rose's (1996b) account of the emergence of advanced liberal rationalities is at pains to stress the role of those who opposed government through the social; but there was, here as elsewhere, no single movement of resistance to power, but rather a conflict of rival programs and strategies (Rose 1996b). The various neo-liberalisms and neo-conservatisms that formed in the 1970s and 1980s were assembled from critiques drawn from across the political spectrum. It is not, then, that studies of governmentality neglect resistance to programs of government, or to techniques for the shaping of conduct; what they do refuse is the idea of resistance derived from the analytical framework of agency versus structure that has haunted so much contemporary social theory. After all, if freedom is not to be defined as the absence of constraint, but as a rather diverse array of invented technologies of the self, such a binary is meaningless. But more than this, structure almost always implies limits to freedom and almost always implies some underlying logic or social force that has to be overcome in order that the structures be breached or transformed. Ironically, by focusing instead on how those who seek to govern imagine their world and seek to fashion it anew, governmentality escapes the cage of structure that itself limits and constrains so much of the sociological imagination.

All of this discussion brings us back to the question of whether governmentality therefore studies only the mind or texts of the programmer. If the alternative is thought to be the sociological study of how programs are actually implemented, or the proportions and numbers of subjects who adopt or refuse governmental problematics and agendas, or whether or not according to their own criteria programs succeed or fail, then there is a limited truth to the statement. Governmental analysis does not aspire to be such a sociology. But there is no reason why it could not be articulated with such work. Those who criticize governmentality for not doing what it never claimed to do can only make their criticism bite to the extent that they imagine governmentality as a systematic theory that can be regarded as having logical incompatibilities with other theories. If, on the other hand, it is regarded as part of an analytical toolbox, good for some purposes but not for others, and capable of being used in conjunction with other tools, then the problem appears more as a limitation of the critique than a critique of the limitations of governmental analyses.

THE LEGACY OF GOVERNMENTALITY

Thirty years on from the initial formulations, the language and approach of governmentality has dispersed, hybridized with other approaches, and gone off in many different ways. This is to be celebrated, especially when its inventiveness is contrasted with the often sterile cookie-cutter approach or the application of a template, a method, or a few catchwords. But what, then, is the legacy? What remains salient and challenging about this approach is its insistence that to understand how we are governed in the present, individually and collectively, in our homes, workplaces, schools, and hospitals, in our towns, regions, and nations, and by our national and transnational governing bodies requires us to turn away from grand theory, the state, globalization, reflexive individualization, and the like. Instead, we need to investigate the role of the gray sciences, the minor professions, the accountants and insurers, the managers and psychologists, in the mundane business of governing everyday economic and social life, in the shaping of governable domains and governable persons, in the new forms of power, authority, and subjectivity being formed within these mundane practices. Every practice for the conduct of conduct involves authorities, aspirations, programmatic thinking, the invention or redeployment of techniques and technologies.

The analytical tools developed in studies of governmentality are flexible and open-ended. They are compatible with many other methods. They are not hard-wired to any political perspective. What is worth retaining above all from this approach is its creativity. We should not seek to extract a method from the multiple studies of governing, but rather to identify a certain ethos of investigation, a way of asking questions, a focus not upon why certain things happened, but how they happened and the difference that that made in relation to what had gone before. Above all, the aim of such studies is critical, but not critique—to identify and describe differences and hence to help make criticism possible.

The *Annual Review of Law and Social Science* is online at http://lawsocsci.annualreviews.org

LITERATURE CITED

Althusser L. 1977. Ideology and ideological state apparatuses (notes towards an investigation). In *Lenin and Philosophy and Other Essays*, pp. 127–86. London: New Left Books

Arnold D, Hardiman D, eds. 1994. *Subaltern Studies VIII: Essays in Honor of Ranajit Guha*. Delhi/Oxford: Oxford Univ. Press

Beck U. 1992. *Risk Society: Towards a New Modernity*. London: Sage

Beck U. 1996. World risk society as cosmopolitan society? Ecological questions in a framework of manufactured uncertainties. *Theory Cult. Soc.* 13:1–32

Beck U. 2000. The cosmopolitan perspective: sociology of the second age of modernity. *Br. J. Sociol.* 51:79–105

Beck U. 2002. The cosmopolitan society and its enemies. *Theory Cult. Soc.* 19:17–44

Beck U, Giddens A, Lash S. 1994. *Reflexive Modernization: Politics, Tradition and Aesthetics in the Modern Social Order*. Cambridge, UK: Polity

Bennett T. 1997. Regulated restlessness: museums, liberal government and the historical sciences. *Econ. Soc.* 26:161–90

Bennett T. 2004. *Pasts Beyond Memory: Evolution, Museums, Colonialism*. London: Routledge

Bhabha HK. 1990. *Nation and Narration*. London: Routledge

Bhabha HK. 1994. *The Location of Culture*. London: Routledge

Burchell G, Gordon C, Miller P, Foucault M.

1991. *The Foucault Effect: Studies in Governmentality: With Two Lectures by and an Interview with Michael Foucault*. London: Harvester Wheatsheaf
Callon M, Latour B. 1981. Unscrewing the big Leviathan: how do actors macrostructure reality. In *Advances in Social Theory and Methodology: Toward an Integration of Micro and Macro Sociologies*, ed. KD Knorr, A Cicourel, pp. 277–303. London: Routledge
Castel R. 1991. From dangerousness to risk. See Burchell 1991, pp. 281–98
Chakrabarty D. 2000. *Provincializing Europe: Postcolonial Thought and Historical Difference*. Princeton, NJ/Oxford: Princeton Univ. Press
Cohen S. 1985. *Visions of Social Control*. Cambridge, UK: Polity
Cohn BS. 1996. *Colonialism and Its Forms of Knowledge: The British in India*. Princeton, NJ/Chichester: Princeton Univ. Press
Corrigan P, Sayer D. 1985. *The Great Arch: English State Formation as Cultural Revolution*. Oxford: Blackwell
Daston L. 1996. *Classical Probability in the Enlightenment*. Princeton, NJ: Princeton Univ. Press
Defert D. 1991. 'Popular life' and insurance technology. See Burchell 1991, pp. 211–33
Donzelot J. 1979a. *The Policing of Families*. New York: Pantheon Books
Donzelot J. 1979b. The poverty of political culture. *Ideol. Conscious.* 5:73–86
Donzelot J. 1981. Pleasure in work. *Ideol. Conscious.* 9:3–28
Ericson R, Barry D, Doyle A. 2000. The moral hazards of neoliberalism: lessons from the private insurance industry. *Econ. Soc.* 29:532–58
Ericson RV, Doyle A. 2004. *Uncertain Business: Risk, Insurance and the Limits of Knowledge*. Toronto/London: Univ. Toronto Press
Ericson RV, Doyle D. 2003. *Risk and Morality*. Toronto: Univ. Toronto Press
Ericson RV, Haggerty KD. 1997. *Policing the Risk Society*. Oxford: Clarendon
Ewald F. 1986. *L'Ètat Providence*. Paris: Grasset
Ewald F. 1991. Insurance and risk. See Burchell 1991, pp. 197–210
Foucault M. 1967. *Madness and Civilization: A History of Insanity in the Age of Reason*. London: Tavistock
Foucault M. 1970. *The Order of Things: An Archaeology of the Human Sciences*. London: Tavistock
Foucault M. 1972. *The Archaeology of Knowledge*. London: Tavistock
Foucault M. 1977. *Discipline and Punish: The Birth of the Prison*. New York: Random House
Foucault M. 1979. Governmentality. *Ideol. Conscious.* 6:5–21
Foucault M. 1982. The subject and power. In *Michel Foucault: Beyond Structuralism and Hermeneutics*, ed. H Dreyfus, P Rabinow, pp. 208–26. Chicago: Chicago Univ. Press
Foucault M. 1997. *Ethics: Subjectivity and Truth. Essential Works of Michel Foucault, 1954–1984*. Vol. 1. New York: New Press
Foucault M, Gordon C. 1980. *Power/Knowledge: Selected Interviews and Other Writings,* 1972–1977. New York/London: Harvester Wheatsheaf
Frankel B. 1997. Confronting neoliberal regimes: the post-Marxist embrace of populism and realpolitik. *New Left Rev.* 226:57–59
Goody J. 1977. *The Domestication of the Savage Mind*. Cambridge, UK: Cambridge Univ. Press
Gordon C. 1987. The soul of the citizen: Max Weber and Michel Foucault on rationality and government. In *Max Weber: Rationality and Modernity,* ed. S Lash, S Whimster, pp. 293–316. London: Allen & Unwin
Gordon C. 1991. Governmental rationality: an introduction. See Burchell 1991, pp. 1–51
Gramsci A. 1971. *Prison Notebooks: Selections from the Prison Notebooks of Antonio Gramsci [Quaderni del carcere]*, ed. transl. Q Hoare, GN Smith. London: Lawrence & Wishart

Guha R. 1997. *A Subaltern Studies Reader, 1986–1995*. Minneapolis/London: Univ. Minn. Press

Hacking I. 1990. *The Taming of Chance*. Cambridge, UK: Cambridge Univ. Press

Hunt A. 1996. *Governance of the Consuming Passions: A History of Sumptuary Regulation*. London: Macmillan

Hunt A. 1999. *Governing Morals: A Social History of Moral Regulation*. Cambridge, UK: Cambridge Univ. Press

Hunter I. 1988. *Culture and Government: The Emergence of Literary Education*. Basingstoke, UK: Macmillan

Hunter I. 1991. *Accounting for the Humanities: The Language of Culture and the Logic of Government*. Brisbane, Aust.: Inst. Cult. Policy Stud., Griffith Univ.

Hunter I. 1993. Subjectivity and government. *Econ. Soc.* 22:123–34

Hunter I. 1994. *Rethinking the School: Subjectivity, Bureaucracy, Criticism*. St. Leonards, NSW: Allen & Unwin

Jones K, Williamson K. 1979. The birth of the schoolroom. *Ideol. Conscious.* 6:59–110

Latour B. 1986. Visualization and cognition: thinking with eyes and hands. In *Knowledge and Society: Studies in the Sociology of Culture Past and Present*, ed. H Kuklick, E Long, pp. 1–40. Greenwich, CT: JAI

Latour B. 1993. *We Have Never Been Modern*. London: Harvester Wheatsheaf

Latour B. 2005. *Reassembling the Social: An Introduction to Actor-Network-Theory*. Oxford: Clarendon

Law J. 1986. On the methods of long-distance control: vessels, navigation and the Portuguese route to India. In *Power, Action and Belief: A New Sociology of Knowledge?* ed. J Law, pp. 196–233. London: Routledge

Meuret D. 1981. Political economy and the legitimation of the state. *Ideol. Conscious.* 9:29–38

Miller P. 1980. The territory of the psychiatrist: review of Robert Castel's *L'Ordre Psychiatrique*. *Ideol. Conscious.* 7:63–106

Miller P. 1981. Psychiatry—the regulation of a territory: a review of F. Castel *La Société Psychiatrique Avancée*. *Ideol. Conscious.* 8:97–122

Miller P. 1986. Accounting for progress—national accounting and planning in France—a review essay. *Account. Org. Soc.* 11:83–104

Miller P. 1990. On the interrelations between accounting and the state. *Account. Org. Soc.* 15:315–38

Miller P, Hopper T, Laughlin R. 1991. The new accounting history—an introduction. *Account. Org. Soc.* 16:395–403

Miller P, O'Leary T. 1987. Accounting and the construction of the governable person. *Account. Org. Soc.* 12:235–65

Miller P, O'Leary T. 1989. Hierarchies and American ideals, 1900–1940. *Acad. Manag. Rev.* 14:250–65

Miller P, O'Leary T. 1993. Accounting expertise and the politics of the product—economic citizenship and modes of corporate governance. *Account. Org. Soc.* 18:187–206

Miller P, O'Leary T. 1994. Accounting, economic citizenship and the spatial reordering of manufacture. *Account. Org. Soc.* 19:15–43

Miller P, Rose N. 1988. The Tavistock program—the government of subjectivity and social life. *Sociology* 22:171–92

Miller P, Rose N. 1990. Governing economic life. *Econ. Soc.* 19:1–31

Miller P, Rose N. 1995. Production, identity, and democracy. *Theory Soc.* 24:427–67

O'Malley P. 1996a. Indigenous governance. *Econ. Soc.* 25:310–26

O'Malley P. 1996b. Risk and responsibility. In *Foucault and Political Reason*, ed. A Barry, T Osborne, N Rose, pp. 189–209. London: UCL Press

O'Malley P. 2004. *Risk, Uncertainty and Government*. London: Cavendish/Glasshouse

O'Malley P, Weir L, Shearing C. 1997. Governmentality, criticism, politics. *Econ. Soc.* 26:501–17

Parton N. 1991. *Governing the Family: Child Care, Child Protection and the State*. London: Macmillan Educ.

Parton N, Thorpe DH, Wattam C. 1997. *Child Protection: Risk and the Moral Order*. Basingstoke, UK: Macmillan

Pasquino P. 1978. Theatrum politicum: the genealogy of capital—police and the state of prosperity. *Ideol. Conscious.* 4:41–54

Poovey M. 1995. *Making a Social Body: British Cultural Formation,* 1830–1864. Chicago/London: Univ. Chicago Press

Poovey M. 1998. *A History of the Modern Fact: Problems of Knowledge in the Sciences of Wealth and Society*. Chicago/London: Univ. Chicago Press

Porter TM. 1995. *Trust in Numbers: The Pursuit of Objectivity in Science and Public Life*. Princeton, NJ: Princeton Univ. Press

Power M. 1995. *Audit and the Decline of Inspection*. London: CIPFA

Power M. 1997a. *The Audit Society: Rituals of Verification*. Oxford: Clarendon

Power M. 1997b. *The Perils of the Audit Society.* London: LSE Public Policy Group

Power M. 2000. *The Audit Implosion: Regulating Risk from the Inside*. London: ICAEW

Procacci G. 1978. Social economy and the government of poverty. *Ideol. Conscious.* 4:55–73

Rose N. 1979. The psychological complex: mental measurement and social administration. *Ideol. Conscious.* 5:5–70

Rose N. 1988. Calculable minds and manageable individuals. *Hist. Hum. Sci.* 1:179–200

Rose N. 1989. *Governing the Soul: The Shaping of the Private Self.* London: Routledge

Rose N. 1992. *Towards a critical sociology of freedom.* Inaug. Lect., Goldsmiths Coll., London, May 5

Rose N. 1996a. The death of the social? Refiguring the territory of government. *Econ. Soc.* 25:327–56

Rose N. 1996b. Governing 'advanced' liberal democracies. In *Foucault and Political Reason*, ed. A Barry, T Osborne, N Rose, pp. 37–64. London: UCL Press

Rose N, Miller P. 1992. Political power beyond the state: problematics of government. *Br. J. Sociol.* 43:173–205

Ruhl L. 1999. Liberal governance and prenatal care: risk and regulation in pregnancy. *Econ. Soc.* 28:95–117

Spivak GC, Landry D, MacLean GM. 1996. *The Spivak Reader: Selected Works of Gayatri Chakravorty Spivak*. New York/London: Routledge

Stoler A. 1995. *Race and the Education of Desire: Foucault's History of Sexuality and the Colonial Order of Things*. Durham, NC: Duke Univ. Press

Tully J. 1993. *An Approach to Political Philosophy: Locke in Contexts*. Cambridge, UK: Cambridge Univ. Press

Valverde M. 1998. *Diseases of the Will: Alcohol and the Dilemmas of Freedom*. Cambridge, UK: Cambridge Univ. Press

Annu. Rev. Law Soc. Sci. 2006. 2:105–23
doi: 10.1146/annurev.lawsocsci.2.081805.110015

First published online as a Review in Advance on June 16, 2006

THE DEATH OF LABOR LAW?

Cynthia L. Estlund
New York University School of Law, New York, NY 10012; email: ce21@nyu.edu

Key Words employment, unions, collective bargaining

■ **Abstract** This review tells three interlocking tales of decline, each with its respective prognosis for recovery: the declines of labor law scholarship, labor law, and organized labor. The relationship between the latter two and the role that a reformed labor law might play in reviving organized labor are matters of continuing controversy. In the meantime, two developments on the ground suggest a way forward for organized labor, labor law, and labor law scholars. Activist unions have found success with a new organizing model: neutrality and card-check agreements. Elsewhere, antisweatshop activists are developing increasingly sophisticated supplier codes and monitoring schemes to improve labor standards in developing countries. Both strategies, with their basically contractual architecture, exemplify what regulatory scholars are calling new governance. These strategies suggest a potential way around the roadblocks that meet labor law reform proposals and toward more agile and responsive forms of workplace governance.

INTRODUCTION

Labor law is clearly ailing, both as a field of law and as a field of study. By labor law, I mean the body of federal law that governs private sector workers' efforts to advance their own shared interests through self-organization and collective protest, pressure, negotiation, and agreement with employers. I thus follow conventional American usage that, somewhat idiosyncratically, distinguishes labor law from the unruly but dynamic hodgepodge of individual employee rights, antidiscrimination laws, tort and contract doctrines, statutory minimum standards, and all the rest that goes under the heading of employment law. Thus defined, the health and vitality of labor law, both as a body of law and as a field of scholarly inquiry, hinges on the vitality of the institutions that define labor law: labor unions and collective bargaining. Therein lies the problem. Organized labor's share of the private sector workforce, and hence the ambit of collective bargaining, has fallen to about 8%—lower than it was before the National Labor Relations Act (NLRA or the Act) was passed in 1935. Labor law has thus become nearly irrelevant to the vast majority of private sector American workers.

In this review I tell three interlocking tales of decline, each with its respective prognosis for possible recovery: the decline (and possible revival) of labor law scholarship, of labor law, and of organized labor. As much as an academic reader might wish otherwise, one must concede at the outset that the decline, and declining prestige, of labor law scholarship is an epiphenomenon of the decline of labor and of labor law. The relationship between those last two developments, by contrast, is a matter of continuing dispute, as are the role that a reformed labor law might play in the rejuvenation of organized labor and the question of whether either of those can happen without the other coming first. Indeed, those disputes sustain and animate much of the labor law scholarship that remains.

Let us begin with a question that is near and dear to labor law academics: Why has the prestige of labor law within the American legal academy fallen so low?[1] From this rather narcissistic starting point, I follow some of the threads that tie together these three lapsarian tales.

THE GLORY DAYS OF LABOR LAW AND ITS SCHOLARSHIP

For much of the twentieth century, labor law scholars were at the forefront of the legal academy. The field drew leading figures in academic law—Robert Hale, Felix Frankfurter, Jerome Frank, and Archibald Cox, for example. One major law school put labor law into its required first-year curriculum; no respectable law school could neglect the area. Nowadays, by contrast, labor law is regarded as a virtual backwater in the legal academy. More than one major law school does not feel the need to have even one labor law scholar on its full-time faculty. How did this happen?

The glory days of labor law scholarship have their origins in the pre–New Deal *Lochner* era, in which the law of the workplace was the primary battleground for the great and absorbing constitutional showdown between the judiciary and the legislatures over the proper allocation of authority over social and economic relations. Legislative efforts to regulate the terms of the labor contract posed frequent and direct challenges to the reigning constitutional construct of liberty of contract (e.g., *In re Debs* 1895, *Lochner v. New York* 1905, *Adair v. U.S.* 1908, *Coppage v. Kansas* 1915). Moreover, labor organizing and protest activity, and the efforts of employers and their governmental allies to suppress it, precipitated pivotal legal contests over the scope of judicial power, and especially equitable power: Government by injunction became a rallying cry for the adversaries of judicial imperialism (Frankfurter & Green 1930). The labor question was one of the most pressing social and economic issues of the age.

The legal academy was deeply engaged in this battle. The leading school of legal academic thought leading up to the New Deal—Legal Realism—formed around the critique of the liberty of contract paradigm that was used to strike down much early twentieth century labor legislation. Robert Hale, Morris Cohen, and their fellow Legal Realists at Columbia and Yale addressed themselves directly and urgently to this building constitutional crisis (Cohen 1928, Cook 1918, Hale 1923,

[1]An earlier rendition of parts of this tale appears in Estlund 2002a.

Hohfeld 1913). Felix Frankfurter, from his elite perch at the Harvard Law School, was central both in building the intellectual case against the labor injunction and in drafting the legislative efforts to contain it (Frankfurter & Green 1930, Pope 2002). And the intellectual foundations of the Wagner Act, still the basic charter of modern American labor law, were partly shaped by legal academics, many of whom were highly engaged public intellectuals (Barenberg 1993).

The stature of labor law within the academy was bolstered by the romance of the labor movement and of the New Deal breakthrough. The Wagner Act was born in a moment of high drama, complete with heroes and villains and plenty of suspense, in the wake of a sweeping electoral mandate for government intervention in the economy and a wave of labor militancy (Bernstein 1970). Its constitutional vindication in 1937 in *NLRB v. Jones & Laughlin Steel* was the climax of a gripping tale of political brinkmanship by the president, the Congress, and the Supreme Court. The storied switch in time that saved the Wagner Act, the New Deal, and on some accounts the Court itself, burnished the epic quality of the Act.

Moreover, the Wagner Act and its constitutional vindication seemed to promise a just and peaceable resolution to the labor question that had plagued American society for generations. This peaceable resolution was not always so peaceable in the making. Labor's still controversial organizing and protest activities elicited from the Court some of its foundational First Amendment decisions (*Hague v. CIO* 1939, *Thomas v. Collins* 1945, *Thornhill v. Alabama* 1940; see Rabban 1997). At the same time, the ranks of organized labor exploded in the years following the Wagner Act and especially during World War II, and collective bargaining became normalized. The scholars and the scholarship that played a part in bringing about that resolution were toiling at the very heart of the public agenda.

The Wagner Act inaugurated a scheme of industrial self-governance informed by decades of trade union practice, energized by the visionary leadership of a new generation of industrial unionists, and filtered through the brilliant statesmanship of Senator Wagner (Barenberg 1993). The animating ideas, reflected in the quasi-constitutional text of the NLRA's basic provisions, were grand and ennobling, for they proposed the extension of freedom and democracy into industrial life (Becker 1993, Summers 1979). The Act articulated fundamental rights, it laid the groundwork for institutions of self-governance within industry, and it reconceived the nature of contract and private ordering within the labor market. All these qualities lent to labor law scholarship the prestige associated with public law and constitutional lawmaking.

But there was more. The new labor law regime required enormous institutional adjustments, both before and after the major antiunion Taft-Hartley amendments of 1947. The NLRA itself brought about a massive shift of decision-making power from state and local law to national law, and from judicial to administrative law-making processes. It also promoted a collective bargaining regime and a system for the resolution of industrial disputes that spawned a body of law about arbitral versus judicial authority in the interpretation and enforcement of collective agreements, and about the reach of collective versus individual contract. The Supreme

Court was necessarily a frequent and leading actor in carrying out these great institutional changes and engaged leading members of the labor law academy in an intense and high-profile dialogue. Archibald Cox himself carried on a remarkable dialogue with the Court (Cox 1948, 1951, 1954a,b, 1957, 1958, 1959; Cox & Dunlop 1950). The law of federal labor preemption, the federal common law of collective bargaining agreements and of deference to labor arbitration, unions' duty of fair representation and the scope of their exclusive representation, and the principles governing judicial review of National Labor Relations Board (NLRB) decisions were among the watershed developments of this period. The labor law scholars of the 1940s, 1950s, and early 1960s could realistically aspire to participating in this high-level dialogue and to making a real mark on what all agreed were fundamental issues of institutional design and public policy.

The nature of those institutional settlements further elevated the stature of labor law and scholarship during this era. The Legal Process school of thought, which held that the law's legitimacy lay in its allocation of decision-making authority to the appropriate institutional actors, was the dominant postwar school of thought among elite law faculties about the nature of legal authority (Eskridge & Frickey 1994, Hart & Sacks 1994). The most important law was the law of who decides. And that was what labor law was all about during this postwar era: It was a highly elaborated jurisprudence of who decides.

THE OSSIFICATION AND DECLINE OF LABOR LAW SINCE THE 1970s

So what happened to push labor law scholarship to the margins of the legal academy? First, of course, there was the steady decline of organized labor to less than 10% of the private sector, a phenomenon to which I return below. There can be no collective bargaining without collective representation. Not surprisingly, the shrinking reach of labor law and collective bargaining brought with it a decline in the prestige and perceived importance of labor law scholarship. But there is more to the story.

Labor and Labor Law in the Civil Rights Era

The 1950s were the best and the worst of times for organized labor. The movement reached its peak in numbers and in ideological diversity and found itself in various quarters battered by the anticommunist, antileft crusade, corrupted by criminal elements, and seduced by the powers that be. The labor movement emerged from the 1950s not only smaller in size, but smaller in spirit. It began to look and act less like a social movement for industrial democracy and basic economic rights and more like a self-interested faction seeking more of the economic pie for itself—indeed, more like the corporate moguls across the bargaining table, but without the enduring advantages of capital ownership or the voracious drive toward expansion. As George Meany became the face of the labor movement, the labor movement became part of the establishment. It did not help that, during the political coming of age of much of the current professoriat, some union leaders cast their lot against both the student peace movement and, in some regions and sectors, against civil rights activists. The resulting gulf between the student activists and the labor movement helped to define what was new in the New Left.

At the same time, the civil rights movement's demands for equal citizenship brought about a new wave of constitutional claims and structural demands, for example for more aggressive judicial protection of individual rights and judicial supervision of public institutions and for greater federal power over states. Those demands claimed much of the moral gravitational force and intellectual space within the legal academy that the labor movement had during the 1930s. *Brown v. Board of Education* (1954) and the legal assault on segregation became the defining conflict around which much of the legal academy elite circled (Black 1960, Brest 1976, Fiss 1976). Even compared with the labor movement of the 1930s, the civil rights movement had the added virtue, from the perspective of the legal academy, of putting lawyers and judges at the forefront of the battle for progress and justice. In the 1930s, judges were seen as the agents of reaction, and progressive lawyers devoted much of their energies to keeping labor disputes out of the courts. But in the 1960s and 1970s, courts were among the main stages of the drama, and lawyers and judges were among its heroes (Bass 1981).

During this period, union leaders often found themselves at odds with the civil rights movement rather than in alliance with it. Some unions had a long history of excluding black members and resisting their entry into the trades. Others, especially the unions of the Congress of Industrial Organizations (CIO), had historically pursued a policy of integration (Cohen 1990). But unions were majoritarian institutions, and the white majority still fought within many local unions and unionized workplaces to maintain the seniority and privileges they had secured in mostly segregated plants against the claims of subordinated black workers for their rightful place within the plants. Organized labor came to be seen as part of the problem that progressive social movements and the emerging public interest legal community sought to address, not as part of the solution. This perception was reflected in labor law scholarship, which began to focus less on the practice and the promise of collective bargaining and more on its oppressive or reactionary potential. Inspired by union dissidents and discontented minority groups, they turned away from the majoritarian core of collective bargaining (e.g., Atleson 1975, Klare 1982).

The Ossification of Labor Law

At the same time, labor law itself began to look less like public law and institution building and more like private law. For one thing, there have been no major statutory reforms since 1947 and almost no statutory changes at all since 1959 (Brudney 1996a, Estlund 2002b). Within about a decade of the last meaningful legislative changes, or at least by 1970, the big structural and institutional issues generated by the labor legislation of the mid-twentieth century were largely settled. The issues that remained were important, but they were mainly important within the shrinking world of collective bargaining. What constituted concerted activity (Finkin 1985, George 1988, Gorman & Finkin 1981)? What did it mean to discriminate against union members, particularly within the context of a labor dispute and the deployment of economic weapons (e.g., Getman 1965, 1967)? What were the permissible bounds of employers' antiunion campaigns (Getman et al. 1976)? These issues were comparatively low profile outside the specialized arena of labor law and did not seem to implicate transcendent issues of public policy and public law.

Indeed, the intellectual agenda that had put labor law at the center of the legal academy in the 1950s, and the very success of the labor law scholars of that era, contributed to the marginalization of labor law in subsequent decades. The whole objective of the "legal process" decisions of the 1950s and early 1960s had been to remove labor law as much as possible from the courts and from politics—from the central institutions of public lawmaking—and to locate it within the domain of experts—labor arbitrators and the NLRB. Once that was done, the Supreme Court's interventions in the elaboration of labor law became less frequent and more incremental.

Indeed, once the major statutes were in place and the major institutional issues were settled in the early 1960s, the core of American labor law became cut off—to a remarkable extent and for a remarkably long time—both from democratic revision and renewal and from local experimentation and innovation. The basic statutory language and many of the intermediate-level principles and procedures through which the essentials of self-organization and collective bargaining are put into practice have been nearly frozen, or ossified, for more than 50 years. The elements of this process of ossification are mostly familiar; yet, once assembled, they make up an impressive set of barriers to innovation (Estlund 2002b).

Most importantly, a longstanding political impasse at the national level has blocked any major congressional revision of the basic text since at least 1959. Nearly the entire text of the NLRA dates from either 1935 or 1947. Needless to say, much has happened since then. The labor force has changed, as women have flooded into the workforce and racial and ethnic diversity has burgeoned. The economy has changed, as manufacturing has shrunk relative to the service sector and the new information sector, and as the technology of transportation and communication has increasingly eroded geographic constraints on product markets and on the location of production. The organization of work has changed, as mass production and stable workplace hierarchies have given way to more flexible, customer-centered production methods and semiautonomous team-based organizations. The surrounding legal landscape has changed, as laws regulating substantive terms of employment and granting individual employee rights have proliferated. And the basic NLRA scheme has become dysfunctional—distorted in some cases by judicial interpretation, but in any case inadequate to the task of protecting the rights of self-organization and collective bargaining under modern conditions.

Beginning in the 1970s, organized labor has mounted several major campaigns for labor law reform and has several times gained a congressional majority. Labor has targeted in particular the rules governing union organizing and representation elections, which effectively sanction aggressive antiunion campaigns; the weak and long-delayed remedies for unfair labor practices; and the legality of the increasingly common practice of permanently replacing strikers. But all such reform bills have gone down to defeat in the face of an exceptionally united employer opposition. In the meantime, the aging and unrevised text of the NLRA and the collectivist ethos that it expresses have begun to sound like a vintage 78 rpm recording—a scratchy voice from the distant past.

The age of the basic text would be striking enough, but that is only the beginning of the story of ossification, for the text itself and the structure it establishes contain additional obstacles to change. First, the original and unrevised federal ban on company unions—broadly worded and broadly interpreted—has inhibited the development of competing, employer-sponsored forms of employee representation, some of which might have been or become viable alternative vehicles of employee voice. Forms of employee representation that are in wide use elsewhere in the developed world, and forms of representation that many U.S. employees say they would favor, are made illegal by this 70-year-old statutory provision (Freeman & Rogers 1999).

Many of the Act's basic provisions, broadly worded as they are, would seem to leave ample room for reinterpretation; yet the Act's mechanisms for reinterpretation are limited and increasingly narrow. The absence of a private right of action by which workers might enforce their rights under the Act—a deliberate choice by a New Deal Congress that was deeply distrustful of courts—excludes the energies of private plaintiffs and their attorneys and the creative role of courts. Private litigation might have produced innovative interpretations of the Act as well as decentralizing and energizing the enforcement of employee rights. Responsibility for adjusting the Act to modern conditions has instead been entrusted to the NLRB; yet the NLRB is itself increasingly constrained by the age of the text, the encrustation of binding precedent, and the growing dissonance between the collectivist premises of the New Deal labor law regime and the prevailing legal-political climate of market and managerial freedom tempered by individual rights (Brudney 1996b).

Potential channels of revision and variation from outside the congressional scheme have also been closed: The broad implied federal preemption of most state and local laws affecting collective labor relations blocks democratically inspired reforms or variations at the state and local level, as well as state common law innovation (Estlund 2002b). Federal labor law preemption was one of the great institutional settlements of the 1950s and 1960s. But the preclusion of state labor law initiatives has come to haunt organized labor as federal law aged and proved resistant to revision. To describe just one example of what might have been, the public policy exception to employment at will under state common law might have generated a wrongful discharge action for terminated union activists, but preemption doctrine bars that cause of action.

Nor has legal change and ferment from above—from the federal Constitution and international human rights law—penetrated the calloused hide of labor law. An unusually sturdy deference to congressional judgment has made labor law largely impervious to constitutional scrutiny and has insulated labor law from an evolving body of norms that have extended robust protection to nonlabor protest and remade the law of public employment. Resistance to transnational legal authority, endemic to American law, has insulated labor law from the potential influence of international human rights or other labor rights such as those that have forced the reexamination of national labor laws in Europe.

So we find that American labor law has been insulated from both internal and external sources of renovation. It has been cut off from revision at the national level by Congress; from market-driven competition by employers; from the entrepreneurial energies of individual plaintiffs and the plaintiff's bar, and the creativity they can sometimes coax from courts; from variation at the state or local level by representative or judicial bodies; from the winds of changing constitutional doctrine; and from emerging transnational legal norms. Even without knowing where any of these potential paths of change might have led, one can surmise that change or experimentation through one or more of these channels might have produced, over the past half-century, a body of labor law that was more responsive to the very different economic and social conditions that workers and employers face today.

Consider, by contrast, the sprawling hodgepodge of employment law, and especially the law of employment discrimination, where real innovation has taken place through multiple channels of legal change. Congress has revisited and revised the law of employment discrimination several times in the past three decades in response to changing social norms. Moreover, employment discrimination law has encouraged rather than prohibited employer-initiated organizational reforms that aim to internalize public law norms; the corporate embrace of norms of nondiscrimination and diversity is one of the great success stories of law reform in the twentieth century. Part of this success story has come about as a result of litigation. Private rights of action abound within employment discrimination law and have brought the energy, ideas, and impatience of private plaintiffs, attorneys, and advocacy groups and the motivating power of litigation and of courts into the process of law reform. And the potential channels of law reform are many, for federal employment discrimination law does not preempt state law, which has produced its own variations on the reach, operation, and enforcement of the antidiscrimination norm—for example, state and local bans on discrimination based on sexual orientation, which federal law still permits. All these sources of dynamism have helped to bring about a remarkable transformation of institutional norms regarding workforce diversity and discrimination. They have also enlivened legal scholarship.

None of this has happened within the traditional confines of labor law for nearly four decades. One may argue that no other major American legal regime—no other body of federal law that governs a whole domain of social life—has been so insulated from significant change for as long as labor law has been. Major legislation continues to face potent roadblocks; yet without major legislation, the other major blockages to reform—especially the lack of private rights of action, the encrustation of Supreme Court precedents constraining the NLRB, the ban on nontraditional forms of employee representation within firms, and the preemption of state and local law—remain locked in place.

So one cause of the decline of labor law scholarship is the decline of labor law itself. There has been little new law to write about and few realistic openings for law reform for several decades now. Underlying both the decline of labor law scholarship and the decline of labor law, of course, is the decline of organized labor. At a minimum, a larger and more powerful labor movement could presumably have broken through some of the political roadblocks and gained some favored statutory reforms. Such a change might have reinvigorated labor law scholarship as well. Instead, scholars of labor law and labor relations have devoted much of their energies to explaining the decline of labor.

Scholars have advanced several explanations, not mutually exclusive but competing for emphasis, for union decline. A favorite theme among legal scholars is the role of increasingly brazen employer resistance and the law's ineffectual response to that resistance (Craver 1993; Freeman & Kleiner 1990; Gottesman 1993; Weiler 1983, 1990). Many underscore, as an additional, alternative, or underlying factor, the role of structural economic change, including deindustrialization, deregulation, and increasingly global and competitive product markets (Craver 1993, Estreicher 1993, Troy 1990). In particular, there are multiple points of friction between traditional unionism and what Stone (2004) calls "boundariless workplaces," or what Hyde (2003) calls "high-velocity labor markets." Others point to a mismatch between traditional adversarial unionism and the preference of employees and employers for cooperative labor relations (Freeman & Rogers 1999). Others point at least one finger at unions themselves—at their lukewarm commitment to organizing for several crucial decades (Getman 1997), or at some unions' corruption and infiltration by organized crime and the relative quiescence of the rest of the union movement in the face of that blight (Jacobs 2006).

These factors do not operate independently. Increasingly competitive and global product markets surely intensify management resistance to unionization and collective bargaining, while undermining workers' confidence that unionization can secure significant economic gains. Increasingly vehement management opposition provokes a combative, adversarial response from unions, undermines the prospects for trust and cooperation, and convinces many employees that the risks from unionization—especially the risk of job loss, whether at the hands of a resentful employer or through the cold logic of competitive markets—outweigh the prospect of pulling concessions from a resistant employer. All in all, however, management opposition—usually aggressive and often illegally coercive—plays a direct and pivotal role in the frustration of many of the organizational campaigns that do get off the ground, and prevents many others from coalescing at all. Or at least management must believe it to be so, given the millions of dollars in antiunion consulting fees and millions of hours of employee work time that are spent every year to defeat unionization campaigns (Logan 2002).

To whatever extent law makes a difference, labor law's ossification has surely contributed to the decline of organized labor (Estlund 2002b): By the ordinary workings of creative destruction in a market economy, existing unionized firms and workplaces are bound to shrink and die every day. And under our labor laws, every new firm and every new workplace start from a nonunion baseline. Given that employees must make an affirmative choice to organize themselves, and that most employers aggressively oppose that choice, it is evident—and it is a basic assumption of the Act—that employees need the law's help in order to have a real choice with respect to self-organization. Yet rigidity in the face of change has crippled the law's capacity to protect employees' associational rights. It has buttressed the nonunion baseline from which all new workplaces begin and allowed the creative destruction and the deliberate deunionization of organized workplaces to outrun the pace of new organizing. For these reasons, the proponents of unions and collective bargaining have mounted several major campaigns for labor law reform, whereas employers' allies have mostly been content to sit back and monitor the aging process.

The Impact on Labor Law Scholarship

Back in the halls of academe, the stagnation of labor law has inevitably taken a toll on labor law scholarship. As the realistic prospects for legal change were confined to fewer and narrower channels, labor law scholarship that stayed within those channels began to look specialized and interstitial. Some in the labor law academy, seeing that labor law was out of sync with emerging economic realities, put forward more ambitious diagnoses of the law's pathology and prescriptions for a cure (e.g., Becker 1993; Craver 1992; Estreicher 1993; Gottesman 1993; Harper 2001; Weiler 1983, 1984). The political impracticability of significant labor law reform fostered a sense of futility among labor law scholars and prompted a movement away from law reform scholarship and toward broad-gauged criticism of the premises of labor law (e.g., Atleson 1983, Klare 1978, Stone 1981). Theorizing the failings of the existing system came to seem more worthwhile to many on the left than constructive criticism and reform proposals that were doomed to failure. This new current of labor law scholarship connected with a different set of conversation partners—not legal decision makers but fellow scholars within an increasingly academic and interdisciplinary legal academy. Of course, those scholarly trends transcended labor law; but for a while in the late 1970s through the 1980s, labor law became a major playing field for critical legal scholarship of this sort. Some of this scholarship was very sophisticated and thoughtful and exposed some fundamental weaknesses in the system of labor law that contributed to its increasingly evident failings. But the appetite of the rest of the legal academy for this kind of incisive pathology diminished as the body of labor law itself grew increasingly cold.

Another perspective on the pathology of labor law came from the other end of the legal-political spectrum: the law-and-economics movement. For some early exponents of law and economics, labor law appeared to be emblematic of the misconceived New Deal–era approach to economic activity: It rejected the elegant logic of the market and of individual contract in favor of collective action and government-sponsored cartelization of the labor market. With the temporary zeal of missionaries, and with as little respect for the local culture, several law-and-economics scholars brought the harsh logic of the neo-classical gospel to labor law and found it hopelessly mired in rent seeking (Epstein 1983, 1984; Posner 1984). In this clash of values, labor law scholars found themselves cast as apologists for the *ancien regime*, whereas the law-and-economics critics mostly moved on to other battlegrounds. The clash proved fruitful in some ways, and it eventually generated more nuanced economic analyses of labor law doctrines (Cohen & Wachter 1988, Dau-Schmidt 1992, Hylton 1993), although it did little to restore the lost prestige of labor law within the academy.

Several issues heated up and briefly generated broader interest—for example, the *Mackay* doctrine permitting permanent replacement of lawful strikers (*NLRB v. Mackay Radio & Telegraph* 1938), which gained prominence after the air traffic controllers' strike in 1981 and was nearly overturned in the early 1990s (Getman 1998); the rise and fall of union rights of access to private property, interred by the Court in *Lechmere v. NLRB* (1992) (Estlund 1994); the 70-year-old ban on many forms of nonunion labor-management cooperation, almost amended by Congress in 1997 (Barenberg 1993). But labor law's moments in the sun became rare and short-lived, and labor law scholarship veered toward despondency.

In the meantime, interest in the law of the workplace within the academy has been both revived and channeled away from traditional labor law by the growth of employment law. For the decline of organized labor and of collective bargaining, and of labor law as a field, has been paralleled by the rise of regulatory regimes such as the Occupational Safety and Health Administration and individual, judicially enforceable employee rights. A very important component of that new body of employment law—antidiscrimination law—arose directly out of the civil rights movement, which grew to encompass not only African Americans but also those of other racial and ethnic minority groups, women, older workers, and the disabled. The centrality of litigation and lawyers in these new legal regimes, as well as the vibrancy and ferment to which they contributed, gave employment law a more salient place in the law school world, and indeed in the legal profession, than what was left of labor law.

This relatively new field of employment law seems unlikely to capture the exalted place that labor law held 50 years ago in the legal academy. There is ample room for useful legal scholarship to bring order to the hodgepodge that is employment law, but that project tends to proceed at a relatively low level of generality and visibility. It rarely engages that most prestigious of conversation partners, the Supreme Court, outside the fields of employment discrimination law and public employment. Ironically, one of the Supreme Court's most important and widely noted interventions into employment law tends both to lower the visibility and to diminish the public character of employment law. The Court's decisions upholding the enforceability of predispute agreements to arbitrate employment law claims, including federal employment discrimination claims, have generated their own profusion of scholarly commentary (Bales 1997, Estreicher 1997, Stone 1996). But the abiding effect of those decisions, like the effect of the labor arbitration decisions of the early 1960s, is to channel workplace disputes away from public institutions and public attention and into private fora with little public exposure.

HOPE FOR REVIVAL?

Is there hope for recovery—of labor law scholarship, of labor law, and of organized labor—from the doldrums in which they have largely languished in recent times? Their fates are linked, although the lines of causation are not always clear. Just as there is debate over the role that weak labor laws have played in the decline of unions, there is room for argument as to whether law reform is the key to a revitalized labor movement or vice versa. And of course it is debatable whether legal scholarship can contribute meaningfully to either. But that will not be for lack of trying among the determined but shrinking core of labor law scholars.

The dramatic origins and high-minded phrasing of the Wagner Act still exert a powerful pull on labor law scholars. Two major recent works harken to a prelapsarian past and show why the Act continues to enthrall. In *Taking Back the Workers' Law: How to Fight the Assault on Labor Rights*, Dannin (2006) argues for a long-term litigation campaign, on the model of the NAACP Legal Defense Fund's campaign against the jurisprudence of separate-but-equal, to overturn decades of judicial precedent that distorts the NLRA's meaning. She rightly takes aim at the multitude of employer rights that courts have read into the Act and that have generated blistering criticism from the academy for many decades, such as the rights to permanently replace strikers, to shut down operations altogether in retaliation for union organizing, and to exclude union organizers from employer property, among others. Anticipating the pessimism that I confess to sharing, Dannin points out that there was little basis for optimism in the depths of 1920s Jim Crow when the Legal Defense Fund began the campaign that culminated in *Brown v. Board of Education* (1954). But at least in hindsight, that legal campaign seems to have been in sync with the times and with other social forces for equal opportunity and desegregation. The social forces that favor union growth and collective empowerment today are at best more obscure and are likely to provide less than fertile ground for law reform along the lines Dannin proposes.

Morris (2005) advances a provocative rereading of the NLRA in *The Blue Eagle At Work: Reclaiming Democratic Rights in the American Workplace*. Morris argues that a true understanding of the NLRA would support the practice of nonexclusive members-only bargaining, which had a solid footing in pre-Act union practice. In members-only bargaining, workers who favor union representation but who make up less than a majority of workers in a bargaining unit would be entitled to form a union and to bargain collectively on their own behalf through that union. The allure of this possibility lies in evidence that up to half of unrepresented workers today would choose union representation if they had the choice (but are too rarely galvanized into a battle-ready supermajority in any given workplace). Members-only bargaining, which would largely circumvent the obstacle course of union representation battles and elections, is thus a tantalizing prospect and one that unions and their allies should explore. There are serious questions, however, about the viability of members-only nonexclusive collective bargaining, as well as about the contemporary viability of Morris's revisionist reading of the Act (True 2005). It thus remains to be seen whether Morris's thesis gains traction either among scholars or on the ground.

Whatever the ultimate payoff of these efforts to excavate and burnish the original meaning of the Act, much of the labor movement appears to be staking its future on a strategy of avoidance rather than reformation of ineffectual labor laws. So although they remain largely committed to a more or less recognizable regime of union organization and collective bargaining, unions that are determined to grow have been experimenting with other instruments for achieving those ends. Some have made creative use of tactics of public protest, publicity, and consumer pressure—tactics that are drawn from labor's historic arsenal but that are lately more associated with the civil rights and antiaparteid movements (Estlund 2005). In recent years, those extralegal pressures have often aimed to induce employers to enter into a neutrality agreement by which the employer agrees to remain neutral toward the union's organizing effort, or to constrain its antiunion campaign, and in many cases to forego an NLRB election in favor of a card check as evidence of majority support for union representation (Brudney 2005).

The neutrality agreement essentially substitutes a quasi-private, contractually based set of ground rules, and usually a private mode of dispute resolution, for the outmoded rules and machinery of the NLRA. It uses contract for the time-honored purpose of constructing private law rules to govern a relationship when external law alone does not meet the parties' needs. These innovations of organized labor, and the scholarship that elaborates their legal dimensions, seek to renew and revitalize labor law from outside its formal boundaries (Brudney 2005). But the NLRB, whose delay- and conflict-ridden regime these agreements seek to avoid, is not clearly prepared to cede its authority over representation disputes. In a long-pending case, the Board is considering the claim that at least some of these agreements violate the Act by depriving employees of the benefits of a no-holds-barred antiunion campaign (*Dana Corp. and Metaldyne Corp.* 2004). It would be a cruel twist on the ossification theme if this became one of the Board's all-too-rare efforts to update the Act in response to changing conditions.

These innovations do not so much transform the nature of labor relations—of unionization, majority rule, and collective bargaining—as they seek to smooth the path that leads there. Moreover, the idea of using contract to create a private law between the parties is in one sense simply a variation on the practice of collective bargaining itself. Yet neutrality agreements do break, or at least work, important new ground. The deployment of the private law instrument of contract to establish the basic rules of engagement between unions and employers calls to mind the development of corporate codes of conduct for the improvement of labor standards in developing countries (Elliot & Freeman 2003, Sabel et al. 2001). In both cases, the failure or absence of conventional regulatory machinery for the protection of workers' rights and interests has led worker advocates to turn to quasi-contractual mechanisms to establish both stronger substantive protections for workers and privatized modes of dispute resolution and enforcement. And in both cases, extralegal pressure from sympathetic consumers and citizens often plays a major part in bringing corporate actors to the bargaining table.

The corporate code of conduct strategy, which was pioneered by global antisweatshop advocates and is still evolving, may point toward a more far-reaching revitalization and transformation of labor law. The problem that both American unions and global antisweatshop activists face is similar: Conventional legal institutions in the relevant jurisdiction are unable or unwilling, for one reason or another, to induce compliance with or enforce standards of acceptable treatment for workers and their associations. Yet the worker advocates in both cases are sometimes able to exert leverage over particular corporate actors to induce entry into a more worker-friendly regime. The leverage may come from firms' sensitivity to brand reputation and the loyalty of consumers whose sympathies can be aroused, or from economic dependence on worker-friendly political institutions. Whatever brings the company to the bargaining table, the result is a kind of contract promising to abide by (or to impose upon contractor/suppliers) more worker-friendly standards of conduct than external law demands.

When unions are parties to these agreements, as in the case of neutrality agreements, they can monitor compliance themselves. In the case of global supplier codes, the agreement usually provides for some form of monitoring by independent auditors. Unfortunately, in many of these codes the content of the promises, the identity of the promisees, the standards governing monitors, and the enforcement mechanisms remain too vague to make the codes effective. But with decades of experience now under their belts, worker allies are refining their strategies and paying greater heed, for example, to the need for independent and effective monitoring and to the vital importance of an ongoing informal monitoring role for the affected workers themselves, without which code compliance may be superficial and episodic (Elliot & Freeman 2003).

As long as consumer and public pressure plays a critical role in inducing corporations to enter into and adhere to a code of conduct, the content of these codes is likely to hew rather closely to norms of fair and decent treatment that are embraced by the wider public and embodied in national or international law. At its worst—that is, without effective monitoring and sanctions—the code of conduct strategy may become a public relations sham. At its best, however, it may evolve into an alternative to, or an alternative form of, collective bargaining, with workers themselves playing a role in the formulation and enforcement of the code (Estlund 2005). It may, in short, become a template for a new kind of labor law, a mechanism by which workers could exercise a collective voice and advance their own shared goals at the workplace, at least to the extent the consuming (or shareholding) public endorses those goals.

This portrait of a possible future for American labor law may seem remote. But it seems no more remote than the holy grail of labor law reform. It has the virtue of engaging many possible actors—corporations with varying interests, unions and other worker advocacy groups, consumers, private monitoring organizations—and many possible points of leverage, legal and nonlegal. Public norms can be located at many different nodes of the hodgepodge that is employment law, and many of those nodes contain private enforcement mechanisms. That means that litigation or the threat of litigation can be among the inducements that may bring reluctant firms to the bargaining table to devise effective systems for the monitoring and improvement of working conditions. And as worker advocates become increasingly aware that efficacy depends on an integral role for the affected workers themselves, we can begin to see in the code of conduct approach the germs of a novel alternative form of employee representation. Indeed, unions and union-like organizations play important but nontraditional roles—as political advocates, litigants, monitors, and watchdogs—in several of the workplace monitoring regimes that have emerged in the United States thus far (Estlund 2005).

Of course, things could go badly. The incentive for firms to devise effective systems of compliance comes from legal and nonlegal pressures. The threat of litigation might be defanged by mandatory arbitration agreements and especially by those agreements that waive the right to participate in class or collective actions in or out of arbitration. Nonlegal pressures from consumers and equity markets might be siphoned off by superficial but ineffectual compliance systems in which workers play no real role. And unions, still the one reliable institutional advocate for the interests of workers themselves, may continue to slide toward debility.

To survive and grow, and to help revitalize labor law in any form, whether recognizable or radically revised, unions will have to reconstruct themselves to play new roles. Unions are quite simply organizations of workers who give collective voice and support to shared worker goals. Those goals were primarily served in the past by unions serving as exclusive representatives within a collective bargaining regime. In the future that is unfolding, unions will have to reshape themselves into new institutional forms that suit the new environment. The new environment is characterized in part by organizations with shifting boundaries and transnational reach and by the extensive use of contingent forms of labor, outsourcing, and insourcing—what Stone (2004) has called the "boundariless workplace." In her book, *From Widgets to Digits: Employment Regulation for the Changing Workplace*, Stone outlines two such institutional forms: New craft unionism, "an occupation-based form of unionism that bargains with industry-wide employer groups to establish minimum standards and provide training, while enabling employees to move freely between employers in the industry," and citizen unionism, "a locality-based form of unionism that uses collective pressure to induce corporations to become good corporate citizens of the geographic area in which they are located" (Stone 2004, p. 219).

Both occupationally based unions and locally based citizen unions can play important roles in the quasi-contractual, code-based regimes sketched above. But they can also play a variety of other roles as the collective voice of workers in the workplace and the society. Whether the resulting institutions and dynamics will resolve themselves into something that can be called labor law is less important than the question of whether workers will end up with decent working conditions, a modicum of economic security, and a real voice in their working lives. And that may depend on whether the institutions and dynamics in which unions and other worker allies invest their efforts are in sync with wider societal currents within the domain of governance.

Many of the same trends that have helped render the New Deal labor law regime an anachronism—trends toward organizational flexibility and fluidity and toward geographically unbounded product markets—pose similar challenges to other domains of regulation, such as environmental law, where command and control was once the order of the day. In the past decade or two, scholars of law and regulation in the United States and abroad have strived to analyze and to name the new forms of decentralized, semiprivatized, collaborative forms of governance that are arising in the face of those developments. Terms such as responsive regulation (Ayres & Braithwaite 1992), negotiated governance (Krawiec 2003), collaborative governance (Freeman 1997), contractarian regulation (Dana 2000), reconstitutive law (Stewart 1986), democratic experimentalism (Dorf & Sabel 1998), and the Renew Deal (Lobel 2004) describe varying strains of these emerging dynamics and mechanisms. We may call this the "new governance" paradigm.

For some of those scholars, the problem of workplace governance is at the periphery of their view. But for others it serves as an archetypal case (e.g., Ayres & Braithwaite 1992, Lobel 2004), as well it should. The competitive race that is capitalism, with its embedded threat of a race to the bottom in costs of production, has always been most vividly and sometimes violently brought to bear on labor. The escalation and expansion of that competitive race in this latest era of globalization has again highlighted the problem of sweatshop labor at the bottom of global production chains. At the same time, the sweatshop problem has spawned some of the most promising experiments with nonstate-centered regulation or governance.

If this growing cluster of new governance theories, strategies, and practices does indeed represent the future of law, then there is hope for a reconstituted labor law, or law of workplace governance, that harnesses those strategies. And there is hope, too, for the growth of new forms of worker involvement in workplace governance. A very incidental beneficiary of this development would be the labor law academy: If the new governance paradigm does represent the future of law, and if it thus becomes a center of gravity within the legal academy, then the scholarship that elaborates and refines that paradigm in the context of workplace governance may yet regain its central place within that corner of the world.

The *Annual Review of Law and Social Science* is online at http://lawsocsci.annualreviews.org

LITERATURE CITED

Adair v. U.S., 208 U.S. 161 (1908)

Atleson J. 1975. Work group behavior and wildcat strikes: the causes and functions of industrial disobedience. *Ohio State Law Rev.* 34: 35

Atleson J. 1983. *Values and Assumption in*

American Labor Law. Amherst: Univ. Mass. Press

Ayres I, Braithwaite J. 1992. *Responsive Regulation: Transcending the Deregulation Debate*. New York: Oxford Univ. Press

Bales RA. 1997. *Compulsory Arbitration: The Grand Experiment in Employment*. Ithaca, NY: Cornell Univ. Press

Barenberg M. 1993. The political economy of the Wagner Act: power, symbol, and workplace cooperation. *Harvard Law Rev.* 106:1379

Bass J. 1981. *Unlikely Heroes: The Dramatic Story of the Southern Judges of the Fifth Circuit Who Translated the Supreme Court's* Brown *Decision into a Revolution for Equality*. New York: Simon & Schuster

Becker C. 1993. Democracy in the workplace: union representation elections and federal labor law. *Minn. Law Rev.* 77:495

Bernstein I. 1970. *Turbulent Years: A History of the American Worker, 1933–1941*. Boston: Houghton Mifflin

Black CL. 1960. The lawfulness of the segregation decisions. *Yale Law J.* 69:421

Brest P. 1976. The Supreme Court 1975 term—Foreword: in defense of the antidiscrimination principle. *Harvard Law Rev.* 90:1

Brown v. Board of Education, 347 U.S. 483 (1954)

Brudney JJ. 1996a. A famous victory: collective bargaining protections and the statutory aging process. *N. C. Law Rev.* 74:939

Brudney JJ. 1996b. Reflections on group action and the law of the workplace. *Tex. Law Rev.* 74:1563

Brudney JJ. 2005. Neutrality agreements and card check recognition: prospects for changing paradigms. *Iowa Law Rev.* 90:819

Cohen GM, Wachter ML. 1988. The law and economics of collective bargaining: an introduction and application to the problem of subcontracting, partial closure, and relocation. *Univ. Penn. Law Rev.* 136:1349

Cohen L. 1990. *Making a New Deal: Industrial Workers in Chicago, 1919–1939*. New York: Cambridge Univ. Press

Cohen M. 1928. Property and sovereignty. *Cornell Law Q.* 13:8

Cook WW. 1918. Privileges of labor unions in the struggle for life. *Yale Law J.* 27:779

Coppage v. Kansas, 236 U.S. 1 (1915)

Cox A. 1948. Some aspects of the Labor Management Relations Act, 1947. *Harvard Law Rev.* 61:274

Cox A. 1951. Strikes, picketing and the constitution. *Vanderbilt Law Rev.* 4:574

Cox A. 1954a. Federalism and the law of labor relations. *Harvard Law Rev.* 67:1297

Cox A. 1954b. Grievance arbitration in the federal courts. *Harvard Law Rev.* 67:591

Cox A. 1957. The duty of fair representation. *Villanova Law Rev.* 2:151

Cox A. 1958. The duty to bargain in good faith. *Harvard Law Rev.* 71:1401

Cox A. 1959. Reflections upon labor arbitration. *Harvard Law Rev.* 72:1482

Cox A, Dunlop J. 1950. Regulation of collective bargaining by the National Labor Relations Board. *Harvard Law Rev.* 63:389

Craver CB. 1992. The National Labor Relations Act must be revised to preserve industrial democracy. *Arizona Law Rev.* 34:397

Craver CB. 1993. *Can Unions Survive? The Rejuvination of the American Labor Movement*. New York: N. Y. Univ. Press

Dana DA. 2000. The new "contractarian" paradigm in environmental regulation. *Univ. Ill. Law Rev.* 2000:35

Dana Corp. and Metaldyne Corp., 341 NLRB No. 150 (2004)

Dannin E. 2006. *Taking Back the Workers' Law: How to Fight the Assault on Labor Rights*. Ithaca, NY: Cornell Univ. Press

Dau-Schmidt K. 1992. A bargaining analysis of American labor law. *Mich. Law Rev.* 91:419

Dorf MC, Sabel CF. 1998. A constitution of democratic experimentalism. *Columbia Law Rev.* 98:267

Elliot KA, Freeman RB. 2003. *Can Labor Standards Improve Under Globalization*? Washington, DC: Inst. Int. Econ.

Epstein RA. 1983. A common law for labor relations: a critique of the New Deal labor legislation. *Yale Law J.* 92:1357

Epstein RA. 1984. In defense of the contract at will. *Univ. Chicago Law Rev.* 51:947

Eskridge WN, Frickey PP. 1994. The Supreme Court 1993 term—Foreword: law as equilibrium. *Harvard Law Rev.* 108:26

Estlund C. 1994. Labor, property, and sovereignty after *Lechmere*. *Stanford Law Rev.* 46:305

Estlund C. 2002a. Reflections on the declining prestige of American labor law scholarship. *Comp. Labor Law Policy J.* 23:789

Estlund C. 2002b. The ossification of American labor law. *Columbia Law Rev.* 102:1527

Estlund C. 2005. Rebuilding the law of the workplace in an era of self-regulation. *Columbia Law Rev.* 105:319

Estreicher S. 1993. Labor law reform in a world of competitive product markets. *Chicago-Kent Law Rev.* 69:3

Estreicher S. 1997. Predispute agreements to arbitrate statutory employment claims. *N. Y. Univ. Law Rev.* 72:1344

Finkin M. 1985. Labor law by Boz—a theory of Meyers Industries, Inc., Sears, Roebuck & Co., and Bird Engineering. *Iowa Law Rev.* 71:155

Fiss OM. 1976. Groups and the equal protection clause. *Philos. Public Aff.* 5:107

Frankfurter F, Green L. 1930. *The Labor Injunction*. New York: Macmillan

Freeman J. 1997. Collaborative governance in the administrative state. *UCLA Law Rev.* 45:1

Freeman RB. 1992. Is declining unionization of the U.S. good, bad, or irrelevant? In *Unions and Economic Competitiveness*, ed. L Mishel, PB Voos, p. 143. Armonk, NY: M.E. Sharpe

Freeman RB, Kleiner MM. 1990. Employer behavior in the face of union organizing drives. *Ind. Labor Relat. Rev.* 43:351

Freeman RB, Rogers J. 1999. *What Workers Want*. Ithaca, NY: ILR Press

George BG. 1988. Divided we stand: concerted activity and the maturing of the NLRA. *George Wash. Law Rev.* 56:509

Getman JG. 1965. Section 8(a)(3) of the NLRA and the effort to insulate free employee choice. *Univ. Chicago Law Rev.* 32:735

Getman JG. 1967. The protection of economic pressure by Section 7 of the National Labor Relations Act. *Univ. Penn. Law Rev.* 115:1195

Getman JG. 1997. Explaining the fall of the labor movement. *St. Louis Univ. Law J.* 41:575

Getman JG. 1998. *The Betrayal of Local 14*. Ithaca, NY: ILR Press

Getman JG, Golberg SB, Herman JB. 1976. *Union Representation Elections: Law and Reality*. New York: Russell Sage Found.

Gorman RA, Finkin M. 1981. The individual and the requirement of "concert" under the National Labor Relations Act. *Univ. Penn. Law Rev.* 130:286

Gottesman MH. 1993. In despair, starting over: imagining a labor law for unorganized workers. *Chicago-Kent Law Rev.* 69:59

Hague v. CIO, 307 U.S. 496 (1939)

Hale RL. 1923. Coercion and distribution in a supposedly non-coercive state. *Polit. Sci. Q.* 38:470

Harper MC. 2001. A framework for the rejuvenation of the American labor movement. *Indiana Law J.* 76:103

Hart HM, Sacks AM. 1994. *The Legal Process: Basic Problems in the Making and Application of Law*, ed. WN Eskridge, PP Frickey. Westbury, NY: Foundation Press

Hohfeld W. 1913. Some fundamental legal conceptions as applied in judicial reasoning. *Yale Law J.* 23:16

Hyde A. 2003. *Working in Silicon Valley*. Armonk, NY: M.E. Sharpe

Hylton KN. 1993. Efficiency and labor law. *Northwest. Univ. Law Rev.* 87:471

In re Debs, 158 U.S. 564 (1895)

Jacobs J. 2006. *Mobsters, Unions, and Feds: The Mafia and the American Labor Movement*. New York: N. Y. Univ. Press

Klare KE. 1978. Judicial deradicalization of the Wagner Act and the origins of modern legal consciousness, 1937–1941. *Minn. Law Rev.* 62:265

Klare KE. 1982. The quest for industrial democracy and the struggle against racism: perspectives from labor law and civil rights law. *Oregon Law Rev.* 61:157

Krawiec KD. 2003. Cosmetic compliance and the failure of negotiated governance. *Wash. Univ. Law Q.* 81:487

Lechmere, Inc. v. NLRB, 502 U.S. 527 (1992)

Lobel O. 2004. The Renew Deal: the fall of regulation and the rise of governance in contemporary legal thought. *Minn. Law Rev.* 89:342

Lochner v. New York, 198 U.S. 45 (1905)

Logan J. 2002. Consultants, lawyers, and the 'Union Free' movement in the USA since the 1970s. *Ind. Relat. J.* 3:197

Morris CJ. 2005. *The Blue Eagle at Work: Reclaiming Democratic Rights in the American Workplace*. Ithaca, NY: ILR Press

NLRB v. Jones & Laughlin Steel Corp., 301 U.S. 1 (1937)

NLRB v. Mackay Radio & Telegraph, 304 U.S. 333 (1938)

Pope JG. 2002. The Thirteenth Amendment versus the Commerce Clause: labor and the shaping of American constitutional law, 1921–1957. *Columbia Law Rev.* 102:1

Posner R. 1984. Some economics of labor law. *Univ. Chicago Law Rev.* 51:988

Rabban DM. 1997. *Free Speech in the Forgotten Years*. New York: Cambridge Univ. Press

Sabel CF, Fung A, O'Rourke D. 2001. Stepping up labor standards. *Boston Rev.* 26:4

Stewart RB. 1986. Reconstitutive law. *Maryland Law Rev.* 46:86

Stone KVW. 1981. The post-war paradigm in American labor law. *Yale Law J.* 90:1509

Stone KVW. 1996. Mandatory arbitration of individual employment rights: the yellow dog contract of the 1990s. *Denver Univ. Law Rev.* 73:1017

Stone KVW. 2004. *From Widgets to Digits: Employment Regulation for the Changing Workplace*. Cambridge, UK: Cambridge Univ. Press

Summers CW. 1979. Industrial democracy: America's unfulfilled promise. *Cleveland State Law Rev.* 28:29

Thomas v. Collins, 323 U.S. 516 (1945)

Thornhill v. Alabama, 310 U.S. 88 (1940)

Troy L. 1990. Is the U.S. unique in the decline of private sector unionism? *J. Labor Res.* 11:111

True JM. 2005. Review essay: the Blue Eagle at work. *Berkeley J. Employ. Labor Law* 26:181

Weiler PC. 1983. Promises to keep: securing workers' rights to self-organization under the NLRA. *Harvard Law Rev.* 96:1769

Weiler PC. 1984. Striking a new balance: freedom of contract and the prospects for union representation. *Harvard Law Rev.* 98:351

Weiler PC. 1990. *Governing the Workplace: The Future of Labor and Employment Law*. Cambridge, MA: Harvard Univ. Press

Annu. Rev. Law Soc. Sci. 2006. 2:125–46
doi: 10.1146/annurev.lawsocsci.2.081805.110011

First published online as a Review in Advance on June 15, 2006

The Crime Drop and Beyond

Alfred Blumstein[1] and Joel Wallman[2]
[1]*H. John Heinz III School of Public Policy, Carnegie Mellon University, Pittsburgh, PA 15213; email: ab0q@andrew.cmu.edu*
[2]*Harry Frank Guggenheim Foundation, 25 W. 53rd St., New York, NY 10019; email: jwallman@hfg.org*

Key Words United States, American, homicide, violence, crime trends

■ **Abstract** Violent crime in the United States has traveled a striking path in the past 20 years, from a sharp spike in the late 1980s to a dramatic drop beginning around 1993 that lasted until a flattening occurred at the beginning of the new century. The upturn of the 1980s was driven almost exclusively by a sharp increase in gun violence among young people, whereas the downturn was a joint product of a turndown in youth violence and a steady drop in violence among adults over 30 that has been ongoing for at least 25 years. These trends have intrigued lay observers and students of crime alike, with advocates of various explanations of crime arguing that the key for the rise, fall, or both lies with one or another favored determinant: prisons, drugs, guns, policing, economics, or demography, including abortion. In this review, we discuss both the crime trends and their candidate explanations, concluding that the most reasonable accounts involve a complex interaction among several of these factors.

INTRODUCTION

Over the past 20 years, the United States has seen dramatic swings in violent crime. Its path can be broken into three periods: a rise, a drop, and a flattening. The rise period began in 1985 when a five-year national decline from 1980 was reversed almost entirely by a sharp spike in violence by adolescent and young adult males. This spike outweighed an ongoing downtrend in violence among the much larger older population that began at least as early as 1980. The rise period ended around 1993 with the beginning of a pronounced and much discussed crime drop in which the murder rate declined by 42% and robbery by 44%, resulting in levels not seen since the 1960s. The drop was succeeded by the third period, a flattening of violent crime rates beginning around 2000.

Understandably, there has been widespread curiosity, among both the public and scholars of crime, about the factors contributing to these sharp changes. Many explanations have been proposed, invoking such varied factors as incarceration, illicit drugs, proliferation of firearms, police practices, the state of the economy, demographic shifts, and even the *Roe v. Wade* Supreme Court decision legalizing abortion.

1550-3585/06/1201-0125$20.00

In this review, we explore the course of recent U.S. violent crime, highlighting the variability by place and population subgroup that underlies the national trends. Then we consider the factors that are most important to understanding these trends. Some of these factors—prison, drugs, guns, and police—are associated in a direct and obvious way with crime and the criminal justice system. Others—the economy and population trends—are less self-evidently pertinent to crime but are arguably equally powerful determinants.

THE TRENDS IN CRIME

The crime decline of the 1990s included property crime, but it was particularly noteworthy in the violent crimes (Figure 1, see color insert). We focus on the two best measured of the serious crimes: murder and robbery. The other two violent crime types, rape and aggravated assault, are much less reliably measured. Rape is significantly underreported, so slight changes in the reporting rate can produce misleadingly large changes in apparent rates of occurrence. Rates of aggravated assault are very much subject to the discretion of police in characterizing assaults as simple (and not counted) or aggravated (and counted). Classification criteria can vary over time and are influenced by local incentives, such as whether a police department wants to look good (and so establishes a higher threshold for aggravated assault) or is seeking additional funding (and so establishes a lower threshold to increase the apparent severity of local crime). Furthermore, shifts in arrest policies, particularly the changes in recent years that encourage arrest for domestic assault, have led to significant increases in designation of such assaults as aggravated in order to warrant an arrest.

From 1993 until 2000, there was a steep annual decline of 7.4% per year in murder rates and 8.0% per year in robbery rates as recorded in the Uniform Crime Reports (UCR) of the FBI, which are based on reports from police departments of crimes reported to them. In contrast, from 2000 to 2004, murder rates were quite flat, decreasing minimally from 5.54 per 100,000 in 2000 to 5.50 in 2004, an annual change over those four years of just 0.2%. Robbery rates over the same period went from 145 in 2000 to 137 in 2004, an annual decline of 1.5%. Burglary rates displayed a rather different pattern. They started a steady decline in 1986, dropped at an annual rate of 4.3% until 2000, and then increased by 1% per year until 2004.

The data from the National Crime Victimization Survey (NCVS), which come from surveys of American households rather than from police reports, are generally consistent with the UCR, especially for the crime-drop period. Aggravated assault peaked in 1993 and simple assault and robbery in 1994, and all dropped by at least 50% through 2000. (The NCVS does not track homicide.) There is a slight divergence between the NCVS and the UCR for the period after 2000. Rather than the flattening seen in the UCR data, the NCVS reports a continuing decline in overall violent victimization of 14%. The year-to-year changes in this period, however, are generally not statistically significant because of reductions in the yearly NCVS sample sizes and the low rates of violent crimes that now prevail.

Although the crime drop of the 1990s was pervasive and evident in most major U.S. cities, not all evinced both a distinct upturn in the 1980s and a downturn phase in the 1990s. Messner et al. (2005) used spline regression to identify breaks in crime curves for the 68 largest cities that have adequate homicide data for the period 1979–2001. They found that slightly over half of the cities experienced a clear rise and fall during these years, with those that did tending to be the larger ones. In addition, they found that among the cities showing this epidemic profile, the ones with denser populations and greater socioeconomic deprivation both began and ended their crime-rise periods earlier than others. Finally, they found that cities in the vanguard of the crime rise tended to be on the West coast, whereas East coast cities typically entered the decline phase earlier.

Just as a consistent national crime trend can obscure such interesting variability across cities, so can city-level trends mask variation across and even within neighborhoods. Weisburd et al. (2004) charted the numbers of police incident reports for each of nearly 30,000 Seattle block segments (i.e., block sides) for the period 1989–2002. Although Seattle underwent an overall drop in incidents of 24%, Weisburd et al. found that the great majority of block segments (84%) showed no change over this period, with downtrends in just 14% accounting for the entire city trend. A full picture of crime trends thus requires looking at both the forest and the trees.

In contrast to the 1990s, when the large majority of cities took part in a pervasive declining trend, the flat period after 2000 did not display a uniform pattern. Rather, crime rates went up in some places and down in others, and many cities changed direction from year to year. The diverse city patterns are thus more indicative of local conditions than of a general national pattern. On the one hand, New York City, whose high homicide rate accounted for about 10% of the nation's total rate in 1993, continued its impressive decline, begun in the mid-1990s, attaining in 2004 its lowest number since 1963. On the other hand, places such as New Orleans had steady rises over most of the period between 2000 and 2004. On the whole, though, few large cities had homicide rates that moved consistently up or down during this period.

An important characteristic of U.S. violent crime in the 1980s and 1990s is the rather distinctive trends by age and ethnicity. The surge of the late 1980s and early 1990s was largely limited to young black men, whereas all demographic sectors shared in the downturn of the 1990s. Figure 2 (see color insert) presents information on age-specific arrest rates in three years. We use 1985, just before the major takeoff in young people's homicide, as the base because rates prior to 1985 display a very similar age pattern to 1985. The upper curve shows the ratio of age-specific arrest rates for murder in 1993 to those in 1985. By 1993, the murder arrest rate had tripled for 15-year-olds and more than doubled for all ages of 20 and under. The figure thus shows the rapid and dramatic increase between 1985 and 1993 among these young ages. In contrast, it also highlights the accompanying decline in the ages older than 30. The lower curve extends the comparison with 1985 to 2001. Note that for all ages, including young people, the murder arrest rate fell below the 1985 rate. Note also that for all ages over 30, the rates continued a decrease begun well before 1985 and that their 2001 rates had dropped to about half the 1985 rates.

Figure 3 (see color insert) shows homicide victimization trends for whites (non-Hispanic), blacks (non-Hispanic), and Hispanics, each partitioned into two age groups: young (15–24) and adult (25–44).[1] Three features of these curves should be noted: (*a*) the large differences across the three ethnic groups in their homicide victimization rates; (*b*) the sharp spike of over 150% among young blacks and the much smaller increases of 40%–50% in homicide victimization among young Hispanics and whites; and (*c*) the sharp decline among all groups, especially blacks, following the 1993–1994 peak.

FACTORS CONTRIBUTING TO THE CRIME TRENDS

Incarceration

Rates of incarceration in the United States were stable from the 1920s until the mid-1970s but then began a prodigious increase, quadrupling by 2000. Many commentators on the crime drop, especially those whose favored response to crime is incarceration, were quick to attribute the drop to the steady increase of incarceration throughout the 1990s. This argument ignores the fact that the crime rise of the late 1980s was also accompanied by a steady increase in incarceration. Indeed, even though crime rates have fluctuated from 1970 through 1990 (see Figure 1), incarceration rates in the United States rose steadily at an annual exponential growth rate of 6%–8% from the mid-1970s until 2000, and only recently has the annual growth rate declined to 2%.

Incarceration controls crime by incapacitating those in prison or jail and also, it is assumed, by deterring would-be offenders through their aversion to incarceration. It is hard to imagine how the massive growth in U.S. imprisonment could not eventually have served to curtail crime. A constant percentage increase means far more additional prisoners when the base figure has reached 1.5 million than when it is only a quarter million. The steady drop in crime among those over age 30 since at least 1980 is very probably related to the fact that the median prisoner age is early 30s.

At the same time, however, a certain inefficiency inheres in augmenting the prison population. The criminal justice system tends naturally to catch and imprison the highest rate offenders first. An increase in the system's inclination to

[1]The data in this figure are from the Supplementary Homicide Reports, which contain detailed information on homicide incidents provided to the FBI by police departments. We use victimization data, although offending data would tell essentially the same story, as homicides typically occur between people of similar demographic characteristics. We truncate the adult category at 44 because the large fraction of the population above that age, together with their low homicide rates, would exaggerate the young/old contrast.

imprison results in a decrease in the average offending rate of those being sentenced. In other words, the crime-reduction benefit of each additional prison bed declines as imprisonment grows. Spelman (2006) takes these dynamics into account in analyzing the contribution of prison growth to the national drop in violent crimes in the 1990s, concluding that roughly 25% of the drop is attributable to the combined effect of incarceration and deterrence. Rosenfeld (2006) takes a very different approach, estimating the number of violent crimes (homicides) a given number of prisoners would have been involved in, as perpetrators or victims, if not incarcerated and thus how many homicides were averted through their incarceration. Although this tack does not capture any deterrence effect of imprisonment, Rosenfeld's analysis yields an estimate for the suppression of homicide during the crime-drop period that is the same as Spelman's estimate for all violent crime: 25%.

In two articles, Blumstein & Beck (1999, 2005) have apportioned the sources of the quadrupling of the U.S. incarceration rates since 1980, demonstrating that it does not follow from increases in crime or in police effectiveness as measured by arrests per crime. Rather, it is almost entirely attributable to policy choices that increased the rates of prison commitments per arrest and lengthened prison terms, including more returns to prison for parole violators.

Departures from prison, through both parole and unconditional release at the completion of a sentence, have climbed to 630,000 persons per year. This has led to much more scholarly attention devoted to the issues of reentry into society and the need to provide some mixture of preparation before release and support after release in order to reduce the frequency of recidivism (Travis & Visher 2005). Two studies by the Bureau of Justice Statistics found rearrest rates of prisoners released in 1983 (Beck & Shipley 1989) and 1994 (Langan & Levin 2002) to be strikingly consistent and distressingly high: about two-thirds over the first three years after release. Rosenfeld et al. (2005b) estimate the arrest rates for ex-prisoners to be fully 30 to 45 times the rate for the general population, depending on crime type, or 7 to 29 times the rate of demographically comparable sectors of the population. In addition to the large absolute number of returnees, several attributes of current release cohorts do not bode well for crime trends. Longer average prison stays, diminished access to prerelease services, and increasing use by the prison system of mandatory release, in which prisoners are automatically released after a set fraction of their sentence rather than being evaluated as ready by a parole board, suggest that, absent significant improvements in corrections policy and practice, high recidivism will continue.

Recent budget crises in the states have led to reconsiderations of both front- and backdoor incarceration policies. A number of states have passed legislation that rescinds or softens mandatory minimum terms and truth-in-sentencing laws, provides for early release, or limits the burgeoning number of parolees returned to prison for technical violations. At least eight states have followed the lead of California's Proposition 36, which was based on the presumption that treatment would be more effective for drug offenders than incarceration. Although it was focused more narrowly on drug users with nonserious criminal histories, this reform certainly reflected a preference for the lower cost and probably more effective option in reducing subsequent drug offending. The incarceration rate for drug offenses has grown by a factor of ten since 1980. Over 20% of state prisoners and over 50% of federal prisoners are now drug offenders, even though there is no indication that drug transactions are diminished by this growth, a finding that is unsurprising given the ready availability of replacements to the markets (Blumstein 1993). Thus, finding safe means of reducing this major component of the prison population could be particularly beneficial.

Illicit Drug Markets

Whereas the adult violence downtrend of the 1990s was a continuation of the previous decade's pattern, a significant fraction of the reduction in youth violence in the 1990s represented an undoing of the growth of youth violence of the late 1980s. Much of this growth resulted from the recruitment of young people into the street marketing of crack (smokable cocaine) and the effect of those markets on youth more generally, effects that dominated much of inner-city life in the late 1980s and early 1990s. The proliferation of firearms was an intrinsic part of the rise of crack, as we discuss more fully below. That the acquisition of firearms spread beyond those directly involved in the crack trade is attested to by youth surveys carried out during this period (e.g., Sheley & Wright 1995). These studies documented a rate of gun-carrying far higher than could be explained in terms of participation in drug sales. Geographic diffusion was evident as well: An upswing in homicide (though of smaller magnitude) occurred among white youth some three years after the rise in the inner cities, and an upturn in violence in smaller cities occurred some two years after the increase in larger ones. It is no accident that the time difference by city size in the surge in violence maps rather well, with a lag of one to three years, onto the time difference across cities in the beginning of juvenile involvement in crack markets (Cork 1999).

Figure 4 (see color insert) shows the trends in drug arrests of four population groups since 1980. The early 1980s saw a rapid increase in arrests of nonwhite adults. This reflects the growth in demand for the then-new drug, crack, which was sold predominantly by African Americans and mainly in street markets.[2] The upturn in adult arrests was initially not accompanied by comparable growth for nonwhite juveniles, but after 1985 there was a steep rise in the arrests of nonwhite juveniles. This is shown in the upper graph of Figure 5 (see color insert), which displays the ratio of drug arrests of nonwhite adults to those of nonwhite juveniles. In the early 1980s, this ratio was quite high (reaching a level of almost 6:1 in 1983), indicating, again, that the crack market in its early years was served primarily by adult sellers. As the demand for crack grew, and especially as the incarceration of crack sellers cut into the pool of adults available on the street, juveniles were

[2]In contrast, marketing of powder cocaine is carried out predominantly by whites and Hispanics.

recruited as additions and replacements in those markets. This pattern is reflected in Figure 4 in the tripling of the arrest rate of nonwhite juveniles between 1985 and their 1996 peak.

Another indication of the growth of the nonwhite juvenile role is depicted in the lower graph of Figure 5, which shows the ratio of nonwhite to white juvenile arrests for drug offenses. In 1980, this ratio was less than 1; throughout the 1970s and until 1981, white juveniles were being arrested at a higher rate than nonwhites. The ratio rose slowly in the early 1980s but quite rapidly after 1985, reaching a peak of more than quadruple in 1991. It then declined just as rapidly, as the demand for crack fell and the young sellers were no longer needed in the markets. This ratio is also affected, of course, by trends in the denominator, i.e., white juvenile arrests, and, in fact, during the peak crack period, those rates declined by about half (see Figure 4). After a 1991 nadir, the white juvenile arrest rate began to rise again, reaching a level in 2003 only about 30% lower than that of the nonwhite juveniles. This uptrend appears to be a function of a steady increase in the rate of marijuana use by white juveniles (Johnston et al. 2003).

By the early 1990s, retail crack markets were contracting, either because they had become too violent for the participants, police tactics against them were succeeding, a new generation of drug users feared the destruction crack had wrought on their older peers, siblings, or parents, or—most likely—a combination of all these factors. The open-air, curb-service markets were being driven underground, with many dealers moving to indoor transactions, a mode of business more feasible with longer-term users. Indoor selling may be inherently less conducive to violence or it may simply entail a reduction in the level of sales, with a consequent reduction in levels of violence. In recent years, this shift has been accompanied by increasing reliance by dealers on technological adjuncts to business, including prepaid phone cards and disposable cell phones (both resistant to tracing) and even the Internet. Open-air drug markets are still abundant in many cities, however. And at least as recently as 2002, crack continued to be the commodity whose sellers and users were most involved in violent crime, followed by sellers of heroin, powder cocaine, methamphetamine, and marijuana (Exec. Off. Pres. 2002).

Johnson et al. (2006) describe the succession in New York City of the crack generation by the marijuana-smoking blunt generation. Evidence for such a transition at the national level can be found in data from the Arrestee Drug Abuse Monitoring (ADAM) program, which tested arrestees for drugs. Among adult male arrestees, cocaine (undifferentiated between powder and crack) was the drug most often detected by urine testing, with marijuana second, from 1990 through 1998. Since then, marijuana has predominated, with cocaine second (except among females, for whom cocaine continues to rank first). Opiates (undifferentiated but mainly heroin) are a distant third, at about a fifth of the frequency of cocaine, and methamphetamine fourth, with a frequency about 20% less than that for opiates. Detection frequencies for these drugs remained constant between 2000 and 2003, except that methamphetamine increased from 1.6% to 4.7% (Natl. Inst. Justice 2002, 2003a,b, 2004).

These figures are based on medians for all 35 of the ADAM cities and thus obscure a good deal of variability by location. Methamphetamine, for example, continued to be a problem primarily of rural areas and western cities, and in those locales rates of detection for methamphetamine are higher than for cocaine and close to those for marijuana. This is the case for Honolulu, Phoenix, and San Diego, among other cities. By 2005, methamphetamine had made inroads into some midwestern and eastern cities, especially Minneapolis and St. Louis, but it had yet to attain a nationwide prevalence. In those places where its use has taken root, however, it is significantly associated with violence, especially domestic violence (Butterfield 2004, Exec. Off. Pres. 2002).

The crack-using population is aging, with no evidence for significant initiation by young people. The heroin picture is somewhat different. There is evidence for an increase in young heroin users in a number of major cities, including Boston, Chicago, Cleveland, Dallas, Los Angeles, Cincinnati, and New York (Exec. Off. Pres. 2004). This suggests at least the potential for a new round in a heroin cycle, created by young users unmindful of the damage wrought on a previous generation (Musto 1999). On balance, though, the heroin-using population appears, like the crack generation, to be an aging group, so that youthful initiates will probably only slow the decline of the group rather than maintain or increase its numbers.

Guns and Gun Control

As mentioned above, firearms, especially guns in the hands of young people, were a crucial part of the violence epidemic of the late 1980s and early 1990s. This is reflected in Figure 6 (see color insert), which depicts the number of murders with handguns for three age groups: juveniles under 18, youth from 18 to 24, and adults from 25 to 44. The numbers are presented as an index in comparison to the numbers in 1985, with the number in 1985 for each age group indexed as 100. These figures are probably the major indicators of the involvement of youth in drug markets and the consequent diffusion of guns into their neighborhoods. We see a factor-of-five growth from 1985 to 1994 in the number of handgun murders by juveniles under 18 and a growth of 2.5 times for youth in the 18–24 age range. By contrast, there was only a slight decrease in nongun killings, so the increase in gun crimes cannot be interpreted mainly as a mere substitution of weapons. In both of the young groups, there was a peak in the use of handguns for homicide in 1994 and a subsequent decline to almost the 1985 (prerise) level by 2002.

The growth in handgun violence in the late 1980s was accompanied by a decline in revolvers and an increase in semiautomatic pistols as the crime weapons of choice. This shift in preference was accommodated, if not driven, by manufacturing trends in the firearms industry, which stepped up production of semiautomatics relative to revolvers in this period and also increased the caliber of the handguns produced. The combination of high-capacity magazines and higher-caliber bullets yielded weapons of considerably greater lethality, an attribute that manifests in a much lower survival rate for victims of these weapons compared with victims of revolvers (Wintemute 2006).

Another trend in the firearms industry that may have facilitated the rise in crime was the proliferation of federally licensed firearms dealers at the same time that the government was carrying out minimal oversight of dealers. (The number of dealers was also on the rise during the first half of the 1980s, when crime was declining, but the total was considerably smaller than during the crime rise.) A federal license to sell firearms, good for three years, could be had for $30, and the Bureau of Alcohol, Tobacco, and Firearms (ATF) was prohibited from inspecting any dealer more than once per year without a warrant. Only a small proportion received even that much attention. By 1992, there were more federally licensed gun dealers in the United States than there were gas stations (Sugarmann & Rand 1992). Although most guns used in crime were not acquired by the perpetrator through purchase from a licensed dealer, a significant fraction were obtained in this way (27%, according to a 1991 survey of prisoners; see Beck et al. 1993).[3] Moreover, crime-gun tracing has revealed that a very small number of licensed dealers are the source of a greatly disproportionate percentage of guns recovered after crimes, weapons that are acquired by offenders through straw purchasers or through a black market supplied by these unscrupulous licensees, if not by direct purchase.

The 1990s saw a number of law enforcement initiatives intended to impede or deter the acquisition of firearms by people who should not have them. Gun buybacks, bans on specific types of firearms, limits on multiple purchases, longer sentences for gun crimes, background checks, waiting periods, and more rigorous regulation of licensed gun dealers all held the potential to reduce gun crime and may therefore have contributed to the crime drop. Only a small number of these initiatives have been properly evaluated, however.

The Brady Handgun Act, which was implemented in 1994, had by 1999 resulted in the denial of over 400,000 handgun purchases by people in categories legally proscribed from possessing handguns. This was a promising figure, but there remained the possibility that some fraction of those denied firearms by licensed dealers would turn to theft or to the unregulated, secondary market, which comprises the estimated 30%–40% of firearms transactions that involve unlicensed sellers within and outside of guns shows (Braga et al. 2002). Although the number of rejected would-be buyers who obtain a firearm elsewhere is still not known, an inference can be drawn from an assessment of the Brady Act's effect on gun violence by Ludwig & Cook (2000). They compared homicide and suicide trends in the 32 states that implemented the background check and waiting period mandated by Brady with the 18 states that already employed such policies and were thus not required to change the practices of licensed dealers. They did find a reduction in gun suicides, suggesting that people intending to commit suicide were unlikely to

[3]A survey of juvenile inmates suggests that direct purchase from retail outlets is substantially less common among youth (7%), although the same survey found that a third of respondents had asked someone to purchase a gun for them at a retail outlet (Sheley & Wright 1993).

turn to the secondary gun market if thwarted in the primary. However, they found no effect on homicides. This was disappointing to those who had hoped that a nationwide policy of screening customers would put a dent in gun violence. If the hundreds of thousands of blocked purchases assessed by Ludwig & Cook had no effect on gun homicides, then the kinds of persons Brady kept from buying guns from licensed dealers—youth, felons, and the mentally ill—must have managed to procure guns in the secondary market. It is also possible, however, that a nonnegligible number of dangerous persons were successfully blocked from acquiring a gun but that this number was too small to affect aggregate homicide rates. This possibility gains credibility from a set of studies reported by Wintemute (2006). For example, Wright et al. (1999) compared handgun purchasers who had a record of felony arrest but had not been convicted (and thus could still purchase under the Brady rules) with convicted felons who tried to purchase but were rejected after a background check. They found that those who were allowed to purchase were 21% more likely to be charged with a gun offense over the next three years.

Another gun-control policy that has since been evaluated is Project Exile. Initiated in 1997 in Richmond, Virginia, this program sent those arrested for a gun crime who had a prior record to the federal justice system for prosecution, where they faced a much more severe sentence than they would have if they had been prosecuted by the local district attorney. The rationale was that carrying a gun is a conscious decision that could be deterred by significantly increasing the potential punishment for using that gun. Following the introduction of Project Exile, Richmond saw an appreciable reduction in its homicide rate, which stimulated interest in pursuing the Exile strategy elsewhere.

Raphael & Ludwig (2003), however, cast doubt on the impact of Project Exile on Richmond's homicide rate, concluding that it had merely followed the pattern seen in other jurisdictions that had evinced especially high rates in the preceding years. But a subsequent evaluation by Rosenfeld et al. (2005a) concluded that the years immediately after deployment of Project Exile (1997–2001) did evince a statistically significant reduction in Richmond's gun homicides. Their study compared Richmond's trend with the average trend for the 95 largest U.S. cities, controlling for a large array of known covariates of crime. Rosenfeld et al. argue that their analysis improves on the Raphael & Ludwig study by including more covariates and extending the intervention time frame from the two years of that study to five.

The larger question raised by Project Exile concerns the potential for deterring gun crime through severe sentences as opposed to preventing gun crime by stanching the flow of firearms to high-risk persons. In any case, Project Exile became the model for the Department of Justice's implementation of Project Safe Neighborhoods, which provided $900 million over three years to the U.S. attorneys' offices around the nation for pursuit of gun crimes.

The publications of John Lott (Lott & Mustard 1997, Lott 2000) arguing for the crime-suppressing virtues of arming the public were not intended as an explanation of the crime drop, as the period he studied, 1977–1992, ends just at the start of the decline. However, Lott's work continues to be perhaps the most controversial area

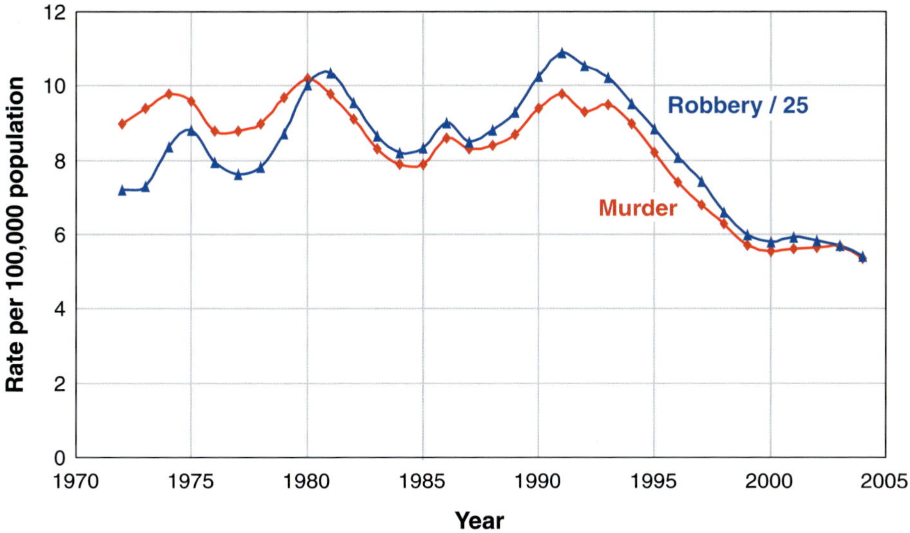

Figure 1 UCR murder and robbery rates.

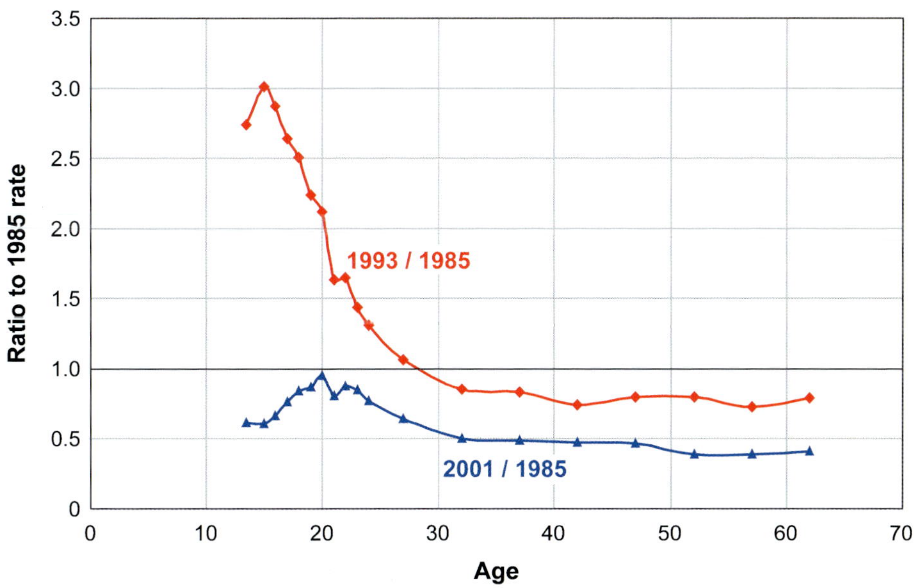

Figure 2 Ratios of age-specific murder arrest rates to 1985 rates.

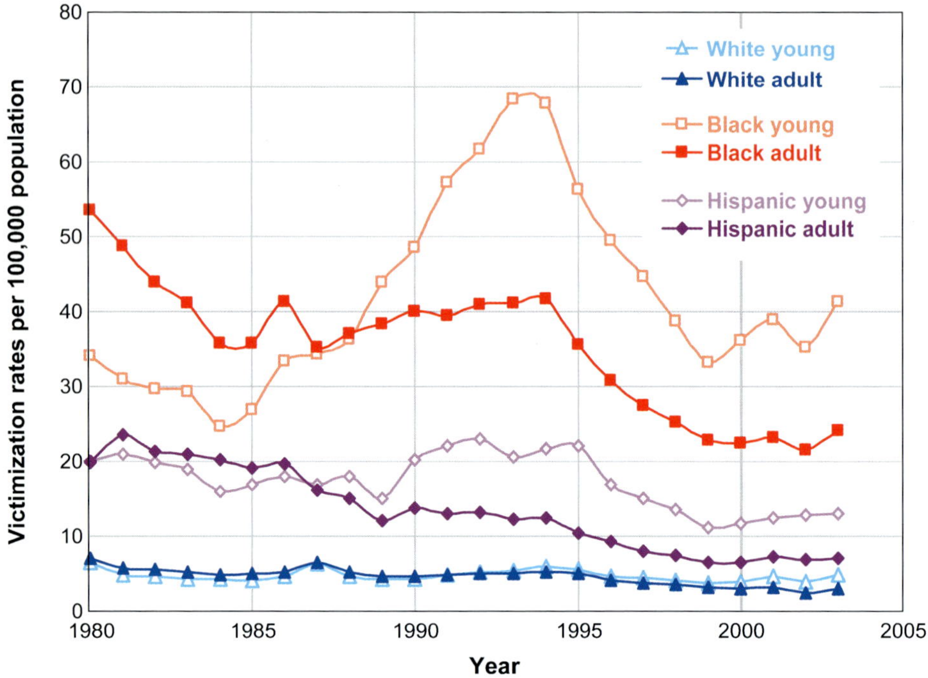

Figure 3 SHR victimization rates for the young (15–24) and for adults (25–44) by race/ethnicity.

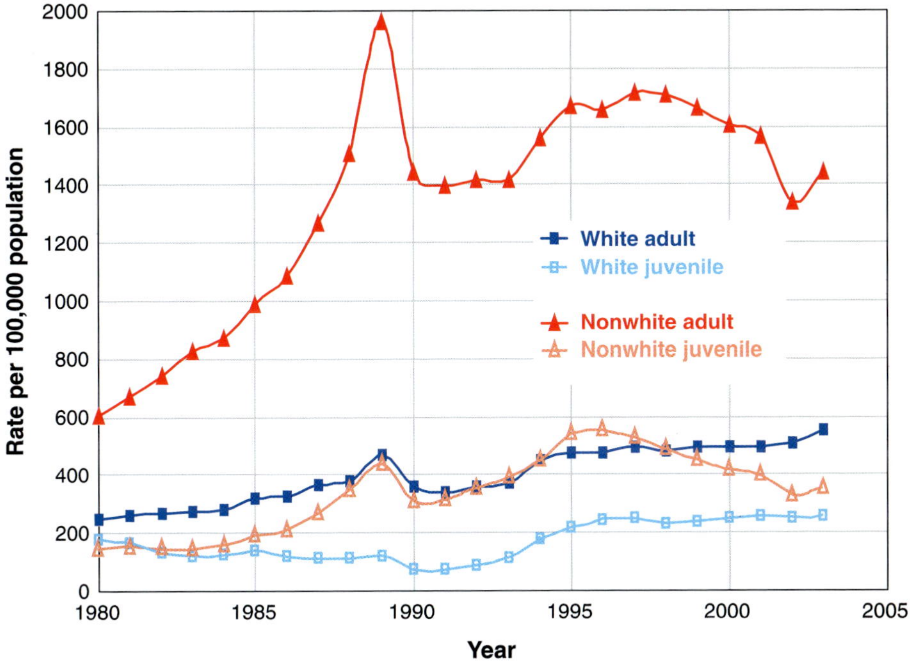

Figure 4 Drug arrest rates by race and age.

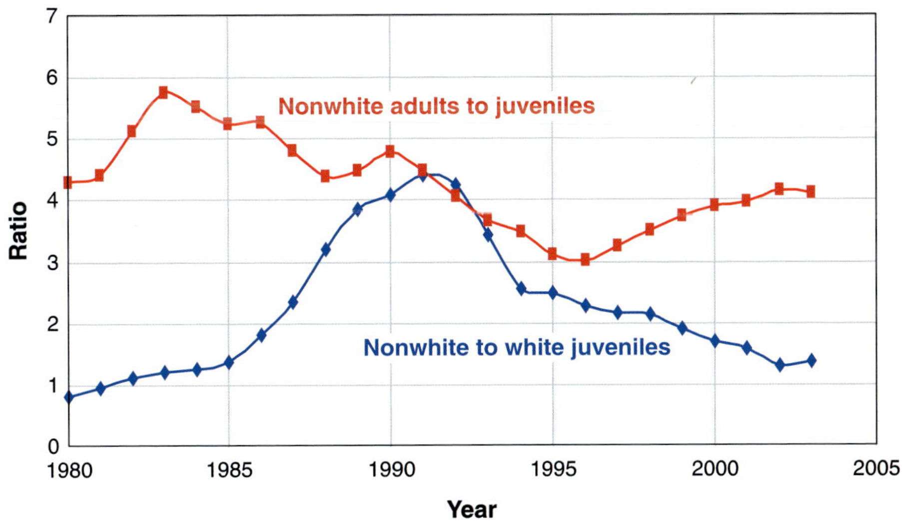

Figure 5 Drug arrest ratios.

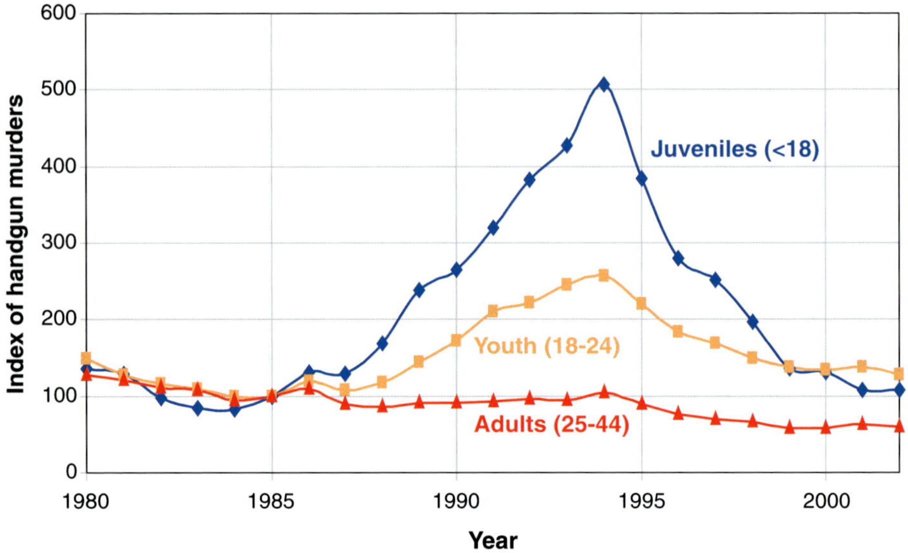

Figure 6 Use of handguns in murder by three age groups (indexed, 1985 = 100).

in the debate over gun control and thus merits mention. Lott's claim is controversial not because there is a substantial division among scholars as to its merits—several researchers have been unable to corroborate his findings, and a number of scholars have shown his studies to be seriously flawed (e.g., Black & Nagin 1998, Ayres & Donohue 2003). Rather, the "more guns, less crime" argument—arming citizens will deter criminals from face-to-face crimes by inducing fear of confronting an armed victim—has engendered controversy because it runs counter to the belief of most analysts of U.S. crime that our extraordinary rate of lethal violence is facilitated by the abundance of firearms in private hands (Miller et al. 2002).

The gist of Lott's analysis is a comparison of crime trends in states that passed shall-issue laws (laws mandating that a gun-carrying permit be issued to any applicant who is not in a proscribed category) with trends in states that did not. His conclusion was that passing such laws resulted in a reduction in most violent crimes but in an increase in certain property offenses. One of the most thorough evaluations of this argument was conducted by Ayres & Donohue (2003). They extended Lott's data set by seven years—well into the crime-drop period—and found that the effect of shall-issue laws on crime is inconsistent across states and that these laws are at least as likely to increase crime as to reduce it. The explanation for this finding may be that the bulk of the states adopting shall-issue policies were relatively rural in attributes and thus did not see the great spike in violent crime that occurred in more urbanized states, which tended not to pass these laws. In the 1990s, however, the years that Ayres & Donohue added to the Lott data set, urbanized states enjoyed a greater drop in crime than rural ones. In the latter period, then, states without shall-issue laws fared relatively better than those with them, and, as a result, the net effect of shall-issue laws over the period from 1977 to 1999 was nil. A National Academy of Sciences panel (Wellford et al. 2004) conducted an extensive review of research on the issue and concluded with similar skepticism toward Lott's findings.

During the crime drop of the 1990s, the gun manufacturing trends of the rise period were reversed, with production of semiautomatic pistols declining by nearly 60% as of 1998 (Wintemute 2006). This trend almost certainly reflected an industry adjustment to declining demand rather than an exogenous factor that reduced crime through diminished access to preferred weapons.

The drop period also saw a reversal of the growth in federal firearms licenses that had occurred since the 1970s. A new policy of active vigilance by ATF as of 1993, including greater use of background checks of applicants, together with an increase in the three-year license fee from $30 to $200, may have been responsible for the reduction in sales licenses from 287,000 in 1993 to 104,000 by 2002 (Insp. Gen. US Dep. Justice 2004).

Policing

If any factor would seem to be self-evidently relevant to understanding the crime drop, policing would be it. Police are the first line of response to crime. Moreover, the period of the crime drop was also an era of substantial innovation in police practice. And yet compelling evidence of a police role in the crime drop is hard to come by.

The 1990s saw the evolution of reforms begun earlier and the implementation of new ones, both generic and specific. Generic changes involved new strategies for controlling crime, whereas specific changes can be thought of as more tactical in nature, focusing on one or more repeaters: offenders, victims, and places (Eck & Maguire 2006). Community policing, which enlists the public in anticrime partnerships, began in the 1980s and thus early enough to be considered as a cause of the crime drop. However, the evidence for the efficacy of such partnerships in reducing serious crime is equivocal at best. Neither Neighborhood Watch nor foot patrols, to take two examples, have been proven effective in reducing violent crime. Order-maintenance, or zero-tolerance, policing, inspired by the "broken windows" philosophy—nip crime in the bud by sanctioning minor infractions—is another influential strategic initiative, often touted as the reason for New York City's especially marked crime drop. Yet here, too, evidence for a role in crime reduction is not abundant. Order-maintenance policing was begun in New York in 1993, but violent crime was already in decline by this point. Moreover, order-maintenance policing was adopted at the same time that several other changes (Compstat, more police) were being put into place, making it very difficult to apportion credit for the crime drop among these various strategies (Eck & Maguire 2006).

Policing changes of a narrower, more tactical nature have in common the deployment of police resources to people and places that have been identified as hot spots of crime. New York City's Compstat program, which tracks incidents via computer and allocates resources accordingly, is the best known such program. As with order-maintenance policing, Compstat was deployed after New York's crime drop was already in progress and simultaneously with other strategic and tactical innovations, so evaluating its efficacy is not a straightforward undertaking. One recent analysis (Rosenfeld et al. 2005a) concludes that New York's homicide rate did not decline significantly following the introduction of Compstat, net of the other factors reducing this rate.

Note that this conclusion does not preclude the possibility that Compstat does, in fact, reduce crime. Compstat is a prominent example of directed patrol, which has been shown in experimental studies to reduce crime (Sherman & Weisburd 1995).[4] Intensive patrol directed specifically at areas of high levels of gun crime has been shown to be effective as well (Sherman & Rogan 1995, McGarrell et al. 2001). What is less certain is how widely adopted such tactics were in the crime-drop period and thus to what extent they should receive credit for the drop.

[4]Compstat entails much more than just directed patrol; it also includes a management change that holds local commanders accountable for the crime in their area and encourages initiative in responding to it. It could as reasonably be categorized a strategic innovation as a tactical one. See Karmen (2000) for a thorough discussion.

In their comprehensive review of the role of policing in the crime drop, Eck & Maguire (2006) conclude that police efforts to impede the drug trade would probably have the most compelling case for an intervention that reduced violence. These efforts preceded the crime drop and arguably played a role in the demise of the crack market and its attendant violence by making life difficult and riskier for both buyers and sellers.

In research on policing and crime, the relationship between number of police and number of crimes is an ongoing occupation. In their treatment of the issue, Eck & Maguire (2006) discuss the challenge of overcoming the simultaneity problem: Increasing police strength may well reduce crime, but crime just as surely causes changes in police strength, as cities bring on or lay off officers in response to crime trends (or at least beliefs about them). This reciprocal causality makes isolating the influence of each variable difficult. In the quest to determine the extent to which more police means less crime, researchers need an instrumental variable—one that affects police numbers but is not itself influenced by police numbers or by crime rates and does not itself directly affect crime rates. Any association between changes over time in that variable and subsequent changes in crime can then be taken as an indication of the causal effect of police numbers on crime.

Levitt's (1997) use of electoral cycles as such an independent instrument is the best known of such studies. Reasoning that incumbent politicians typically hire more police as elections near, Levitt first demonstrated, with a sample of 52 cities, that both mayoral and gubernatorial election years do see a small but significant increase in the rate of police hiring. He then completed the causal linkage with regressions assessing the effect of year type (election or no) on change in crime rates in that and the following year. He found that violent crime was appreciably reduced, whereas property crime was essentially unaffected. However, in an effort to replicate Levitt's study, McCrary (2002) found an error in Levitt's weighting of crime types. When McCrary used correct weightings, he found no effect of police staffing. Levitt (2002) acknowledged the error but offered a new analysis in which he employed a different instrumental variable as a proxy for police numbers. Instead of using elections as a cause of changes in police numbers, he used a correlate, changes in number of firefighters, which he showed do tend to accompany changes in police numbers, presumably because they result from the same political and budgetary considerations. Growth and decline in firefighters should not be affected by or affect crime rates, so, given the correlation between numbers of firefighters and police officers, changes in firefighters can be used as markers of changes in police numbers that are independent of crime. The result, in theory, is a means of assessing the subsequent impact of those changes on crime. Levitt found that both violent and property crime were suppressed by growth in police, with 1% more police reducing crime by close to 0.5%. Levitt (2004) attributes 5%–6% of the 1990s crime drop to police growth in that period.

Levitt's finding that murder was the crime most responsive to increased police numbers is somewhat surprising, as murder is among the most passionate of crimes and therefore among those one would expect to be least deterrable by fear of police detection and subsequent punishment. Murders might be suppressed by growth in police because there are more police available to intervene in conflicts. If that were the case, then one would expect police numbers also to affect less serious violence. Although Levitt does report a suppression of robbery, aggravated (i.e., serious) assault actually increased. The latter result could be a consequence of a trend toward a more inclusive definition of assault by police agencies during the study period, as discussed earlier.

A potentially significant recent development in policing is changes in policies and force deployments enacted in the aftermath of the September 11, 2001, terrorist attacks in New York City and Washington, DC. On the one hand, police control of common crime may have suffered, especially in the major cities, as a result of reassignments of police personnel to tasks related to antiterror efforts. (Such a decline in police efficacy would not necessarily result in increased crime rates, as the decline might be negated by changes in the other factors that affect crime.) If, on the other hand, policing responses to the terrorist threat entailed moving personnel from off-street duties to patrol and thus increasing the number of police on the street, then the terrorist attacks might have stimulated an increase in police effectiveness. This scenario assumes that, as argued by Levitt, increasing the number of officers on the street does reduce crime.

Economics

Research on the influence of economic conditions on crime rests on the assumption that criminal behavior, at least the acquisitive sort, is shaped by rational motivations. Crime involves decisions, and these decisions are a product of both positive and negative incentives. Whether to engage in crime and how much time and effort to devote to it as opposed to legitimate work is a function, in part, of the comparative returns of each, weighed against the perceived risk and severity of punishment for crime. All else being equal, a reduction in the expected payoff from legal work because of a decline in the availability of jobs, in rates of pay, or in both should increase the likelihood or extent of illegal economic activity, both for individuals and, therefore, for society.

Grogger (2006) presents evidence for the validity of this model. His analysis of youth participation in crime found an inverse relationship between the hourly wages of a young worker's legitimate efforts and the extent of their criminal work. The quantitative relationship was one-to-one: a 1% drop in wages yielded a 1% rise in time devoted to property crime. This elasticity more than explained the 18% growth in youth property crime in the 1980s, as the 22% decrease in their wages predicted a 22% rise in their crime. Clearly, other factors were militating against the criminogenic effect of wage decline, but wages do appear to have had a role in the uptrend in property crime in the 1980s and possibly the downturn of the 1990s as well.

Freeman & Rodgers (1999) assessed the relationship between unemployment and crime for young, noncollege-educated men in the 1980s and 1990s, using labor data for metropolitan areas and state crime rates. They concluded that a 1% decline in youth unemployment reduced youth crime by 1.5%.

Raphael & Winter-Ebmer (2001) related state unemployment to major crimes for the period from 1971 to 1997. Their analysis included controls for a number of demographic and economic variables that might vary with unemployment and thus confound the effect of unemployment on crime. They found that a 1% drop in unemployment was associated with reductions in overall property crime ranging from 1.6% to 5%. Between 1992 and 1997, they concluded, 28% of the decline in burglary, 82% of that in larceny, and 14% of that in vehicle theft were due to declining unemployment. Their overall estimate is that 40% of the drop in property crime was attributable to the economic boom of the 1990s.

Gould et al. (2002) carried out a similar analysis but focused on the low-wage sector (noncollege-educated men), relating state trends in unemployment and wages to county crime rates for 1979 to 1997. They determined that more than 60% of the demographically adjusted growth in property crime in the 1980s and 1990s resulted from the steady drop in wages among low-skilled workers. Although this group saw a rise in wages in the mid- to late 1990s, Gould et al. credit a decrease in unemployment after 1993 with much of the post-1992 crime drop. Their calculated elasticity of property crime with respect to unemployment of noncollege-educated males predicted a property crime drop of 7.5%; the actual decline, adjusted for population changes in age, sex, and race, was 7.6%.

The proposition that declining economic conditions engender more property crime is consonant with common sense. That an economic downturn would produce an increase in violence is less self-evidently tenable. Each of the studies mentioned here, however, either finds evidence for such an effect or finds one plausible. Grogger (2006) argues that poor job prospects in the 1980s might have influenced the calculus of unskilled young men in decisions about legal work versus work in the drug trade. Given the violence that inheres in illegal markets, and especially the crack business, economic trends could thus have played a role in the spike in violence. Equally, the flattening of the low-skill wage drop in the mid-1990s and upturn in wages toward the end of that decade may have tilted the balance toward the legitimate economy for many young men.

Raphael & Winter-Ebmer (2001) had mixed findings for the effect of unemployment on violent crime. However, the type of violent crime that is closest in motivation to purely acquisitive crimes—robbery—showed the strongest and most consistent positive relationship to unemployment. They concluded that 14% of the drop in robbery was due to declining unemployment. Gould et al. (2002) likewise found that the drop in robbery was significantly affected by economic factors, but they found assault to be so as well, whereas Raphael & Winter-Ebmer did not. Because of the numeric predominance of robbery and assault within the general category of violent crime, in the Gould study between 40% and 60% of the decrease in violent crime is accounted for by the combination of dropping unemployment and rising wages.

Not all analysts accord as much causal weight to the economy. Levitt (2004), for example, sees a more modest elasticity of property crime on unemployment of around 1.0 and is unconvinced that unemployment or wages affect violent crime. Freeman (2001), on the other hand, reviews the same evidence and revises his earlier, more conservative estimates, crediting the improved economy with a third of the crime drop.

Demographics

It is well recognized that crime rates differ considerably across demographic characteristics of gender, age, and ethnicity. If crime rates within each such demographic subgroup remained stable—if crime were not influenced by the social and economic forces and law enforcement practices discussed here—then aggregate crime rates could be predicted with great accuracy based on the per capita rates of those subgroups and their changing numbers. However, the 1980s and 1990s offer a clear lesson that changes in those within-group rates (see Figure 4) outweigh changes in group numbers, as the aggregate crime spike of the late 1980s and early 1990s was driven by a sharp rise in the violent crime rate of young men despite their decreasing proportion in the population. And, conversely, the national decline of the 1990s occurred despite growing numbers of young men because their per capita crime rate declined markedly.

The most provocative contribution to the crime-drop debate was an article by Donohue & Levitt (2001) arguing that at least half of the drop was a result of the upsurge in abortions following the Supreme Court's *Roe v. Wade* decision in 1973 overturning bans on abortion. The logic of the argument starts with the premise that children born to mothers in adverse circumstances—young, poor, unmarried—are often unwanted and so suffer developmental deficits and are thus at increased risk of eventual criminal offending. This assumption, combined with the belief that pregnant girls and women in such situations are more likely than others to avail themselves of abortion, leads to the inference that the *Roe v. Wade* decision led to the termination of millions of such unwanted pregnancies in the ensuing years. And this, in turn, would mean that cohorts born in these years, having passed through what might be called an abortion filter, should produce less crime than cohorts born prior to 1973. Abortion might reduce crime also just by reducing the size of birth cohorts.

Donohue & Levitt cite several lines of evidence in support of their thesis. Five states legalized abortion three years earlier than the 1973 national legalization, and these states began their crime drops earlier than the others. And those states with higher abortion rates in the 1970s saw greater reductions in crime in the 1990s.

Critics of the abortion hypothesis have taken its authors to task for ignoring the powerful influence of the crack-related spike in youth homicide of the 1980s, which had a varying role across states in the timing of the crime drop. This criticism is relevant both to the early onset of the drop in the states that legalized abortion early and to the correlation between state abortion rates and crime rates. The five early legalizing states were dominated by New York and California, whose major cities—New York and Los Angeles—underwent their crack periods earlier than elsewhere (Cork 1999) and thus experienced an earlier start to the crime drop. New York and California are also among the states with the highest abortion rates. And, in general, states with large cities have higher rates of abortion, and large cities met the crime drop sooner. Given the urban focus of the crack phenomenon, the correlation invoked by Donohue & Levitt between abortion rate and extent of crime decline becomes less compelling.

In one of the most thorough of the responses to the abortion hypothesis, Joyce (2004) questions one of its indispensable tenets—that an increase in abortions indicates a corresponding increase in the rate at which unwanted pregnancies are ended. Were this assumption valid, we would expect fertility rates to decline with increases in abortion. Or, if abortions entailed not a decline in women's lifetime fertility but rather a means of forestalling childbirth until later, then at least fertility in younger women should decline as abortions increase. Joyce found no such correlations for the period after national legalization. In other words, state fertility rates—both overall and for teenage girls—did not decline as abortion rates increased. This suggests that an important part of the increase in documented abortions post-*Roe* represents either a substitution of legal for previously illegal abortions or a partial replacement of less drastic means of birth control, i.e., abstinence and contraception, or some combination of both. If, as Joyce contends, trends in abortion do not represent trends in the rate of unwanted births, then the abortion hypothesis founders.

It happens, however, that fertility rates did decline in the states that legalized abortion in the three years prior to *Roe.* In these states and this period, then, abortions may have been employed to avoid unwanted children. Joyce (2004) employs this fact in an approach that avoids confounding the crime effects of crack with possible changes in criminal propensities of successive age groups because of differing exposure to abortion. The strategy involves comparing crime rates of two cohorts of a given age group, one of which was born prior to legalization and one after, the latter thus filtered through legal abortion. For example, 18-year-olds born in 1969 and in 1971 turned 18 in 1987 and 1989. Differences in the offending rates of these two cohorts will reflect the combined influence of their differing exposure to abortion (no for the 1969 group and yes for the 1971 group) plus any differing period effects operating on the two groups, such as crack-related crime trends. In order to subtract out the period effects to yield an estimate of the abortion factor, a similar exercise is conducted with two other age cohorts, as close to age 18 as possible, but neither of which was born after legalization. For example, the offending-rate difference between 19-year-olds in 1987 and 1989, born in the prelegalization years of 1968 and 1970, should reflect only period effects, i.e., differences between the two years in prevailing criminogenic influences. A greater difference in crime rates between the two 18-year-old groups than between the two 19-year-old groups could then plausibly be ascribed to abortion. All these comparisons are conducted within states to control for cross-state variation in period influences. The upshot of Joyce's analysis is a strong and consistent finding of no effect of abortion on crime rates.

Foote & Goetz (2005) also stress the importance of controlling for the varied timing of the crack epidemic across cities, which, to reiterate, could confound an effect of abortion on crime. They examined the multivariate regression program used by Donohue & Levitt (2001) and discovered that they had failed to include a state-by-year interaction term, essential for controlling for between-state variation in the crack effect. Running the regression with state-year interactions included, Foote & Goetz found that the association of abortion with crime was reduced by half. They also criticize Donohue & Levitt's use of total arrests per cohort as the outcome measure rather than arrests per capita, which would seem the proper test of the claim that abortion acts as a filter, resulting in individuals less given to crime. Total arrests per cohort will be a function not just of any such filtering effect but also of cohort size. Although, as Donohue & Levitt observed, excellent data on population by age for the years between decennial censuses are not available, reasonable interpolations do exist. Foote & Goetz employed such information and found that replacing total arrests with arrests per capita eliminates the remaining apparent filtering effect of abortion (although it could still reduce crime simply by reducing the size of the crime-prone age groups).

In the final analysis, even if a general crime-suppressing function of legalized abortion were established, it could not explain much of the crime drop because the advent of legal abortion and the crime drop are out of synch (Cook & Laub 2002). During the crime rise of the late 1980s, both property and violent crime were markedly elevated for the age range from 13 to 24. The first cohort of 13-year-olds to pass through the abortion sieve after national legalization attained that age in 1986, yet property crime did not decline for youth until 1994, or eight years later than it should have. Adolescent violent arrest rates were increasing through 1993. And the upswing was greatest for black adolescents, even though black women were having more abortions per capita than women of other racial groups.

SUMMARY AND CONCLUSIONS

The American crime drop of the 1990s is a tale of two trends, one for people younger than their late 20s and one for those older. Both segments partook of the drop. In the case of the older one, though, the downtrend was a continuation of a decrease in violence that had begun at least as early as 1980. The decline among the younger groups, by contrast, occurred only after their sharp upturn in violence, which began after 1985. The differing histories of the two parts of the population suggest that although they moved in the same direction in the 1990s, the causes of their downtrends were quite different.

Incarceration is one factor that certainly deserves different causal weightings with respect to youth and their elders. The relatively long-term pacification of the U.S. adult population is partly explicable by the massive growth in the rate of imprisonment over roughly the same period, whereas the same cannot be true of the violence decline among those under 18, for whom punishment rarely entails imprisonment. It is equally clear, however, that the magnitude of the adult decrease exceeds the crime-suppressing capacity of even as great a growth in incarceration as occurred in the United States. It is conceivable, as Rosenfeld (2006) has suggested, that some of the adult decline reflects a shift in the American ethos, a reduced tolerance for interpersonal violence.

It also seems reasonable to conclude that for all age sectors, no single factor can explain all or even most of the decline in violence. This is not to say that all factors were equally important. As we have related in this review, there is no lack of arguments for the primacy of a single factor, such as incarceration, the economy, or abortion. But, generalizing across all sectors, the crime drop does appear to derive from some beneficial synergies, mutual reinforcements among the factors we have discussed. For example, the waning of the crack markets resulted from some combination of erosion by successful tactical adaptations in policing and rejection of crack by a new generation. At the same time, a strong economy in the 1990s was able to absorb many of those displaced by the shrinking crack markets.

It is interesting to note that although the crime drop has undone the spike in violence among youth, reducing their levels to what had prevailed before the upturn, their patterns of violence and contribution to the national burden of violence still evince traits of the rise period (Cook & Laub 2002). The perennially disproportionate contribution of youth and young adults to the aggregate rate became even greater during the rise period, and this increase in the youth/adult ratio is still in evidence. Similarly, the disproportionate involvement of black Americans in violent crime became even more pronounced in the rise period, an elevated ratio that persists. And the striking increase in the ratio of gun to nongun youth crime during the rise period has not declined to prerise levels. Cook & Laub (2002) invoke these hangovers as reasons to doubt the ebbing of crack as the source of the crime drop. But it seems quite reasonable to interpret the carrying over of the high black-white and gun-nongun ratios as unsurprising inertial consequences of the diffusion of gun carrying by young people, especially in inner-city areas, in association with the rise of crack. And the persistence of the elevated role of youth in violent crime despite their reversion to their prerise rates would be expected, given that adult rates declined during both the youth rise and the youth drop.

The crime drop has been followed by a leveling off and a trendless first few years of the new century. The causes of this apparent end to the drop, as with the drop itself, cannot be discerned with certainty, as it is early yet to gain an analytic foothold. But we are not without tenable linkages. The flourishing economy of the 1990s was succeeded by a largely stagnant one, with fewer opportunities for young people of low education lacking skills suited to the contemporary information economy. Legitimate employment has always served as an important termination point for teenage offending, so the slowing of the economy may be related to the ending of the decline in youth offending. Governmental revenue at state and city levels has been waning, and the federal government, an important source of funding for a wide variety of services that presumably militate against crime, such as job training, has reduced such outlays in the face of record deficits brought on by large tax cuts and military expenditures in Iraq. Police activities in major cities have been reoriented, to varying degrees, from controlling conventional crime to averting terrorism. The crime-reduction effect of incarceration has been diminished as the steady growth in per capita imprisonment has slowed to less than one-third of the growth rate of the 1980s and 1990s. Crack, a technological innovation that made the pleasures of cocaine affordable to low-income citizens, took root in the U.S. inner city in the 1980s, engendering heightened violence and fueling massive imprisonment, the latter persisting even after the ebbing of crack and its attendant violence in the 1990s. As crack has waned, methamphetamine has increased its toll, although, by contrast with crack, its users are predominantly white and its geographic focus still mainly rural. The crimes associated with the sale and consumption of this drug could become more violent as the Mexican drug cartels increase their involvement in its manufacture and distribution (Zernike 2006).

If interpreting the present is challenging, predicting the future of crime is daunting. The logic of using changing demographic composition to limn the future is unassailable but, as we have seen, this predictor has been of little use recently because of the large changes in per capita crime rates within demographic groups. We have presented some of the best evidence for the role of economic variables in crime trends, but demonstrating such a connection is one thing, predicting where the economy will be in five years quite a different, and less credible, one. It cannot even be said with great confidence that the crime drop has ended. Although it was a certainty that crime rates could not continue their decline forever, it is not certain that U.S. crime has arrived at its irreducible minimum. Present rates have declined to those of the 1960s, but crime rates have been even lower in U.S. history. If the recent crime drop was a correction not to the rise of the 1980s but rather to the more protracted increase that began in the 1960s (LaFree 2000), then perhaps the natural equilibrium of American crime is closer to the good old days of the 1950s than to the bad old days of the 1980s.

LITERATURE CITED

Ayres I, Donohue JJ III. 2003. Shooting down the "more guns, less crime" hypothesis. *Stanford Law Rev.* 55:1193–212

Beck A, Gilliard D, Greenfeld L, Harlow C, Hester T, et al. 1993. *Survey of State Prison Inmates, 1991*. Washington, DC: US Dep. Justice. NCJ 136949

Beck AJ, Shipley BE. 1989. *Recidivism of Prisoners Released in 1983*. Washington, DC: US Dep. Justice. NCJ 116261

Black DA, Nagin D. 1998. Do right-to-carry laws deter violent crime? *J. Leg. Stud.* 27:209–19

Blumstein A. 1993. Making rationality relevant: the American Society of Criminology presidential address. *Criminology* 31:1–16

Blumstein A, Beck AJ. 1999. Population growth in U.S. prisons: 1980–1996. In *Crime and Justice: A Review of Research*, ed. M Tonry, J Petersilia, 26:17–62. Chicago: Univ. Chicago Press

Blumstein A, Beck AJ. 2005. Reentry as a transient state between liberty and recommitment. See Travis & Visher 2005, pp. 50–79

Blumstein A, Wallman J, eds. 2006. *The Crime Drop in America*. New York: Cambridge Univ. Press. Rev. ed.

Braga A, Cook PJ, Kennedy DM, Moore MH. 2002. The illegal supply of firearms. In *Crime and Justice: A Review of Research*, ed. M Tonry, 29:319–52. Chicago: Univ. Chicago Press

Butterfield F. 2004. Across rural America, drug casts a grim shadow. *NY Times*. Jan. 4, p. A10

Cook PJ, Laub JH. 2002. After the epidemic: recent trends in youth violence in the United States. In *Crime and Justice: A Review of Research*, ed. M Tonry, 29:1–37. Chicago: Univ. Chicago Press

Cork D. 1999. Examining space-time interaction in city-level homicide data: crack markets and the diffusion of guns among youth. *J. Quant. Crim.* 15:379–406

Donohue JJ III, Levitt SD. 2001. The impact of legalized abortion on crime. *Q. J. Econ.* 116:379–420

Eck JE, Maguire ER. 2006. Have changes in policing reduced violent crime? An assessment of the evidence. See Blumstein & Wallman 2006, pp. 207–65

Exec. Off. Pres. 2002. *Pulse Check: Trends in Drug Abuse, November 2002*. Washington, DC: Off. Natl. Drug Control Policy. NCJ 197242

Exec. Off. Pres. 2004. *Pulse Check: Trends in Drug Abuse. January 2004*. Washington, DC: Off. Natl. Drug Control Policy. NCJ 201398

Foote CL, Goetz CF. 2005. *Testing economic hypotheses with state-level data: a comment on Donohue and Levitt 2001*. Work. Pap. 05–15, Fed. Res. Bank Boston

Freeman RB. 2001. Does the booming economy help explain the fall in crime? In *Perspectives on Crime and Justice: 1999–2000 Lecture Series*, pp. 23–43. Washington, DC: Natl. Inst. Justice. NCJ 184245

Freeman RB, Rodgers WM III. 1999. *Area economic conditions and the labor market outcomes of young men in the 1990s expansion*. Work. Pap. 7073, Natl. Bur. Econ. Res.

Gould ED, Weinberg BA, Mustard DB. 2002. Crime rates and local labor market opportunities in the United States: 1979–1997. *Rev. Econ. Stat.* 84(1):45–61

Grogger J. 2006. An economic model of recent trends in violence. See Blumstein & Wallman 2006, pp. 266–87

Insp. Gen. US Dep. Justice. 2004. *Inspections of Firearms Dealers by the Bureau of Alcohol, Tobacco, Firearms and Explosives*. Washington, DC: US Dep. Justice Rep. No. I-2004–05

Johnson BD, Golub A, Dunlap E. 2006. The rise and decline of hard drugs, drug markets, and violence in inner-city New York. See Blumstein & Wallman 2006, pp. 164–206

Johnston LD, O'Malley PM, Bachman JG. 2003. *Demographic Subgroup Trends for Various Licit and Illicit Drugs, 1975–2002*. Monitoring the Future Occas. Pap. No. 59. Ann Arbor, MI: Inst. Soc. Res.

Joyce T. 2004. Did legalized abortion lower crime? *J. Hum. Resourc.* 39:1–28

Karmen A. 2000. *New York Murder Mystery*. New York: N. Y. Univ. Press

LaFree G. 2000. Explaining the crime bust of the 1990s. *J. Crim. Law Criminol.* 91:269–305

Langan PA, Levin DJ. 2002. *Recidivism of Prisoners Released in 1994*. Washington, DC: US Dep. Justice. NCJ 193427

Levitt SD. 1997. Using electoral cycles in police hiring to estimate the effect of police on crime. *Am. Econ. Rev.* 87:270–90

Levitt SD. 2002. Using electoral cycles in police hiring to estimate the effects of police on crime: reply. *Am. Econ. Rev.* 92:1244–50

Levitt SD. 2004. Understanding why crime fell in the 1990s: four factors that explain the decline and six that do not. *J. Econ. Perspect.* 18:163–90

Lott JRJ. 2000. *More Guns, Less Crime:*

Understanding Crime and Gun-Control Laws. Chicago: Univ. Chicago Press. 2nd ed.

Lott JRJ, Mustard DB. 1997. Crime, deterrence, and right-to-carry concealed handguns. *J. Leg. Stud.* 26:1–68

Ludwig J, Cook PJ. 2000. Homicide and suicide rates associated with implementation of the Brady handgun violence prevention act. *J. Am. Med. Assoc.* 284:585–91

McCrary J. 2002. Using electoral cycles in police hiring to estimate the effect of police on crime: comment. *Am. Econ. Rev.* 92:1236–43

McGarrell EF, Chermak S, Weiss A, Wilson J. 2001. Reducing firearms violence through directed police patrol. *Crim. Public Policy* 1:119–48

Messner S, Deane GD, Anselin L, Pearson-Nelson B. 2005. Locating the vanguard in rising and falling homicide rates across U.S. cities. *Criminology* 43:661–96

Miller M, Azrael D, Hemenway D. 2002. Rates of household firearm ownership and homicide across US regions and states, 1988–1997. *Am. J. Public Health* 92:1988–93

Musto DF. 1999. *The American Disease: Origins of Narcotic Control*. New York: Oxford Univ. Press. 3rd ed.

Natl. Inst. Justice. 2002. *Drug Use and Related Matters Among Adult Arrestees, 2001*. Washington, DC: US Dep. Justice

Natl. Inst. Justice. 2003a. *2000 Arrestee Drug Abuse Monitoring: Annual Report*. Washington, DC: US Dep. Justice. NCJ 193013

Natl. Inst. Justice. 2003b. *Preliminary Data on Drug Use and Related Matters Among Adult Arrestees and Juvenile Detainees, 2002*. Washington, DC: US Dep. Justice

Natl. Inst. Justice. 2004. *Drug and Alcohol Use and Related Matters Among Arrestees, 2003*. Washington, DC: US Dep. Justice

Raphael S, Ludwig J. 2003. Prison sentence enhancements: the case of Project Exile. In *Evaluating Gun Policy: Effects on Crime and Violence*, ed. J Ludwig, PJ Cook, pp. 251–86. Washington, DC: Brookings Inst. Press

Raphael S, Winter-Ebmer R. 2001. Identifying the effect of unemployment on crime. *J. Law Econ.* 44:259–83

Rosenfeld R. 2006. Patterns in adult homicide: 1980–1995. See Blumstein & Wallman 2006, pp. 130–63

Rosenfeld R, Fornango R, Baumer E. 2005a. Did Ceasefire, Compstat, and Exile reduce homicide? *Crim. Public Policy* 4:419–49

Rosenfeld R, Wallman J, Fornango R. 2005b. The contribution of ex-prisoners to crime rates. See Travis & Visher 2005, pp. 80–104

Sheley JF, Wright JD. 1993. *Gun Acquisition and Possession in Selected Juvenile Samples*. Washington, DC: US Dep. Justice

Sheley JF, Wright JD. 1995. *In the Line of Fire*. New York: Aldine de Gruyter

Sherman LW, Rogan DP. 1995. Effects of gun seizures on gun violence: "hot spots" patrol in Kansas City. *Justice Q.* 12:673–93

Sherman LW, Weisburd DA. 1995. General deterrent effects of police patrol in crime "hot spots": a randomized, controlled trial. *Justice Q.* 12:625–48

Spelman W. 2006. The limited importance of prison expansion. See Blumstein & Wallman 2006, pp. 97–129

Sugarmann J, Rand K. 1992. *More Gun Dealers than Gas Stations: A Study of Federally Licensed Firearms Dealers in America*. Washington, DC: Violence Policy Cent.

Travis J, Visher C, eds. 2005. *Prisoner Reentry and Crime in America*. New York: Cambridge Univ. Press

Weisburd D, Bushway S, Lum C, Yang SM. 2004. Trajectories of crime at places: a longitudinal study of street segments in the city of Seattle. *Criminology* 42:283–321

Wellford CF, Pepper JV, Petrie CV. 2004. *Firearms and Violence: A Critical Review*. Washington, DC: Natl. Acad. Press

Wintemute G. 2006. Guns and gun violence. See Blumstein & Wallman 2006, pp. 45–96

Wright MA, Wintemute GJ, Rivara FP. 1999. Effectiveness of denial of handgun purchase to persons believed to be at high risk for firearm violence. *Am. J. Public Health* 89:88–90

Zernike K. 2006. Potent Mexican meth floods in as states curb domestic variety. *NY Times*. Jan. 23, p. A1

Annu. Rev. Law Soc. Sci. 2006. 2:147–64
doi: 10.1146/annurev.lawsocsci.2.081805.105856

First published online as a Review in Advance on August 22, 2006

ECONOMIC CONTRIBUTIONS TO THE UNDERSTANDING OF CRIME

Steven D. Levitt[1] and Thomas J. Miles[2]
[1]*Department of Economics, University of Chicago, Chicago, Illinois 60637; American Bar Foundation, Chicago, Illinois 60611; email: s-levitt@uchicago.edu*
[2]*University of Chicago Law School, Chicago, Illinois 60637; email: tmiles@law.uchicago.edu*

Key Words deterrence, incapacitation, criminal justice

■ **Abstract** The past decade has seen a sharp increase in the application of empirical economic approaches to the study of crime and the criminal justice system. Much of this research has emphasized identifying causal impacts, as opposed to correlations. These studies have generally found that increases in police and greater incarceration lead to reduced crime. The death penalty, as currently used in the United States, does not appear to lower crime. We also review the evidence on three other crime-related debates in which economists have played a central role: racial profiling, concealed weapons laws, and the impact of legalized abortion.

INTRODUCTION

The casual observer might expect that economics has little to contribute to the understanding of criminal activity. Economics is a discipline seemingly concerned with market-based transactions in which parties act purposefully to realize the benefits of exchange. In contrast, many criminal acts, such as homicide and theft, are inherently nonconsensual, even coercive. Moreover, many crimes appear to be acts of impulse or emotion rather than the kind of rational decision making associated with market behavior. Despite this apparent mismatch of methodology and subject matter, the economic approach has made significant contributions to the study of crime, and in the past decade, the pace of these contributions has accelerated. In this review, we examine some of the recent contributions that economics has made to the understanding of crime, and, as much of the recent work by economists on crime is empirical rather than theoretical, we emphasize empirical research over theory. The discussion is organized around two broad categories of influences on criminal behavior: (*a*) the criminal justice system and (*b*) other legal rules that, although distinct from the criminal justice system, nonetheless potentially influence criminal behavior.

As an initial matter, it is worth clarifying what we mean by the phrase economic approach. We believe four characteristics distinguish the economic approach to the study of crime from that of other social sciences. These characteristics are (*a*) an emphasis on the role of incentives in determining the behavior of individuals, whether they are criminals, victims, or those responsible for enforcing the law; (*b*) the use of econometric approaches that seek to differentiate correlation from causality in nonexperimental settings; (*c*) a focus on broad, public policy implications rather than evaluation of specific, small-scale interventions; and (*d*) the use of cost-benefit analysis as the metric for evaluating public policies.[1]

The emphasis on incentives in determining behavior arises from the assumption in economics that individuals maximize their utility subject to constraints. While counterexamples of this assumption surely exist, particularly in the context of criminal behavior, a plausible generalization about human behavior is that most individuals do the best they can with what they have. Becker (1968) presented the first modern economic model of criminal behavior. In it, actors prospectively compare the expected costs and expected benefits of offending. They commit crimes when the expected gains exceed the expected costs, and otherwise refrain from criminal acts. The model incorporates the criminal justice system as part of the offender's expected costs, with policing influencing the probability of punishment and fines representing the criminal sanction. In the model, the criminal justice system therefore reduces crime through deterrence. Since Becker's influential article, a large and active literature on the theory of deterrence has developed, with many elaborations and refinements of the core Becker model [see Kaplow & Shavell (2002) and Polinsky & Shavell (2006) for comprehensive reviews].

The emphasis in economics on identifying true causal impacts of particular crime-control policies also distinguishes it from other modes of research. Questions, such as the impact of the size of police forces or the scale of imprisonment on crime, are vexingly difficult to answer because crime rates influence the formation of public policies that combat crime. For example, if police reduce crime, but crime leads to the hiring of police, standard correlational statistical approaches such as ordinary least squares estimation do not capture the causal impact of these policies. Rather, these estimates suffer from what econometricians term simultaneity bias. Despite this formidable challenge, economists have enjoyed significant progress in recent years in addressing these issues. In so doing, they have found various components of the criminal justice system to be effective, but not always cost-effective, means of reducing crime.

The third distinguishing feature of the economic analysis of crime is the emphasis on broad, public policy implications rather than on the assessment of particular, small-scale policy interventions. Economists typically conduct analyses at the level of geographic aggregates, which serve as a proxy for individual behavior and permit comparisons across jurisdictions with different criminal justice

[1]Not all economic studies of crime are done by economists. A number of researchers who are not economists have done research that fits our broad definition of the economic approach (e.g., Bushway 2004).

policies. This emphasis on a broader level of analysis does not discount the importance of context. Rather, for economists interested in testing Becker's prediction that criminal actors respond to incentives in the form of deterrence, the goal is to understand human behavior in general rather than in particular settings. Similarly, for economists interested in evaluating policy, a frequent objective is to provide analysis that is sufficiently general to assist policy makers in numerous contexts.

The fourth defining characteristic of the economic approach to crime is the use of cost-benefit analysis. In economic theory, a widely used normative criterion is Pareto efficiency, the condition in which no reallocation of resources can make one person better off without leaving another person worse off. In practice, economists typically assess the desirability of a social program by weighing its costs and benefits, relative to other alternatives. These comparisons necessarily involve counterfactuals or predictions of the outcomes that would be achieved under the alternative, and what is especially useful in making these predictions are the arguably causal estimates provided by empirical economic analysis. Moreover, cost-benefit comparisons express the many dimensions of a decision in a single metric of price or money. The idea of a common unit of measurement has its limits; even many economists would resist the notion that all human values can be reduced to monetary equivalents. Despite these limitations, cost-benefit analysis furnishes a coherent normative criterion that is especially appropriate in the context of crime control, where the menu of policy alternatives is extensive and hundreds of millions of dollars are expended.

The remainder of this review is structured as follows. The next section discusses the economic literature regarding the effectiveness of three specific aspects of the criminal justice system: police, prisons, and capital punishment. In addition to examining the impact of the criminal justice system on crime rates, some economists have studied how the criminal justice system itself operates. Although a complete review of economic research on the operation of the criminal justice system is not possible here, a topic that has received much attention recently is racial profiling, and thus the next section also describes the work on racial profiling. The third section reviews the economic contributions of two determinants of crime outside the criminal justice system: the victim precaution of concealed weapons and the influence of legalized abortion. Both of these issues have been active areas of academic debate in recent years.

MEASURING THE IMPACT OF THE CRIMINAL JUSTICE SYSTEM ON CRIME

The Bureau of Justice Statistics estimates that nearly $200 billion is spent each year in the United States to catch, prosecute, and punish offenders (Bauer & Owens 2004). Measuring the effectiveness of this spending is a critical input into the development of good public policy, both in terms of allocating criminal justice dollars and of determining whether money is better spent on punishing today's offenders or on resources to lower the criminality of future cohorts.

As mentioned in the introduction, the key issue in measuring the impact of components of the criminal justice system is the identification of causal relationships. A step in isolating a causal effect of a criminal justice policy is to exclude the influence of other factors bearing on the frequency of criminal activity. To do so, economists often mimic the empirical design of medical studies. They compare outcomes in a set of jurisdictions that adopted a particular policy or law before and after its implementation. Consciously analogizing to medical research, economists typically refer to persons who receive and the jurisdictions that adopt the particular policy or law as the treatment groups. Economists also draw these comparisons relative to a set of jurisdictions that did not adopt the particular treatment, and this second set of jurisdictions acts as a control group. This empirical design draws comparisons across two dimensions—before and after, and treatment and control—and is therefore known as difference-in-differences.

The application of a difference-in-differences framework does not assure the accurate measurement of a causal impact because, unlike treatment groups in medical experiments, the set of jurisdictions adopting a particular crime-control policy is not randomly selected for two reasons. First, the crime-fighting policies that jurisdictions adopt are often themselves products of crime rates. For example, the amount of resources allocated to the criminal justice system is typically greater when crime is higher. Crime-fighting policies set the incentives to engage in crime and at the same time respond to the incidence of crime. Second, the social and historical factors that influence the adoption of specific laws and enforcement policies may also affect the incidence of crime directly. Social norms in the South, for instance, might lead southern states to use more freely capital punishment, and aside from any impact of capital punishment, these norms may directly affect southern crime. Econometricians refer to the simultaneous determination of policies and outcomes as the simultaneity problem, and this problem bedevils measurements of the impact of crime-control policies on crime rates. A failure to control for such biases risks serious mismeasurement of the impact of crime-control policies. We therefore review empirical attempts to deal with these difficult questions topic by topic. We begin with studies estimating the impact of police on crime, before examining the scale of imprisonment and the enforcement of the death penalty.

Measuring the Impact of Police on Crime

The first generation of empirical research on police and crime consisted of cross-sectional studies that compared policing and crime rates across jurisdictions, typically cities or states, at a point in time. In his comprehensive review of the literature, Cameron (1988) reported that a majority of these papers found either no relationship or a positive relationship between the level of police and crime rates. The cross-sectional methodology of these papers provided a poor test of the causal effect of police on crime because it failed to correct for the simultaneity problem. Jurisdictions with higher crime rates typically respond by hiring more police, whereas jurisdictions with lower crime rates need to employ fewer police. The failure of early contributors to this literature to recognize or grapple with the simultaneity problem prompted Fisher & Nagin (1978), as part of a National Academy of Sciences report, to criticize the cross-sectional approach severely.[2]

A second generation of research emerged in the 1990s. Two methodological innovations characterize this generation of scholarship. First, researchers employ larger and richer data sets. Rather than investigating a single year of data from a set of jurisdictions, second-generation researchers typically examine multiple years of data from the set of jurisdictions. These so-called repeated cross-sectional data sets allow economists to track patterns in crime rates within a jurisdiction over time as well as across jurisdictions. Thus, both sources of variation in crime rates—across different jurisdictions and within a single jurisdiction over time—may help identify the impact of police on crime. Estimates from repeated cross sections enjoy greater precision owing to the larger number of observations. They also are less prone to bias from unobserved heterogeneity because repeated cross-sectional data permit the inclusion of year and jurisdiction fixed effects as control variables.

The second feature of this wave of literature was the explicit recognition of the simultaneity problem and the use of relatively sophisticated econometric techniques to overcome it. Economists have primarily used two techniques: Granger causality (Granger 1969) and instrumental variables or natural experiments. The first of these methods, Granger causality, refers to a temporal relationship between variables rather than actual causation. One variable "Granger causes" another when changes in the first variable generally precede changes in the second.[3] The first to apply the technique of Granger causality to the question of police and crime were Marvell & Moody (1996). These authors studied a repeated cross section first of states and then of cities that spanned 20 years. They also controlled for sundry demographic and economic characteristics of these jurisdictions. Their estimates revealed that increases in police preceded declines in crime. In other words, police "Granger cause" crime drops. Their estimates implied that a 10% increase in an urban police force produced a 3% long-term decline in total crime.

Marvell & Moody (1996) used annual observations of police and crime, but annual data may miss short-term fluctuations and produce an understatement of the actual relationship between police and crime. For example, an increase in

[2]An early quasi-randomized experiment in Kansas City (Kelling et al. 1974) that also found little impact of police was not subject to these critiques, although it has been criticized by Larson (1976) for having inadequate power.

[3]A frequently cited example of the difference between actual causation and Granger causality is Christmas cards (Kennedy 1998). Christmas cards arrive in mailboxes before December 25, and thus they Granger cause Christmas. But the true causation is the reverse: the imminent arrival of Christmas causes individuals to mail Christmas cards. Forward-looking behavior produces a divergence between actual causation and Granger causation.

crime at the beginning of a year may later in the year prompt authorities to hire more police. With annual observations, any increase in crime and police appears contemporaneous rather than sequential, and the short-term causal effect is not observed. The resulting estimate of the impact of police on crime is biased toward zero in that circumstance. Higher frequency data, or data with a finer degree of temporal disaggregation, can remedy this problem. Corman & Mocan (2000) tested for the presence of these shorter-term fluctuations using nearly 30 years of monthly data from New York City. They found evidence that the governmental response to higher crime occurs rapidly. After an increase in crime, the hiring of more police occurs within six months. They also found evidence that offending rates similarly react quickly to greater policing. Employing the Granger causality method, Corman & Mocan (2000) estimated that a 10% increase in police resulted in a 10% drop in crime rates. These estimates suggest a considerably stronger effect of police on crime than the annual data indicated.[4]

Another econometric technique employed by contributors to the second generation of economic research on police and crime was instrumental variables or natural experiments. Instrumental variables help an econometrician break the simultaneity of policies and outcomes. Here, a valid instrument is a variable correlated with the criminal justice policy of interest but otherwise uncorrelated with crime rates. Unlike laboratory scientists, economists cannot assign subjects randomly to treatment and control groups. Instead, economists often look for naturally occurring phenomena that create nearly random exposure to particular public policies. They seek natural rather than laboratory experiments. In effect, economists employ such naturally occurring phenomena as instrumental variables.

Levitt (1997) proposed that the timing of mayoral and gubernatorial elections was a valid instrumental variable. He reported that police forces in major cities grew during election years, presumably because expanding the ranks of police forces provides an electoral advantage to incumbents. Thus, peculiar timing in the growth of police was plausibly exogenous to the incidence of crime because, after controlling for other factors, an election is not otherwise apt to influence the incentives for street crime. The elections were effectively a natural experiment that induced movement in the size of police forces but were otherwise exogenous to crime rates. Applying this methodology to a repeated cross section of cities covering more than 20 years, Levitt (1997) estimated that an increase of 10% in the police force led to a 3% to 10% reduction in crime rates. These estimates are very close to those of Marvell & Moody (1996).[5]

---

[4]Another dimension of disaggregation is geography. Di Tella & Schargrodsky (2004) pursued this approach and investigated a reallocation of police in Buenos Aires at the level of city blocks. When police were posted to temples and mosques in response to terrorist threats, automobile thefts on these blocks diminished. But beyond the immediate vicinity of these buildings, the incidence of automobile thefts was unchanged.

[5]Economists have continued to investigate the relationship of police and crime. McCrary (2002) disputed that electoral cycles induced sufficient variation in the size of police forces to measure the impact of crime. He argued that when properly measured, the imprecision of

In sum, the second generation of research by economists provides persuasive evidence on the behavioral question of whether police reduce crime. In view of this evidence, economists have also addressed the normative question of whether additional increases are worth it. Using estimates derived from his sample that terminated in 1992, Levitt (1997) claimed that the marginal benefit in reduced crime from employing another city police officer exceeded the costs. Marvell & Moody (1996) noted a similar calculation, but believing that additional costs (such as the attendant court and prison expenditures) could not be quantified, they declined to conduct a full cost-benefit analysis. Despite this hesitation, the estimates from this research indicate that the marginal benefit in reduced crime associated with hiring an additional police officer in large urban environments likely exceeds or equals the marginal cost.

Measuring the Impact of the Scale of Imprisonment on Crime

Research on the effect of the scale of incarceration on crime followed a similar path as research on the impact of policing. The first generation of scholarship gave insufficient attention to the issue of causal direction and drew normative conclusions on the basis of relatively limited data sets, such as single cross sections or national time series. In the 1990s, a second generation of research, conducted by economists, emerged. As with research on policing, the next wave of incarceration scholarship examined larger and richer data sets and applied econometric techniques that attempted to isolate causal direction. With respect to data, repeated cross sections again became standard, and with respect to techniques, Granger causality and instrumental variables again furnished estimates that more persuasively reflected causal effects.

Marvell & Moody (1994) applied the technique of Granger causality to almost 20 years of state-level data on incarceration and crime rates. They found that increases in incarceration precipitated drops in crime. Their estimates indicated that a 10% increase in prison populations led to a 1.5% reduction in crime rates. Evidence from instrumental variables or natural experiments also suggested that the scale of incarceration had a crime reducing effect. Levitt (1996) argued that lawsuits challenging overcrowded conditions in state prisons constituted a valid instrumental variable. He demonstrated that when these suits resulted in injunctions to alleviate overcrowding, state authorities complied by releasing prisoners or by declining to incarcerate convicts who otherwise would have been imprisoned. The suits were plausibly exogenous to crime rates because, after controlling for other factors, the suit would not affect the incentive to commit crime, except through the channel of prison populations. In other words, prison litigation was arguably

the instrument precluded inferences about the causal effect of police on crime. In response, Levitt (2002) showed that even with an alternative instrumental variable, the number of firefighters, estimates of the impact of police on crime are negative and sizable. Also, W. Evans and E. Owens (unpublished manuscript) found estimates similar to those of Marvell & Moody (1996) and Levitt (1997, 2002) by examining the impact of recent federal subsidies on the hiring of local police.

a natural experiment that produced nearly random variation in incarceration rates in certain states but left other states unaffected. Applying this technique to over 20 years of annual, state-level data, Levitt (1996) found that increases in crime occurred simultaneously with litigation-induced reductions in state prison populations. His estimates implied that the reduction in crime from incarcerating an additional prisoner was two to three times larger than that predicted by Marvell & Moody (1994). According to Levitt's (1996) analysis, the release of an additional prisoner produced an additional 15 crimes annually.

Another test of the responsiveness of offending rates to the magnitude of penalties was Levitt's (1998) study of the severity of the transition from the juvenile to the adult criminal justice system. The estimation of the causal impact of this transition is complicated by the fact that crime propensities rise and fall with age and by the difficulty in making absolute comparisons between expected punishments in juvenile and adult systems. Levitt (1998), however, exploited the fact that in certain states the criminal justice system was substantially more punitive than the juvenile system, whereas in other states this was less true. States where the transition to the adult system was severe did not appear correlated with other factors influencing crime, and thus the pattern of transitions approximated a natural experiment in the severity of punishments. Applying a difference-in-differences methodology, Levitt (1998) observed that in states where the severity of the adult system is greatest relative to the juvenile system, both violent and property crime fell almost 30% at the age of majority relative to the states where the transition to adulthood engenders the smallest increases in punishment.

Incarceration is an expensive penalty. Although the estimates are already several years old, the most recent comprehensive estimates of the annual cost of incarcerating an offender range from \$25,000 (DiIulio & Piehl 1991) to \$35,000 (Donohue & Siegelman 1998). Economists who estimated the number of crimes reduced by incarcerating the marginal prisoner used their forecasts, together with these cost figures and estimates of the monetary loss associated with criminal offenses, to conduct cost-benefit analyses of incarceration. In the early to mid-1990s, when the second generation of economic studies of incarceration appeared, a frequent conclusion was that the benefits of incarceration outweighed the costs. However, in the intervening decade, prison populations have nearly doubled again. Economists' now decade-old estimates of the number of crimes reduced by the marginal offender have limited application in conducting a current cost-benefit analysis. If the two-millionth prisoner incarcerated is less dangerous than the one-millionth prisoner, the net social benefits of incarceration today are likely less than those of a decade ago. For the most reasonable set of assumptions, the current scale of incarceration is apparently at or above the socially optimal level.

Measuring the Impact of Capital Punishment on Crime

Academics, policy makers, and the general public have long debated capital punishment. Empirical economists have also contributed to the debate by attempting to determine whether capital punishment reduces crime. Economic research on this topic divides again into two generations. As with the other research questions discussed above, the first generation of economic research on capital punishment consists of studies of national time series and state cross sections, and the second generation examines repeated cross sections. Unique to the study of capital punishment is that a dramatic and brief policy change, the Supreme Court's moratorium on the application of the death penalty, separates the two generations.[6] In addition, economic research on the deterrent effect of the death penalty has not produced a consensus.

The most prominent national time-series study that claimed to find evidence of the death penalty's deterrent effect was Ehrlich (1975). He claimed that over the period 1932–1970, each execution prevented between one and eight homicides, as well as numerous robberies, assaults, and property crimes. Other researchers disputed Ehrlich's claim, and Cameron (1994) reviews the large body of work on the topic.[7] Perhaps the most troubling criticism was that if the sample period is extended to include later dates or truncated to exclude the late 1960s, no effect on crime rates is found (Passell & Taylor 1977, Klein et al. 1978, Leamer 1983).

Studies of cross-sectional data fared no better in persuading researchers. Ehrlich (1977) examined two cross sections of states and reported estimates similar to those of his earlier time-series study. Cameron (1994) reviews the criticisms of this work as well. Perhaps most important is that, as seen in the research on policing and incarceration, cross-sectional estimates may not reliably identify a causal effect because a particular state's criminal justice policies, such as capital punishment, may themselves be functions of a state's crime rate. Moreover, the concentration of executions in southern and western states strongly suggests that the use of the death penalty is nonrandom. In addition, researchers who explored other tests of the hypothesis that the death penalty deters found contrary evidence. Bailey (1982), for example, reports no effect of the death penalty on the frequency with which police officers are killed. Because killers of police officers are much more likely to face capital punishment than murderers of civilians, the absence of an effect there is troubling.

The second generation of economic research on capital punishment began within the past five years, as data on executions in the postmoratorium period

---

[6]In *Furman v. Georgia* (1972), the Supreme Court held that Georgia's death penalty statute was constitutionally deficient because it created a substantial risk that it would be imposed in an arbitrary and capricious manner. In *Gregg v. Georgia* (1976), the Court held that the death penalty does not always constitute cruel and unusual punishment and that the revisions to the Georgia statute remedied its constitutional deficiencies.

[7]Even the Supreme Court, in *Gregg v. Georgia* (1976), which held that capital punishment could comport with the Eighth Amendment, commented on the debate. In reference to the estimates on the deterrent effect, the Court observed, "[s]ubstantial attempts to evaluate the worth of the death penalty as a deterrent to crimes by potential offenders have occasioned a great deal of debate. The results have simply been inconclusive" (*Gregg v. Georgia* at 184–85, footnotes omitted).

became available. All these studies employ repeated cross-sectional data, but the range of estimates they present is even wider than that of the earlier studies. Mocan & Gittings (2003) investigated the effect of commutations, as well as of executions, in a monthly, state-level panel spanning 1977–1997. They reported that the marginal execution spared five homicides, and each commutation caused five homicides. Contrary to Ehrlich's (1975) findings, their estimates indicated that executions and commutations had no effect on other categories of crime, such as assaults, robberies, and property offenses. Dezhbakhsh et al. (2003) applied a simultaneous equations methodology to annual, county-level data and reported that, with a margin of error of 10, each execution prevents an astonishing 18 homicides. The lower end of this estimated impact, 8 homicides, matches the highest of Ehrlich's (1975) estimates. Shepherd (2004) used a monthly, state-level panel covering 1977–1999 to estimate the effect of the death penalty on different types of homicides. Her estimates indicated that each execution deterred approximately three murders, including so-called crimes of passion. More recently, Shepherd (2005) reported that the impact of the death penalty varies by state, reducing homicides in some states and increasing it in others. Rather than attribute these differences to the weakness of the empirical test, she hypothesizes that capital punishment deters in some states and brutalizes or fosters brutal violence in others.

In contrast to these authors, Katz et al. (2003) studied state-level panel data covering the 1950–1990 period and detected no effect of the death penalty on crime rates. Katz et al. (2003) found instead that a proxy for prison conditions, the death rate among prisoners, correlated negatively with crime rates. Donohue & Wolfers (2006) present the most exhaustive review of the recent empirical literature on capital punishment and are highly critical of the existing studies. Their reanalysis of recent studies finding a deterrent effect of the death penalty exposes a range of empirical weaknesses and demonstrates the sensitivity of these results to minor changes in specification. Donohue & Wolfers (2006) conclude that there is no compelling evidence of a deterrent effect of executions.

The Donohue & Wolfers conclusion is not particularly surprising given the relatively modest use of the death penalty. In 1999, 98 prisoners were executed, more than any other year since the Supreme Court's 1976 reinstatement of capital punishment. However, relative to the 3540 prisoners under a sentence of death in 1999, the number of executions constituted 3% of death row. Since then, the number of death row inmates has steadily grown while the pace of executions has slowed. For example, the 59 executions in 2004 implied an execution rate of 1.8%. The execution rates on death row are only slightly larger than the risk of accidental and violent death for African American males aged 15 to 34. The new death sentences as a percentage of the homicides in a particular year, a rough proxy for the risk of receiving a death sentence conditional on having committed a homicide, is also low—hovering between 0.8% and 1.8% in recent years. Note also that most criminals sentenced to death will never actually be executed, so this number dramatically overstates the true risk of execution. For a person regularly participating in crime, the risk of violent death is surely higher. Kennedy et al.

(1996) estimate that annual violent death rates among gang members in Boston are between 1% and 2%. Levitt & Venkatesh (2000) find that the death rate among street-level drug dealers in an urban gang was 7%. Individuals who readily bear such risks as part of their criminal activity are unlikely to be influenced by the relatively low risk of capital punishment. Ironically, to the extent the death penalty has any deterrent effect on homicide, it is unlikely to be the rational criminal who is deterred but rather an irrational criminal who mistakenly overstates the expected punishment associated with the death penalty.

Racial Profiling

In addition to testing the economic model of deterrence and assessing the costs and benefits of particular crime-control policies, economists have studied the operation of the criminal justice system itself from a rational choice perspective [see Levitt & Miles (2006) for a review of that literature]. An aspect of the operation of the criminal justice system that has received considerable attention from the public and academics is racial profiling, the practice by police of using the race of the driver as a criterion in choosing whether to stop and search automobiles. Knowles et al. (2001) developed an empirical test of whether racial prejudice or the goal of maximizing the number of successful searches explains the racial disparity in searches. Their test distinguishes two economic accounts of discrimination. Becker's (1957) model describes racial prejudice as a preference or taste for disfavoring members of a particular race. In contrast, Arrow's (1973) model describes actors who statistically discriminate by using race to predict outcomes and then rely on these predictions in their decision making. Arrow's information-based model differs from Becker's in that its actors are not necessarily racially prejudiced. As applied to stops and searches, the Arrowian framework presents police as seeking to maximize the number of searches in which contraband is found. If being black correlates with the likelihood of possessing contraband, police, even if they are not racially prejudiced, in an Arrowian equilibrium will search blacks more often [see Persico (2002) for a model of police searches that includes a notion of fairness and a stigma of search].

Knowles et al. (2001) compare the probabilities that searches of members of each racial group yield contraband. If police are not racially prejudiced and merely maximize the number of successful searches, the rates at which searched persons are found carrying contraband should be equal across racial groups. Knowles et al. (2001) tested their hypothesis using a data set obtained from the ACLU containing all vehicle searches along an interstate highway in Maryland over a four-year period. The authors could not reject equality across racial groups in the rates at which police found contraband during searches. They also could not reject equality in the rates of successful searches across various other dimensions, such as gender, age of the vehicle, whether the vehicle is a luxury model, and whether the search occurred during the day or at night. The estimates of Knowles et al. (2001) suggest that racial disparities in vehicle searches result from a desire to maximize successful searches rather than from racial prejudice.

Several economists have criticized the Knowles et al. (2001) finding. Dharmapala & Ross (2003) argued that in a more generalized model, including varying offense levels and imperfect observation of offenders, the appropriate test requires stratifying the data by offense severity. Using the Knowles et al. (2001) data, Dharmapala & Ross (2003) found that blacks have higher guilty rates for felonies and whites have higher guilty rates for misdemeanors. Antonovics & Knight (2004) also argue that the ability of the Knowles et al. (2001) model to distinguish preference-based discrimination from statistical discrimination is not robust to generalization. Antonovics & Knight (2004) instead predicted that, if officers engaged only in statistical discrimination, search decisions should be independent of an officer's race (assuming police are randomly assigned geographically by race). Using data from the Boston Police Department, they found that they were not. A consensus about the explanation for racial disparities in search rates has not emerged among economists, and the questions of race and policing are likely to remain an active and contentious area of research.

All the papers described in this section focus on the issue of whether or not the police unfairly target minorities. Heaton (2006), in contrast, investigates the impact that racial profiling has on criminal activities. In particular, Heaton exploits the fact that highly publicized cases in both New Jersey and Maryland led to wholesale changes in police practices, resulting in sharp reductions in the relative likelihood that black motorists would be stopped and searched in these states. Heaton finds evidence that, in response to these alterations in police strategy, motor vehicle thefts by blacks rise relative to thefts by whites, although he does not find evidence that other dimensions (motor vehicle crashes, failure to properly restrain children) of black driving behavior changes. And, as would be expected, changes in vehicle searches have no discernible impact on nonvehicle-related crimes such as burglary.

MEASURING THE IMPACT OF FACTORS OTHER THAN THE CRIMINAL JUSTICE SYSTEM ON CRIME

The incidence of criminal activity is a product of many factors, of which the criminal justice system is only one, and economists have also studied many of these other factors. Although a complete review is well beyond the scope of this paper, this section discusses two such factors: concealed weapons laws and abortion legalization. We focus on these topics because they have received considerable attention recently and because they involve laws, albeit not criminal laws.

Measuring the Impact of Concealed Weapons Laws on Crime

In the late 1990s, the debate over gun policy partly shifted away from measures designed to limit the availability of guns to laws that expand the availability of guns, especially concealed guns. This change resulted from a series of studies (Lott & Mustard 1996, Lott 1998, Lott & Landes 1999) that claimed that a greater availability of concealed weapons reduced, rather than increased, crime. Their hypothesis was that a potential victim's surreptitious gun possession has a general deterrent effect because it was an unobservable precaution that raised the risk of criminal activity. Lott and his coauthors employed the difference-in-differences methodology. They compared county-level crime rates before and after a state's passage of concealed weapons laws, relative to other states without these laws. They asserted that once a state enacted a concealed weapons law, the rates of certain types of crimes decline sharply.

At the time of the Lott studies, the existing literature on guns and crime focused on gun control policies. Much of this earlier research by economists casts doubt on the efficacy of these policies and hypothesized that they were unsuccessful because the vast secondary markets in guns implied that gun control measures did not effectively constrain the availability of guns [Cook et al. (2002) provide a thorough review of that literature]. Despite this evidence, the Lott hypothesis assumed the opposite: that concealed weapons laws could reduce crime because they could increase the availability of guns.

A large number of researchers challenged the Lott findings by criticizing the empirical weakness of the estimates and by reporting that additional tests of the unobservable precaution hypothesis yielded contrary evidence. First, Duggan (2000) showed that the basic Lott & Mustard (1996) estimates lack statistical significance when the assumption of the statistical independence of counties within the same state is relaxed. Second, the Lott estimates also appeared to suffer from omitted variable bias. Duggan (2000) demonstrated that crime rates in states that adopted concealed weapons laws began to decline before the passage of the laws. Donohue & Levitt (2001) reported that after controlling for abortion rates, the laws do not correlate with crime rates. Third, Ayres & Donohue (1999) extended the original Lott sample to include more recent enactments of concealed weapons laws, and in this larger sample they found no correlation between the law and crime rates. Fourth, other researchers conducted further tests of the behavioral implications of the concealed weapons hypothesis. For example, a victim's potential possession of a concealed weapon should have the greatest deterrent effect on crimes involving the criminal's direct confrontation of a stranger victim. Street robbery is the prime example of such a crime. However, the original Lott & Mustard (1996) estimates featured large effects on homicide and rape and a much smaller effect on robbery. But, in Ayres & Donohue's extended sample, the concealed weapons laws correlated positively with robbery. Moreover, Ludwig (1998) predicted that the laws should induce criminals to substitute victims who cannot take the precaution. Because the laws do not authorize possession of concealed weapons by juveniles, the laws should prompt criminals to seek younger victims. Ludwig (1998) found evidence to the contrary. He reported that passage of these laws is associated with larger declines in juvenile victimizations than adult victimizations.

Measuring the Impact of Legalized Abortion on Crime

The overwhelming majority of research by economists on crime has focused on the near-term impact of criminal justice and public policy interventions on crime. Donohue & Levitt (2001) presented evidence suggesting that a much earlier change in policy—the legalization of abortion in the 1970s—may also have played an important role in influencing the unprecedented declines in American crime in the 1990s. The theory underlying an abortion-crime link is straightforward. A substantial body of social scientific research suggests that growing up unwanted puts a child at risk for adverse life outcomes, including criminal involvement (Dagg 1991). If the legalization of abortion led to the birth of fewer unwanted children, then two decades later when those cohorts reached peak crime ages, there would be fewer individuals at risk for crime.[8]

Donohue & Levitt (2001) put forth six different types of empirical evidence in support of this conjecture: (*a*) a calibration exercise based on pre-existing estimates of the impact of abortion and the distribution of women seeking abortions; (*b*) the national time-series data; (*c*) a comparison of the crime paths of early legalizing states and those in which abortion only became legal with *Roe v. Wade* (1973); (*d*) differences in crime patterns in states with high and low abortion rates after abortion became legal nationwide; (*e*) isolation of the reductions in crime in high-abortion states to those born after abortion legalization; and (*f*) a correlation between arrest patterns by single year of age and abortion exposure. The findings of each of these analyses were consistent with the proposed theory. Donohue & Levitt estimated that legalized abortion lowered crime by 10%–15% in the 1990s relative to a counterfactual in which abortion had remained illegal.

These findings have generated substantial controversy, inside and outside of academia. A number of papers have confirmed and extended the initial findings. A. Sen (unpublished paper) found a similar relationship between abortion and crime in Canadian data, as did Leigh & Wolfers (2000) using Australian data. Pop-Eleches (2006) demonstrated that a ban on abortion in Romania led to increased criminal activity in that cohort, consistent with the theory. Charles & Stephens (2006) analyzed the Monitoring the Future survey data and uncovered evidence that exposure to legalized abortion was associated with lower rates of illicit drug use as a teenager. Sorenson et al. (2002) argued that legalized abortion led to decreases in homicides of young children.

Joyce (2003) is the only published study to date that directly challenges the link between abortion and crime. Joyce (2003) contended that legalized abortions largely replaced illegal abortions such that one would not expect to see an impact on crime rates. He argued that the national time-series fluctuations in arrests by age were not supportive of the abortion hypothesis, and he showed that when the sample

[8]In addition to this change in the composition of the cohort, it is also the case that the absolute number of children fell by approximately 5% after legalization (Levine et al. 1999), which will further reduce crime in a mechanical way.

was restricted to the 1985–1990 time period, the abortion-crime link disappeared. Donohue & Levitt (2003) responded to Joyce's claims and presented evidence that legalization indeed increased the number of abortions. They noted that the other two results in Joyce (2003) were likely an artifact of the crack epidemic, which hit just as the first cohort exposed to legalized abortion reached peak crime age. Joyce estimated a difference-in-differences approach that compared those born before and after legalization in states that did and did not legalize abortion before *Roe v. Wade* (1973). Joyce reported results using only crime rates for 1985 and 1990. When Donohue & Levitt carried out the same exercise on the same birth cohorts but expanded the sample to include data from all available years, the results were consistent with their initial claims; Joyce's contrary findings appear to be a function of his limiting the sample to the peak crime years.

In a recent and widely publicized working paper, Foote & Goetz (2005) challenged one of the six pieces of evidence in Donohue & Levitt (2001), namely the analysis done on arrests by single year of age. Foote & Goetz correctly noted that the final table in the original Donohue & Levitt paper was mislabeled—the text implies that the analysis included controls for state-year interactions, when none were included. Foote & Goetz proceeded to show that when examining arrests by single year of age, a specification that combined three features—the inclusion of state-year interactions as controls, the use of log of per capita arrests (rather than the log of the number of arrests), and the extension of the data set beyond the original years covered in Donohue & Levitt (2001)—eliminated any effect of legalized abortion. Donohue & Levitt (2006) responded by arguing that the combination of poorly measured abortion rates and the high demands on the data associated with the inclusion of state-year interactions removed virtually all the signal from the abortion rates. They demonstrated that even when the preferred specification of Foote & Goetz (2005) is employed, three adjustments—the use of more precise abortion data (which measures abortions by the state of residence of the women, as opposed to the state in which the procedure is performed), the correction for cross-state mobility between birth and adolescence, and more careful matches of the ages in the arrest data to abortion exposure—led to estimates as large as or larger than those reported in the original Donohue & Levitt (2001) paper.

CONCLUSION

The past decade has seen a renaissance in the application of empirical economic approaches to issues of crime. Substantial progress has been made in understanding the impact of elements of the criminal justice system such as police, prisons, and the death penalty. In addition, new hypotheses related to racial profiling, concealed weapons, and legalized abortion have emerged as contentious and widely publicized debates. In some cases, such as the impact of adding more police, a consensus has developed among economists. For most other questions, substantial uncertainty remains, ensuring that the subject will be a fertile area of study for the foreseeable future.

LITERATURE CITED

Antonovics KL, Knight BG. 2004. *A new look at racial profiling: evidence from the Boston Police Department*. Work. Pap. No. 1063.4, Nat. Bur. Econ. Res., July

Arrow KJ. 1973. The theory of discrimination. In *Discrimination in Labor Markets*, ed. O Ashenfelter, A Rees, pp. 3–33. Princeton, NJ: Princeton Univ. Press

Ayres I, Donohue JJ III. 1999. Nondiscretionary concealed weapons laws: a case study of statistics, standards of proof, and public policy. *Am. Law Econ. Rev.* 1:436–70

Bailey WC. 1982. Capital punishment and lethal assaults against police. *Criminology* 19:608–28

Bauer L, Owens SD. 2004. *Justice Expenditures and Employment in the United States, 2001*. Washington, DC: US Dep. Justice, Off. Justice Programs

Becker GS. 1957. *The Economics of Discrimination*. Chicago: Univ. Chicago Press. 137 pp.

Becker GS. 1968. Crime and punishment: an economic approach. *J. Polit. Econ.* 76:169–217

Bushway S. 2004. Labor market effects of permitting employer access to criminal history records. *J. Contemp. Crim. Justice*: *Spec. Issue Econ. Crime* 20:276–91

Cameron S. 1988. The economics of deterrence: a survey of theory and evidence. *Kyklos* 41:301–23

Cameron S. 1994. A review of econometric evidence on the effects of capital punishment. *J. Socio-Econ.* 23(1):197–214

Charles KK, Stephens M Jr. 2006. Abortion legalization and adolescent substance abuse. *J. Law Econ.* In press

Cook PJ, Moore MH, Braga AA. 2002. Gun control. In *Crime*, ed. JQ Wilson, J Petersilia, pp. 291–330. San Francisco: Inst. Contemp. Stud. 705 pp.

Corman H, Mocan HN. 2000. A time-series analysis of crime and drug use in New York City. *Am. Econ. Rev.* 90:584–604

Dagg PK. 1991. The psychological sequelae of therapeutic abortion—denied and completed. *Am. J. Psychiatry* 148(5):578–85

Dezhbakhsh H, Rubin PH, Shepherd JM. 2003. Does capital punishment have a deterrent effect? New evidence from postmoratorium panel data. *Am. Law Econ. Rev.* 5(2):344–76

Dharmapala D, Ross SL. 2003. *Racial bias in motor vehicle searches: additional theory and evidence*. Work. Pap. No. 2003–12R, Dep. Econ., Univ. Conn., Dec.

DiIulio J, Piehl AM. 1991. Does prison pay? The stormy national debate over the cost-effectiveness of imprisonment. *Brookings Rev.* 9(Fall):28–35

Di Tella R, Schargrodsky E. 2004. Do police reduce crime? Estimates using the allocation of police forces after a terrorist attack. *Am. Econ. Rev.* 94:115–33

Donohue JJ III, Levitt SD. 2001. The impact of legalized abortion on crime. *Q. J. Econ.* 116:379–420

Donohue JJ III, Levitt S. 2003. Further evidence that legalized abortion reduced crime: a reply to Joyce. *J. Hum. Resourc.* 39(1):30–49

Donohue JJ III, Levitt S. 2006. *Measurement error, legalized abortion, and the decline in crime: a reply to Foote and Goetz 2005*. Work. Pap. 11987, Nat. Bur. Econ. Res.

Donohue JJ III, Siegelman P. 1998. Allocating resources among prisons and social programs in the battle against crime. *J. Leg. Stud.* 27:1–43

Donohue JJ III, Wolfers J. 2006. Uses and abuses of empirical evidence in the death penalty debate. *Stanford Law Rev.* 58:791–846

Duggan M. 2000. More guns, more crime. *J. Polit. Econ.* 109(5):1086–114

Ehrlich I. 1975. The deterrent effect of capital punishment: a question of life and death. *Am. Econ. Rev.* 65:397–417

Ehrlich I. 1977. Capital punishment and deterrence: some further thoughts and additional estimates. *J. Polit. Econ.* 85(4):741–88

Fisher F, Nagin D. 1978. On the feasibility of identifying the crime function in a simultaneous equations model of crime and sanctions. In *Deterrence and Incapacitation: Estimating the Effects of Criminal Sanctions on Crime Rates*, ed. A Blumstein, D Nagin, J Cohen, pp. 361–99. Washington, DC: Natl. Acad. Press

Foote C, Goetz C. 2005. *Testing economic hypotheses using state-level data: a comment on Donohue and Levitt 2001*. Work. Pap. No. 05–15, Fed. Reserve Bank of Boston

Furman v. Georgia, 408 U.S. 238 (1972)

Granger C. 1969. Investigating causal relations by econometric models and cross-spectral methods. *Econometrica* 37:424–38

Gregg v. Georgia, 428 U.S. 153 (1976)

Heaton P. 2006. *Understanding the effects of anti-profiling policies*. Work. Pap., Univ. Chicago. http://home.uchicago.edu/~psheaton/workingpapers/workingpapers.htm

Joyce T. 2003. Did legalized abortion lower crime? *J. Hum. Resourc.* 38(1):1–37

Kaplow L, Shavell S. 2002. Economic analysis of law. In *Handbook of Public Economics*, ed. AJ Auerbach, M Feldstein, 3:1661–784. New York: Elsevier

Katz L, Levitt SD, Shustorovich E. 2003. Prison conditions, capital punishment, and deterrence. *Am. Law Econ. Rev.* 5:318–43

Kelling G, Pate T, Dieckman D, Brown C. 1974. *The Kansas City Preventative Patrol Experiment: A Summary Report*. Washington, DC: Police Found.

Kennedy P. 1998. *A Guide to Econometrics*. Cambridge, MA: MIT Press. 468 pp.

Kennedy D, Piehl A, Braga A. 1996. Youth violence in Boston: gun markets, serious youth offenders, and a use-reduction strategy. *Law Contemp. Probl.* 59:147–96

Klein L, Forst B, Filatov V. 1978. The deterrent effect of capital punishment: an assessment of the estimates. In *Deterrence and Incapacitation: Estimating the Effects of Criminal Sanctions on Crime Rates*, ed. A Blumstein, D Nagin, J Cohen, pp. 336–60. Washington, DC: Natl. Acad. Press

Knowles J, Persico N, Todd P. 2001. Racial bias in motor vehicle searches: theory and evidence. *J. Polit. Econ.* 109(1):203–32

Larson R. 1976. What happened to patrol operations in Kansas City? *Evaluation* 3:117–23

Leamer E. 1983. Let's take the con out of econometrics. *Am. Econ. Rev.* 73:31–43

Leigh A, Wolfers J. 2000. Abortion and crime. *Aust. Q: J. Contemp. Anal.* 72(4):28–30

Levine PB, Staiger D, Kane TJ, Zimmerman D. 1999. *Roe v. Wade* and American fertility. *Am. J. Public Health* 89(2):199–203

Levitt SD. 1996. The effect of prison population size on crime rates: evidence from prison overcrowding litigation. *Q. J. Econ.* 111:319–25

Levitt SD. 1997. Using electoral cycles in police hiring to estimate the effect of police on crime. *Am. Econ. Rev.* 87(3):280–90

Levitt SD. 1998. Juvenile crime and punishment. *J. Polit. Econ.* 106:1156–85

Levitt SD. 2002. Using electoral cycles in police hiring to estimate the effects of police on crime: Reply. *Am. Econ. Rev.* 92(4):1244–50

Levitt SD, Miles TJ. 2006. The economic analysis of criminal punishment. In *The Handbook of Law and Economics*, ed. AM Polinsky, S Shavell. Amsterdam: North Holland/Elsevier Sci. In press

Levitt SD, Venkatesh S. 2000. An economic analysis of a drug-selling gang's finances. *Q. J. Econ.* 115:755–89

Lott JR Jr. 1998. *More Guns, Less Crime*. Chicago: Univ. Chicago Press. 225 pp.

Lott JR Jr, Landes W. 1999. *Multiple victim public shootings, bombings, and right-to-carry concealed handgun laws: contrasting private and public law enforcement*. Work. Pap. No. 73, Univ. Chicago Law Sch., John M. Olin Law Econ. Program

Lott JR Jr, Mustard DB. 1996. Crime, deterrence, and right-to-carry concealed handguns. *J. Leg. Stud.* 26(1):1–68

Ludwig J. 1998. Concealed-gun-carrying laws and violent crime: evidence from state panel data. *Int. Rev. Law Econ.* 18:239–54

Marvell T, Moody C. 1994. Prison population growth and crime reduction. *J. Quant. Criminol.* 10:109–40

Marvell T, Moody C. 1996. Specification problems, police levels, and crime rates. *Criminology* 34:609–46

McCrary J. 2002. Using electoral cycles in police hiring to estimate the effect of police on crime: comment. *Am. Econ. Rev.* 92(4):1236–43

Mocan HN, Gittings RK. 2003. Getting off death row: commuted sentences and the deterrent effect of capital punishment. *J. Law Econ.* 46:453–78

Passell P, Taylor J. 1977. The deterrent effect of capital punishment: another view. *Am. Econ. Rev.* 67:445–51

Persico N. 2002. Racial profiling, fairness, and effectiveness of policing. *Am. Econ. Rev.* 92(5):1472–97

Polinsky AM, Shavell S. 2006. Public enforcement of law. In *The Handbook of Law and Economics*, ed. AM Polinsky, S Shavell. Amsterdam: North Holland/Elsevier Sci. In press

Pop-Eleches C. 2006. The impact of an abortion ban on socio-economic outcomes of children: evidence from Romania. *J. Polit. Econ.* In press

Roe v. Wade, 410 U.S. 113 (1973)

Sorenson S, Wiebe D, Berk R. 2002. Legalized abortion and the homicide of young children: an empirical investigation. *Anal. Soc. Issues Public Policy* 2(1):239–56

Shepherd JM. 2004. Murders of passion, execution delays, and the deterrence of capital punishment. *J. Leg. Stud.* 33:283–322

Shepherd JM. 2005. Deterrence versus brutalization: capital punishment's differing impacts among states. *Michigan Law Rev.* 104:203–55

Annu. Rev. Law Soc. Sci. 2006. 2:165–86
doi: 10.1146/annurev.lawsocsci.1.041604.115922

First published online as a Review in Advance on July 5, 2006

ISLAMIC LAW AND SOCIETY POST-9/11

Susan F. Hirsch
Institute for Conflict Analysis and Resolution, George Mason University, Washington, DC 20016; email: shirsch4@gmu.edu

Key Words Islam, legal ethnography, political violence, religion

■ **Abstract** After the events of September 11, 2001, scholars rushed to contribute to the growing public debate about religion and political violence, including to counter stereotypic depictions of Islamic law and to raise questions about its role in the social and political life of Muslim and non-Muslim nations. The same period also witnessed the publication of much scholarship on Muslim personal or family law. This review focuses on these works and highlights their sophisticated theoretical treatments of social theory in critical areas, such as the interaction of normative orders, constructions and intersections of identity, human agency in the legal process, law reform and social movements, state uses of law, and the challenges facing globalizing societies. These theories provide grounding for scholars, activists, and policymakers in addressing the pressing issues emerging after 9/11.

INTRODUCTION

Socio-legal scholarship on Islamic law was proceeding with great vigor just prior to the events of September 11, 2001. Most of it focused on personal law, often glossed as family law, the substantive area of Islamic legal practice most prevalent in the world today. Major research efforts were about to result in comprehensive portraits of Muslim personal law (An-Na'im 2002b, WLUML 2003). Several scholars had just published or reissued influential studies of Islamic law and gender, a dynamic area of inquiry for several decades (e.g., Ali 2000, Mir-Hosseini 2000, Moors 1995, Tucker 1998). Researchers in anthropology, political science, history, and religious studies were producing ever more refined analyses on such topics as judicial reasoning, law reform, and law's relation to custom, culture, and politics. Certain substantive legal areas were gaining attention, including Islamic finance, child custody, and conflict of laws, at the same time as long-standing debates continued over the scope of Islamic law, the mutability of legal principles and jurisprudence, the authority of particular texts and interpreters, and the problem of whether text or social context is the proper focus for scholarship. One authority noted that the increased attention to the vibrancy of Islamic law, including its flexibility throughout history, had invigorated scholarship (Hallaq 2003, p. 1711). All this activity attested to the field's maturity and the productivity of its contributors.

Without question, however, the events of September 11, 2001, had an impact on scholarly and popular discussions of Islamic law. Experts on Islamic law were among those who contributed to the groundswell of reaction to 9/11 through editorials, public talks, listserv postings, or on the Internet, some of which were subsequently collected into readers that conveyed the urgency and high stakes of a moment when so many academics felt compelled to speak out. As vitriolic and ill-informed discussions by pundits of Islamic concepts, including Islamic law, filled public discourse, scholars wrote to correct false impressions and found themselves positioned as public intellectuals. Post-9/11 Islamic law was implicated in the need for new constitutions in majority Muslim nations, in the significant movement of Muslims across borders, in higher scrutiny of Muslims and their actions globally, in new questions about Islamic practices, and in calls for reforms—political, religious, and legal. Among the consequences of 9/11 and its aftermath was the certainty that the future of Islamic law would be more highly politicized than previously.

At the same time, the slow pace of scholarly publication ensured that what had been written just prior to 9/11 would appear in print later, probably much later, albeit with a hastily written preface or afterword mentioning 9/11. This scholarship focuses primarily on Muslim personal law, and, accordingly, the bulk of this review addresses that topic. Muslim personal law encompasses matrimonial issues, child custody, and legitimacy, among other topics. Personal law is one among several areas of civil law, which also includes litigation, commercial transactions, trusts, and estates. Criminal delicts and penalties and the regulation of devotional matters (e.g., prayer, alms, and fasting, among others) represent the two other major areas of Islamic legal literature, although they are afforded less attention here.

In this review, I argue that the recent scholarship on Muslim personal law, though mentioning 9/11 only in passing, in fact speaks to the thorny social and political challenges that have emerged in the wake of 9/11. Specifically, these works offer sophisticated treatments of social theory in critical areas, such as the interaction of normative orders, constructions and intersections of identity, human agency in the legal process, law reform and social movements, state uses of law, and the challenges facing globalizing societies, and these discussions provide grounding for scholars, activists, and policymakers in addressing the pressing issues emerging after 9/11.

Given the amount and diversity of scholarly writing on Islamic law and the constraints of a review, some caveats are in order. For one, the object of study in this review is Islamic law, yet no definition is offered. Many of the works discussed herein note that conceptualizing Islamic law poses a challenge. Mir-Hosseini (2000, p. xiii) captures its contrast with other legal traditions: "Law in Islam has a transcendental dimension—in Muslim belief its source is divine revelation—but its prime purpose is that of molding human reality." Islamic law's transcendental dimension leads some scholars to focus their studies on the Qur'an as well as the hadith (or stories from the Prophet Mohammed's life) and leads some believers to insist on these as the only relevant sources. While acknowledging the power of these texts, this review does not focus on divinely revealed sources. Relatedly, the object of study is Islamic law rather than shari'a, also a much contested term. Islamists in particular would argue that shari'a invokes the divinely inspired dimension and not the creations of humans, such as the Islamic legal principles of current legal systems or even, for some, the schools of jurisprudence (madhhab) that have figured so prominently in Islamic legal scholarship. Legal reasoning, or fiqh, is a major secondary source of Islamic law. With its origins in revelation and human reason, and yet with its creation or, better, its institutionalization in the nineteenth century as part of colonial legal systems, Islamic law exhibits an elusive character (Khalafallah 2001). For Khalafallah, the invented space in which Islamic law is conceptualized routinely includes two landmarks: "a fixed Islamic law and a modern Western legal system that stand tensely at opposite and necessarily conflicting poles" (Khalafallah 2005, p. 38), which leads her to emphasize the shifting meaning of Islamic law.

As a second caveat, the bulk of this review focuses on socio-legal scholarship, largely empirical and attentive to Islamic law's role in social life. My background as a cultural anthropologist leads me to embrace Dupret's (2006, p. 167) neatly articulated guidance: "To the question, What is Islamic law? we should substitute the question, What do people do when referring to Islamic law?" In this review, citations of social science perspectives outnumber those of religious textual studies, legal treatments of jurisprudence, and historiography. Given the premise that a political event might influence a scholarly field, a focus on law's role in social life, including political uses of Islamic law after 9/11, seems most appropriate. Third, as mentioned above, Islamic family law gains the most attention, while important areas are largely neglected, such as criminal law and finance. A fourth caveat, and perhaps the main limitation of this review for specialists, is the emphasis on works written for a Western audience. A tremendous amount of scholarship produced in Arabic, Urdu, German, and other languages was not considered, although the review covers many geographic areas. The field's breadth is evident; however, some pieces are singled out for in-depth treatment in order to demonstrate my contention that the value of this scholarship lies as much in its contributions to social theory as it does in shaping understandings of Islamic law.

A review of scholarship from a post-9/11 perspective offers the opportunity to think anew about the relationship among political acts and our practices and obligations as scholars. The next two sections briefly trace scholars' responses to the 9/11 attacks and their aftermath, including the prominent emergence of a liberal reformist vision of Islamic law and society designed to address the controversies over Islamic law that followed 9/11. Subsequent sections review scholarship on Muslim personal law with the goal of highlighting work that could prove useful as scholars and activists envision new approaches to Islamic law. The conclusion briefly reconsiders the politics of scholarship in the post-9/11 era.

RESPONSES TO 9/11: EXPLAINING AND JUSTIFYING

In the rush to explain the violence of 9/11 and to preempt, espouse, or justify particular responses, many pundits and scholars made reference to Huntington's (1997) "clash of civilizations," which assumes deep division between two definable opponents—the attackers and their ideology (often read as Islam) and those attacked (the West)—with violence as the main modality of relationship. Among the many who have contested this influential perspective, Hallaq (2003, p. 1705) charges that such essentialist scholarship, "sometimes propounded by highly politicized academics who had spent decades studying Islamic history and culture," has "imputed to the religion and culture certain qualities, nearly genetic in nature, which make it inherently hostile and violent." In the heady weeks after 9/11, images of violence at the core of the attackers' ideology, and by implication congruent with Islam, were deployed to justify a retaliatory invasion that never seemed in doubt. Although these images tended to blur differences between al Qaeda, the Taliban, and, at times, the Afghan nation, the Taliban's violent history and policies received special attention, including their discrimination against and violence toward women, rule of law, prior aggressors, neighboring nations, and religions other than Islam.

Scholars who supported the invasion of Afghanistan by U.S. and coalition forces justified their perspective by positioning Islamist violence as a nihilistic and destructive force that had to be confronted through a "just war." Elshtain (2003), for instance, condemned Edward Said who, among many other academics, dared to criticize the call for war in response to the attacks. Though careful to distinguish Islamist fundamentalism from the rest of Islam, Elshtain could hardly guard against the slippage that assumes causal links between the religion and instances of violence. Public disagreements also emerged over whether the Taliban's treatment of Afghan women constituted an appropriate additional reason for invasion. In rejecting attempts to use the plight of women to justify violence (see, generally, Hawthorne & Winter 2003), particularly violence with a neocolonial resonance, some feminists argued that the U.S.-backed Northern Alliance—guilty of ill-treating women in the past—might do so again (Delphy 2003) and that an invasion had little chance of loosening the overlapping political and social controls on Afghan women (Moghadam 2003).

At their most strident, the debates seemed to pit the justness of a victimized West against the lawlessness of al Qaeda, the Taliban, and other extremist aggressors. Negative stereotypes of Islamic law as inflexible, arbitrary, and discriminatory and of Islamic legal institutions as oppressive, coercive, and incompatible with democracy further established the difference between Western (rule of) law and Islamic law. Although this false dichotomy has emerged repeatedly in scholarship and in the commentary of political and religious leaders over the centuries, its stark terms gain new currency in periods of high conflict, such as the post-9/11 era. For instance, calls by the Taliban, al Qaeda, or anyone for a return to shari'a were readily interpreted as acts of coercion. In a climate in which moderate Muslims were repeatedly expected to articulate ideologies that would distinguish them from extremists, taking a position on Islamic law carried grave risks.

It is precisely the forced choice between being a good Muslim or a bad Muslim in the post-9/11 era that compelled Mamdani (2002, 2004) to advocate focusing not on the internal politics of Islamic societies but on the influence of U.S. foreign policy in creating the conditions for violent groups to emerge. Mamdani sought to counter an approach that he believed was forcing Muslims into civil wars without ever locating the root of the problem in the complex politics and history with the West (cf. Elshtain 2003).

With somewhat different conclusions in mind, Hallaq, an expert on Islamic law (e.g., Hallaq 2005), also insists that political history holds the key to explaining the violence behind 9/11, which, following others, he glosses as "Muslim rage" (Hallaq 2003). In a major address, Hallaq locates the cause(s) of 9/11 in the decimation of Islamic law over the past few hundred years. The centrality of Islamic law to Muslim social life and its oft-mentioned status, following Schacht (1964), as the "kernel of Islamic civilization" mean that inattention to its role in relation to the political system wreaks havoc for Muslim populations. Law's decimation through colonization, secularization, and the fall of the Ottoman Empire left Muslims vulnerable to nation-states that, in Hallaq's view, have been both exploitative and largely ineffective at providing justice satisfying to Muslim believers. This perspective insists that political events of the last century or so—especially the fall of the Ottoman Empire and the secularization of Turkey and other majority Muslim nations—have posed new challenges to the continuity of Islam. Evidence of the inability of nation-states to incorporate Islamic law effectively is found in the heated and sometimes violent struggles in the last century among the supporters of distinct reformist perspectives: traditionists who seek to expand the "necessity" doctrine to justify altering legal practices, Islamists who insist on returning to shari'a, and liberalists who seek to enhance Muslims' ability to draw on the spirit of revealed texts while also adhering to other normative systems (Hallaq 2003, p. 1717). As the next section shows, intellectuals of the latter persuasion took prominent positions in the public debates after 9/11.

RESPONSES TO 9/11: DEFENDING ISLAMIC LAW

As the Afghanistan conflict wound down, the U.S.-led war on terror intensified and spread, violent attacks multiplied, and public opinion in the Islamic world (and elsewhere) of the United States turned increasingly negative, some scholars' responses went beyond condemning the attacks, or explaining them, to modifying Islam's image in public and scholarly discourse. For instance, scholars writing about jihad or martyrdom—with considerably more subtlety than pundits—identified its multiple meanings and their connection to contexts of use (Feldman 2003, Freamon 2003, Lawrence 2002, Moaddel & Talattof 2002, Sachedina 2002).

The impulse to write about 9/11, and against too-stark dichotomies and misconceptions, was familiar to me. When the 9/11 attacks occurred, I was in the midst of writing about my own experience of al Qaeda terrorism, which had left me a surviving victim of the bombing of the U.S. Embassy in Tanzania and the widow of a deceased victim, Abdurahman Abdalla. Simultaneous blasts in Dar es Salaam and Nairobi on August 7, 1998, killed over 200 people and injured thousands, mostly East Africans. During the trial of four men accused of murder, conspiracy, and other terror-related crimes, I decided to write an essay about the difficulties of participating in a capital case for victims who, like myself, oppose the death penalty (Hirsch 2002). After 9/11, my project broadened beyond reflecting on my experience to respond to issues raised by 9/11, including misperceptions of Islamic law (Hirsch 2006). Toward that end, my book addresses the restrictions on the death penalty throughout Muslim history, Islam's emphasis on granting mercy, and the politics behind punishment in contemporary Muslim societies (see, e.g., Ismail 2002, Layish & Warburg 2002). Such observations counter the all-too-common link between Islamic law and violence through, for instance, media accounts of Nigerian women who faced death sentences for moral infractions. Scholars' analyses of the cases of Amina Lawal, Saffiyatu Husseini, and others caution against reducing the problem to either Islamic law or gender oppression alone, given that local politics play an important role (Ezeilo & Afolabi 2003, Harvard Law Rev. Assoc. 2004, Kalu 2003, Peters 2006; for a variety of perspectives on Islam and law in Nigeria, see Ilesanmi 2001, Oba 2002, Toda 2002).

Among the prominent Muslim scholars to write against negative portrayals of Islamic law, Abou el Fadl (2002) did so by emphasizing its stature as a normative system capable of coexisting with other legal and political traditions because of the commitment to tolerance at its core (see also Abou el Fadl 2003, Abou el Fadl et al. 2004). Throughout history, Islamic societies have marginalized intolerant perspectives or factions, a point also made by Abdullahi An-Na'im. Even as he rejects the "clash of civilizations" perspective, An-Na'im (2003) offers a trenchant criticism of fundamentalist movements of recent years in that they profess concern for the self-determination of Muslim people yet lack mechanisms for resolving competing perspectives. An-Na'im concludes that these groups fail to sustain their own claims: "To impose the views selected by the leadership of a fundamentalist movement as a matter of law and official state policy, even if against the beliefs of other Muslims, is a violation of the right of Muslims themselves to self-determination" (An-Na'im 2003, p. 35), and of non-Muslims as well (see also An-Na'im 2002a). An-Na'im's reformist agenda proposes a "framework for constructive interdependence" that would recognize a range of collective and individual rights and provide mechanisms for reconciling competing claims.

The pluralistic perspectives on reform offered by Abou el Fadl, An-Na'im, Hallaq, and other Muslim and non-Muslim intellectuals gained public attention after 9/11 (see also Rauf 2004, Safi 2003), and they were among the many challenged to come up with answers to the questions that had become more urgent: What role should Islamic law (or any religiously based law) play in democratic societies? What kinds of legal and political arrangements are tolerable/feasible/appropriate for Muslim believers or anyone else living in a majority Muslim nation? Who should be vested with the authority to interpret and apply Islamic law? How should Muslims in non-Muslim nation-states be treated? Answering these normative questions is an especially tough task. Pluralist approaches generally contend that satisfying answers come through open, deliberative processes involving national governments, local communities, and civil society organizations through which divergent perspectives are debated. In my view, those participating in such processes would benefit from consulting well-analyzed depictions of existing legal arrangements and their implications. As demonstrated below, scholars have laid this groundwork, perhaps at an opportune moment.

ISLAMIC FAMILY LAW, POST-9/11

The publication of two sourcebooks in Islamic family law is evidence of the considerable amount of scholarship and data on this topic and indicative as well of a mature and vibrant field (An-Na'im 2002b, WLUML 2003). Information collected and consulted to produce these sourcebooks included analyses of religious texts, legal codes, statutes, and decisions, ethnographic and sociological case studies, and jurisprudence, all from multiple perspectives including feminist, liberal, normative, and religious. Taken together with other recent scholarship of a survey nature (Engineer 2001, Esposito & DeLong-Bas 2001, Iqbal 2004, Welchman 2004), these sourcebooks ensure that the only generalizations one can make about Islamic family law—given its presence and use in a wide range of contexts and its various substantive and procedural forms—emphasize its diversity in practice.

The global resource book edited by An-Na'im (2002b) documents Islamic family law in countries with majority Muslim populations located in south, central, and east Asia, the Near and Middle East, and parts of Africa. Broad discussions of the history, politics, and culture of each region provide the context for descriptions of law in specific nations. Plenty of facts and figures establish how individual national governments have dealt with the main areas of Islamic family law: marriage, maintenance and other spousal obligations, divorce, custody, inheritance, and related issues, not all of which apply in every context. The second sourcebook emerged out of long-term research conducted by the international activist network, Women Living Under Muslim Laws (WLUML), whose numerous publications promote law reform and legal protections for Muslim women (WLUML 2003). Compared to An-Na'im's volume, the WLUML sourcebook synthesizes less information, yet it draws attention to specific issues such as instances of gender oppression through law. Although both volumes sacrifice depth for coverage, together they facilitate comparisons of trends in regions and legal areas, including those that have seen recent volatility (e.g., wives' consent to polygamous marriages, age of marriage, and parental rights). Relatedly, these works belie any attempts to depict Islamic family law as unchangeable, at least in contemporary practice.

An-Na'im credits many colleagues for their contributions to the sourcebook, yet he carefully claims sole credit for the volume's provocative introduction. His plainly stated reformist agenda is a call "for the transformation of family law into a normative system that is guided by modern notions of social policy as well as Islamic precepts, but not bound by Shari'a, or represented as such" (An-Na'im 2002b, p. 1). An-Na'im argues that shari'a—understood as divine and unchangeable—has never been achieved by practicing Muslims who have always had to rely on legal understandings mediated by human actors. Thus, Islamic family law as practiced by humans by definition falls short of the ideal represented by shari'a and, when instituted by a state, should never be called such. Those who would insist that states adopt shari'a embrace the inseparability of political institutions and religion as central to Islamic society, a view that is contested by An-Na'im and others. Other scholars similarly endeavor to move beyond the long-standing question of whether shari'a can or should be revived in its originally intended form (see, e.g., H.M. Khan 2002) to focus on avenues for reform. An-Na'im risks condemnation for his emphasis on the crucial role of human agency in the practice and development of law, but his approach is both pragmatic and consistent with the liberalist reform agenda in its sensitivity to self-determination and gender equality (see also Ali 2003). At the same time as he advocates reforms that will acknowledge the position of Islamic family law within legal systems that are primarily secular, An-Na'im notes that Islamic family law remains a religious symbol of deep importance to Muslims.

The sourcebooks highlight the incorporation and expression of Islamic family law in the legal codes of contemporary nation-states, which beg the question of how Islamic family law has any influence in the absence of such codes. Drawing on research in Turkey, where secular legal codes replaced Islamic law decades back, Yilmaz (2002) reveals that when people marry, divorce, or engage related activities, many choose to follow Islamic principles. Turkish Muslims' desire to use Islamic family law leads Yilmaz to argue that their strategies to achieve this goal constitute an "unofficial" Islamic law. Relatedly, the Turkish population in Britain makes use of a hybrid secular/religious law, even as many Turks seek assimilation in other spheres of daily life (Yilmaz 2001, 2004). These studies, and others described in the later sections, suggest that reform of Islamic family law might be taking place with little ideological elaboration (see also Kucukcan 2003).

As the next sections show, detailed case studies focused on Turkey, Britain, Israel, Jordan, Malaysia, and other contexts illustrate most directly the depth and sophistication of socio-legal scholarship on Islamic family law by deepening knowledge of Islamic law and practice and at the same time contributing to the development of socio-legal theory.

COMPETING NORMATIVE ORDERS

Whether institutionalized or invoked informally, Islamic principles of family law invariably operate amid multiple normative orders that can include customary practices, customary law, European-modeled civil and criminal law, and other religious legal systems. Custom (in its various incarnations) exists in nearly constant tension with Islamic law, particularly in those contexts where the matrilineal or bilateral kinship reckoning of an ethnic group meets the patrilineal assumptions of Islamic legal principles. Neat designations, such as religious courts or customary law set up by colonial powers and often retained in the postcolonial era, blur in practice. For example, the colonial (mis-)designation of Islamic law as customary law has led to increased support among some Muslims for a literalist Islamic law in Nigeria in order to ensure the distinction between religion and custom (Oba 2002).

Keebet and Franz von Benda-Beckman and other scholars from the Netherlands, Indonesia, and elsewhere have long found the complex interweaving of Islamic law with Indonesia's adat system—a set of principles for regulating social, economic, and political life and for managing disputes—rich ground for theorizing the interaction of normative orders. In a monograph on the history and political stakes of this interaction, anthropologist Bowen (2003, p. 13) depicts adat as ranging from "rules or practices of social life, to feelings and a sense of propriety, or to a somewhat thinner sense of tradition and custom" and charts its intersections with Islamic law at local, regional, and national levels of society. His approach is an "anthropological account of public reasoning" designed to illuminate the justifications used by various actors as they grapple with multiple value systems in the midst of, and in relation to, political movements that, depending on the moment, call for Islamicization or a return to tradition or a New Order or the overthrow of that Order. In a place where adat and Islam are pitted against one another on some issues, and where reasoning takes different forms at different social levels, the results can mean institutionalizing some local norms while abandoning others; ingenious reconciliations of widely varying schemas sometimes produce a "boot-strapped *fiqh*" (Islamic legal reasoning) acceptable to religious leaders, traditionalists, and secularists. For instance, Bowen shows in intricate detail how marital property—about which both adat and Islam are ambivalent—becomes enshrined in judicial decision making. Through careful ethnography, Bowen follows certain reforms up the decision-making ladder to regional and national courts, yet he repeatedly draws attention to the mutual influence of different levels. Bowen's complex example offers important theoretical and methodological innovations that illuminate the relations among law, adat, culture, politics, and circumstance but, as he rightly concludes, might also guide approaches to clashing normative orders in other contexts. Those who turn to Western political theory for perspectives on reconciling competing normative systems will welcome Bowen's review of major approaches in his final chapter, yet it is his detailed ethnography of how these details are worked out in practice that provides the real blueprint for how multiple normative orders might be sustained in a nation-state.

As one would expect of an anthropologist, Bowen refuses to gloss adat as culture. His explicit attention to culture is more limited than that of Geertz, Rosen, Greenhouse, and others who have shaped socio-legal understandings of the concept. For instance, Rosen (2000) has shown in fine ethnographic detail the deep imbrication of cultural motifs (e.g., bargaining) on Islamic law in Morocco.

Theories of culture's interaction with law have been an important contribution of socio-legal theory that should not be lost as attention to national and global normative orders pulls the purview of legal anthropology away from the local, where cultural analyses have been most often pursued. At the same time, in an innovative monograph on Islamic banking (and other forms of alternative currency), Maurer (2005) calls into question the most basic assumptions about social scientists' abilities to represent culture or law.

CONSTRUCTIONS AND INTERSECTIONS OF IDENTITY

The clear distinctions between men and women made in Qur'anic verses and other source texts have led feminists and their interlocutors to scrutinize Islamic law's construction of gender identity, in its sense as social position or role (see, e.g., Badlishah 2003). In past decades, scholars were forced to position themselves on one side or another of a dichotomy that either vilified Islamic law as subordinating women or argued that women could find means within the law to contest subordination (Keddie 2002; see also Ali 2003). Choosing among these was painful for some scholars, especially Muslim feminists. Later studies of Muslim women's position(s) exposed the dichotomy's artificial and polemical nature by highlighting the multiplicity of gender roles within and across societies and, relatedly, the intersection of gender with other aspects of identity, such as class, ethnicity, citizenship, familial role, culture, and age.

Although theoretical perspectives that bring "intersectionality" to the foreground mitigate against universalist measures of women's position under Islam, gender hierarchy and women's subordination remain important topics, albeit treated with increased nuance. For instance, Sonbol (2003b) argues that Jordanian women were eventually restricted from labor markets not by shari'a law intended to curtail their movements outside the home but by other factors, such as labor regulation. A comparative study of postcolonial Tunisia, Morocco, and Algeria demonstrates that women's position depends less on Islamic law than on whether powerful agnatic lineages can be controlled, including by the state (Charrad 2001). As Keddie (2002) notes, the shift to a greater role for the conjugal family over the natal, as experienced across Muslim societies, has consequences for women's position; it remains for scholars to explore the legal correlates of that transformation and thus to refine even further theories of law's contribution to social change, including in gender relations.

In her introduction to a rich edited volume on women in Muslim societies, Sonbol (2005a) cautions against continuing two tendencies in historians' accounts: (*a*) an overreliance on scriptural sources that freeze women's social position, and (*b*) an uncritical assumption that Muslim women require enlightenment from their Western sisters. Contributors to the volume avoid the first tendency by mining understudied sources of data, such as fatwas (legal decrees) (Tucker 2005). In reaction to the second, contributors write against the Orientalist paradigm (see Said 1979) and, in the process, reveal unusual juxtapositions of Western and Islamic influences on gender roles (see, e.g., Khalafallah 2005).

Scholarly and popular discourses on Muslim women's position invoke the language of rights with a frequency that parallels the growth of human rights discourse globally. Yet the invocation of rights, even women's rights, is not the sole province of feminist or liberal reformists. As but one among numerous examples, a pamphlet distributed by the Islamic Propagation Office in Saudi Arabia highlights the many rights afforded women under Muslim law in contrast to their lack of rights in other religions and nations and in pre-Islamic contexts (al-Sheha 2000). A woman's rights to financial maintenance from her spouse is generally mentioned in such tracts. From contrasting perspectives, the assessment of rights has become a common way of configuring women's position (see, e.g., Elmadmad 2002, Engineer 2004, WLUML 2003). A complex and provocative example comes from Osanloo's (2006) study of law in postrevolutionary Iran. As Iranian women make use of a hybridized Islamico-civil legal system, they bring to life a "relegitimated rights discourse." Just after the revolution, such language had been dismissed as too Western, and Osanloo's genealogy of rights confirms the role of women's agency in the emergence of a new discourse (Osanloo 2006; see also Osanloo 2004). The Iranian example disrupts yet another dichotomy by helping scholars to "better understand how women embody and perform citizenship in modern Islamic states, allowing us to cultivate visions of women's rights in such societies that are more complex than the seemingly bifurcated debates between liberal rights talk and Islamic culture talk" (Osanloo 2006, p. 204). (For a more cynical perspective, see Mayer 2003.)

Mirroring trends in postmodernist thought, the literature on Muslim women has shifted from a focus on identity as social role to its sense as subjectivity. For instance, women's experience of their own complex identities within pluralist and other systems has gained attention through the reflexive writings of such scholars as Fatima Mernissi, Leila Ahmed, Amina Wadud, Asra Nomani, and Aziza al-Hibri, who have shared insights into their own positioning as they advance influential agendas with respect to law and law reform.

COURTS, INTERPRETATIONS, AND AGENCY

In the past several years, the study of Islamic courts has come into its own through dissertations, monographs, and a notable edited volume focused on qadis (Islamic judges) and their courts (Masud et al. 2006). With 21 chapters from historical, anthropological, and other perspectives, this volume is the law-in-action companion to an earlier collection on muftis (jurists) and legal doctrine (Masud et al. 1996). The volume's introduction summarizes changes in the institutional framework of Islamic law in the modern period (Masud et al. 2006, p. 33):

> 1. abolition of discretionary criminal justice . . . and the promotion of respect for the rule of law; 2. bureaucratization of the shariah courts; 3. codification of the shariah; 4. the emergence, in most countries, of a dual judiciary composed of (a) secular, national courts that apply Western-style legal codes; and (b) shariah courts that apply Islamic legal doctrine in fields such as family relations and inheritance; 5. the gradual integration of the shariah court system into the national court system.

These institutional trends, although enormously consequential for the delivery of justice, have received less scholarly attention than the substance of legal decisions. Court records of decisions and related archival material can reveal trends in both substantive law and, to a lesser extent, institutional organization, yet scholars note their limitations (al-Khowli 2005; Sonbol 2003a, 2005a). That said, the study of Ottoman-era court records continues with great energy (see, e.g., al-Qattan 2002, Sonbol 2003a, Yazbak 2002). In a trenchant review of a much cited sourcebook on Muslim family law (Pearl & Menski 1998), Carroll laments that scholars in the West are challenged by the dearth and inaccuracy of available material on South Asian case law (Carroll 2001; see also Carroll 2002). Similar limitations confront scholars with interests in other geographic areas and thus complicate comparative analysis.

Much recent literature on Islamic courts consists of ethnographic studies in a wide range of societies, such as Zanzibar (Stiles 2003, 2006), Indonesia (Bowen 2003), and Malaysia (Peletz 2002). The great value of this work is that each explores the court's operation as part of ongoing social life. And because ethnographers of courts follow disputes in and out of legal arenas, their work facilitates assessments of the impact of legal processes on individuals' daily lives, which is less possible when using archival case material. Several ethnographies direct considerable attention to women's agentive use of courts, a theme addressed in earlier work (see, e.g., Hirsch 1998, Mir-Hosseini 2000). Across widely varying contexts, Muslim women file cases in court, accuse relatives, appear as witnesses, rely on family members, strategize around restrictions, and, more often than not, win their claims. Such activities characterized courts in earlier periods as well (see, for example, Sonbol 2003a,b; Tucker 1998). As this research accrues, old questions remain unanswered. For instance, how have the changes in institutional framework identified above, such as the dual judiciary (whereby secular law courts operate alongside Islamic law courts), influenced court use, legal consciousness, and the development of law? As another example, is it still the case that decisions obtained in courts are not always enforced (Moors 1995)? At a broader level, the increased availability of ethnographic and historical information about Muslim women's use of courts warrants a reappraisal of theories of agency. What constitutes an agentive act? Is legal success required? What about legal consciousness? The answers, which are beyond the scope of this review, might be obtained through matching statistical data on court use (which is scattered among the studies at present) with in-depth ethnographic depictions. It may be the case that as scholarly attention has turned to theorizing social movements (including civil society groups organizing for law reform as discussed below), interest in the agency of individuals has waned.

Wide variation in the use of courts and in the substance of legal decisions makes such studies invaluable complements to doctrinal discussions in that they can illuminate trends in whole areas of law, such as divorce, which has been an especially volatile area of legal development. Sourcebooks identify the multiple forms of divorce (e.g., unilateral talaq by a husband, a khul agreement), the differences among the legal schools (e.g., the Maliki school offers women the most opportunity for dissolving marriage), and general reforms characterizing the last century (see, e.g., Sonbol 1996). As to the latter, Welchman (2000, p. 62) notes that across Arab states "there has been a broad tendency to widen the grounds on which the wife may seek dissolution while restricting the unilateral power of talaq held by the husband." In *Beyond the Code,* her monograph on law in the Palestinian West Bank, Welchman (2000) relies on legal decisions to show how men and women make use of and are positioned through these options. Given transformations in legal codes and institutions, scholars may find that Muslim men's agency in using Islamic law and ideology in and out of court requires new attention (Peletz 2002).

The Masud et al. (2006) volume examines cases in areas other than family law, such as commercial law (Messick 2006) and charitable endowments. Scholars contributing to this volume and elsewhere address foundational concepts that impinge on the legal process and decision making, such as fairness (Bowen 2006), intent (Messick 2001, Stiles 2003), and evidence (Messick 2002; see also the special issue of *Islamic Law and Society* on evidence [Haykel 2002]). Comparing these concepts with so-called Western notions remains an important endeavor given the claims that deep differences distinguish Islamic law from other legal traditions.

Attention to court clerks—who tend to be powerful, sometimes chimerical characters—appears throughout studies of courts. Female court personnel warrant additional study as their roles raise interesting questions about gender, agency, and Islamic law. Ultimately, though, qadis (judges) receive the most scholarly attention (see, generally, Masud et al. 2006). How qadis collaborate on legal decision making or political action is especially intriguing though rarely discussed (Ramadhan 2003). And dealing with the legacy of Weber's much interpreted and misinterpreted depiction of kadi-justice continues to warrant considerable commentary (see, e.g., Peletz 2002, Sonbol 2003a).

LAW REFORM AND SOCIAL MOVEMENTS

Legal reforms are on the agenda of many different Muslim constituencies (see, generally, Hallaq 2003, H.M. Khan 2002, Roberson 2003). Although, in Hallaq's view, the liberalist perspective holds the most promise, nation-states have generally proven unable to institute acceptable reforms, with endless interpretation the inevitable (unacceptable) result (Hallaq 2003). Nonetheless, the liberalist perspective has fueled many efforts at reform over the past few decades. Generated by Muslim groups and individuals, by governmental bodies, and by activist organizations of all stripes, many reform efforts—whether of statutory law or constitutions or through judicial opinion—endeavor to expand the rights of Muslim women as part of the broader emphasis on protecting human rights (for an overview, see Moors 2003). Certain substantive laws (e.g., inheritance and divorce law) viewed as disadvantaging Muslim women have been targeted for change. For instance, a study by Fawzy (2004) examines reactions to Egyptian Law No. 1 of 2000, which altered several key features of personal status (for a related discussion, see Dupret 2006).

Scholarship on legal reform across Muslim populations points to areas of enduring contention in family law and also illuminates the politics of reform. An issue of the journal *Islamic Law and Society* brings together case studies of public debates over law reform in Mali (Schulz 2003), Yemen (Würth 2003), and Morocco (Buskens 2003). In the introduction, Moors (2003) notes that law reform generated considerable heat in the 1990s, and women activists were vocal participants. Yet, women expressed the full range of political perspectives, which Moors attributes to the effects of class. As Schulz (2003) describes for Mali, the dynamics of law reform create tenuous alliances among unlikely partners, such as state officials and religious leaders, and networks among activists, who might find a way to gloss over divergent beliefs. Given the political intricacies and the high stakes of law reform efforts, additional explicitly comparative studies could yield findings that might guide new efforts or at least indicate pitfalls. Such a comparison would ideally draw parallels with other social movements and would benefit from more explicit engagement with highly developed social movement theory (Jamal 2001).

Situations of political transformation or instability are fertile ground for attempts to reform family law, as demonstrated by Welchman's analysis of law reform in occupied Palestine (Welchman 2004). When members of KARAMAH (Muslim Women Lawyers for Human Rights) realized that the detentions and security sweeps targeting American Muslim communities after 9/11 were precipitating a rise in domestic violence in families debilitated by the stress, they turned their scholarly and activist attentions to the problem. Their approach carefully interprets Qur'anic passages, such as the "chastisement principle," that have been misused to justify men's violence and, at the same time, insists on the criminality of domestic violence (al-Hibri 2003). The group directs new attention to informal mechanisms for resolving domestic conflict as counseled in the Qur'an and advocates strengthening community support for such processes (see http://www.karamah.org). Their efforts to raise legal consciousness and similar projects undertaken by networks of Muslim activists lend support to the notion that situations of political turmoil can spawn innovative approaches to law and legal change.

STATES AND THE POLITICAL USES OF ISLAMIC LAW

Islamic law and legal institutions have long been focal points for political projects undertaken by states, activists, and religious factions. Broad political and social transformations occur through the legal system, as Peletz (2002) demonstrates in *Islamic Modern,* an engaging ethnography of the cultural politics of Malaysian courts in recent decades. Partly in reaction to the demand of religious leaders that it demonstrate Islamic credentials (a demand facing many Muslim nations), the Malay state supported strengthening the Islamic courts. And yet, as is also true across Muslim nations, these efforts collided with the fruits of their other political projects, as "the cultural logics of Islamic jurisprudence are subject to the transforming gaze of the state apparatuses in which they are embedded . . . which are almost always strongly secular in terms of their modern origins and contemporary institutional design" (Peletz 2002, p. 126). This juxtaposition, and the generally forward-looking orientation of the state, resulted in court decisions that have streamlined the extended family and eroded cultural practices deemed traditional. At the same time, by using courts that valorize such modern constructs as the individual and the contract, Malay Muslims constitute themselves as citizens participating in a larger effort to build state legitimacy and civil society. Peletz makes the intriguing point that the particular coalescence of ideologies in the Malay legal system emphasizes citizens' responsibilities, not their rights.

By situating the Malay courts at the nexus of national, regional, and global discourses, Peletz offers a constructive approach to theorizing the political uses of Islamic law. In drawing on this perspective, scholars should be mindful of Peletz's insistence that the manipulation of symbols and meanings associated with courts is integral to their political efficacy. This point is especially apparent in his deft discussion of the criminalization of nonheterosexual sex practices and identities, which had the effects of addressing religious leaders' calls for tightening up morality at the same time as it symbolized the state's refusal to be penetrated by putative Western practices and, even further, accomplished the political objectives of leaders struggling to maintain power. That courts and law play such roles in multilayered discourses is not unique to Malaysia, and additional studies from this perspective would strengthen theories of Islamic law's role in state-building processes. Hajjar's (2004) comparative analysis of state responses to domestic violence is an important contribution toward this end.

CHALLENGES IN THE POST-9/11 ERA

Wars on terror and other military actions promulgated in the wake of 9/11 have led to the development of new constitutions in majority Muslim nations. Those creating constitutions in Afghanistan and Iraq have grappled with the highly charged issue of how to incorporate Islamic law, with scholars—from Islamic academies to Washington think tanks—offering their perspectives (Benard 2003). These deliberations raise the broader question of conceptualizing Islamic democracy that engages numerous scholars (see, e.g., Abou el Fadl et al. 2004, Mernissi 2002, Norris & Inglehart 2002). No doubt this area will continue to evolve as the efficacy of the new constitutions in dispensing justice and building viable states is weighed against the theories that envisioned them.

The growth of Muslim populations in largely non-Muslim nations in recent years, though unrelated to 9/11 per se, also generates new challenges (see, generally, Haddad & Smith 2002, Quraishi & Syeed-Miller 2004). For instance, in Ontario, Canada, Muslim leaders faced harsh reactions, including from Muslim women, when they requested formalized protection of their right, since 1991, to use Islamic principles to arbitrate family disputes in the province (Bakht 2004). Their insistence that the Canadian Charter sanctioned the use of religious law was countered by concerns over potential negative effects on individual rights. Women's organizations, legal practitioners, and government officials were prominent opponents of the effort to maintain recognition for religious law. The strident debate over a long-standing practice perhaps reflected the inflammatory atmosphere surrounding Islamic law post-9/11. Debate over such issues will arise with increasing frequency in nations with minority Muslim populations, as will concerns over religious images, headscarves, punishing apostasy, and other issues that have fueled controversy.

Sorting out conflicts over laws is similarly made difficult in a post-9/11 era, when collaboration among individual nations can be strained and questions of citizenship raise concerns about sovereignty and security. Drawing on migrants' accounts of their legal difficulties, Rosen (2002) highlights the vulnerability of individuals caught amid multiple legal orders, especially when the notions that they hold of custody, marriage payment (Blenkhorn 2002), or divorce (Berger 2002) fail to reflect those in the country to which they migrate. Rosen offers recommendations to reconcile the divergent legal approaches. For one, he argues for recognizing Islamic law as a form of common law, not civil law, which would encourage greater sensitivity to its contextualized practice (see also Sonbol 2005b).

As much of the scholarship reviewed in this chapter reveals, equally challenging difficulties remain in majority Muslim nations, particular if the reformist visions of An-Na'im, Hallaq, al-Hibri, Mernissi, and others are to have any influence. Additional concrete analyses of the complex politics in which nation-states are embedded, combined with further development of theories of the state in the midst of globalization (as is proceeding in social science more generally), might address the concerns of Hallaq and others who charge that nation-states, particularly in the Muslim world, are inadequate contexts for interpreting and deploying Islamic law. Undertaken in the post-9/11 era, when processes of economic and social globalization bear the effects of other global processes, such as the war on terror and the expansion of international legal bodies, such studies might reveal new configurations of nation-states and new ideas for their capacity with respect to Islamic law. Potential areas for study, which are beyond the scope of this review, include Islamic finance (the citations here are simply too numerous to list), international human rights (Ali 2000, Baderin 2003, M.A. Khan 2002), and new legal institutions, such as the International Criminal Court (Clarke 2006).

CONCLUSION

Facing the challenges discussed here, as well as others present in societies where multiple perspectives on religious law await reconciliation or some other resolution (which is most every society), is made less daunting by the availability of detailed, well-analyzed examples of how such debates over different perspectives have played out in other contexts. The examples reviewed here could contribute as liberalist reformers develop new legal systems or new forms of debate that might productively channel differences in values and commitments. Even as I place faith in the liberatory possibilities of social analysis, I am mindful of Sherman Jackson's (2003) caution that, in their emphasis on the flexibility of law and possibilities for systemic change, social science studies of Islamic law generally fail to appreciate that Islamic law is fundamentally conservative in its recognition of prior authority, as are legal systems generally. Over and over again, the multiple backward-looking (in Jackson's terminology) qualities of Islamic law have served to empower jurists who continue to hold tremendous power over interpretation, espouse conservative interpretations, and demand allegiance of nation-states. The relation between jurists and nation-states has been at the root of skepticism about Islam's compatibility with democracy and the related question of Islamic law's compatibility with pluralism and equality. To move beyond this impasse, Jackson advocates rethinking the role of the nation-state with respect to Islamic law, including perhaps decentralizing government control over religious law. Overcoming his objections gives new vigor to two additional progressive political projects.

For one, scholars will no doubt continue to expand the notion of jurist in Islam to include many individuals authorized to reinterpret source texts, jurisprudence, and legal rulings and, more broadly, participate in the public reasoning through which legal decisions and policies are shaped and implemented (Peters 2003). Arkoun (2002) urges an expanded role for intellectuals, particularly in transforming civil society to accommodate new perspectives on law. Ovid Safi and contributors to a valuable 2003 volume take a similar approach: "To introduce an Islamic term, one might state that the progressive Muslim project represents an ongoing attempt at an Islamic ijtihad, or committed critical thinking based on disciplined but independent reasoning, to come up with solutions to new problems. This progressive ijtihad *is* our jihad" (Safi 2003, p. 8). Safi and others acknowledge that this process will result in a series of experiments, not the one global solution that fundamentalists repeatedly pursue. A second, related project would involve Muslim and non-Muslim scholars in the continued production of socio-legal scholarship on Islamic law of the sort that would offer blueprints for reforms and diagnoses of situations that need attention. In the several years since 9/11, many scholars have stepped back from public discourse, perhaps to focus on producing the in-depth scholarship called for above. Yet, there remains an urgent need to address distortions in understandings about Islam and Islamic law as well as to provide the public with a vision of a pluralist society where widely divergent perspectives coexist, if only to inform them, gently, that such a vision will doubtless include a "restless, endless process of deliberation" (Bowen 2003).

ACKNOWLEDGMENTS

With gratitude I acknowledge the contributions made to this piece by research assistants Julia Hirsch, Talha Kose, and Min Zaw Oo.

LITERATURE CITED

Abou el Fadl K. 2002. The place of tolerance in Islam. In *The Place of Tolerance in Islam*, ed. J Cohen, I Lague, pp. 3–23. Boston: Beacon

Abou el Fadl K. 2003. Islam and the challenge of democratic commitment. *Fordham Int. Law J.* 27:4

Abou el Fadl K, Cohen J, Chasman D. 2004. *Islam and the Challenge of Democracy*. Princeton, NJ: Princeton Univ. Press. 139 pp.

al-Hibri AY. 2003. An Islamic perspective on domestic violence. *Fordham Int. Law J.* 27:195–224

Ali K. 2003. Progressive Muslims and Islamic jurisprudence: the necessity for critical engagement with marriage and divorce law. See Safi 2003, pp. 163–89

Ali SS. 2000. *Gender and Human Rights in Islam and International Law: Equal Before Allah, Unequal Before Man?* The Hague/Boston: Kluwer Law Int. 358 pp.

al-Khowli R. 2005. Observations on the use of shari'a court records as a source of social history. See Sonbol 2005a, pp. 139–51

al-Qattan N. 2002. Litigants and neighbors: the communal topography of Ottoman Damascus. *Comp. Stud. Soc. Hist.* 44:511–33

al-Sheha AR. 2000. *Woman in the Shade of Islam*. Riyadh: Islamic Propag. Off.

An-Na'im AA. 2002a. 'The best of times' and 'the worst of times': human agency and human rights in Islamic societies. *Muslim World J. Hum. Rights* 1:1–12

An-Na'im AA. 2002b. *Islamic Family Law in a Changing World: A Global Resource Book*. London/New York: Zed Books. 320 pp.

An-Na'im AA. 2003. Islamic fundamentalism and social change: neither the end of history nor a clash of civilizations. In *Freedom to Do God's Will: Religious Fundamentalism and Social Change*, ed. J Busuttil, pp. 25–48. London/New York: Routledge

Arkoun M. 2002. *The Unthought in Contemporary Islamic Thought*. London: Saqi. 352 pp.

Baderin MA. 2003. *International Human Rights and Islamic Law*. Oxford/New York: Oxford Univ. Press. 279 pp.

Badlishah HNN. 2003. *Islamic Family Law and Justice for Muslim Women*. Malaysia: Sisters in Islam

Bakht N. 2004. Family arbitration using sharia law: examining Ontario's Arbitration Act and its impact on women. *Muslim World J. Hum. Rights* 1:1–24

Benard C. 2003. *Civil Democratic Islam: Partners, Resources, and Strategies*. Santa Monica, CA: RAND. 72 pp.

Berger MS. 2002. Conflicts law and public policy in Egyptian family law: Islamic law through the backdoor. *Am. J. Comp. Law* 50:555–95

Blenkhorn L. 2002. Islamic marriage contracts in American courts: interpreting *mahr* agreements as prenuptuals and their effect on Muslim women. *South. Calif. Law Rev.* 76:189–234

Bowen JR. 2003. *Islam, Law and Equality in Indonesia: An Anthropology of Public Reason*. Cambridge, UK: Cambridge Univ. Press. 289 pp.

Bowen JR. 2006. Fairness and law in an Indonesian court. See Masud et al. 2006, pp. 117–42

Buskens L. 2003. Recent debates on family law reform in Morocco: Islamic law as politics in an emerging public sphere. *Islam. Law Soc.* 10:70–131

Carroll L. 2001. Adoption in Pakistani law: repercussions in UK immigration law: a critique of David Pearl and Werner Menski, *Muslim Family Law* (3rd ed.) London: Sweet & Maxwell, 1998. *Islam. Q.* 45:161–72

Carroll L. 2002. The Pakistan Federal Shariat Court, section 4 of the Muslim Family Laws Ordinance, and the orphaned grandchild. *Islam. Law Soc.* 9:70–82

Charrad M. 2001. *States and Women's Rights: The Making of Postcolonial Tunisia, Algeria, and Morocco*. Berkeley: Univ. Calif. Press. 341 pp.

Clarke KM. 2006. Internationalizing the statecraft: the ICC, religious revivalism, and the cultural politics of genocide. *Loyola Los Angeles Int. Comp. Law Rev.* In press

Delphy C. 2003. A war for Afghan women? See Hawthorne & Winter 2003, pp. 333–47

Dupret B. 2006. The practice of judging: the Egyptian judiciary at work in a personal status case. See Masud et al. 2006, pp. 143–68

Elmadmad K. 2002. Women's rights under Islam. In *The Human Rights of Women: International Instruments and African Experiences*, ed. W Benedek, EM Kisaakye, G Oberleitner, pp. 243–67. London/New York: Zed Books

Elshtain J. 2003. *Just War Against Terror: The Burden of American Power in a Violent World*. New York: Basic Books. 240 pp.

Engineer A. 2001. *Islam, Women, and Gender Justice*. New Delhi, India: Gyan Publ. House. 370 pp.

Engineer A. 2004. *The Rights of Women in Islam*. Elgin, IL: New Dawn. 188 pp.

Esposito JL, DeLong-Bas N. 2001. *Women in Muslim Family Law*. Syracuse: Syracuse Univ. Press. 195 pp.

Ezeilo J, Afolabi AA. 2003. *Sharia and Women's Human Rights in Nigeria: Strategies for Action*. Nigeria: Women Advocates Res. Doc. Cent. (WARDC). 140 pp.

Fawzy E. 2004. Muslim personal status law in Egypt: the current situation and possibilities of reform through internal initiatives. See Welchman 2004, pp. 15–94

Feldman N. 2003. *After Jihad: America and the Struggle for Islamic Democracy*. New York: Farrar, Strauss, Giroux. 260 pp.

Freamon BK. 2003. Martyrdom, suicide, and the Islamic law of war: a short legal history. *Fordham Int. Law J.* 27:299–369

Haddad YY, Smith JI, eds. 2002. *Muslim Minorities in the West: Visible and Invisible*. New York: Altamira. 306 pp.

Hajjar L. 2004. Religion, state power, and domestic violence in Muslim societies: a framework for comparative analysis. *Law Soc. Inq.* 29:1–38

Hallaq WB. 2003. Justice Matthew O. Tobriner memorial lecture: "Muslim rage" and Islamic law. *Hastings Law J.* 54:1705–20

Hallaq WB. 2005. *Authority, Continuity, and Change in Islamic Law*. Cambridge, UK: Cambridge Univ. Press. 265 pp.

Harvard Law Rev. Assoc. 2004. Saving Amina Lawal: human rights symbolism and the dangers of colonialism. *Harvard Law Rev.* 117:2365–86

Hawthorne S, Winter B. 2003. *After Shock: September 11, 2001/Global Feminist Perspectives*. Vancouver, BC: Raincoast Books

Haykel B. 2002. Theme issue: evidence in Islamic law. *Islam. Law Soc.* 9:129–31

Hirsch SF. 1998. *Pronouncing and Persevering: Gender and the Discourses of Disputing in an African Islamic Court*. Chicago: Univ. Chicago Press

Hirsch SF. 2002. Victims for the prosecution: a survivor of the embassy bombings on the limits of victim impact testimony. *Boston Rev.* 27:21–25

Hirsch SF. 2006. *In the Moment of Greatest Calamity: Terrorism, Grief, and a Victim's Quest for Justice*. Princeton, NJ: Princeton Univ. Press

Huntington S. 1997. *The Clash of Civilizations and the Remaking of World Order*. New York: Simon & Schuster

Ilesanmi SO. 2001. Constitutional treatment of religion and the politics of human rights in Nigeria. *African Aff.* 100:529–54

Iqbal S. 2004. *Woman and Islamic Law*. New Delhi, India: Adam Publ. Distrib. 316 pp.

Ismail R. 2002. *Hudud in Malaysia: The Issues at Stake*. Petaling Jaya, Selangor, Malaysia: Ilmiah. 210 pp.

Jackson S. 2003. Shari'ah, democracy, and the modern nation-state: some reflections on Islam, popular rule, and pluralism. *Fordham Int. Law J.* 27:88–107

Jamal A. 2001. Engendering state-building: the women's movement and gender-regime in Palestine. *Middle East J.* 55:256–76

Kalu OU. 2003. Safiyya and Adamah: punishing adultery with sharia stones in twenty-first-century Nigeria. *African Aff.* 102:389–408

Keddie NR. 2002. Women in the limelight: some recent books on Middle Eastern women's history. *Int. J. Middle East Stud.* 34:553–73

Khalafallah H. 2001. The elusive 'Islamic law': rethinking the focus of modern scholarship. *Islam Christ. Muslim Relat.* 12:143–52

Khalafallah H. 2005. Muslim women: public authority, scriptures, and "Islamic law." See Sonbol 2005a, pp. 37–52

Khan HM. 2002. Nothing is written: fundamentalism, revivalism, reformism and the fate of Islamic law. *Mich. J. Int. Law* 24:273–345

Khan MA. 2002. *Human Rights in the Muslim World: Fundamentalism, Constitutionalism, and International Politics*. Durham, NC: Carolina Acad. 489 pp.

Kucukcan T. 2003. State, Islam, and religious liberty in modern Turkey: reconfiguration of religion in the public sphere. *Brigham Young Univ. Law Rev.* 2003:475–502

Lawrence BB. 2002. Conjuring with Islam, II. *J. Am. Hist.* 89:485–97

Layish A, Warburg G. 2002. *The Reinstatement of Islamic Law in Sudan Under Numayri: An Evaluation of a Legal Experiment in the Light of its Historical Context, Methodology, and Repercussions*. Leiden/Boston: Brill. 348 pp.

Mamdani M. 2002. Good Muslim, bad Muslim: a political perspective on culture and terrorism. *Am. Anthropol.* 104:766–75

Mamdani M. 2004. *Good Muslim, Bad Muslim: America, the Cold War, and the Roots of Terror*. New York: Pantheon. 304 pp.

Masud MK, Messick B, Powers DS, eds. 1996. *Islamic Legal Interpretation: Muftis and their Fatwas*. Cambridge, MA/London: Harvard Univ. Press. 431 pp.

Masud MK, Peters R, Powers DS, eds. 2006. *Dispensing Justice in Islam: Qadis and their Judgments*. Leiden/Boston: Brill. 591 pp.

Maurer B. 2005. *Mutual Life, Limited: Islamic Banking, Alternative Currencies, Lateral Reason*. Princeton, NJ: Princeton Univ. Press. 217 pp.

Mayer AE. 2003. Islamic law as a core for political law: the withering of an Islamist illusion. See Roberson 2003, pp. 117–42

Mernissi F. 2002. *Islam and Democracy: Fear of the Modern World*. Cambridge, MA: Perseus. 197 pp.

Messick B. 2001. Indexing the self: intent and expression in Islamic legal acts. *Islam. Law Soc.* 8:151–78

Messick B. 2002. Evidence: from memory to archive. *Islam. Law Soc.* 9:231–70

Messick B. 2006. Commercial litigation in a shari'a court. See Masud et al. 2006, pp. 195–218

Mir-Hosseini Z. 2000. *Marriage on Trial: A Study of Islamic Family Law: Iran and Morocco Compared*. London/New York: Tauris. 245 pp.

Moaddel M, Talattof K. 2002. *Modernist and Fundamentalist Debates in Islam: A*

Reader. New York: Palgrave Macmillan. 382 pp.
Moghadam V. 2003. Women, the Taliban, and the politics of public space in Afghanistan. See Hawthorne & Winter 2003, pp. 290–315
Moors A. 1995. *Women, Property, and Islam, Palestinian Experiences, 1920–1990*. Cambridge, UK: Cambridge Univ. Press. 274 pp.
Moors A. 2003. Public debates on family law reform participants, positions, and styles of argumentation in the 1990s. *Islam. Law Soc.* 10:1–11
Norris P, Inglehart R. 2002. Islamic culture and democracy: testing the "clash of civilizations" thesis. *Comp. Sociol.* 1:235–63
Oba A. 2002. Islamic law as customary law: the changing perspective in Nigeria. *Int. Comp. Law Q.* 51:817–51
Osanloo A. 2004. Doing the "rights" thing: methods and challenges of fieldwork in Iran. *Iran. Stud.* 37:675–84
Osanloo A. 2006. Islamico-civil "rights-talk": women, subjectivity, and law in Iranian family court. *Am. Ethnol.* 33:191–209
Pearl D, Menski W. 1998. *Muslim Family Law*. London: Sweet & Maxwell
Peletz MG. 2002. *Islamic Modern: Religious Courts and Cultural Politics in Malaysia*. Princeton, NJ/Oxford: Princeton Univ. Press. 339 pp.
Peters R. 2003. From jurists' law to statute law or what happens when the shari'a is codified. See Roberson 2003, pp. 82–95
Peters R. 2006. The re-Islamization of criminal law in northern Nigeria and the judiciary: the Safiyyatu Hussaini case. See Masud et al. 2006, pp. 219–44
Quraishi A, Syeed-Miller N. 2004. No altars: a survey of Islamic family law in the United States. See Welchman 2004, pp. 177–230
Ramadhan MA. 2003. Judicial activism of the Shari'ah Appeals Court in Israel (1994–2001): rise and crisis. *Fordham Int. Law J.* 27:254–98
Rauf FA. 2004. *What's Right with Islam: A New Vision for Muslims and the West*. San Francisco: HarperSanFrancisco. 314 pp.
Roberson BA, ed. 2003. *Shaping the Current Islamic Reformation*. London/Portland, OR: Frank Cass. 262 pp.
Rosen L. 2000. *The Justice of Islam: Comparative Perspectives on Islamic Law Society*. Oxford: New York. 234 pp.
Rosen L. 2002. *The Culture of Islam: Changing Aspects of Contemporary Muslim Life*. Chicago: Univ. Chicago Press. 230 pp.
Sachedina AA. 2002. From defensive to offensive warfare: the use and abuse of *jihad* in the Muslim world. In *Religion, Law and the Role of Force: A Study of Their Influence on Conflict and on Conflict Resolution*, ed. JI Coffey, CT Mathewes, pp. 23–38. Ardsley, NY: Transnational
Safi O, ed. 2003. *Progressive Muslims: On Justice, Gender, and Pluralism*. Oxford: Oneworld. 351 pp.
Said E. 1979. *Orientalism*. New York: Vintage. 368 pp.
Schacht J. 1964. *An Introduction to Islamic Law*. Oxford: Clarendon. 304 pp.
Schulz D. 2003. Political factions, ideological fictions: the controversy over family law reform in democratic Mali. *Islam. Law Soc.* 10:132–64
Sonbol AEA, ed. 1996. *Women, Family, and Divorce Laws in Islamic History*. Syracuse: Syracuse Univ. Press. 357 pp.
Sonbol AEA. 2003a. Women in shari'ah courts: a historical and methodological discussion. *Fordham Int. Law J.* 27:225–53
Sonbol AEA. 2003b. *Women of Jordan: Islam, Labor and the Law*. Syracuse: Syracuse Univ. Press. 300 pp.
Sonbol AEA. 2005a. *Beyond the Exotic: Women's Histories in Islamic Societies*. Syracuse: Syracuse Univ. Press. 522 pp.
Sonbol AEA. 2005b. Mixed and other courts: women and modern patriarchy. See Sonbol 2005a, pp. 198–226
Stiles EE. 2003. When is a divorce a divorce? Determining intention in Zanzibar's Islamic courts. *Ethnology* 42:273–88
Stiles EE. 2006. Broken *edda* and marital mistakes: two recent disputes from an Islamic court in Zanzibar. See Masud et al. 2006, pp. 95–116

Toda M. 2002. Religion and politics in Nigeria: the real cause of the sharia conflict in 2000. *J. Asian Afr. Stud. (Tokyo)* 64:217–36

Tucker J. 1998. *In the House of the Law: Gender and Islamic Law in Ottoman Syria and Palestine*. Berkeley: Univ. Calif. Press. 221 pp.

Tucker J. 2005. "And God knows best": the *fatwa* as a source for the history of gender in the Arab world. See Sonbol 2005a, pp. 165–79

Welchman L. 2000. *Beyond the Code: Muslim Family Law and the Shari'a Judiciary in the Palestinian West Bank*. Hague/Boston: Kluwer Law Int. 444 pp.

Welchman L. 2004. *Women's Rights and Islamic Family Law: Perspectives on Reform*. New York: Zed Books. 300 pp.

WLUML. 2003. *Knowing Our Rights: Women, Family, Laws and Customs in the Muslim World*. London: WLUML. 360 pp.

Würth A. 2003. Stalled reform: family law in postunification Yemen. *Islam. Law Soc.* 10:12–33

Yazbak M. 2002. Minor marriages and *khiyar al-bulugh* in Ottoman Palestine: a note on women's strategies in a patriarchal society. *Islam. Law Soc.* 9:386–409

Yilmaz I. 2001. Law as chameleon: the question of incorporation of Muslim personal law into the English law. *J. Muslim Minor. Aff.* 21:297

Yilmaz I. 2002. Secular law and the emergence of unofficial Turkish Islamic law. *Middle East J.* 56:113–31

Yilmaz I. 2004. Marriage solemnization among Turks in Britain: the emergence of a hybrid Anglo-Muslim Turkish law. *J. Muslim Minor. Aff.* 24:57–66

Annu. Rev. Law Soc. Sci. 2006. 2:187–210
doi: 10.1146/annurev.lawsocsci.2.081805.105933

FIELDWORK ON LAW

Carol J. Greenhouse
Department of Anthropology, Princeton University, Princeton, New Jersey 08544; email: cgreenho@princeton.edu

Key Words regulation, rights, war on terror, hegemony, neoliberalism

■ **Abstract** Based on a review of field-based scholarship on law published in English in 2004 and 2005, this review focuses on themes most strongly emergent across the disciplines of law and the social sciences: state regulation of the private sector, rights (individual rights, indigenous rights, and human rights), and security. These developing areas of field research show the impact of neoliberalism on the social fields of law, an impact intensified by the war on terror. They also point to fresh theoretical horizons in relation to issues of identity, hegemony, and the discursivity of state power. Although disciplines retain their distinctive questions and approaches, they reveal common attention to discourse and practice—particularly in relation to critical events in the war on terror and new forms of executive power, especially in the United States. Current literature thus points not only to new terrain for field research on law, but also, correspondingly, to the changing nature of the field itself as a methodological object.

INTRODUCTION

Fieldwork is a relational practice linking knowledge production to the historical and local specificity of experience. Field studies of law therefore make a broad subject, not just because of their quantity and variety, but also because of the mutual embeddedness of legal and social concepts. Changes in the social fields of law in turn affect what constitutes fieldwork. The strong emergence of discourse, narrative, performance, and practice as "found objects" [to borrow from Riles (2004, p. 776) in a related context] blurs any easy distinction between what is "in" some "field" or outside of it. Indeed, what counts as fieldwork shifts as legality moves in and out of visibility in actual historical and political circumstances; it is never wholly accessible (because there is no whole) as an object for field study or theorizing (see Latour 2004).[1]

The sources of contemporary transdisciplinary shape shifting in this sense lie in major developments that unsettle legal consciousness in relation to place and time: denationalization of law through the neoliberalization of institutional infrastructures under privatization as well as through the transnational private sector, the

[1]By discourse, I refer to ways of representing the world in language and other symbols, as well as the worlds built up from those representations, making the literary literal.

"relocation of politics into the legal domain" (Comaroff & Comaroff 2005, p. 13), and the security crisis usually labeled as the war on terror (see also Comaroff & Comaroff 2004, pp. 538–40). In this review, I develop the connection between the temporal and political regrounding of law and current directions in field studies through a field exercise of my own: mapping the terrain from its most vivid interdisciplinary intersections.[2] Reading across disciplines, I focus on emergent openings for field study (see Hacking 2004; Sarfaty 2005, especially, p. 1818; Scheppele 2004b, p. 391; Suchman et al. 2002; Vick 2004).

While socio-legal research traditions are methodologically and theoretically keyed to stable institutions and discourses, they are also available as resources for those scholars who turn to the field in response to current—even very immediate—events. As the temporal field becomes more compressed (e.g., around the beginning of the war in Iraq in March 2003, or the revelation of torture at Abu Ghraib in May 2004, or Hurricane Katrina in 2005), scholars' field projects become more discourse- and practice-centered, whatever their discipline. In these and other respects, the field traditions of the subject disciplines associated with legal study, as well as academic law, clearly remain vital resources for comparative and theoretical work within and across disciplines.

Before moving on to the specifics of these engagements, and by way of preface, I offer the following observations of the field as I found it: One striking observation of current field studies is how much scholars appear to have abandoned the effort to equate law and culture, or law and society, as being in some way generalized reflections of each other. Contemporary processes of citizenship—including consent, dissent, and claims-making—appear to have escaped the bounds of generality in this regard. Current field studies of law, whatever their disciplinary foundation, are specific and concrete in their attention to the dynamic specificity of institutional and interpretive practices and the interests and social consequences these entail. In many respects, they obviate a distinction between empirical and interpretive work, as they probe social conditions, knowledge production, and legal practice (broadly speaking).

The romanticism of earlier generations of socio-legal scholars for whom society was inherently legal retains its traces but nowadays appears primarily as an evocation of democratic possibility, as a claim to rights revindicated by cultural communities pressing their interests in courts of law, or as an irony. In current field studies, this discursive shift is evident, especially in the treatment of identity in relation to "stateness" (Hansen & Stepputat 2001), most notably as citizenship emerges as an actively contested domain (especially, in current literature, in relation to rights and to migration).

In a related vein, while legal pluralism remains an important fact of contemporary social life, the concept is undergoing some revision (if tacitly) as scholars turn

[2]To be sure, journals, Internet-based outlets, and book publication continue to expand, and even the narrow historical window I have taken as my purview in this article (2004–2005) admits far more relevant material than could be synthesized in essay form. See the Appendix for more information on the sources that inform this review.

to the layerings of interests and powers (not all of them legal) in play within and across social fields and the recognition practices associated with legal domains and law practice.

In field studies of law, the reformist commitment remains strong. I follow the lines of these observations as an exercise in cumulative reading "out of school" (Cavell 1984), an effort to convey the sorts of issues that are driving socio-legal scholars onto new ground. Today, it seems, field study of law is changing hands: Anthropologists are working on legal doctrine, and lawyers are working on cultural practice. Field studies of law abound in the regional and specialist professional journals (e.g., in education, information law, urban studies, African and Asian studies), yet are relatively few in the social science subject discipline journals. Law reviews are just beginning to publish articles on the legalities of the so-called war on terror, but the Social Science Research Network's Legal Scholarship Network Research Paper Series contains ample evidence of work in progress on war, its makings, and its consequences. Government is a major focus of field study, if not generally of fieldwork in the conventional ethnographic or sociological sense. It is also a major source of field studies. The neoliberal state extends market values to policymaking, strengthening government mandates for evidence-based policy in the United States and elsewhere; this, too, accounts for some of the current breadth of socio-legal fieldwork.[3]

THEMES FROM RESTRUCTURED LEGAL FIELDS

On all fronts, current literature shows important signs of innovation and improvisation in the face of new and sometimes unexpected developments. The social

[3]The very nature of recent developments in the world and in academic publication precludes bright methodological lines, say, between field studies and law-related scholarship of other kinds (e.g., of legal doctrine or professional practice). In seeking a basis for delimiting my own efforts, I included working papers, articles, and books based on ethnography, field surveys conducted by the author, and studies of discourse, rhetoric, texts, and other media; I did not review the field of legal history, although much of that literature would fit well within the criteria I set for myself. I emphasized social science journals, although humanities journals and law reviews also contain relevant material (cited illustratively in the text). Although the expansion of empirical legal studies has been an important development in law scholarship in recent years, I ultimately set aside studies based on data sets acquired from external sources. I included studies of the legal profession but set aside works on legal advocacy as such unless there was a field component. I included discursive analyses of legalities in the context of the war on terror and accounts of their production and practice, but not doctrinal analyses of their legality. I considered articles on the impact of new security regimes and other laws on citizens' identities, but not articles on identity or citizenship as such. A major limitation is the restriction of my review to publications in English. These distinctions emerged over time as the project's pragmatic limits, but I do not defend them as epistemological, thematic, or methodological boundaries. The contemporary problematics of such a defense is part of the point.

fields around and under law appear to be in the midst of significant restructuring. Major thematic concentrations in this regard are along the following lines:

1. Neoliberal reform and the marketization of major social institutions affect the contexts and conditions of personal agency and legal efficacy, particularly in the nexus of citizenship, mobility, consumption, and debt (see Chikwendu 2004; Coutin 2002, 2005; Fassin 2005; Maurer 2005a,b; Moran 2006; Petryna 2002; Roitman 2005; Taussig 2003; Ticktin 2006). Under such conditions, legality may or may not be primarily associated with the state (see Shvarts 2003 on the Russian mafia).
2. Transnational institutions, nation-states, regions, cities, and private sector enterprises (e.g., multinational firms) are neither continuous nor neatly layered socio-legal fields, but are, in practice, distinct and even disconnected legal and political topographies with extremely varied means of articulation and internal control (see Grattet & Jenness 2005).
3. The situation described in Theme 2 makes for a slippery regulatory landscape in which the enforceability of law runs well short of critical areas of the private sector (see Shamir 2004) and of the state itself (see Gross 2003, 2004).
4. Important new work suggests that there are new litigants working those verges and margins: indigenous and ethnic communities (Comaroff & Comaroff 2005); human rights activists (Merry 2005, Wilson 2005); business managers involved in interenterprise disputes (Hendley 2004); and state officials, turning to courts to resolve structural and other conflicts within the government itself (Scheppele 2004a)—the latter being the context for much of the current studies addressed to the war on terror (see below). In general, legal arenas are increasingly forums for political contestation (Comaroff & Comaroff 2004, 2005).
5. New scholarship shows the emergence of new debates in the field of human rights, such as the efficacy of rights, the legitimacy of state authority, the etiology of violence, the nature of cultural difference, as well as fresh assessments of formerly taken-for-granted tensions between advocacy and value-neutral social science (see especially Goodale 2006, Jean-Klein & Riles 2005, Visweswaran 2004; see also Strathern 2004).
6. Movements for law reform remain strongly embedded in rights discourse, but are also keyed to other registers, notably judicial administration (e.g., in the context of the death penalty; Sarat 2005, Sarat & Boulanger 2005) and administrative law (as a restraint on globalization; Aman 2004), but also the arts (see Sarat et al. 2005b). Major new volumes examine cause lawyering—activist advocates who "construct and transform the boundary between law and politics, fabricating political action with legal tools and legal action that respond to political necessity" (Sarat & Scheingold 2005, p. 9; see also Sarat & Scheingold 2004 and contributions to Sarat & Scheingold 2005).

7. The pressures of events and the pervasive sense of crisis in the context of the war on terror have pushed open new field projects and methods well beyond the already wide circuits of law and society scholarship. The social and legal apparatus of security as well as critical assessments of the legal authority for war and key elements of the Bush administration's war on terror yield prominent themes across the disciplines, including academic law (see Dudziak & Volpp 2005; Gross 2003, 2004; Levinson 2004; Sarat et al. 2005a).

These issues are evidence above all of a critical polarity in the neoliberal state. The ideologization of neoliberal reform—in particular the politicization of privatization—over the course of the 1980s and 1990s made the executive branch structurally dominant (Aman 2004). Shifts in regulation and rights enforcement can be understood in relation to this history, if sometimes indirectly, as discussed below.

A large new literature addresses the war on terror. The policy commitment to war in Iraq and the international counterterrorism effort unfolded before the public primarily as a series of questions involving legal powers, especially presidential authority in the United States and the authority of the United Nations. The political and diplomatic process leading to the war in Iraq took place selectively in concert among the main coalition partner countries. The public face of the buildup to war and other central elements of the war on terror (the USA PATRIOT Act, military tribunals, and detention camps, among other things) was a series of intra- and intergovernmental legal maneuvers, against a backdrop of new security practices (coded alerts, heightened surveillance at transit checkpoints, and so forth).

With respect to war powers, the U.S. executive branch now operates as a private sector within the government itself, defining its own interests, eschewing external checks, and emphasizing its capacity for self-regulation. But far from being unique, this situation only underscores the extent to which, quite apart from the context of counterterrorism or emergency, neoliberal governmentality retains the option of a "state of exception" (Agamben 2005) within the state itself, as an internalization of the principle of privatization through law.

In this context, it may seem odd to insist on the theoretical significance of the war on terror, but in important ways, the war on terror involves more than a series of events and pragmatic responses. It challenges the recent cultural theory of the state, while at the same time consolidating a picture of the field effects of contemporary legality around the relative autonomy of the transnational private sector—the model on which the coalition appears to have been organized (albeit through states) and the war in Iraq managed (through select private contractors). The compression of events and the intensity of the performativity of text in relation to the buildup to war and other aspects of the war on terror challenge the conventional distinctions between text and practice, discourse and event, and even legality and authority.

Although most of the studies I cite in the discussion of the war on terror (below) are not field studies in the usual sense, I take them as such because they take their openings from events themselves, as explorations of social conditions affecting the production of knowledge and meaning, and vice versa. In this sense they have everything in common with the longest socio-legal traditions in which law features as both the theoretical subject and methodological object of inquiry—and the subject and object of democratic reform. Although the war is a vivid demonstration of the limitations of any theoretical equation or conflation of law and society, its theoretical significance for socio-legal scholars might emerge from the very necessity of reworking the knowledge relations (i.e., the connections between knowledge, interpretation, identity, and social action) on which, and about which, field studies are, at the most general level, premised (see Strathern 2005, pp. 90–91).

In a review of this scope, I can do no more than touch on these themes. I do so by concentrating on their interrelationships where legality is most enmeshed in revisions in the constitution of time and place characteristic of the present moment. Accordingly, the following sections address issues of regulation, rights, and the war on terror.

RIGHTS AND REGULATION

Current field studies of law point to new developments in the broad area of regulation and rights. They emphasize new uses of law and new law users, as well as contexts where individuals and communities are exposed to the unmediated power of their governments, employers, and other major private sector actors. In this section, I review literature on state regulation of private sector firms with respect to rights and responsibilities, individual rights, indigenous rights, and human rights. These issues are related in the pervasive effects of neoliberal reform on conditions of life, the diminished mandate (or efficacy) of certain state institutions (e.g., regulatory agencies), and the relatively ready accessibility of courts.

Regulation

New field studies of regulation yield a vivid image of the frailty of the neoliberal state relative to the powers of the private sector, both in relation to regulation aimed at private sector entities (notably but not only multinational corporations) and in presenting intended or unintended obstacles to the rights claims of employees, consumers, and others. Private sector evasions of regulation are a recurring theme (Gezelius 2002, He 2005, Endeshaw 2004, Middleton 2005). Shamir's (2004) study of multinational corporations in relation to the Alien Tort Claims Act maps the debate surrounding the "responsibilization" of multinationals (p. 660) as a conflict between human rights activists (who seek legal regulation and enforcement mechanisms) and the multinationals themselves, whose advocacy of self-regulation would make corporate social responsibility "essentially" beyond the law (p. 636). In this context, Shamir notes an irony in the fact that the classic sociocultural literature—with its emphasis on the self-regulating aspects of community—supports the position of the multinationals (p. 660).

Indeed, read cumulatively, the new field studies of regulation and rights do present a very mixed picture of the efficacy of top-down regulation—generally celebrated in the context of human rights but assessed more negatively in other areas, e.g., in relation to the regulation of schools (see discussion, below) or criminalization of various forms of consumption (on drugs, crime, and criminalization, see Allaste & Lagerspetz 2005, Garland 2005, Parnell & Kane 2003). Merry (2006, chapter 7, especially p. 223) notes as a "conundrum" the fact that the "vernacularization" of human rights law requires and expands state power. In light of these studies of the extent to which the transnational private sector escapes state regulation, relatively impoverished and weak states may embrace human rights law as an alternative means of legitimizing their legality, given constraints on delivering goods in either literal or figurative terms.

Studies of the corporations' evasions of law lend some additional substance to analyses of the expanding market orientation of political and economic infrastructure in terms of neoliberal reform (Henisz et al. 2005, Brady et al. 2005). Questions of trust in government become a trenchant question in relation to the relative efficacy of public sector and private sector power (Wallace & Latcheva 2006, Dalton 2005).

These and the studies of rights discussed below underscore the theoretical importance of understanding neoliberalism as a significant shift in the relative powers of states and private entities, with consequences for both the market for law and the relevance of law to the very framing of social problems in the public sphere (see Benson & Saguy 2005, Jennings 2003). In other words, rights consciousness (or legal consciousness) does not face law as its sole referent. As new studies make clear, social embeddedness as well as the nexus of institutional powers confronting individuals and communities (e.g., state versus corporate) are crucial to making commitments to rights actualities, and indeed to the self-identity of rights-bearing subjects.

Individual Rights

Current field studies of rights consciousness—as evidenced in what Engel (2005, p. 470) calls "injury narratives"—suggest the nature of the crosscurrents that shape the contemporary terrain of rights claims. On the one hand, individuals appear to be aware of their rights (Albiston 2005, Engel 2005, Hoffmann 2005, Marshall 2005). On the other hand, rights claims constitute only one option among other courses of action that may be more compelling for various reasons. In her study of the impact of the U.S. Family and Medical Leave Act on workers' claims against employers, Albiston (2005, p. 11) notes that rights are "not always the dominant normative system, [but] legal entitlements help make the contradictions in workers' circumstances more visible." Hoffman's (2005) study of dispute resolution in a worker cooperative shows strong gender effects. Men are reluctant to confront supervisors in formal processes, and they use their informal networks to pursue complaints. Women's preferences are similar, but they nonetheless tend to use formal processes because they lack informal networks for resolving grievances. Remedial processes set in place as implementation of state policy might be accessible yet unproductive; Marshall's (2005) study of women's efforts to press sexual harassment claims in the workplace shows them to be thwarted by obstacles arising from the procedures themselves.

Workplace health care is also a subject for field studies of law in relation to the unintended consequences (or outright failures) of policies in place to protect workers [see Absar (2003) and the special issue of the *British Journal of Sociology* (Heath & Button 2002)]. In this context, mass injury and AIDS/HIV are read as signs of social crisis as well as a crisis of citizenship (Fortun 2001, Petryna 2002, Chikwendu 2004). Education, particularly in primary and secondary schools, also emerges as a broad field site for examining the effects of exposure of vulnerable populations (children and adolescents) to law through curriculum, language policy, and multicultural policy, as well as discipline and policing (including drug testing, exclusions, searches, and surveillance) (Aumeerally 2005, Parry 2005, Essex 2005, Monk 2005, Montgomery 2005, Russo & Maurdsley 2004, Varnham 2005).

In short, social embedding cannot guarantee the efficacy of rights, yet without some localized community supportive of rights discourse (not to speak of forums for pressing rights claims), individual rights consciousness drifts into other idioms of justice, e.g., health or religion (among other things). Engel's (2005) study of the transformation of legal consciousness in northern Thailand compares current findings with his field data from 30 years ago. Focusing on the effects of globalization on legal consciousness "at ground level" (p. 471), Engel challenges the commonplace premise that globalization means the export of American and European ideas, muting cultural differences with homogenizing effects. On the contrary, Engel's findings confirm "a trend *away* from liberal legalism among ordinary people in Thailand and a diminished regard for and use of law and legal institutions" (Engel 2005, p. 472). Although his interviewees acknowledge rights and law, new forms of social distance between states and citizens on the one hand and among individuals on the other make legal rights relatively abstract compared with the immediacy of a justice discourse derived from personal religious belief. Engel emphasizes the eclectic and improvisatory nature of individuals' interpretive frameworks, yet also their intensity.

In sum, without local institutions that support rights claims as a basis for interpreting injury and seeking redress, individuals appear unlikely to invoke even those rights of which they are well aware. And even when such institutional conditions hold, constraints arising from workplace hierarchies and lack of employment alternatives may exert a powerful draw toward informal procedures or toward nonaction. Although this latter point is not in itself new, its contemporary relevance is a commentary on how much private sector enterprises elude substantive demands of rights. Read together, these and other field studies of rights in action underscore the extent to which the pervasive marketization of former state sectors, privatization, and the restructuring of employment alter conditions of life and work in ways that profoundly affect people's understandings and expectations of their own status as citizens or aliens (see Abdullah 2005, Bauman 2005, Coleman 2004, Gilbert 2005, Golden & Sabbagh 2005, Ho et al. 2002, Keil & Boudreau 2005, Kong 2005, Kruegger 2004, Marwell 2004, Nichols 2003, Nyers 2006, Pieterse 2004, Reed 2005, Thomas 2004).

Current scholarship offers much evidence that urban life overexposes individuals to naked power and violence (Goldstein 2004, Taussig 2003; cf. Fassin 2005, Peteet 2005). The pragmatics of everyday living entail dependence on private and public institutions for material provision and other forms of security, thereby subjecting individuals and communities to a wide and varied range of social controls apart from law. These appear to intensify the discriminatory effects of status differences (gender, age, nationality, indigeneity, etc.), with only the most uneven—if any—protection of law (on difference and vulnerability, see Bedford 2005; Douglas 2005; Hagan et al. 2005; Jacobs et al. 2005; Mason 2005; May & Smart 2004; Messner et al. 2004, 2005; Nijhawan 2005; Soule & Olzak 2004; Ungaro 2005).

At the same time, urban field studies also point strongly to the importance of cultural policy and municipal initiatives (especially in the arts) as offering new contexts for self-identification, democratic participation, and innovative collective endeavors (e.g., McGuigan 2005, Hughson 2004, Bailey et al. 2004; cf. Jennings 2003). From this standpoint, it is perhaps not surprising that it is in municipalities that citizenship, subjectivity, and state legality appear to be most thickly entwined in the operations of the public sphere (see West 2005), for good or for ill, and where legal polycentricity has active social support in at least some areas of personal rights (e.g., same sex marriage, Doms 2004).

Indigenous Rights

Although individuals' energies and options for pursuing rights claims may be constrained in the ways mentioned above, an important new body of field-based scholarship points to the emergence of new legal claimants and claims in indigenous and ethnic communities. Indigenous and ethnic groups are increasingly turning to state (i.e., national) courts to assert and defend collective interests in intellectual property, land, language rights, and sovereignty (Comaroff & Comaroff 2005). In their ethnographic study of postapartheid South Africa, Comaroff & Comaroff (2004) point to a new "culture of constitutionalism, legality and rights" (p. 521), positing a dialectical interdependence of cultural identity and state formation in courts' mediations of cultural practices associated with witchcraft and related forms of violence. In the "neoliberal epoch," the legalization of politics is, they suggest, endemic to "postcolonial nation-states," lending them "their delicate sense of unity and coherence" (p. 539).

Indeed, mutual if highly asymmetrical investments of states and indigenous claimants may be a condition of postcolonial constitutionalism: "The language of legality" lends "postcolonial regimes, bereft of many of the political and economic resources of modern governance" an expedient means of "delineat[ing] the moral frontiers of civil society" (Comaroff & Comaroff 2004, p. 539), putting postcolonial states on "both sides of an unresolvable equation" between "moral relativism and liberal universalism, of cultural difference and legal rationality" (p. 540).

If litigation offers claimants an arena in which they might secure cultural (or more broadly, community) recognition, that process is complicated by tensions between relatively impoverished states and a powerful transnational private sector. Culture and tradition are contested ground between them (Coombe 2005, pp. 35–37). New field studies show indigenous claimants to be knowledgeable if not always successful legal players in relation to powerful global industries—notably pharmaceutical bioprospecting and tourism—seeking to capitalize on their cultural and material resources (for a field study of pharmaceutical firms' involvements in clinical trials among indigenous communities and other marginalized groups, see Petryna 2005). Indigenous groups challenge those agendas in courts of law—defending their rights in cultural knowledge as intellectual property, asserting claims to land, and in other registers (see Brown 2003, Comaroff & Comaroff 2005, Conklin 2002, Dombrowski 2002, Errington 2003, Glaskin 2003, Hale 2006, Haviland 2003, Hodgson 2002a,b, Richland 2005, Sylvain 2002, Visarro & Bastine 2003, Whiteley 2003; intellectual property rights are the subject of new field studies beyond the indigenous context; see Akalemwa 2005, Griffin 2005, Pottage & Mundy 2004, Rose 2005). In the United States, casinos and gaming have become inextricably tied to broader claims to territorial rights and sovereignty (Cramer 2005, Steinman 2005). More generally, as Coombe (2005, p. 52) observes, "under conditions of neoliberalism, culture is being repositioned within as well as differentiated from market forces in state practices, international policy-making, and social movements that make strategic recourse to law as they challenge its current limitations." Such developments alter the pragmatics of legal pluralism, as well as the interpretive frameworks through which legal pluralism might be understood in comparative and theoretical terms (e.g., see Habtu 2004 on ethnic pluralism in Ethiopia, Shahrani 2002 on political conflict in Afghanistan).

Human Rights

Current debates in the realm of human rights are a vivid reflection of the shifting social and political contexts of rights claims outlined above, the desedimentation of state bureaucracies under pressures of neoliberalism and war, and the reflexive challenges to received ideas about the universality of legal rationality. Given the foregoing discussion, one should not be surprised that these debates are located primarily in anthropological literature, given the populations marked out as potential beneficiaries, as well as the issues of cultural translation associated with the reception of international human rights law at the local level (for reviews of these debates, see Merry 2006 and contributions to Goodale 2006). Recent field studies concentrate around two related debates. One debate involves questions about rights, remedies, and access to law, framed ethnographically around the processes by which international human rights law attains local meaning and efficacy. Yet framing human rights in terms of local reception of an external legality raises further debate surrounding the questions of whether the local and the global are distinct levels, and indeed whether the concept of culture entails an inside and outside (e.g., as distinct spheres). Contemporary ethnography points in the direction of "no" to both of these questions; legal practice, however, anchored to notions of national sovereignty, points in the direction of "yes." Riles's intensely reflexive analysis of human rights as disciplinary knowledge practice takes up this contradiction as an ethnographic object in itself, exploring the disciplinary epistemologies of anthropology and law and their associated professional practices (including professional ethics).

Riles uncovers a mutual imbrication of law and anthropology in their common discourse of the means and ends of knowledge (Riles 2006). The discourse of rights tends to conceal such elisions under a generalized notion of individual subjectivity and citizenship (individual recognition linked to territorial states). There is much to be explored in the selectivity of such notions in practice, not only as studies of gaps between ideas and practices (as in earlier socio-legal scholarship of a reformist bent) but also as a reflexive critique of their cultural and regionalist premises.

Indeed, the very meaning of the category "culture" is today inseparable from a moral geography of human rights in which culture is featured as the rupture of some universal ideal. Thus, Visweswaran (2004, p. 484) explores the salience of gender violence as a trope through which "the language of universal feminism and human rights recreates patterns of cultural deviance which fall disproportionately upon some nations and geographical areas, and not upon others" (see also Gatens 2004, West-Newman 2005). Recent symposium issues of *Political and Legal Anthropology Review* and *American Anthropologist* present major collections on human rights themes, valuable both for the originality of their ethnography and their fresh theorizing beyond the universalist-particularist paradigm [see Speed & Sierra (2005) on human rights in neoliberal governance, Jean-Klein & Riles (2005) on human rights administration, and Goodale (2006) on the implications of human rights for anthropological practice]. Wilson's (2005) edited volume on human rights in the context of the war on terror takes human rights debates in a different direction, emphasizing international human rights as "democratic political values" (p. 28), the implementation of which would set some checks on war-making powers, as well as on the conduct of war, treatment of prisoners, and counterterrorism (including burdens on military and civilian civil liberties; see also Agozino 2004, Dabbagh 2004, Davis & Silver 2004, Huddy et al. 2005, Kilshaw 2004, Nafi 2004).

Recent field studies of rights, and especially human rights, underscore how much the conditions of social life, including the lifeways of law, make fieldwork urgent and, at the same time, preclude a neutral point of observation. The latter theme is explicit in the new accounts by anthropologists (cited above). The collapse of an external perspective should not be misunderstood as an abandonment of scientific rigor, but, quite the contrary, as a sign of the way state power itself operates unevenly and ambiguously in relation to the political communities in whose name it functions and in which field research is critically embedded. Socio-legal scholars once imagined all social relations as encompassed by law, or, critical of that notion, resistant to it; however, these recent field studies reflect the ethnographic specificity of those claims and the political assumptions (and historical contingencies) implicit in a presumed antithesis between local and translocal legal fields.

THE WAR ON TERROR

Blurring the distinction between activism and social analysis is most vivid in the context of the war on terror. As in the human rights context, this situation should not be read (or read not only) in terms of the pull of partisanship; as in that other context, that would be too superficial a reading, one that fails to take into account the theoretical significance of current research. Rather, the new terms of engagement suggest a discursive shift in the law-society relation such that the new public discourse leaves little in the way of neutral ground. One measure of this new state of affairs in the field of discourse is the difficulty of finding some alternative to the very phrase "war on terror" that does not immediately plunge discussion into contest over the war and its history in policy on and off the fields of battle.

But in broader terms, too, the condensation of analytic vocabulary into political discourse is noteworthy as a development at once ethical and epistemological. To illustrate with just one pair of examples: In a world where the term culture now bears powerful connotations of "the clash of civilizations" (Huntington 1996) or of "friend" and "enemy" (Schmitt 1996), and where law rests on claims as to totalizing demands of security (construed as the physical surface of all of society), those who labor in the fields of the human sciences cannot but find themselves caught out in their efforts to hold onto culture as an analytical term reserved for their own craft. Academic lawyers—attuned to the legal technicalities of the new situation, accustomed to theorizing state practice, and socialized to a professional practice that is explicitly evaluative and normative—are, not surprisingly, in the broad vanguard of a new literature on the production of legality in the context of the war on terror. The new security scenario, likely to remain an ongoing state of affairs for some time, will no doubt affect the ways scholars conceptualize their endeavors and debate their merits (Lutz 2002).

Current writing on the war on terror in the law field is strongly text- and practice-based, reflecting the extent to which the legality of the war on terror rests on specific constructions of legal texts. The legal strategy of the war focuses on issues of interpretive authority, textual meaning, and specialized forms of knowledge. Accordingly, fieldwork on the war on terror leans strongly in the direction of these same issues as constituting politicized forms of social action—i.e., toward the institutional and official practices (including contestation) that account for law's discursive production, and indeed the discursive production of specific laws.[4] My review of law school working papers and law reviews was largely restricted to U.S. materials—their focus, not surprisingly, on the George W. Bush administration. Studies are broadly divided in focus between war powers and security issues beyond the war in Iraq and are almost uniformly critical of the administration's justifications of special executive powers and modifications of checks and balances.

The legality of the war and the treatment of detainees are major themes (see Drumbl 2005; Gross 2003, 2004; Jonakait 2005; Levinson 2004; Margulies 2003; McCormack 2005; Muller 2002; Murphy 2004; O'Connell 2006; Roach & Trotter 2005; Smith 2003; Strauss 2006; Vladeck 2004; see also Davies 2004). Security issues focus primarily on domestic law, such as racial profiling (Ellman 2002–2003, Hellman 2003), civil liberties (Bellia 2005, Chesney 2003, Scheppele 2004c), community response (Umbreit et al. 2003), emergency preparedness (Gross 2003, 2004), surveillance (Ventura et al. 2005), prosecutions (Chesney 2005), deportations (Kanstroom 2005), presidential powers (Damrosch 2005), and even the category of terrorism itself (Richman 2003).

The war is also the context for assessments of the contemporary status of the rule of law (Mullins et al. 2004, Rothe & Muzatti 2004, Russell 2005, Welch 2004; see also Dudziak & Volpp 2005 and Sarat et al. 2005a on the limits of law, the *Journal of Human Rights* theme issue on the Iraq war (Cushman 2005), and the *Cambridge Review of International Affairs* theme issue on security policy in practice (Farmanfarmaian 2003). Glickman (2003) and Adebajo (2003) explore the stakes for Africans (including Africans in diaspora) in the U.S. national security strategy and its implications for U.S. Africa policy. The war is also context for studies of the rule of law in relation to human rights (Gearty 2005, Kanstroom 2005, Wilson 2005) and international law (Mansell 2004, Russell 2005, Ventura et al. 2005), as well as for studies of the role of the press (Korn 2004).

The war on terror consolidates particular forms of legality relevant beyond the security context, especially as they bear on policing and criminal justice, state accountability, the importance of transnational institutions within domestic administration (Aman 2004), the cooptation of political parties, and other conditions affecting the articulation of political communities within national states (Greenhouse 2005b). These developments—perhaps even more than the war itself—suggest the contemporary inadequacy of theorizing hegemony as a top-down force field that draws people's aspirations into line with the major interests of state and capital. Today, hegemony involves not only the power of state over society, but also—illuminated by circumstances of war's making—a redirection of the state's performative alignment with the moral discourse of its principal constituent communities

[4]Among lawyers whose attention is drawn to field study, this methodological ambiguity is by no means new to this subject matter, nor is the extent to which field studies are keyed to specific events [such as court opinions, new legislation, or, in this case, presidential orders and questions of administrative policy (see contributions to Dudziak & Volpp 2005, Levinson 2004, Sarat et al. 2005a)].

(Greenhouse 2005a) as a substitute for their active political participation and representation). In the scenarios of privatization and contracting out, the politicization of moral discourse—indeed, the politicization of discourse *as* moral—deflects and reworks politics especially through consumption. Seen in this light, the discursivity of law is central to state hegemony but primarily as a political function. Legal discourse is not necessarily produced by the state, nor does it necessarily govern state power; this is the essence of hegemony's "double-sided nature" (Beckett & Hoffman 2005, pp. 164–65).

Reconceptualizing hegemony to take account of this disjunction within neoliberal states would return us, better equipped, to the point of theoretical "impasse" presciently noted by Hall (1985, pp. 102–3)—i.e., where the ideological construction of the subject elides the very conditions that preclude subjects' political agency. Imagining hegemony as a top-down structuring of social action errs in rendering the state as an abstraction, in effect constituted by discourse, as if internalized by ordinary men and women (Abrams 1988, Mitchell 1991). That abstraction—produced discursively in the contest between welfare liberalism and emergent neoliberalism in the 1980s—nowadays functions politically as a practically limitless basis for claiming authority for states in the counterterrorism scenario. Reading the war on terror across current field studies of law—with their emphasis on the regulatory autonomy of private sector capitalism and the parlous conditions affecting rights in practice—clarifies the context in which it can be productively theorized.

CONCLUSIONS

Current field studies of law point to shifts in the theoretical and methodological terrain of socio-legal scholarship, drawing disciplines into dialogue over issues of discourse and practice. I have suggested that these should be read as signs of shifts in the social terrain of law. In this concluding section, I turn to the question of how discourse features in field studies of law, as both means and ends (to borrow Riles's phrase again), that is, as both analytical object and interpretive technique. A theory of discourse helps to account for how states are rendered social through language and the interplay of subjective experience among ordinary people in their everyday lives, as well as how states figure in history through collective identities created in these very processes. As formulated by Corrigan & Sayer (1985, p. 180), "the enormous power of 'the State' is not only external and objective; it is in equal part internal and subjective." The present moment seems above all to beg for some further precision in this regard, if only to distinguish between language that is conversationally produced and the pragmatic effects of the textual artifacts of governing (whether through states or other entities).

From the mid-1980s through the 1990s, Foucauldian concepts of discourse and governmentality tended to blur this distinction, as discourse in a sense replaced the state as a theoretical object for cultural theorists concerned with politics (Abrams 1988; Mitchell 1991; cf. Schmitt 1996, p. 19, and Weber 1978). A new canon emerged around the interplay of imagination and identity as elements of "stateness." As more recent critical syntheses of that cultural turn emphasize, the relevance of the state to social theory in effect shifted to its salience as *a* discourse, i.e., the idea of the state (Axel 2002, Hansen & Stepputat 2001, Steinmetz 1999). Today, the "state idea" (Abrams 1988) may still be inseparable from contemporary practices of collective self-identity, but it is clear that states reciprocate this gesture only when pressed, as the studies of new litigation by indigenous and ethnic claimants suggest. In other contexts, it is not at all clear that the state is available as an addressee. As noted, current field studies yield evidence of a broad transition in this regard, as personal self-identity withdraws from the state, and communities form around nonstate arenas such as arts and sports.

In the mid-1980s, discourse and governmentality displaced the state as theoretical objects for cultural theorists at the precise historical juncture when liberalism reached its maximum point of tension within the emergent neoliberal state in the United States (and in different terms in the United Kingdom). The ideological commitment to bringing an end to big government and state regulation under Reagan and Thatcher made privatization the cornerstone not just of the new economic order but also of a new political and social order in which identity was to be specifically devalued as a basis for rights claims and collective representation. The idea that the state had become an abstraction, internalized as social effects or merged with political identity, can perhaps be accounted for, in retrospect, in the novelty of privatization and the intensity of the competition for markets of cultural expression in the 1980s.

In its generality, discourse theory preserved the form of an organic connection between state and society past its actuality as a political limit, rendering identity ambiguously and ambivalently public and private.[5] Foucault's concept of governmentality adjoins the state to identity through a conceptual merging of legality and social knowledge (Foucault 1978; 1980, especially chapters 5 and 10; Santos 1995, pp. 3–4, 405). From this vantage point (i.e., ambiguously fused to social identity), state power is theoretically inexhaustible. Indeed, identity is precisely what the current security discourse takes as its most public idiom—positively as the moral community of citizens, negatively as the terrorist. This is key to the functionality of state hegemony: the superficially unlimited capacity of government spokesmen to take up and deploy community discourses in justification of state action outside of representative institutions (i.e., legislatures and the local workings of political parties). Such claims to knowledge relations may at a certain point reach the limits of tolerable doubt (e.g., as questions of actionable intelligence), but whether such doubts limit state power is a political, rather than a theoretical, question. Field studies of law perhaps above all represent an affirmation of the salience of such critical junctures, regrounding and reclaiming them for theoretical work.

[5]Ethnographers' and socio-legal scholars' concerns with identity, representation, agency, and discourse in the terrains of everyday legal and political practice at this time may be read as specialized articulations of these same social currents—in effect tracking the escape of neoliberal legality into the categories of everyday life.

By their very attention to the contemporary fields of discursive production and deployment, current field studies demonstrate that discourse neither explains nor expresses the state. The state is not an actor; it does not speak. State agency is not bound to the rules of syntax nor of discursive coherence in the way that political agency for individuals or represented groups might be (e.g., in making a legal claim). Theorizing discourse requires acknowledgment of these zones of silence, secrecy, and the unknown, and their potential salience in channeling discourse and discursive opposition toward particular ends. Field studies of law are especially valuable in this context because only in the field can such zones be seen emerging in the midst of fully tenanted social spaces, against the light of construable alternatives. Current field studies show that law is not a unified field in this regard. They also show that state action is not automatically congruent with legality, nor is state law necessarily the highest power for individuals suffering injury or injustice, although it may be the best recourse available at a given moment, depending on the circumstances.

APPENDIX

This review is based on sources published in print or on the Internet in English—a significant limitation—for the most part since 2004 (exceptions are noted). In addition to references cited in the text, I developed my baseline, so to speak, from an extensive literature accessed initially online. I began by reviewing the entire set of abstracts (3143) published by the Social Science Research Network's Legal Research Institutes Research Papers Series (2001–2006) (http://www.ssrn.com). Through Ingenta Connect (http://www.IngentaConnect.com), I was able to review a database consisting of 952 publications in the social sciences; of these titles, I selected a subset (some 50 titles) that I either knew contained or deemed likely to contain field studies, selecting articles from an initial scan of tables of contents and relevant abstracts for all issues published in 2004 and 2005 (exceptions are noted below, with variations depending on online availability and relevance of journal content). The list of journals follows here; asterisks indicate journals in which I found articles that inform this review, some of which are cited in the references section: *Acta Juridica Hungarica* (2000–2001); **Acta Politica* (2003–2004); **Acta Sociologica* (2002–2005); **Africa* (2003–2005); **African Affairs*; **American Journal of Political Science* (2003–2006); **American Sociological Review* (2003–2005); **Anthropological Forum* (2002–2006); **Anthropology and Medicine* (2003–2005); **Arab Law Quarterly* (2003–2004); *Asia Pacific Journal on Human Rights and Law* (2002–2005); **Asian Journal of Social Science* (2002–2005); *Artificial Intelligence and Law* (2001–2004); **British Journal of Criminology* (2005); **British Journal of Social Work*; **British Journal of Sociology* (2002–2003); **Child and Family Law Quarterly*; *Cities*; **City: Analysis of Urban Trends, Culture, Theory, Policy, Action*; *Cambridge Review of International Affairs* (2003–2005); **Crime, Law and Social Change*; **Critical Criminology*; **Contemporary Justice Review*; **Contemporary Political Theory; Computer Law & Security Report*;

**Dialectical Anthropology* (2003–2005); **Discourse*; *Disasters*; **Economy & Society*; **Education and the Law*; *Educational Research*; **Information and Communications Technology Law; Inquiry; International and Comparative Law Quarterly; International Journal of Constitutional Law*; **International Journal of Cultural Policy*; **Ethnos; European Law Journal; European Studies* (2005); **Europe-Asia Studies* (formerly *Soviet Studies*) (2006); *Family Law*; **Feminist Legal Studies; History and Anthropology* (2005); *International Journal of Law and Information Technology*; **International Journal of the Sociology of Law* (2002–2003); *International Review of Sociology*; **Islamic Law and Society* (2004–2006); **Journal of Asian and African Studies* (2002–2003); *Journal of Conflict and Security Law* (2005); *Journal of Criminal Justice* (2003); *Journal of Empirical Legal Studies; Journal of Environmental Law; Journal of Gender Studies; Journal of Human Rights*; **Journal of Latin American Cultural Studies* (2005); **Journal of Law & Society* (2005); *Journal of Popular Culture; *Journal of Southern African Studies; Oxford Legal Studies; Political Science Quarterly; Review of Central and East European Law; *Security Studies*. In addition, I reviewed 2004 and 2005 volume years of *American Anthropologist, American Ethnologist, Cultural Anthropology, Journal of the Royal Anthropological Institute, Law & Policy, Law & Social Inquiry, Law & Society Review*, and *Political and Legal Anthropology Review*. I also reviewed the most recent two years of current catalogs for major academic and commercial presses with lists in socio-legal studies or relevant subject disciplines. I pursued key word, subject, and author searches through Princeton's Firestone Library catalog and accepted suggestions (gratefully) from faculty and student colleagues. Even with these extensive resources at hand, I make no claim to have accomplished a comprehensive or wholly systematic review of the field(s) of law in the field. Any alert reader will notice omissions, but I hope it will nonetheless serve as a rough guide toward conversations and sources of which they might not have been previously aware.

ACKNOWLEDGMENTS

I gratefully acknowledge constructive collegial readings by Annelise Riles, John Comaroff, Hendrik Hartog, and Richard Wilson. My thanks, too, for permission to draw on unpublished work by Jean and John Comaroff, and Richard Wilson. Errors, including errors of omission, are my own.

The *Annual Review of Law and Social Science* is online at http://lawsocsci.annualreviews.org

LITERATURE CITED

Abdullah N. 2005. Foreign bodies at work: good, docile and other-ed. *Asian J. Soc. Sci.* 33(2):223–45

Abrams P. 1988. Notes on the difficulty of studying the state. *J. Hist. Sociol.* 1(1):58–89

Absar SS. 2003. Health hazards and labor laws in Bangladesh: a narrative-based study of women garment workers. *Asian J. Soc. Sci.* 31(3):452–77

Adebajo A. 2003. America in an age of terror. *J. Asian Afr. Stud.* 38(2–3):175–91

Agamben G. 2005. *State of Exception*. Transl. K Attell. Chicago: Univ. Chicago Press

Agozino B. 2004. The Iraq war did not take place: sociological implications of a conflict that was neither a just war nor just a war. *Int. Rev. Sociol.* 14(1):73–88

Akalemwa N. 2005. The nature of the international intellectual property system: universal norms and values or Western chauvinism? *Inf. Commun. Technol. Law* 14(1):59–79

Albiston CR. 2005. Bargaining in the shadow of social institutions: competing discourses and social change in workplace mobilization of civil rights. *Law Soc. Rev.* 39(1):11–50

Allaste AA, Lagerspetz M. 2005. Drugs and doublethink in a marginalized community. *Crit. Criminol.* 13(3):267–85

Aman AC Jr. 2004. *Democracy Deficit: Taming Globalization with Law Reform*. New York: NY Univ. Press

Aumeerally NL. 2005. The ambivalence of postcolonial Mauritius. *Int. J. Cult. Policy* 11(3):307–23

Axel B. 2002. *From the Margins: Historical Anthropology and Its Futures*. Durham, NC: Duke Univ. Press

Bailey C, Miles S, Stark P. 2004. Culture-led urban regeneration and the revitalization of identities in Newcastle, Gateshead and the north east of England. *Int. J. Cult. Policy* 10(1):47–65

Bauman Z. 2005. Seeking shelter in Pandora's box. *City: Anal. Urban Trends Cult. Theory Policy Action* 9(2):161–68

Beckett K, Hoffman B. 2005. Challenging medicine: law, resistance, and the cultural politics of childbirth. *Law Soc. Rev.* 39(1):125–70

Bedford K. 2005. Loving to straighten out development. *Fem. Leg. Stud.* 13(3):295–322

Bellia P. 2005. Spyware and the limits of surveillance law. *Berkeley Technol. Law J.* 20:1283–344

Benson R, Saguy AC. 2005. Constructing social problems in an age of globalization: a French-American comparison. *Am. Sociol. Rev.* 700(2):233–59

Brady D, Beckfield J, Seeleib-Kaiser M. 2005. Economic globalization and the welfare state in affluent democracies, 1975–2001. *Am. Sociol. Rev.* 70(6):921–48

Brown M. 2003. *Who Owns Native Culture?* Cambridge, MA: Harvard Univ. Press

Cavell S. 1984. *Themes Out of School: Effects and Causes*. Chicago: Univ. Chicago Press

Chesney R. 2003. Civil liberties and the terrorism prevention paradigm. *Mich. Law Rev.* 101:1409–50

Chesney R. 2005. The sleeper scenario: terrorism-support laws and the demands of prevention. *Harvard J. Legis.* 42(1):1–89

Chikwendu E. 2004. AIDS/HIV—when the state fails: NGOs in grassroots AIDS care. *Dialect. Anthropol.* 28(3–4):245–59

Coleman R. 2004. Images from a neoliberal city: the state, surveillance and social control. *Crit. Criminol.* 12(1):21–42

Comaroff J, Comaroff J. 2004. Policing culture, cultural policing: law and social order in postcolonial South Africa. *Law Soc. Inq.* 29(3):513–45

Comaroff J, Comaroff J. 2005. *Ethnicity, Inc.* Presented to the Program Law Public Aff., Princeton Univ., Oct. 24

Conklin BA. 2002. Shamans versus pirates in the Amazonian treasure chest. *Am. Anthropol.* 104(4):1050–61

Coombe RJ. 2005. Legal claims to culture in and against the market. *Law Cult. Human.* 1(1):35–52

Corrigan P, Sayer D. 1985. *The Great Arch: English State Formation as Cultural Revolution*. Oxford: Blackwell

Coutin SB. 2002. *Legalizing Moves: Salvadoran Immigrants' Struggle for U.S. Residency*. Ann Arbor: Univ. Mich. Press

Coutin SB. 2005. Being en route. *Am. Anthropol.* 107(2):195–206

Cramer RA. 2005. Perceptions of the process: Indian gaming as it affects federal tribal acknowledgment law and practices. *Law Policy* 27(4):578–605

Cushman T, ed. 2005. Theme issue on the war in Iraq. *J. Hum. Rights*, Vol. 4, No. 1

Dabbagh NT. 2004. Narrative expressions of despair under occupation. *Anthropol. Med.* 11(2):201–20

Dalton R. 2005. The social transformation of trust in government. *Rev. Sociol.* 15(1):133–54

Damrosch LF. 2005. Comment: war and uncertainty. *Yale Law J.* 114(6):1405–17

Davies P. 2004. Intelligence culture and intelligence failure in Britain and the United States. *Cambridge Rev. Int. Aff.* 17(3):495–520

Davis DW, Silver BD. 2004. Civil liberties versus security: public opinion in the context of the terrorist attacks on America. *Am. J. Polit. Sci.* 48(1):28–46

Dombrowski K. 2002. The praxis of indigenism and Alaska native timber politics. *Am. Anthropol.* 104(4):1062–73

Doms K. 2004. Cultural emergence, legal polycentricity and same-sex couples' right to marry. *J. Gend. Stud.* 13(3):271–74

Douglas H. 2005. "She knew what was expected of her": the white legal system's encounter with traditional marriage. *Fem. Leg. Stud.* 13(2):181–203

Drumbl MA. 2005. *Guantanamo, Rasul and the twilight of law.* Washington and Lee Univ. Leg. Stud. Res. Pap. 05–04 (http://ssrn.com/abstract = 685624)

Dudziak ML, Volpp L, eds. 2005. Legal borderlands: law and the construction of American borders. *Am. Q.* 57(3) Special issue

Ellman S. 2002–2003. Racial profiling and terrorism. *NY Law School Law Rev.* 46:675–730

Endeshaw A. 2004. Internet regulation in China: the never-ending cat and mouse game. *Inf. Commun. Technol. Law* 13(1):41–57

Engel DM. 2005. Globalization and the decline of legal consciousness: torts, ghosts, and karma in Thailand. *Law Soc. Inq.* 30(3):469–514

Errington J. 2003. Getting language rights: the rhetorics of language, endangerment, and change. *Am. Anthropol.* 105(4):723–32

Essex N. 2005. Student privacy rights involving strip searches. *Educ. Law* 17(3):105–10

Farmanfarmaian R, ed. 2003. Theme issue on security policy in practice. *Cambridge Rev. Int. Aff.*, Vol. 16, No. 3

Fassin D. 2005. Compassion and repression: the moral economy of immigration economies in France. *Cult. Anthropol.* 20(3):362–87

Fortun K. 2001. *Advocacy After Bhopal: Environmentalism, Disaster, New Global Orders.* Chicago: Univ. Chicago Press

Foucault M. 1978. *The History of Sexuality.* Vol. 1: *An Introduction.* Transl. R Hurley. New York: Pantheon

Foucault M. 1980. *Power/Knowledge: Selected Interviews and Other Writings, 1972—1977.* Transl. ed. C Gordon. New York: Pantheon

Garland D. 2005. Penal excess and surplus meaning: public torture lynchings in twentieth-century America. *Law Soc. Rev.* 39(4):793–33

Gatens M. 2004. Can human rights accommodate women's rights? Towards an embodied account of social norms, social meaning, and cultural change. *Contemp. Polit. Theory* 3(3):275–99

Gearty C. 2005. 11 September 2001; counter-terrorism and the Human Rights Act. *J. Law Soc.* 32(1):18–33

Gezelius SS. 2002. Do norms count? State regulation and compliance in a Norwegian fishing community. *Acta Sociol.* 45(4):305–14

Gilbert L. 2005. Resistance in the neoliberal city. *City: Anal. Urban Trends Cult. Theory Policy Action* 9(1):23–32

Glaskin K. 2003. Native title and the 'bundle of rights' model. *Anthropol. Forum* 13(1):67–88

Glickman H. 2003. Africa in the war on terrorism. *J. Asian Afr. Stud.* 38(2–3):162–74

Golden D, Sabbagh C. 2005. Immigration and justice: the allocation of goods to newcomers from the (former) Soviet Union in Israel. *Contemp. Justice Rev.* 8(3):251–64

Goldstein D. 2004. *The Spectacular City: Violence and Performance in Urban Bolivia.* Durham, NC: Duke Univ. Press

Goodale M, ed. 2006. In focus: human rights in a new key. *Am. Anthropol.* 108(1):1–83

Grattet R, Jenness V. 2005. The reconstitution of law in local settings: agency discretion, ambiguity, and a surplus of law in the policing of hate crime. *Law Soc. Rev.* 39(4):893–941

Greenhouse CJ. 2005a. Hegemony and hidden transcripts. *Am. Anthropol.* 107(3):356–68

Greenhouse CJ. 2005b. Nationalizing the local: comparative notes on the recent restructuring of political space. In *Human Rights in the 'War on Terror,'* ed. RA Wilson, pp. 184–208. Cambridge, UK: Cambridge Univ. Press

Griffin J. 2005. The need for a new paradigm in IP law: a focus on authorship. *Inf. Commun. Technol. Law* 14(3):267–78

Gross O. 2003. Chaos and rules: should responses to violent crises always be constitutional? *Yale Law J.* 112(5):1011–35

Gross O. 2004. Are torture warrants warranted? Pragmatic absolutism and official disobedience. *Minn. Law Rev.* 88(6):1481–555

Habtu A. 2004. Ethnic pluralism as an organizing principle of the Ethiopian Federation. *Dialect. Anthropol.* 28(2):91–123

Hacking I. 2004. Between Michel Foucault and Erving Goffman: between discourse in the abstract and face-to-face interaction. *Econ. Soc.* 33(3):277–302

Hagan J, Shedd C, Payne MR. 2005. Race, ethnicity and youth perceptions of criminal injustice. *Am. Sociol. Rev.* 70(3):381–407

Hale C. 2006. Activist research v. cultural critique: indigenous land rights and the contradictions of politically engaged ethnography. *Cult. Anthropol.* 21(1):96–120

Hall S. 1985. Signification, representation, ideology: Althusser and poststructuralist debates. *Crit. Stud. Mass Commun.* 2(2):91–114

Hansen TB, Stepputat F. 2001. *States of Imagination: Ethnographic Exploration of the Postcolonial State*. Durham, NC: Duke Univ. Press

Haviland JB. 2003. Ideologies of language: some reflections on language and U.S. law. *Am. Anthropol.* 105(4):764–74

He X. 2005. Why do they not comply with the law? Illegality and semilegality among rural-urban migrant entrepreneurs in Beijing. *Law Soc. Rev.* 39(3):527–62

Heath CC, Button G, eds. 2002. Special issue on workplace studies. *Br. J. Sociol.*, Vol. 53, No. 2

Hellman D. 2003. *Classification and fair treatment: an essay on the moral and legal permissibility of profiling*. Univ. Maryland Pub-Law Res. Pap. No. 2003-04. http:/ssrn.com/abstract = 456460

Hendley K. 2004. Business litigation in the transition: a portrait of debt collection in Russia. *Law Soc. Rev.* 38(2):305–48

Henisz W, Zelner BA, Guillen MF. 2005. The worldwide diffusion of market-oriented infrastructure reform, 1977–1999. *Am. Sociol. Rev.* 70(6):871–97

Ho KC, Baber Z, Khondker H. 2002. "Sites" of resistance: alternative websites and state-society relations. *Br. J. Sociol.* 53(1):127–48

Hodgson D. 2002a. Introduction: comparative perspectives on the indigenous rights movements of Africa and the Americas. *Am. Anthropol.* 104(4):1037–49

Hodgson D. 2002b. Precarious alliances: the cultural politics and structural predicaments of an indigenous rights movement in Tanzania. *Am. Anthropol.* 104(4):1086–97

Hoffmann EA. 2005. Dispute resolution in a worker cooperative: formal procedures and procedural justice. *Law Soc. Rev.* 39(1):51–82

Huddy L, Feldman S, Taber C, Lahav G. 2005. Threat, anxiety, and support of antiterrorism politics. *Am. J. Polit. Sci.* 49(3):593–608

Hughson J. 2004. Sport in the "city of culture." *Int. J. Cult. Policy* 10(3):319–30

Huntington SP. 1996. *The Clash of Civilizations and the Remaking of World Order*. New York: Simon & Schuster

Jacobs D, Carmichael JT, Kent S. 2005. Vigilantism, current racial threat, and death sentences. *Am. Sociol. Rev.* 70(4):656–77

Jean-Klein I, Riles A. 2005. Introducing discipline: anthropology and human rights administrations. Symposium:

anthropology and human rights administrations: expert observation and representation after the fact. *Polit. Leg. Anthropol. Rev.* 28(2):173–202

Jennings MK. 2003. Local problem agendas in the Chinese countryside as viewed by cadres and villagers. *Acta Polit.* 38(4):313–32

Jonakait RN. 2005. Rasul v. Bush: unanswered questions. *William & Mary Bill Rights J.* 13:1103–38

Kanstroom D. 2005. Legal lines shifting in the sand: immigration law and human rights in the wake of September 11. *Boston Coll. Third World Law J.* 25:1–12

Keil R, Boudreau JA. 2005. Is there regionalism after municipal amalgamation in Toronto? *City: Anal. Urban Trends Cult. Theory Policy Action* 9(1):9–22

Kilshaw S. 2004. Friendly fire. *Anthropol. Med.* 11(2):149–60

Kong L. 2005. The sociality of cultural industries. *Int. J. Cult. Policy* 11(1):61–76

Korn A. 2004. Israeli press and the war against terrorism: the construction of the 'liquidation policy.' *Crime Law Soc. Change* 41(3):209–34

Kruegger O. 2004. The Internet as distributor and mirror of religious and ritual knowledge. *Asian J. Soc. Sci.* 32(2):183–97

Latour B. 2004. Scientific objects and legal objectivity. In *Anthropology and the Construction of the Social: Making Persons and Things*, ed. A Pottage, M Mundy, pp. 73–114. Cambridge, UK: Cambridge Univ. Press

Levinson S, ed. 2004. *Torture: A Collection.* Oxford: Oxford Univ. Press

Lutz C. 2002. Making war at home in the United States: militarization and the current crisis. *Am. Anthropol.* 104(3):723–35

Mansell W. 2004. Goodbye to all that? The rule of law, international law, the United States, and the use of force. *J. Law Soc.* 31(4):433–56

Margulies P. 2003. Judging terror in the 'zone of twilight': exigency, institutional equity, and procedure after September 11. *Boston Univ. Law Rev.* 84:383–443

Marshall AM. 2005. Idle rights: employees' rights consciousness and the construction of sexual harassment policies. *Law Soc. Rev.* 39(1):83–124

Marwell NP. 2004. Privatizing the welfare state. *Am. Sociol. Rev.* 69(2):265–91

Mason G. 2005. Hate crime and the image of the stranger. *Br. J. Criminol.* 45(6):837–59

Maurer B. 2005a. Due diligence and 'reasonable man,' offshore. *Cult. Anthropol.* 20(4):474–505

Maurer B. 2005b. *Mutual Life, Limited: Islamic Banking, Alternative Currencies, Lateral Reason.* Princeton, NJ: Princeton Univ. Press

May V, Smart C. 2004. Silence in court? Hearing children in residence and contact disputes. *Child Fam. Law Q.* 16(3):305–15

McCormack W. 2005. Emergency powers and terrorism. *Mil. Law Rev.* 185:69–148

McGuigan J. 2005. Neo-liberalism, culture and policy. *Int. J. Cult. Policy* 11(3):229–41

Merry SE. 2005. Anthropology and activism: research human rights across porous boundaries. *Polit. Leg. Anthropol. Rev.* 28(2):240–57

Merry SE. 2006. *Human Rights and Gender Violence: Translating International Law into Local Justice.* Chicago: Univ. Chicago Press

Messner SF, Baller RD, Zevenbergen MP. 2005. The legacy of lynching and southern homicide. *Am. Sociol. Rev.* 70(4):633–55

Messner SF, Baumer EP, Rosenfeld R. 2004. Dimensions of social capital and rates of criminal homicide. *Am. Sociol. Rev.* 69(6):882–907

Middleton DJ. 2005. The legal and regulatory response to solicitors involved in serious fraud. *Br. J. Criminol.* 45(6):810–36

Mitchell T. 1991. The limits of the state: beyond statist approaches and their critics. *Am. Polit. Sci. Rev.* 85(1):77–96

Monk D. 2005. (Re)constructing the head teacher: legal narratives and the politics of school exclusions. *J. Law Soc.* 32(3):399–423

Montgomery K. 2005. Imagining the antiracist state: representations of racism in Canadian history textbooks. *Discourse* 26(4):427–42

Moran MH. 2006. *Liberia: The Violence of Democracy*. Philadelphia: Univ. Pa. Press

Muller E. 2002. 12/7 and 9/11: war, liberties, and the lessons of history. *West Va. Law Rev.* 104(2):571–92

Mullins C, Kauzlarich D, Rothe D. 2004. The International Criminal Court and the control of state crime: prospects and problems. *Crit. Criminol.* 12(3):285–308

Murphy S. 2004. Assessing the legality of invading Iraq. *Georgetown Law J.* 92(2):173–257

Nafi BM. 2004. Fatwa and war: on the allegiance of the American Muslim soldiers in the aftermath of September 11. *Islamic Law Soc.* 11(1):78–116

Nichols T. 2003. Signs of change in Turkey's working class: workers' age-related perceptions in the modern manufacturing sector. *Br. J. Sociol.* 54(4):527–46

Nijhawan M. 2005. Deportability, medicine and the law. *Anthropol. Med.* 12(3):271–85

Nyers P. 2006. The accidental citizen: acts of sovereignty and (un)making citizenship. *Econ. Soc.* 35(2):22–41

O'Connell M-E. 2006. Affirming the ban on harsh interrogation. *Ohio State Law J.* 66(6):1231–67

Parnell PC, Kane SC, eds. 2003. *Crime's Power: Anthropologists and the Ethnography of Crime*. New York: Palgrave Macmillan

Parry G. 2005. Camera/video phones in schools: law and practice. *Educ. Law* 17(3):73–85

Peteet J. 2005. *Landscape of Hope and Despair: Palestinian Refugee Camps*. Philadelphia: Univ. Pa. Press

Petryna A. 2002. *Life Exposed: Biological Citizenship After Chernobyl*. Princeton, NJ: Princeton Univ. Press

Petryna A. 2005. Ethical variability: drug development and globalizing clinical trials. *Am. Ethnol.* 32(2):183–97

Pieterse JN. 2004. Capitalisms: Asian-European dialogue after Enron. *Asian J. Soc. Sci.* 32(2):274–89

Pottage A, Mundy M, eds. 2004. *Law, Anthropology, and the Constitution of the Social: Making Persons and Things*. Cambridge, UK: Cambridge Univ. Press

Reed A. 2005. "My blog is me": texts and persons in UK online journal culture (and anthropology). *Ethnos* 70(2):220–42

Richland JB. 2005. "What are you going to do with the village's knowledge?" Talking tradition, talking law in Hopi Tribal Court. *Law Soc. Rev.* 39(2):235–71

Richman DC. 2003. *From violent crime to terrorism: the changing basis of the federal, state and local law enforcement dynamic*. Fordham Sch. Law, Pub-Law Res. Pap. No. 31. http://ssrn.com/abstract=450840

Riles A. 2006. Skepticism, intimacy and the ethnographic subject: human rights as legal knowledge. *Am. Anthropol.* 108(1):52–65

Roach K, Trotter G. 2005. Miscarriages of justice. *Pa. State. Law Rev.* 109(4):967–1041

Roitman J. 2005. *Fiscal Disobedience: An Anthropology of Economic Regulation in Central Africa*. Princeton, NJ: Princeton Univ. Press

Rothe D, Muzatti S. 2004. Enemies everywhere: terrorism, moral panic, and U.S. civil society. *Crit. Criminol.* 12(3):327–50

Russell S. 2005. Since September 11, all roads lead to Rome. *Crit. Criminol.* 13(1):37–53

Russo C, Maurdsley R. 2004. The Supreme Court and the pledge of allegiance: a hollow victory. *Educ. Law* 16(4):261–67

Santos BS. 1995. *Toward a New Common Sense: Law, Science and Politics in the Paradigmatic Transition*. New York: Routledge

Sarat A. 2005. *Mercy on Trial: What It Means to Stop an Execution*. Princeton, NJ: Princeton Univ. Press

Sarat A, Boulanger C, eds. 2005. *The Cultural Lives of Capital Punishment: Comparative Perspectives*. Stanford, CA: Stanford Univ. Press

Sarat A, Douglas L, Umphrey MM, eds. 2005a. *The Limits of Law*. Stanford, CA: Stanford Univ. Press

Sarat A, Douglas L, Umphrey MM, eds. 2005b. *Law on the Screen*. Stanford, CA: Stanford Univ. Press

Sarat A, Scheingold SA. 2004. *Something to Believe In: Politics, Professionalism, and Cause Lawyering*. Stanford, CA: Stanford Univ. Press

Sarat A, Scheingold SA. 2005. The dynamics of cause lawyering—constraints and opportunities. In *The Worlds Cause Lawyers Make: Structure and Agency in Legal Practice*, ed. A Sarat, SA Scheingold, pp. 1–34. Stanford, CA: Stanford Univ. Press

Sarfaty G. 2005. The World Bank and the internationalization of indigenous rights norms. *Yale Law J.* 114(7):1701–818

Scheppele KL. 2004a. A realpolitik defense of social rights. *Univ. Tex. Law Rev.* 82:1921–61

Scheppele KL. 2004b. Constitutional ethnography: an introduction. *Law Soc. Rev.* 38(3):389–406

Scheppele KL. 2004c. Other people's PATRIOT Acts: Europe's response to Sept 11. *Loyola Law Rev. New Orleans* 50:89–148

Schmitt C. 1996. *The Concept of the Political*. Transl. G Schwaab. Chicago: Chicago Univ. Press

Shahrani N. 2002. War, factionalism, and the state in Afghanistan. *Am. Anthropol.* 104(3):715–22

Shamir R. 2004. Between self-regulation and the Alien Tort Claims Act: on the contested concept of corporate social responsibility. *Law Soc. Rev.* 38(4):635–64

Shvarts A. 2003. The Russian mafia: expulsion of law. *Contemp. Justice Rev.* 6(4):363–82

Smith EM. 2003. The laws of war and humanitarian law: a turbulent vista (review essay) *Glob. Gov.* 9(1):115–34

Soule SA, Olzak S. 2004. When do movements matter? The politics of ERA. *Am. Sociol. Rev.* 69(4):473–97

Speed S, Sierra M-T, eds. 2005. Theme issue: critical perspectives on human rights and multiculturalism in neoliberal Latin America. *Polit. Leg. Anthropol. Rev.* 28(1):1–50

Steinman EW. 2005. Legitimizing American Indian sovereignty: mobilizing the constitutive power of law through institutional entrepreneurship. *Law Soc. Rev.* 39(4):759–91

Steinmetz G. 1999. Introduction: culture and the state. In *State/Culture: State-Formation After the Cultural Turn*, ed. G Steinmetz, pp. 1–49. Ithaca, NY: Cornell Univ. Press

Strathern M. 2004. Social property: an interdisciplinary experiment? *Polit. Leg. Anthropol. Rev.* 27(1):23–50

Strathern M. 2005. *Kinship, Law and the Unexpected: Relatives Are Always a Surprise*. Cambridge, UK: Cambridge Univ. Press

Strauss M. 2006. Lessons of Abu Ghraib. *Ohio State Law J.* 66(6):1269–310

Suchman L, Trigg R, Blomberg J. 2002. Working artifacts: ethnomethods of the prototype. *Br. J. Sociol.* 53(2):163–79

Sylvain R. 2002. 'Land, water, and truth': San identity and global indigenism. *Am. Anthropol.* 104(4):1074–85

Taussig M. 2003. *Law in a Lawless Land: Diary of a Limpieza in Colombia*. Chicago: Univ. Chicago Press

Thomas H. 2004. Identity building and cultural projects in Butetown, Cardiff. *City: Anal. Urban Trends Cult. Theory Policy Action* 8(2):274–78

Ticktin M. 2006. Where ethics and politics meet: the violence of humanitarianism in France. *Am. Ethnol.* 33(1):33–49

Umbreit M, Lewis T, Burns H. 2003. A community response to a 9/11 hate crime: restorative justice through dialogue. *Contemp. Justice Rev.* 6(4):383–91

Ungaro D. 2005. Ecological democracy. *Rev. Sociol.* 15(2):293–303

Varnham S. 2005. Citizenship in schools: the gap between theory and practice. *Educ. Law* 17(1–2):53–64

Ventura H, Miller J, DeFlem M. 2005. Governmentality and the war on terror: FBI Project Carnivore and the diffusion of disciplinary power. *Crit. Criminol.* 13(1):55–70

Vick DW. 2004. Interdisciplinarity and the discipline of law. *J. Law Soc.* 31(2):163–93

Visarro LA, Bastine NA. 2003. The role of law in the rule of economics: a critical study of Ghana's labor laws. *J. Asian Afr. Stud.* 38(1):52–70

Visweswaran K. 2004. Gendered states: rethinking culture as a site of South Asian human rights. *Hum. Rights Q.* 26(2):483–511

Vladeck SI. 2004. Emergency power and the militia acts. *Yale Law J.* 114(1):149–94

Wallace C, Latcheva R. 2006. Economic transformation outside the law: corruption, trust in public institutions and the informal economy in transition countries of central and eastern Europe. *Eur.-Asia Stud.* 58(1):81–102

Weber M. 1978. *Economy and Society*, ed. G Roch, C Wittich. Transl. E Fischoff, H Gerth, AM Henderson, F Kolegar, CW Mills, et al., Vols. 1–2. Berkeley: Univ. Calif. Press

Welch M. 2004. Trampling human rights in the war on terror: implications to the sociology of denial. *Crit. Criminol.* 12(1):1–20

West MD. 2005. *Law in Everyday Japan: Sex, Sumo, Suicide, and Statutes*. Chicago: Univ. Chicago Press

West-Newman CL. 2005. Feeling for justice? Rights, laws and cultural contexts. *Law Soc. Inq.* 30(2):305–35

Whiteley P. 2003. Do 'language rights' serve indigenous interests? Some Hopi and other cases. *Am. Anthropol.* 205(4):712–22

Wilson RA. 2005. Human rights in the "war on terror." In *Human Rights in the "War on Terror,"* ed. RA Wilson, pp. 1–36. Cambridge, UK: Cambridge Univ. Press

Annu. Rev. Law Soc. Sci. 2006. 2:211–29
doi: 10.1146/annurev.lawsocsci.1.041604.120026

First published online as a Review in Advance on August 21, 2006

NETWORKING GOES INTERNATIONAL: An Update

Anne-Marie Slaughter[1] and David Zaring[2]
[1]*Woodrow Wilson School, Princeton University, Princeton, New Jersey 08540; email: slaughtr@princeton.edu*
[2]*Washington and Lee University School of Law, Lexington, Virginia 24450; email: zaringd@wlu.edu*

Key Words international law, international relations, regimes, transgovernmentalism

■ **Abstract** This literature review asks three questions of the scholarship on the regulatory networks that have so transformed global governance. First, what are these networks good for? We summarize the state of the literature on regulatory races, the fit between networks and the process of globalization, and the crucial role of the revolution in communications in the development of networks, introducing the topics with a brief intellectual history of regulatory network analysis in international relations and international law scholarship. Second, we examine how we can make sure that regulatory networks are good by asking this question: How might necessary and appropriate accountability mechanisms for the networks be constructed? The answers to these questions are at the foundation of a global administrative law, which is itself the subject of a burgeoning scholarly literature. Our third question concerns the way regulatory networks fit into a world where traditional intergovernmental relations and formally constituted international organizations are still important. We conclude by identifying different ways in which networks and international organizations can complement each other and by spotlighting questions for future research.

INTRODUCTION

The study of regulatory networks is entering adulthood. Legal scholars and political scientists have identified, described, and classified many such networks. The descriptive achievement has been impressive. As a result, the cutting edge of international regulatory network research will be directed toward answering three broad questions. First, what are these networks good for? Second, how can we make sure that they are good? And finally, how do and should they interact with traditional international institutions?

Networks scholarship grew out of a proud but not always prominent oeuvre of scholarship on transgovernmentalism; we begin this review with a survey of that history. As scholars began to consider the different ways that governments interacted with one another—and as it became clear that the paradigmatic form of interaction, through executive officials with claims to represent the interests of their states as a whole and through formal processes—only represented part of the rich story of government interaction, network theory became an ascendant way of understanding these processes of interaction. We discuss some of the underpinnings of that theory and explore some of its applications in the second part of the review.

We then turn to the three broad questions outlined above. With the first question—what are these networks good for?—we inquire about the conditions under which regulatory networks are likely to be most effective. These issues are primarily the concern of political scientists working within the broader category of regime design; their appropriateness for certain tasks varies depending on the observer. Some scholars, like Charles Sabel, think that networks can and do handle the widest possible range of government functions; others are less sure.

The second question—can we make sure that networks are good?—raises a range of accountability issues. These issues primarily attract lawyers and political theorists. Here, the question is how to achieve the traditional goals of administrative law, including responsiveness, transparency, and good government, in the face of a new and informal form of regulation. Some of the traditional mechanisms of administrative law risk destroying the very attributes of informal network regulation that make them attractive to the participants.

Tackling issues of accountability is vital to prescribing and designing regulatory networks that address specific governance problems. Moreover, accountability is impossible without an understanding of how networks fit together with more traditional international organizations. The ultimate architecture of global governance in what Robert Keohane has described as a "partially globalized world" will be a complex mix of formal and informal, global and regional, vertical and horizontal institutions. Where and how government networks best fit into this architecture is an important question of regime design. These issues also raise questions of legal and political strategy on the part of the would-be architects.

We briefly conclude with a recommendation. Scholars currently face the substantial challenge of having to draw together the multiple types of regulatory networks that have been described in myriad subspecialties—global financial regulation, antitrust, environmental law, and international criminal law—and to analyze their common features as part of a toolkit of global governance. We suggest some fruitful avenues for the broader, more synthetic work that will help scholars respond to the challenge.

A BRIEF INTELLECTUAL HISTORY OF TRANSGOVERNMENTAL RELATIONS

The study of networks grew out of work in international relations that began, somewhat cautiously, to unpack the state—traditionally the relevant and unitary actor in international affairs—into its constituent parts. In 1974, Robert Keohane and Joseph Nye defined transgovernmental relations, or international relationships between government officials "that are not controlled or closely guided by the policies of the cabinets or chief executives of those governments," as an important component of international relations (Keohane & Nye 1974, pp. 39, 42; for a history of transgovernmentalism, see Slaughter 2001). They also identified a broader category of transnational relations, which they defined as "contacts, coalitions, and interactions across state boundaries that are not controlled by the central foreign policy organs of governments" (Nye & Keohane 1972, p. xi).

Legal scholars had long accepted the idea that transnational law—law regulating international relationships between nonstate actors—was worthy of study (Jessup 1956). The legal process theorists produced articles and casebooks in the 1950s and 1960s that looked at the entire web of state and nonstate actors involved in international legal incidents. For example, Chayes and coauthors (1968) created case studies that analyzed the chicken trade war[1] between the United States and the European Economic Community in the early 1960s with reference to the constituents on both continents who pushed that conflict (pp. 249–306) and to the nonstate actors involved in Argentina's abrogation of its oil contracts with American companies in the 1960s[2] (pp. 805–77). By the 1970s, the legal focus shifted more to the private side of international legal relationships, with a particular emphasis on the role of multinational corporations. Steiner & Vagts's (1976) casebook entitled *Transnational Legal Problems* was the forerunner of law school course offerings that today fall under the rubric of international business transactions.

In both law and political science, these early ventures into the transnational and transgovernmental realm were driven primarily by the observation that theoretical models of the international system in both disciplines focused only on states, although the world around them teemed with many additional actors. Keohane & Nye's (1977) landmark *Power and Interdependence* did not deny the realities of power, but it did insist on the importance of the forces resulting from growing interdependence—precisely the web of transgovernmental and transnational relations—in shaping international outcomes.

By the 1980s, international relations scholars confronted the apparent puzzle posed by the declining hegemony of the United States in the international system, as new powers such as Japan and Germany claimed their place. Yet international regimes and institutions, established in the late 1940s and early 1950s when the United States could simply impose them on other states, persisted. The central research question moved from which actors mattered in international relations to

[1]This trade war gave agency to chicken producers from both sovereigns, to the press that covered the war, and to the various actors involved in the negotiations and litigation over trade in chickens.

[2]In the view of Chayes et al. (1968), the oil contracts dispute could best be understood with reference to internal Argentine politics as well as international questions over compensation for contracts with sovereigns. In addition to this work by Chayes, the American Society of International Law published an "International Crisis and the Role of Law" series of monographs that examined crises like the oil contracts dispute with reference to the many actors, both within and outside of the state apparatus, that played roles in the matters (e.g., Chayes 1974, Bowie 1974, Ehrlich 1974, Abi-Saab 1978, Fisher 1978).

how they interacted. Specifically, Keohane (1984) asked, "[H]ow was sustained cooperation possible in the absence of a hegemon?"

Scholars began to consider the mechanisms that states might use to constrain and regulate their behavior. The result was regime theory: the study of "sets of implicit or explicit principles, norms, rules, and decision-making procedures around which actors' expectations converge in a given [issue area]" (Krasner 1983, p. 2; see also Keohane & Nye 1977, p. 19). But here again, a focus on unitary states as principal actors proved limiting. A second wave of regime theorists such as Young (1997) looked not just to states but to other actors, such as nongovernmental organizations (NGOs), as important participants in international regimes (see also Keck & Sikkink 1998). Early in the 1990s, Haas (1992) moved even further away from the state-centered paradigm in international relations. He pioneered the concept of the "epistemic community," which he defined as "a network of professionals with recognized expertise and competence in a particular domain and an authoritative claim to policy-relevant knowledge within that domain or issue area" (Haas 1992, p. 3). The epistemic community was united by four characteristics: (*a*) a "shared set of normative and principled beliefs" that provides them with a "value-base rationale" for undertaking socially relevant action; (*b*) "shared causal beliefs" illuminating the underlying relationship between the available policies and the preferred outcomes; (*c*) "shared notions of validity" that are employed to identify admissible knowledge in the subject area of concern; and (*d*) "a common policy enterprise" that comprises particular sets of social issues and the policy instruments ordinarily used to manage them within the domain at issue (Haas 1992).

More broadly still, constructivist scholars brought back an emphasis on the logic of socialization as an alternative to the rationalist insistence on the logic of calculation. The processes of socialization, persuasion, and ideation can be identified and observed far more readily among actual state officials operating on behalf of parts of states rather than among states as aggregate actors, providing a fertile climate for a renewed focus on government networks in specific issue areas (see, e.g., Porter 1993; Picciotto 2000, 1996–1997). The result was a new burst of scholarship that finally gave pride of place to the kind of actors that Keohane & Nye had recognized were important in 1974 (Spiro 2004, p. 197; see also Stewart 2003, p. 455).

The move in political science to look beyond formal international organizations to the more elastic regime concept had no counterpart in international law. Many of the regimes of interest to political scientists had no formal expression at all; they could simply be sets of norms and practices, or informal agreements like memoranda of understanding (Zaring 2005). Yet according to *The Restatement of the Law Third, Foreign Relations Law of the United States*, section 221, an international organization imbued with legal personality would be "created by an international agreement and has a membership consisting entirely or principally of states." Moreover, legally binding international agreements were presumed to be treaties or executive agreements formally negotiated and approved by two or more states. The black letter law was simply silent regarding the rules of less formally constituted international actors.

At the same time, however, legal scholars in areas such as international financial regulation and environmental law became increasingly aware of the proliferation of new types of structured cooperation in response to the practical necessities of international economic and political interdependence. As Slaughter noted in 1995, international lawyers and political scientists were already "collaborating on joint studies of environmental regimes, trade regimes, and the general subject of regime management and compliance. The world cooperated, holding out new vistas of international cooperation and law-making" (Slaughter 1995, p. 717). These new relationships were principally horizontal, relatively informal, and driven by the basic need of government officials in one country to interact with their counterparts in another to regulate increasingly mobile and global private actors. The chroniclers and analysts of this new phenomenon thus focused on regulatory competition to the top or the bottom; they lacked an overall conceptual framework for analyzing the resulting interactions as part of international law.

THE PHENOMENOLOGY OF NETWORKS

The unifying framework that has emerged to understand all these entities is the network. Although defined differently depending on the writer and the context, networks may be understood as informal institutions linking actors across national boundaries and carrying on various aspects of global governance in new and informal ways. In their transgovernmental form, these networks exhibit "pattern[s] of regular and purposive relations among like government units working across the borders that divide countries from one another and that demarcate the 'domestic' from the 'international' sphere" (Slaughter 2004, p. 14). They allow domestic officials to interact with their foreign counterparts directly, without much supervision by foreign offices or senior executive branch officials, and feature "loosely-structured, peer-to-peer ties developed through frequent interaction rather than formal negotiation" (Raustiala 2002, see also Risse-Kappen 1995). In this section, we focus on network theorists and identify some particularly important developments in international relations that fit the network theory rather well.

Networks exhibit low-key characteristics of informal collaboration, but they also, crucially, demonstrate a compliance or inertial pull as the network develops and grows. As Raustiala (2002, p. 68) has put it, "the existence of a network strengthens incentives for jurisdictions to seek convergence because convergence allows for deeper and broader cooperation."

As networks have grown in size and importance and taken on increasingly more important tasks, their aspect has changed, and in many cases they have become more formal. Since arriving on the scene, many have adopted some of the administrative trappings—notice and comment, transparency through the electronic publication of minutes and reports—that are traditionally marked as features of democratically governed domestic systems of administrative law (Zaring 2005).

And they are everywhere. By the close of the twentieth century, these networks had proliferated into almost every area of government regulation. They have been used to address the leading problems of the day, ranging from high politics questions of national security and official corruption (Krahmann 2003, Tarullo 2004) to more mundane issues such as common policies on airplane regulation (Saba 2002). Legal scholars have identified and considered the implications of regulatory cooperation in tax (Park 2004), antitrust (Whytock 2005, Gerber 2004, Smitherman 2004, McGinnis 2003, Piilola 2003, Fox 2000), food and drug[3] (Noah 2000), and telecommunications regulation (Bermann 1996), as well as in other areas (e.g., Mulqueeny 2004). Indeed, in the European Union alone, C.F. Sabel & H. Zeitlin (unpublished manuscript) have documented disaggregated forms of coordinative governance (which to them are network-like, but branded as examples of "directly-deliberative polyarchy") in privatized network infrastructure, public health and safety, employment and social protection, other forms of regulation, and even rights-sensitive areas like the protection of race, gender, and disabled status, all after combing carefully through an exhaustive literature.

Of particular interest is the proliferation of networks in the global criminal arena. In *Policing the Globe,* Andreas & Nadelmann (2006) describe a "transnational criminal law enforcement community based on expanding governmental networks with shared technical and investigative expertise." Naim (2002), on the other hand, documents the demand side of this phenomenon, chronicling an extraordinary rise of illicit trading networks in money laundering, of trafficking in arms, drugs, and people, and of intellectual piracy. Naim acknowledges the existence of many government networks designed to counter the criminal networks, but calls for many more (Naim 2002, pp. 15–17).

The simple counting of case studies creates a rather imposing picture. Even international law skeptics such as Posner (2005, p. 838) now concede that transgovernmental relations are a vibrant and growing norm-creating phenomenon. But, of course, a series of case studies makes for quite issue-specific work, which is particularly surprising given that the network form itself is not issue-dependent.[4]

---

[3]The Codex Alimentarius Commission is one of the primary, but not only, organizations around which labeling and food safety standards are harmonized. For information, see Codex Alimentarius Commission, Codex Alimentarius, at http://www.codexalimentarius.net. The FDA and the USDA both send representatives to the Codex process, with the USDA's Food, Safety, and Inspection Service in charge of coordinating the participation of American regulators on the process (see USDA: Regulations and Policies: International Affairs: Codex Alimentarius, http://www.fsis.usda.gov/Regulations_&_Policies/Codex_Alimentarius/index.asp).

[4]Not everyone agrees. Pollack & Shaffer (2001) think, at least in the context of transatlantic regulatory networks, that "Slaughter's new world order of governance by transgovernmental networks is limited to specific issue areas, such as competition policy, in which regulators on each side of the Atlantic enjoy considerable de facto or de jure independence from their political masters and are guided by sufficiently similar regulatory laws and cultures."

Other scholars have focused on particular governance structures rather than on issue areas, concluding that now "networks of national government officials are one of the principal forms of European governance" (Bignami 2005, Cappellin et al. 1993), that they play a large role in ASEAN (Mulqueeny 2004), and that they affect the nature of regulatory collaboration between the United States and Europe (Bermann et al. 2001, Slaughter 2003). Indeed, Slaughter argues that the most interesting actors in world politics now include the same types of government institutions that are important in domestic politics, such as administrative agencies, courts, and legislatures and the networks they create with one another[5] (Slaughter 2000a, p. 178).

All this work has been essential in developing an understanding of just what networks do, but it has risked obscuring a larger picture of the overall network phenomenon. Although we make no claim to comprehensiveness here, we note three aspects of network governance that repeatedly characterize the form that issue- and institution-specific network governance takes.

An Alternative to the Regulatory Race

Networks offer an alternative to the paradigm of a regulatory race to the top or bottom (Esty & Geradin 2001, p. 5). In many areas of scholarship, but particularly in corporate law, competition between jurisdictions that regulate has been the dominant paradigm through which legal rules have been evaluated.[6] But network regulation avoids the race. Instead of competing with one another, regulators who participate in networks work to create common standards among the diverse jurisdictions with regulators through agreement and copying. Antitrust, for example—an area in which the competition between regulators to attract business might be expected to be fierce—is rife with informal cooperation. The now close ties between the United States and European Union competition officials is an example, as is the more global work being done through the International Competition Network (Fox 2000).

Similar transatlantic examples of network cooperation as a way around regulatory competition may be found in environmental protection, securities regulation, and other forms of cooperation. The cooperation is so pervasive that Esty & Geradin (2000) refer to it as "co-optition," under a "New Transatlantic Agenda," pursuant

[5]Other observers see networks everywhere, and not only in international regulation. The scholarship identifies networks in less regulatory but still norm-enforcing processes, such as the use of gossip to disclose information and make judgments (Strahelevitz 2005, p. 922). Indeed, some observers argue that networks are at the root of communities that can be defined by a broad, almost limitless, range of affinities, from public to private, and including ties based not just on the state but also on ethnicity, religion, and indeed one's weltanschauung (Berman 2005).

[6]Corporate race literature in the United States began with the debate between William Cary and Ralph Winter (Cary 1974, Winter 1977) and has been an incredibly fertile topic of scholarship ever since.

to which the United States and European Union "have agreed to consult each other in the early stages of drafting regulations, and to rely to a greater extent on each other's technical resources and expertise" (p. 41). In this way, the network literature offers a new means of evaluating unexamined notions of jurisdictional competition in a number of different contexts.

A New Way to Address Globalization

That problems of governance have become increasingly global is a truism. But it is worth remembering that globalization is not the result of an agreement by important heads of state but rather is something that has resulted from the increasingly global outlook of businesspeople, bureaucrats, lawyers, and laypeople. Networks comport with deep-seated intuitions about how globalization really works. Many writers have recognized that regulatory matters—for example, protection of the environment or supervision of financial institutions—necessarily cross borders, along with pollution and finance. Regulatory networks parallel and comport with the disaggregated but powerful way that globalization has actually happened. We think two implications of the fit between networks and globalization are particularly worth noting. First, thinking about globalization from a disaggregated, networked perspective challenges claims about homogenization and centralization of power and allows for at least the possibility of continuing diversity in implementing common standards. But second, where traditional power relations continue to operate, as they surely must, they must now operate in a networked rather than a centralized context.

The Information Revolution

Finally, the network literature continually emphasizes how the revolution in communication has enlarged the promise and even the possibility of networks. There has been, as Woods (2000, p. 31) observed, a "change in the way governments interact. Modern communications systems mean that national (or even subnational) decision makers can interact horizontally with officials in other countries." The growth of the Internet has also publicized transgovernmental networks; many informal regulatory organizations have created websites that announce their accomplishments and agendas for the future. They have become more real, to their participants and the broader public, by becoming virtual.

In sum, the study of government networks is here to stay, both for legal and political specialists in specific areas of regulation and for students of global governance more generally. They both reflect and contribute to larger global trends. And they exhibit common characteristics, common capacities, and common problems.

THE EFFECTIVENESS OF GOVERNMENT NETWORKS

In 1990, Walter Powell theorized that network forms of organization should be more effective than either markets or hierarchies in situations requiring know-how, demanding speed, and involving relatively homogeneous groups of actors likely to trust one another. Powell was writing about forms of industrial organization rather than of governance, but he captured essential features of networks in both contexts. Of particular importance is his analysis of why networks are particularly good at coping with change, which he attributed to "their ability to disseminate and interpret new information." Because they are "based on complex communication channels," networks are able not only to communicate information but also to generate new meanings and interpretations of the information transmitted, thereby providing "a context for learning by doing" (Powell 1990, p. 325). In this section, we review some of the recent literature that takes up where Powell left off, literature that largely concludes that regulatory networks are effective and powerful forms of global (and national, for that matter) governance.

Sabel and coauthors have largely proved Powell right in a series of articles that analyze networks in a number of different contexts, ranging from within the European Union to domestic institutional reform litigation (Sabel & Simon 2004, Cohen & Sabel 2003, Dorf & Sabel 1998). They focus not on networks per se, but rather on processes of disaggregated decision making that rely on bottom-up experimentalism as a path to convergence around ever better rules. Dorf & Sabel have gone so far as to advocate a theory of democratic experimentalism, championing participation in local problem-solving experiments under the discipline of mandatory minimum performance standards set—and regularly improved—by a central authority (Dorf & Sabel 1998). As they explain, democratic experimentalism points to ways that "central authority and decentralized actors can together explore and evaluate solutions to complex problems that neither alone would have been likely to identify, much less investigate or address, without the exchanges with the others" (Dorf & Sabel 2000, p. 834).

Networks combine central authority and decentralized actors, at least when they are constituted, as they increasingly are in the European Union, with a central node that functions as a secretariat and clearinghouse. In new work, Cohen & Sabel (2006) describe an entire class of problems in which "actors have to learn what problem they are solving, and what solution they are seeking, through the very process of problem solving." These problems begin with the inflow of raw data—data about an uptick in individuals presenting themselves at hospitals with a particular set of symptoms, about the direction of capital flows, about levels of chatter across terrorist networks, or about levels of ozone or the melting rate of glaciers. Pooling these data is the first step; analyzing them to determine whether they indicate a problem or an opportunity is the second; working through potential solutions or optimization strategies is the third—all in real time, as these data are continually updated.

Equally important are the problems that are created by the absence of coordination in virtually every policy area imaginable, from trade and security to education and health care. In traditional coordination games, government officials can see that they would be better off if they could coordinate with their foreign counterparts; in a global economy and society, however, the effectiveness of the solutions an individual government adopts individually depends at least in part on how well it meshes with the solutions adopted by other governments to the same problem.

Thus, the fact of interconnectedness creates its own set of problems that must be worked out collectively.

Cohen & Sabel (2006) argue that these kinds of problems require "deliberative coordination: deliberation among units of decision-making directed both to learning jointly from their several experiences, and improving the institutional possibilities for such learning—a system with continuous discussion across separate units about current best practice and better ways of ascertaining it." The results of such deliberation are distributed along a particular network, as well as among members of a distinct public that helps create and is created by the network and its regulatory domain. The public is a site not only for contesting and commenting on the results of the deliberation among network members, but also for communicating and complying with the results of that deliberation.

To know precisely the conditions under which networks can be most effective, researchers must develop a new branch of game theory that can identify more precisely the kinds of problems for which the formation of a network is an optimal solution. [Current game theory tells us that cooperative institutions are necessary to solve collective action (prisoner's dilemma) problems and that traditional coordination institutions, which establish a fixed standard that all members agree on, are required to solve coordination problems (Martin 1992, Krasner 1983).] We might think of problems requiring networked solutions as "complex coordination and deliberation problems," arising more often in an age of instant information and intense interconnectedness.

A final and simpler key to network effectiveness is the increasing value of credible information in an age of information overload. As Keohane & Nye (1998, p. 88) observed, "A plenitude of information leads to a poverty of attention.... Editors, filters, interpreters, and cue-givers become more in demand, and this is a source of power." To the extent that regulatory networks are sources of codes of best practices and credible information in a particular regulatory domain generally, they have the kind of knowledge that is power in the information age.

THE ACCOUNTABILITY OF GOVERNMENT NETWORKS

For government networks to be effective, they must also be accountable. The literature has focused on two particular accountability concerns. The first is one of unconstrained technocratic governance, and it invokes classic administrative law concerns that the interactions of putatively expert regulators risk the development of a regime with little or no public check on administrative action. The second accountability concern turns on a fear that the informal nature of regulatory networks means that they are particularly likely to mask unequal power relationships. We explore the initial forays scholars have made into these accountability issues with particular reference to the efforts to develop some paradigms of "global administrative law" that might help to resolve them.

Scholars concerned with technocracy see regulatory and judicial networks as networks of unelected officials who are not accountable at the level of national voters. These unelected officials are regulated through carefully worked out procedures at home—notice and comment requirements, for instance—but are entirely free to pursue their technocratic projects with their peers offshore.

The concern over unequal bargaining power focuses on the ability of officials from wealthy and advanced states to make decisions without consulting officials from weaker and poorer states and thus to have little accountability at the level of the state system. These officials may develop codes of best practices and points of coordination that they then impose unilaterally on other states.

Slaughter (2000a) originally raised the technocratic objection by asking whether regulatory government networks were comprised of "agencies on the loose." Kingsbury et al. (2005) expand on this point, noting that networks often operate semi-publicly at best, leading, they and others fear, to a transgovernmental democratic deficit. The transparency of the networks is by no means assured, given that their flexible informality makes for a number of meetings of public import outside of the public eye. And the difficulties are real for outsiders in identifying the locus of decision on an administrative action in which domestic rulemakers, international negotiators, and, on occasion, private parties may be involved.

More classically, Macey (2003) has suggested that informal harmonization is subject to many of the familiar problems of public choice, such as capture and unrepresentative agency action. His story is principally one of regulatory turf building, as regulators seek to do internationally what they might not be able to do domestically; he also questions whether it is clear that regulators acting internationally will serve public interests or private ones.

In response to this concern, Kingsbury et al. (2005) ask whether there is, or ought to be, a "global administrative law." Their project is gratifyingly broad. They note that international administration includes a wide variety of forms of bureaucratic action, ranging from the international regulations governing the bureaucracies of international organizations to the less formal work of regulatory networks, to the legally hazy status of semi-public international standard-setting organizations. As they have explained, global administrative bodies include "formal intergovernmental regulatory bodies, informal intergovernmental regulatory networks and coordination arrangements, national regulatory bodies operating with reference to an international intergovernmental regime, hybrid public-private regulatory bodies, and some private regulatory bodies exercising transnational governance functions of particular public significance" (Kingsbury et al. 2005, p. 17). Their global administrative project has produced a book, a website with a helpful bibliography (http://www.iilj.org/global_adlaw/gal_bibliography.htm), and a number of case studies [including one contributed by one of us (Zaring 2005)]. Their project not only describes this wide range of international regulation, including the network paradigm that we think is particularly prevalent; they also consider what sort of constraints might be imposed on these sorts of governance.

Regulatory networks could be subjected to the traditional paradigms of administrative law: transparency, participation, notice before action, as Kingsbury et al. (2005) recommend (see also Aman 2004). But more work needs to be done on the merits or debits of limited institutionalization. We can imagine an international version of the federal register, or a formally constituted international organization charged with gathering the charters of informal networks and reporting on their activities. But developing a treaty-style process would, of course, be rife with difficulties and delay (Esty 2006). We see some promise in the development of an expert group of arbitrators or dispute settlers who could evaluate network-driven regulatory initiatives without ossifying them. But much more work needs to be done to establish a set of both flexible but constraining principles that experienced network analysts might use to curb excesses.[7]

Alternatively, and perhaps riskily, we could do nothing, or not much, to limit the freedom of networks to develop and operate. We could trust the network form not to veer too far into secrecy and countermajoritarianism: Even though networks *could* create many countermajoritarian problems, there is little indication so far that they *will* create those problems. Some regulatory networks have, for example, adopted principles of process that any American administrative lawyer would find familiar, and in some cases they have opened up their work to NGO participants, at least in part. The Basel Committee's revision to its capital accord is an example. In this way networks increasingly exhibit characteristics that are consistent with a disclosure-oriented paradigm of regulatory control.

Moreover, as global actors networks may be constrained by the global milieu in which they operate. That milieu includes traditional state action, such as treaties, when networks fail or pursue undesirable policies. It also includes the web of domestic accountability mechanisms that already constrain agencies in their normal activities and that also cover agency participation in networks. We do not mean to suggest that benign neglect is a complete answer. But some scholars think that limited reform of networks is the most that is required. Drahos (2004), for example, looks to the fostering of nodes as a way of managing networks. Nodes

---

[7]Some network constraint solutions would turn away from international solutions and bolster internal state remedies—such as the American Administrative Procedure Act—for international regulatory initiatives that go too far. Proponents of this view might urge courts to take a hard look at international initiatives by agencies in light of their procedural shortcomings. As Garland (1985) has explained, "hard look" review in the United States has both a procedural and a substantive component—procedurally, courts insisted on "adequate" consideration and "reasoned" explanation, along with evidentiary support for policy decisions, and substantively, courts focused on the reasonability of the agency's ultimate policy choice. Hard look review of agency action that turned in part on network-based initiatives would be something that courts could adopt of their own volition. It is therefore a relatively implementable prescription for network control, and it could be communicated from court to court. However, the hard look doctrine, at least as applied in the United States, began to look like a process whereby courts tried to second chair regulators in complicated domestic regulatory contexts. With the advent of deferential judicial review of agency decisions—the famous *Chevron* doctrine—the hard look doctrine has fallen into domestic disfavor, and proponents of a vigorous domestic solution to the problems of international rulemaking would have to grapple with these issues.

are the places in the network where the various parts of the network meet; they accordingly are the places where the information and agreement necessary for networked governance to occur happen. Ensure the existence and the publicity of the things that happen in the nodes, Drahos suggests, and network governance will prosper.

Along these lines, we think more work could be done to examine whether and how networks can check networks. For example, legislators responsible for securities laws could work with their foreign counterparts to ensure that agency-driven international securities harmonization initiatives are monitored effectively. NGO networks, which are quite vibrant, as Keck & Sikkink (1998) have shown, might also serve to check regulatory networks. The idea is similar to that of the separation of powers, in which one branch of government checks the power of another (or the fourth branch—the press—might serve this function). The proliferation of networks to counterbalance networks might get complex, but we note that it would not necessarily be inconsistent with other paradigms of democratic accountability. As Slaughter (2003, chapter 6) has observed, the disaggregated, decentralized nature of networks is not inconsistent with basic principles of democratic accountability.

The prescriptive possibilities for enhanced control over network regulation are all problematic. Some scholars have effectively thrown up their hands at the possibility of true international democratic oversight and looked for second-best, satisficing mechanisms of checking power on the international level, without fetishizing the democratic deficit (Grant & Keohane 2005). For example, Grant & Keohane (2005) propose a focus on accountability above all else—requiring that international administrative initiatives be publicized and checked by the rigors of reaction from civil society, markets, and the traditional state system, and would not go much further.

Cohen & Sabel (2006), on the other hand, have more faith in the possibility of democratic control, which they see arising from the linked publics affected by issue-specific regulatory initiatives. As networks develop regulation, in other words, they may create stakeholders in regulatory schemes that can coalesce to check the prescriptions of horizontal regulatory initiatives.[8] Over time, as these initiatives grow in size and scope, Cohen & Sabel envision the potential growth of nothing less than a global polity comprised of the stakeholders in issue-specific

[8]Tim Buthe, in contrast, has studied the delegation of rulemaking power to private authorities, and has concluded that the decision about whether to regulate through public and private process is a very political one (http://www.duke.edu/~buthe/research/standards_regulation.html#delegation). In his view, the adoption of traditional mechanisms of administrative law may be unnecessary in cases in which regulation by private standard-setters is effective; his case study is the setting of accounting standards by private and semi-private accounting standards boards in the United States and elsewhere. To him, it is by no means inevitable that linked publics will be mobilized; rather, the nature of the participation will depend on the positive political relationships in the particular issue area at issue (Buthe & Mattli 2005).

areas of network regulation. In each of these areas, stakeholders would be able to exercise genuine accountability.

These broader views of the appropriate limitations on global administration turn, of course, on what the process of regulation looks like. And here, the facts on the ground—the existence and prominence of networks in global regulation—may affect the kind of accountability deemed required. The questions for future research are more fine-grained. Given the nature of the existing system and the precise problems that have to be tackled, which parts of the global networks of administrative law should be subjected to traditional mechanisms of administrative accountability, and which to mechanisms specifically designed for network control?

GOVERNMENT NETWORKS AND TRADITIONAL INTERNATIONAL INSTITUTIONS

The title of Keohane & Nye's (1974) article was "Transgovernmental Relations and International Organizations." This choice was not accidental; Keohane & Nye were explicitly writing against Huntington's (1973) claim that because of the rise of transnational relations, "internationalism [defined as agreements among nation-states] is a dead end" (p. 368). Keohane & Nye argued exactly the reverse, that transgovernmental relations—defined as "direct bureaucratic contacts among governmental sub-units"—had the potential to "create opportunities for international organizations to play significant roles in world politics." The idea was driven in part by domestic turf wars unlikely to be resolved by strong executive rule: In Keohane & Nye's view, transgovernmental relations were most likely to take place "when sub-units build coalitions with like-minded agencies from other governments against elements of their own administrative structure" (Keohane & Nye 1974, p. 44).

When Slaughter first wrote about transgovernmental relations, or, in her parlance, "government networks," she sounded more like Huntington, arguing that "[t]he state. . .is disaggregating into its separate, functionally distinct parts. These parts—courts, regulatory agencies, executives, and even legislatures—are networking with their counterparts abroad, creating a dense web of relations that constitutes a new, transgovernmental order" (Slaughter 1997, p. 184). Raustiala and others challenged her view.[9] Raustiala (2002), in particular, argued that

[9]For example, Posner (2005, p. 813) has noted that "interagency cooperation may make it easier for governments to cooperate, or it may make it easier for governments to comply with international law. But it also may merely be a result of governments wanting to cooperate with each other, and directing their agencies to implement legal or nonlegal cooperative agreements."

networks offer a mechanism of organizing international relationships that coexists with more traditional accounts of state-to-state treaty style relationships. By 2004, however, Slaughter had come around to this view as well. In her revised view, government networks and traditional international organizations fit together in three principal ways: Although the networks can stand alone, they can also complement the efforts of traditional international institutions by facilitating convergence, or "deeper cooperation through more formal international agreements," by enhancing compliance with existing treaties and other international agreements, and by improving "the quality and depth of cooperation across nations" (Slaughter 2003, p. 169).

As a legal matter, transgovernmental networks operate in environments with widely varying grants of legal authority. Sometimes they come into being after the conclusion of executive agreements, such as with the series of executive agreements between the United States and European Union authorizing networks to develop a transatlantic agenda (Slaughter 2004, pp. 46–47). Sometimes they develop within treaty arrangements—the relatively formal Open Method of Coordination in the European Union is an example (Cohen & Sabel 2003). And sometimes they arise spontaneously, as has been the case for the increasingly elaborate financial regulatory networks, such as the Basel Committee and the International Organization of Securities Commissions (IOSCO) (Zaring 2005; Braithwaite & Drahos 2000, p. 27). These different legal foundations can make it harder or easier to integrate government networks with existing international organizations or perhaps ultimately to transform them into new ones.

In still other situations, networks provide forms of interaction for parts of governments that would be unlikely to interact in any more formal institutions, such as courts, for instance. The rapid growth of judicial networks of various kinds, resulting in what some observers and participants have called a global constitutional dialogue, requires that the judges themselves remain part of distinct national and international institutions (Slaughter 2000a, 2004, 2005; Martinez 2003, p. 111; Berman 2004, p. 111; Koh 2005; Michelman 2005). It is difficult to imagine how this function could be performed by a formal international organization, even though the informal cooperation by judges across jurisdictions has strengthened the enforcement of traditional international law and even helped to define its content (Waters 2005; Ahdieh 2004; Dubinsky 2005; Knop 2000, pp. 518–24).

The challenge for global governance generally is not simply to design multiple institutions to meet multiple challenges, but also to determine how they can best fit together. As long as world government remains infeasible and, for many, undesirable, then the world's capacity to govern itself collectively on those issues that require collective decision will depend on a patchwork of different kinds of institutions: formal and informal, intergovernmental and transgovernmental, state-based and society-based, durable and flexible. Where transgovernmental networks fit into this picture, or pictures, and how they can best be deployed to strengthen, foreshadow, or replace intergovernmental institutions are rich topics for research and analysis.

CONCLUSION

As the study of networks has moved from the edges of international relations and international law scholarship to the center, and as network regulation has been identified in a plethora of issue-specific areas to a more universal, if still fuzzy phenomenon, the questions confronting network scholars will change. Descriptively, a fuzzy but very broad picture is gradually coming into focus. We know more about different types of networks, when and how they arise, and when they are most effective. We recommend moving from the descriptive and explanatory to the normative and prescriptive. In the process, lawyers and political theorists can begin arguing *for* the creation of networks as valuable mechanisms of global governance in some circumstances, particularly in various different relationships to traditional intergovernmental institutions, and *against* them in others where they appear unlikely to be successful, or where the governance costs do not look like they would be worth the benefits.

The *Annual Review of Law and Social Science* is online at http://lawsocsci.annualreviews.org

LITERATURE CITED

Abi-Saab G. 1978. *The United Nations Operation in the Congo, 1960–64*. Oxford/New York: Oxford Univ. Press

Ahdieh RB. 2004. Between dialogue and decree: international review of national courts. *NY Univ. Law Rev.* 76:2029–2163

Aman AC. 2004. *The Democracy Deficit: Taming Globalization Through Law Reform*. New York: NY Univ. Press. 253 pp.

Andreas P, Nadelmann E. 2006. *Policing the Globe: Criminalization and Crime Control in International Relations*. Oxford/New York: Oxford Univ. Press. In press

Bermann G. 1996. Regulatory cooperation between the European commission and U.S. administrative agencies. *Admin. Law J. Am. Univ.* 9:968

Bermann G, Herdegen M, Lindseth P. 2001. *Transatlantic Regulatory Co-Operation: Legal Problems and Political Prospects*. Oxford/New York: Oxford Univ. Press. 656 pp.

Berman PS. 2004. Judges as cosmopolitan transnational actors. *Tulsa J. Comp. Int. Law* 12:109–21

Berman PS. 2005. From international law to law and globalization. *Columbia J. Transnatl. Law* 43:485–556

Bignami F. 2005. Transgovernmental networks vs. democracy: the case of the European Information Privacy Network. *Mich. J. Int. Law* 26:809

Bowie RR. 1974. *Suez 1956*. London/New York: Oxford Univ. Press

Braithwaite J, Drahos P. 2000. *Global Business Regulation*. Cambridge, UK: Cambridge Univ. Press

Buthe T, Mattli W. 2005. Global private governance: lessons from a national model of setting standards in accounting. *Law Contemp. Probl.* 68:225

Cary W. 1974. Federalism and corporate law: reflections upon Delaware. *Yale Law. J.* 83:663

Cappellin R, Batey P, Cappellin TR, eds. 1993. *Regional Networks, Border Regions and European Integration*. London: Pion. 256 pp.

Chayes A. 1974. *The Cuban Missile Crisis*. London/New York: Oxford Univ. Press

Chayes A, Ehrlich T, Lowenfeld A. 1968. *The International Legal Process*. New York: Little, Brown

Cohen J, Sabel C. 2003. Sovereignty and solidarity in the EU. In *Governing Work and Welfare in a New Economy: European and American Experiments*, ed. J Zeitlin, D Trubek, 13:691–750. Oxford: Oxford Univ. Press

Cohen J, Sabel C. 2006. *Norms and global institutions*. Prepared for Princeton Global Governance Workshop, Princeton Univ., April 16–18

Dorf MC, Sabel CF. 1998. A constitution of democratic experimentalism. *Columbia Law Rev*. 98:267–371

Dorf MC, Sabel CF. 2000. Drug treatment courts and emergent experimentalist government. *Vanderbilt Law Rev*. 53:831–83

Drahos P. 2004. Intellectual property and pharmaceutical markets: a nodal governance approach. *Temple Law Rev.* 77:401

Dubinsky PR. 2005. Human rights law meets private law harmonization: the coming conflict. *Yale J. Int. Law* 30:211–17

Ehrlich T. 1974. *Cyprus, 1958–1967*. London/New York: Oxford Univ. Press

Esty DC. 2006. Good governance at the supranational scale: globalizing administrative law. *Yale Law Rev.* 115:1490–562

Esty DC, Geradin D. 2000. Regulatory co-optition. *J. Int. Econ. Law* 3:235

Esty DC, Geradin D, eds. 2001. *Regulatory Competition and Economic Integration*. Oxford/New York: Oxford Univ. Press

Fisher R. 1978. *Points of Choice*. Oxford/New York: Oxford Univ. Press

Fox EM. 2000. Antitrust and regulatory federalism: races up, down, and sideways. *NY Univ. Law Rev*. 75:1785–87, 1802–7

Garland M. 1985. Deregulation and judicial review. *Harvard Law Rev.* 98:505

Gerber D. 2004. Prescriptive authority: global markets as a challenge to national regulatory systems. *Houston J. Int. Law* 26:302, 308

Grant R, Keohane R. 2005. Accountability and abuses of power in world politics. *Am. Polit. Sci. Rev.* 99:29–44

Haas PM. 1992. Introduction: epistemic communities and international policy coordination. *Int. Organ.* 46:1–35

Huntington SP. 1973. Transnational organizations in world politics. *World Polit*. 25:333–68

Ignatieff M, ed. 2005. *American Exceptionalism and Human Rights*. Princeton, NJ: Princeton Univ. Press

Jessup C. 1956. *Transnational Law*. New Haven, CT: Yale Univ. Press. 113 pp.

Keck ME, Sikkink K. 1998. *Activists Beyond Borders: Advocacy Networks in International Politics*. Ithaca: Cornell Univ. Press. 228 pp.

Keohane R. 1984. *After Hegemony: Cooperation and Discord in the World Political Economy*. Princeton, NJ: Princeton Univ. Press

Keohane R, Nye J. 1974. Transgovernmental relations and international organizations. *World Polit.* 1:39–42

Keohane R, Nye J. 1977. *Power and Interdependence: World Politics in Transition*. Boston: Little, Brown. 273 pp.

Keohane R, Nye J. 1998. Power and interdependence in the information age. *Foreign Aff.* 77:81–94

Kingsbury B, Krisch N, Stewart RB. 2005. The emergence of global administrative law. *Law Contemp. Probl.* 68:15–61

Knop K. 2000. Here and there: international law in domestic courts. *NY Univ. J. Int. Law Policy* 32:501–35

Koh H. 2005. America's Jekyll-and-Hyde exceptionalism. See Ignatieff 2005, 5:145–47

Krahmann E. 2003. *Multilevel Networks in European Foreign Policy*. Aldershot, UK: Ashgate. 224 pp.

Krasner SD. 1983. *International Regimes*. Ithaca, NY: Cornell Univ. Press

Macey J. 2003. Regulatory globalization as a response to regulatory competition. *Emory Law J.* 52:1353

Martin L. 1992. Interests, power, and multilateralism. *Int. Organ.* 46:765–92

Martinez J. 2003. Towards an international judicial system. *Stanford Law Rev.* 56:429–529

McGinnis JO. 2003. The political economy of international antitrust harmonization. *William & Mary Law Rev*. 45:551

Michelman F. 2005. Integrity-anxiety? See Ignatieff 2005, 9:241–77

Mulqueeny K. 2004. Regionalism, economic integration and legalisation in ASEAN: what space for environmental sustainability? *Asia Pac. J. Environ. Law* 8(1-2):5

Naim M. 2002. The fourth annual Grotius lecture: five wars of globalization. *Am. Univ. Int. Law Rev.* 18:1–18

Noah BA. 2000. Adverse drug reactions, harnessing experiential data to promote patient welfare. *Catholic Univ. Law Rev.* 49:500–1

Nye J, Keohane R, eds. 1972. *Transnational Relations and World Politics*. Cambridge, MA: Harvard Univ. Press. 428 pp.

Park I. 2004. International finance and state sovereignty: global governance in the international tax regime. *Annu. Surv. Int. Comp. Law* 10:167

Picciotto S. 1996–1997. Networks in international economic integration: fragmented states and the dilemma of neo-liberalism. *Northwest. J. Int. Law Bus.* 17(1996–97):1014–56

Picciotto S. 2000. Liberalization and democratization: the forum and the hearth in the era of cosmopolitan post-industrial capitalism. *Law Contemp. Probl.* 63:157–78

Piilola A. 2003. Assessing theories of global governance: a case study of international antitrust regulation. *Stanford J. Int. Law* 39:208

Pollack M, Shaffer G. 2001. *Transatlantic Governance in the Global Economy*. Lanham, MD: Rowman & Littlefield. 368 pp.

Porter T. 1993. *States, Markets, and Regimes in Global Finance*. Basingstoke: Macmillan/New York: St. Martins

Posner E. 2005. International law and the disaggregated state. *Fla. State Univ. Law Rev.* 32:842

Powell W. 1990. Neither market nor hierarchy: network forms of organization. *Res. Org. Behav.* 12:295–336

Raustiala K. 2002. The architecture of international cooperation: transgovernmental networks and the future of international law. *Va. J. Int. Law* 43:1–92

Risse-Kappen T. 1995. Introduction. In *Transnational Relations Back In*, ed. T Risse-Kappen. New York: Cambridge Univ. Press. 323 pp.

Saba J. 2002. Aviation safety in crisis: the option of the international financial facility for aviation safety. *Transp. Law J.* 30:1

Sabel CF, Simon WH. 2004. Destabilization rights: how public law litigation succeeds. *Harvard Law Rev.* 117:1015–101

Sabel CF, Zeitlin H. 2006. *Learning from difference: the new architecture of experimentalist governance in the European Union.* Presented at ARENA Seminar, Cent. Eur. Stud., Univ. Oslo, June 13. http://www.arena.uio.no/events/seminarpapers/2006/Zeitlin_June06.pdf

Slaughter AM. 1995. Liberal international relations theory and international economic law. *Am. Univ. J. Int. Law Policy* 10:717–43

Slaughter AM. 1997. The real new order. *Foreign Aff.* 76:183–97

Slaughter AM. 2000a. Governing the global economy through government networks. In *The Role of Law in International Politics. Essays in International Relations and International Law*, ed. M Byers, 9:177–205. Oxford/New York: Oxford Univ. Press

Slaughter AM. 2000b. Judicial globalization. *Va. J. Int. Law* 40:1103–24

Slaughter AM. 2001. The accountability of government networks. *Indiana J. Global Legal Stud.* 8:347, 350–55

Slaughter AM. 2003. Global government networks, global information agencies, and disaggregated democracy. *Mich. J. Int. Law* 24:1047

Slaughter AM. 2004. *A New World Order*. Princeton, NJ: Princeton Univ. Press. 368 pp.

Slaughter AM. 2005. A brave new judicial world. See Ignatieff 2005, 10:277–304

Smitherman CW. 2004. The future of global competition governance: lessons from the transatlantic. *Am. Univ. Int. Law Rev.* 19:770

Spiro P. 2004. Disaggregating U.S. interests in international law. *Law Contemp. Probl.* 67:197

Steiner HJ, Vagts DF. 1976. *Transnational Legal Problems*. Mineola, NY: Found. Press. 1429 pp. 2nd ed.

Stewart R. 2003. Administrative law in the twenty-first century. *NY Univ. Law Rev.* 78:455

Strahelevitz L. 2005. A social networks theory of privacy. *Univ. Chicago Law Rev.* 72:919–88

Tarullo D. 2004. The limits of institutional design: implementing the OECD Anti-Bribery Convention. *Va. J. Int. Law* 44:701

Waters M. 2005. Mediating norms and identity: the role of transnational judicial dialogue in creating and enforcing international law. *Georgetown Law J.* 93:487–574

Whytock C. 2005. A rational design theory of transgovernmentalism: the case of E.U.-U.S. merger review cooperation. *Boston Univ. Int. Law J.* 23:51

Winter R. 1977. State law, shareholder protection, and the theory of the corporation. *J. Legal Stud.* 6:251

Woods N, ed. 2000. *The Political Economy of Globalization*. London: Macmillan

Young OR. 1997. Rights, rules, and resources in world affairs. In *Global Governance: Drawing Insights from the Environmental Experience*, ed. O Young, 1:1–23. Cambridge, MA: MIT Press. 364 pp.

Zaring D. 2005. Informal procedure, hard and soft, in international administration. *Chicago J. Int. Law* 5:547

Annu. Rev. Law Soc. Sci. 2006. 2:231–55
doi: 10.1146/annurev.lawsocsci.2.032406.145708

First published online as a Review in Advance on July 24, 2006

FROM THE COLD WAR TO KOSOVO: The Rise and Renewal of the Field of International Human Rights

Yves Dezalay[1] and Bryant Garth[2]
[1]*Centre National de la Recherche Scientifique & Centre de Sociologie de l'Education et de la Culture of Paris, 75270 Paris, France; email: dezalay@msh-paris.fr*
[2]*Southwestern Law School, Los Angeles, California 90005; email: bgarth@swlaw.edu*

Key Words international relations, legalization, Amnesty International, Human Rights Watch

■ **Abstract** This review explores the creation and transformation of the field of international human rights in the period after World War II. The narrative proceeds through an examination, based on documentary evidence and interviews, of three generations of human rights nongovernmental organizations: the International Commission of Jurists, Amnesty International, and Human Rights Watch. Each was created in part to overcome the limitations of the previous generation, and the process, linked to developments in the U.S. field of state power and U.S. activities abroad—especially in Latin America—gradually produced a field with substantial legal autonomy. At the same time, however, the structure of the field moved increasingly close to U.S. power and the issues and strategies that would gain credibility in the United States. The autonomy is therefore structurally close to U.S. power.

INTRODUCTION

The protection of human rights around the globe is a central concern of international relations today (Klug 2005, p. 99; see Sikkink 2002). A substantial body of scholarship has explored the rise of the human rights movement and the successes and limitations of efforts to expand enforcement through such entities as international war crimes tribunals (e.g., Hagan 2003, Hagan & Levi 2005, Sikkink 2002). The focus of much scholarship and activism is now on the conditions that can facilitate the mission of spreading and enforcing international human rights (e.g., McClymont & Golub 2000). There is now, as Klug (2005) has noted, a relatively autonomous field of transnational human rights. We seek in this review to explore the dynamics of the field of human rights using the tools of structural sociology associated with Pierre Bourdieu (see generally Dezalay & Garth 1996, 2002).

To understand the logic of the field, we examine how it was built and what ingredients became a part of it. This sociological and historical approach reveals power relationships that are obscured in words like "the international community," "norms," and the "law" (Risse & Sikkink 1999, p. 35). The "rules of the game" of the field determine the kinds of arguments, ideas, and actors that will be capable of transforming the field, or particular aspects of it. U.S. influence, as discussed below, created a transnational field that not only privileges legalization, but also places U.S. campuses, the U.S. media, and the U.S. power centers of New York and Washington, DC, at the top of the hierarchy of actors and organizations.

Our narrative is organized around the evolution of three major nongovernmental organizations (NGOs) in the period after World War II: the International Commission of Jurists (ICJ), Amnesty International, and Human Rights Watch (HRW). Our general narrative traces the movement of actors and an emerging expertise in international human rights from one major organization to the next, showing both the origins and the transformation of the field.

A study of the creation and activities of the most important NGOs helps to reveal the mechanisms of power and influence. The internal story of the leading NGOs can be related to their historical context, to internal political struggles in the most powerful states, especially the United States, and to the creation of a relatively legalized transnational field (Dezalay & Garth 2002, 2006). The use of the term nongovernmental obscures the fact that NGOs are created by actors with national backgrounds, with strategies and approaches developed in national settings, and with political orientations formed mainly in the context of national political struggles. This relationship of the NGOs to U.S. internal political battles is essential to understanding an apparent paradox: Those most opposed to using law and human rights as bases for foreign policy—the realists who controlled foreign policy in the 1950s and 1960s—were transformed into the leading proponents of the human rights strategy. A focus on contested internal U.S. politics and their relationship to NGOs, moreover, allows us to see how the promotion of human rights was transformed from an instrument of U.S. domestic opposition to a staple of established U.S. foreign policy.

The histories of particular NGOs, including the ICJ (Tolley 1994), Amnesty International (Power 2001), and HRW (Laber 2002, Neier 2003), have been documented in a number of useful scholarly, journalistic, and autographic studies (Korey 1993, 1998; Keck & Sikkink 1998). We draw on these studies, but we also use interviews that we undertook as part of our work on the transformation of Latin American states (Dezalay & Garth 2002) to show the relationship between the organizations and U.S. domestic politics. The story is of human rights organizations but also more generally of the Cold War, the breakup of the Cold War consensus, the transformation of the Ford Foundation, and the rise of the New Right and a new kind of media-oriented politics. We show how human rights organizations changed in relation to each other and to these larger political events and contests. We also see a story of legalization in the increase in the relative autonomy of the law, but at the same time we recognize the close relationship of the transnational field to U.S. political power. Closely related to developments in the United States, political developments in Chile in the early 1970s are highlighted here. Developments in Chile combined with those in the United States to promote the autonomy of human rights activities from the narrow Cold War fight.

As a history, this account is necessarily incomplete. The concentration on Latin America and the U.S. field of state power excludes much of the important activity that took place outside of these settings. For example, drawing especially on Korey (1998; see also Korey 1993, Laber 2002, Neier 2003), we make some references to parallel developments in other countries where human rights became central to the opposition to authoritarian states. The influx of support for human rights from organizations and funds linked to Northern European and Scandinavian countries is also important. The focus on leading NGOs also shifts attention from the many local variations of the human rights movement (for parallel European accounts, see Madsen 2005, 2006). Nevertheless, this emphasis shows how the human rights field developed autonomy from the positions of the Cold War, explains the development and activities of the most important global human rights organizations, and reveals how the field's center of gravity became oriented toward the U.S. state and politics—and toward establishment law.

A COUNTEROFFENSIVE ON THE TERRAIN OF THE GREAT LEGAL PRINCIPLES

The end of World War II brought considerable attention to the possibility that universal human rights could help protect against genocide and other atrocities identified with the Nazis. After the enactment of the Universal Declaration of Human Rights in 1948, however, the escalation of the Cold War led both sides in that conflict away from a human rights focus toward competition in international arenas. The most prominent human rights group within the United States at that time was the International League for the Rights of Man (founded in 1942 and which became the International League for Human Rights in 1976) set up by Roger Baldwin, the first chair of the American Civil Liberties Union (ACLU) (which had been founded in 1919). Baldwin took as his model the French Ligue Français pour la Defense de Droits de l'Homme et du Citoyen, which was formed in response to the Dreyfus affair in 1902. The International League drew on leaders who had immigrated to the United States during World War II. In addition, Eleanor Roosevelt was on the board, along with other notables, recruited from an "old boy network." The New York–based League was active in the United Nations and involved early in the effort to attack apartheid in South Africa (Korey 1998, pp. 99–104). Under the leadership of Jerome Shestak, the League in the 1970s developed close ties to Andrei Sakharov, the leader of Soviet dissidents and winner of the Nobel Peace Prize in 1975. The League appears to have been perceived by the Soviets as a Cold War organization, and they sought to expel it from consultative status with the UN in the late 1960s (Korey 1998, p. 87). The contemplated affiliation with Freedom House in the early 1970s, in addition, suggests a Cold War orientation (see Wiseberg & Scoble 1977, p. 300). The League was initially divided, but it took stands against the military dictatorships in Chile and Paraguay in the 1970s (Wiseberg & Scoble 1977).

The first of the prominent human rights groups in the postwar period, the ICJ, was constructed to provide an NGO that could serve U.S. interests in the Cold War. As detailed by Tolley (1994), the ICJ was created in 1952 by powerful lawyers from the United States, in particular those identified with the Council on Foreign Relations. The immediate cause of the initiative was the desire to mount a counterattack against a rival organization, the International Association of Democratic Jurists (IADJ), launched in 1946 by French lawyers who had been connected to the resistance. In the name of legal principles, the IADJ overtly attacked McCarthyism and supported the defense of the Rosenbergs.

Recognizing that the United States was vulnerable on its civil rights record (Dudziak 2000), John J. McCloy, the so-called "Chairman of the Establishment" (Bird 1998) and then the high commissioner for Germany, and a small group of political lawyers close to him, including Allen Dulles, president of the Council on Foreign Relations and deputy director of the CIA, decided to engage in battle on the terrain of law. Pro-Soviet organizations such as the IADJ, according to this group, had "stolen the great words—Peace, Freedom, Justice." The objective of the U.S. counterattack, accordingly, was to create international organizations that would, in Tolley's (1994, p. 34) words, "mobilize the forces—in particular the juridical forces—of the free world for the defense of our fundamental legal principles, and in doing so to organize the fight against all forms of systematic injustice of the Communist countries."

The directors of the ICJ's parent organization belonged to the elite of the New York bar. Characterized by a strong sense of noblesse oblige, they mobilized the establishment of gentlemen lawyers and their friends for the defense of the free world according to the same logic that pushed them to invest in domestic public affairs. They recruited their counterparts from abroad and located the ICJ in Geneva. According to Tolley (1994, p. 36), "The committee selected only men with high standing and considerable experience in public life—cabinet ministers, parliamentary deputies, appeal court judges." Consistent with this elitist strategy, the ICJ was limited to 25 members who were nominated for life. Drawing on the status of the jurists, the commission represented a kind of high international court that authenticated the criticisms made by lawyers expelled from communist countries and rejected the claims of the new communist regimes to the great universals of Western law. These judgments were used by the media and diffused through adherents and sympathizers of the national sections that had been organized as part of the general enterprise.

To increase its credibility, the ICJ, whose funds and powerful administrative secretary were provided by the CIA, recruited well-known persons from the academic and diplomatic worlds to serve as secretary general. Those who served included Norman S. Marsh, barrister and fellow of University College Oxford; Jean Flavien Lalive, an eminent Swiss jurist who had held leading positions in the International Red Cross, the United Nations, and the Court of Justice at the Hague; Sir Leslie Munro, ambassador from New Zealand and president of the UN General Assembly; and then, in 1963, Sean McBride. McBride, one of the founders of the

Council of Europe and a signatory of the European Convention on Human Rights, was especially active until his dismissal in 1967 when the CIA's involvement was made public.

This human rights strategy was inseparable from the Cold War strategy linked to the so-called foreign policy establishment and implemented in all the major institutions of and around the U.S. state. There was little difference in this respect between the Ford Foundation and the CIA. Both were enlisted in part as a search for high-prestige friends who would fight communism and reinforce the power of their counterparts back in the United States. Law was relatively unimportant in the struggle at the time. The ICJ was reactive, created to provide a counterpoint to the IADJ. But the approach was the same one taken generally by leading U.S. actors in and around the state during the Cold War. They looked for political allies with whom they could identify and work in a shared cause.

Despite the relative lack of importance of the law, except for the legitimacy and cover it might provide for politically motivated activities, the ICJ did develop legal expertise and a group of individuals schooled and invested in human rights. They were willing to take that learning and experience to other organizations where their expertise would be valued and where they could aspire to a greater role for human rights ideals.

AMNESTY INTERNATIONAL: FROM ELITIST MORALISM TO MASS ORGANIZATION

This profile of the ICJ is essential for understanding the development of Amnesty International. Those who invested in the human rights concerns of the ICJ knew the limitations that came from its close connection to the Cold War. They saw that the credibility and effectiveness of human rights activism could be strengthened by creating vehicles that would allow a distance from the Cold War politics of the ICJ and the IADJ. The founders of Amnesty International in 1961 in the United Kingdom thus sought to construct a mass organization financed exclusively by activists[1] and characterized, according to one former Amnesty official, by "a quasi-obsessional identification with neutrality." This same Amnesty official described Amnesty's approach as follows:

> There were academics, there were lawyers but there were also. . .people from all walks of life,. . .usually from the. . .liberal end of the political spectrum but there were some Republicans; there were conservatives. . . . [W]e had an organizer who went around the country. . .[who] would announce. . ., "Amnesty's

[1]According to one former Amnesty official, "Amnesty didn't take money from foundations and it didn't take money from governments. So, all of its money had to come from ordinary folk and. . .it didn't have that many large donors" (quoted in Dezalay & Garth 2002; see also Korey 1998, Clark 2001, Power 2001).

> forming a group and anyone's welcome" so who would show: teachers, housewives, the local journalists,...people who just cared[,] who were looking for some way to respond to the horrors that were in their newspaper[,] and [they] saw Amnesty as a safe way...[a] nonpolitical way.... [T]he strength of it was...to have a sort of mix of left and right;...every adoption group had cases from both sort of left wing countries and right wing countries so it was balanced. But also...for a while, we had both Joan Baez and William Buckley on our board, and we would trumpet that to the press.

Rather than acting more discreetly through personal relations, Amnesty's founders sought systematically to focus the attention of the media on their campaigns and activities. More specifically, from the launching of the first great international campaign in *The Observer* and *Le Monde*, Peter Benenson, a London barrister and founder of Amnesty, proposed the notion of three networks: Amnesty groups were to adopt simultaneously three political prisoners from the three great blocs of countries—communist, Western, and Third World—and thus affirm their total impartiality. This same purpose of demarcating the organization from its more political predecessors led Amnesty to limit very strictly its objectives and mandate.[2] It gave priority to prisoners of conscience punished for the expression of their opinions, and it excluded those who had committed or encouraged acts of violence (Clark 2001, pp. 12–16).

Although the founders of Amnesty initially encountered reluctance among journalists and editors, they sought to mobilize public opinion on behalf of their campaigns. Amnesty had to work hard to gain general credibility with journalists: "Amnesty was usually not the story[,] but it would fit into a story and...we did a campaign where we actually went around to editorial boards [to] convince people that [we] were credible[,] that [we]...were not pushing an agenda[,] and that was hard to do.... Nonideological journalists very quickly liked the...way we were operating because they could rely on us" (quoted in Dezalay & Garth 2002). Ultimately, the media not only opened their columns, but they also financed the first investigative missions.

These innovations were important, but the break between the first and second postwar generations of human rights was not absolute. Certainly, a clear difference was that the notables of the ICJ privileged battles on the terrain of legal standards, whereas the mass campaigns had more concrete ambitions. But continuities are quite evident in the personal relations between Amnesty and the ICJ. Most Amnesty founders were leaders of Justice, the British chapter of the ICJ. Indeed, Justice and McBride, the secretary general of the ICJ, publicly supported the new organization, and McBride was part of the first fact-finding mission to Czechoslovakia in 1962 (see Korey 1998, p. 163). McBride also went on to be chairman of Amnesty in

[2]This strict policy was debated at some length as Amnesty grew and prospered: "[T]here were all kinds of struggles on its mandate because people began to say that what Amnesty was doing was human rights and if Amnesty wasn't doing it...it wasn't human rights" (interview with former Amnesty official; see Desmond 1983).

the early 1970s. The innovations were nevertheless significant. The founders of Amnesty clearly reacted to the excesses of a too open partisanship in the name of human rights. They sought a new organization to promote their effort to give more legitimacy to human rights.

As with the ICJ, Amnesty's political autonomy was not always maintained in practice. For example, the relative ambiguity of the relationship between Amnesty and the British state became public in 1966–1967. A report, entrusted to the Amnesty Swedish section, examined acts of torture committed by the British Army in Aden (a Yemen port that was controlled as a British crown colony from 1937 to 1967). The report was hidden by Amnesty's secretary general, Robert Swann, who preferred to use his connections at the British Foreign Service to exert more discreet pressure on the government to improve its practices. Peter Benenson, taking the opposite position, quarreled with Swann and then with McBride. This internal dispute then became a more public scandal when the press revealed that Swann had worked for the British intelligence service and that Benenson had accepted funds from the British government for a mission to Rhodesia. All this happened, in fact, before the revelations in 1967 of the ICJ's financing from the CIA.

Whereas the ICJ's public scandals triggered a complete revision of its objectives and its mode of operation, Amnesty was able to get through its crisis with the support of its militant base, which was already large and active. Amnesty's obsession with neutrality helped to build its legitimacy in the 1960s (Korey 1998, pp. 168–69; Power 2001; Neier 2003, p. 151) and allowed the organization to take advantage of a series of events and crises that occurred in the late 1960s and early 1970s.

THE VICARIATE IN CHILE: AN INTERNATIONAL LABORATORY FOR HUMAN RIGHTS

Chile occupies a central place in the development of the international human rights movement both because of what happened in Chile and because of what Chile meant for politics in the United States (Keck & Sikkink 1998, pp. 88–92; Clark 2001, pp. 51–52). For example, with regard to Amnesty International's development, "[w]hat enormously facilitated Amnesty's purpose were developments in Chile. . . . The torture appeal of Amnesty took on a sense of immediacy and urgency" (Korey 1998, p. 172). Sean McBride, the new secretary general of Amnesty, had announced a campaign against torture in 1972. At the time of the coup that toppled Allende in 1973, issues such as the legality of torture or disappearances were largely absent from political debates. Lawyers mainly supported the coup, and there was no autonomous human rights movement or discourse through which lawyers could gain any distance from politics. A petition that was circulated among Chilean lawyers to mobilize opposition to the military coup in 1973 gained, according to one signer, only 12 signatures. Nevertheless, there was a very strong legally trained elite in Chile, and legal legitimacy had long been important for the Chilean state.

The focus on human rights in Chile began with an alliance between opposition politicians (especially Christian Democrats) and the Roman Catholic Church, which still contained many holdovers from Catholic progressive social thought (see generally Snyder 1995; Clark 2001, p. 52). As a well-placed informant noted, "only churches remained to provide some umbrella." According to another, the judiciary "didn't matter;" judges served only as "doormats." Some bishops joined with a group of lawyers and activists to form the Peace Committee, which later evolved into the Vicariate of Solidarity. The Vicariate became, according to Aryeh Neier, former executive director of HWR and the ACLU, "the flagship of human rights groups in Latin America, the class act" (Graham 1989). The Peace Committee established a legal department, initially headed by Jose Zalaquett, who was soon arrested and held for six weeks. By March and April 1974, the government was targeting "enemies" in unions, political parties, and faculties and using disappearances to get rid of perceived enemies.

The legal department of the Peace Committee, which soon grew to some 75 people, drew on the discredited but nevertheless existing legal tradition, filed habeas corpus petitions in every case possible, and also helped to provide lawyers for defense in the military courts. Some individuals oriented toward political action asked at the beginning whether they were legitimating the system by using the courts, but as another noted, "we didn't have any other forum." While the courts granted at most two or three writs in total, it turned out that the writs often served the collateral purpose of leading to information on the status of particular individuals.

Chile's place in the development of the field of human rights relates to its importance in the Cold War and to the internal struggles in the United States and elsewhere. It was the site of international contestation and concern about Allende and democratic transitions to socialism, and it remained so after the Pinochet coup: "*Le Monde*, *Time*, the UN, Amnesty International," and others "were coming by every day. . . . Chile was news," according to a Chilean human rights activist (see Dezalay & Garth 2002). This attention helped Chilean activists to internationalize their strategies. The people at the Peace Committee began to network with Amnesty International, which visited first in 1973 with a team that included Frank Newman (who had also worked with the ICJ and with Amnesty in Greece in 1967). They also became connected to the ICJ, the Organization of American States, and the international human rights instruments that had been created under UN auspices and were, in some cases, just coming into effect. This international focus made Chile the hot case of the day.

Some of the dynamics of this transformation in Chile and elsewhere can be seen in the biography of Jose Zalaquett. He graduated from law school in 1967 and became a law professor and criminal defense lawyer, activities consistent with careers of the traditional legal elite in Chile—lawyers from leading families who tended to serve as professors and also occupy the leading positions in the state and in the economy. But as a Christian Democrat linked to the progressive wing of Catholic thought, he also briefly worked on agrarian reform in the Allende government. After the coup, he became part of the Peace Committee. The Peace

Committee had quickly gained the support of a number of lawyers, the large majority of whom, typified by Zalaquett, had sympathized with the Allende government and joined the Peace Committee as a way to save jailed comrades. These Chilean lawyers tended to be left of center politically, but they began to move from political tactics to professional strategies, in effect turning politics into law. As Chilean activists learned that human rights talk had universal appeal—that is, that it gained widespread international support—they modified their rhetoric, from speaking of the constitution or the rights of defendants to speaking of human rights. They began, for the first time, to seek systematically to activate UN machinery.

Thus, when Zalaquett was expelled from Chile in 1976 after his second arrest, he went to work for Amnesty International, which was not yet part of the international mainstream. He became a board member of the U.S. section in 1977, began service on the international executive committee in 1978, and ultimately became chair in 1979. He moved from politics to human rights along with the field. More specifically, he went in the direction of the international strategy that gave him and others forced out of political involvement in their home countries the greatest local leverage and credibility.[3]

Amnesty's investment in Chile and other authoritarian states in the 1970s further helped to legitimate Amnesty and increase its membership. Several indicators illustrate this evolution. In the 1960s, 900 prisoners were the focus of campaigns by Amnesty, which had a staff of only one full-time and one part-time salaried person and a budget of only £10,000. By 1976, the staff had grown to about 40. Amnesty's success was evident in the fact that in 1981 it supported the campaigns of 4000 prisoners, had 250,000 members, a budget of £2 million, and a staff of 150 persons. Amnesty's growing respectability was also recognized and bolstered by the receipt of the Nobel Peace Prize in 1977 [Korey 1998, p. 179 (citing especially the work in Argentina); Power 2001].[4]

In sum, the field of international human rights developed in part out of the successes that came from political/legal investment in Chile and elsewhere in Latin America. Amnesty shaped its agenda to fit the particular developments in Latin America and to present them in ways that would build membership and gain support in the north. The weakening of the Cold War consensus in the United States, as is discussed in the next section, made the time ripe for this less politicized focus on human rights norms. It was no longer enough in the United States to simply link Chile with socialism and therefore with the wrong side of the Cold War. The

[3]Owing in part to the relative success of the international focus on Chile, the worst part of Chilean repression ended in 1978 when the secret police force (DINA) was disbanded. Pinochet governed in the 1980s without the former degree of terror, although he proclaimed amnesty for all violations except the murder of Orlando Letelier, exempted under U.S. pressure.

[4]The organizations' growth further accelerated, largely through the influx of Americans. From 1974 to 1976, U.S. membership went from 3,000 to 50,000 (Wiseberg & Scoble 1977, p. 290). The number of members tripled to 400,000 from 1985 to 1989.

authority of Cold War arguments declined, making space for other approaches, especially ones built on norms that made sense to the U.S. public—and that, indeed, had been promoted in the fight against communism.

DIVISIONS IN U.S. POLITICS: DOVES IN CONGRESS AND THE FORD FOUNDATION

Investment by human rights organizations in Chile grew out of struggles in the north and in particular in the United States. By the late 1960s, as evidenced by the student movements against the Vietnam War, the foreign policy establishment and its aggressive Cold War strategy were under considerable attack and internally divided. The U.S. executive branch support for the coup in Chile in 1973 was also symptomatic of the political divisions that already existed over Vietnam. The Democratic Party had split in 1968, which paved the way for the election of Richard Nixon. The liberal Democrats or Cold War doves in Congress began to mobilize new arguments that could be used to attack the Nixon administration's involvement in Chile. They drew upon the emerging discourses of human rights, produced a report on "Human Rights and the World Community" (U.S. Congress 1974), and enacted legislation calling for the State Department to deny assistance to countries "committing serious violations of human rights" (Foreign Assistance Act of 1973, section 32).

The congressional mandate to take human rights into account in foreign policy was sponsored by Donald Fraser, a Minnesota congressman who had been a leading liberal protégé of Hubert Humphrey. Reacting to the revelations of the role of the CIA in the fall of Allende, he and some activist congressmen, including Father Robert Drinan, sought to "put the country on the side of angels by using human rights as the touchstone of U.S. foreign policy." The initiative in Congress "came because we in Congress were very, very annoyed at the administration, particularly after we found out that the Nixon administration had destabilized the regime of. . .President Allende of Chile" (interview with Robert Drinan, quoted in Dezalay & Garth 2002).[5]

Academic idealists who had been promoting the Universal Declaration of Human Rights, and who had made some connections with Amnesty International and the ICJ, were essential in the strategy of the congressional doves (and their young staffs). Largely owing to the efforts of the existing organizations, especially the International League for the Rights of Man and the ICJ, the UN Commission on Human Rights had also passed the International Covenant on Economic, Social, and Cultural Rights and the International Covenant on Civil and Political Rights

[5]These efforts by Congress continued under the Carter administration. In March 1976, three congressmen from the U.S. went to Chile. They brought the Carter human rights message and talked to some of the Vicariate activists.

in 1966. These instruments went into effect in the mid-1970s (Korey 1998, p. 72). Furthermore, the International League for the Rights of Man and the Washington Office on Latin America had ties to the National Council of Churches and to the movements of Solidarity with Chile and Argentina (Korey 1998, p. 186). In precisely the same way as the Vicariate in Chile, these academics mobilized the neutral principles of the international law scholars, including especially Europeans (focusing on the Council of Europe and the European Convention on Human Rights), and the existing organizations, including Amnesty and the ICJ, in a series of congressional hearings. International law scholars in the United States had begun to write articles and books suggesting that the soft law of the Universal Declaration on Human Rights and the UN Charter might come to constitute a customary law of human rights and that UN machinery should be reformed to allow at least some measures of enforcement. At the time, however, international human rights law was still relatively marginal in the United States—the domain of a few immigrant-scholars with personal histories and connections that made them especially interested in the field. The first casebook on international human rights was published in 1973 by Louis Sohn and Thomas Buergenthal, both of whom had been refugees from the Nazis.

Frank Newman, although not traditionally an international law scholar, was a key figure in linking the academics and the Democratic doves. Newman had been the dean at the Law School of the University of California at Berkeley prior to taking a sabbatical in Geneva, ostensibly to explore the administrative law of the UN. He became connected to the ICJ and contributed to its activities against the Greek colonels brought before the Council of Europe. Similarly, other scholars, such as Thomas Buergenthal, drew on the experience of the Council of Europe and the European Court of Human Rights to promote new developments in the Inter-American Commission.

The linking of these academic idealists, the few existing human rights organizations, and the doves in Congress helped to build the international human rights movement as a response to the U.S. division over such regimes as that in Chile. Just as the Chilean opposition had been able to gain some power and credibility within Chile through its connection to a discourse of human rights coming largely from the north, those in the north who were questioning the traditional Cold War strategies could build their own positions by investing in the same discourse and the struggles in Chile and elsewhere. They were sufficiently successful to persuade Jimmy Carter to make human rights rhetoric an essential part of his 1976 presidential campaign and subsequently of his foreign policy.

The development and universalization of human rights activity was greatly accelerated by the activities of large philanthropic organizations, especially the Ford Foundation, where similar divisions between Cold War doves and hawks existed. The conversion of the Ford Foundation to the cause of human rights did not come easy. Even as late as 1976, according to one human rights supporter from the new generation within the Foundation, "some of our colleagues back at the Ford Foundation still believed. . .[that] Amnesty International. . .was a communist front organization" (Dezalay & Garth 2002). Despite Amnesty's efforts, the political valence of the human rights rhetoric still placed obstacles in the way of endeavors to build credibility. In the context of the Cold War, human rights rhetoric was seen as simply part of the arsenal of arguments that each side made against the other side.

The transformation within the Ford Foundation grew out of the developmental assistance in the 1960s that was geared toward upgrading social science, including economics. Economic reform and development were part of the Alliance for Progress's effort to mollify the discontent fueling leftist movements. Contrary to the specific advice of the CIA, however, which strongly opposed Allende when elected in 1970, a younger generation in the Ford Foundation office in Chile was unwilling to stop aid just because it might be helping the left. They decided to work with the Allende government rather than seek to destabilize it. After the coup, the Foundation then had to decide what to do with the pro-Allende social scientists it had funded. The survival of social science and the social scientists was now threatened.

The Ford people in Chile thus naturally asked themselves, "[W]hat can we do in a repressive regime?" The support of human rights grew out of what one former Ford Foundation official described as "a natural transition from previous times, you know before the crisis. . . . [We were] protecting our investments, past investments." The independent centers for research that Ford funded after the coup led to the support of human rights organizations that were both linked and analogous in their approaches. As another former official stated (see Dezalay & Garth 2002), the initial beneficiaries in the mid-1960s were mostly the academic elites:

> We were helping those people who were under threat of life or at least livelihood get out of the country and things like that. So, in a certain sense, that was a human rights oriented or at least influenced kind of activity. We began to broaden that in the Brazilian context and then we went squarely into supporting groups that would have to be called human rights groups in the Chile post-1973 period.

The Vicariate was already gaining prominence, but it did not fit the Ford Foundation's program. The Santiago office of the Ford Foundation recognized the need for distance from Pinochet, but in human rights—a term that was still not very prominent—the Foundation did not know what to do. The growing respectability in the international community of the Vicariate made it possible for the local Ford Foundation people to make the Vicariate part of their strategy against the repressive Pinochet regime and the Cold War tactics that supported the regime. Local Foundation officials debated internally how to support the Vicariate without getting involved in politics. Was supporting the Vicariate human rights or partisan politics?

The impressive documentation at the Vicariate—"people could pull out empirical data"—impressed the Ford Foundation trustees when they visited Chile. It was comparable to public interest law firms that the Foundation was then funding aggressively in the United States. The Vicariate was "not just people yelling and screaming" but rather was "curiously legalistic." The Foundation was willing for the first time to treat human rights as a neutral norm to be used against noncommunist U.S. allies as well as opponents.

By the mid- to late 1970s, therefore, the Ford Foundation had converted to the cause of human rights, at least as represented by the relatively legalistic and respectable Vicariate. Not coincidentally, the Foundation came to promote this model—recognizable in the United States—elsewhere. The Foundation encouraged the building of international networks in the domain of human rights. Citing the history of Zalaquett, a Ford Foundation official in Chile observed that by the late 1970s the model was in place and worked in Chile. By 1977, they had a formal program in human rights, and in 1981 "Human Rights and Governance" became one of the Foundation's five program areas (Keck & Sikkink 1998, p. 101).

The export of this model inspired by the Vicariate in Chile influenced other groups. Peter Bell, who helped work on the Ford Foundation's human rights program, then made human rights the centerpiece of the Inter-American Foundation, which he headed from the late 1970s until early in the 1980s (Keck & Sikkink 1998). William Carmichael, who also started in Latin America with human rights, became vice president of the Ford Foundation and later brought the model to South Africa, among other places. Both Bell and Carmichael also became active in human rights organizations during the 1980s and 1990s. There was also considerable investment from Canadian entities and from entities close to the Northern European and Scandinavian countries. The export of the model does not mean that it took root in the same way in other places. It depended on local conditions. Nevertheless, the program helped define what could be considered worthy of funding from the north. In this manner, the field grew enormously and attracted local groups seeking international credibility and resources elsewhere. According to Keck & Sikkink (1998, p. 99), the total U.S. investment in human rights organizations went from $1 million in 1977 to just over $3 million in 1982. Among the new organizations created with the help of the Ford Foundation were the Lawyers Committee for Human Rights[6] and the International Human Rights Law Group, both formed in 1978, reflecting the focus on more legal legitimacy seen in Chile and in the U.S. Congress. The increase in the number of organizations and the expansion of the field increased the competition between organizations. This growing legitimacy of human rights also helped to strengthen human rights strategies used against the Soviet Union and the countries of southern and eastern Europe (Laber 2002).

Along with growth and competition came a movement toward professionalization and increasing legalization. The Ford Foundation itself tended to fund

[6]The Lawyers Committee—now called Human Rights First—was a direct outgrowth of both the civil rights movement and the International League for Human Rights, linked especially through Jerome Shestak, the chair of the International League and one of the founders of the Lawyers Committee (Korey 1998, p. 157). It also reflected the League's strategy of responding to the success of Amnesty (Wiseberg & Scoble 1977, p. 308). The International League, it should be noted, appeared to be divided sharply by the Pinochet coup (Wiseberg & Scoble 1977, p. 300). One of its affiliates strongly defended the coup and Pinochet.

projects only when they put together respectable governing boards akin to those mandated for public interest law firms in the United States. Amnesty International progressively upgraded its London staff as the field grew (Page 1992). A team of professionals who focused on collecting and organizing information gradually replaced an earlier generation of distinguished amateurs, and there were some tensions between the two generations. Some of the tensions are reflected in the story of the establishment of HRW. Again, we see the reaction to predecessor organizations—the internal human rights story—and a reaction to changes in the political landscape in the United States. The next section focuses on the political landscape.

COMPETITION AND PROFESSIONALIZATION IN THE MARKET OF CIVIC VIRTUE

The increased competition and professionalization in the field of human rights must be understood in relation to the change that took place generally in the field of state power in the United States. The key element—which shaped subsequent developments in the field—was the conservative counterrevolution. We have already described the split in the Cold War consensus and its impact on the human rights field. The split in that consensus led to the election of Richard Nixon, but it did not challenge the essentially reformist nature of U.S. politics since the New Deal. Changes in the economy and in business began to unleash a conservative dynamic with profound consequences. Indeed, as the liberal establishment had done, conservatives from the United States also sought to build their power by investing their ideas in Chile. The famous "Chicago Boys," who became Pinochet's economists, formed a foreign beachhead for monetarist ideas that at the time were still not part of the mainstream in the United States. The Chicago economic ideas then became part of the conservative counterrevolution in the United States—attacking the activist state and various social programs. The activism of the Ford Foundation domestically now became quite controversial. This activism was especially apparent under the Foundation presidency of McGeorge Bundy, which began in 1966. Bundy was a perfect representative of the eastern establishment and a diehard cold warrior. He was also a strong domestic reformer and helped the Ford Foundation turn toward the civil rights movement and public interest law (Bird 1998). Bundy presided over the Ford Foundation's conversion to human rights as a revised basis for building and protecting American friends abroad.

The Conservative Counterrevolution

The progressive reformers of what had by then become the "liberal establishment" (Kabaservice 2004), which had long dominated domestic politics, became the scapegoats of a conservative counterrevolution, which mimicked the Ford Foundation's own strategy of mobilizing the academic world and the ideas connected to it in the service of a political project. This mimicry is captured in an account of the history of the conservative movement. Paul Weyrich, one of the founders and the first president of the Heritage Foundation, created in 1973, reported that he attended "a civil rights strategy meeting" as a member of the staff of a Republican senator in 1969. He claimed that "[t]here before my eyes was unveiled how the other side operated.... The meeting drew together disparate groups from the Left—among them, the Brookings Institution, the liberal National Committee for an Effective Congress, the ACLU—to discuss how to pool their discrete resources into an effort to torpedo a Nixon Administration housing initiative" (quoted in Lowry 1995). Weyrich and a small group of friends finally found funding from Joseph Coors to establish the Heritage Foundation.[7]

According to the director of research of the Heritage Foundation, who began there in 1977, "[W]e had one major goal in mind: to create a think tank unlike any Washington had previously known.... One of the most important decisions we made right at the start was to run Heritage like a business. That meant identifying our market niche, creating a unique product and aggressively marketing it.... The third thing we did is go out and recruit the best and brightest researchers and marketing professionals we could afford" (Heritage Foundation 1996). James Piereson, executive director of the Olin Foundation, which invested substantially in law and economics and in the right-wing think tanks, stated that "[w]e invested at the top of society, in Washington think tanks and the best universities, and the idea is this would have a much larger impact because they were influential places" (People for the American Way 1996, p. 8).

The effects of this conservative strategy (linked also to the neo-liberal economic revolution that gained power at the same time) were contradictory. On the one hand, the development of right-wing activism moved the left-leaning reformers linked to the liberal establishment—which had lost power when it divided over Vietnam—to protect the social movements representing the disadvantaged, polarizing domestic politics. On the other hand, the engagement of the strategies of the New Right with the practices of the more liberal foundations helped to remake domestic politics. Politics in the United States became more competitive, more adversarial, and more media-oriented. This change had major implications for the field of human rights as well.

When Reagan became president in 1980, he brought to power a very conservative coalition that rejected the social programs and political approaches that had long been the center of the federal government. The new politics, in addition, put a premium on the ability to package news, to develop catchy sound bites, and to be flexible and address issues as they came up. Not surprisingly, contrary to the developments seen in the establishment of Amnesty, the succeeding generation of actors and institutions in the field of human rights became more politically oriented and more willing to adopt an elitist profile.

---

[7]The American Enterprise Institute (AEI), another prominent think tank of the right, was founded much earlier, in 1943. A description of the AEI in 1995 describes it as having "twice as much history and half the funding as Heritage but prides itself on original research and the eminence of its senior scholars" (Burton 1995). There is, of course, a parallel in the conservative histories to the story of the notables of the foreign policy establishment.

The emerging terrain of human rights provided a legitimate means to contest the orientations of the Reagan administration. The right was fighting—at home in the guise of neo-liberalism and abroad in the name of an anticommunist crusade—against the human rights professionals' institutional bases in the social state. Those who had been linked to the reformist and antiwar movements of the 1960s and 1970s sought to mobilize their social capital of personal relations as well as the professional institutions that they controlled. For example, the chairman of the U.S. Helsinki Watch Committee was Robert Bernstein, the president of Random House. The two other officers, Orville Schell and Adrian DeWind, were partners in leading Wall Street law firms and had been or were at the time presidents of the New York City Bar. DeWind's career includes serving as the chair of the Natural Resources Defense Council, one of the most active NGOs in the domain of the environment. Schell was also a member of the select Council for Public Interest Law funded by the Ford Foundation in the mid-1970s. Along with this group associated with Helsinki Watch were presidents of major universities including Chicago, MIT, and Columbia; leaders of banks, including Lazard Freres and Salomon Brothers; representatives of the literary world, including the authors E.L. Doctorow, Toni Morrison, and Robert Penn Warren and well-known editors and literary critics (see Laber 2002). As Aryeh Neier (2003, pp. 153–54) wrote about Orville Schell, the first chair of Americas Watch, "he understood very well that I wanted to trade on his establishment credentials. As senior partner at a leading Wall Street law firm, counsel to major corporations, and a past president of the Association of the Bar of the City of New York, those credentials were impeccable.... Orville brought patrician respectability to our efforts."

A civil rights strategy abroad was designed to curb the Reagan crusade and maintain the value of a civil rights expertise that had been depreciated as rent-seeking by special interests. In fact, in several important respects this strategy served to bolster the declining domestic political fortunes of the lawyers associated with the civil rights movement, which was losing momentum in the United States in the new era of conservatism. According to one law professor who went into human rights in the late 1970s:

> I did all sorts of First Amendment work and a lot of other sorts of cases. But as the '70s wore on, the tide began to turn against us and we started to repeat ourselves and. . .I just got tired of it. And, so I was offered this job here teaching. . .about the time. . .[that] international human rights became a hot issue about which I knew absolutely nothing. I mean I didn't even know what the documents were that set forth the rights, initially. But. . .people who have been mixed up in civil rights, you know, public interest people have tended to siphon into human rights.

Aryeh Neier made a similar move from the ACLU in the 1970s to HRW in the 1980s. The ACLU underwent a substantial decline in the late 1970s, from 270,000 members in 1974 to 185,000 in 1978 (Garey 1998, p. 177). Human rights therefore provided a strategic opportunity and terrain for a political fight in the United

States between the new conservative holders of state power and their supporting foundations and a large coalition of opponents from the civil rights movement and liberal foundations.

This new version of the reformist establishment fought the authoritarian free market in Chile, just as the cold warriors around Kissinger had sought to counter the potential domestic influence of Democratic Socialism in Chile in the early 1970s. The symbolic target in the United States was Jeanne Kirkpatrick, a former Humphrey Democrat isolated by the left turn of the Democratic Party in 1972. After 1972, this group, calling themselves the Coalition for a Democratic Majority, found themselves shut out of the decision-making process: Humphrey, Daniel Moynihan, Kirkpatrick, and others, who were characterized as neoconservative (Conaway 1981). Kirkpatrick became affiliated with the American Enterprise Institute and maintained close ties to *Commentary*, the leading neo-conservative publication. Her rationale for supporting Pinochet, as well as the Argentine generals in that country's authoritarian regime, hearkened back to the Cold War. Such support by Democrats of authoritarian regimes in Latin America provided an opportunity for human rights activists: Human rights became a means to fight this U.S. political battle abroad. Aryeh Neier was reported in *The New Republic* as saying that "when Jeanne Kirkpatrick. . .suggested treating friendly authoritarian regimes more charitably than hostile totalitarian ones, 'We felt that the only way we could be credible in dealing with human rights in the Soviet Union, and not subject to the charge of waging a cold war attack, was if we were even handed and were concerned with human rights abuses in friendly authoritarian countries'" (Kondracke 1988). HRW emerged in this context.

Human Rights Watch

The forerunner of HRW, the U.S. Helsinki Watch Committee, was initially created at the instigation of Arthur Goldberg in 1979 to support the actions of the Helsinki monitors in the United States. Goldberg was the key figure in taking the Helsinki Accords into the public forum to attack the treatment of dissidents. He asked Robert Bernstein and the U.S. Helsinki Watch Committee to become involved in Helsinki monitoring (Laber 2002). According to Korey (1998, p. 238), "Goldberg saw the need for a responsible and highly regarded American NGO that could provide detailed information about Communist repression that might sensitize Western public opinion.... [H]e met with the President of the Ford Foundation, McGeorge Bundy, and prevailed upon him to form an appropriate NGO." Ford's initial grant was $500,000 to Bernstein to "establish liaison" with groups formed or that could be formed in the wake of Helsinki. The U.S. Helsinki Watch Committee began by using human rights strategies to support the emerging opposition in eastern and central Europe, helping to build the language of the Helsinki Accords into a network of opposition groups united under the banner of human rights (Laber 2002). This reshaping of the Cold War strategy was consistent with the growing credibility of human rights but not so different from the strategy pursued initially by the ICJ. The real change, however, came with the election of Ronald Reagan.

The U.S. Helsinki Watch Committee was transformed in 1982 into HRW, along with a new branch termed Americas Watch. Aryeh Neier, who had been a prominent leader of the ACLU, became director, and the early board included establishment lawyers identified with opposition to the Vietnam War. Neier described Americas Watch as "founded in reaction to the arrival of the Reagan administration. 'Those of us who created Helsinki Watch,' he said, felt that it [the Reagan administration] 'threatened to undercut Helsinki Watch because it politicized the issue of human rights in the Soviet Union'" (Kondracke 1988). The focus of HRW was on the state at home even though the investigations were conducted abroad: "[W]e were oriented toward Washington, D.C. at the time" (interview with U.S. human rights activist). For example, Bernstein was quoted in Korey (1998, p. 343) as saying that, in comparison to Amnesty, "We're much more involved with the U.S. government. We're in all parts of it." According to Neier (2003, p. 168), "Human Rights Watch's rise to international eminence derived in part from its role as an organization based in the United States that exercised influence over U.S. policy." The focus on the United States as the key actor, in other words, was what defined HRW internationally.

This new elite of human rights—which flourished in institutions like HRW—included a number of the important lawyers from the beginning, but the early initiative came from the publishing industry. Robert Bernstein, in particular, came to Helsinki Watch through a concern that began in the 1960s to protect the freedom of expression of Soviet and Eastern European dissidents. Bernstein created the Fund for Free Expression in 1964 to have a forum that could be more aggressive than the Association of American Publishers was willing to be (Korey 1998, p. 341; see also Laber 2002). The dissidents' work was published by Random House, where Bernstein was president.

This anchor of human rights in the literary and journalistic world helped to reinforce the strategy of mediatization increasingly practiced by Amnesty, but the new context was at the same time more political and more elitist. As NGOs multiplied in number, moreover, the competition increased in the media and in the domain of philanthropy. The competition was exacerbated because the success of NGOs in gaining exposure in the media in large part determined their visibility, their capacity to recruit, and finally even their budget. The individual contributions made to these enterprises and, to a certain extent, their support from the foundations, were closely connected to their notoriety. In this new political context, linked to the rise of the New Right and its more aggressive media strategy, the professionals that the human rights groups recruited were anxious to operate with the objectives and methods that appeared to be most effective pursuant to this media-oriented strategy.

In the same way that Amnesty International constructed its identity in opposition to the ICJ, therefore, the new organizations for the protection of human rights, developed after the Helsinki Accords, were defined in relation to what they perceived as problems in Amnesty's type of mass mobilization. According to a veteran activist in human rights,

> [T]he fundamental difference. . .is that Human Rights Watch didn't see itself as a membership organization, which is probably why it could move very quickly. . . . Amnesty's strength was also one of its limits[,] because. . .it couldn't change without the consent of its membership, which grew larger and larger. . . . Human Rights Watch saw that and very consciously decided it didn't want to be bogged down by having to consult with members when it wanted to do something and it had this tremendous freedom. . . . [T]ake an example, humanitarian law. Amnesty was very careful and still is very careful about. . .working in the area of armed conflict and citing humanitarian laws. . . . Human Rights Watch said human rights [violations] are occurring in the context of armed conflict, we're going to start citing. . .humanitarian law and we're going to work on armed conflict situations like in Chechnya[,] and they were able to do that (quoted in Dezalay & Garth 2002).

HRW was particularly successful in using the press as a tool on behalf of human rights. "We pride ourselves in being able to present human rights information in a way that is interesting to the press, and that is a regularly evolving process—and one that requires knowing what journalists revere as pushing the envelope and interesting to the readers and beyond what they could have done on their own so that they will be inclined to incorporate this information" (U.S. human rights activist, quoted in Dezalay & Garth 2002). Further, drawing on elite foundation support, HRW emphasized a flexible and professional staff. They "consciously saw Amnesty as a model, tried to take the best of what Amnesty had in terms of its accuracy, its reporting, its impartiality[,] but felt that Amnesty had too limited a mandate and moved too slowly. The new structures like HRW sought to be lighter in order to have the power to invest more easily in new and more political and policy-oriented terrains, such as humanitarian law, and to develop new strategies and modes of action like trade sanctions or boycott campaigns. They also emphasized their technical skills and links to cutting-edge law, making them less reliant on legal notables. HRW thus reportedly relied on Theodor Meron of NYU Law School and Robert Goldman at American University: "[T]hey introduced us to the laws of war. They guided us through the complex set of commandments and got us comfortable in dealing with something that was really not considered a human rights issue." Indeed, the media emphasis and increased competition made using other kinds of celebrities to gain attention to particular causes and concerns increasingly important. "In the beginning we were very careful about. . .a list of advisory committee members who were very prominent people[,] who could open doors for us. And so that kind of personal diplomacy built on sort of pre-existing relationships was much more important in the early years. As time went on we didn't need others to create access for us. It came. . .through respect for our work. . .[and] the fact that we were going to be able to get to the press. I mean it was clear that we had credibility with the press. And so policymakers understood that they ignored us at their peril" (interview with U.S. human rights activist, quoted in Dezalay & Garth 2002).

While the new breed of activist NGOs could act with commando-like swiftness, they were also dependent on the philanthropic foundations.[8] Indeed, they owed their existence to the symbiotic relationship between the professionals of activism and the managers of philanthropy. The foundations made their decisions by consulting the judgment of peers, in this case the small network of professionals and intellectuals of philanthropic activism, both for the selection of projects and for their evaluation. They also contributed to the education of new generations of professionals. Activities included financing seminars about human rights, courses on the campuses, and granting intern fellowships to young graduates who wanted apprenticeships in NGOs—thus creating local paths for the development of leaders for the often related transnational NGOs. With the active support of the foundations, therefore, the human rights field and its transnational networks developed further.

Within the emerging field of international human rights, as in other fields, competition fostered development and professionalization under the direction of policy entrepreneurs. The adversarial marketing that helped the conservative think tanks attack the foundations and the liberal think tanks' strategy of gradual reformism matched perfectly with the new generation of human rights organizations epitomized by HRW. In particular, the human rights field prospered enormously in the 1980s from the widely reported debates between Reagan administration officials, especially Elliot Abrams, and human rights advocates such as Aryeh Neier and Michael Posner. An article in *The New Republic* noted that, "As combatants go, you could not ask for a better match—in terms of intelligence, assurance, activism, sometimes savage partisanship, and argumentative skills, than Abrams and Neier" (Kondracke 1988). The media success on both sides of these debates ensured that, in the words of a *New York Times* editor, "the American public has made it fairly clear that it sees human rights as an absolute good—a universal aspiration to be pursued for its own sake" (Jacoby 1986). Ultimately, the debates helped to turn Reagan against Pinochet and toward support of elections that led to Pinochet's defeat. The debates also forced the human rights movement to balance its reporting across countries and to upgrade the quality of its work:

> Americas Watch. . .was designed to show that we were going to apply the same standards not only to the communist governments that had been the subject of Helsinki Watch but also to the right-wing governments that were subject of Americas Watch in Latin America. And that movement into head on confrontation with the Administration in Washington over its human rights policy[,] be it supporting the Salvadoran regimes, supporting the Contras in Nicaragua,. . .tolerating Pinochet in Chile or the Junta in Argentina, that very adversarial relationship was very interesting to the press[,] and we found that

[8]In addition to the Ford Foundation, other major funding sources in the 1980s were the MacArthur Foundation, the Revson Foundation, the J.M. Kaplan Foundation, and George Soros, who ultimately hired Aryeh Neier to head his own foundation.

> the argument. . .because the Reagan Administration couldn't say human rights are irrelevant or "we don't mind if we're supporting human rights abusers," they tended to try to apologize for and defend the human rights records of these very repressive right-wing governments[,] and they did it by lying about the facts. And so. . .that sort of pushed us into our methodology which was to be absolutely certain that we got our facts right[,] and it forced us to be much more sophisticated, to go out into the field in the middle of the war zone and get the firsthand witnesses who can reliably tell you what happened and then to put that information out in a way that could affect the policy debates in Washington about whether to continue funding the Contras or whether to cut off aid to the Salvadoran government" (interview with U.S. human rights activist; see also Neier 2003, pp. 169, 174–221).

The adversarial media campaign organized around human rights also gave legitimacy and importance to law and to lawyers in debates around U.S. foreign policy. In the words of a *New York Times* editor, this "public disputation" on many occasions "seemed to serve a useful purpose, conferring new legitimacy on human rights issues and providing the noisy background clamor—the evidence of domestic American concern—that was often needed to give some meaning to the Administration's quiet diplomacy" (Jacoby 1986, p. 1082). Neier and Abrams argued both about facts and about the legal requirements.[9] The expertise of the new generation of lawyers (and journalists) gained a more prominent place.

The human rights field gained autonomy in relation to these and similar debates, which led both conservatives and relatively liberal activists to occupy the same field. These investments also legalized the field to a much greater extent, and the leading human rights organizations began to recruit increasingly from the most elite law schools—which cemented their relationships through human rights programs and internships. As a lawyer in HRW stated, "the goal is to try to enforce the law without a legal system in any traditional sense. If you have a functioning legal system[,] you can call on organizations that look more like the ACLU, where there is a prominent role for lawyers. But most of the countries where we work. . .have much more rudimentary if any legal systems[,] and so the challenge of the human rights movement is to create surrogate forms of protection pending the establishment of legally based rights[,] and the process of doing that doesn't require a law degree. I mean a law degree is very helpful but if you look at sort of

---

[9]Ehrman (1995, pp. 155–62) provides a fascinating account of how Elliot Abrams used human rights as a platform to assert the importance of law and his own importance with respect to Jeanne Kirkpatrick and the Reagan administration. Abrams's campaign on the terrain of law was successful enough to lead the administration to invest in democracy more generally, including the creation of the National Endowment for Democracy in 1983 (Erhman 1995, pp. 163; see generally Guilhot 2005). The revival of what can be termed a new law and development movement in Washington owes much to this revival of interest in law as a tool of foreign policy in the 1980s (Carothers 1991, 1998).

our employees, maybe a third of them are lawyers but the rest are journalists, they are regional experts." HRW leaders noted that they tended to get the top people from the top law schools. As of 2006, some 40 members of the Yale Law School student body spend the summer after their first year working on a human rights mission as part of the Orville H. Schell, Jr. Center for International Human Rights. The relative autonomy of this field is indicated in part through the circulation of individuals. There is mobility within the human rights community, between the human rights community and the foundations that support it, and between the elite human rights organizations and the legal academy.[10] With the arrival of the Clinton administration in 1992, in addition, there was much more circulation between the human rights community and the state. Human rights discourse by that time had moved from a combination of marginal soft law and mainly instrumental politics in the 1950s to a field characterized by many institutions and organizations competing to unmask human rights violations and to redefine human rights categories to make them relevant to emerging foreign policy issues central to Washington, DC, decision making.

This relative autonomy does not mean that the arguments are not used strategically. The terrain of international human rights, as with respect to the terrain of law in the United States, is less that of virtue and great principles and more that of realpolitik. Recourse to public opinion and legalistic pronouncements are above all arguments in a negotiation. There can be an implicit or explicit blackmail behind the arguments, but arguments can also be addressed less to the dictators than to all those who have political and economic relations with them—from the State Department to the multilateral financial institutions to leaders of multinational corporations. As a professor in the Harvard Graduate School of Business recently described:

> When U.S. corporations go abroad, they take more than their capital and technology with them. They also take their brand names, their reputations, and their international images. They bring in their wake the scrutiny of U.S.-based activist groups and the international media. When U.S. corporations are caught engaging in unfair or abusive practices, these groups spring into action, casting a shadow of scorn.... On the Internet, grassroots activism has, quite literally, been electrified.... Suddenly, the advantages of lower-cost labor or lower-cost inputs must be weighed against the crush of negative publicity, the cost of public relations, and the possibility of consumer protests (Spar 1998, p. 8).

[10]"We get a lot of people who come to Human Rights Watch who've worked for another human rights group," reported a U.S. human rights activist. Korey (1998) reports many such career moves: Gay McDougall from the Southern Africa project of the Lawyers Committee for Civil Rights under Law to director of the International Human Rights Law Group; Reed Brody from deputy director of the ICJ in Geneva to director of the International Human Rights Law Group to HRW; Holly Burkhalter from HRW to Physicians for Human Rights; Felice Gaer from the Ford Foundation to the International League to the Blaustein Institute, with service as a public representative to the Beijing Conference.

These actors have some leverage over countries that can be portrayed as human rights violators, and influence in New York and Washington—and media attention in those centers of power—is essential to get that leverage. As Neier (2003, p. 200) noted about innovations that he helped generate at HRW, including those in international humanitarian law, "These additions were needed for our reports to carry weight in Washington. . .to mobilize members of Congress to confront the Reagan administration."

CONCLUDING OBSERVATIONS

Paradoxically, the process of internal transformation and autonomization in the field of international human rights has allowed the field to serve the interests of the United States better than in the days of the Cold War. The growing global market in expertise—including in human rights expertise—is structured around the human rights industry and the institutions that support it in the United States. As the supporters of the NGOs that promote international human rights are quick to point out, the move from the original version of the ICJ to HRW and others can be seen as a story of growing autonomy from the state, including the United States. The instrumental Cold War strategy of the early ICJ is long gone. The movement from the grand old men to the technocrats here, as elsewhere, led to an institutionalization and rationalization. But the relative autonomy that emerged remains structured around the U.S. state and the strategies that are used in U.S. politics, especially legal and media strategies. The issues that are put on the international human rights agenda, through the same logic, are issues that can gain attention in the media and in the academies of the United States—human rights, the environment, ethnic cleansing, and violence against women are scrutinized today as were torture, apartheid, and disappearances tied to U.S.-supported dictatorships in Latin America in an earlier day. The human rights rhetoric that played a small part in the war against communism in the 1950s became the central discourse and source of legitimacy for the war in Kosovo in the 1990s.[11] The war in Iraq lacks the consensus that supported the war in Kosovo, but it is instructive that the Bush administration—despite its own reluctance to invest in treaties or compliance with international law—increasingly relied on the rhetoric of human rights and democracy to justify the U.S.-led invasion.

---

[11]One young HRW lawyer provided an account, celebrated by his alma mater, Stanford Law School, of the relationship between HRW, *The New York Times*, and the war in Kosovo. Two HRW experts in 1998 brought a *New York Times* reporter to see three corpses and to do interviews on some 13 deaths of Albanians. The reporter "wrote a front-page story in *The New York Times*, for which the editors made the rare decision to run explicit photographs of the victims. . . . After the war, Richard Holbrooke, the American diplomat, was quoted as saying that the *Times* story. . .helped galvanize U.S. intervention[,]. . . strengthened by the expertise. . .and the authority of Human Rights Watch on the scene" (Fisher 2002).

LITERATURE CITED

Bird K. 1998. *The Color of Truth: McGeorge Bundy and William Bundy, Brothers in Arms.* New York: Simon & Schuster

Burton D. 1995. To win the battle of ideas, send in the conservative think tanks. *Insight News*, March 6, p. 16–17

Carothers T. 1991. *In the Name of Democracy: U.S. Policy Toward Latin America in the Reagan Years*. Berkeley: Univ. Calif. Press

Carothers T. 1998. The rule of law revised. *Foreign Aff.* 77(2):95–106

Clark AM. 2001. *Diplomacy of Conscience: Amnesty International and Changing Human Rights Norms*. Princeton, NJ: Princeton Univ. Press

Conaway J. 1981. Jeane Kirkpatrick: the ambassador from *Commentary* magazine. *Wash. Post Mag.*, Nov. 1, p. 11

Desmond L. 1983. *Preservation East and West: Human Rights, Political Prisoners and Amnesty*. Harmondsworth: Penguin

Dezalay Y, Garth B. 1996. *Dealing in Virtue: International Commercial Arbitration and the Construction of a Transnational Legal Order*. Chicago: Univ. Chicago Press

Dezalay Y, Garth BG. 2002. *The Internationalization of Palace Wars: Lawyers, Economists, and the Contest to Transform Latin American States*. Chicago: Univ. Chicago Press

Dezalay Y, Garth BG. 2006. From the foreign policy establishment to the legalization of foreign policy. In *Cambridge History of American Law*, ed. M Grossberg, C Tomlins. Cambridge, UK: Cambridge Univ. Press. In press

Dudziak M. 2000. *Cold War Civil Rights: Race and the Image of American Democracy*. Princeton, NJ: Princeton Univ. Press

Ehrman J. 1995. *The Rise of Neoconservatism: Intellectuals and Foreign Affairs 1945–1994*. New Haven, CT: Yale Univ. Press

Fisher I. 2002. Making the world unsafe for dictators. *Stanford Lawyer* Summer:18–23

Garey D. 1998. *Defending Everybody: A History of the American Civil Liberties Union*. New York: TV Books

Graham B. 1989. Chilean oppressed turn to Vicariate. *Wash. Post*, May 2, p. G12

Guilhot N. 2005. *The Democracy Makers: Human Rights and the Politics of the Global Order*. New York: Columbia Univ. Press

Hagan J. 2003. *Justice in the Balkans: Prosecuting War Crimes in the Hague Tribunal*. Chicago: Univ. Chicago Press

Hagan J, Levi R. 2005. Crimes of war and the force of law. *Soc. Forces* 83:1499–534

Heritage Foundation. 1996. *Annual Report*. Washington, DC: Heritage Found.

Jacoby T. 1986. The Reagan turnaround on human rights. *Foreign Aff.* 64:1071–72

Kabaservice G. 2004. *Kingman Brewster. His Circle, and the Rise of the Liberal Establishment*. New York: Henry Holt

Keck M, Sikkink K. 1998. *Activists Beyond Borders*. Ithaca, NY: Cornell Univ. Press

Klug H. 2005. Transnational human rights: exploring the persistence and globalization of human rights. *Annu. Rev. Law Soc. Sci.* 1:85–103

Kondracke M. 1988. Broken watch: human rights or politics. *New Repub.*, Aug. 22, p. 8

Korey W. 1993. *The Promises We Keep: Human Rights, the Helsinki Process, and American Foreign Policy*. New York: St. Martin's

Korey W. 1998. *NGOs and the Universal Declaration of Human Rights: A Curious Grapevine*. New York: St. Martin's

Laber J. 2002. *The Courage of Strangers: Coming of Age with the Human Rights Movement*. New York: Public Affairs

Lowry R. 1995. How the right rose. *Natl. Rev.*, Dec. 11, p. 66

Madsen MR. 2005. *L'emergence d'un champ des droits de l'homme dans les pays européens: enjeux professional et strategies d'etat au Carrefour du droit et de la politique (France, Gran-Bretagne, et pays scandinave, 1945–2000)*. PhD thesis. L'Ecole de hautes études en science socials, Paris

Madsen MR. 2006. From Cold War instrument to European Supreme Court: the European Court of Human Rights at the crossroads of international and national law and politics. *Law Soc. Inq.* In press

McClymont M, Golub S, eds. 2000. *Many Roads to Justice: The Law Related Work of Ford Foundation Grantees Around the World*. New York: Ford Found.

Neier A. 2003. *Taking Liberties: Four Decades in the Struggle for Rights*. New York: Public Affairs

Page N. 1992. Workers for freedom. *Legal Bus. Mag.*, June, pp. 28–31

People for the American Way. 1996. *Buying a Movement*. Washington, DC: People for the American Way

Power J. 2001. *Like Water on Stone: The Story of Amnesty International*. Boston: Northeast. Univ. Press

Risse T, Sikkink K. 1999. The socialization of international human rights norms into domestic practices: introduction. In *The Power of Human Rights: International Norms and Domestic Change*, ed. T Risse, SC Ropp, K Sikkink, pp. 1–38. Cambridge, UK: Cambridge Univ. Press

Sikkink K. 2002. *Mixed Signals: U.S. Human Rights Policy and Latin America*. Ithaca, NY: Cornell Univ. Press

Singer A. 1987. Human rights defender Michael Posner. *Am. Lawyer*, Sept., p. 97

Snyder M. 1995. *Transforming Development: Women, Poverty and Politics*. London: Intermed. Technol. Publ.

Sohn L, Buergenthal T. 1973. *International Protection of Human Rights*. Indianapolis: Bobbs-Merrill

Spar D. 1998. The spotlight and the bottom line. *Foreign Aff.* 77(2):7–12

Tolley HJ. 1994. *The International Commission of Jurists: Global Advocates for Human Rights*. Philadelphia: Univ. Penn. Press

U.S. Congress. House. Foreign Affairs Committee. 1974. *Human Rights in the World Community: A Call for U.S. Leadership, Report of the Subcommittee on International Organizations and Movements*. 93d Cong., 2d Sess., March 27

Valdes JG. 1995. *Pinochet's Economists: The Chicago School in Chile*. Cambridge, UK: Cambridge Univ. Press

Wiseberg L, Scoble H. 1977. The International League for Human Rights: the strategy of a human rights NGO. *Georgia J. Int. Comp. Law* 7:289–314

Annu. Rev. Law Soc. Sci. 2006. 2:257–77
doi: 10.1146/annurev.lawsocsci.2.061206.074644

First published online as a Review in Advance on July 31, 2006

EMERGENCY POWERS

William E. Scheuerman
Department of Political Science, Indiana University, Bloomington, Indiana 47405; email: wscheuer@indiana.edu

Key Words state of emergency, rule of law, terrorism

■ **Abstract** This review considers competing models of emergency legal regulation in the aftermath of the terrorist attacks of September 11, 2001. Drawing on research in political science and political sociology, it criticizes recent debates about emergency powers among legal and constitutional scholars for ignoring the institutional dynamics of modern executive power, especially in presidential regimes. Constitutional relativists (e.g., Harvey Mansfield, Michael Stokes Paulsen, John Yoo), defenders of the extralegal model of emergency action (Oren Gross, Mark Tushnet), and common lawyers (David Cole, David Dyzenhaus) are criticized for failing to consider the pathologies likely generated by their proposals in an institutional context in which the executive possesses incentives for declaring, perpetuating, and exploiting emergency situations. Only a legal formalist perspective on emergency government (e.g., Bruce Ackerman) pays sufficient attention to the institutional dynamics of the contemporary executive.

INTRODUCTION

The terrorist attacks of September 11, 2001, quickly altered not only ordinary political debate in the United States and many other liberal democracies, but also legal scholarship. There is perhaps no better example of this shift than the dramatic revival of interest in the question of emergency powers. What special powers need to be given the executive in the context of a dire threat to the political order, and how might we best regulate those powers to preserve the rule of law and constitutionalism?[1] How can the executive both take on potentially unprecedented forms of discretionary legal authority and use it solely for the purpose of reestablishing legal normalcy? As the annals of both political theory and history quickly confirm, the dilemmas at hand are enormous. Jurists and political theorists have struggled to develop models that claim to square the circle of emergency rule, offering up a variety of ideas about how the executive might garner vast exceptional power without necessarily leading to authoritarian rule. Yet too often rulers

[1]Both the rule of law and constitutionalism are contested terms. For the purposes of this review, I see them as interlocking parts of a general attempt to ensure that government action rests on norms that take a general, relatively clear, stable, and prospective form for the sake of guaranteeing both individual liberty and democratic accountability.

exploit crisis situations to augment their personal and institutional power, relying on emergencies to transform the constitutional system for the worse (Freeman 2003, Franklin 1991, Lobel 1989, Loveman 1993, Rossiter 2002 [1948]). Historical experience leads us to question what the most astute mid-century students of emergency power dubbed "constitutional dictatorship," according to which substantial augmentations of emergency executive authority could successfully buttress rather than diminish liberal democratic legal and constitutional aspirations (Rossiter 2002 [1948], Watkins 1940).

Unfortunately, the post-9/11 debate about emergency powers has done little better at squaring the circle of emergency power. Socio-legal scholarship has raised vital questions about the structural roots of emergency government, linking its growth to the dynamics of colonialism, militarism, imperialism, capitalism, globalization, the "risk society," and even the high-speed temporality of contemporary society (Brandon 2005; Jayasuriya 2002; Hussain 2003; Lobel 1989; Neumann & Kirchheimer 1996; Scheuerman 1999, 2004; Schneiderman 2001). Yet socio-legal researchers have avoided tackling the pressing normative and institutional question of how emergency power might be rendered congruent with the rule of law and constitutionalism. In contrast, traditional legal and constitutional scholars have tackled this puzzle. Four main positions have been staked out in the ongoing debate, each of which supports an expansion of emergency discretionary power while hoping to employ it for the sake of preserving the rule of law and constitutionalism. Constitutional relativists see the possibility of freewheeling emergency prerogative as built into constitutionally based notions of the executive power. In contrast, extralegalists follow the seventeenth century philosopher John Locke in insisting that emergency prerogative rightly operates outside the boundaries of the normally functioning legal and constitutional order. Like the constitutional relativists, the common lawyers believe that emergency authority should be conceived as resting on the law, but they look to the traditional methods and virtues of a judiciary schooled in the common law in order to counteract its dangers. Finally, the legal formalists posit that only well-designed formal emergency powers clauses, along the lines already found in some liberal democratic constitutions, provide a reasonable opportunity to square the circle of emergency power.

Yet this otherwise impressive jurisprudential debate suffers from a familiar weakness: It focuses on legal and normative arguments and fails to give sufficient consideration to the broader social and political context in which competing conceptions of emergency government operate. In what follows, I summarize and then criticize the present debate by bringing social factors—more specifically, the institutional dynamics of the modern executive—back into the story. I argue that any plausible vision of emergency government must adequately consider a body of empirical research in political science and sociology about the modern executive. In the U.S. context, special attention must be paid to critical analyses of presidentialism (Ackerman 2000, Arato 2002, Finer 1960, Linz 1994, O'Donnell 1994, Rudalevige 2005). As I show in this review, only the legal formalists acknowledge satisfactorily the dangers posed by executive power in a historical context in which it already possesses a stunning array of political and legal weapons.

CONSTITUTIONAL RELATIVISM

Constitutional relativism became influential within the Bush administration and among its partisan academic defenders in the immediate aftermath of 9/11. This is not surprising: It provided a ready justification for the extraordinary examples of executive prerogative along the lines most U.S. citizens seemed willing to embrace. Its outlines can be discerned in a series of internal Bush administration memos authored by Jay Bybee, Alberto Gonzales, and John Yoo (Danner 2004), in recent Supreme Courts briefs penned by Justice Clarence Thomas (see Dyzenhaus 2005), as well as in scholarly works published by conservative intellectuals like the political theorist Harvey C. Mansfield (1989, 2006) and legal scholar Michael Stokes Paulsen (2004). Yet its deeper roots lie in the emergence of the modern imperial presidency (Lobel 1989, Rudalevige 2005, Schlesinger 2005).[2]

Although differing on some crucial points, the constitutional relativists endorse two main theses. First, they believe that the executive possesses constitutionally based authority to undertake discretionary emergency action. Bybee and Yoo, for example, refer to the commander-in-chief clause; Paulsen looks to the presidential oath clause and the executive's duty to protect, preserve, and defend the constitution; and Mansfield locates the president's special authority to respond in unprecedented ways to novel circumstances in the overall structure of the executive power clause. At least in the U.S. constitutional system (with which this group of analysts is preoccupied), the argument goes, executive-based emergency government rests on constitutional foundations. Why does the executive possess a privileged position in this scheme? It alone supposedly embodies the requisite capacities for "decision, activity, secrecy, and dispatch" famously described by Alexander Hamilton (see Rossiter 1961, pp. 424). The constitutional relativists rely on a traditional account of the unitary executive and its alleged institutional merits, despite empirical and normative questions about the viability of that account (Scheuerman 2006b).

Second, the constitutional relativists attribute far-reaching and potentially awesome emergency authority to the executive. To be sure, they describe possible institutional and legal restraints on executive discretion. For example, Yoo notes that Congress can always refuse to finance presidential wars. Yet the clear thrust of this theoretical genre is to downplay the overall significance of many of the familiar constitutional checks on executive power described by mainstream legal scholars. Yoo goes so far as to dispute the conventional view that only Congress possesses the constitutional right to declare war, interpreting the declare war clause as little more than a polite formality according to which Congress should inform

---

[2]I borrow here from Lobel's (1989) useful description of what he labels the "relativistic" model of emergency power.

other countries that the United States has commenced hostilities with them. In Yoo's highly tendentious reading of the constitutional founding, the declare war clause offers no real impediments to wars initiated by the executive (Yoo 2005; see also Cole 2005).

The relatively open-ended wording of the relevant constitutional basis is then adduced as evidence that the scope of executive power is effectively indefinable during a serious crisis. Because emergency power must always be relative to the particularities of the crisis at hand, and because we cannot a priori eliminate the possibility of a life-threatening existential threat, the constitution must allow for no less ambitious forms of undefined executive emergency action. In this vein, Bybee and Yoo argued in internal administration memos that President Bush is permitted to ignore longstanding congressional prohibitions on torture as part of his authority as commander in chief (see Danner 2004, pp. 144–66). Paulsen posits that the president's special responsibility as "Lord Protector of the Constitution" means that he holds legitimate authority to override even specific constitutional norms when they prevent him from protecting the constitutional order as whole. Both unilateral preemptive invasion and the denial of basic civil liberties to U.S. nationals who have taken up arms against their government potentially fall under the rubric of legitimate emergency executive power (Paulsen 2004, pp. 1272–75). Paulsen concedes that one historically counterintuitive implication of his view of executive power, considering that Americans once rebelled against monarchical rule, is that the president is permitted some exercises of power "not traditionally recognized as belonging to the British King" (Paulsen 2004, p. 1288). Even though an executive outfitted with more discretionary prerogative than a monarch may not have been the framers' subjective intention, it nonetheless was the necessary result of the constitutional mechanisms they established. In Mansfield's version of the argument, the genius of the U.S. framers stems from the fact that the "executive power represents necessity in the form of response to emergencies. It anticipates that events will occur and situations will arise that we cannot anticipate through our laws" (Mansfield 2006). Consequently, the president holds constitutional authority to act independently of and even against the legislature if necessary for the sake of tackling unprecedented crises. In sharp contrast to John Locke and other of the framers' British constitutionalist predecessors, the U.S. framers provided a constitutional basis for necessity and emergency discretion, rather than envisioning them as operating beyond the law. They broke categorically with what Mansfield derisively describes as the "small-r" republican view, according to which emergency government must always be neatly contained by prospective legal devices and the rule of law.

What then should we make of this model of emergency powers? It certainly provides substantial opportunities for the executive to act flexibly and rapidly in the face of emergencies. However, as I suggest in my introductory comments, any normatively attractive vision of emergency government must also demonstrate how it can deter executive discretion from becoming a permanent state of affairs in which the rule of law and constitutionalism are put at peril. Squaring the circle of emergency power means not only acknowledging the possible advantages of far-reaching executive action, but also ensuring that executive discretion can ultimately be reined in.

Constitutional relativism relapses to clichés when explaining how its demiurge-like emergency executive can itself be prevented from becoming an existential foe to the rule of law and constitutionalism. The relativists are eager to let loose emergency executive discretion, but they say little about how to contain it once the emergency has subsided. Not only can we legitimately question their often tendentious interpretation of the origins of the U.S. system (Fisher 2004, Prakash 2004), but we can also observe that they seem remarkably uninterested in an impressive critical literature on the U.S. model of emergency government. According to this model, the long-term tendency among presidents to claim vast constitutional authority to combat internal and external threats has generated highly discretionary forms of law, blurred any meaningful distinction between ordinary and emergency law, undermined civil and political liberties, and dramatically shifted the focus of decision making from the legislature to the executive (Cole 2003a, Gross 2003, Lobel 1989, Scheppele 2004, U.S. Congress 1974). They also ignore a sizable literature from political sociology and political science showing that where a relatively strict separation of powers obtains between the legislature and executive, with both possessing independent bases of electoral support, they typically find themselves engaged in a zero-sum rivalry for political power and influence. In this context, the executive faces numerous institutional incentives for declaring and even perpetuating emergencies, because only then might a potentially recalcitrant legislature likely defer to executive rule (Ackerman 2000, Arato 2002, Linz 1994, O'Donnell 1994). In the orthodox and still influential view, the unitary executive alone possesses the requisite dispatch and energy necessary for managing crises. Even under normal conditions, "ongoing competition between House, Senate, and Presidency for control over the administrative apparatus has created an excessively politicized style of bureaucratic government, transforming the executive branch into an enemy of the rule of law" (Ackerman 2000, p. 641). The relativist interpretation of the executive as the bearer of an intrinsic constitutional authority to protect and preserve the political order as a whole, trumping subordinate powers granted to the legislature and judiciary, can only encourage the proliferation of emergency executive discretion.

This gap in the literature is by no means surprising because the constitutional relativists lack a convincing story about how the familiar dangers of executive emergency power can be combated. Revealingly, they prefer to engage in historical cherry picking, associating their ideas about emergency government with presidential giants like Abraham Lincoln or Franklin Roosevelt. Yet this rhetorical move tends to obscure the old political truism that we cannot always count on wise and virtuous political leaders committed to the rule of law or constitutionalism, particularly in an emergency context in which the executive has an interest in its continuation. They also respond to understandable legalistic anxieties about their proposals with a conceptual sleight of hand. For example, Mansfield points out that the U.S. framers placed emergency discretion within the executive power clause and thus at the core of the constitutional order. This placement might imply that emergency power is also contained by traditional constitutional mechanisms; we need not worry about the dangers of the emergency executive because it is now subsumed within the constitutional system. In fact, constitutional relativists generate nothing more than legal pretense for unmitigated executive prerogative: As they repeatedly suggest, the open-ended language of the executive power, presidential oath, and commander-in-chief clauses constitutes no severe restriction on highly discretionary employments of executive power during a crisis. What we find here is not an attempt to guarantee that emergency power is consistent with the traditional idea of the rule *of* law, but instead an implicit transformation of that complex and multifaceted idea into the related but cruder notion of the rule *by* law. Rule of law has traditionally implied substantial legal restraints on the exercise of political power, whereas rule by law simply asserts that political officials can do whatever they want as long as some reasonable basis in the legal order can be found (Tamanaha 2004). In this model, vast emergency discretion that potentially derides conventional rule-of-law virtues (e.g., legal generality, publicity, clarity, stability, and prospectiveness) is justified by vague constitutional language, while neither statutory nor constitutional law is allowed to check executive authority.

EXTRALEGAL EMERGENCY POWER

A second group of authors embrace the weaknesses of constitutional relativism as virtues. For example, if constitutional relativism stumbles in part because constitutional language fails to tame executive power, why not abandon recourse to constitutional norms altogether? Constitutional provisions always "provide executive officials with a fig leaf of legal justification for the expansive use of sheer power. What appears to be emergency power limited by the rule of law is actually unlimited emergency power" (Tushnet 2005a, p. 49). So why not sacrifice the charade of law and concede that emergency power inevitably tends to explode the confines of the legal and constitutional system? No constitutional or legal norm can fully capture the possible exigencies of the emergency situation. Given the diversity of real-life crisis scenarios, how could law ever realistically succeed in doing so? In other words, one must envision executive emergency power as inherently extralegal, as operating beyond the boundaries of the legal order as a whole. This conceptual path has been pursued most systematically by the legal scholar Oren Gross, but sympathy for at least some of its attributes can be found among prominent practitioners of Critical Legal Studies as well (Gross 2003, 2005; Tushnet 2005a). This approach to emergency powers synthesizes Locke's famous view of prerogative power as extralegal with a deep and characteristically contemporary skepticism about the capacity of law to contain political power, typically molded by the right-wing German jurist Carl Schmitt's views of emergency legal regulation (Dyzenhaus 2005, Scheuerman 2006a).

In the face of dire emergencies, Gross argues, political officials should be permitted to pursue potentially extreme measures. We simply cannot presuppose that preexisting legal materials will anticipate what the particular dictates of the emergency situation might demand of the executive. Even if the law clearly prohibits violent measures (e.g., torture), it may be necessary to pursue them in the face of cataclysmic threats (Gross 2004). But officials at least should be required to do so openly, underscoring that their actions have no support from the legal order. Because emergency power can never be neatly cabined within the law, it is best that officials stop pretending otherwise. In Gross's account, the refusal to acknowledge the necessary extralegality of emergency action conflates ordinary and emergency law, undermines civil liberties, and generates an overall process of legal decay in which the rule of law and constitutionalism are polluted by discretionary emergency law (Gross 2003). Paradoxically, the optimal way to preserve the rule of law and constitutionalism is by neatly cordoning off extralegal emergency law and then subjecting extralegal emergency action to severe public scrutiny. An official might face criminal or civil charges in court, be forced to resign, suffer impeachment, or simply be replaced by a hostile electorate. Alternately, extralegal executive activities might get indemnified by the legislature or courts, or garner endorsement by conventional political mechanisms (e.g., a landslide reelection victory). Strict requirements for publicity and some ex post facto determination of the legitimacy of executive emergency action advances popular debate as well as individual accountability, discouraging the executive from acting unnecessarily or irresponsibly. If the executive must act openly while knowing that she can claim no legal basis for her actions and risks severe retrospective political or legal censure, she will avoid repressive action.

Gross's innovative ideas have generated substantial debate (Ackerman 2006, pp. 88–89; Cole 2003b; Dyzenhaus 2005; Huq 2006; Scheuerman 2006a). His model fails to square the circle of emergency power, however. Like constitutional relativism, the extralegal model opens the door to expeditious executive emergency action. However, it similarly fails to close the door when the crisis situation comes to an end. As in constitutional relativism, insufficient attention is paid by Gross and his allies to the institutional dynamics of modern executive power. Much of their polemic is directed at the supposedly unrealistic endeavor to subordinate executive action to traditional legal devices. Yet Gross's account of the operations of the contemporary executive proves no less unrealistic.

Gross hopes that a series of ex post facto checks on emergency action can forestall unacceptable executive discretion. In light of the impressive institutional advantages enjoyed by the modern executive, however, this seems naive. Throughout modern history, executives have relied on emergencies, real or otherwise, to undertake dramatic measures that rapidly transform basic attributes of the political and social status quo (even Locke worried that extralegal emergency acts undertaken by wise and virtuous kings might serve as dubious legal precedents for less virtuous rulers; see Fatovic 2004). Modern executives, armed with an impressive array of institutional and legal weapons, quickly close down newspapers, clamp down on opposition parties, pursue controversial public policies, and even transform the political and constitutional rules of the game. In the context of a foreign attack, internal disorder, or severe economic downturn, a climate of fear typically inconsistent with reasonable public deliberation tends to emerge. A politically astute holder of executive power will use that climate to advance his or her political agenda, especially in socially divided polities where the executive hopes to advance significant change. Recent history includes myriad examples of executive-driven constitutional reform undertaken in the context of (real or alleged) crises: De Gaulle's France (1958), Indira Gandhi's India (1975), Yeltsin's Russia (1993), Menem's Argentina (1994), and perhaps even Franklin Roosevelt's United States (1933–1944), where emergency authority was employed to break with constitutionally based laissez-faire (Levinson 2006; Scheuerman 2004, pp. 71–104). The executive has obvious political incentives to use, manufacture, and perpetrate crisis situations, because the traditional view of the unitary executive as best able to act with energy and dispatch necessarily means that most political actors will look to the executive for political leadership during an emergency. The executive then will inevitably find herself particularly well positioned to pursue otherwise controversial political, social, and constitutional change. These dangers are especially pronounced in presidential systems based on a strict separation of powers, yet they arguably represent a universal feature of contemporary institutional life (Ackerman 2000, Arato 2002).

Whatever its weaknesses, the traditional notion that emergency executive action requires legal sanction at least forces the executive prospectively to provide legal or constitutional justification for her actions. Contrary to Gross and others, this familiar feature of contemporary liberal emergency government helps restrain the executive. Of course, the executive will typically offer additional political and moral justifications as well. Gross effectively reduces the burden of proof placed on an executive initiating emergency action by permitting her to do so without providing legal or constitutional grounds. When undertaking emergency action, fewer justificatory restraints function than is the case under existing emergency legal regimes. In effect, Gross condones controversial forms of emergency action that at least under the present system may be seen as legally and constitutionally suspect. To be sure, executives commonly make cynical use of ambiguous legal and constitutional norms to justify controversial actions. Yet even when relying on the most cynical constitutional justifications, they inadvertently permit legal argumentation in which those worried by executive action can respond in kind. Only the most dogmatic brand of legal skepticism can discount the virtues of such legal argumentation, seeing in it nothing more than a series of strategic political games. Even if such debate fails to put an immediate stop to the executive's actions, it helps generate a discursive and argumentative field upon which later critics can build.

In Gross's view, his model nonetheless does a superior job providing retrospective checks on executive action. Yet this assertion obscures the possibility that a fast-moving executive may very well have altered the rules of the political game even before any ex post facto tests have to be met. The executive may already have effectively modified core elements of the original political universe from which such checks might have emerged. Political opponents have perhaps been imprisoned, exiled, or, in the extreme case, executed; opposition newspapers that might once have raised critical questions about the executive's actions have been closed down or at least intimidated, fearful of appearing out of sync with a nervous public eager to "rally 'round the flag." Faced with an executive making daily reminders of imminent perils in a climate of widespread anxiety, opposition politicians are likely to remain quiet as well. Of course, at some point, the public may tire of the executive's incessant crisis rhetoric and fearmongering. Yet it may suddenly find that its political, social, and constitutional system has dramatically changed. The retrospective corrective mechanisms described by Gross might then be mobilized, at least where basic democratic procedures remain intact, but those checks will be exercised in a new political environment in which the opposition must operate at least partially according to the executive's program and preferences. Is it any surprise that history provides so many examples of legally dubious executive emergency actions that go unpunished? Even modest attempts to censure legally suspect executive action retrospectively often meet with deep hostility because they emerge in a novel political universe that the executive has helped create.[3]

As with constitutional relativism, the advocates of extralegal emergency power eagerly countenance emergency executive discretion but prove no more successful at explaining how to contain it. Their model excuses legally dubious emergency rule without evincing possible institutional checks. Like the constitutional relativists, they ignore some of the more troubling realities of modern executive power.

COMMON LAW EMERGENCY OVERSIGHT

In response to such weaknesses, an otherwise intellectually diverse group of recent writers proposes a resuscitation of traditional common law ideals of emergency regulation (Cole 2003b, 2004; Dyzenhaus 2001, 2003, 2004, 2005; Tribe & Gudridge 2004). After all, the great common lawyer, Sir Matthew Hale, claimed that the gradual accretion of customary law, in which a slow organic progression of reason and experience could be traced, provides a better instrument for tackling the exigencies of unforeseen crises than abstract reasoning. The case-oriented approach of the common law, in which sage judges could both learn from and build on the lessons of their historical predecessors, would best deal with "the multitude of successive Exigencies and Emergencies, that in a long Tract of Time will offer themselves" (cited in Fatovic 2004, p. 291). Although breaking with the more idealized features of this view, contemporary analysts build on its core elements.

[3]Think, for example, of the recent domestic spying scandal in the United States, in which even partisan Democrats distanced themselves from Senator Russ Feingold's modest proposal to censure President Bush.

Like constitutional relativism, and in stark contrast to Gross, the common lawyers envision emergency law as part and parcel of the legal order. Yet they reject constitutional relativism's tendency to reduce the rule of law to rule by law, instead insisting that the rule of law should be interpreted as expressing a robust set of substantive moral and legal values, including ideals of fairness, reasonableness, and equality before the law (Dyzenhaus 2005, p. 89). In this way, they hope to subject emergency action to strict legal tests and ward off the creation of a regime of exception operating outside the confines of the law.

As David Dyzenhaus energetically argues, unprecedented emergencies may require equally novel legal and regulatory innovations. However, institutional experiments with emergency government need to remain faithful to the basic values of the rule of law. All institutions of government are expected to cooperate in realizing the law's underlying commitment to "important moral values" and especially respect for the "fundamental interests of the individual," but judges have a special role to play as guardians of the rule of law during emergencies (Dyzenhaus 2004, p. 248). Because both the legislature and executive then tend to embrace regulation incongruent with the core values of the rule of law, the task of protecting those values necessarily falls to the courts. This means in practical terms that the courts should rigorously scrutinize emergency law to make sure that it pays proper fidelity to basic legal values, always remembering that "the law that rules is not just positive law; the law includes values and principles to do with human dignity and freedom" (Dyzenhaus 2003, p. 13). Even if some courts lack the formal authority to overturn onerous emergency legislation, they are compelled to declare its inconsistency with rule-of-law values. By doing so, they may force the legislature and executive to reconsider and revise it, or at least raise public awareness of its ills. Against those troubled by the dangers of excessive judicial intervention, Dyzenhaus argues that the separation of powers doctrine should be seen as instrumental to the broader normative aspiration to realize fundamental moral values in the law. The orthodox view that judges should regularly defer to the legislature or executive represents an anachronistic impediment to the effective maintenance of rule-of-law virtues in emergency contexts (Dyzenhaus 2003, 2004, 2005).

This ambitious substantive interpretation of the rule of law thus generates a preeminent role for the judiciary in overseeing emergency law. In David Cole's version, clear echoes of the traditional common lawyer's preference for the judiciary over the legislature, as well as particularistic, case-oriented reasoning over formalistic abstract thinking, can be discerned. "Courts take up issues of emergency powers not in the abstract . . . but in the context of specific cases" (Cole 2004, p. 1763). Because emergencies inevitably occur in various forms, courts are institutionally best suited to grapple with the exigencies of emergency rule. General legal norms inevitably prove too heavy-handed (Cole 2004, Tribe & Gudridge 2004). From this perspective, the competing extralegal model rests on legitimate skepticism that prospective legislation can successfully anticipate future emergency scenarios. Yet Gross and his allies miss the possibility of an alternative, case-oriented, common law view. For many reasons, the courts bring more foresight and wisdom to the difficult legal questions than do competing institutional actors. For example, the courts typically weigh in on the merits of emergency measures long after the measures have been promulgated and are therefore less likely to succumb to irrational crisis-related anxiety than the executive or legislature. The courts base their rulings on principled reasons intended to bind future decision makers and also pay attention to longstanding legal precedents. In the process, courts participate in a gradual process of judicial learning and the "measured development of rules in the context of specific cases" (Cole 2003b, p. 2577). Most important, courts are relatively insulated from immediate political pressures and are thus less susceptible to fear and more likely to reach deliberate and well-considered rulings (Cole 2003b, pp. 2576–77).

Much can be said in favor of this approach to emergency government. The common lawyers acknowledge the unavoidability of executive emergency action, but they seek to contain it by the tried and tested methods of a judiciary committed to a thick interpretation of the rule of law. They certainly go further than either the constitutional relativists or theorists of extralegality in squaring the circle of emergency power. To be sure, one might legitimately ask whether their proposals would not result in a political system in which "judges are the ultimate decision-makers with respect to the specification and enforcement of fundamental values" (Campbell 2003, p. 33), especially in light of Dyzenhaus's view of the rule of law as consisting of abstract and contestable political and moral ideals. Whether a resurrected model of the common law can do justice to either modern pluralism or modern democracy remains a legitimate worry. Even if we bracket such fundamental jurisprudential reservations, however, deep immanent flaws plague the common law approach.

The common lawyers oscillate between empirical description and normative prognosis. That is, they mix descriptions of the actual workings of those legal systems (e.g., the United States, Canada, the United Kingdom) in which common law traditions remain vibrant with normative proposals for reform. On one level, this seems fair enough: Their general point is that common law traditions already at work within existing legal systems offer untapped potentials for critique and reform. Yet this oscillation generates certain conceptual ambiguities. Like constitutional relativists, the common lawyers sometimes provide an inappropriately defensive description of the system of emergency regulation as presently practiced in Anglo-American legal systems (Tribe & Gudridge 2004). In this version of their argument, they offer little more than an unconvincing apology for a system whose weaknesses—e.g., the fusion of emergency and ordinary law, the dramatic expansion of executive prerogative, and the concomitant decline of the legislature—have been widely documented. Because some of these writers simultaneously acknowledge the existence of dreary legal trends in the common law world, their positive description of the common law model necessarily appears inconsistent, or at least peculiar (Cole 2003a). Others rigorously acknowledge the ugly warts of emergency rule in the United States or United Kingdom. Yet they tend, not altogether convincingly, to attribute such weaknesses to elements of the legal order incongruent with common law aspirations. So Dyzenhaus delights in attributing the weaknesses of the British system to what he describes as the formal separation of powers, according to which the courts defer to the executive on fundamental issues of national security and foreign affairs, and he argues that such deference conflicts with the fundaments of the common law. Yet he makes things too easy for himself: Many flaws of emergency law in the United States or United Kingdom are directly linked to core facets of the common law approach (Dyzenhaus 2003, 2005).

If we look again at Cole's traditionalistic interpretation of judicial oversight, the sources of this failing becomes clear. The judiciary is necessarily limited to ex post facto review, meaning that judges typically weigh in on the merits of a legislative or executive action "long after they have been adopted" (Cole 2003b, p. 2577). This may buttress Cole's expectation that the courts are likely to prove less susceptible to irrational fear. Yet this judicial virtue represents at best a double-edged sword. The delayed character of the judicial response provides plenty of time for the other branches of government (and most likely the executive) to have already undertaken damaging forms of far-reaching emergency action. As noted earlier, such actions potentially generate significant transformations to the political and legal universe. When courts finally manage to respond to emergency rule, they not only operate in the context of a political world altered by executive emergency action, but they necessarily focus on individual cases, meaning that they are typically limited to dealing with egregious and by no means typical violations of civil liberties or infringements on the rule of law. In many situations, the judiciary will only achieve useful but necessarily constrained ex post facto corrections to the most extreme government measures. The cautious and institutionally conservative mindset of the jurist schooled in the common law tradition undoubtedly tends to discourage dramatic challenges to unjust government action as well. Although I cannot demonstrate this point conclusively here, the instinctive common law preference for gradual and cautious legal evolution, and by no means idiosyncratic views about the separation of powers per se, has contributed to some of the great injustices of modern emergency government.

Dyzenhaus seems insufficiently alert to the fact that some common law systems long ago abandoned the so-called formal separation of powers that he holds responsible for the ills of emergency government.[4] Presidential and semipresidential regimes, like the United States, expressly outfit the unitary executive with distinct legislative power, and courts there can defer to the executive for legitimate constitutional reasons. At the very least, an investigation of whether common law mechanisms operate differently in parliamentary than in presidential versions of liberal democracy would be useful. Especially in presidential regimes, where institutional

[4]In this model, "the legislature makes policy decisions, public officials implement those decisions, and judges make sure . . . [they] are limited by constitutional principle" (Dyzenhaus 2005, p. 78).

rivalry between the executive and legislature encourages the executive to declare and perpetuate crises, real or otherwise, the slow-moving common law judiciary may find itself unable to respond coherently to the dynamic of executive-driven emergency government. Built-in structural incentives that drive the president continually to expand emergency discretion mean that the courts tend to lag behind, their review powers continually outpaced in an institutional race that they cannot possibly hope to win: Before our cautious common law judges have even begun to grapple with the legal ramifications of the last round of presidential emergency measures, the executive has already undertaken new ones. In presidential regimes, where the executive is driven by immanent institutional mechanisms to exploit crisis situations to demonstrate his or her capacity for effective leadership and gain leverage against a potentially hostile legislature, common law emergency oversight seems destined to fail. As Arato (2002, pp. 457, 463) accurately observes, the "constitutional under-regulation of emergencies" in the context of a legal system with a strong common law orientation, in conjunction with the poorly defined constitutional powers of a plebiscitary president, tends to increase the likelihood of illegal and unconstitutional emergency government.

Cole restates the traditional view that judges not only are expected to build on legal precedents but also typically envision their own rulings as potentially binding on future judicial actors, the happy outcome being a "measured development of rules in the context of specific cases." However, when an emergency is unprecedented and thus truly novel, precedent will provide little guidance to judges. Nor will judges' own highly specific rulings provide much help to future judges facing quite different emergency scenarios. In short, judicial rulings are likely to take on a highly discretionary form in the context of emergency regulation. In this context, the common lawyers' definition of the rule of law proves revealing: Commitments to fundamental yet necessarily open-ended ideals such as reasonableness, individual liberty, or equality before the law inevitably allow for a vast range of distinct and arguably conflicting legal outcomes. This model of the rule of law hardly provides a sturdy legal basis for hindering any but the most blatantly authoritarian and illiberal forms of executive emergency rule.

Cole might nonetheless respond that the courts' political insularity encourages them to exercise discretion in a relatively reasonable manner because they are less subject to the anxious climate of emergency rule. Yet here as well, a familiar judicial virtue proves ambiguous. Judges in common law systems prove just as irrational, prickly, and deferential to authority as the rest of us: The history of common law jurisdictions is littered with the wreckage of bad legal rulings. Although judicial independence sometimes contributes to measured legal responses, the opposite results can occur as well. A politically secure judiciary may remain relatively unscathed by the excesses of emergency rule. Federal judges have little to fear from Draconian post-9/11 antiterror measures, for example, whereas recent immigrants, Muslims, politically active civil libertarians, and their legal advocates do. Such constituencies might appropriately respond to executive measures with outrage, whereas tenured judges announce politically quiescent and legally smug rulings: The recent U.S. Supreme Court, for example, "has invoked repressive precedents from the gravest wars of the past as if they were applicable to our present predicament," despite fundamental differences between the "war on terror" and previous U.S. military engagements (Ackerman 2006, p. 20). Is it any surprise that the real-life history of common law systems offers at best a mixed record at circumventing the excesses of emergency executive rule (Ewing & Gearty 2001, Scheppele 2006, U.S. Congress 1974)? Or that so much of the common law literature takes a hortatory tone, as its defenders incessantly scold the courts for jettisoning the critical resources of the common law (Dyzenhaus 2003)? Common law judges fail to rein in executive emergency power neither because of outdated ideas about the separation of powers nor because of a failure to tap into the critical resources of their own legal traditions, but instead because basic institutional attributes of contemporary liberal democracy discourage them from doing so.

EMERGENCY LEGAL FORMALISM

Only a final group of scholars concentrates competently on the central dilemmas of emergency government. These writers, who share a commitment to strict formal constitutional mechanisms as a way of regulating emergency executive discretion, start with a hard-headed analysis of what Ackerman (2006, p. 7) describes as the "presidentialist war dynamic," according to which the president is most likely to dominate the political game by effectively exploiting crisis situations. In fact, some of the most astute advocates of this approach—most notably Ackerman (2000)—have authored important critical works on presidentialism. Successful emergency government must allow for executive discretion while minimizing the possibility of problematic unilateral executive prerogative that some versions of liberal democracy tend to invite. Given recent technological innovations and the global free market in weapons technology, advanced liberal democracies should probably expect future terrorist attacks. Such attacks would likely contribute to the proliferation of executive prerogative. The central question for institutional architects therefore becomes "how can an emergency constitution constrain the abuse of presidential power when the homeland is repeatedly shaken, at unpredictable moments, by the shock waves of terrorist assault?" (Ackerman 2006, p. 38).

The legal formalist position is endorsed by a diverse range of scholars, yet all take inspiration from classical Roman ideals of emergency government, to which they typically amend modern liberal legal sensibilities (Ackerman 2006, Arato 2002, Negretto & Rivera 2000, Rossiter 2002 [1948], Scheppele 2004, Scheuerman 2006a).[5] The main thrust of this genre is to advocate properly designed formal

[5]The authors included under the rubric of legal formalism do not use this term, probably because the term "formalism" has become something of a bogeyman in recent jurisprudence. But for reasons that should become clear in my exposition, I consider it appropriate.

constitutional emergency power devices. They alone supposedly establish useful prospective or ex ante legal guidelines for emergency authority, help create a clear separation between ordinary and emergency law, and set up standards by which we can delineate legal from illegal emergency government. Exceptional powers "that can be called up during an emergency are fixed in advance of the emergency itself" by constitutional clauses that establish basic rules for their exercise (Ferejohn & Pasquino 2004, pp. 210, 235). Constitutional provisions alone determine when and how emergency power is to be put into effect. No emergency action is permitted to take on a permanent legal character and thereby blur the boundary between ordinary and exceptional law; legally codified time restrictions should be placed on its exercise. Formal constitutional devices should also "enumerate a formidable set of fundamental rights that must be respected during crises," although allowing for some notable diversions from legal normalcy (Ackerman 2006, p. 68). Such relaxations of ordinary legal standards are only legitimate when precisely specified conditions and constitutional tests have been met, however. In Ackerman's version of the argument, for example, the executive is permitted to request special emergency power only in the immediate aftermath of a violent domestic terrorist attack. If the legislature decides to delegate emergency authority, the executive can detain suspected terrorists for a predetermined period of no more than two to three months according to legal standards less strict than those normally operating in the law. When the initial state of emergency has passed, the executive can only continue to employ exceptional power upon the express renewal of "an escalating cascade of supermajorities: 60% for the next two months, 70 for the next, and 80 for each subsequent period" (Ackerman 2006, p. 80). Decisions to institute, as well as end, emergency government can never be left in the hands of those who exercise and potentially benefit from it politically.

Legal formalism goes further than its competitors in squaring the circle of emergency power. First, formalism allows for emergency discretion while subjecting it to significant legal and constitutional controls—the rule of law is never discarded altogether. Dire crises require augmenting executive prerogative, yet crisis situations need not generate legal black holes in which executive discretion is effectively unlimited. The ever looming specter of an emergency dictator with an obvious political interest in preserving his or her awesome power position even after a crisis has subsided is at least mitigated. For this reason, it should prove easier to reestablish legal normalcy once the emergency situation has passed. Second, this approach underscores the importance of maintaining strict, institutionally backed, temporal limits on emergency power, which similarly work to prevent it from becoming a permanent state of affairs. Third, by allowing for judicial supervision of emergency rule, formalism integrates the virtues of the common law model while recognizing its intrinsic limitations. For the legal formalists, judicial supervision plays an indispensable role in ensuring that basic rule-of-law virtues are upheld in emergency contexts. Yet the unavoidably ex post facto character of judicial supervision needs to be complemented by clear retrospective or ex ante emergency legal devices. The rule of law, after all, requires not only judicial review, but also relatively stable and clear general legal norms on which state action is based. By necessity, such norms will have been set up prior to the occurrence of a crisis. We can thus reasonably expect that they might help achieve greater impartiality and evenhandedness than even the most impressive judicial rulings delivered in the aftermath of a state of emergency: like every form of general prospective rule making, emergency constitutional clauses will be promulgated without advanced knowledge of the specific political interests or constituencies likely to gain from their employment. To be sure, one might wonder whether prospective constitutional emergency clauses can ever fully anticipate the exigencies of novel forms of crisis. Yet the familiar dilemma of hard cases is by no means limited to the sphere of emergency regulation. The fact that no general norm can ever perfectly capture every conceivable case it was originally meant to cover hardly forces us to abandon the effort to subject the exercise of political power to law (Scheuerman 2006a).

Even more fundamentally, strict ex ante legal devices counter the troublesome institutional dynamic by which the executive unilaterally defines, declares, and potentially gains from emergency situations. In this model, prospective standing constitutional rules specify how and when emergencies can be declared, and the executive is forced to rely on other decision-making organs (chiefly the legislature) to set up emergency government. Of course, some executives will inevitably manipulate even the strictest system of constitutional norms, seeking to use it to their political advantage. Yet legal formalism offers plausible reasons for suggesting that we might diminish the perils posed by this ubiquitous feature of political existence. A fourth main strength of legal formalism is its quest for an effective system of institutional checks and balances. To garner emergency power, the executive needs the unambiguous support of the legislature. By itself, this presents few obstacles to a politically astute holder of executive power. In a parliamentary system, the executive is likely to have been chosen by the legislature and probably exercises de facto political control of his or her party and its elected representatives. In a presidential system with a strict separation of powers, during a violent crisis even members of hostile political parties tend to turn to the executive for political guidance. Thus, the mere fact that executive action requires legislative endorsement may function as no more than a rubber stamp for familiar forms of executive-centered prerogative.

Legal formalism makes two ingenious proposals to help ward off this hazard. First, inspired by the example of the South African Constitution,[6] Ackerman (2006) advocates a supermajoritarian escalator according to which every (temporally limited) extension of emergency power would require more extensive legislative support than previous promulgations. Subsequent legislative reauthorizations demand that the executive gain the support of ever more numerous supermajorities. The aim of this proposal is to ensure that emergency government is no mere partisan weapon

[6]After 21 days, extensions of emergency power have to be approved by 60% of the National Assembly, and a state of emergency can never be extended for more than three months.

of a sitting executive and instead proves reasonably "representative of every part of the citizenry interested in the defense of the existing constitutional order" (Rossiter 2002 [1948], p. xiii.). By subjecting the executive's most problematic acts to the will of ever decreasing proportions of the legislature, the supermajoritarian escalator functions as a direct institutional check on controversial and unreasonable executive discretion. The familiar peril of the executive using emergencies to advance controversial social, political, or constitutional change would presumably be reduced.

For example, immediately following 9/11 most U.S. citizens were willing to delegate extensive emergency discretion to President Bush and even seemed to throw their political support behind his broader right-wing political and social agenda. However, many of the administration's more repressive measures (e.g., indefinite detentions, some features of the USA PATRIOT Act, the Guantanamo Bay detention center) rapidly became controversial. A supermajoritarian escalator undoubtedly would have made pursuing these measures more difficult for the Bush administration: If within a mere year or two the renewal of special emergency power required the support of as much as 80% of elected representatives, even a coherently acting minority of Senate Democrats would have been able to threaten the administration with an effective veto. At the very least, significant modifications to administration policy might have resulted. As the initial emergency passes and the general climate of fear subsides, opposition legislators will discover their own political reasons for questioning controversial, repressive, emergency measures.

Second, during an emergency situation, "members of opposition political parties should be guaranteed the majority of seats on the [legislative] oversight committees" so as further to reduce the perils of partisan manipulation of executive emergency power (Ackerman 2006, p. 85). Although unfamiliar to the U.S. political system, other countries have experimented with minority control of legislative committees; some empirical evidence implies that it works well as a device for preventing committees from becoming mere lapdogs for the executive. Historically sensitive analysts similarly suggest that emergency government proves both politically successful and legally praiseworthy when it takes the form of a "cabinet government" in which all significant political constituencies are well represented (Rossiter 2002 [1948]).

CONCLUSION

One could easily squabble about the details of the various proposals proffered by the legal formalists. Yet it would be a mistake to become mired in the idiosyncrasies of Ackerman's ideas, for example, and ignore the considerable insights underlying legal formalism as a whole. As I have tried to show, legal formalism begins with an empirically astute understanding of the institutional dynamics of the modern executive, and its indisputable achievement is to focus debates about institutional design on the need to counter the most disturbing structural perils of executive-dominated emergency government. Whatever the flaws of legal formalism's specific proposals, no competing paradigm identifies the fundamental dilemmas of emergency government with comparable acumen.

Similarly, readers sympathetic to constitutional relativism or even extralegal emergency government might respond that legal formalism fails at squaring the circle of emergency power for another reason: It proves unable to justify sufficiently far-reaching modes of emergency executive discretion. Legal formalism, in short, squares the circle of emergency power but only at the cost of trivializing the necessity of executive prerogative. I have argued above that constitutional relativism reduces the ideal of the rule of law to rule by law, according to which the executive need only appeal to vague constitutional clauses to unleash vast discretion potentially inconsistent with classical rule-of-law commitments to generality, clarity, publicity, and stability in the law. In contrast, legal formalism, and to a less successful degree the common law model, pursue a rigorous legalization of the emergency situation by subjecting executive discretion to strict legal and constitutional tests. From the perspective of those who believe that emergency situations potentially demand vast expressions of executive discretion, a legally shackled executive of this type might seem unduly handicapped in the face of life-or-death emergency threats.

This is a serious rejoinder requiring careful consideration. For now, I conclude by mentioning two reasons for skepticism. First, it would be an error to understate the extent of legal formalism's concession that emergencies must allow for significant executive discretion. For example, Ackerman permits emergency security services to arrest and detain suspected terrorists on the standard of reasonable suspicion, which is less demanding than the traditional probable cause required by the ordinary criminal law (Ackerman 2006, p. 46). Only the most authoritarian perspective could dismiss the potentially far-reaching implications of this relaxation of criminal law. Some critics of Ackerman in fact worry that he allows for too much executive discretion in detaining suspected terrorists (Cole 2004, Tribe & Gudridge 2004). Second, lurking in the background of those arguments favoring far-reaching abrogations from normal legality is the old idea that emergencies typically constitute existential threats to the physical well-being and survival of the political community as a whole. When the body politic faces physical elimination, can it not rightfully undertake even the most authoritarian and violent actions to ward off attackers, even at the risk of sacrificing the luxuries of the rule of law or constitutionalism? This familiar imagery obscures two important facts, however. First, many and perhaps most crisis or emergency situations constitute serious threats, but by no means entail the prospect of the physical elimination of the political community. Al Qaeda killed thousands of U.S. civilians and undoubtedly hopes to kill more, but it is an exaggeration to assume that its activities pose a life-or-death challenge to the survival of the United States (Ackerman 2006, Scheuerman 2006b). Second, political communities are not physical organisms for which the question of what constitutes survival can be understood in relatively clear-cut terms. Political communities are always defined fundamentally by shared normative commitments. Even if the United States were to continue to maintain the inviolate status of its existing physical borders, it very well might undergo a massive alteration to its political identity by shedding longstanding legal and constitutional commitments. It is precisely this danger, and by no means primarily the threat of physical elimination, that we Americans face today, as our government continues to sacrifice fundamental liberal democratic legal and constitutional practices in the name of a vaguely defined and temporally unlimited war on terror. An American Republic in which Guantanamo Bay, indefinite detentions, or wiretapping at the whim of the executive were allowed to become part of ordinary law would no longer be the same political community brutally attacked by Al Qaeda on September 11, 2001.

The *Annual Review of Law and Social Science* is online at http://lawsocsci.annualreviews.org

LITERATURE CITED

Ackerman B. 2000. The new separation of powers. *Harvard Law Rev.* 113:642–729

Ackerman B. 2006. *Before the Next Attack: Preserving Civil Liberties in an Age of Terrorism*. New Haven, CT: Yale Univ. Press

Arato A. 2002. The Bush tribunals and the specter of dictatorship. *Constellations* 9(4):457–76

Brandon M. 2005. War and the American constitutional order. See Tushnet 2005b, pp. 11–38

Campbell T. 2003. Blaming legal positivism: a reply to David Dyzenhaus. *Aust. J. Leg. Philos.* 28:31–38

Cole D. 2003a. *Enemy Aliens: Double Standards and Constitutional Freedoms in the War on Terrorism*. New York: New Press

Cole D. 2003b. Judging the next emergency: judicial review and individual rights in times of crisis. *Mich. Law Rev.* 101:2565–95

Cole D. 2004. The priority of morality: the emergency constitution's blind spot. *Yale Law Rev.* 113:1753–800

Cole D. 2005. What Bush wants to hear. *NY Rev. Books* 52(18):8–12

Daniels R, Macklem P, Roach K, eds. 2001. *Security of Freedom: Essays on Canada's Anti-Terrorism Bill*. Toronto: Univ. Toronto Press

Danner M. 2004. *Torture and Truth: America, Abu Ghraib, and the War on Terror*. New York: NY Rev. Books

Dyzenhaus D. 2001. The permanence of the temporary: can emergency powers be normalized? See Daniels et al. 2001, pp. 21–37

Dyzenhaus D. 2003. Humpty dumpty rules or the rule of law: legal theory and the adjudication of national security. *Aust. J. Leg. Philos.* 28:1–30

Dyzenhaus D. 2004. Intimations of legality and the clash of arms. *Int. J. Const. Law* 2(2):244–71

Dyzenhaus D. 2005. The state of emergency in legal theory. See Ramraj et al. 2005, pp. 65–89

Ewing K Gearty C. 2001. *The Struggle for Civil Liberties: Political Freedom and the Rule of Law in Britain, 1914–45*. Oxford: Oxford Univ. Press

Fatovic C. 2004. Constitutionalism and contingency: Locke's theory of prerogative. *Hist. Polit. Thought* 25(2):276–97

Ferejohn J, Pasquino P. 2004. The law of exception: a typology of emergency powers. *Int. J. Const. Law* 2(2):210–39

Finer H. 1960. *The Presidency: Crisis and Regeneration*. Chicago: Univ. Chicago Press

Fisher L. 2004. *Presidential War Power*. Lawrence: Univ. Kansas Press

Franklin D. 1991. *Extraordinary Measures: The Exercise of Prerogative Powers in the United States*. Pittsburgh: Univ. Pittsburgh Press

Freeman M. 2003. *Freedom or Security: The Consequences for Democracies Using Emergency Powers to Fight Terror*. Westport: Praeger

Gross O. 2003. Chaos and rules: should responses to violent crises always be constitutional? *Yale Law Rev.* 112:1011–134

Gross O. 2004. The prohibition on torture and the limits of the law. In *Torture: A Collection*, ed. S Levinson, pp. 229–56. Oxford: Oxford Univ. Press

Gross O. 2005. Stability and flexibility: a dicey business. See Ramraj et al. 2005, pp. 90–106

Huq A. 2006. Uncertain law in uncertain times: emergency powers and lessons from South Asia. *Constellations* 13(1):89–107

Hussain N. 2003. *The Jurisprudence of Emergency: Colonialism and the Rule of Law*. Ann Arbor: Univ. Mich. Press

Jayasuriya K. 2002. September 11, security, and the new post-liberal politics of fear. In *Critical Views of September 11: Analyses from Around the World*, ed. E Herschberg, C Calhoun, pp. 131–50. New York: New Press

Levinson S. 2006. Preserving constitutional norms in times of permanent emergencies. *Constellations* 13(1):59–73

Linz J. 1994. Presidential or parliamentary democracy: does it matter? In *The Failure of Presidential Democracy*, ed. J Linz, A Valenzuela, pp. 3–87. Baltimore, MD: Johns Hopkins Univ. Press

Lobel J. 1989. Emergency power and the decline of liberalism. *Yale Law Rev.* 98:1386–433

Loveman B. 1993. *The Constitution of Tyranny: Regimes of Exception in Spanish America*. Pittsburgh: Univ. Pittsburgh Press

Mansfield H. 1989. *Taming the Prince: The Ambivalence of Modern Executive Power*. Baltimore, MD: Johns Hopkins Univ. Press

Mansfield H. 2006. The law and the president: In a national emergency, who you gonna call? *Weekly Stand.* 11(17):12

Negretto G, Rivera J. 2000. Liberalism and emergency powers in Latin America: reflections on Carl Schmitt and the theory of constitutional dictatorship. *Cardozo Law Rev.* 21:1797–824

Neumann F, Kirchheimer O. 1996. *Rule of Law Under Siege: Selected Essays*, ed. W Scheuerman. Berkeley: Univ. Calif. Press

O'Donnell G. 1994. Delegative democracy. *J. Democr.* 5(1):55–69

Paulsen M. 2004. The constitution of necessity. *Notre Dame Law Rev.* 79:1257–98

Prakash S. 2004. The constitution as suicide pact. *Notre Dame Law Rev.* 79:1299–320

Ramraj V, Hor M, Roach M. 2005. *Global Anti-Terrorism Law and Policy*. Cambridge, UK: Cambridge Univ. Press

Rossiter C, ed. 1961. *The Federalist Papers*. New York: New Am. Libr.

Rossiter C. 2002 (1948). *Constitutional Dictatorship: Crisis Government in the Modern Democracies*. New Brunswick, NJ: Transaction

Rudalevige A. 2005. *The New Imperial Presidency: Renewing Presidential Power After Watergate*. Washington, DC: Brookings Inst.

Scheppele K. 2004. Law in a time of emergency: states of exceptions and the temptations of 9/11. *Univ. Penn. J. Const. Law* 6:1001–80

Scheppele K. 2006. North American emergencies: the use of emergency powers in Canada and the United States. *Int. J. Const. Law.* 4(2):213–43

Scheuerman W. 1999. Globalization, exceptional powers, and the erosion of liberal democracy. *Radic. Philos.* 93:14–23

Scheuerman W. 2004. *Liberal Democracy and the Social Acceleration of Time*. Baltimore, MD: Johns Hopkins Univ. Press

Scheuerman W. 2006a. Emergency powers and the rule of law after 9/11. *J. Polit. Philos.* 14(1):61–84

Scheuerman W. 2006b. Rethinking crisis government. In *Terror, Culture, Politics: Rethinking 9/11*, ed. T Nardin, D Sherman, pp. 214–35. Bloomington: Indiana Univ. Press

Schlesinger A. 2005. *War and the American Presidency*. New York: Norton

Schneiderman D. 2001. Terrorism and the risk society. See Daniels et al. 2001, pp. 63–72

Tamanaha B. 2004. *On the Rule of Law*. Cambridge, UK: Cambridge Univ. Press

Tribe L, Gudridge P. 2004. The anti-emergency constitution. *Yale Law Rev.* 113:1801–70

Tushnet M. 2005a. Emergencies and the idea of constitutionalism. See Tushnet 2005b, pp. 39–54

Tushnet M. 2005b. *The Constitution in Wartime*. Durham, NC: Duke Univ. Press

U.S. Congress. Senate Special Committee on National Emergencies. 1974. *A Brief History of Emergency Powers in the United States*. 93d Cong., 2d sess. Washington, DC: GPO

Watkins F. 1940. The problem of constitutional dictatorship. In *Public Policy*, ed. C Friedrich, E Mason, pp. 324–80. Cambridge, MA: Harvard Univ. Press

Yoo J. 2005. *The Powers of War and Peace: The Constitution and Foreign Affairs After 9/11*. Chicago: Univ. of Chicago Press

Annu. Rev. Law Soc. Sci. 2006. 2:279–97
doi: 10.1146/annurev.lawsocsci.2.081805.105913

First published online as a Review in Advance on August 1, 2006

THE LAW AND ECONOMICS OF INCOMPLETE CONTRACTS

Robert E. Scott
Columbia University School of Law, New York, NY 10027-7297;
email: rscott@law.columbia.edu

Key Words contract theory, commercial law

■ **Abstract** Individual actors want to make their promises enforceable in order to motivate mutually profitable investments. But parties cannot easily design contracts that maximize beneficial investments and also respond appropriately to changing conditions. Although economists have designed theoretical models that maximize joint welfare both ex ante and ex post, these mechanisms depend on a perfectly functioning and costless system of enforcement. In the real world, parties must expend substantial resources to enforce commitments legally, and, in many cases, courts lack information to assess the parties' actions. This review examines one of the main insights of the theory of incomplete contracts: that legal enforcement alone cannot ensure the full realization of jointly beneficial cooperative ventures. Legal enforcement, supported by the coercive power of the state, is only one mechanism for inducing cooperation, and in many relationships it typically has only a limited role to play. Complex contracts do lend themselves to effective formal enforcement. But parties often choose to write simple contracts that look to renegotiation once the future is known. Simple contracts require enforcement by informal mechanisms, such as reputation, repeated dealings, and norms of reciprocity in order to motivate both beneficial investment ex ante and adjustment ex post.

INTRODUCTION[1]

The institution of voluntary commitment is the time-honored mechanism for pursuing cooperative goals that benefit the collective interest of parties whose particular interests may diverge. Contract is the means for attaching legal consequences to such commitments. This link between the mechanisms of private contracting and the social goals of facilitating productive cooperation between individuals has long been recognized. But policymakers and scholars often invoke this link only rhetorically. One of the primary objectives of the law and economic approach to contracts is to draw out these linkages carefully and explicitly.

[1]This review draws in part on chapter 3 of Scott & Stephan 2006.

1550-3585/06/1201-0279$20.00

Although contract law has a long and distinguished pedigree, only in recent years has the underlying theory of contract been systematically explored. In this review, I survey the economic theory of contract and, in particular, theories predicting what types of contracts parties will elect to write under conditions of imperfect information and incentives to behave opportunistically. The economic approach begins with the assumption that parties act rationally, within the constraints of their environment, in the sense that they wish to contract if they believe the arrangement will make them better off and not otherwise. Thus, we ask how contracting parties might deal rationally with known and anticipated information deficiencies and with private incentives to exploit the arrangement at the expense of joint benefits.

Parties who enter into contracts typically face a conundrum. They want to write a contract that is optimal ex ante, that is, one that at the time of contracting encourages each party to invest in the contractual relationship so as to maximize the anticipated joint benefits. In particular, parties wish to make credible (i.e., enforceable) promises to motivate their contracting partners to invest in jointly profitable activities. They also want to write a contract that is optimal ex post, that is, one that is still value maximizing after all future uncertainties have been resolved as of the time of performance.

But the uncertain future and problems of private information present substantial obstacles to the accomplishment of both of these goals. Owing to uncertainty, parties cannot easily design contracts that maximize jointly beneficial investments and also respond appropriately to changing conditions. For example, each contracting party would like to ensure the commitment of the other party so as to protect investments in the cooperative enterprise. But subsequent events may render inflexible commitments inconsistent with the contractual objective of maximizing the joint surplus. Suppose that, owing to unforeseen circumstances, the cost of completing a promised investment will exceed the value the promisee expects to obtain from the contract. Anticipating this, the parties would want the flexibility to adjust the level of investment whenever future circumstances make the contract no longer profitable. But if the contract is written to accommodate this desire to change its terms, the credibility of the promisor's commitment to invest in the enterprise is undermined. This, in turn, may lead the promisee to decline to undertake her reciprocal obligations under the contract. Thus, each party wants not only to preserve the flexibility to adjust to future uncertainties but also to insure that all commitments are credible. This tension between the need for commitment and the need for flexibility influences the parties' decisions whether or not to contract and, if so, what kind of contract to write.

The law and economic theory of incomplete contracts (hereafter contract theory) has developed a set of analytic tools for understanding how this contracting conundrum might best be resolved. These tools rely on advances in the economics of information, a field that is less than 30 years old but that has already produced three Nobel laureates. The task for legal academics is to test the predictions of this theory by searching for real-world applications, taking as a given the particular structure of existing legal institutions. In this review, I present a brief overview of the tools of contract theory and sketch their application to ordinary commercial contracts. Contracts involving individual consumers raise separate issues that challenge the assumption that their commitments are voluntary, rational, and informed. This discussion, therefore, is limited to contracts in which those assumptions are more plausible.

Traditionally, the legal analysis of contracts has taken an ex post perspective. That approach analyzes the rights and obligations of the parties after the contracted-for performance has come due and one party or the other has failed to comply with its commitments. From this perspective, contract law appears to be a system of rules that imposes obligations on the promisor and specifies remedies available to the promisee for breach of those obligations.

This ex post perspective is not surprising. In general, the analysis of private law has tended to focus on litigated disputes and judicial decisions resolving those disputes as the key elements in the state's decision to interfere in private relationships. Thus, courts and commentators have tended to view contract from the lens of the litigants. Once a contract is breached, the injured party seeks to recover for losses incurred in reliance on the broken promise. A court judgment for the injured party is logically seen as compensation for the wrong that the breaching promisor did to the promisee. This analogy to tort law—that breach is compensation for harm inflicted by the broken promise—reflects the history of the common law action in assumpsit for breach of contract, which judges initially borrowed from tort law and which provided legal redress for a wrongful failure to perform a promised undertaking (Ames 1913, Simpson 1986).

The first major conceptual advance in the law and economics of contracts was to shift the focus of analysis from the ex post judicial decision enforcing the contract to the ex ante decision to enter into the contract in the first place. The ex ante perspective has enormous payoffs for advancing our understanding of how and why people enter into contracts. It forces the analyst to recognize that contract regulates a consensual activity, and thus the parties have choices over whether or not to contract and, if they do, whether to accept the legal obligations that a court will impose on the parties should the deal break down. For the most part, the obligations of contract law are only default rules—terms that will be implied in the contract in the absence of a contrary agreement. Thus, the parties must determine whether to accept these default terms or to contract out of the legal defaults and negotiate their own alternative terms. Instead of asking the ex post question (What do courts do?), the ex ante perspective asks: Why do parties write the contracts that they do in light of what courts (and other legal entities) do?

From this ex ante perspective, then, one can isolate the key analytical questions: Why do parties enter into legally binding contracts? What factors determine whether they choose to write a complex contract (one that seeks to specify outcomes in many possible states of the world) or a simple contract (one that leaves many contingencies unaddressed and looks to renegotiation once the unknown future states are realized)? And, how do the parties deal with the central problem that each party may have private information that the other does not have, and that some information known to both of the parties (i.e., information that is observable) may not be provable to a court (i.e., the information is not verifiable)? The balance of this review offers a primer on the answers that contract theory provides to these basic questions.

WHY DO PARTIES CONTRACT?

Why do parties enter into legally binding contracts? After all, much cooperative behavior goes on without contracting. Many people can and do enter into relationships that are enduring and effective but do not contemplate legal coercion if either party departs from the cooperative understanding. Indeed, parties frequently make agreements that they specifically intend not to be legally binding. These agreements rely on informal (or nonlegal) mechanisms to motivate the cooperation necessary for parties to achieve a welfare-enhancing objective (Klein 1996, Scott 2003). But sometimes these informal mechanisms fail to work effectively. When that happens, parties may consider the alternative of a legally binding contract.

A contract contemplates a commitment regarding future cooperative behavior. This commitment has an intertemporal aspect: Parties promise today to do something tomorrow. When parties choose to make a binding contract, therefore, they invoke the power of the state to coerce performance (or require a monetary substitute) from a promisor who later comes to regret having made the promise. Moreover, the fact that regret was caused by circumstances not expressly contemplated by the parties generally will not excuse the disappointed promisor. In this sense, then, contractual liability is a form of strict liability.

The intertemporal aspect of transactions makes contract law's strict liability highly salient. Contract involves an unconditional promise to do something in the future and the future is unknown. Inevitably, therefore, such a commitment entails risks. The promise may be more costly to perform than the promisor anticipated, or the promise may not have the value to the promisee that was anticipated at the time of contracting. Thus, an initial question arises: Why don't parties simply wait until the future unfolds and then act on current knowledge to acquire the goods and services that they need? After all, a legal regime that respects and protects property rights is sufficient to support current, spot market exchange transactions.

If promises were cost-free, then obviously a party who will rely on the actions of another would prefer to receive a promise in advance of a contemplated future activity. A promisee can always better plan for the future having received a credible promise from a promisor. The problem, of course, is that in a reciprocal relationship each party is both a promisee and a promisor. To obtain a promise from you, I must make a reciprocal commitment. So, why would anyone exchange a risky promise—where she is legally obligated to perform despite unanticipated hardships—in order to receive a return promise from someone else?

The most plausible answer is that this exchange of promises produces a welfare surplus. In simple terms, an exchange of promises will be, in expectation, a win/win situation for both parties (assuming that the promises are rational, voluntary, and informed). If the welfare gains that both parties anticipate are greater than the expected costs, including the predicted costs of regret, then both parties will be better off, in terms of expectations, if they mutually bind themselves. This is simply another way of expressing the idea that cooperative behavior can be mutually beneficial to all the participants in the cooperative enterprise, even when the cost of a promised investment is borne individually and the resulting returns are shared.

PROTECTING RELATION-SPECIFIC INVESTMENTS

One obvious instance in which parties might contract, despite the risks, is when the desired objective requires a specific investment by either (or both) of the parties in a joint activity. The initial motivation for a party to cooperate derives from a determination that, following the planned investment, the resulting joint venture is potentially more profitable (however one defines profit) than any alternative use of her time and resources. If this determination is well founded, then each promisor's investment will be either wholly or partially relation-specific, that is, the resources constituting each party's investment will generate more valuable products if they are deployed in the relationship than if used for other purposes (Schwartz & Scott 2003).

But there is an inherent dilemma for parties who contemplate such joint activity. Each party bears the full burden of her own investment in the cooperative enterprise but must share the future returns from that investment with her partner(s). This means that once a party undertakes a relation-specific investment, she is vulnerable to exploitation if her contracting partner fails to reciprocate fully (Che & Hausch 1999, Segal 1999).

These specialized investments can be of any sort. They might require the production of customized goods, or perhaps an investment in human capital to perform a particular service, or even investments by the parties in information, say, about future price fluctuations. As an example, assume that a seller of software systems produces off-the-shelf software that is suitable for many business needs. The seller also takes on special orders for individual customers, creating specialized software systems that are designed for a single buyer's needs. Buyer is interested in purchasing one of these systems. Assume that Seller can produce either system (but not both) in time to meet Buyer's needs. The specialized software system configured to fit Buyer's particular business needs would cost \$70,000 to produce and would be worth \$100,000 to Buyer. Seller could also provide Buyer her off-the-shelf system at a cost of \$40,000. Because the market for off-the-shelf business software is competitive, Seller would sell that system to Buyer at the market price of \$40,000. The off-the-shelf system is worth \$50,000 to Buyer. If the parties did contract for the specialized system and Buyer subsequently breached, Seller could only resell that system on the market for \$20,000 (the specialized system is tailored to the needs of Buyer and, thus, is not as valuable to another buyer). There are two key questions: What agreement would be socially desirable for these parties to make? Second, what agreement would they make were contracts not enforceable?

The answer to the first question is easy. Recall that social welfare is the sum of the parties' gains from contracting. Thus, the total surplus is the difference between Buyer's valuation and Seller's cost. The off-the-shelf contract would produce a surplus of $10,000 ($50,000 Buyer's valuation less $40,000 Seller's cost). A contract for the specialized software would create a surplus of $30,000 ($100,000 Buyer's valuation less $70,000 Seller's cost). Therefore, joint welfare would be maximized if the parties contract to produce the specialized software system.

But in the absence of legal enforcement (and assuming the absence of any informal means of enforcement), Seller would never agree to produce the specialized software system. To see why, suppose that Seller did agree to produce the specialized system for a price of $85,000. Now consider the parties' positions after Seller has already incurred the $70,000 production cost. Buyer now knows that if he refuses to pay the agreed-upon price, he can still purchase an off-the-shelf system on the market for $40,000 and receive a gain of $10,000. Seller knows that if Buyer breaches her only recourse is to sell the specialized machine on the market for $20,000 and incur a $50,000 loss. On these facts, unless Buyer is concerned about loss of reputation or other informal sanctions, he will propose to renegotiate the price (perhaps offering some pretext such as unanticipated hardship). The potential surplus from a renegotiation is $80,000 [the difference between the value of the system to Buyer ($100,000) and its value to Seller ($20,000)]. One plausible result of a renegotiation is for the parties to agree to split the surplus equally. A renegotiated price of $60,000 achieves this division.

This example illustrates why, absent legal enforcement, the parties would not contract for the specialized system in the first place. A seller who is not myopic would realize that, because the buyer will renegotiate the price after the seller invests, her true payoff under this contract will be a loss of $10,000, rather than the anticipated gain of $15,000 that the contract initially promises. Therefore, Seller will only produce and sell the off-the-shelf system. Seller's decision not to make a specialized system follows directly from the fact that Buyer's initial promise to pay $85,000 is not credible. Both parties would realize at the time of contracting that the buyer will have an incentive to renege later. Because Seller cannot resell the specialized software system for a price above cost—this is the definition of a relation-specific investment—the specialized contract would yield an expected negative payoff for Seller.

What are the implications of this vulnerability for the legal enforcement of contracts? In the jargon of contract theory, the investing party, our hypothetical Seller, risks being held up by a promisor such as Buyer, who can renege on his promise and force a renegotiation of the contract. This threat will be credible if Seller's investment cannot be used for other purposes outside the relationship. In that case, Seller's sunk cost investment will increase the risk that Buyer will threaten to walk away from the deal unless Seller agrees to renegotiate the initial contract terms (Ayres 2003).

This vulnerability points to one of the key insights of the ex ante perspective. Legal enforcement of contracts is traditionally understood to protect an injured promisee by awarding compensation for her reliance on a promise. Of course this is true, but the traditional understanding misses the main purpose of legal enforcement. If contracts were not enforceable—that is, if promises were not credible because there was no effective means of ensuring performance—then parties would decline to put themselves in situations in which they could be exploited by the other party's failure to perform. Instead, prospective investors who fear being exploited (such as Seller in our example) would elect to redirect their energies and resources to interactions that would not lead to such vulnerability. By invoking a mechanism that commits him to perform as promised in the future, a promisor can enhance the credibility of his promise and thus can secure in return a valuable investment from a prospective contracting party. Otherwise, the prospective investor might choose not to make the proposed investment and instead walk away from the deal.

SOCIAL NORMS AND REPUTATION

But surely, a skeptic might respond, many parties would never behave strategically even when they are legally free to do so. Instead, they will be constrained by social norms, a desire to maintain their reputation in the relevant community, or the hope that they might deal with the promisee again in the future. Of course this is true. In many instances, therefore, the agreement between Seller and Buyer will be self-enforcing in the sense that the desire to protect a good reputation or possible future business dealings with Seller will motivate Buyer to perform even in the absence of legal coercion compelling performance (Klein 1996, Scott 1987).

Although reputation and future business prospects are important ingredients of successful contracting, these traditional means of self-enforcement have their limits. Consider reputational incentives first. Social esteem and a reputation for keeping one's word are powerful motivations whenever other potential trading partners are able conveniently to learn why the parties' deal broke down. Reputation is an effective mechanism in small trading communities, especially those with ethnically homogeneous members or other cooperation-inducing structures, where everything that happens soon becomes common knowledge, and boycotts of bad actors are readily enforced (Landa 1981, Grief 1998). Reputational sanctions also can be effective in industries that establish trade associations because the associations can create a collective memory of the contracting behavior of their members (Bernstein 1996, 2001). Reputations are difficult to establish, however, in large, heterogeneous economies in which particular contracting parties often are anonymous.

Contract theory also recognizes that agreements will be self-enforcing to the extent that the parties anticipate the prospect of future dealings. Specifically, when parties contemplate making a series of contracts, neither party will breach an early contract if the gains from that breach are lower than the expected profits from future contracts that a breach would eliminate. But this incentive has natural limits. Unfortunately, ongoing relationships inevitably come to an end. When parties realize that the relationship is soon to terminate (say when the promisor contemplates retirement or otherwise withdrawing from the trading community), the threat that the other party will no longer deal with the promisor is insufficient to induce performance. Thus, all repeated interactions are subject to a familiar end-game problem. Indeed, in the limiting case, the anticipation of the last transaction may cause the entire cooperative pattern to unravel as each party anticipates that the next interaction will be the last interaction and that the promisor might defect (Axelrod 1984, Scott 1987).

Despite these limitations, there are strong reasons to believe that powerful norms of reciprocity enhance and extend the reach of reputation and repeat dealings as means of self-enforcement (Rabin 1993, Levine 1998). Experimental evidence shows that a preference for reciprocity—the willingness to reward cooperation and punish selfishness—can motivate cooperation even in arms-length interactions between complete strangers (Fehr & Schmidt 1999, Fehr et al. 1997). Nevertheless, even enhanced by norms of reciprocity, informal enforcement mechanisms rely upon transparent interactions between the parties and are less effective in controlling complex, interactive relationships (Scott & Stephan 2004). Therefore, formal legal mechanisms matter when informal enforcement does not constrain the incentive to breach. In such an environment, legal enforcement is necessary to make a promise to perform credible and thus to induce valuable cooperation.[2]

PROBLEMS OF ADVERSE SELECTION, MORAL HAZARD, AND VERIFICATION

One of the challenges parties seek to overcome when contracting is that, quite simply, prospective contracting partners do not know everything about each other. Rather, each party has private information about himself that the other does not know. We can illustrate this point with a simple example. Assume Buyer wishes to purchase a product—say, a new machine—from Seller, but Buyer is unsure about the quality of the goods or services that are being offered. In our example, Seller knows the quality of the machine that she has contracted to sell, but Buyer does not. To illustrate the problems that result from this asymmetry of information, assume that the sellers in this market fall into two groups: high-quality sellers and low-quality sellers. If quality varies among sellers, then buyers face a problem. Our

[2]Contract theory recognizes more functions for contract than inducing specific investments. A contract can have a risk management function by shifting a risk to someone who can bear it at a lower cost. For fuller discussion, see Schwartz & Scott (2003), Scott & Triantis (2004), and Triantis & Triantis (1998).

Buyer does not know whether Seller's machine is of a high quality or a low quality. Unless the problem can be solved, Buyer has an incentive to offer only a blended price for the machine (a price less than the value of a high-quality machine but more than the value of one of low quality) reflecting the probability that Seller's goods are either high or low quality. Over time, this reluctance to pay full value will drive the high-quality sellers out of the market because the blended price would not permit them to recover their higher costs. As a result, only low-quality sellers will remain in the market. This example illustrates the famous lemons problem caused by the adverse selection of low-quality sellers (Akerloff 1970).

Parties can respond to this problem of hidden information in several ways. One familiar method is for the high-quality sellers to offer warranties to their buyers. Because high-quality goods perform better and last longer, a warranty of replacement or repair would cost the high-quality sellers less to provide compared with their low-quality competitors. Warranties thus serve as valuable signals of quality to the extent that low-quality sellers cannot readily copy them. An effective signal creates a separating equilibrium in which both high- and low-quality sellers can exist in the same market.

But warranties are not a perfect signal because they are not self-executing. Rather, a buyer must be able to prove to a court that the seller has breached its warranty of quality. This merely moves the problem of hidden information one step further up the chain of the legal process. To understand this problem, we need to distinguish between what the buyer cannot observe, what the buyer can observe for himself, and what he will be able to prove in court. To return to our example, absent a warranty, the quality of Seller's machine may remain completely private, in the sense that no prospective buyer will be able to observe the condition or quality of the goods prior to the sale. But once Buyer purchases the goods with a warranty, he will then be able to perceive whether the condition or quality of the machine matches the warranty, thus making the information observable. But for the legal process to be effective, information must not only be observable but verifiable, in the sense that Buyer can, at a reasonable cost, convince a court or other arbiter that his observation is valid.

In short, not all observable information is verifiable, and only verifiable conditions or qualities can be used to specify an obligation that a court can enforce. So, if Seller gives a warranty of quality and Buyer claims that the machine fails to meet the warranty standard, then Buyer bears the burden of proving to a court that the machine does not conform to the agreed standard. Even if Buyer can observe for himself that the goods fail to meet the warranty that they "are fit for the ordinary purposes for which such goods are used" [see Uniform Commercial Code sect. 2-314(2)(c)], he still must bear the additional burden of proving or verifying that fact to a court or other third party (Hart 1995).

In addition to the problem of adverse selection caused by hidden information regarding the attributes or characteristics of a contract performance, the parties must also cope with the problem of moral hazard caused by the hidden actions or behavior of a contracting partner. Assume in our example that Seller warrants to use her best efforts to modify the contracted-for machine should Buyer encounter any problems in adapting it to Buyer's particular requirements. If Buyer is unable to monitor Seller's efforts to adapt the machine, then Seller's hidden actions create a problem of moral hazard. Buyer faces a risk that Seller will not fully exert her best efforts as promised, but rather will (immorally) chisel on or shirk a portion of her responsibility (Klein et al. 1978). And even if Buyer can observe Seller's actions, once again he faces the difficult task of verifying to a court that the efforts actually undertaken by Seller fall short of the standard of best efforts.

Information asymmetries caused by hidden information and hidden action thus operate at two distinct levels. Between the parties, hidden information or action may prevent the uninformed party from observing a key fact or condition (in our example, the level of quality of the goods or the efforts undertaken by Seller). But even if the information known to one party is observable in the sense that her contracting partner can perceive it as well, it may not be verifiable in the sense that the observing party is unable at reasonable cost to establish the fact sufficiently to convince a neutral third party such as a court (Milgrom & Roberts 1992).

Note, however, that verifiability is not a dichotomous concept, i.e., a fact is not either completely verifiable or completely unverifiable (Hadfield 1994). Rather, proof to a court is a matter of degree. The ability to verify a condition of the contract will be determined by the interactive evidentiary strategies of the parties and the rules allocating burdens and standards of proof. At the conclusion of any litigation, a court makes a factual determination by comparing its confidence in the truth of a given fact against a standard of proof (such as the typical civil standard of "more likely than not"). The costs of verification thus vary because the parties bear their own costs of evidence production as they fight over a fixed amount at stake (Scott & Triantis 2006).

USING RULES AND STANDARDS TO AMELIORATE THE VERIFICATION PROBLEM

One way that parties can reduce the burden of verification is by specifying substitutes or proxies for the underlying fact or condition in question. For example, qualitative performance obligations (such as the duty of care or the obligation to exert efforts) may seem at first blush to be unverifiable. Even though contracting parties can observe each others' effort or level of care, the costs of proving a contracting partner's failure to exert a promised level of effort may seem greater than the gains from tying the contract performance directly to the level of those efforts. But courts typically do not search for direct measures of effort. Instead, they employ evidentiary proxies for the desired performance. For example, rather than assessing Seller's efforts directly, a court may rely on evidence of Buyer's profits as a signal of Seller's effort. Proxies such as these serve to reduce evidentiary cost, even at some sacrifice in accuracy (Scott & Triantis 2006).

The utility of evidentiary proxies turns largely on the ability of the parties to translate contract-specific standards into objective equivalents. Damages for contract breach provide a familiar illustration of how this translation works. Suppose that contracting parties wish to set damages so that the breaching party internalizes the expectation loss inflicted on the promisee. The parties initially have a choice between negotiating a liquidated damages provision or delegating to a court the task of applying the legal standard of expectation damages (Edlin 1998). A liquidated damages clause typically will specify a fixed sum, readily verifiable to a court. But assume the contract is enforced instead by expectation damages. This alternative does not require a promisee to verify the vague standard of expectation damages directly. Indeed, a court will reject difficult-to-verify evidence based on the promisor's costs or the promisee's valuation. Instead, the court will invite the parties to select verifiable, market-based proxies for the value of the promisee's lost expectation. For example, assume that a buyer breaches a contract to purchase goods from a seller and the seller sues to recover damages for breach. The seller will receive her contractual expectation without offering any evidence of her production costs (which are unverifiable). Rather, the court will measure the expectation damages standard by requiring proof of the difference between the contract price and the prevailing market price of the contract goods, a readily verifiable fact [see, e.g., Uniform Commercial Code sect. 2-708(1); sect. 2-713(1); sect. 2-723(2) (proof of market damages)]. The parties' choice, therefore, is not whether to condition the contract on a verifiable liquidated damages clause or unverifiable expectation damages. Rather, the choice is between two more or less efficient proxies for the promisee's expected losses from breach (Scott & Triantis 2006).

As the preceding example illustrates, a core feature of contract design is the decision of how best to allocate resources between the drafting and the enforcement stages of contracting. Because there is inevitably a trade-off between the front-end and the back-end costs of the contracting process, this decision requires the allocation of resources between the two stages. Anticipating future litigation, the parties might elect to invest resources in negotiation and drafting by, for instance, contracting directly on key evidence—such as a liquidated damages clause—that establishes the existence or nonexistence of a particular condition (the expected losses from breach). Such a contract might instruct a court to compel the defendant to pay $10,000 when the parties present evidence of a specific instance of nonperformance.

But the number of possible future states of the world and the corresponding contractual performances mean that the up-front cost of drafting such a term may exceed any expected gains. Alternatively, the parties can instead express their obligations in more general terms and rely on a court to assign outcomes based on the evidence presented at trial. A vague term (such as an obligation to make a good faith effort to deliver goods on a certain date) gives the court much more discretion than a precise or specific term.

Accordingly, one can divide contract terms into two categories—precise terms and vague terms or, to follow the convention in characterizing legal regulation, rules and standards (Kaplow 1992). Evidence at trial proves directly whether a contractual rule is satisfied. In contrast, contractual standards are one step further removed from the evidence. Proof at trial establishes whether a proxy is satisfied, and then the court must determine what weight to give to the proxy in the enforcement of the relevant standard. The choice between rules and standards in contracts thus concerns who chooses the evidentiary proxies for the desirable behavior and when the choice is made. Rules permit the parties to choose the proxy at the time of contracting, whereas standards delegate the choice of proxies to the court at the time of trial.

The choice between rules and standards in contracting turns on the trade-off between two different kinds of informational advantage. The parties know better than any court what objectives they desire from the contract and what actions are required to achieve those objectives. But the parties do not know what the future holds, whereas the court has the benefit of hindsight. Thus, parties are motivated to specify in precise terms a proxy for a desired performance or contractual contingency when the proxy's accuracy is less likely to be affected by the future state of the world. Alternatively, parties will tend to use contractual standards and delegate to a court the later choice of those proxies that are more likely to be contingent on unknown future events.

When parties choose to delegate the selection of proxies to a court, they can constrain judicial discretion by using combinations of rules and standards to define more carefully the space within which a court may later choose the relevant proxies. For example, the parties can combine their description of a standard—say, the obligation to undertake a prescribed action in good faith—with precise terms that exemplify the good faith standard. Relying on maxims of interpretation, courts will then select proxies under the good faith standard only to the extent that they are similar in kind or classification to the enumerated examples. Moreover, the good faith standard itself aids in interpreting the meaning of the exemplar terms. When a broad standard is added to a listing of precise terms, it communicates the underlying contractual objective and helps the court interpret the precise terms in light of that general purpose.

The process of specifying contract terms thus proceeds along a continuum that extends from narrow rules to very broad standards. The ultimate objective is to lower contracting costs (or to improve the incentive gains from contracting) by shifting investments in contracting costs between the front- and back-end of the process. In short, the goal is to "maximize the incentive bang for the contracting cost buck" (Scott & Triantis 2006).

This analysis suggests some caution when analyzing the optimal enforcement of contractual commitments according to whether or not the relevant conditions are verifiable. The question, at bottom, turns on whether appropriate proxies for the desired condition can be specified ex ante or whether a court or other third party can be trusted to make such a selection ex post. The fundamental point is that verification necessarily requires the use of evidentiary substitutes for the underlying behavior or contingency. The availability of good substitutes, in turn, depends largely on whether the contractual condition at issue can be translated (without significant losses in accuracy) into relatively accessible objective equivalents. Therefore, in assessing whether or not a particular contractual commitment can be verified (and thus legally enforced), parties must consider both the cost of formal adjudication as well as the loss in accuracy occasioned by resort to the particular proxies in question.

SIMPLE CONTRACTS AND THE PROBLEMS OF INCOMPLETE CONTRACTING

The preceding discussion illustrates how parties cope with the problems involved in verifying contractual commitments. It highlights the key fact that, at the time of contracting, parties will balance current investments in negotiating and drafting against prospective investments in enforcement. In theory, of course, parties can elect to invest entirely in the drafting process by identifying every possible state of the world that might materialize and by specifying an appropriate contractual solution to each state. But, in reality, contracting parties confront a vexing problem: The future is unknown and unknowable. As a result, when the level of uncertainty is high, it simply costs too much for contracting parties to foresee and then describe appropriately the contractual outcomes for all (or even most) of the possible states of the world that might materialize. Under these circumstances, the ideal of the efficiently complete contingent contract—one that specifies the efficient payoffs for every relevant action and the corresponding sanctions for nonperformance—cannot be realized. Contracts will be incomplete in the sense that they will fail to discriminate between states of the world that optimally call for different obligations (Hart 1998, Hart & Moore 1999).

It is important to emphasize what is meant by efficient completeness. Parties can easily write an inefficient complete contract simply by specifying, for example, that no matter what circumstance may arise in the future, the buyer must always pay the seller the contract price. In such a contract, the parties know at the time of contracting that in many of the realized states of the world the contract will generate less surplus than their joint venture could have achieved. The challenge is to write an efficient complete contract, one that specifies the best outcome for both parties under all possible circumstances. This they cannot do.

Facing high uncertainty and high contracting costs, how should parties formulate the terms of their contracts? One option is to specify a simple contract with precise rules, i.e., determinate outcomes that would apply across the board regardless of the state of the world that actually obtains. Returning to our earlier example, the parties could provide that Seller, who agrees to manufacture a customized machine for Buyer, will deliver the machine to Buyer at a fixed price regardless of any subsequent events that might increase Seller's costs or reduce the value of the machine to Buyer. The advantage of a contract with such "hard" terms is that it binds each party to their respective commitments, thus ensuring the credibility of their promises. And, as we have seen, the promises' credibility will motivate each party as promisee to undertake relation-specific investments or to take precautionary steps to reduce anticipated risk-bearing costs.

But unless the parties can fully and accurately anticipate the conditions that will exist at the time of performance, a contract containing only hard terms will always turn out to be suboptimal once the future arrives. Under conditions of uncertainty, any outcome that is based on expected values (i.e., one that is optimal "on average") will always tend to be wrong in the particular situation that ultimately materializes (Goetz & Scott 1981). In short, once conditions change, a contract with hard terms will lead to outcomes that are less desirable than those the parties would have agreed to had they known the uncertainties in advance. Moreover, the prospect of incurring a loss ex post means that the parties will enjoy a smaller ex ante surplus. Each party will have an incentive to undertake costly precautions (purchasing insurance and the like) to guard against the risk of unfavorable future states. One solution to this problem is for the parties to renegotiate the contract ex post. But renegotiation raises the risk of a holdup to the extent that parties have made sunk cost investments in the contract (Klein 1988, Hart & Moore 1990).

Alternatively, if initial contracting costs are high, the parties might consider another option. They could draft a simple contract with vague standards, i.e., "soft" terms that invite subsequent adjustment to take account of new facts on the ground. Thus, for example, the parties might agree to adjust in good faith the price term in the contract if subsequent events imposed significant hardship on one party or the other. By agreeing to good faith adjustment, the parties seek to ensure that their contract is efficient ex post and that the resulting surplus is shared in some manner between both of them.

Assume, for example, that an unanticipated event causes the costs to Seller of manufacturing the machine specified in the contract to rise above the contract price. If Buyer nonetheless insists on performance, Seller would suffer a loss. Anticipating the prospect of a loss in certain states of the world will lead Seller to take costly precautions, including in the extreme case deciding not to proceed with the contract. Assume, however, that Seller can produce a substitute machine at the original cost that is only slightly less valuable to Buyer. If so, one solution for the parties is for the contract to contain a standard of good faith adjustment by which Seller is authorized to provide the lower-cost substitute, perhaps with a price reduction for Buyer. A good faith adjustment standard would reduce, if not eliminate, the need for precautions against unfavorable conditions that do not materialize.

But a contract that uses such soft terms may create the moral hazard problem identified earlier. Moral hazard results because a promisor who has the flexibility to adjust his performance in the future as conditions change will always choose the best alternative for him, even though it may not be best for the promisee or best for both parties in terms of joint welfare. Assume, in our example above, that Seller proposes to substitute an alternative machine at the original contract price because, as things turned out, her cost of producing the substitute machine is 10% less than the cost of producing the contract machine. Buyer values the substitute goods 20% less than the contract goods, yet still values those goods above Seller's cost and needs Seller's performance to fulfill his own obligations to third parties. Buyer, therefore, agrees to the adjustment. The contract as performed still produces a surplus that the parties can share. But this comes at a cost. The effect of the good faith adjustment is that Seller can capture a larger share of a smaller surplus. Viewed ex ante, Seller's actions reduce joint welfare because the reduction in Buyer's share of the surplus under the renegotiated deal is greater than Seller's gain.

Note that this particular moral hazard problem exists even when Buyer can monitor and observe Seller's actions under the contract to determine whether Seller's representations regarding her costs are true. The particular problem with soft terms such as good faith adjustment is one of verification. If a third party verifying the contract performance under a broad standard of good faith adjustment would permit the promisor to select a lower-cost proxy for the contract performance (say, by tendering the substitute machine), the promisor will do so even when this action results in an overall reduction in joint welfare.

The moral hazard problem is exacerbated whenever the seller's actions are effectively hidden from the buyer. In cases in which the buyer cannot observe the seller's costs (or use any reliable proxy as a check on claims of increased cost), the seller has an incentive to claim hardship even when none has occurred so as to capture a larger share of the contractual surplus. In short, if a third party cannot determine when a claim of good faith adjustment is genuine and when it is pretextual, the promisee is vulnerable to false claims of adjustment. Such a contract is inefficient because the buyer, anticipating the subsequent claim for good faith adjustment, will take costly precautions (such as entering into contingent contracts with other suppliers) that will reduce the contract surplus (Schwartz & Scott 2003).

Flexible (or soft) contract terms thus invite a party who is obligated to perform under an incomplete contract to attempt to reduce its investment so as to capture a larger share of the surplus from that investment. This happens because each party bears the full cost of its own investments but must share the resulting contractual surplus with its contracting partner. These moral hazard risks are often minimized by norms of trust, reciprocity, and desire for esteem, all of which bind people to perform obligations even when they share benefits. But, as we have indicated, in many arms-length transactions between strangers, these self-enforcing mechanisms may be inadequate to reduce the moral hazard risk.

CAN THE HOLDUP AND MORAL HAZARD PROBLEMS BE SOLVED?

Economic theorists have devised ways of surmounting the moral hazard and holdup problems that result from ex post adjustment or renegotiation. For example, they have imagined contractual mechanisms that induce truthful revelation of private information. These mechanisms, properly specified, can eliminate the incentive to exploit party vulnerability while retaining the flexibility to adapt to new information arising during the course of contract performance (Maskin 1999, Tirole 1999, Hermalin & Katz 1993). Other strategies include dividing the power to renegotiate, either explicitly, by the assignment of property rights, or by using external factors to determine renegotiating capacities (Grossman & Hart 1986, Hart & Moore 1990, Edlin & Reichelstein 1996). All these devices assume the existence of strong powers on the part of courts and other enforcement bodies to compel truthful testimony and/or police renegotiation. In reality, of course, courts do not have such power.

We should not dismiss these formal models even though they assume a hypothetical legal system unlike any that exists today. Even so, economic theorists have made important contributions to our understanding of optimal contracting strategies by showing that parties can indeed write complete, complex contracts, under carefully prescribed conditions, that produce both efficient ex ante investment and efficient ex post trade and that are invulnerable to renegotiation. Alternatively, the models show that parties can write simple contracts with hard terms that anticipate renegotiation and yet can constrain the renegotiation so as to limit the risk of holdup.

The lessons from this work can be simplified as follows: If, on the one hand, the parties can sustain the costs of writing complex (i.e., efficiently complete) contracts, they would prefer to invoke an enforcement mechanism that precluded renegotiation because the ex ante contract, by definition, would have provided for the optimal outcome in all possible states of the world. On the other hand, if the costs of contracting are high (because, for example, uncertainty is high) the parties will be motivated to write simple contracts that either anticipate an ex post renegotiation or delegate discretion to enforcing bodies ex post. If the simple contract contains precise terms, the parties would anticipate renegotiation and would want the renegotiation process to be constrained so as to limit the holdup risk (Schwartz 1998, Schwartz & Watson 2004). If the simple contract contains vague standards, the parties would anticipate adjustment and would want the adjustment process to be constrained so as to limit the moral hazard risk.[3]

Unfortunately, existing legal mechanisms cannot preclude renegotiation in the case of complex contracts, nor can they effectively regulate either the renegotiation or the adjustment process in the case of simple contracts. Individuals generally have the freedom to renegotiate their commitments, regardless of agreements to the contrary in the contract, and courts lack the power to compel only truthful claims of ex post adjustment (Schwartz & Scott 2003). Under these circumstances, parties can (and do) turn instead to informal mechanisms of self-enforcement.

---

[3]Some scholars suggest that, in a world of private information, parties will renegotiate more efficiently when the contract term is a vague standard rather than a precise rule (Ayres & Talley 1995, Johnston 1995). Bernstein (2001) suggests, on the other hand, that precise rules provide more efficient renegotiation.

Thus, for example, private firms can limit their power to renegotiate to some extent through internal governance rules, such as by requiring many layers of consent as a prerequisite to the assumption of a legal obligation. In addition, the law imposes some external limits on a firm's renegotiation autonomy, e.g., by regulating conflicts of interest on the part of firm officials and in some cases allowing firm stakeholders to challenge transactions infected by such conflicts. In the case of simple contracts, reputation, repeat dealings, and norms of reciprocity provide the best available means of regulating the inevitable renegotiation and/or adjustment process so as to protect the vulnerabilities of both parties. If the parties can rely upon these informal mechanisms for enforcing promissory commitments, they can approximate in practice the theoretical goal of writing contracts that achieve efficient trade without compromising investment efficiency.

CONCLUSION

The lesson from contract theory is that actors can best solve contracting problems by employing the full range of enforcement methods (both self-enforcement and formal legal enforcement). When transactions costs are low, the parties can write a complex, contingent contract. Such a contract will frequently require the parties to make sequential, interactive investments in a joint venture. The individual components of these more complex contracting strategies tend to be opaque, thus making it hard for either party to characterize accurately their partners' actions as cooperative or not. Complex contracts, therefore, often require third party arbiters, such as courts, to unpack the parties' respective obligations in the particular circumstances that unfold. Such contracts anticipate that the arbiter can verify the responses appropriate to the particular contingencies and states of the world specified in the contract.

When transactions costs are high relative to the gains from contracting, parties will choose to write simple contracts that lump together many future states of the world so that their respective obligations are transparent and iterative. But simple contracts create moral hazard and holdup risks. Parties will either write simple contracts with soft contract terms (using standards such as best efforts or good faith adjustment) and anticipate opportunistic claims for adjustment, or they will write simple contracts with hard terms and anticipate the risk of holdup. In either case, exclusive reliance on formal legal enforcement of such agreements creates an enforcement risk that courts and arbiters cannot easily police. In the case of simple contracts with soft terms, the risk is that the investing party will substitute an alternative performance that reduces joint welfare or will otherwise seek to shirk or chisel on the obligation to perform. In the case of simple contracts with hard terms, the risk is that the investing party will be exploited strategically in a subsequent renegotiation. This exploitation is hard for third parties to police because a demand to renegotiate often will reflect a party's alternatives to the original deal, which typically rest on private information. In the face of the evident shortcoming of legal enforcement to ensure efficient renegotiation and/or adjustment, parties to simple contracts thus have an incentive to use informal means of enforcement to enhance contractual incentives to perform.

The *Annual Review of Law and Social Science* is online at http://lawsocsci.annualreviews.org

LITERATURE CITED

Akerloff G. 1970. The market for "lemons": quality uncertainty and the market mechanism. *Q. J. Econ.* 84:488–500

Ames JB. 1913. *Lectures on Legal History and Miscellaneous Legal Essays.* Cambridge, MA: Harvard Univ. Press

Axelrod R. 1984. *The Evolution of Cooperation.* New York: Basic Books

Ayres I. 2003. Valuing modern contract scholarship. *Yale Law J.* 112:881–902

Ayres I, Talley E. 1995. Solomonic bargaining: dividing an entitlement to facilitate Coasian trade. *Yale Law J.* 104:1027–78

Bernstein L. 1996. Merchant law in a merchant court: rethinking the code's search for immanent business norms. *Univ. Pa. Law Rev.* 144:1765

Bernstein L. 2001. Private commercial law in the cotton industry: creating cooperation through rules, norms and institutions. *Mich. Law Rev.* 99:1724

Che YK, Hausch D. 1999. Cooperative investment and the value of contracting. *Am. Econ. Rev.* 89:125–47

Edlin AS. 1998. Breach remedies. In *The New Palgrave Dictionary of Economics and the Law*, ed. P Newman, pp. 174–79. London: Macmillan

Edlin AS, Reichelstein S. 1996. Holdups, standard breach remedies, and optimal investment. *Am. Econ. Rev.* 86:478

Fehr E, Gächter S, Kirchsteiger G. 1997. Reciprocity as a contract enforcement device: experimental evidence. *Econometrica* 65: 833

Fehr E, Schmidt K. 1999. A theory of fairness, competition and cooperation. *Q. J. Econ.* 114:817–68

Goetz CJ, Scott RE. 1981. Principles of relational contracts. *Va. Law Rev.* 67:1089

Grief A. 1998. Informal contract enforcement: lessons from medieval trade. In *The New Palgrave Dictionary of Economics and Law*, ed. P Newman, pp. 287–95. London: Macmillan

Grossman SJ, Hart OD. 1986. The costs and benefits of ownership: a theory of vertical and lateral integration. *J. Polit. Econ.* 94:691–791

Hadfield GK. 1994. Judicial competence and the interpretation of incomplete contracts. *J. Leg. Stud.* 23:159–86

Hart OD. 1995. *Firms, Contracts and Financial Structure.* Oxford: Oxford Univ. Press

Hart OD. 1998. Incomplete contracts and the theory of the firm. *J. Law Econ.* 119–37

Hart OD, Moore J. 1990. Property rights and the nature of the firm. *J. Polit. Econ.* 98:1119–58

Hart OD, Moore J. 1999. Foundations of incomplete contracts. *Rev. Econ. Stud.* 66:115–38

Hermalin B, Katz M. 1993. Judicial modification of contracts between sophisticated parties: a more complete view of incomplete contracts and their breach. *J. Law Econ. Organ.* 9:230–55

Johnston J. 1995. Bargaining under rules versus standards. *J. Law Econ. Organ.* 11:256

Kaplow L. 1992. Rules versus standards: an economic analysis. *Duke Law J.* 42:557–629

Klein B. 1988. Vertical integration as organizational ownership: the Fisher Body-General Motors relationship revisited. *J. Law Econ. Organ.* 4:199–212

Klein B. 1996. Why hold-ups occur: the self-enforcing range of contractual relationships. *Econ. Inq.* 34:444–63

Klein B, Crawford RG, Alchian A. 1978. Vertical integration, appropriable rents, and the competitive contracting process. *J. Law Econ.* 21:297–326

Landa J. 1981. A theory of the ethnically homogenous middleman group: an institutional alternative to contract law. *J. Leg. Stud.* 10:349–62

Levine K. 1998. Modeling altruism and spitefulness in experiments. *Rev. Econ. Dyn.* 1:593–622

Maskin E. 1999. Nash equilibrium and welfare optimality. *Rev. Econ. Stud.* 66:23–38

Milgrom P, Roberts J. 1992. *Economics, Organization and Management*. Englewood Cliffs, NJ: Prentice Hall

Rabin M. 1993. Incorporating fairness into game theory and economics. *Am. Econ. Rev.* 83:1281–302

Schwartz A. 1998. Incomplete contracts. In *The New Palgrave Dictionary of Economics and the Law*, ed. P Newman, pp. 277–83. London: Macmillan

Schwartz A, Scott RE. 2003. Contract theory and the limits of contract law. *Yale Law J.* 113:541

Schwartz A, Watson J. 2004. The law and economics of costly contracting. *J. Law Econ. Organ.* 20:2–31

Scott RE. 1987. Conflict and cooperation in long-term contracts. *Calif. Law Rev.* 75:2005

Scott RE. 2003. A theory of self-enforcing indefinite agreements. *Columbia Law Rev.* 103:1641

Scott RE, Stephan PB. 2004. Self-enforcing international agreements and the limits of coercion. *Wis. Law Rev.* 2004:551

Scott RE, Stephan PB. 2006. *The Limits of Leviathan—Contract Theory and the Enforcement of International Law*. Cambridge, UK: Cambridge Univ. Press

Scott RE, Triantis GG. 2004. Embedded options and the case against compensation in contract damages. *Columbia Law Rev*. 104:1428

Scott RE, Triantis GG. 2006. Anticipating litigation in contract design. *Yale Law J.* 115:814–79

Segal I. 1999. Complexity and renegotiation: a foundation for incomplete contracts. *Rev. Econ. Stud.* 66:57

Simpson AWB. 1986. *A History of the Common Law of Contract*. Oxford: Oxford Univ. Press

Tirole J. 1999. Incomplete contracts: where do we stand. *Econometrica* 67:741–81

Triantis GG, Triantis AJ. 1998. Timing problems in contract breach decisions. *J. Law Econ.* 41:163–207

Annu. Rev. Law Soc. Sci. 2006. 2:299–340
doi: 10.1146/annurev.lawsocsci.2.081805.105756

First published online as a Review in Advance on August 4, 2006

AFTER POSTCOMMUNISM: The Next Phase

Martin Krygier and Adam Czarnota
Faculty of Law, University of New South Wales, Sydney NSW 2052, Australia; email: m.krygier@unsw.edu.au, a.czarnota@unsw.edu.au

Key Words transition, rule of law, transitional justice

■ **Abstract** This is a review, from a social scientific perspective, of law-related transformations in the formerly communist parts of Europe. It draws particularly on developments in East Central Europe. The frame of the discussion is a specific and interrelated group of questions: What are the distinctive features of these transformations, to what extent do these features endure, and what would it mean to say that the postcommunist region has entered a new phase? The review discusses the utility of the concepts "postcommunism" and "transition"; the goal of the rule of law, in the name of which many legal reforms have been made; particular problems that have arisen in relation to the judiciary, constitutional courts, and former secret police; and questions about "dealing with the past" as they have been asked about past institutions, people, and property rights. It concludes with a consideration of the likely impact of "joining Europe" on those countries that have been accepted as members of the European Union, on those that have not yet been accepted, and on those that are unlikely ever to be accepted.

INTRODUCTION

When asked to discuss the topic "after postcommunism—the next phase," our first instinct was to insert two question marks, one after each phrase. We have left the title as we received it, but we regard it as a provocation rather than a conclusion. What is/was postcommunism that it might be thought to have passed so quickly? What reasons exist to believe that it has passed, or will any time soon? What are some of the features that characterize(d) postcommunism? Have they gone? If so, do traces remain? With what effects? Have they been added to, replaced? If so, with what, and with what consequences?

The next phase? Like the experience of postcommunism itself, the phrase is laced with assumptions, or at least questions, about time and development. What are the interrelations between past, present, and future, both in the world of postcommunism as its inhabitants live it (or, in the next phase, might recall it), and in commentators' discussions, distillations, and characterizations of it. Should we anticipate a momentum, whereby what was once present—communism, postcommunism—has been/will be/can be superseded? What might that momentum be, and how would what it led to relate to what went before?

Our concern is with law in postcommunist society, particularly what is distinctive about it, and whether and in what ways its roles might be said to, thought to, made to differ now from what it once was. We discuss the rule of law, the judiciary, secret services, dealing with the past, and the implications of European enlargement. But we begin with two key and connected terms: postcommunism and transition. These terms, though used in relation to law, have been applied to much else as well, indeed to pretty well everything that has happened over the 17 years since the collapse of the communist empire in Europe. They are now almost unavoidable, and they seem simple enough, but they embody assumptions that their obviousness and simplicity conceal. Those assumptions have been held by many actors within and observers of the region. They frame discussions, even when—perhaps especially when—they themselves are not discussed. They do not have to mislead, but they can. Certainly, they can set or reflect agendas, all the more powerful for being unexamined.

POSTCOMMUNISM?

"In 1989," Ken Jowitt writes, "the Soviet bloc became extinct; communist parties in every Eastern European country added the loss of political power to their earlier loss of ideological purpose during the phase of 'real socialism'; and the Soviet Union . . . not only tolerated but instigated its collapse. The result is a gap in Europe's 'conceptual geography' no less significant than that of 1918" (Jowitt 1992, p. 284). What might fill that gap became a matter of much guesswork, many experiments, some more and some less controlled, and not a little apprehension. In many ways these uncertainties remain, both within the redrawn map of Europe and more generally in our geographically reconceptualized world. But a lot has happened in the meantime.

It has been common to characterize the region whose legacy was communism as postcommunist. That might seem simple common sense, since the region was but is no longer run by parties that called themselves communist. However, the label is not innocent. It represents a choice and raises several points of contention. We mention just a few.

The first is whether, in the hybrid postcommunism, emphasis should lie on the prefix or the suffix. It makes a difference. If the region is seen as primarily *post*communist, we can regard the communist past as some sort of dream or nightmare, which dissipates on waking. Many newly minted experts and advisors from the West tended to favor this interpretation, often unreflectively. Communism was the past and perhaps had left rubbish that needed to be removed, but *post*communism is the present and future. The more you believe this, the less you need to understand communism. But if you take it to matter that the region is post*communist,* there is a clear suggestion that the communist past, or its legacies, retain present effects. Then it will seem folly to try to understand or act in the present without understanding what preceded it. Wisdom lies in determining not which of these polar options should be chosen, but what mix of them illuminates the complexities, constraints, and choices of the postcommunist world.

Second, there is a striking gap or bias in the term. A period and a state of affairs are defined in terms of what preceded them—by what they are presumed to be post—rather than by what they are. That is no accident. We knew, or at least thought we knew, the nature of communism. We did not know the nature of what was to follow, nor is it clear that we know today.

Third, to call the region postcommunist is to choose as significant one element of the past rather than others. Although many scholars have taken that choice to be natural, it is not self-evident. After all, the states in the region will always be chronologically postcommunist, but they are post many other things as well, and arguably some of those things, too, remain significant in the present. Thus, in a recent collection (Přibáň et al. 2003), the overarching concern is to explore the interplay between "[r]evolutionary changes and recent transformations in postcommunist Central Europe . . . [and] under the surface of rapid constitutional changes . . . much slower processes of institutional and cultural changes in which continuity and persistence play a much more substantial role" (p. 1). In most of the book's chapters, not merely communism but earlier pasts are shown to have bequeathed heavy legacies to the law-related present. Communism was not the whole of any country's presently relevant past but just its most recent stage. What went before differed from place to place, although there were commonalities, particularly deriving from the dominance of the Ottoman and Austro-Hungarian Empires in the precursors of several postcommunist countries, Prussia in others, Russia in many (partitioned Poland was for 120 years the beneficiary of the last three of these four). Each of these imperial legacies differed from the others, but all had in common backwardness in relation to Western Europe (see Janos 2000, Jedlicki 1990). That was a profoundly important inheritance of the countries that were taken over by communist parties, and one that the latter tried, lustily but at great cost, to overcome. As a result, postcommunism was from the start as much or more plagued by misdevelopment as by underdevelopment.

But although communism imposed common and crucial systemic features on every country in the bloc, communism was not identical in every country. It came to Central Europe much later than to the Soviet Union, and it differed in many ways there from its parent and model. The Balkans were different, too, and within the Balkans, Yugoslavia differed greatly from Romania, Bulgaria, and Albania. And we have not even mentioned any "stans."

What, then, is special about the communist past? We do not usually call contemporary Europe postfeudal, though of course, considered in the *longue durée* that is precisely what it is. However, it is no longer considered salient to remind people of that fact, still less to name the present in terms of it. A sign that postcommunism has reached a next phase—that is, that it has become post-post—might be that people cease to call it "post" at all. What is it that gives specific substance and identity to the period in between?

One palpable aspect of this in-between period is that much that existed under communism has stayed around. In several languages of the region, the term postcommunist is used to refer specifically to parties that emerged from former communist parties, as distinguished from non- or anticommunist parties, like those after and including Solidarity, that emerged from such opposition as had existed. Following that logic (which is absent in English, where we speak of excommunist parties), to call a state postcommunist is, at least subliminally, to suggest that elements of the communist past retain some special significance. And many people have suggested that.

Communism in power created a "system" (Frentzel-Zagórska 1997), aptly described by Ernest Gellner as Caesaro-Papist-Mammonist (Gellner 1991, p. 495; 1994, pp. 4, 196). The system aimed at, and to an unparalleled extent achieved, monopoly control over the polity, ideology, and economy. That control also extended to law and to society as a whole. No other system of government sought so completely to obliterate institutions and activities independent of central domination and to fill the space with itself.

The central truth in the label postcommunist is that that system has ended. However, most of its personnel at every level, and many of its institutions, practices, and thoughtways certainly did survive. Not only are there parties still operating in the new multiparty systems that are direct descendants of the old communist parties, but there are judges who have not changed, bureaucracies with the same bureaucrats, and local leaders who also never changed. These are typically referred to as legacies of communism. How significant they are and what that significance amounts to remain matters of hot contention, both in political debate and in academic analysis. A large literature devoted to communist legacies and their short- and long-term implications began to arise almost as soon as walls began to fall (see Jowitt 1992, Holmes 1995, Ekiert 1999), although the size of the literature varies by discipline. On the one hand, economists tend to ignore historical legacies until they are embarrassed by them, as do behavioral sociologists and political scientists, although social scientists impressed by path dependence might go back to Lenin, or at least Gorbachev. On the other hand, historians, particularly from the region, are likely to trace older and allegedly deeper legacies that they believe still dominate contemporary and superficial variations (Jedlicki 1990; and see, for a similar argument from a nonhistorian, Gray 1993).

There are controversies both about the extent of continuities and their significance. In relation to positive law, however, there is less room for controversy about the fact of continuity, although there is plenty of room for disputes in the evaluation of the fact. For these were predominantly "self-limiting revolutions" (see Staniszkis 1986; 1991, pp. 215–25), where it makes sense to talk of revolutions at all (on this point, see Garton Ash 1999). Speaking only of formal law, the continuities—of personnel, institutions, and laws—were vast. Laws remained valid unless explicitly replaced or found to be unconstitutional under new constitutions. The old hierarchy of regular courts stayed intact, with some additions, such as constitutional courts, implemented as separate in function, personnel, and hierarchical position. Even with these, sometimes important, supplements, the traditional system hardly changed, particularly at lower levels. Whatever academics make of these continuities, they are the stuff of lively and bitter controversy in the political debates of the region. And if this is true of formal law, a social scientist might anticipate, it is all the more so of informal law-related practices and assumptions occurring in the shadow of, or arguably overshadowing, legal forms.

But in law there has been a lot of replacing and borrowing, too, and this raises socio-legal conundrums in acute form. Enthusiasts who imagine that legal regime change, wherever it occurs, simply involves putting right things in place of wrong ones have often been embarrassed, and they continue to be. There are many reasons for such embarrassment, but one is that a lot stays around to complicate, penetrate, and at times subvert any novel initiative. What persists includes hardware on the ground and software in people's heads, institutions, and attitudes, ways of doing and ways of thinking. Old hardware is everywhere, but examples of dated software are also easy to find. Thus, Kim Scheppele cites the system for tracking judicial mistakes that was created in Russia in Soviet times and persists today. Judicial promotions still depend (inversely) on the number of cases a judge decides that were overturned on appeal. In Hungary, she also notes, the Supreme Court thought it could go on issuing guiding explanations for years until the Constitutional Court told the justices they could not do so any more. Durable, too, is "the cluelessness of the defense bar in many places where changes in criminal procedure finally allowed them to introduce evidence for the defense" (K. Scheppele, personal communication). None of this is easy to shift or remold. The persistence of such legacies does not mean that nothing new can or should be tried, nor that past legacies determine present and future possibilities. But it does mean that the past matters, always. Indeed, the history of postcommunist transitions suggests that L.P. Hartley was quite wrong to suggest that "the past is another country. They do things differently there." Often it is just the same country, and they do the same things. More apposite is Faulkner's observation that "the past is never dead. It's not even past." We return to this theme later.

A fourth issue has to do with the dating of postcommunism. Scholars have not clearly dated when it began, let alone when it will end. After all, many of the changes that became publicly manifest in Central Europe in 1989 or in the Soviet Union in 1991 or elsewhere even later (Serbia in 2000, Ukraine in 2005)—in the economy, in the polity, in social relations, in ideological controls, in the role of law—were already happening before communist elites started to negotiate with, or run away from, or become, postcommunist elites. The Hungarian justice ministry had already drafted a new constitution in 1988, which turned out to be most of what was accepted by the opposition in 1989, and in other countries other struggles for the separation of party and state had been successfully waged by communists for communists since the start of perestroika in 1985. Because social processes, large-scale revolutions apart, do not provide bright-line markers of their phases of development, there can be and has been endless controversy about whether and when communism became post and whether postcommunism has or will become something else. Obvious points of departure or closure, such as the entry of many countries of the region into NATO and later the European Union (EU), do change some processes, even significantly, but not all. And most former communist countries are not participants in them.

And finally, in relation to any of these matters, indeed virtually all matters, one must remember that postcommunism is not a uniform phenomenon. There is enormous diversity among and within its components. Twenty-eight countries with 400 million inhabitants constitute a region in name only (although many within the region have old regional connections and are used to thinking of themselves as part of it, which is a social fact of considerable importance). These countries have very different pasts, and they will have increasingly diverse and probably divergent futures. Among these differences is likely to be the weight of the communist past in the present. These countries had one enormously important factor in common: They were ruled by communist parties as parts of imposed systems, almost all backed by force from Moscow. Much stemmed from that fact: enforced models of institutional hardware and ideological software, identities, connections, networks, a host of what Durkheim called "manières d'agir et de penser." But although that rather large fact about their past contributes to their present and gives them many common problems, it does not determine what they do about those problems or what new things happen to them. Thus, two postcommunist neighbors, Poland and Belarus, are actually very far apart in almost every interesting respect except their borders. To a much lesser extent, that remains true of other neighbors, such as Romania and Moldova, as it was until 1998 of Slovakia and Hungary, and until 2005 of Ukraine and Poland. There are reasons for these differences that a catch-all label does nothing to disclose. Moreover, diversity is found not merely among states but also within them: diversity of regions, classes, ethnic groups, age cohorts, social and political processes, winners and losers, winners who will be losers, and losers who will be winners (see Rychard 1996). Not only do these diversities exist, but they are differently affected by the panoply of processes we call postcommunism. Some works attempt a general overview (Holmes 1997, Sakwa 1999) of postcommunism. Some of the best (Elster et al. 1998) are more selective.

TRANSITION?

In response to such controversies and diversities, how have scholars responded in their attempts to understand the period? We identify three tendencies, although there are many others.

The first and probably dominant trend, at least among Western observers, is the vast literature of transition. The significance of this word bears an odd mirror-like similarity to that of postcommunism. Here, too, the present is absent. However, whereas postcommunism defines the present in relation to the past, transition characterizes it in terms of its putative future. Indeed, from the perspective of transitology's teleological history, questions about what postcommunism is and what it is likely to become merge. On this view, the key fact about postcommunism is that it is in transition to what it will be: when the transition is over, when new institutions and practices are consolidated, when a new social and economic order and a new legal and political system have gelled. In the meantime, postcommunism is a way station between a known point of departure to a hoped-for and well-defined destination, via a rather volatile and undefined present. For some time, scholars typically asked how the transition was going, what obstacles stood in the way of its passage, how it might be facilitated, and whether it would succeed. Less typical was asking whether it was occurring at all.

The early years after 1989 were dominated by the language of transition, or rather a particular combination of transitions—to the market, democracy, and the rule of law, typically thought of as a package deal. The very distinctive predicament of postcommunism, scholars argued, was that all three futures had to be approached at once, called the simultaneity problem (Dahrendorf 1990, Elster et al. 1998). A world-historical struggle between two models of development had ended, and the Western variant—capitalist, liberal democratic, law-governed—had emerged as victor and model for other states, the 28 states that arose where the alternative model had been overthrown. Their teleological confidence put commentators and experts in the curious position of appearing to know much more about where the region was going and what it would find on arrival than they could tell us about where it actually was, not to mention what the trip would be like.

One reason for this confidence was that the discourse was not only teleological but also imitative. The teleology had a curious back-to-the-future quality about it, summed up in the common slogan of the time: No Experiments. So in curious parody of Lincoln Steffens's remark about the Soviet Union of the 1930s—"I've seen the future and it works"—transitologists saw the future of the region in the present of somewhere else and assumed that what worked there would work here too. And so, as Timothy Garton Ash wrote in 1990:

> In politics they are all saying: There is no "socialist democracy," there is only democracy. And by democracy they mean multi-party, parliamentary democracy as practised in contemporary Western, Northern, and Southern Europe. They are all saying: There is no "socialist legality," there is only legality. And by that they mean the rule of law, guaranteed by the constitutionally anchored independence of the judiciary (Garton Ash 1990, p. 21).

There are now numerous centers and institutions and countless studies of transitional justice (see, e.g., the studies listed at http://userpage.fu-berlin.de/~theissen/biblio/), all staffed by multilingual mini-Aristotles, from Berlin to Vladivostok, in no doubt about their subjects' proper *telos,* if less confident about whether or how it will be reached. Indeed, the tendency of such works has been doubly imitative because not only is the goal thought to have been reached elsewhere, but so too the means. Thus, there have been frequent crossovers between transitologists who have studied postdictatorships in other parts of the world (e.g., Linz & Stepan 1996) and those whose data are just beginning to appear but whose hypotheses and even conclusions are often well honed. Whether this is the best way to analyze the trajectories of countries with long and complex histories, and many variations, is a matter of some debate (Schmitter & Karl 1994, Bunce 1995), but it is certainly common. Transitological teleology is reflected in the tone of the majority of black letter constitutional lawyers in the region, and also legal theorists who have quickly transitioned from their earlier theories of state and law in the service of the "democratic rule-of-law state" (Mołdawa 2003, Safjan 2005).

Transition, however, is not simple. That is true in general, and it is true particularly in relation to law. What do you need to know? How does a good legal institution work where it works? But transplanted laws and institutions are typically uprooted from much of what their working might depend on when they are called upon to travel. They land in territory where much that is already firmly embedded is often quite unfamiliar and not always welcoming. Are there examples of successful transplantations elsewhere? But why imagine that every transplant will encounter the same reception, wherever it is sent? Should we then stick to local knowledge? But "the way we do things here" is often the problem. Moreover, changes happen and can be made to happen, and often it is better that they do. We are not always impotent, nor is history just a recycling of familiar patterns. And among the things that can be learned from history is that some things long done are better undone. But how? Regimes purportedly in transition are fascinating precisely because they pose these questions with urgency, in contexts where every choice is inescapably enmeshed in complex and dialectical interplays of legacies and initiatives, familiar and novel, local and exotic. Many things, often in tension, compete simultaneously for attention. Too often we attend to too few of them, following our particular national and/or disciplinary provenance, experience, biases (see Krygier 1999b).

In light of such persistent sources of puzzlement, one can find, in contrast to confident transitologies, a plethora of individual studies and edited collections that deal with particular aspects of this elephantine subject while remaining agnostic about the overall character of the animal(s) in question. A signal of such self-conscious agnosticism is use of the word "transformation" instead of the originally ubiquitous "transition." As countless essays have noted in their first paragraphs, transition suggests we know where things are going. Transformation just tells us the joint is rocking. Many such essays have appeared in collections (e.g., Přibáň & Young 1999; Přibáň et al. 2003), among them our own (Krygier & Czarnota 1999, Czarnota et al. 2005, Sadurski et al. 2006), that bring together a variety of perspectives on particular problems, suggesting common themes, including transitological themes, but not generating univocal paradigms of description, evaluation, or prescription. There is wisdom in this caution, and in the preference for the essay over the book. Many quick and confident judgments of the development and direction of postcommunism have dated rather swiftly (see Krygier 1999b); there is something appropriately tentative about the essay.

Of course, reluctance to speak of transition is not always a sign of caution. It might be a sign of disagreement (see especially Carothers 2002). Transition is a situation, a condition, a predicament if you will, on a kind of indeterminate but

Whiggishly inclined trajectory from hateful past to liberal future. But in that space people make decisions, make mistakes, seek to serve their interests, etc., for many different reasons. Some are concerned with that trajectory, others not much or at all. Citizens and elites have many purposes, some of them arguably not related merely to getting us from disreputable point A in the transition to liberal destination B. Thus, Stark & Bruszt (1998) emphasize that the morning after the revolution, people were not wondering how to transit to the market, democracy, and the rule of law. Rather they were trying to make do with the resources they had. For many, and especially the more successful, these included the networks necessary to make things work, at least for them, under communism. The region is full of people not especially interested in the transition and its normative changes but in making a buck, even a killing, with the resources and connections and opportunities at their disposal (for an excellent, and still rare, sociological case study of such networks in action, see Gadowska 2002). And often those with such resources—at times not very post at all—benefit from early moments of transition, to stifle further changes that might threaten their positions, for example, by capturing the state, or attractive parts of it (see Hellman 1998). Differences between approaches in different transitional countries may have as much to do with different elites with different resources, facing different obstacles, choosing different solutions, for different reasons, even where observers might see common problems, as they have to do with the *telos*-driven exigencies of the transitional moment.

Some critics simply wish to deflate the pretensions of transitology, without offering an overarching counternarrative. A more ambitious third approach goes further in this critical direction, to argue that postcommunism is a specific social formation, structurally distinct from communism though significantly its heir, but distinct also from liberal democratic states of the West (Staniszkis 1999, 2001a,b; Krasnodębski 2003). On this view, the main problem of postcommunism as a specific social-political structure is the attempt to modernize societies that are at once postcommunist and peripheral, at a time of globalization. This particular combination is unprecedented. It generates a predicament, the argument suggests, less like that of a chrysalis struggling to shed its carapace to become a beautiful and familiar butterfly than of some different species altogether, mutant perhaps, that needs to be understood in its own morphological terms.

Thus, Staniszkis (1999, 2001a) claims that postcommunist peripheral capitalism differs systematically both from nonperipheral capitalism in the developed West and also from non-postcommunist peripheries such as those of Latin America, both because of differences in its institutional structure and in the historical moment of its emergence. Staniszkis points to institutional changes, new networks of power, hierarchically organized markets, and transformed forms of hybrid property, neither quite public nor quite private (also emphasized by Stark & Bruszt 1998). She analyzes the problem of transformed rationalities in the former communist states, as well as the incompleteness of the changes in state capitalism following the collapse of communism. She emphasizes basic elements in the creation of a new system, not from the ashes of communism but built out of rearranged bricks of the communist system. There have been rearrangements, and there are new bricks as well, but the resulting postcommunist amalgam is specific and needs to be understood in its own terms.

Her approach has considerable heuristic usefulness from a socio-legal point of view, particularly by comparison with a naive faith in institutional transplantation and in the redeeming power of Western legal and political institutions. Staniszkis argues that the new institutions often cannot act in transitologically predicted ways because of internal features of this postcommunist context, which are not part of the transitological script but are no less important than those that are, and in some respects and circumstances are able to make over new institutions to old, or anyway not transitological purposes. Although law is not her focus, her ideas brim with implications for legal transitology.

These differences of perspective are not merely semantic. How one characterizes the next phase is likely to depend materially on what one understands postcommunism to have been about. If transition, then the questions are whether or when the *telos* has been closely enough approached, when the market, democracy, and the rule of law have been stably institutionalized, or in the term of transitological art, consolidated. But agnostics might not expect any such stage, or conversely, might not consider the passage a failure if the predefined destinations are not reached. And peripheralists never expected the region to make the transition anyway because that was not where it was going.

Transitologists and postcommunist peripheralists, although they differ over what they expect to find there, do agree on some of its elements. Thus, both agree that the next phase will amount to the consolidation of a new order different from what went before. They also agree that such consolidation depends on the economic modernization of countries that were formerly communist and their entry into the global sphere of exchange on the best conditions possible. In Central Europe, more prosaically, they see both entry into the Atlantic security sphere and into the economic structures of the EU as important stages in the developments they identify. They differ, however, because although the former looks forward to a familiar capitalist economy, with democratic institutions and the rule of law, the latter sees a quite different, and idiosyncratic constellation emerging. In Russia, Eurasia, Belarus, the Caucasus, Azerbaijan, and at least until very recently Ukraine (see Riabczuk 2004), moreover, the idiosyncrasies prevail over the similarities. That the idiosyncrasies include authoritarian government, not simply as a difficult legacy but as a central part of elite commitment and design, is increasingly evident. These members of what Kotkin (2002) calls "Trashcanistan" are not obviously in transition toward anything modeled in the West, nor do their elites necessarily have any such ambitions. One or other paradigm might be right, or, more likely, one or other applies more or less well to different countries among those lumped together as postcommunist. Because labels bear (and hide) assumptions, it is worth getting these things straight.

There is a sociological lesson here. Much of transitology in general, and legal transitology in particular was, in effect, presociological. It did not reckon with local structures, traditions, networks, incentive structures, institutions, and practices. In the world of legal transitology, its failure to appreciate these issues is becoming increasingly evident to some of the most perceptive former enthusiasts and practitioners of transplantation and reform (e.g., Jensen & Heller 2003, Carothers 2006). Many legal institutions seem devilishly hard to transplant, or at least to make grow and bloom in ways to which the transplanters are accustomed. If this is so in places where there is a will to emulatory transition, then it is all the more dramatically so where that will is absent (see Bernardo & Neier 2006). Indeed, scholars increasingly have a reason to believe that the next phase of postcommunism will witness considerable effort by some elites, particularly those of former Soviet republics, to push back against precisely those reforms in law and politics that are most associated with transitological ambitions.

That does not in itself mean that the goals of transitologists are nowhere applicable or reachable (although that may turn out to be true of some of the goals everywhere and of all of them somewhere). People often achieve what they do not understand, let alone what they do not intend. And sometimes they even get what they want. But the number of surprises that transitologists have experienced do, at the very least, suggest that a bit more modesty, sociology, and attention to particularity than was first brought to the region might be useful. However, insistence on local uniqueness can threaten to essentialize local peculiarities, to transform hard facts into insuperable obstacles, thus cutting a region's moorings in and relationships to common human predicaments and wider human history, possibilities, and achievements (see di Palma 1990, Krygier 1999a). Discussion has often foundered between these false extremes. That means are found to bridge them may mark a new phase.

In this survey, we come across tensions of this sort frequently. We examine them by starting with the rule of law, which is the announced general goal prescribed by all legal transitologists, and subscribed to, at least rhetorically, by most elites. We then trace the fate of more specific domains of legal development that most centrally raise questions of past, present, and future.

RULE OF LAW

The overarching legal goal of transition was commonly said to be establishment of the rule of law or, in more local idioms, a law-governed state. Massive programs of aid have been devoted to the rule-of-law project. The whole initiative is a remarkable demonstration of a lawyers' project (which was adopted) that ran into difficulties that might have been predicted by a socio-legal understanding (which was rarely in evidence). For example, Hendley et al.'s (1999) fascinating work in Russia investigates what use factory managers make of legal institutions. Contrary to the "Field of Dreams" expectation that "if you build it they'll come," the question remains unanswered whether a supply of legal institutions, even of adequate quality, generates a demand for and use of legal services. Yet this question is crucial if the law is to matter. How much citizens are able and willing to use and to rely upon legal institutions to protect and advance their interests varies, again within and between societies and over time. In one study, Hendley et al. (1999) argue that adequate institutions were built in Russia, but few people came. The extent to which this is true, even in Russia, Hendley makes clear, varies by location, institution, and actor, and there are enormous variations within the region as a whole. How enormous is not clear because socio-legal research in the region on demand for law—that is, the different circumstances in which official law is regarded as salient to the solution of social problems, where, by whom, how, and with what consequences—is in its infancy (Murrell 2003). One would hope that the next phase will see more of it.

Bulgarians have a saying that "the law is like a door in the middle of an open field. Only a fool would go through the door." If one agrees that changing this way of thinking is important, then even an exemplary career in commercial law, say, or in any other necessary branch of law, is unlikely to prepare one for changing the deep realities that underlie this way of thinking (see Kurkchiyan 2003). For the question is not what sorts of institutions work best in circumstances where legal institutions are a fundamentally important part of normative social guidance, but rather what might make the law important in this way. Lawyers from legally well-equipped countries are rarely especially skilled to answer these sorts of questions. Quite the contrary.

What Holmes (1999) has observed of Russia can be generalized in principle, although not every country in the region faces problems of the same magnitude, and the elites of several countries, Russia now included, do not seem to regard them as problems. In particular, when our question is asked by someone concerned with how law might be encouraged to count, we should keep in mind that

> Lawyers are trained to solve routine problems within routine procedures. They are not trained to reflect creatively on the emergence and stabilization of the complex institutions that lawyering silently presupposes. Ordinary legal training, therefore, is not adequate to the extraordinary problems faced by the manager of a legal-development project in Russia. The problem is not Russian uniqueness and exceptionalism, but the opposite. In Russia, as everywhere else, legal reform cannot succeed without attention to social context, local infrastructure, professional skills, logistic capacities, and political support.... So legal knowledge alone is never enough (Holmes 1999, p. 71).

Where the law really does count, we can foreshorten the question why, as lawyers commonly do, and answer it in terms of the provisions and institutions of the law. When the law is socially and politically significant, the legal position will bear closely on the factual position, and then the hour of the lawyer is at hand. But that is only because what lawyers do not know—the conditions of legal effectiveness—gives significance to what they do know: the law.

What does it mean for law to count in a society in such a way that we feel confident saying that the rule of law exists there? A difficulty we have is that many social scientists are unconfident—because inexpert—to say much about law, whereas the experts, lawyers, are often confident but incompetent on this question. There are many questions about law too serious to be left to lawyers, who are typically specialists merely in law. One such question is what makes law count as an effective frame for the exercise of power. It asks about the social reach and weight of law. As Galanter (1992, p. 24) has observed in another context, "The answer will not yield to the most painstaking study of the law, for the deep fountains of change are outside it." This is not because the law has no significance, but because the nature and extent of that significance is outside the lawyer's special expertise. Answers depend on what the law itself depends on, not just on its terms. Those answers, whatever they are, will have to attend to matters of sociology and politics, as much as of law.

Indeed, social and political questions are central ones to ask about the place of law in a society, and they will be answered differently in different societies, whatever the written laws say or have in common. Moreover, because there are differences both within and between societies in this regard, one needs to think not just about people or societies in general, but about particular features of particular societies. No one doubts that these issues go beyond law on the books. But they also go beyond the law in action, where law in action is understood to refer to the way official law is implemented rather than to the many unofficial sources of normative order and disorder in social life (see Nelken 1984). We need to consider not merely how formal legal institutions operate when "in action," but also how individuals, groups, and entrenched networks respond or, especially, how they do not bother to respond. Do they fail to respond because the formal law does not reach them, because they consider it unimportant, because they consider other things more important, or because they can get away with ignoring it?

It is hard to generalize about these socio-legal matters in the region, first because we do not yet have much data, and second because of the inherent complexity and variety of the issues to be investigated. Of course, the salience of law varies considerably among classes, races, religious groups, and regions in all societies. However, there are some distinctive complexities in the postcommunist world. For example, Örkény & Scheppele (1999) write intriguingly about what they call "the complexity of legality in Hungary." The data are local, but the implications are more general. They distinguish between three levels: constitutional, state-citizen, and citizen-citizen. At the first level (and most discussed in the West), they find the rule of law astonishingly well established. The first generation Hungarian Constitutional Court, which they describe as "the most powerful high court in the world," had struck down an enormous number of laws; at one stage it struck down about one in three laws passed by the Parliament in two different elected governments. And *mirabile dictu,* Parliament continually, meekly, if at times resentfully, complied. And the Court was very popular. A true success story.

At the other levels, however, the story is different and much closer to familiar stories of relations under communism between citizen and state and among citizens. And we should remember that in the postcommunist world, Hungary has one of the longest and deepest traditions of legality. Nevertheless, administrators do not yet have this commitment. And at the level of citizen-citizen relations, life goes on very much as it did before the political changes of 1989—i.e., only a fool goes through the door. If this is true in Hungary, we are prepared to speculate, *a fortiori* it is truer the further east and south one travels from Budapest. Whether that is in fact the case is something only to be answered after detailed research in many parts of the region, of the sort Hendley does in Russia.

Of course, as all students of law and society know, there are parallels to this in every society. Differences are usually of degree, but those differences, and what might account for them, are often crucial. Transitologists have often ignored them.

Not only might institutionalizing the rule of law after postcommunism be harder than enthusiasts once thought, but certain efforts might turn out to harm precisely what they are supposed to help. Thus, Kleinfeld (2006, p. 53) points out:

> Most pernicious, depending on how they are implemented, institutional reforms carried out under the banner of rule-of-law reform can actually undermine rule-of-law ends. For instance, in Romania, businessmen have pleaded for an end to legal reform: They can live with bad laws, but the constant "improvement" of key property laws by various bilateral and multilateral aid agencies creates an unpredictable legal environment. An end good of the rule of law—a stable, predictable legal system—has been undermined by the so-called reform process.

Indeed, we can threaten the rule of law by exaggerating its significance, not merely by deriding or ignoring it. Thus, in a sparkling piece of contrarian analysis, Krastev (2005) examines the use of the rule of law, everyone's favorite remedy, to combat corruption, everyone's most easily condemned vice. The rule of law, Krastev (2005) contends, has become "the white myth of transition. After some years of flirting with the ideas of democracy and market economy, now rule of law is the magic phrase in Eastern Europe. It is rule of law and not democracy that brings foreign investors, it is rule of law that secures development and protects rights" (p. 323). Pitted against this "white myth" there is an even more widespread "black myth" that corruption is "the explanation of last resort for all failures and disappointments of the first postcommunist decade" (p. 323). It is not only that the rule of law is taken to be good and corruption bad, but that they are believed to be precisely each other's Other—if one rises the other must fall. And so the promotion of the rule of law is sought through anticorruption campaigns, corruption is fought by measures claimed to build the rule of law, and these campaigns become a currency of political virtue. While corruption is allegedly everywhere and the rule of law nowhere, who speaks for the former or against the latter?

So great is the hold of such rhetoric on the public mind that today the call for anticorruption campaigns is nearly irresistible: "If at the beginning of the campaign the suspicion is that corruption is almost everywhere, already in the middle of the campaign the suspicion is that corruption is almost everything. The final stage is the conviction that almost everybody is corrupt" (Krastev 2005, p. 336). Krastev (2005) is skeptical about this development for many reasons, among them anti-corruption campaigners' inability to deliver their loudly proclaimed goal, the rule of law. Because corruption is very hard to prove, the determination to prosecute in ever-increasing circles for corruption exposes the legal system to ridicule: If everyone is corrupt and so few are convicted for corruption, then what is wrong with the legal system? And if the legal system is remodeled on the best Transparency International (http://www.transparency.org/) models, and still everyone is corrupt, what hope exists for the rule of law? Rather than promote the rule of law, obsession with corruption might just undermine the possibility of it (see also Mungiu-Pippidi 2005, p. 47).

This argument jibes with a deeper issue raised at several places in this review. Is the rule of law to be regarded as primarily a legal institutional achievement, judged by the forms and properties of legal institutions, or is it rather to be seen as a complex social and political state of affairs in which the law counts—has depth and salience in a significant range of social practice? Such a state of affairs depends in part on legal institutions, to be sure, but on much else as well, and familiar institutional recipes are not self-evidently necessary or sufficient to produce it. The argument in this review is that the second interpretation is the more useful, and that one should not get carried away with formal-legal prescriptions at the expense of social and political realities. To do so is to mistake means for ends, and at the same time threaten those, and perhaps other, valuable goals in whose name one is purporting to act. So, just as corruption is not necessarily reduced by an obsession with it, the rule of law is not necessarily served. Mechanistic attempts to institutionalize the rule of law fall under similar suspicion to those voiced by Krastev (2005, p. 337) about anticorruption campaigns: "[W]hat postcommunist societies need are policies that reduce corruption, but not a rhetoric that leads to corruption-centered politics."

Even worse, some argue, are the potential antilegal consequences of formal legality. Thus, one of the basic constitutional principles asserted by postcommunist states was that they had become democratic and law-governed. In Poland, for example, this became a fundamental interpretive principle of the judgments of the Constitutional Tribunal, as it did of the Constitutional Court in Hungary (see Sadurski 2005, pp. 102–3, 135, 146, 244, 262), as well as a main constitutional principle. Fairly early, voices complained that the introduction of these principles had occurred too early, too early in that the legalism to which the democratic, law-governed state was reduced by the practice of the institutions of justice turned out to preserve and reposition old communist elites, together with illegally or extralegally gotten gains, now privately owned, under the new regime. In Zybertowicz's (2005) view, as is discussed further below, the period of postcommunist transformation is characterized by the advance and interconnection of the interests of former secret servicemen, politicians, and businessmen in so-called postcommunist networks.

One significant reflection of these problems in local legal literatures is a debate formulated as between a material and formal conception of the rule of law (see Morawski 1994; Nowacki 1995; Czarnota 2001, p. 17) and the contrast between the formal conception of the Hungarian Constitutional Court and the material conception of the Czech court, each deciding whether law could deal retrospectively with an evident but past injustice, or between a positivist and nonpositivist conception of the rule of law (Morawski 2005, pp. 228–41). On the one hand, postcommunist lawyers have generally adopted a narrowly interpreted conception of the rule of law, namely as fulfillment of formal legal requirements literally interpreted. Scholars have argued, however, that such a narrowly and formalistically conceived idea of the rule of law can prove to be helpful in the defense of people tied to the communist regime—in particular, the former communist *nomenklatura* allegedly shielded by what Adam Podgórecki called "hidden structures of law" (see Łoś 1996, pp. 275–322; Podgórecki 1996, pp. 29–33). On the other hand, any invocation of substantive considerations threatens retroactivity, the bane of many formal conceptions of the rule of law. The debate has not been concluded, but one may say that at the level of law creation and application, highly formalistic and positivistic approaches have been dominant (see Zirk-Sadowski 2005), at least in East-Central Europe. This is not merely an academic debate because it goes to questions of relations between the new system and the communist one, and to the necessity (or lack thereof) of dealing with the past by measures such as decommunization, lustration, and restitution.

JUDICIAL FUNCTIONS AND DYSFUNCTIONS

A key role in the implementation of the rule of law, as distinct from instrumental rule by law (which is common among dictatorships and existed in the later phases of communism), is supposed to be played by the judiciary. For the judicial branch to play an effective role in restraining other branches of power, including political power, its decisions must be able to affect socially important relationships and it must have the power to dispose of cases before it with real independence from other centers of social power. Further, the reasons for judicial decision must have some routine, institutionalized relationship to plausible interpretation of public laws, rather than stem from caprice, willfulness, external pressures, or secret directions. Such a legal result depends on a complex array of legal, sociological, cultural, and political preconditions.

Regular Courts

Lawyers typically emphasize the need for an independent judiciary, but the needs go far deeper, and all postcommunist countries face (or do not face) significant challenges in this area. There are, to be sure, familiar political and legal analyses of sources of judicial weakness under and before communism, and there is no doubt that judicial dependence had a long tradition in the region. Traditions of legal independence had much greater significance in Austria-Hungary than in, say, Russia, but it is also true that "[t]ypically, power in this region was either not restrained by legal measures, or only slightly bound, and there is also a long tradition of evading law" (Přibáň et al. 2003, p. 123). This remained true during the brief period of interwar independence, brought to its shocking end by World War II and Nazi occupation (or in Slovakia, Hungary, and Croatia, collaboration). After the war, communism introduced the doctrine that Lenin had called "the unity of power"—law was conceived as one among a range of instruments of power, all subservient to the party. Institutions, among them courts in a rather minor and dependent way, were vehicles, transmission belts, of power. There was in principle no room for notions of independence or institutions of restraint.

That doctrine was preached everywhere. In all communist states, subordination of the law to dictates of the party was a matter of principle and telephone justice; common practice was published and unpublished Guidelines, Viewpoints, Common Viewpoints, Supreme Court Informations, Orientations, Resolutions to be applied by judges or rebukes for deviation in subsequent political discussions, court inspections, and other conformity-inducing devices (see Markovits 1995, pp. 24ff, 71ff). As Markovits observes of East Germany, "In this network of permanent communication, it was not difficult 'to know what they wanted'" (Markovits 1995, p. 71). The extent of the practice and the zeal with which it was pursued varied in different places and at different times. These were greatest in areas deemed politically sensitive. These in turn were not stable, but changed at the discretion of the rulers.

Ambitious transitologists might predict that all this would change with the collapse of communism, and indeed there have been changes and new institutions, some of which work. However, not all of them have moved in the direction hoped, nor have all the weaknesses of the judicial arm come from expected sources. To start with the most obvious source, political interference with the administration of justice remains an important problem in many postcommunist states, though not all. In most, some ideological pressures remain or have resurfaced, but with nothing like the comprehensive and institutionalized force of communist ideology (apart, perhaps, from nationalism in parts of the former Yugoslavia). There are religious and nationalist forces that have affected court decisions in several countries, however, and the law has been a common object of populist antipathies to postcommunist states.

Direct political interference is perhaps most blatant in Belarus, in several of the Eurasian republics, in Croatia under Tuđman, Serbia under Milošević, and Ukraine under Kuchma. It can take the form of direct interference in the judicial process, as has often occurred, but it can start earlier, with the framing of favorable laws, for example, as has often been alleged of Russian oligarchs, or by destroying an embarrassing procurator, as Yeltsin did in Russia in 1999, or by using the procuracy and judiciary to undertake false investigations and prosecutions of foes. And charges do not even have to be false. In a climate of widespread networks of "dirty togetherness," to use Podgórecki's (1994, pp. 131–32) evocative phrase, there may well be legal grounds for prosecution. However, not those legal grounds but rather political mobilization of the legal and judicial apparatus explains why some are prosecuted and others not. Such political instrumentalization of law is alleged to be common practice in Russia and, at least until recently, in Ukraine (on Ukraine as a "blackmail state," see Riabczuk 2004, pp. 58–61). This practice, too, can be seen as a legacy of communism where, as Scheppele (personal communication) has observed, "the rules were so complicated that following them all was impossible. As a result, the state always had the possibility of prosecuting those it did not favor because everyone was always in violation of some law." Formal democracy is not in itself a cure for these tendencies, although it can help in combating some. But even when dictators are deposed, their appointees and arrangements remain problematic, and they may well become the material or the model for successor regimes.

Moreover, with the collapse of the party's monopoly of power, independence of the administration of justice was not always the result. Other potential external sources of threat exist. Powerful economic actors or networks of political and politico-economic actors and relationships have in various ways and with varying degrees of success sought to capture, lean on, or bypass the state: oligarchs (Russia), tycoons (Croatia), wrestlers (Bulgaria). Personal clientelistic networks (Sajó 1998) that are commonly embedded in social power arrangements are often politically significant, and sometimes legally so. When applied to the legal system, they exert pressure to override formal constraints with informal and antiformal considerations: to make exemptions, to stall or discontinue cases, to minimize penalties, to make favorable decisions. Among their sources are secret police networks established under the previous regime and new or *nomenklatura*-linked criminal-economic networks. Their workings are often secret. In these cases, as in many others, the sources of judicial independence and effectiveness, and the lack thereof, are largely nonlegal.

How might such sources of pressure on the judiciary be lessened or resisted? One solution, obvious to many lawyers, is to institutionalize an independent judiciary from the very start. In many countries there have been decisive moves in that direction. Not all of them have served the ends of the rule of law. One difficulty is that measures designed to enhance institutional autonomy, or at least measures justified in those terms, might well shield incompetence, political affiliations, and corruption. Thus, several postcommunist countries, among them Poland, quickly institutionalized complete judicial independence from outside interference, as though their ideal of having a substantively autonomous judiciary would best be reached by imagining it had already been attained. A by-product of such initiatives, whether intended or not, has been to make immovable the old, incompetent, corrupt, and badly formed holdovers from earlier times. In Bulgaria, and most likely elsewhere as well, the same measure—rendering judges irremovable—was clearly intended, by the first unrenovated excommunist leaders, to result in maintaining their people on the bench even if the excommunist leaders themselves lost electorally (Magalhães 1999; see also Mungiu-Pippidi 2005, p. 52).

A better tactic might have been to sack or not to reappoint existing judges and appoint an independent commission to rehire, including such members of the former cadres as qualified, as was done with the Polish Supreme Court (but not the wider judiciary). In this way, one would not assume what still needed to be proved, that judges shielded from sacking would perform their tasks in competent, independent, and substantively autonomous ways. However, this strategy brings with it a further danger because if, as in Croatia under Tuđman, the appointment committee is not truly independent, then new political appointees with tenure are brought into the judiciary. Not only the judges but also those who appoint them should combine competence with impartiality and institutional security. Candidates with such a combination of qualities do not grow on trees.

In any event, institutional independence is only part of the story. Not all judicial pathologies come from outside, so independence is not enough. For institutional autonomy to yield good and independent legal decisions, there must be a good and independent legal and judicial culture and profession and competent professionals. Attaining these has preconditions, some of them internal to the culture and profession, and some dependent on wider social and cultural conditions. A common postcommunist dilemma, for example, is that, on the one hand, there are many judges with bad judicial socialization, training, and experience (where old cadres were not replaced, or long judicial experience was made a criterion for appointment, which amounts to the same thing), while on the other hand, if such cadres are purged, the alternative, particularly in the early years of postcommunism, was often judges with very little relevant experience. Among these were raw recruits prematurely appointed, for lack of respectable alternatives, both because of the bad quality of what exists and the emigration to higher paid private practices of lawyers (among them judges) of talent. In all postcommunist countries, there are few cadres in reserve.

Again, we are dealing in part with strong legacies of the past. Thus, Eliška Wagnerová, former chief justice of the Czech Supreme Court and current vice-president of the Constitutional Court, and Alexander Bröstl, justice of the Slovak Constitutional Court, both concur in the former's judgment that

> [t]he role of judges in the 1948–89 period was a demonstration of the dominance of the political power of the state over the judges. The greatest demand on the judges was a readiness to adapt. . . . In such an environment, the development of independent personalities, willing to serve justice, was impossible. The law was defined only according to the exercise of power and a formal gown which could cover any unjustice [sic] . . . . Czechoslovak and Czech history has shaped a judge as an obedient and subordinate civil servant. Provided s/he was sufficiently dexterous or cynical, or at least careless of the destiny of individuals, s/he could successfully move high in his or her career, regardless of the vertiginous changes in the political system (Wagnerová 2003, pp. 168, 177–78).

Both Wagnerová and Bröstl stress that the attitudes formed in these times did not simply disappear in 1989. On the contrary, Bröstl (2003, p. 144) observes,

> the real problem is to change the enduring old mentality. "Crooked paths" became almost standard and part of life in place of established and well-functioning institutions. They were connected with a relevant "know-how." . . .

> That was the beginning of a vicious circle of "services" and "counter-services," of "advantages" and "counter-advantages" destroying the aim and the basis of the competence-founded activity of state authorities and institutions. The problem is how to uncover the rotten foundations of such a state and how to transform them into the bases of a functioning system.

This is no small problem.

Some of the problems faced by the judiciaries in these countries might be considered merely transitional, fated to disappear over time, perhaps in some next phase. But there is no strong reason to believe that that will happen quickly. In all the post-communist countries, judges and judicial institutions are likely to remain among the central problems of institutional transformation. Moreover, one need not look for pathologies to find problems. Even standing operating procedures might cause problems if the context in which they are used undergoes radical change. Arguably, the problem is less one of corruption among judges, although that is not rare, than of their inadequate professional preparation. In the region, a judge has been and is treated as a state official, mechanically applying rules of law. This approach in legal education, both in law schools and in the ethos of the judiciary, has lasted until today. And because the context of judging is changing in the postpost era, this is likely to be a matter of considerable importance. Thus, many judges fear applying constitutional provisions directly, although in several countries they have the legal authority to do so. Again, early postcommunist governments changed the domestic laws so frequently in the 1990s that even well-intentioned and well-trained judges could not have kept up with the changes. The problem was accentuated more recently in those countries that prepared to accede to the EU. Thousands of pieces of European legislation have been adopted in great haste, but local and especially lower court judges are not well prepared to digest, still less apply, the mass of European law they have just acquired, with its many exotic and soft provisions. This unpreparedness will probably continue for some time. This is a somewhat poignant incapacity because accession to the EU carries the heaviest burden of expectations that postcommunism can be left behind for the next phase.

The problems faced by judges cannot be fixed merely by increasing legal knowledge or basic legal competence. At least as important are trained and practiced conceptions of the role of law and of its interpreters that judges themselves bring to bear in interpretation. For example, socio-legal exploration of the insider observations of Marek Zirk-Sadowski, a Polish legal philosopher and judge of uncommon intelligence and perceptiveness, would be interesting. He offers a disturbing account of the way not-altogether-European law functions in now-European Poland. Zirk-Sadowski (2005) argues that at least in Poland there is little conception, either among citizens or among lawyers, of law as an argumentative tradition, a discourse, mastery of which might enable disciplined, convergent but yet often novel legal responses to new situations. Rather, law is seen socially as a source, at one stage, of oppressive rules and, at another stage, of potential bonuses to be grabbed. In either case, law is "still regarded as 'received' and not resulting from negotiations or discussions," but in neither case is it recognized as a hermeneutic practice in which lawyers and citizens themselves are legitimately involved. Law is viewed purely instrumentally and as an elite imposition or gift, sometimes for elite purposes, sometimes foisted on the country by the arbiters of Europeanness (Zirk-Sadowski 2005, pp. 306–11).

Apart from this discursive incompetence, Zirk-Sadowski (2005) implies, nothing much else is good in the practice of Polish law either. Underfunded, overworked judges watch delays mount and can do nothing about them. Society had naive hopes that postcommunism would bring them justice; instead, as an East German dissident complained, "[W]e wanted justice; we got the rule of law." But the Poles did not even get an effective version of that. And like every other arm of state, the judicial arm withers, while people watch with scorn and without sympathy, and with increasing anomie. The result of these layers of pathology is a paradoxical sort of "disintegration in legal consciousness . . . [;] there exists a sense of the presence of law, of its validity[,] but it is accompanied by the sense of destruction of normativity. Law is a collection of texts, a source of certain goods[,] but it is not a duty . . . . Law exists, as do legal institutions[,] but there is no legal order" (Zirk-Sadowski 2005, p. 307). And Polish lawyers, primitive positivists all, he alleges, are themselves bereft of the argumentative equipment to interpret law. They simply know how to apply rules, apparently with machine-like precision and lack of imagination; "they did not presume that a new role in the social discourse was required of them, and especially of judges" (p. 308). This makes them particularly inept receivers of European law, quite unable to deal with soft law and more generally the kind of argumentative participation in legal discourse that it demands. Instead of a language, all they have is a book of rules. And another paradox of integration is that a form of law that depends on all these discursive and semantic capacities that Poles lack has been introduced in a way that leads "to the strengthening of the tendency to instrumentalise law. The disintegration of legal order is a result of the narrow understanding of the harmonisation of law as the implementation of new texts. They were introduced to Polish legal order without a reference to the achievements of the European legal discourse. The consequences of this primitive implementation of law have led today to alarming phenomena" (p. 311). Of course, these are impressionistic and engaged judgments, not the result of surveys or controlled experiments. They may well be overdrawn. They do, however, draw on local knowledge and wisdom that socio-lawyers would do well to heed and explore.

There is another way in which too much emphasis on judicial independence might mislead, for legal culture and performance can be threatened as much by lack of support as by overbearing interference. There are problems of salaries, infrastructure, working conditions, caseload (in Poland some thousands of cases sat in the courts until they lapsed because of statute of limitations problems). Where support is lacking, even a good judge may need to be a saint to stay good, and saints are in short supply. In postcommunist states, supports for the nonsaintly have often been lacking.

More soft but arguably no less significant in the region is the weakness of traditions of respect for the judicial vocation. This lack of respect can be found within the vocation itself, by those happy to lean on it, by other public officials, and by ordinary citizens with memories, who still need persuasion to trust the judiciary and be prepared to enlist its services. All these factors militate against an ethos of office that combines judicial independence with integrity and responsibility. They also militate against expectations by procurators, litigants, and citizens that they will be dealt with by judges who share such an ethos. Not only are judicial institutions weak, but they are expected to be weak and not much liked.

In all the countries of the region, citizens have traditionally tended to see the law as an instrument, but of purposes other than their own, so much so that the normativity of law was dramatically low (see Kurczewski 1993, Kurkchiyan 2003, Zirk-Sadowski 2005). Law was imposed, and one might have to deal with it, even take it seriously as an element in, or a hurdle in the way of, one's aims, but not as a normative resource or morally reinforced constraint. This perception of law is another inheritance that has not vanished.

Indeed, it is not at all clear that these are problems of the past, nor that we will quickly enter a phase in which they disappear. Take the example where data are best known to us: Poland. It is a good example for the whole of the postcommunist world because no one suggests that respect for law in Poland is, within that particular frame of comparison, peculiarly low. In the 1990s, there was a distinct increase in negative opinions about courts and judges. There was a noticeable connection between these negative opinions and the introduction of the new constitution of 1997. The connection is significant because that constitution strengthened the position of legal institutions, and particularly courts, as the third branch of power. A Polish study (Borucka-Arctowa & Pałecki 2003) gives results of surveys of public opinion, and particularly negative opinion about courts and their judgments, as well as the reasons for this state of affairs. According to one-third of the society, the quality of the courts' work had not changed in the preceding five years, 31% said it had worsened, and only 9% suggested it had improved. Close to 88.5% of those who saw no improvement claimed that courts do not treat both sides impartially; respondents thought that judges were leaned on. As causes of this state of the judiciary, respondents nominated corruption (56%), bad law (51%), and too many cases (34%). These figures suggest a chronic lack of trust in the courts. The research, which was a continuation of repeated investigations of the prestige of courts, suggests that law has a marginal role as regulator of many social activities. If judges are widely regarded as corrupt, then why turn to courts to resolve legal problems?

And yet, if transitological optimism is often naive, so too is pessimism often caught short. We simply do not yet know enough, although given the confidence of many analysts one might be forgiven for thinking otherwise. Consider the wise observations of the political scientist Venelin Ganev (personal communication):

> What does the postcommunist experience demonstrate? Well, the picture is confusing, indeed. There are the failures—countries that have constitutions

but no constitutionalism. And there are stunning successes—where, against all odds and in defiance of macabre predictions, robust constitutionalism emerged. How to account for this variation—this is a central question that, in my view, has not been addressed in a satisfactory manner. More broadly, the issue at stake is the saliency of cultural, historical and social factors: if they matter so much, how come countries like Bulgaria and Romania could nourish their "Rule of Law" regimes? If they do not matter so much and hence the possibility that a group of "founding fathers" may create the fundament of constitutionalism, then how do we explain Russia and central Asia? While the former regimes are by no means perfect, they are vastly superior to the latter—and we are yet to figure out why. All in all, in my view the series of postcommunist constitutional reforms demonstrated that the chances of "survival" of Western "transplants" are greater than we expected, but I am not sure what to make of this empirical finding: whether to assert that a non-Western cultural milieu is not as inimical to the Rule of Law as we thought it is going to be, or to redefine, retroactively, countries like Bulgaria and Romania as much more Western than we thought they in fact were in the 1990s.

Constitutional Courts

There is one apparent bright spot in this sorry picture: the constitutional courts. Once formed, these were largely staffed by academics, rather than the regular judiciary, precisely because of doubts about the independence and competence of regular judges. And many other measures were taken to ensure that constitutional courts stood out and apart from the regular judicial system. They are all, for example, with the merely apparent exception of Estonia, independent of the regular court structure, separately created, housed, and staffed. Reformers argued that the ordinary courts were tainted by compulsory conformity, routine obedience to political directives, and negative selection of the communist past. Many were incompetent, and the prestige of the judiciary was low.

On many readings, constitutional courts are, by contrast to the regular judiciary, the legal success story of the region. Before 1989, only two countries in the communist world had them, and neither was, to put it gently, of critical significance. Now every country in the region has one, many are well endowed with legal artillery, and in several countries—Hungary, Poland, the Czech Republic, Slovenia, and Bulgaria—they have become important legal and political forces. In other countries (the usual suspects), they have not.

Throughout the region, lawyers, at least, almost take for granted that a strong constitutional court is essential and central for the rule of law (see Sólyom & Brunner 2000), and the stronger the better. And some constitutional courts have been very strong and prepared to exercise their strength. Indeed, according to Scheppele (2005, p. 44), an expert on, and enthusiast for, the work of the first Hungarian court, for its first six years the court was "virtually running the country." That, she believes, was a good thing. Many Western experts agree (see Brzezinski

2000, Schwartz 2000, Skach 2005) and believe that a strong, independent, separate constitutional court is an essential protector of constitutionalism, the rule of law, and liberal values more generally, the stronger the better, particularly in a region so long and recently dominated by the executive. They applaud the first Hungarian Constitutional Court for its boldness, courage, and vision and were bored and disappointed with its successor for its lack of the same. They are relieved that with the ouster of the right-wing FIDESZ government in 2002, the court has retained some more assertive members and regained some of its earlier boldness. They were unhappy that the pre-1997 Polish Constitutional Tribunal could be overridden by a two-thirds majority in the *Sejm* [Parliament] and are pleased now that the tribunal's decision is final. These experts are suspicious that governments will always tend to be overmighty, and they rely on courts to cut overmighty governments down to size. They note cases that have occurred in Albania and Bulgaria, not to mention Belarus and Russia, where governments have retaliated against recalcitrant jurists, and they heap praise on the judges who do not bend, let alone break. It is an uplifting story, with heroic judges at its core, and venal, dangerous politicians in the wings.

Some observers are more skeptical, however. Such skeptics argue, for example, that now as before in the region we are witnessing, at the top, a traditional distrust of the people and their representatives, and from below, a long-lived regional culture of complaint and reliance on experts, rather than self-generated political action and democratic accountability. Again Sadurski (2005) is surprised that while postcommunist constitutional courts have borrowed so much from their Western counterparts, they have left the Western controversies over their roles behind. But why? What about the effects of such powerful courts on weak, newly emerging legislatures? What about their potential anesthetizing effects on the population? Should these issues be left to the experts? What of the wars between the regular courts and the constitutional court in Poland and the Czech Republic? What of the extraordinary power of the courts, with their abstract power of review, given vague constitutional provisions and a willingness to mold them according to the judicial imagination or its special access to the invisible constitution? What of the fact that such a court, exercising such a power, is not really a court at all, nor a third-party dispute settler, but another level of government? If so, by what right, with what democratic credentials? What of the incompetence of judges in deciding matters of complex social and economic policy? What of their designed political irresponsibility?

We do not have a clear preference in this debate. Instead, we suggest two socio-legally inclined cautions, one about evaluations of the work of such courts and the other about their importance. First, 17 years is a short time in the history of institutions, unless they fail quickly, and it might be too short for confident generalizations and predictions to be warranted. Too much is sometimes made of general predictive or normative principles, on the one hand, and of generalizations from single success stories or failures, on the other. Too little attention is devoted to the particular texture, problems and challenges and to ways of meeting them that have occurred in particular countries at particular times. We utter these platitudes, not because we imagine them profound, but because we are struck that lawyers do not always heed them and because we are impressed by one example, that of Bulgaria, as interpreted by a keen observer, Venelin Ganev. For the establishment of the rule of law and democracy, Bulgaria seemed to have nothing going for it: an inhospitable past, impoverished present, and location in the benighted Balkans. Many observers and theorists uttered gloomy prognostications, and some have proved accurate. But not with regard to constitutionalism. As Ganev demonstrates, in the Bulgarian situation about which few legalists write, "[A]t the end of the 1990s Bulgaria emerged as a consolidated, constitutionally governed democracy with a devastated economy and a stolen future" (Ganev 2003, p. 609). The bright spot in that mixed assessment is the constitutional court, unprecedented, viciously attacked by government opponents, yet a crucial player in the consolidation of both democracy and the rule of law, a "story of success that defies initial anticipations." Until we are confident why such successes have occurred, and what in them can be generalized, we should generalize warily, and continue to watch.

Second, it is not clear to us whether constitutional courts warrant the attention they receive. How do court decisions or the existence of the court, or its character, contribute to the spread of the rule of law or more generally affect law-related behavior in the society? It is, after all, a socio-legal truism that most people, most of the time, stay away from courts of any sort, and if they have to deal with them have a lot more to do with ordinary than with constitutional courts. That remains the case even with the Hungarian *actio popularis,* that allows anyone to petition the constitutional court directly. Yet the incentives for competent, well-trained and disciplined lawyers to flood into the socially visible and closer-to-the-ground branches of the judiciary are small. However, from the point of view of social significance, the understandable attention of the best and brightest scholars to the best and brightest jurists in the best, brightest, and highest courts—to their judgments, their reasoning, their relationships with the executive—at times might better have been devoted to the tawdry operations of the shabby remainder of the court system. But this, as socio-lawyers have often complained, is a set of priorities hard to shift among legal scholars.

THE POST-POLICE STATE

Some sorts of institutional and personal continuities and legacies, such as those we have been discussing, are among the expected results of regime change anywhere except in the most brutal of circumstances, and probably even there too. Since the original Adam, there has never been a clean slate. There are differences of degree, and they matter, but there are less often differences of kind. However, one of the most interesting approaches and potential spheres of social research in relation to transformation of postcommunism relates to a specific element of the institutional structure of the communist state: the place of the secret police and machinery of surveillance of communist societies.

If one thing haunts the memory of postcommunist citizens, it is the secret police. Its significance, pervasiveness, and scale of operations were unparalleled in any other political formation known, and on some views it has bequeathed legacies of profound, if characteristically hidden, significance in the postcommunist present. One approach to postcommunism is to investigate whether and, if so, how this most central of communist institutions has come to influence the creation of the postcommunist institutional structure.

Seventeen years after the collapse of communism, the problem of the files still exists and plays a role, particularly before parliamentary elections. People in the West learned, for example, from Garton Ash's (1997) *The File* (see also Funder 2002), of the East German *Stasi* and its archives, together with the infiltration of the whole of the society with its agents. The so-called Gauck Commission presides over 140 kilometers of files, notwithstanding that a portion was systematically destroyed in the last days of communism in the former German Democratic Republic (DDR). Doubtless, scholars of that period will take many years to comprehend fully the activities and role of secret services of the most significant institution in the communist prerogative state. The Romanian Securitate, similarly, yielded 20 kilometers of files, and questions about those files still play a role in parliamentary and local government elections. Somewhat surprisingly, the Romanian law on disclosure of files is so constructed that it allows members of the Ministry of Internal Affairs, rather than officials independent of the intelligence apparatus, to take such decisions.

We stress that the problem is one of dealing with the whole of the secret services and their past, and not merely a problem of access to archives. Countries have dealt in various ways. As Noel Calhoun has aptly entitled his survey of accounting with the past in Germany, Poland, and Russia, the role, character, and legacies of these institutions lead to a host of "dilemmas of justice" in Eastern Europe's democratic transitions (Calhoun 2004).

Thus, questions of lustration (dealing with erstwhile informers to the secret police) and decommunization (dealing with former, usually higher, party officials) are running sores: What should postcommunists do about the presence of the past and particularly about the former activities of secret services? Perhaps a sign of the next phase will be that the sores have healed. They are commonly treated as primarily moral questions of retributive justice, which of course they also are. However, there is a significant sociological dimension to them, as is most strongly argued by Łoś & Zybertowicz (2000), for the questions of lustration and decommunization involve core questions about building a new political and legal order. They are thus not merely matters of criminal law and criminology, but equally ones of public law, or *droit politique*—that is, the principles, structures, and institutions that constitute a new regime and a new polity.

The thesis of Łoś & Zybertowicz is expressed in the title of their book, *Privatizing the Police State*. It is closely related to the Staniszkis characterization of postcommunism, discussed above. The process of transformation—that is, of both exit from communism and the beginnings of the new structures, particularly those connected with the new distribution of property—was to a significant degree, they claim, controlled by members of the former secret services. Writing primarily of Poland, but claiming more general applicability, they claim that "[a] well orchestrated party/army/police strategy allowed the most powerful *nomenklatura* networks to maintain a relatively high degree of informal control over the multiple, unexpected processes of change that turned an attempted reform into a systemic transformation" (Łoś & Zybertowicz 2000, p. 217). Particularly worth noting are their analyses of the influence of the special services on economic changes and the connections between postcommunist transformations, secret police skills, and access to information and networks, with processes of globalization.

The implications of this analysis for a socio-legal understanding of the quality and actual functioning of law are considerable. If one follows Ehrlich (2002 [1936], p. lviv) in believing that "the center of gravity of legal development lies not in legislation, nor in juristic science, nor in judicial decision, but in society itself," then tracing the specific character of particular social orders, and the particular ways they impinge on (and are affected by) the formal legal order, would seem an obvious necessity. But with regard to the posthumous operations of the secret police of these police states, tracing the activities of these organizations has rarely been done, partly because it is extremely hard (and can be dangerous) to do (these were not called secret services for nothing) and partly because the problem has often been assumed away. From a socio-legal viewpoint, however, as also from that of the truly agonizing normative dilemmas of transformation, the following thesis is key:

> A degree of police-state privatization seems inevitable in any peacefully negotiated transformation of a police state into a democratic state. The creation of democratic institutions does not in any way prevent the continuation of co-operation, or even consolidation, of the informal power networks of the previous regime. On the contrary, *an early proclamation of the transforming state as a fully democratic state, based on the rule of law, practically guarantees the undisturbed operation of those informal, secret forces within the new state and economy. Being trained and conditioned to act in secrecy and to engage in conspiratorial practices, they could only be detected and restrained through massive surveillance and repression* (Łoś & Zybertowicz 2000, p. 223, emphasis in the original).

One might agree with Łoś & Zybertowicz that, in a situation of controlled change, otherwise known as negotiated revolution, the rule of law too early declared *de haut en bas* can lead to a façade form of justice. Less clear, however, is whether their thesis about the necessity for mass repression, surveillance, and control has a universal character in postcommunist circumstances, or whether it could ever be realized, particularly under the circumstances of a negotiated revolution, or that it should be. There is little account of variation in their analysis, and yet, as Ganev (2003) pointed out above, and as anyone who travels from Poland to Russia or Kazakhstan will quickly sense, variations within the postcommunist region, precisely in the pervasiveness of the trends Łoś & Zybertowicz stress, are profound. Russia is publicly run by a former KGB agent and his former colleagues in a political system for the moment emptied of opposition, but Hungary is not. That likely makes a difference. How much of a difference is a question to which we do not have definitive answers. In any event, if professedly liberal institutions can be so easily bent to illiberal purposes, why trust that illiberal ones will prove more resistant? Perhaps some risks just have to be taken. But, and this is a credit to the somewhat marginalized analyses of Łoś & Zybertowicz, at least one should be aware that they are risks. Often that awareness has not developed until the risks have eventuated.

TRANSITIONAL JUSTICE: DEALING WITH THE PAST

The past does not merely figure as subtext of much that happens in the post-communist present. Put most sweepingly, we can characterize the whole epoch of transformation as one great process of dealing with the past. This is often neglected by outside observers and commentators, inclined to regard reference to the communist past as anachronistic and immaterial, without present relevance or role. Our view, as is by now apparent, is different. We are struck by the weight of the past in the present, a weight well captured in Istvan Rev's (2006) recent study of *Retroactive Justice. Prehistory of Postcommunism.* As he explains,

> [T]he object of my study is the *remake*: the remake of the dead, the martyr turned unknown soldier and back again, the criminal who is redeemed as innocent, holy days banalized, cemeteries reconstructed, and unremarkable figures presented as historical monstrosities, ordinary places rebuilt as sites of horror. My book is not devoted to traces of times gone by or representation of past events, but to *phantoms*. It deals with the bodies and objects that are presented as visibly, even tangibly, incarnate. Instead of the notion of substitution, I study manipulation by hand: undoing by remaking (Rev 2006, pp. 7–8).

Although Rev is primarily concerned with Hungary, his sensitivity to the ways in which the past is pervasively and compulsively enlisted in remaking the postcommunist present has a wider and continuing relevance throughout the postcommunist region.

Within that whole, the concept of transitional justice focuses on legal practices and problems faced by states and societies under transformation, particularly stemming from the fact that law is typically required to serve two ambitions, often in significant tension with each other: to function both as a stable framework of transformation and as a (frequently changing) means of achieving it (see especially Teitel 2000). In principle, tensions are often thought to flow from the different demands of seeking to instantiate the rule of law in the present, to repair its absence in the past, and to establish conditions for it in the future. Each of these aims may pull in quite different directions from those to which the others tend (see, e.g., interview with J.M. Rokita, quoted in Krygier 1994, pp. 114–17). Not every country has faced these tensions, however, because not all lawmakers share these three aims, or any of them.

The main line of division exists between the states that emerged from the collapse of the Soviet Union itself and the former satellites of East-Central Europe. Legal strategies to "undo the wrongs of the communist past" are an issue for societies that seriously engaged themselves in transformation and release from the iron embrace of communist institutions. Such strategies do not feature, however, in the present Russian Federation, Kazakhstan, Kyrgyzstan, Azerbaijan, or even Georgia. Why? That is too serious a problem to dispose of in a few sentences, but there are several obvious social conditions one can point to: the longer period that communism existed in these countries; the depth to which communist institutions, practices, and thoughtways had soaked into the society; the complicated problem of nationalities and, in the central Asian republics, the role of tribal connections in the exercise of state power.

Of particular interest is the position of Russia. Apart from the period immediately after 1992, when the problem of coming to terms with the past was at least mentioned in public discourse, after Vladimir Putin took power there was a period of normalization and elimination of questions to do with the past, except occasionally to praise it. Indeed, at the symbolic level Putin's Russia seeks to stress continuities with the USSR. These are not as far-reaching as in Belarus under Lukashenko, but they are strong and evident. They do not spell a return to communism as a system, but perhaps to a much older Russian tradition of state-centered authoritarianism that at times sought to borrow from the West, even heavily, but resisted contamination by it. Raeff (1983) memorably dubbed the ambitions of those times the "well-ordered police state," and whether or not he knows the phrase, Putin seems keen to continue the tradition.

In this connection, the situation of Ukraine is interesting. The real anticommunist revolution in Ukraine was the Orange Revolution of 2005 and the events in Kiev's Independence Square. After the moral awakening that this revolution symbolized, the problem of dealing with the past, or rather the need to face it, began to feature in public discourse. One might suggest the hypothesis that an effective postcommunist transformation, let alone a transition from communism, depends on at least the possibility of public discussion of the communist past. That this will occur in Ukraine is not yet clear (Riabczuk 2004, pp. 136–49).

The problem of dealing with the past does not, however, merely involve dealing with the remnants or legacies of former communist regimes. Transitional justice in postcommunist states is also a constitutional problem for new postcommunist social, political, and legal systems. Dealing with the past as a constitutional question is a problem of creating social conditions for the new social-political order, as well as regenerating damaged moral bonds in the society. This makes dealing with the past, or the limitation or impossibility of doing so, a socio-legal problem par excellence.

The transitional justice problem in all postcommunist countries that have taken an active approach to these matters can be divided into two main issues:

1. Relations between new and old regimes (the problem of legal continuity); and
2. The problem of decommunization (legal means for removal of communist legacies from the state and society). This problem in turn can be subdivided into three categories, namely:

a. retributive justice for crimes committed under the former regimes (lustration),
b. rehabilitation and compensation for victims of communist regimes, and
c. restitution of property after communism.

Relations Between Old and New Regimes

The type of exit from communism determined the approach taken to this problem. In the countries of East-Central Europe, exit from communism was institutionalized via roundtable talks (see Elster 1996). Countries that did not even simulate such an institutionalized passage generally accepted a straightforward continuation of the former regime.

The roundtable talks established a point of connection between the old communist and new postcommunist regimes. The agreements established a base for legal continuity between regimes, with consequences for the new legal and political order. Symbolically, a new law-governed state, as stated in amendments to the constitutions, was born as a legitimate child of a communist regime that typically had been installed illegally and had operated with no respect for law. This combination of discontinuity with continuity has created tensions between the demands of legality and those of preserving the revolutionary ethos, with its commitment to material justice, where they existed. Such tensions still exist. One could argue that the existence of such tensions is a positive extension of the self-limiting nature of the revolutions that ended communism, at least in Central Europe, and that their persistence has had a positive significance. The Hungarians called this the revolution of the rule of law—the revolutionary part was that existing law would be taken seriously (see Sólyom 2000). Those tensions between the formal demands of law and material justice allowed those revolutions to avoid the flaw at the heart of most previous revolutions, where the logic of righteous virtue and morality justified everything. In the countries of East-Central Europe, a clear choice has not been made, and this salutary tension continues.

Decommunization and Lustration

Some new postcommunist regimes (e.g., Poland) tried to address the problem of continuity and at the same time stress discontinuity by adopting, with rather meager results, a policy of drawing a so-called thick line between the present and the past. The idea was to integrate all citizens in the process of building a new political and social order after communism, while also stressing that it would be a new political and social structure, not a simple continuation of the former regime. It has proved impossible to sustain such a policy. Instead, discussion of decommunization and lustration has recurred.

The terms are often confused with each other, and confusing for everyone. At its broadest, decommunization can refer to all political and legal strategies, the aim of which is eradication of the legacies of communism in a social and political system. This would include both a narrower conception of decommunization (focusing on elimination of personnel) and lustration (focusing on informers). But these terms are often used interchangeably. Sadurski (2005, p. 245) injects some clarity on these matters by reconstructing the meaning of these categories in political discourse in East-Central European postcommunist countries:

> "Lustration" applies to the screening of persons seeking to occupy (or actually occupying) certain public positions for evidence of involvement with the communist regime (mainly with the secret security apparatus), while "decommunization" refers to the exclusion of certain categories of ex-Communist officials from the right to run for, and occupy, certain public positions in the new system. However, in the public debate on the moral and legal rationales for and against the policies covered by these concepts, the two have been often lumped together.

Even this does not get us all the way, for a question formulated as broadly as lustration usually includes three problems: lustration proper (screening of former collaborators and members of secret services), access to secret services files, and decommunization. Quite often, separating them even analytically, especially lustration from decommunization, is difficult.

Lustration and decommunization became an issue in all East-Central European postcommunist countries when a real struggle for the future social and institutional structure began (see de Grieff 2006; Wildstein 2000; Grzelak 2005; Calhoun 2004, pp. 92–131). That struggle shows that, contrary to the dominant perception, lustration and decommunization are not backward-looking but forward-looking. They were and are part of the political process and political struggle. The peculiar character of the postcommunist negotiated revolution, when all elements of social life are undergoing radical change at the same time, is a type of transformation in which dealing with the past cannot be reduced to the question of what to do with the hangman. It is not just a response to gross violation of human rights, retributive justice, compensation and restitution of property, and truth telling. Lustration and decommunization became legal and political tools in rearrangement of the constitutional setting of the society and state.

However, the legal strategies of decommunization and lustration play a rather limited role in postcommunist societies. They have been used mainly in political battles, where they serve to curtail discourse on the operation of the communist system. Instead of serious societal discussion, public discourse is limited by attacks on a few scapegoats.

Access to Secret Police Files

The problem is not just what to do about people, for there are also the files, all those millions of them. In 1992, Germany became the first former communist country to open up secret police files to citizens. Other postcommunist countries followed and passed similar legislation, for instance Hungary in 1994 and Bulgaria in 1998. This was not possible everywhere, owing to both economic and organizational limitations. In Poland the issue was discussed only in 1997 in connection with a presidential lustration law project in which it was suggested that a civic archive be established within the framework of the state archives. In the wake of the election held in September 1997, this idea was absorbed into the governmental project of a law, introduced in July 2000, that created an Institute of National Remembrance. The law regulates access of interested persons to information collected about them by the secret services between 1944 and 1989.

Communist regimes were based on control of society not only through the party cells in all factories and organizational units but also through permanent surveillance by the secret police and its collaborators. The scale was not the same in each country in the communist camp—some barracks were under more relaxed surveillance—but nevertheless the problem of the files exists everywhere.

Legal strategies adopted by particular countries vary. The most radical was the strategy adopted in the former DDR. Each person, not only citizens, has a right to have access to his/her own file with names of secret collaborators visible—not erased. Although we occasionally learn about the personal tragedies when brother spied on brother and a husband on his wife, and although such a strategy might clear the atmosphere of universal suspiciousness, it is not clear that granting this open access stimulates public discussion about the mechanisms of the past and citizens' involvement in sustenance of the regime. Access to files still has a private character. It involves a private citizen having access to his/her file through the Gauck Commission.

Other countries, such as Poland, adopted a middle-of-the-road approach, based on separation of the archival substance of the secret services in the Institute for National Memory. Each citizen now has a right to apply to have access to his/her file, but the decision to grant access is made by authorities on the basis of evidence of victimization. This only began in 2000, and that might already have been too distant from the beginning of the transformation to be useful. Hungary allows everyone to see his/her own file, but with the name of the spies redacted because of a constitutional court decision that even spies have privacy rights. If a former spy runs for office, however, a three-judge panel will publish the contents of the spy's files so that people know who they are voting for or against. If the spy stays in private life, the files remain sealed.

The peculiar type of exit from communism that occurred in each country—such as through roundtable talks and then through partly free elections, as in Poland, or through fully free elections after 1989, as in many other countries—shows that even the communists were not conscious of the volatility of the files issue. They did not demand sunset clauses for access laws or general amnesty for former spies. They did not destroy all the files, although we know that they destroyed many during 1989 and 1990.

Retributive Justice

An important step in historical retributive justice was taken in some countries (among them Poland) that identified communist crimes as crimes against humanity, similar to genocide. Communist crimes were not subject to a statute of limitations. Similarly, some countries established institutes for national remembrance with prosecutorial powers. The main aim of these institutes is to document and prosecute the crimes committed by the functionaries of the communist regimes. In all postcommunist countries, despite the large number of inquiries, the courts have received a very small number of indictments. Prosecution was ultimately abandoned for lack of satisfactory documents and the impossibility of identifying perpetrators. If trials started at all, they were often prolonged, to the frustration of former victims.

Restitution of Property

Restitution of expropriated and nationalized property, sometimes called reprivatization, is one of the most burning issues (only partly resolved by postcommunist regimes) because communist regimes were based on nationalization of property. The question of what to do with property created under communism (new factories, housing blocks, etc.), particularly if these were built over previously privately owned property, is also critical. After the collapse of communism, there was a need to create a new system of property rights. In most cases, restitution of property was impossible, so compensation for lost property, in percentages and forms deemed affordable in particular countries, was attempted.

However, economic and political aims often conflict with the moral claims of providing restitution; different logics and moralities are in play. In many cases, the restitution of property has an ethical dimension, especially in the case of ethnic minorities, religious communities' property, and Jewish property. Pogany (1997, p. vii) writes that reprivatization "offers a principal means to redress some of the worst and most heinous injustices to the past." He is treating the question of reprivatization not merely as a technical economic question about what and how to privatize and reprivatize, but also as a question about how to achieve restorative or compensatory justice.

Specialists in property law, however, approach this as a technical problem. For two reasons, we want to draw attention to another approach to the problem of privatization. The first reason has to do with the socio-legal dimensions of the problem and the second with its connection to the next phase. Systematic research has been undertaken on the problem in selected postcommunist countries, and one of the senior researchers, Grażyna Skąpska, has recently summarized some results of this work (Skąpska 2005). She reveals the complicated historico-geographic situation of property in this part of the world and reminds us that expropriation of property by communists after World War II had been, in parts of Central Europe, preceded by the Nazi expropriation of property. If the Nazi expropriation had purportedly been made for public purposes, then the succeeding postwar communist regimes did not return properties so confiscated to their original owners. Also, after the war, a new phase of ethnic cleansing began, exemplified by the forced expulsion of Germans in the former eastern Prussia, Silesia, and western Pomerania, as well as the expulsion and confiscation of property of the Sudeten Germans from Czechoslovakia and Hungarian property in Slovakia, under the Beneš decrees.

Skąpska (2005) emphasizes that the expropriation of property also liquidated communities and dehumanized societies. For these reasons, the problem of property restitution postcommunism must be approached as an ethical problem—restoration of the possibilities of functioning for religious (Jews, Byzantine Catholics, Orthodox, Protestants) or ethnic (Jews, Lemkos, Germans, Silesians) communities destroyed by communism and its Nazi predecessors.

Skąpska (2005) suggests that acceptance of a strategy of reprivatization can provide a moral impulse necessary in societies undergoing transformation. However, the only country that has made a principled general commitment to reprivatization is Germany after reunification. As a result, 95% of state-owned property was reprivatized. The other postcommunist countries have not treated privatization as a matter of key importance, but rather have directed themselves largely by the dictates of economic doctrine. As a result, a large proportion of cases brought before the European Court of Human Rights concern restitution of property. There is also considerable pressure from institutions outside the region (among them the American courts and Congress). Even if the will were clear, however, there is a host of questions that are and will remain hard to answer: How far back to go? To what year? At whose expense? In what manner? On the basis of what criteria? Declaring eligibility to claim property restitution, limiting it to citizens, or permanent residents, for example, inflames emotions and generates the sort of sentiment expressed in the disappointed postcommunist aphorism quoted earlier, "we wanted justice; we got the rule of law."

Reprivatization is a key element of the economic constitution (distribution of property rights) of postcommunist societies. On the one hand, acceptance of a drastic form of restitution would limit the possibilities of control over property by *nomenklatura* networks. On the other hand, restitution in a strict sense is impossible because of the complicated, mixed-up property rights involved over the (often considerable) passage of time. This leads to "facts on the ground" that are often regarded as unjust.

Whoever decides on the criteria of reprivatization has enormous power. These are decisions with very long-term effects, even though they are often presented as merely matters of technical expertise. They have significance for the nature and quality of democracy and the rule of law because issues of the legitimacy of new regimes, problems of alienation or inclusion and social justice, in other words acceptance of the new system, are connected with the issue of restitution of property. In this sense, property is too important to be left to economists.

After 17 years of transformation, problems regarding restitution exist in every former postcommunist country, but not every country has the same problems. In all of them, however, there is an evident split between beneficiaries of the transformation and those who have lost from it. Indeed, as Rychard (1996) has forcefully pointed out, given the complexity of the changes, there are winners who will be losers, and losers who will be winners, and who is who is unclear and changing (Rychard 1996). These distinctions, although they are played out in the economic domain, have political significance, and they influence the process of democratization of the society and political system, as well as the quality of the functioning of law and legal institutions.

The groups who come to consider themselves losers of the transformation must be connected to the democratic institutions. Populist slogans, common in this part of Europe, need to be combated, not just by words, but by inclusive operations of democracy and legal institutions. Some consider connection and inclusion to be the promise of the EU, through its structural funds, the process of negotiation and accession (for those invited), and the whole process of adaptation of law and institutions to so-called European standards. The ambitions are huge. If they are achieved, this will indeed be a new phase, not just for those postcommunist societies that benefit, but for Europe as a whole. Of course, even in the best case, there will be many parts of the postcommunist world left out.

JOINING EUROPE

If one process might be thought to signal movement from postcommunism to a new phase, it is accession to the EU. Of course, most postcommunist states are not in the running, but eight have been members of the EU since 2004, and at the time of writing two, Romania and Bulgaria, are waiting anxiously in the wings. These two countries both received warnings from the EU in late 2005 that major areas are still wanting, including their justice systems and protection of human rights, as well as progress in rooting out organized crime and high-level corruption. They will nevertheless almost certainly be accepted in 2007, which will leave more anxious applicants worried about European enlargement fatigue; some hostile neighbors who will never be invited and look to Russia to find alternative sources of solace, support, and emulation; and a few, like Ukraine and Georgia, anxiously seeking to assert their independence and eligibility.

The European project represents an even more ambitious teleology than does transition. The project is intended at once to reinforce, or even complete, transition and also to close that gap in conceptual geography that the collapse of communism had opened. There is no doubt that its influence will be substantial, and in numerous intertwined domains, for the story of European enlargement is a story of multiple interactions, between nations, states, economies, regions, social structures, and political and legal systems. So far it has been largely a matter of negotiations between elites, but the ambition is that the consequences will be broad and deep. Like postcommunism itself, but more deliberately embarked upon, integrating postcommunist countries into the EU is an experiment likely to have huge consequences for millions of people over an indefinite period of time. But what those consequences will be is today anybody's guess.

The mere functioning of the EU together with the ambitions of so many countries of Central and Eastern Europe to join it have and continue to have deep impacts on the postcommunist world. Accession to the EU was a complicated process that depended on enlargees satisfying enlargers that they had fulfilled the so-called Copenhagen criteria of 1993—political, economic, and legal. At a formal level, although one cannot speak of unification of laws, harmonization is well advanced among the old and new members. The Union has influenced changes in law and its application, through its system of monitoring prior to accession and, to a lesser extent afterwards, through criticism of delays in introducing agreed-upon reforms.

Legislative alignment required compliance with the 80,000 pages of the *acquis communautaire,* and the Copenhagen criterion most directly related to law, article 4, makes a country's admission dependent on its achieving "the stability of institutions guaranteeing democracy, the rule of law, human rights and the respect for and protection of minorities." Eight postcommunist countries have been held to have complied with the *acquis* and satisfied this and the other criteria; two more are on the way to doing so. It is an interesting question for social science what such compliance might mean. Undoubtedly, many institutional forms have been decreed, and written laws have been rewritten, supplemented, deleted, replaced, and whatever else can be done by eager emulators with active computers, but what is the relation between such emulation and the generation of "the stability of institutions guaranteeing the rule of law" and other good things? That, as we have seen, is a socio-legal question par excellence, but it has not been so treated by those elites who have embarked on this ambitious venture.

Note, for example, the success language of the criterion. To qualify for accession, a country needs to ensure that its institutions are stable, and it must provide a guarantee. How a country can ensure stability of its institutions in a very short period, let alone know it has done so, is hard to see. But more striking is the requirement of a guarantee, extraordinarily ambitious for things as complex as democracy, the rule of law, human rights, and respect and protection for minorities. Such a requirement assumes (for otherwise the criterion would be otiose) that the institutions had been in less-than-perfect shape hitherto, as is indeed the case. But then whence the confidence that all this can be changed in a few years?

Moreover, the institutions themselves are to do all this good work. Given the significance of the many extra-institutional forces stressed in this review, that is not an innocent assumption, though it is a common one. It focuses attention on those most easily identified features of the legally relevant landscape, perhaps thereby blinding reformers to often hidden and important structures and networks that remain undisturbed. It is a long time since Sally Falk Moore (1978, p. 76) noted that, although "those parts of the social system that are most visible to and are considered most accessible to legislative (or other official action) are often the formal parts of the system," less formal sources of advantage and power "may be far less immediately accessible to formal legal action, and may have great durability over time." Her insight has not always been heeded by impatient law reformers. Galanter (1981) once observed that, just as health is not found primarily in hospitals, so legal institutions are not necessarily the first place one should look to find law. Such an observation has a rather long Central and Eastern European socio-legal pedigree, stretching from the Bukovina (Eugen Ehrlich) through Cracow (Bronisław Malinowski) to St. Petersburg and later Warsaw (Leon Petrażycki). Whatever one thinks about Galanter's remark as applied to law writ large, it has particular pertinence to the rule of law, human rights, minority protection, and so on. Whoever wants these things wants a social and political outcome, not just a bunch of laws drafted and institutions crafted to meet the stringent but sociologically innocent requirements of EU bureaucrats and their supplicants. They want certain ways of behaving to be established and generalized and above all normative. They want the norms on which these thing depend to count, in people's heads and in their acts, as reliable restraints on, and resources and channels for, the ways in which social and political power are routinely exercised and contested. As we have seen, decrees and institutional reforms are uncertain and on their own insufficient means to such ends.

There is here, too, a tension between the view that institutional change will necessarily draw after it behavioral modifications of the sort preferred, and the view, more sociological and skeptical, that formal transformations might well come to seem more like Potemkin villages than the tips of icebergs. And, speaking of Potemkin, while Europe might serve as a model and magnet for those keen and likely to join it, Russia is clearly aiming to serve as a countermodel and magnet for those left out.

For all these cautions, however, accession to the EU is a major event. Changes are likely to flow from many things besides institutional renovations: new incentives and disincentives; potential expansion of horizons, contacts, and networks; potential dilution of the importance of old ones; new models; and a progressive seeping in of changes in consciousness, including legal consciousness. How much progress occurs and in what ways are matters for detailed empirical observation rather than legalistic assumption. Progress is unlikely to be smooth, linear, or across the board, but enlargement is a notable, and arguably noble, venture.

THE NEXT PHASE?

Predictions are perilous, and we do not hazard any. Instead, we resort to an analogy and a metaphor. Laqueur (2006, p. 3) has recently observed that "cultural memory depends on meaningful relationships of facts, both to one another and to surrounding places, artefacts and practices; memories and facts standing alone have no authority; they evaporate." The same may be said not only of cultural memory but of social orders, among them postcommunism. Slowly, certain elements of postcommunism will simply evaporate because they have ceased to have any significance. Their existence in the sea of legal-institutional novelty is impossible. Others, however, are strongly rooted and stay around, sometimes with surprisingly lingering effects. The mix will decide whether, to what extent, and in what ways one may speak of a next phase. Whatever we decide, we have little reason to doubt that traces of postcommunist, communist, and other pasts will continue. They will not determine what happens in the present but rather, if we adapt Karl Marx to a context he affected but did not envisage, will bathe the whole in a "pervasive light, a special atmosphere."

And yet, 17 years after the dramatic birth of postcommunism, the situation bears similarities to that, mentioned earlier, of Europe after feudalism. Postcommunism has increasingly become a chronological, rather than a substantively rich category. What links postcommunist countries is the fact that they once were communist, later—in 1989 or 1992 or 1998 or 2000 or 2003 or 2005—they became postcommunist. Then, and for the next few years, there was much that linked them, both institutionally and in aspects of social structure. During these 17 years, however, such differentiation and variation has occurred that, in fact, little links, say, the Czech Republic and the Republic of Kyrgyzstan, other than that people live in both places and they are both on planet Earth.

Postcommunism as an analytical category has become increasingly multivalent, where it is not empty. Just as scholars have begun to talk of multiple modernities, perhaps we should now speak of plural postcommunisms and their various social, political, and institutional instantiations. Undoubtedly, the countries of Central and Eastern Europe have retained a good deal from their pasts, but the level of communism in their postcommunism is altogether thinner than, and different from, that in Russia or Kazakhstan. The major difference is that, notwithstanding the incompleteness and façade-like character of many East-Central European countries' democratic and legal institutions, their institutions and social structures have undergone considerable differentiation. Subsystems, such as the economy, law, and politics, have developed their own relative autonomy. They are not quite, and certainly not all, the normal societies dreamed of in late-communist years, but then that was always a normative more than a sociological category. The autonomy of subsystems, by comparison with the communist system where everything depended on political dictate, or with the postcommunist system of Belarus or even Russia, where the political sphere dominates and does not allow the development of autonomy, shows that the system in some postcommunist countries has been radically transformed. Doubtless one must understand a good deal about postcommunism, and prepostcommunism too, to grasp the specifics of these countries, but to analyze their functioning we might do better to abandon the category. Or at least expect it to do less and less useful work.

LITERATURE CITED

Bernardo L, Neier A. 2006. Russia: the persecution of civil society. *NY Rev. Books*, April 27, pp. 35–37

Borucka-Arctowa M, Pałecki K, eds. 2003. *Sądy w Opinii Społeczeństwa Polskiego* (Courts in the Opinion of Polish Society). Kraków: Wydawnictwo Polpress

Bröstl A. 2003. At the crossroads on the way to an independent Slovak judiciary. See Přibáň et al. 2003, pp. 141–59

Brzezinski M. 2000. *The Struggle for Constitutionalism in Poland*. London: Macmillan

Bunce V. 1995. Should transitologists be grounded? *Slavic Rev.* 54(1):111–27

Calhoun N. 2004. *Dilemmas of Justice in Eastern Europe's Democratic Transitions*. New York: Palgrave/Macmillan

Carothers T. 2002. The end of the transition paradigm. *J. Democr.* 31(1):5–21

Carothers T, ed. 2006. *Promoting the Rule of Law Abroad: In Search of Knowledge*. Washington, DC: Carnegie Endow. Int. Peace

Czarnota A, ed. 2001. Ius and Lex in East Central Europe. Socio-legal conditions of the rule of law amid post-communist transformation. *East Cent. Eur.– l'Eur. Cent.-Est. Eine wiss. Z.* Vol. 28

Czarnota A, Krygier M, Sadurski W, eds. 2005. *Rethinking the Rule of Law after Communism*. Budapest: Cent. Eur. Univ. Press

Dahrendorf R. 1990. *Reflections on the Revolution in Europe: In a Letter Intended to Have Been Sent to a Gentleman in Warsaw*. New York: Times Books

de Grieff P, ed. 2006. *Vetting and Transitional Justice*. New York: Int. Cent. Transit. Justice. In press

de Palma G. 1990. *To Craft Democracies. An Essay on Democratic Transitions*. Berkeley: Univ. Calif. Press

Ehrlich E. 2002 [1936]. *Fundamental Principles of the Sociology of Law*, trans. WL Moll. New Brunswick, NJ: Transaction

Ekiert G. 1999. *Do legacies matter? Patterns of post-communist transition in Eastern Europe*. Occas. Pap. No. 53, Woodrow Wilson Cent., Washington, DC, June

Elster J, ed. 1996. *The Roundtable Talks and the Breakdown of Communism*. Chicago: Chicago Univ. Press

Elster J, Offe C, Preuss U. 1998. *Institutional Design in Post-Communist Societies*. Cambridge, UK: Cambridge Univ. Press

Frentzel-Zagórska J. 1997. *Society and the system. Transformation in East Central Europe as seen in the making*. Occas. Pap., Contemp. Eur. Res. Cent., Melbourne Univ.

Funder A. 2002. *Stasiland*. Melbourne: Text Publishing

Gadowska K. 2002. *Zjawisko klientelizmu polityczno-ekonomicznego. Systemowa analiza powiązań sieciowych na przykładzie przekształceń sektora górniczego w Polsce* (The phenomenon of politico-economic clientelism. A systematic analysis of network connections on the example of the transformation of the mining sector in Poland). Kraków: Wydaw. Uniw. Jagiell.

Galanter M. 1981. Justice in many rooms: courts, private ordering, and indigenous law. *J. Leg. Plur.* 19:1–47

Galanter M. 1992. Law abounding: legalisation around the world. *Mod. Law Rev.* 55(1):1–24.

Ganev V. 2003. The Bulgarian constitutional court: a success story in context. *Eur. Asia Stud.* 55(4):597–611

Garton Ash T. 1990. Eastern Europe: the year of truth. *NY Rev. Books,* Feb. 15, p. 17–23

Garton Ash T. 1997. *The File. A Personal History*. New York: Vintage

Garton Ash T. 1999. *We the People*. London: Granta

Gellner E. 1991. Civil society in historical context. *Int. Soc. Sci. J.* 129:495

Gellner E. 1994. *Conditions of Liberty. Civil Society and Its Rivals*. London: Hamish Hamilton

Gray J. 1993. From post-communism to civil society: the reemergence of the Western model. *Soc. Philos. Policy* 10(2):26–50

Grzelak P. 2005. *Wojna o lustrację* (*The War over Lustration*), Warsaw: Trio

Hellman JS. 1998. Winners take all: the politics of partial reform in postcommunist transitions. *World Polit.* 50(2):203–34

Hendley K, Holmes S, Åslund A, Sajo A, Pistor K. 1999. Demand for law. *East Eur. Const. Rev.* 8(4):88–108

Holmes L. 1997. *Postcommunism: An Introduction*. Cambridge, UK: Polity Press

Holmes S. 1995. *Cultural legacies or state collapse? Probing the postcommunist dilemma.* Public Lect. No. 13, Coll. Budapest/ Inst. Adv. Study, Oct. 17. http://www.colbud.hu/main/PubArchive/PL/PL13-Holmes.pdf

Holmes S. 1999. Can foreign aid promote the rule of law? *East Eur. Const. Rev.* 8(4):68–74

Janos AC. 2000. *East Central Europe in the Modern World. The Politics of the Borderlands from Pre- to Postcommunism*. Stanford, CA: Stanford Univ. Press.

Jedlicki J. 1990. The revolution of 1989: the unbearable burden of history. *Probl. Communism* July-Aug.:39–45

Jensen E, Heller TC, eds. 2003. *Beyond Common Knowledge. Empirical Approaches to the Rule of Law*. Stanford, CA: Stanford Law Polit.

Jowitt K. 1992. *The New World Disorder. The Leninist Extinction*. Berkeley: Univ. Calif. Press

Kleinfeld R. 2006. Competing definitions of the rule of law. See Carothers 2006, pp. 31–74

Kotkin S. 2002. Trashcanistan. A tour through the wreckage of the Soviet Empire. *New Repub.*, April 15, pp. 26–38

Krasnodębski Z. 2003. *Demokracja Peryferii* (Peripheral Democracy). Gdańsk: Słowa/ Obraz Terytoria

Krastev I. 2005. Corruption, anti-corruption sentiments and the rule of law. See Czarnota et al. 2005, pp. 323–39

Krygier M. 1994. Four visions of communist law. *Aust. J. Polit. Hist.* 40:104–20

Krygier M. 1999a. Institutional optimism, cultural pessimism and the rule of law. See Krygier & Czarnota 1999, pp. 77–105

Krygier M. 1999b. Traps for young players in times of transition. *East Eur. Const. Rev.* 8(4):63–67

Krygier M, Czarnota A, eds. 1999. *The Rule of Law after Communism*. Aldershot, UK: Ashgate/Dartmouth

Kurczewski J. 1993. *The Resurrection of Rights in Poland*. Oxford: Clarendon

Kurkchiyan M. 2003. The illegitimacy of law in post-communist societies. In *Law and Informal Practices. The Post-Communist Experience*, ed. B Galligan, M Kurkchiyan, pp. 25–46. Oxford: Oxford Univ. Press

Linz JJ, Stepan A. 1996. *Problems of Democratic Transition and Consolidation: Southern Europe, South America, and Post-Communist Europe*. Baltimore, MD: Johns Hopkins Univ. Press

Łoś M. 1996. In the shadow of totalitarian law: law-making in post-communist Poland. In *Totalitarian and Post-Totalitarian Law*, ed. A Podgórecki, V Olgiati, pp. 275–322. Aldershot, UK: Dartmouth

Łoś M, Zybertowicz A. 2000. *Privatising the Police-State. The Case of Poland*. New York: Macmillan

Laqueur T. 2006. Unquiet bodies. *London Rev. Books,* April 6, p. 3

Magalhães P. 1999. The politics of judicial reform in Eastern Europe. *Comp. Polit.* 32(1):43–62

Markovits I. 1995. *Imperfect Justice. An East-West German Diary*. Oxford: Oxford Univ. Press

Mołdawa T, ed. 2003. *Zagadnienia konstytucjonalizmu krajów Europy Środkowowschodniej* (Problems of Constitutionalism in the Countries of East Central Europe). Warsaw: Dom Wydawniczy ELIPSA

Moore SF. 1978. *Law as Process. An*

Anthropological Approach. London: Routledge/Kegan Paul

Morawski L. 1994. Spór o pojęcie państwa prawnego (The debate over the rule of law). *Państwo i Prawo* 4:3–17

Morawski L. 2005. *Główne problemy wspólczesnej filozofii prawa. Prawo w toku przemian (Main problems of contemporary legal philosophy. Law in the course of transformation)*. Warsaw: Wydawnictwo Prawnicze LexisNixis

Mungiu-Pippidi A. 2005. Shapes in search of substance. European enlargement and democratic performance. *Roman. J. Polit. Sci.* 5(2):39–56

Murrell P, ed. 2003. *Assessing the Value of Law in Transitional Economies*. Ann Arbor: Univ. Mich. Press

Nelken D. 1984. Law in action or living law? Back to the beginning in sociology of law. *Leg. Stud.* 4:157–74

Nowacki J. 1995. *Rządy Prawa* (The Rule of Law). Katowice

Örkény A, Scheppele KL. 1999. Rules of law: the complexity of legality in Hungary. See Krygier & Czarnota 1999, pp. 55–76

Podgórecki A. 1994. *Polish Society*. Westport, CT: Praeger

Podgórecki A. 1996. Polish communist and post-communist *Nomenklaturas*. In *Totalitarian and Post-Totalitarian Law*, ed. A Podgórecki, V Olgiati, pp. 323–40. Aldershot, UK: Dartmouth

Pogany I. 1997. *Righting Wrongs in Eastern Europe*. Manchester, UK: Manchester Univ. Press

Přibáň J, Roberts P, Young J, eds. 2003. *Systems of Justice in Transition*. Aldershot, UK: Ashgate

Přibáň J, Young J, eds. 1999. *The Rule of Law in Central Europe: The Reconstruction of Constitutionalism, the Rule of Law and Civil Society in the Post-Communist Societies*. Aldershot, UK: Ashgate/Dartmouth

Raeff M. 1983. *The Well-Ordered Police State: Social and Institutional Change Through Law in the Germanies and Russia, 1600–1800*. New Haven, CT: Yale Univ. Press

Rev I. 2006. *Retroactive Justice. Prehistory of Postcommunism*. Stanford, CA: Stanford Univ. Press

Riabczuk M. 2004. *Dwie Ukrainy* (Two Ukraines). Wrocław: Kolegium Europy Wschodniej

Rychard A. 1996. Beyond gains and losses: in search of "winning losers." *Soc. Res.* 63(2):465–85

Sadurski W. 2005. *Rights Before Courts. A Study of Constitutional Courts in Postcommunist States of Central and Eastern Europe*. Dordrecht: Springer

Sadurski W, Czarnota A, Krygier M. 2006. *Spreading Democracy and the Rule of Law*. Dordrecht: Springer

Safjan M. 2005. *Prawa Polska* (Polish Law). Warsaw: Rosner i Wspólnicy

Sajó A. 1998. Corruption, clientelism, and the future of the constitutional state in Eastern Europe. *East Eur. Const. Rev.* 7(2):37–46

Sakwa R. 1999. *Postcommunism*. Buckingham: Open Univ. Press

Scheppele KS. 2005. Democracy by judiciary. See Czarnota et al. 2005, pp. 25–60

Schmitter P, Karl T. 1994. The conceptual travels of transitologists and consolidologists: How far to the east should they attempt to go? *Slavic Rev.* 53(1):173–85

Schwartz H. 2000. *The Struggle for Constitutional Justice in Post-Communist Europe*. Chicago: Univ. Chicago Press

Skach C. 2005. Rethinking judicial review: shaping the toleration of difference? See Czarnota et al. 2005, pp. 61–74

Skąpska G. 2005. Restitutive justice, rule of law, and constitutional dilemmas. See Czarnota et al. 2005, pp. 211–34

Sólyom L. 2000. Introduction to the decisions of the Constitutional Court of the Republic of Hungary. See Sólyom & Brunner 2000, pp. 1–64

Sólyom L, Brunner G, eds. 2000. *Constitutional Judiciary in a New Democracy. The Hungarian Constitutional Court*. Ann Arbor: Univ. Mich. Press

Staniszkis J. 1986. *Poland: Self-Limiting Revolution*. Princeton, NJ: Princeton Univ. Press

Staniszkis J. 1991. *The Dynamics of the Breakthrough in Eastern Europe. The Polish Experience*. Berkeley: Univ. Calif. Press

Staniszkis J. 1999. *Post-Communism. The Emerging Enigma*. Warsaw: Inst. Polit. Stud., Polish Acad. Sci.

Staniszkis J. 2001a. *Postkomunism. Próba opisu* (Postcommunism. An attempt at description). Gdańsk: Słowo/obraz terytoria

Staniszkis J. 2001b. *Władza Globalizacji* (The Rule of Globalization). Warsaw: Wydaw. Naukowe SCHOLAR

Stark D, Bruszt L. 1998. *Postsocialist Pathways*. Cambridge, UK: Cambridge Univ. Press

Teitel R. 2000. *Transitional Justice*. New York: Oxford Univ. Press

Wagnerová E. 2003. Position of judges in the Czech Republic. See Přibáň et al. 2003, pp. 163–79

Wildstein B. 2000. *Dekomunizacja której nie było* (Decommunization which didn't happen). Kraków: Ksigarnia Akademicka

Zirk-Sadowski M. 2005. Transformation and integration of legal cultures and discourses—Poland. See Sadurski et al. 2006, pp. 299–311

Zybertowicz A. 2005. Anti-development interest groups (preliminary outline). *Polish Sociol. Rev.* 1(149):69–90

Annu. Rev. Law Soc. Sci. 2006. 2:341–57
doi: 10.1146/annurev.lawsocsci.2.050306.102350

First published online as a Review in Advance on August 7, 2006

Conspiracy in International Law

Jens Meierhenrich
Department of Government and Committee on Degrees in Social Studies, Harvard University, Cambridge, Massachusetts 02138; email: jmeierhenrich@gov.harvard.edu

Key Words international courts and tribunals, criminal organization, joint criminal enterprise

■ **Abstract** This review examines the function of conspiracy in international law, with particular reference to the jurisprudence of international ad hoc tribunals. It compares and contrasts the function of conspiracy law in the prosecution of international crimes before the International Military Tribunal (IMT) at Nuremberg following World War II, where the concept gave rise to a remarkably innovative and highly controversial conspiracy theory that revolved around the concept of "criminal organization," and the function of conspiracy law in the prosecution of international crimes before the International Criminal Tribunal for the Former Yugoslavia (ICTY) at The Hague, where the concept has left a mark on a similarly innovative and equally controversial conspiracy theory that revolves around the concept of "joint criminal enterprise." By tracing the function of conspiracy, this most controversial of U.S. legal transplants, in the international system, the review illuminates the significance of group dynamics in international law.

INTRODUCTION

Recent studies have shown that more than 25% of all federal criminal prosecutions in the United States involve conspiracy charges. In 1997, for example, 20,132 of 70,114 defendants in federal court faced charges under one of three such provisions of the U.S. Code (Davis & Vitullo 2001, p. 778, fn. 9).[1] According to some, these data bespeak a larger trend in legal scholarship, "one that trains its eye on groups instead of on individuals" (Katyal 2003, p. 1311). As Katyal (2003, p. 1311) writes,

> In corporate law, Eric Talley, Lynn Stout, and Margaret Blair have drawn much attention to the team-production problem; in torts and business organizations, Lewis Kornhauser, Reinier Kraakman, Alan Sykes, and others have usefully analyzed vicarious liability and gatekeepers, and Donald Langevoort has similarly studied employer monitoring; and in civil law, David Schkade,

[1]Of the 20,132 defendants mentioned in the study, 4,502 were charged under 18 U.S. Code sect. 371, and 15,630 under 21 U.S. Code sect. 846 or sect. 963.

> Cass Sunstein, and Daniel Kahneman have developed an understanding of the jury system based on group dynamics.[2]

As a contribution to this emerging literature, which is concerned primarily with group dynamics in municipal law, this review examines the function of conspiracy in international law, with particular reference to the jurisprudence of international ad hoc tribunals.

The review compares and contrasts the function of conspiracy law in the prosecution of international crimes before the International Military Tribunal (IMT) at Nuremberg, where the concept gave rise to a remarkably innovative and highly controversial conspiracy theory that revolved around the concept of "criminal organization," and the function of conspiracy law in the prosecution of international crimes before the International Criminal Tribunal for the Former Yugoslavia (ICTY) at The Hague, where the concept has left a mark on a similarly innovative and equally controversial conspiracy theory that revolves around the concept of "joint criminal enterprise." By tracing the function of conspiracy, this most controversial of U.S. legal transplants, in the international system, the review illuminates the significance of group dynamics in international law. Such an analysis is all the more relevant given that recent jurisprudence from the ICTY and the International Criminal Tribunal for Rwanda (ICTR) has relied on liability theories that are cognizant of the logic of collective action in the commission of international crimes, ranging from modes of individual criminal responsibility (joint criminal enterprise, command and superior responsibility) to substantive crimes (conspiracy to commit genocide, complicity in genocide, direct and public incitement of genocide). As one scholar writes, "recourse to generous—and at times somewhat vicarious—liability theories becomes eminently understandable insofar as these theories permit the tribunals to ascribe individual guilt in cases where violence has several, and often murky, organic sources" (Drumbl 2005, p. 1309).

By tracing the influence of inchoate liability in international law, the review sheds light on the procedural challenges facing international courts and tribunals, notably the ICTY, thus illuminating some of the least understood aspects associated with the prosecution of international crimes. For, as Meron (2004, p. 520) writes,

> Discussions of the ICTY's many contributions to the development of international criminal law tend to focus on the development of substantive doctrines of international criminal responsibility. Less often considered are the significant steps taken within the ICTY to craft a procedural framework for international criminal prosecutions. In my view, the path that the Judges of the ICTY have blazed in the area of international criminal procedure will have just as much influence on future international criminal prosecutions as the

[2]For important contributions, see Kornhauser (1982), Sykes (1984), Schkade et al. (2000).

> substantive doctrine of criminal law that the ICTY enunciates in its decisions and judgments.

This inquiry into the function of conspiracy cuts across the substantive-procedural divide in international law. By reflecting on an emergent mode of responsibility in international law, joint criminal enterprise, and one historical antecedent, criminal organization, the article is rooted in the literature on substantive law (e.g., Eser 2002). By reflecting on the process of synthesizing rules and procedures from different legal traditions in the construction of this mode of responsibility, notably Anglo-American common law and Western European civil law, the review is rooted in the literature on procedural law (e.g., Findlay 2001).

A larger theme of this review, which the analysis of conspiracy theories in international law is meant to illustrate, is the function of methodological individualism in the study of law, which Fletcher (2002, pp. 40–41; see also Meierhenrich 2006) regards as an "egregious shortcoming" of legal studies:

> The liberal (or reductionist) bias pervades everything lawyers say and do. Our concepts are geared toward individuals, their rights and responsibilities. Corporations are reduced to persons under the Fourteenth Amendment. Countries become individuals under international law . . . . We even affirm corporate criminal liability as though the complex organism of the corporation could be reduced to a single actor liable for committing a crime. The polycentric collective as a subject is basically foreign to the legal way of thinking. The generalization holds in our legal system as well as in the civil law tradition: Collective entities, their actions, their responsibility, and their guilt—these are ideas that run afoul of the methodological commitments of the legal mind. Our common-law exception is the law of conspiracy, which seems to address the peculiar danger represented by collective criminal action.

It is against this philosophical and methodological background that the analysis unfolds. The remainder of this review examines (*a*) the function of conspiracy in U.S. law; (*b*) the function of conspiracy in international law, focusing on the doctrines of criminal organization and joint criminal enterprise; and (*c*) the implications of conspiracy for the study of international law.

THE FUNCTION OF CONSPIRACY

Traditionally defined, the crime of conspiracy connotes an agreement between two or more individuals entered into for the purpose of committing an unlawful act. If we follow sect. 5.03 of the Model Penal Code, "the act of combining with another is significant both psychologically and practically, the former because it crosses a clear threshold in arousing expectations, the latter because it increases the likelihood that the offense will be committed. Sharing lends fortitude to purpose. The actor knows, moreover, that the future is no longer governed by his will alone;

others may complete what he has had a hand in starting, even if he has a change of heart." In *U.S. v. Recio* (2003, p. 822; see also *Callanan v. U.S.* 1961), the U.S. Supreme Court echoed this sentiment, declaring conspiracy a "distinct evil," and, quoting from a 1961 case, found that a conspiracy "poses 'a threat to the public' over and above the threat of the commission of the relevant substantive crime—both because the '[c]ombination in crime makes more likely the commission of [other] crimes' and because it 'decreases the probability that the individuals involved will depart from their path of criminality.'"

Insights from economics and psychology are frequently invoked to provide a rationale for the doctrine of conspiracy, especially in the United States. The reasoning underlying the doctrine is that the additional liability introduced by way of conspiracy law has both a deterrent effect and a destabilizing effect. The argument regarding the deterrent effect is that the existence of conspiracy law will prevent some potential participants from joining a conspiracy by raising the cost of membership. The deterrent effect is believed to materialize because "a criminal takes her chances when she joins a conspiracy, in that she is liable for all the crimes that are within the scope of the organization" (Katyal 2003, p. 1372). Scholars argue that this is so regardless of whether liability can be established by the law of complicity (on the law of complicity, see Kutz 2000). The argument regarding the imputed destabilizing effect is founded on insights from psychology:

> Psychological experiments have shown that uncertainty leads to less trust: in situations where a bad apple could poison a group, trust is weak. Lawful partnerships operate under similar precepts since each member is liable for what the others do. Such arrangements work well when the members of the firms are homogenous, practice the same trade, have similar educational backgrounds, and are subject to the same ethical rules (such as law firms), but they become unwieldy and inefficient once heterogeneity is introduced. The criminal conspiracy, often composed of relatively heterogeneous members who lack the same reputational mechanisms to secure trust among each other, will face particular problems from joint liability (Katyal 2003, p. 1373).

What is the essence of conspiracy law, as applied in U.S. courts? As we have seen, conspiracy law criminalizes the agreement to commit a punishable offense. The agreement constitutes the *actus reus* of conspiracy, whereas the intention to commit the punishable offense constitutes conspiracy's *mens rea*. If X and Y agree to commit a bank robbery, they incur liability from the moment of agreement. It is irrelevant whether or not X and Y actually commit the robbery. It is further irrelevant whether or not the commission of the robbery was at all possible. As the U.S. Supreme Court held in *U.S. v. Rabinowich* (1915, p. 86), "A person may be guilty of conspiring, although incapable of committing the objective offense" (for a recent affirmation of this interpretation, see *U.S. v. Recio* 2003, p. 822). This, then, is what is meant by "inchoate liability." The concept refers to an individual's responsibility for criminal conduct that is preparatory or preliminary to unlawful offenses. If X and Y commit the robbery, they incur additional liability for any substantive offenses.

The law of conspiracy has its origins in the reign of Edward I and was unknown to the early common law. The doctrine of conspiracy was expanded twice in the seventeenth century, notably by the Court of Star Chamber in the 1611 *Poulterers' Case*, and in their jurisprudence nineteenth century courts in England and the United States advocated an even broader interpretation (Sayre 1922). Indicative of the steady expansion of conspiracy law is the fact that by the early 1970s some 28 statutory provisions in the U.S. Penal Code declared specific types of conspiracies federal offenses, ranging from conspiracies to overthrow the government to conspiracies to defraud the Tennessee Valley Authority (Hoskins 1973, pp. 246–47). Two critical junctures marked the rise of conspiracy law in twentieth-century America: the *Pinkerton* doctrine of 1946 and the Racketeer Influenced and Corrupt Organizations Act of 1970 (RICO), both of which were billed as powerful crime-fighting weapons.

The evolution of conspiracy law took an important turn in *Pinkerton v. U.S.* (1946). The controversial case revolves around a defendant who had conspired with his brother to operate an illegal still and who was convicted for his brother's later acts of operating the still, notwithstanding the fact that the defendant at that point had been in prison for another offense. The case remains the focal point in the longstanding debate over the promise and limits of U.S. conspiracy law. Most important, for the purpose of this review, *Pinkerton* expands the liability of individuals "to those crimes 'reasonably foreseeable as a natural consequence of the unlawful agreement.' This doctrine is similar to the natural-and-probable-consequence rule of accomplice liability, although without its limiting dictum, broader liability is obviously authorized" (Saltzman 1983, p. 1598). The expansion of liability in *Pinkerton* is worth emphasizing because the language of *Pinkerton* resurfaces, almost verbatim, 50 years later in the joint criminal enterprise jurisprudence of the ICTY.

The notion of enterprise in the U.S. context was first defined in the RICO statute that Congress passed as Title IX of the Organized Crime Control Act. According to RICO, which was amended in sections of the U.S. Code, the term enterprise includes "any individual, partnership, corporation, association, or other legal entity, and any union or group of individuals associated in fact although not a legal entity" [RICO, sect. 1961(4)]. RICO, like conspiracy law more generally, has been the subject of great controversy. The subtleties of this controversy need not concern us here (for recent analyses of RICO's relevance, see Wolff 1995, Mastin 2001). However, some objections to the law of conspiracy are worth considering in this context because they are also applicable—albeit in different ways and to different degrees—to the doctrines of criminal organization and joint criminal enterprise.

Burke & Kadish (1983, p. 236) enumerated the most important objections:

> Liability for substantive crimes is predicated on the loose evidentiary standards of conspiracy law; liability attaches for crimes not actually intended or even necessarily foreseen, and holding each member of a conspiracy liable for all crimes committed by the group without regard to the character of that person's role within the group yields overly broad liability without penal justification. This is particularly true in those jurisdictions that allow the finding of a single conspiracy, rather than several smaller ones, in case of large, sprawling, and loosely confederated criminal enterprises.

Some studies have gone as far as calling for the abolition of conspiracy law (Johnson 1973). Space constraints prevent a comprehensive analysis of U.S. conspiracy law. Suffice it to say that the doctrine has, from its inception until the present, drawn the ire of many. With this in mind, I turn to the function of conspiracy in international law, where one finds substantial traces of U.S. influence.

THE FUNCTION OF CONSPIRACY IN "CRIMINAL ORGANIZATION"

In addition to the conspiracy provision contained in Article 6, the charter of the IMT at Nuremberg made punishable, in Article 9, membership in a criminal organization (IMT 1947a). This part of the review is concerned with the function of conspiracy in the construction and reconstruction of the theory of criminal organization. The focus is not on the conspiracy provision relating to the formulation or execution of a common plan or conspiracy to commit any of the three crimes in the IMT Charter: crimes against peace, war crimes, and crimes against humanity (the most insightful analysis of this provision, the inclusion of which was intimately related to U.S.-led efforts at prosecuting a "war of aggression," remains Pomorski 1990).

When the IMT curtailed the theory of criminal organization in its judgment (IMT 1947b, p. 256), delivered on October 1, 1946, it made particular reference to conceptual similarities between the newly minted concept and the Anglo-American law of conspiracy: "A criminal organization is analogous to a criminal conspiracy in that the essence of both is cooperation for criminal purposes. There must be a group bound together and organized for a common purpose." This dictum is a useful starting point, for it points not only to a conceptual relationship between the theory of conspiracy and the theory of criminal organization, but also to a conceptual relationship between these theories and the theory of joint criminal enterprise, for the latter is also known as the law of common purpose (see, e.g., *Prosecutor v. Duško Tadić* 1999, paragraphs 193, 195, 204, 225).

But let me begin with the function of conspiracy in criminal organization. Aside from the Allied effort to demonstrate a Nazi conspiracy to wage aggressive war, much of the prosecution's work in the wake of World War II was consumed with the construction of criminal organization as a theory of collective criminality. The idea to rely on the law of conspiracy derived in part from a memorandum drawn up by Lieutenant Colonel Murray C. Bernays, a lawyer in the U.S. Department of War.[3] The so-called Bernays Memorandum formulated the rationale for the theory of criminal organization thus:

> Behind each Axis war criminal . . . lies the basic criminal instigation of the Nazi doctrine and policy. It is the guilty nature of this instigation that must be established, for only thus will the conviction and punishment of the individuals concerned achieve their true moral and juristic significance. In turn, this approach throws light on the nature of the individual's guilt, which is not dependent on the commission of specific criminal acts, but follows inevitably from the mere fact of voluntary membership in organizations devised solely to commit such acts (Bernays 1982 [1944], p. 35).

This justification is not dissimilar from the rationale underlying U.S. conspiracy law, as discussed above. The Bernays Memorandum served as the foundation for Article 9 of the IMT Charter, which resulted in the indictment of six Nazi organizations, namely the Reich Cabinet, the Leadership Corps of the NSDAP, the SS including SD, the Gestapo, the SA, and the General Staff and High Command of the German Armed Forces. The importance of both documents notwithstanding, prosecutors at the time still faced "the task of developing a precise and complete theory of collective criminality and liability, as distinguished from individual criminal responsibility and liability" (Jørgensen 2000, p. 62). Here, we encounter the function of conspiracy more directly. The justification of the theory of criminal organization offered by Robert H. Jackson, the U.S. prosecution team's chief of counsel, in open court on February 28, 1946, is reminiscent of the reasoning concerning the presumed deterrent effect of U.S. conspiracy law.

"These organizations," declared Jackson, "are the carriers from this generation to the next of the infection of aggressive and ruthless war . . . . The next war and the next pogroms will be hatched in the nests of these organizations as surely as we leave their membership with its prestige and influence undiminished by condemnation and punishment" (IMT 1947c, pp. 355–56). Further evidence of the function of conspiracy in criminal organization exists. In his justification of the theory of criminal organization, for example, Jackson invoked the Alien Registration Act (1940), also known as the Smith Act. The act provided for the prosecution of conspiracies aimed at overthrowing or destroying the government of the United States. Or, as Jackson put it before the IMT (without mentioning the act by name),

> The Congress of the United States also has enacted legislation outlawing certain organizations. A recent example was on the 28th of June 1940, when the Congress provided that it shall be unlawful for any person, among other

[3]Frequently overlooked in this context is the work of United Nations War Crimes Commission, which sought to turn the notion of criminal organization into a justiciable concept in the run-up to the proceedings of the IMT. See UN War Crimes Comm. (1948); see also Meierhenrich (2005).

> things, to organize or help to organize any society, group, or assembly of persons to teach, advocate, or encourage the overthrow or destruction of any government in the United States by force or violence, or to be or become a member of, or affiliate with, any such society, group, or assembly of persons, knowing the purposes thereof (IMT 1947c, pp. 361–62).

The invocation of the Smith Act by Jackson is once again illustrative of the function of conspiracy in criminal organization [for the current version of the Smith Act, see 18 U.S. Code sect. 2385 (2001)]. "Even in RICO, however, one finds nothing so demanding as Nuremberg's insistence that the enterprise display formally defined boundaries, clearly distinguishing members from others, such as those who may have endorsed its goals or even assisted it occasionally in minor ways" (Osiel 2005, pp. 1792–93). This notwithstanding, "[t]here is no doubt," as Pomorski (1990, pp. 219–20) notes, "that the doctrinal underpinnings of the idea [of criminal organization] were supplied by the conspiracy doctrine. The proponents of the plan viewed Nazi organizations as groups drawn together by common criminal objectives, and consequently, considered membership of these organizations as 'evidence of conspiracy.' This attempt to meet a unique political task of denazification through judicial, rather than administrative action, was, therefore, inspired by a concept well familiar to the common law world." What were the consequences of this for international law?

In the estimation of many, "the imposition of the straightjacket of 'the conspiracy-criminal organization plan"' on the IMT proceedings "amounted to an imposition of justice on history. Nazi documents were collected and filtered without benefit of historical expertise or—consequently—proper contextual analysis and interpretation. Here 'justice' and 'history' were part of the same judicial bag carried by the tribunal's prosecutors—who apparently sought truth in justice and *vice versa*.... Within limits, Nuremberg succeeded in delivering justice. But it failed to capture the true nature of the Nazi state and the Holocaust" (Haberer 2005, p. 493). This is an inherent danger in the adjudication of international crimes, which brings us to a related, yet largely unexamined feature of international law: the central role of prosecutors in the transformation—and deformation—of international law.

Prosecutors, like Jackson, are regularly at the forefront of innovation in international law, a fact that underlines the contribution of judicial networks in the international system (e.g., Slaughter 2004). Yet the controversial innovations of prosecutors, both at the IMT and, as we shall see, the ICTY, raise important questions about the costs of judicial networks, especially U.S.-led networks, in the international system. Telford Taylor, who served on the American prosecution team at Nuremberg, spoke to these costs when reflecting on the theory of criminal organization. "[I]t has also become clear," remarked Taylor (1992, p. 637) after the IMT proceedings, "that what might be called 'the Bernays additions' did more harm than good. In the upshot they did little or no damage to Nuremberg defendants, but they left a black mark on the prosecution's judgment."

Ironically, Jackson himself, the principal proponent of the theory of criminal organization, as a justice of the U.S. Supreme Court in 1949, cast doubt on U.S. conspiracy law, which, as we have seen, had informed the Allied effort at prosecuting collective criminality. As Jackson observed in his concurring opinion in *Krulewich v. U.S.* (1949, pp. 446–47, 449)

> The modern crime of conspiracy is so vague that it almost defies definition. Despite certain elementary and essential elements, it also, chameleon-like, takes on a special coloration from each of the many independent offenses of which it may be overlaid.... The more radical proposition also is well-established that at common law and under some statutes a combination may be a criminal conspiracy even if it contemplates only acts which are not crimes at all when perpetrated by an individual or by many acting severally.

Yet, as the next section of this review demonstrates, Jackson's *volte face* and misgivings about U.S. conspiracy law had little effect on the function of conspiracy in international law. Traces of the controversial doctrine can be found in the theory of joint criminal enterprise, this latest effort at punishing collective criminality in international law.

THE FUNCTION OF CONSPIRACY IN "JOINT CRIMINAL ENTERPRISE"

In his important survey of international adjudication, Mettraux (2005, pp. 287–88) correctly remarked that, ten years after the inception of the ICTY and ICTR, "joint criminal enterprise still remains one of the most contentious issues in their jurisprudential life and its contours have fluctuated a great deal over the years." If we believe recent scholarship, the doctrine of joint criminal enterprise "is historically and conceptually related both to conspiracy and to the prosecution of criminal organizations" (Danner & Martinez 2005, p. 110). Because the jurisprudence of the ICTY denies any such linkages, it is important to consider the matter in more detail.

The doctrine of joint criminal enterprise, as developed in the jurisprudence of the ICTY and, to a lesser degree, in the jurisprudence of the ICTR, distinguishes three categories of what has become a most influential—and controversial—mode of liability in international law. This section does not propose to rehearse the subtleties of this jurisprudence, which originated with the appeal judgment in *Prosecutor v. Duško Tadić* (1999). Instead, it is devoted to exploring the similarities and differences between this and antecedent efforts at prosecuting collective criminality, with particular reference to the influence of U.S. conspiracy law.

The *actus reus* for all categories of joint criminal enterprise is constituted by a plurality of persons, the existence of a common plan that amounts to or involves the commission of a crime provided for in the statutes of the ad hoc tribunals, and participation of the accused in the perpetration of the common plan. The *mens rea* is a more complicated affair and varies with the category under consideration. The first and second categories (the latter is a variant of the first) require, in essence, the intent to perpetrate a certain crime. The third category requires the intent to participate in and further the common plan and to contribute to the joint criminal enterprise or in any event to the commission of a crime by the group. In addition, and this is what makes the third category so controversial, if a crime was committed that fell *outside* the plan of the joint criminal enterprise, liability may attach to an individual provided that the further crime was a possible consequence in the execution of the joint criminal enterprise and that the accused willingly took the risk that one or other members of the joint criminal enterprise might perpetrate a crime outside of the original plan. Regarding the third category, the Appeal Chamber recently provided an illustration in *Prosecutor v. Mitar Vasiljević* (2004, paragraph 99):

> An example is a common purpose or plan on the part of a group to forcibly remove at gun-point members of one ethnicity from their town, village or region (to effect 'ethnic cleansing') with the consequence that, in the course of doing so, one or more of the victims is shot and killed. While murder may not have been explicitly acknowledged to be part of the common purpose, it was nevertheless foreseeable that the forcible removal of civilians at gunpoint might well result in the deaths of one or more of those civilians.

For some defense counsel at the ICTY, the doctrine of joint criminal enterprise apparently represents a form of "sub rosa conspiracy." Osiel (2005, p. 1792) notes that, aside from the Nuremberg influence, "the contemporary notion of an 'enterprise' gone criminally astray has also been filtered through the later U.S. jurisprudence of RICO, which first employs this term expressly." Whereas the jurisprudence of the IMT is replete with references to U.S. conspiracy law, the jurisprudence of the ICTY is conspicuously silent on the function of conspiracy in the evolution of joint criminal enterprise. What, then, are we to make of assertions that RICO has played a role in the evolution of the doctrine of joint criminal enterprise, as currently practiced in the ad hoc tribunals?

According to David Hunt, who previously served as a member of the Appeals Chamber and presiding judge of Trial Chamber II at the ICTY, the assertion that the concept of joint criminal enterprise is a form of conspiracy is "entirely fallacious" (*Prosecutor v. Milan Milutinović* et al. 2003a, paragraph 23). Maintained Hunt in his separate opinion in a recent interlocutory appeal:

> Conspiracy is not a mode of individual criminal responsibility for the commission of a crime. Conspiracy is itself a crime (of an inchoate nature) which is complete once the agreement between the conspirator has been reached. No step needs to have been taken in furtherance of that agreement before the crime of conspiracy has been committed. On the other hand, joint criminal enterprise is available as one mode of individual criminal responsibility by which a crime may be committed, but only where the agreed (or contemplated)

> crime has been in fact committed (*Prosecutor v. Milan Milutinović* et al. 2003a, paragraph 23).

Aside from this distinction, the existence of a conspiracy is easier to prove than joint criminal enterprise, "in that it is not necessary to show that the agreement to perpetrate the crime actually resulted in its commission by any party to the agreement" (Powles 2004, p. 613). Or, as the ICTY Appeals Chamber put it in a recent decision on a defendant's motion challenging jurisdiction, "[w]hilst conspiracy requires a showing that several individuals have agreed to commit a certain crime or set of crimes, a joint criminal enterprise requires, in addition to such a showing, that the parties to that agreement took action in furtherance of that agreement" (*Prosecutor v. Milan Milutinović* et al. 2003b, paragraph 23).

As important as these differences are, they should not distract from underlying similarities, conceptual and functional, between conspiracy and joint criminal enterprise. Consider in this context once again *Pinkerton v. U.S.*, the Supreme Court decision that provided, in 1946, an important impetus to the law of conspiracy. In the case, the petitioners were convicted of a conspiracy to violate the Internal Revenue Code and of several substantive offences. In a nutshell, the Supreme Court stated in *Pinkerton* that "a member of a continuing conspiracy incurs not only conspiracy liability, but also vicarious substantive liability for offenses committed during the conspiracy and in furtherance of it by coconspirators. Liability exists if the act was within the foreseeable scope of the agreement which the defendant intentionally joined, even though he did not agree to—or even know about—the particular act" (Ickler 1983, p. 594). This reasoning underlying the U.S. law of conspiracy is remarkably similar to the reasoning underlying the extended form of joint criminal enterprise in the jurisprudence of the ICTY. There, as we have seen, liability attaches if a joint criminal enterprise existed and one or more participants have committed an international crime that, although being outside of the original agreement of the joint criminal enterprise, was nevertheless a natural and foreseeable consequence of the agreement. As Osiel (2005, p. 1785) remarks, "This resembles U.S. rules on *Pinkerton* conspiracies."

Other scholars concur, describing the function of conspiracy in joint criminal enterprise in similar terms. Barrett & Little (2003, p. 42), for example, contend that the descriptions of criminal behavior used in the ICTY jurisprudence, notably in the appellate judgments in *Prosecutor v. Duško Tadić* (1999) and *Prosecutor v. Anto Furundžija* (2000),

> draw a picture difficult to distinguish from conspiracy, which focuses on agreements to commit a criminal act. One may even ask whether the ICTY treats proof of a "common plan" as the same as proof of an agreement to commit a crime. The Appeals Chamber's statement that a common purpose may materialize "extemporaneously" suggests that a common plan is no more challenging to establish than a conspiratorial agreement. Language in at least one ICTY opinion actually treats agreement and common plan as coextensive.

In other words, we have *prima facie* evidence of the function of conspiracy in joint criminal enterprise. Whether or not we conclude, on the basis of the aforementioned jurisprudence, that the ICTY Statute de jure embraces conspiracy as a form of criminality, it is indisputable that the law of conspiracy has de facto played an important role in the evolution of joint criminal enterprise. What are the implications of this conceptual and functional relationship?

Even though important differences distinguish the doctrine of joint criminal enterprise from the doctrine of conspiracy, the attendant dangers are comparable. With some justification, Danner & Martinez (2005, p. 137) argue that "[j]oint criminal enterprise raises the specter of guilt by association and provides ammunition to those who doubt the rigor and impartiality of the international forum. If conspiracy is the darling of the U.S. prosecutor's nursery, then it is difficult to see how [joint criminal enterprise] can amount to anything less than the nuclear bomb of the international prosecutor's arsenal." This brings us once again to the role of judicial networks in international law.

Hagan (2003) found that in terms of U.S. influence in judicial networks, U.S. prosecutors at the ICTY provided important leadership in the construction of the Office of the Prosecutor (OTP) and the international ad hoc tribunal more generally. One of his respondents claimed that "the Americans who were here in the first two or three years were the real backbone of the tribunal. I mean, not exclusively by any means, a lot of people contributed, but there were some very key Americans here who were the real pushers behind the scenes and made a lot of things happen" (quoted in Hagan 2003, p. 67). One of the things that Americans pushed in the OTP was most likely U.S. conspiracy law. Circumstantial evidence for this argument can be gleaned from research conducted by Osiel (2005) according to which (*a*) ICTY prosecutors trained in the civil law tradition expressed concern about conspiracy and its surreptitious cognates; and (*b*) only one ICTY prosecution team, led by Canadian William Fenrick, resisted an overreliance on the doctrine of joint criminal enterprise. "When he retired in 2003, the restraint he had long exercised on others in the Office of the Prosecutor disappeared, and its members began to employ the doctrine more aggressively before the Tribunal" (Osiel 2005, p. 1794, fn. 202).

The enormous elasticity with which the doctrine of joint criminal enterprise has been used by the OTP is reminiscent of the problems that Allied prosecutors faced in identifying the essence of criminal organization in the proceedings of the IMT, and the ongoing challenges that U.S. prosecutors face in state and federal courts. The preceding analysis points to a relationship not only between the concepts of conspiracy and joint criminal enterprise, but also between the concepts of criminal organization and joint criminal enterprise. "Both Bernays's description of the purposes of the criminal organization charge and the IMT's lukewarm endorsement of the concept share important similarities with JCE [joint criminal enterprise]. Each of these doctrinal stratagems serves to expand the potential liability of defendants far beyond their physical perpetration of crimes. Each harnesses the criminal liability of the defendants to the acts committed within the scope of the enterprise and, in the case of Category Three JCEs, to those beyond the scope of the criminal purpose" (Danner & Martinez 2005, p. 117; for a different interpretation, see *Prosecutor v. Milan Milutinović* et al. 2003b, paragraph 25).

Interestingly, the United Nations War Crimes Commission, in 1949, anticipated the functional equivalence between the concept of criminal organization and joint criminal enterprise, while negating the function of conspiracy in criminal organization:

> [T]he history of the development of the concept of membership [in a criminal organization] suggests strongly that what it was to punish was no mere conspiracy to commit crimes but a knowing and voluntary membership of organisations which did in fact commit crimes, and those on a wide scale. Viewed in this light, membership resembles more the crime of acting in pursuance of a common design than it does that of conspiracy (UN War Crimes Comm. 1949, pp. 98–99).

The trial chamber in *Prosecutor v. Milomir Stakić* (2003, paragraph 433), in turn, recently disputed any such similarities, arguing that "joint criminal enterprise can not be viewed as membership in an organisation because this would constitute a new crime not foreseen under the Statute and therefore amount to a flagrant infringement of the principle *nullum crimen sine lege*." The reasoning underlying this argument, however, is flawed. Although legitimate reasons exist to distinguish the concept of criminal organization from the concept of joint criminal enterprise, these reasons are unrelated to the ICTY statute. Just because the concept of criminal organization is not commensurable with the ICTY statute, it does not follow that the concept cannot resemble, in important respects, the concept of joint criminal enterprise. Some scholars agree, finding that the doctrine of criminal organization "may rule us surreptitiously from the grave through its enduring influence (albeit unacknowledged) on enterprise participation" (Osiel 2005, p. 1792).

Inasmuch as the evolution of joint criminal enterprise is subject to contention, the effects of joint criminal enterprise are less contested: "Unless narrowly construed, this form of liability could come dangerously close to assigning guilt for mere membership in a group (be it a political party, the main staff of an army, the crisis staff of a region, or a ministry) and de facto place the burden upon the accused to establish that, despite its belongings to such a group or despite his association with members of that group, he did not partake in a criminal purpose that was assisted or pursued by that group" (Mettraux 2005, p. 293). This assessment, shared by an increasing number of scholars and practitioners, points not only to the ways in which substantive law and procedural law intersect, but also to the inherent dangers involved in turning the "polycentric collective" (Fletcher 2002) into a subject of international law. From Nuremberg to The Hague, all extant efforts have raised the specter of collective guilt.

CONCLUSION

This review has been concerned with the unacknowledged influence of U.S. conspiracy law on theories of criminality in international law. The analysis of two conspiracy theories—the first revolving around the concept of criminal organization, the second around the concept of joint criminal enterprise—has shown that legal doctrines, in municipal and international law alike, are saturated with assumptions about the logic of collective action. In making choices about legal doctrines in their indictments and judgments,

> prosecutors and courts are therefore tacitly and haphazardly taking a stand on such large questions. Debate among international lawyers over the respective merits of [legal] doctrines nonetheless takes no account of the considerable scholarship on the extralegal issues. In fact, prosecutors frequently make decisions about which doctrine to employ with an acute awareness of how the choice affects their own professional prospects. They may be forgiven for displaying little curiosity about the nature of the sociological assumptions implicit in their legal approaches. Still, an open mind would begin not by asking what legal doctrines offer precedents to cope quickly with this new challenge, but rather, what kind of influence do participants in such collective criminality actually exercise over one another, through what organizational devices and interactional dynamics (Osiel 2005, p. 1768)?

The fact that the doctrinal underpinnings of the theories of criminal organization and joint criminal enterprise were, to a substantial degree, supplied by the law of conspiracy also sheds new light on the operation of judicial networks in international law. In recent years, international lawyers have touted the benefits of these networks. The analysis of the function of conspiracy in international law and the role of U.S. prosecutors therein, however, forces us to take seriously the costs of judicial networks. The promotion of theories of collective criminality by U.S. prosecutors, as exemplified by the function of conspiracy in the evolution of the theories of criminal organization and joint criminal enterprise, points to some of these potential costs. The danger arises that the principle of individual criminal responsibility—a fundamental principle of international law—is hollowed out by an uncritical reliance among prosecutors on theories of collective criminality. Particularly problematic in this context is "the proliferation across indictments of various 'joint criminal enterprises' which—although relating to the same period and frequently many of the same incidents and facts, and sometimes many of the same principle [sic] participants—are however described inconsistently in different indictments issued at different times. The indictments against leadership figures before the ICTY are all characterized by heavy reliance on the joint criminal enterprise theory, but there appears to have been little thought about how the same interconnected events should be charged in different cases" (Mettraux 2005, p. 292).

It is for these reasons that the study of group dynamics in international law ought to become a preoccupation for scholars of law and social science. Interdisciplinary scholarship can contribute to our understanding of the promise—and limits—of holding individuals responsible for international crimes, especially when committed by another. By studying not merely the effects of international adjudication, but also its evolution, interdisciplinary scholarship has an important role to play in improving international justice, both our understanding and practice of it. But let me return to the function of conspiracy in international law.

When contemplating the function of conspiracy in international law, and the theories that the doctrine has inspired, international lawyers would be well advised to recall Judge Learned Hand's cautionary remarks concerning the function of conspiracy in U.S. law. In *U.S. v. Falcone* (1940, p. 581), the eminent jurist was disturbed that "so many prosecutors seek to sweep within the drag-net of conspiracy all those who have been associated in any degree whatever with the main offenders. That there are opportunities of great oppression in such a doctrine is very plain, and it is only by circumscribing the scope of such all comprehensive indictments that they can be avoided." At Nuremberg, the jurisprudence of the IMT successfully navigated many opportunities of great oppression by limiting the function of conspiracy in criminal organization. At The Hague, the jurisprudence of the ICTY has refused to acknowledge the function of conspiracy in the evolution of joint criminal enterprise. Although, as we have seen, important differences distinguish the two doctrines, the increased prosecutorial use of joint criminal enterprise since century's end has raised in international law the specter of Learned Hand's drag-net, particularly so because the doctrine of joint criminal enterprise "has even fewer limits than already expansive domestic conspiracy law" (Danner & Martinez 2005, p. 164).

A growing number of scholars believe that "further restructuring of extant thinking is required in order for international criminal law truly to be transformative" (Drumbl 2005, p. 1328). To assist this process, law and social science must pay closer attention to the logic of collective action in the commission of international crimes, notably the myriad ways in which international courts and tribunals have sought to come to terms with the phenomenon. The study of international law as well as its practice have plainly been marred by a disregard for group dynamics, due largely to "legalistic and microeconomic concerns with individual behavior" (Katyal 2003, pp. 1397–98). To overcome this limitation, we must reconsider the nature of international law and the place of individuals therein. Or, as Fletcher (2002, p. 214) writes,

> Who acts in the world? Individuals act. As the Romantics have taught us, groups and nations also act. And we act through them. The questions of agency and guilt will remain contested. May the debate begin anew—with firm recognition that ours is not a simple world of individuals but a more complicated world in which we seek agency in solidarity with others.

This, then, is the challenge that the adjudication of international crimes poses for law and social science. What is required to truly understand the dynamics of international law is what we do not yet possess—a sociology of international law.

The *Annual Review of Law and Social Science* is online at http://lawsocsci.annualreviews.org

LITERATURE CITED

Barrett R, Little LE. 2003. Lessons of Yugoslav rape trials: a role of conspiracy law in international tribunals. *Minn. Law Rev.* 88:30–85

Bernays MC. 1982 (1944). Trial of European war criminals (by Colonel Murray C. Bernays, G-1). In *The American Road to Nuremberg: The Documentary Record 1944–1945*, ed. BF Smith, pp. 33–37. Stanford, CA: Hoover Inst. Press

Burke JA, Kadish S. 1983. Conspiracy. In *Encyclopedia of Crime and Justice*, ed. SH Kadish, 1:23138. New York: Free Press

Callanan v. U.S., 364 U.S. 587 (1961)

Danner AM, Martinez JS. 2005. Guilty associations: joint criminal enterprise, command responsibility, and the development of international criminal law. *Calif. Law Rev.* 93:75–169

Davis BA, Vitullo J. 2001. Federal criminal conspiracy. *Am. Crim. Law Rev.* 38:777–17

Drumbl MA. 2005. Pluralizing international criminal justice. *Mich. Law Rev.* 99:1295–328

Eser A. 2002. Individual criminal responsibility. In *The Rome Statute of the International Criminal Court: A Commentary*, ed. A Cassese, P Gaeta, JRWD Jones, 1:767–822. Oxford: Oxford Univ. Press

Findlay M. 2001. Synthesis in trial procedures? The experience of international criminal tribunals. *Int. Comp. Law Q.* 50:26–53

Fletcher GP. 2002. *Romantics at War: Glory and Guilt in the Age of Terrorism*. Princeton, NJ: Princeton Univ. Press

Haberer E. 2005. History and justice: paradigms of the prosecution of Nazi crimes. *Holocaust Genocide Stud.* 19:487–519

Hagan J. 2003. *Justice in the Balkans: Prosecuting War Criminals in the Hague Tribunal*. Chicago: Univ. Chicago Press

Hoskins RJ. 1973. A comparative analysis of the crime of conspiracy in Germany, France, and the United States. *NY Univ. J. Int. Law Polit.* 6:245–70

Ickler NL. 1983. Conspiracy to violate RICO: expanding traditional conspiracy law. *Notre Dame Law Rev.* 58:587–615

IMT. 1947a. Charter of the International Military Tribunal. In *Trial of the Major War Criminals before the International Military Tribunal, Nuremberg, 14 November 1945–1 October 1946*, 1:10–16. Nuremberg: IMT

IMT. 1947b. Judgment. In *Trial of the Major War Criminals before the International Military Tribunal, Nuremberg, 14 November 1945–1 October* 1946, 1:171–364. Nuremberg: IMT

IMT. 1947c. Proc., 20 Feb. 1946–7 March 1946. In *Trial of the Major War Criminals before the International Military Tribunal Nuremberg, 14 November 1945–1 October 1946*, 8:1–630. Nuremberg: IMT

Johnson PE. 1973. The unnecessary crime of conspiracy. *Calif. Law Rev.* 61:1137–88

Jørgensen NHB. 2000. *The Responsibility of States for International Crimes*. Oxford: Oxford Univ. Press

Katyal NK. 2003. Conspiracy theory. *Yale Law J.* 112:1307–98

Kornhauser LA. 1982. An economic analysis of the choice between enterprise and personal liability for accidents. *Calif. Law Rev.* 70:1345–92

Krulewich v. U.S., 336 U.S. 445–447 (1949) (J. Jackson concurring)

Kutz C. 2000. *Complicity: Ethics and Law for a Collective Age*. Cambridge, UK: Cambridge Univ. Press

Mastin YM. 2001. RICO conspiracy: dismantles the Mexican mafia and disables procedural due process. *William Mitchell Law Rev.* 27:2295–344

Meierhenrich J. 2005. *The concept of "criminal organization" in international law:*

a reconstruction. Work. Pap., Dep. Gov., Harvard Univ.

Meierhenrich J. 2006. A question of guilt. *Ratio Juris* 19:314–42

Meron T. 2004. Procedural evolution in the ICTY. *J. Int. Crim. Justice* 2:520–25

Mettraux G. 2005. *International Crimes and the Ad Hoc Tribunals*. Oxford: Oxford Univ. Press

Osiel M. 2005. The banality of good: aligning incentives against mass atrocity. *Columbia Law Rev.* 105:1751–862

Pinkerton v. U.S., 328 U.S. 640 (1946)

Pomorski S. 1990. Conspiracy and criminal organization. In *The Nuremberg Trial and International Law*, ed. G Ginsburgs, VN Kudriavtsev, pp. 213–48. The Hague: Kluwer

Powles S. 2004. Joint criminal enterprise: criminal liability by prosecutorial ingenuity and judicial creativity? *J. Int. Crim. Justice* 2:606–19

Prosecutor v. Anto Furundžija. 2000. Case No. IT-95-17/1-A, July 21. ICTY Appeals Chamber. Judgment

Prosecutor v. Duško Tadić. 1999. Case No. IT-94-1-A, July 15. ICTY Appeals Chamber. Judgment

Prosecutor v. Milan Milutinović, Nikola Šainović and Dragoljub Ojdanić. 2003a. Case No. IT-99-37-AR72, May 21. ICTY Appeals Chamber. Separate Opinion of Judge David Hunt on Challenge by Ojdanić to Jurisdiction—Joint Criminal Enterprise

Prosecutor v. Milan Milutinović, Nikola Šainović and Dragoljub Ojdanić. 2003b. Case No. IT-99-37-AR72, May 21. ICTY Appeals Chamber. Decision on Dragoljub Ojdanić's Motion Challenging Jurisdiction—Joint Criminal Enterprise

Prosecutor v. Milomir Stakić. 2003. Case No. IT-97-24-T, July 31. ICTY Trial Chamber. Judgment

Prosecutor v. Mitar Vasiljević. 2004. Case No. IT-98-32-A, Feb. 25. ICTY Appeals Chamber. Judgment

Saltzman A. 1983. Vicarious liability. In *Encyclopedia of Crime and Justice*, ed. SH Kadish, 4:1597–600. New York: Free Press

Sayre FB. 1922. Criminal conspiracy. *Harvard Law Rev.* 35:393–427

Schkade D, Sunstein CR, Kahneman D. 2000. Deliberating about dollars: the severity shift. *Columbia Law Rev.* 100:1139–75

Slaughter A-M. 2004. *A New World Order*. Princeton, NJ: Princeton Univ. Press

Sykes AO. 1984. The economics of vicarious liability. *Yale Law J.* 93:1231–80

Taylor T. 1992. *The Anatomy of the Nuremberg Trials: A Personal Memoir*. New York: Knopf

UN War Crimes Comm. 1948. *History of the United Nations War Crimes Commission and the Development of the Laws of War*. London: HMSO

UN War Crimes Comm. 1949. *Law Reports of Trials of War Crimin*als, Vol. 15. London: HMSO

U.S. v. Falcone, 109 F.2d 579 (1940)

U.S. v. Rabinowich, 238 U.S. 78 (1915)

U.S. v. Recio, 123 S.Ct. 819 (2003)

Wolff D. 1995. The frontier of RICO standing: interpreting RICO's conspiracy provision to realize Congress' goal of creating a powerful crime-fighting weapon. *J. Legis.* 21:147–54

Annu. Rev. Law Soc. Sci. 2006. 2:359–85
doi: 10.1146/annurev.lawsocsci.2.081805.105925

Law and the Labor Market

Christine Jolls
Yale Law School, New Haven, Connecticut 06520; christine.jolls@yale.edu

Key Words employment law, workplace safety, workplace privacy, benefits mandates, employer-employee relationship

■ **Abstract** Legal rules governing the employer-employee relationship are many and varied. This review is concerned with the economic analysis of such rules. The review focuses on areas of employment regulation that have not been reviewed elsewhere from an economic perspective. Topics considered in the review include workplace safety regulation, privacy protection in the workplace, fringe benefits mandates, targeted mandates such as medical and family leave, and rules requiring that employees receive overtime pay. Both economic theory and empirical evidence are considered.

INTRODUCTION

In a modern economy, individuals usually rely on paid work to meet their basic material needs. The present review is concerned with the economic analysis of laws governing this ubiquitous employer-employee relationship. Such laws have proliferated in both number and scope across nations, and economic analysis of these laws' desirability and effects has accordingly attracted significant attention.

Within a pervasively unionized economy, the body of what is referred to in the United States as "labor law" plays an important role in regulating the employer-employee relationship. This body of law governs the practices and treatment of labor unions. In countries with only moderate levels of unionization, however, the central responsibility for legal regulation of the employer-employee relationship falls to what is referred to in the United States as "employment law." Employment law governs the treatment of individual employees regardless of their union status. Areas of regulation include workplace safety and privacy, employee fringe benefits, workplace leave, and the payment of wages. The present review is concerned with the economic analysis of these employment law rules.

An obvious but critical starting point in the economic analysis of employment law is that legal regulation of the treatment of employees typically takes place against the backdrop of a market relationship. This market relationship often imposes significant limits on the prospects for using employment law purely for the purpose of transferring power, wealth, or other entitlements to employees—although employment law is often enacted with such motives as the law's declared purpose. In the area of mandated leave from employment, for instance, if employment law seeks to better employees' situation by specifying minimum entitlements to leave from work, it is possible that the end result will be to worsen employees' situation as wages or employment levels adjust in response to the new legal requirements. Because of the way in which the market constrains the prospects for using employment law purely to effect transfers of resources, the economic analysis of employment law in this review gives primary emphasis to market failures in the employer-employee relationship. In the presence of a market failure, legal intervention through employment law may both enhance efficiency and make employees better off.

This review situates major areas of employment law within this market-failure analytic framework; importantly, it also identifies certain areas in which legal intervention may help targeted employees even in the absence of market failure (see the section on targeted mandates below). At the broadest level, the review seeks to describe both theoretically and empirically the degree to which major forms of legal regulation of the employer-employee relationship may enhance efficiency and make employees better off. The opening section below presents the basic analytic framework used throughout much of the review. The next five sections consider specific areas of employment law, including workplace safety regulation, privacy protection in the workplace, fringe benefits mandates, targeted mandates such as medical and family leave, and rules requiring overtime pay.[1]

FRAMEWORK OF ANALYSIS

As suggested above, the analysis in this review rests on the assumption that employment law operates to regulate market relationships between employers and employees. Obviously, it is possible to organize an economy in which wages and conditions of employment are set not by private actors in employment markets but instead by a central planner; such nonmarket settings would naturally require a different analysis.

Within a market setting, when wages and conditions of employment are determined by the interaction of labor supply and labor demand, legal intervention not tied to an identified market failure will often, although not always, reduce both efficiency and employee welfare. The present section first briefly reviews the reasoning for this claim and then provides an overview of important market failures in the employer-employee relationship.

---

[1]Other major areas of employment law have been reviewed elsewhere within the type of economic framework used in this review and, thus, are not discussed further below. These other areas include employment discrimination law, covered by Cain (1986) and Donohue (2007); minimum wage requirements, covered by Brown (1999); unemployment insurance systems, covered by Krueger & Meyer (2002); and rules governing discharge from employment, covered by Blau & Kahn (1999) and Jolls (2007).

Employment Law in the Absence of Market Failure

Most of the rules of employment law considered in this review reflect the imposition of a legally prescribed term governing the conditions of work into the parties' employment contract. This subsection describes the typical effects of such rules in the absence of market failure. The section on targeted mandates below shows how the analysis differs for rules that target the work conditions of discrete, identifiable subgroups of employees. Note that the framework described here does not apply to the rules establishing minimum wage and overtime pay requirements or to the rules governing discharge of employees because these forms of legal regulation directly operate on the wage or employment level in the regulated employment markets rather than on the conditions of work; overtime pay regulation is covered in the section on overtime pay requirements below.[2]

In speaking of legally prescribed terms within a contract, it is important to distinguish between mandatory and default terms. Mandatory terms are ones that cannot be changed by the parties even if they express a desire to do so. For instance, if the Occupational Safety and Health Act (OSHA), which regulates workplace safety in the United States, requires that a particular safety measure be adopted, employers and employees may not avoid the requirement simply by agreeing through contract that it does not apply. Default terms, by contrast, are terms that apply unless the parties reach a contrary agreement. Most employment law rules are mandatory rules, and the analysis to follow assumes that the rule in question is a mandatory one. The specific employment law rules discussed in the remainder of this review are all mandatory ones.

The legally prescribed terms that employment law specifies for the employer-employee relationship typically require employers to provide something of value—a safer workplace; privacy; certain fringe benefits; leaves from work in specified circumstances—to employees. Accordingly, within a simple labor supply and demand framework with no market failure of any sort, these rules will produce a downward shift in the labor supply curve by the amount of the value of the mandated benefit and a downward shift in the labor demand curve by the amount of the cost of the mandated benefit (Summers 1989). These effects are depicted graphically in Figure 1.

Within this simple framework, the effects of a particular employment law rule on efficiency and employee welfare will turn on the relative magnitude of the labor supply and labor demand shifts. If the downward shift in the labor supply curve (S° to S' in Figure 1) is less than the downward shift in the labor demand curve, then the wage will fall by more than the value of the legally mandated benefit to employees in the employment market in question, and employment (and, with it, efficiency and employee welfare) will fall (Figure 1, *top*). If, by contrast, the downward shift in the labor supply curve is larger than the downward shift in the labor demand

[2]As noted just above, minimum wage requirements and rules governing discharge from employment have been covered elsewhere.

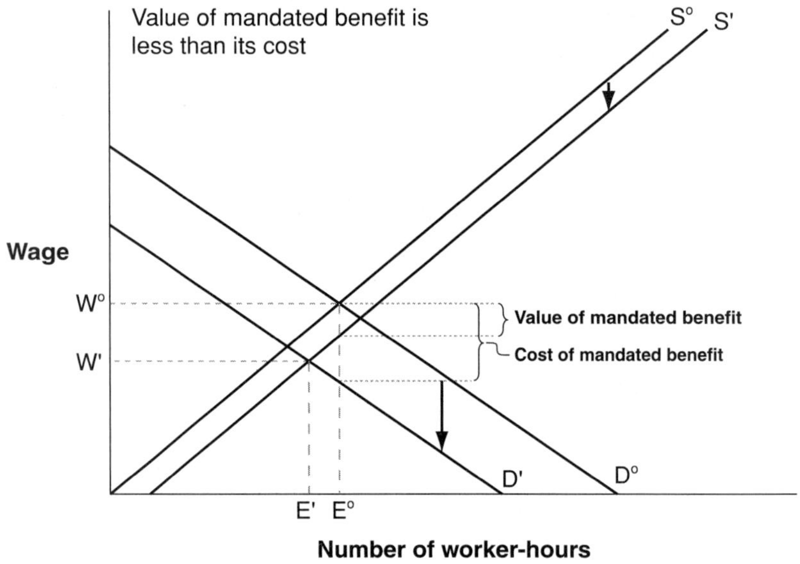

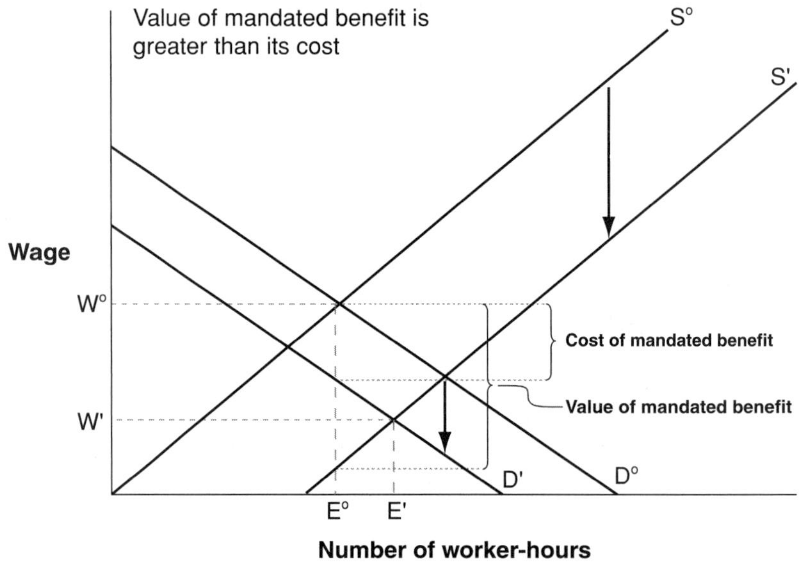

Figure 1 Labor market effects of legally mandated benefits in the absence of market failure. Employees are assumed to be demanded and paid in accordance with their marginal revenue product of labor (rather than, for example, earning efficiency wages), and the mandated benefit is assumed to be a variable-cost rather than a fixed-cost one.

curve, then the wage will fall by less than the value of the legally mandated benefit to employees, and employment (and with it, efficiency and employee welfare) will rise (Figure 1, *bottom*). But if that were the case, then, given the assumed lack of any form of market failure, employers would have offered the benefit without any need for a legal mandate.[3]

Thus, in the absence of market failure, employment law rules will generally reduce both efficiency and employee welfare. However, employment markets may fail for a variety of reasons. The next subsection describes the most commonly discussed market failures in the employer-employee relationship.

Market Failures in the Employer-Employee Relationship

As described above, market failures provide an organizing paradigm for the analysis of many major areas of employment law. This section describes the three forms of market failure that have featured most heavily in economic analysis of employment law.

INFORMATION FAILURES Of central importance in the employment setting are possible information failures. Information failures occur when some market participants lack information that bears upon their decisions in that market. In employer-employee relationships, both parties may suffer from information failures.

Employee-side information failures Some aspects of the employment relationship are likely to be relatively transparent to employees. Wages, for instance, are an aspect of the relationship about which employees will usually have good information. By contrast, the magnitude of the risk of long-term occupational disease is something about which employees will often not be well informed.

Employee-side information failures may be modeled in two distinct ways. One possibility is that employees with limited information are aware of their informational limits and take rational steps in response to those limits. As described below, this type of modeling assumption is often adopted in analyzing employer-side information failures. A second possibility is that employees with limited information either are not aware of their informational limits or do not change their behavior in response to such awareness. This is the usual modeling assumption adopted in analyzing employee-side information failures and is the assumption used in this review for analyzing such information failures.

If employees are unaware of some aspect of the employment relationship that would affect their willingness to supply labor, then observed labor supply will differ

[3]This analysis assumes that there is no binding legally specified minimum wage in the employment market in question. At least in the United States, the minimum wage is sufficiently low in most jurisdictions that it is not binding in most employment markets. With a binding minimum wage (meaning the market wage is near or below the legally prescribed minimum wage), the effects of legally mandated terms would be felt in employment levels rather than wages.

from employees' "true" willingness to supply labor. In the case of workplace safety, for instance, employees may lack adequate information about risks and harms and, as a result, may oversupply labor at a given wage rate. In terms of Figure 1 above, the labor supply curve is shifted toward S′, and employees behave *as if* their workplace were covered by an employment term fostering safety even though it is not. In such cases, the information failure means that some transactions that take place are inefficient—because the cost of supplying labor (measured by S° in Figure 1) in these transactions exceeds the marginal revenue product of labor (measured by D°); it also means that employees are worse off than they would be in a well-functioning market—because they are engaging in some transactions in which the cost of supplying labor exceeds the wage they earn. Employee-side information failures are discussed further in the sections on workplace safety and workplace privacy below.

Employer-side information failures Employers will frequently have only imperfect information about the attributes of their employees. This is particularly likely to be true at the point of hiring but may be true later on as well. A large literature in labor economics examines the consequences of such employer-side imperfect information for labor markets (e.g., Greenwald 1986, Gibbons & Katz 1991).

As noted above, the usual modeling assumption in the case of an employer-side information failure is that employers are aware of the limits on their information and respond rationally to these limits. Thus, the employers' information problem is typically modeled as a situation of adverse selection. Employer-side information failures and the resulting adverse selection problems are discussed further in the section on fringe benefits mandates below.

EXTERNALITIES A second potential failure in employment markets arises from the external effects of some decisions by market participants. If, for instance, an employee is killed or injured on the job, it is not only the employee (and possibly employer) who may suffer harm. Family members will typically suffer, though employees may usually take such effects into account. Systems of social support will often be affected as well. Although externalities are obviously a classic form of market failure, they have received less attention than information failures in the existing literature on the economics of employment law and, thus, receive relatively limited attention below.

EMPLOYEE-SIDE COGNITIVE BIAS A third potential failure in employment markets arises from the possibility that even employees with good general information will exhibit distorted labor supply decisions as a result of various forms of cognitive bias. A substantial literature shows that many individuals exhibit optimism bias, adjudging their personal probability of facing bad outcomes to be lower than the average probability of facing such outcomes (Weinstein 1980). Many people, for instance, believe that their chances of having an auto accident are significantly lower than the average person's chances of experiencing this event (DeJoy 1989), although of course these beliefs cannot all be correct, for if everyone were below "average," then the average would be lower. There is also evidence that people underestimate their absolute as well as relative (to other individuals) probability of experiencing negative events such as auto accidents (Arnould & Grabowski 1981, pp. 34–35; Camerer & Kunreuther 1989, p. 566).

From a modeling standpoint, optimism bias among employees is similar to the employee-side information failures discussed above. Parallel to the case of such information failures, the most natural assumption, and the one that will be utilized in this review, is that employees with optimism bias either are not aware of the bias or do not change their behavior in response to the bias.[4] Thus, as with information failures, if employees exhibit optimism bias in relation to some aspect of the employment relationship that affects their willingness to supply labor, then observed labor supply will differ from employees' true willingness to supply labor. In the case of workplace safety, for instance, optimism bias may lead even employees who have full information about the general risks and harms in their workplace to underestimate the probability that they personally will experience negative outcomes, and, as a result, they may oversupply labor. The effects of this were described in the discussion of employee-side information failures above. Optimism bias is discussed further in the sections on workplace safety and workplace privacy below.

WORKPLACE SAFETY MANDATES

The remainder of this review analyzes several of the major forms of legal regulation of the employer-employee relationship, beginning with the legal regulation of workplace safety.[5] Because many individuals spend a substantial fraction of their waking hours at work and often encounter risks in the course of work, workplace safety is a central issue of public policy, and many features of employment law are concerned with enhancing workplace safety. Legal regulation in this area includes both direct mandates of safe work conditions, as under OSHA in the United States, and indirect channels for improving workplace safety through the employer incentives created by mandated compensation for workplace injuries. This section emphasizes the first basic approach, whereas the second basic approach is covered by Krueger & Meyer (2002).

The general starting point for economic analysis of workplace safety regulation is the observation that in the absence of market failure, less safe working conditions

[4]Akerlof & Dickens (1982), by contrast, analyze workplace safety under the assumption that employees are aware of their tendency to believe (in Akerlof and Dickens's model, because of cognitive dissonance) that the workplace is safer than it is. Because of such awareness, employees in their model take action in response to their biased tendencies.

[5]The treatment offered below seeks to describe and synthesize the most influential economic analyses in each major area of employment law discussed, rather than to catalog in a comprehensive manner all existing economic analyses in each area.

should be fully compensated by higher wages—an application of the theory of equalizing wage differentials.[6] Viscusi (1978) and Viscusi & O'Connor (1984), among others, present evidence of adjustments in wages in response to workplace risks. However, as is widely acknowledged, the evidence on risk-based adjustments in wages is limited in two important ways. First, without some independent way of monetizing the cost of a higher-risk job, at most the empirical evidence can tell us that wages move in a particular *direction* in relation to risk; it cannot tell us whether wages adjust *by the right amount* (given the employee's underlying preferences) in light of workplace risks. Movement in one direction or the other is ultimately a fairly weak test of the theory of equalizing wage differentials. The second limitation is that sources of credible identification of empirical effects are extremely difficult to find in this area because employees who select into different types of jobs with different levels of associated risk may differ along important dimensions that are not observed by the analyst; and moreover, the jobs into which employees select may also differ along dimensions that are not observed by the analyst. If either individual or job characteristics that are unobservable by the analyst are correlated with job risks, then correlations between risks and wages may be entirely spurious. Employment law, not satisfied that equalizing wage differentials fully address the issue of workplace safety, has chosen to regulate workplace safety in both the direct and indirect ways noted above.

Theoretical Analysis of Workplace Safety Mandates

The most direct form of workplace safety regulation is workplace safety mandates. These mandates require particular workplace practices intended to enhance workplace safety. In the United States, as previously noted, OSHA imposes a range of such mandates, which are described in detail in, for instance, Smith (1976) and Mendeloff (1979).

Within economic analysis, workplace safety mandates are typically justified on the ground that either information failures or optimism bias on the part of employees leads them to oversupply labor at a given wage rate. Frequently employees will not be aware of the risks of a particular workplace, and even employees who have good information about the general risks of their workplace may overoptimistically assume that those risks do not apply to them personally.

As noted in the earlier discussion of market failures in the employer-employee relationship, an oversupply of labor because of information failures, optimism bias, or both means that some inefficient transactions are taking place and that employees are worse off than they would be in a well-functioning market. Workplace injuries may also have important externality effects, but the informational and cognitive problems have been central in the existing literature. In the presence of such problems, workplace safety mandates can in theory improve both efficiency and employee welfare by eliminating the inefficient and detrimental (to employees)

[6]Brown (1980) offers a general treatment of the topic of equalizing wage differentials.

transactions described in the discussion of employee-side information failures above. If observed labor supply under a mandate matches the "true" willingness to supply labor (because the workplace is safe, consistent with employees' belief), then only efficient transactions will occur, and employees will accept employment only to the extent that the wage equals or exceeds their "true" cost of supplying labor. Of course, in the real world the mandated levels of workplace safety may not match employees' beliefs or may be exorbitantly expensive; responding to even a genuine employee-side informational or cognitive problem does not guarantee that efficiency and employee welfare will rise under a workplace safety mandate. Ultimately, the effects of a workplace safety mandate are an empirical question.[7]

Empirical Analysis of Workplace Safety Mandates

As just noted, the central question about workplace safety mandates concerns their empirical effects on wages, employment levels, and, of course, workplace safety. A large empirical literature (comprehensively surveyed through the early 1990s by Smith 1992) has attempted to identify such effects. This literature has focused on workplace injuries (in the sense of immediate negative health effects), as distinguished from longer-term health risks from work; this focus is reflected in the discussion below. As the discussion below will make clear, the overall body of empirical evidence suggests modest (at best) effects of workplace safety mandates on observed levels of workplace safety, and, presumably because of the limited evidence of effects on the basic level of workplace safety, wage and employment effects of workplace safety mandates have generally not been studied. Most of the empirical evidence on the effects of workplace safety mandates comes from the United States, and that focus is reflected in the discussion below.

Workplace safety mandates in the United States operate at the federal level, and, as a result of OSHA's status as a federal law, state law variation generally cannot be used to identify OSHA's effects.[8] Ruser & Smith (1988) offer a limited exception to this statement. They examine the effects of the initiation of a records-check procedure in some but not all states on the level of reported workplace injuries; they

[7]Not addressed in this discussion is the possibility that workplace safety mandates may affect the degree of precautionary behavior by employees. Rea (1981) offers related discussion, although his analysis is primarily focused on compensation systems for workplace injuries (such as workers' compensation) rather than on workplace safety mandates.

[8]Much empirical work in employment law, including the work described in several of the sections below as well as much work in the employment discrimination area (e.g., Neumark & Stock 1999, Jolls 2004, Jolls & Prescott 2004), exploits variation in legal innovation across states to identify the effects of such innovation. With change over time but no cross-state variation—as with a federal law such as OSHA—it is often difficult to disentangle the effects of the law's enactment from other unobserved changes occurring at the same time. Indeed, as Smith (1992) notes, even a simple national-level before-after comparison of injury rates in relation to OSHA's enactment is not possible because OSHA significantly changed the manner of collecting data on workplace safety.

find a lower level of reported injuries with the records-check procedure in place, but they are unable to determine from their data whether this results from a true reduction in injury rates or (the interpretation they emphasize) an increase in the frequency of underreporting because under the records-check procedure underreporting would reduce the likelihood of costly safety inspections. Ruser & Smith's study is largely concerned with effects on reporting levels rather than the more basic issue of effects on workplace safety. Morantz (2003) also makes use of state law variation in the OSHA context. Morantz examines how injury rates among construction workers vary with federal versus state enforcement of OSHA's substantive provisions and finds significantly lower injury rates in states with federal enforcement. Although the injury rate data do not go back far enough to allow Morantz to examine changes over time with the move from federal to state enforcement (so that, in contrast to Ruser & Smith, identification is based on cross-state variation only, rather than variation across both states and time), Morantz's empirical approach does attempt to control comprehensively for other cross-state differences, apart from federal versus state enforcement, that could be influencing injury rates.

Other empirical work on OSHA has examined variation in its enforcement over time or across industries (rather than across states) as a source of identification of the law's effects on workplace safety. In light of the low financial penalties for the typical OSHA violation and the low likelihood of OSHA inspections (Viscusi 1979, Weil 1996), many have questioned whether OSHA is likely to have any effect on workplace safety at all, regardless of variation in enforcement within the low observed ranges of penalties and inspection frequencies. Viscusi (1979) and Bartel & Thomas (1985), for instance, find limited or no relationship between measures of OSHA enforcement and injury rates, while Viscusi (1986) finds at best a modest relationship.

Scholz & Gray (1990) have suggested, however, that the limited effects of OSHA on injury rates in many empirical studies reflect the overly generalized approach of these studies. Scholz & Gray focus on the firms most likely to be affected by OSHA—large, frequently inspected firms—and find significant effects of OSHA enforcement on injury rates in their sample. Unlike earlier studies, Scholz & Gray's study uses plant-level rather than industry-level data on OSHA enforcement levels and injury rates. However, a recent study by Gray & Mendeloff (2005) using a methodology similar to that in Scholz & Gray (1990) found that the significant effects of OSHA on injury rates lasted only through the early 1990s and were not apparent in data for most of the 1990s.

While the central variable of policy interest in studying OSHA's effects is the workplace injury rate, several studies have examined the relationship between the level of OSHA enforcement and the degree of firms' observed compliance with OSHA's requirements. Bartel & Thomas (1985) and Weil (1996), for instance, find evidence of significant effects of enforcement on compliance with OSHA's requirements, notwithstanding the general evidence, noted above, of very limited levels of OSHA enforcement. By contrast, Weil (2001) finds only limited effects of enforcement activity on compliance in the construction industry.

Ultimately, the existing empirical work provides relatively little evidence of effects of OSHA on injury rates, with slightly more evidence of compliance effects. The lack of variation across states has, not surprisingly, impeded efforts to pin down the effects of OSHA's workplace safety mandates more definitively. While the theory suggesting the likelihood of market failure in the workplace safety context seems strong, direct empirical evidence on the effects of OSHA has, at least thus far, not provided a clear basis for concluding that this law has enhanced efficiency and employee welfare or, even more basically, that the law has decreased workplace injuries.

WORKPLACE PRIVACY MANDATES

A very rapidly growing area of employment law—particularly with the increasing presence of computers and the associated monitoring possibilities in the workplace—is workplace privacy. Issues of workplace privacy span a broad array of domains. Questions include the degree to which employers may videotape or audiotape their employees' activities in the workplace, the restrictions (if any) on drug and alcohol testing of employees, the degree to which employers may engage in various forms of monitoring of employees' activities on computers, and the limits on employers' disclosure of medical and other personal information about employees. Workplace privacy mandates require employers to conduct activities of this sort in specified ways, if at all. This section briefly highlights the central issues in the economic analysis of such workplace privacy mandates.

Theoretical Analysis of Workplace Privacy Mandates

From an economic standpoint, the possible market failures in the workplace privacy setting parallel the main potential market failures in the workplace safety context. One potential market failure is an employee-side information failure; for some forms of privacy-related employer behavior, the employee may simply have no idea that the behavior is occurring. Employees may assume that their privacy is protected at work, just as they may assume that their workplace is safe. Examples in the privacy context include video or audio monitoring and the monitoring of employees' computers—practices of which employees may be entirely unaware. In other settings, by contrast, an employee may know when a particular invasion of privacy occurs; an example is urine testing for drug use—an employer practice that obviously cannot be done without the employee's knowledge.

Even employees who have accurate information about an employer's general practices in relation to workplace privacy may be led by optimism bias to underestimate the likelihood that the at-issue employer behavior will be undertaken in relation to, or have a negative effect upon, them as opposed to other employees. The analysis is again parallel to the workplace safety context, in which employees may underestimate their personal likelihood of workplace risks. Note that in the workplace privacy context, the risks of market failure related to optimism bias will tend to be greater when there is more uncertainty in the employer's policy. For instance, employees may underestimate the likelihood that they will be subjected to a drug test under an employer policy permitting drug testing of employees involved in a workplace accident, simply because employees may tend to underestimate the likelihood that they will be involved in such an accident. By contrast, if an employer policy provides that employees will be subjected to ongoing video or audio monitoring as a matter of course, then optimism bias is likely to be less important—although optimistically biased employees could still underestimate the likelihood that the monitoring will detect a prohibited behavior on their part.

Parallel to the discussion of workplace safety above, a workplace privacy mandate may address an employee-side information failure or cognitive bias by eliminating the gap between observed labor supply and the "true" willingness to supply labor (because privacy is now protected at the workplace, consistent with employees' expectation). Of course, as above, whether any given workplace privacy mandate actually has positive effects on efficiency and employee welfare is ultimately an empirical question.

Empirical Analysis of Workplace Privacy Mandates

Very little empirical evidence currently exists on the effects of workplace privacy mandates. However, in the case of the United States, the existence of variation in these mandates across states and time suggests the potential value of empirical inquiry in this area. Whether wages and employment levels would ever move to a discernible degree in response to workplace privacy mandates is unclear, but effects on observable outcomes other than wages and employment levels may be easier to detect. Jacobson (2003), for instance, presents evidence of better safety outcomes in safety-sensitive occupations in states that enacted legislation clarifying the permissibility of drug testing for safety-sensitive positions than in states that did not enact such legislation. There is some suggestion of preexisting trends in the enacting states, so the results should be viewed with some caution, but Jacobson also finds improved safety outcomes after the imposition of federally mandated drug testing for certain safety-sensitive positions. Jacobson's findings suggest that some forms of workplace privacy mandates (especially in the drug testing context) may have the unfortunate effect of worsening safety outcomes. Additional empirical work on the effects of workplace privacy mandates is likely to appear as these mandates become increasingly common.

FRINGE BENEFITS MANDATES

Employers may be responsible not only for improved workplace conditions—including safety and privacy—but also for the provision of important fringe benefits. Fringe benefits are usually understood to include such benefits as health insurance and pensions. The present section focuses on the legal regulation of health insurance, the great majority of which is provided through the employment relationship (although this is less true outside the United States). Pension-related mandates are not considered in this review because there is very little existing literature on the effects of such mandates on wages, employment levels, or other labor market outcomes.[9]

With respect to health insurance mandates, the Medicare program in the United States requires compulsory payroll deductions by employers and offers government-provided health insurance to (primarily) retirement-aged individuals. Under this program, individuals see a deduction from their paychecks during their working years and then are entitled to health insurance financed by the federal government during their retirement. (By contrast, the Medicaid program in the United States is targeted to the needy and is not linked to the employment relationship in any way.) The Medicare system is covered by Currie & Madrian (1999) and Cutler (2002); the focus of the present section is other types of health insurance mandates.

Both federal and state law in the United States play a role in structuring the system of health insurance mandates considered in this section. The federal role here is twofold. First, ERISA broadly preempts, or renders inapplicable, all state-level health insurance mandates insofar as employer-provided health insurance is concerned, unless the employer-provided insurance is procured from an insurance company. Thus, any employer that self-insures—as many now do—is not subject to any health insurance mandates imposed at the state level. Second, federal law imposes a few limited mandates on health insurance plans. One such mandate is contained in the Consolidated Omnibus Budget Reconciliation Act (COBRA), which requires that, above a certain employer-size threshold, employees be allowed to continue purchasing health insurance through their former employer for up to 18 months after leaving that employer. A second source of federal health insurance mandates is the Health Insurance Portability and Accountability Act (HIPAA), which imposes a variety of requirements on employers and other health insurance providers, including mandated coverage for preexisting conditions.[10]

State-level health insurance mandates, to the extent that their application is not preempted by ERISA, also impose a variety of requirements on health insurance

[9]The central law governing pensions in the United States is the Employment Retirement Income Security Act (ERISA), a federal law that broadly displaces potential state-level regulation of pensions and, thus, leaves little opportunity for credible identification (through state-level variation in legal innovation) of the effects of legal regulation of pensions. See Ippolito (1988) for further discussion of the effects of the pension-related mandates imposed by ERISA.

[10]Moreover, recently enacted HIPAA regulations impose a series of privacy-related requirements on employers concerning the disclosure of medical information; those requirements may be analyzed under the framework set forth in the section on workplace privacy above. An additional federal law regulating health insurance is the Mental Health Parity Act. As explained in the discussion of targeted mandates below, this law is best viewed as a targeted mandate and, thus, is discussed below.

plans; for instance, some state laws impose continuation coverage mandates similar to the mandate in COBRA (see Gruber & Madrian 1994). State-level regulation is discussed briefly below where its mandates overlap with federal requirements, but, because of the preemption issue noted above, the focus of this section is on federal health insurance mandates.[11]

Theoretical Analysis of Fringe Benefits Mandates

Several potential market failures, including employee-side information failures and cognitive biases, may be relevant to analysis of the health insurance mandates noted just above, but perhaps the most obvious employment market failure in this context involves employer-side imperfect information. (For discussion of the broader issue of provision of health insurance through, rather than independently of, the employment relationship, see Currie & Madrian 1999.) For instance, an individual employer opting unilaterally to offer continuation coverage of the sort required by COBRA might disproportionately attract employees who are less likely to remain employed (especially those who simultaneously have concerns about their future health) and, thus, who are particularly focused on the issue of continuation coverage. The problem of adverse selection here is straightforward.

If the value to employees of a particular form of health insurance coverage (such as continuation coverage) exceeds the cost of providing such coverage, then mandating such coverage may efficiently respond to the adverse selection problem just described. Of course, in the case of continuation coverage, employers in an ideal world might offer not this type of coverage but, instead, employee-specific packages of wages and health insurance tailored to each employee's individual costs and needs (Gruber & Madrian 1994). However, as Gruber & Madrian note, the barriers to such an approach—whether achieved voluntarily or through legal regulation—in the real world are clear, and thus mandated continuation coverage, as under COBRA, may be a good second-best solution. Empirical evidence on the effects of both mandated continuation coverage and mandated coverage for preexisting conditions is noted in the next section.

Empirical Analysis of Fringe Benefits Mandates

Empirical evidence on the effects of continuation coverage mandates on a variety of employment-related outcomes is examined in Currie & Madrian (1999); the discussion there of the studies by Gruber & Madrian (1994, 1995, 1996, 1997) of both COBRA and state-level continuation coverage mandates is especially relevant. On balance, continuation coverage mandates appear to increase both separation and retirement from work by employees; effects on overall wage and employment

[11]Economic analyses of the effects of various state-level health insurance mandates include Gruber (1994a), Kaestner & Simon (2002), and Simon (2005); Cutler (2002) also offers discussion of these mandates.

levels (which would permit conclusions about the welfare effects of continuation coverage mandates) presumably were not large enough to be studied empirically.

With respect to preexisting conditions coverage mandates, Cutler (2002) discusses the effects of various state-level health insurance mandates, including preexisting condition coverage mandates, on health insurance coverage rates. In addition, recent studies by Kaestner & Simon (2002) and Simon (2005) have also examined the effects of state-level health insurance mandates, including preexisting condition coverage mandates, while Sanz-de-Galdeano (2006) has studied the effects of HIPAA, which (as noted above) includes a preexisting conditions coverage mandate. The body of existing empirical work suggests that these mandates have limited or no effects on insurance coverage rates, wage and employment levels, or other outcomes.

TARGETED MANDATES

While the employment law mandates discussed in the previous sections are mandates predominantly directed to employees as a whole rather than to any discrete subgroup of employees, other employment law mandates are targeted to particular demographic subgroups. Indeed, many employment law mandates—including much of employment discrimination law (examined from an economic perspective in the employment-related portions of Donohue 2007), as well as rules such as mandated workplace leave (covered in this section)—are targeted in this way. The direct effects of these targeted mandates will be felt primarily or exclusively by demographic subgroups of employees, such as individuals with disabilities, women, or members of particular racial groups, rather than by employees as a whole.

Of course, no benefits mandate may be entirely untargeted; many mandates may tend to benefit some demographic groups more than others. Thus, the difference between general and targeted mandates is probably best viewed as a difference in degree rather than a difference in kind.

The importance of distinguishing between general and targeted mandates arises from the fact that the subgroups to which targeted mandates are directed are generally groups whose wages and employment opportunities are legally required to match those of the nontargeted employees. In the absence of such requirements (or if such requirements were not binding),[12] the targeted subgroup could simply be treated as a separate labor market, and the same basic sort of analysis as was discussed in the previous sections would continue to apply. However, in the presence of binding restrictions on differential treatment across groups, the analysis of targeted mandates proves to be quite different from the analysis employed until this point in the review. As described more fully below, employment law rules targeted to demographic subgroups of employees constitute an important exception

[12]More precisely, if restrictions on wage differentials between the two groups were not binding. See Jolls (2000) for further discussion.

to the general focus in this review on market failure as a necessary condition for employment law regulation to enhance employee welfare. If the goal of a targeted mandate is to enhance the welfare of targeted employees—as it often is—then the desired result may obtain wholly apart from any sort of market failure. Because of the importance of this point, and for the sake of analytical clarity, this section will analyze targeted mandates on the assumption of no market failure of any sort. The analysis below could readily be adjusted to incorporate market failure in combination with a targeted rather than general mandate.[13]

Theoretical Analysis of Targeted Mandates

With a targeted mandate and no market failure of any sort, labor supply with the mandate in place will shift exclusively or disproportionately for the targeted employees, rather than (as in the previous sections) for employees as a whole. Meanwhile, on the employer side, the total marginal revenue product of labor (reflecting, among other things, the cost of the mandated benefit) will shift exclusively or disproportionately for the targeted group. If, for instance, employers are legally required to provide leave from work following the birth of a child, as they are in many countries, then both the willingness to supply labor and the total marginal revenue product of labor are likely to shift disproportionately for female employees.

Because of the differential effects of a targeted mandate across groups of employees, it is important for purposes of the analysis of such mandates to separate out two distinct labor markets: the market for employees targeted by the mandate and the market for the remaining employees. Each market will have its own labor supply and demand functions (although, as described below, the demand functions will end up being the same if restrictions on wage and employment differentials are binding). And, because the demand for employees of one type will depend, among other things, on the demand for employees of the other type, it will no longer be possible to capture the full set of dynamics on a single, two-dimensional labor supply and demand diagram, as in Figure 1.

In this environment, the effects of a targeted mandate depend very much on the degree to which restrictions on wage and employment differentials are binding. One possibility is that restrictions on wage differentials are not binding (and restrictions on employment differentials are or are not binding); in this case, as noted above, a targeted mandate may be analyzed within the basic type of framework used in the previous sections. A second possibility is that restrictions on wage differentials are binding, while restrictions on employment differentials are not; in this case targeted employees will effectively be more expensive to employ

[13]This section emphasizes that targeted mandates may improve targeted employees' welfare even in the absence of a market failure. Minimum wage rules represent another example of employment law regulation that can help employees (in the sense of raising total employee income) even in the absence of a market failure. As noted above, Brown (1999) provides further discussion of minimum wage rules.

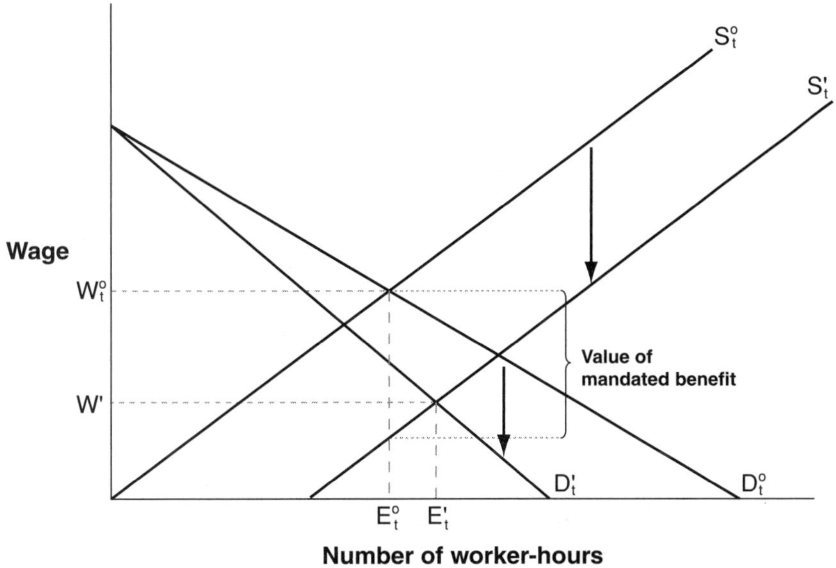

Figure 2 Effects of a targeted mandate on wages and employment of targeted employees.

(as they must earn the same wage but cost the employer more), and employers will thus tend to reduce their hiring of targeted employees. The final possibility, and the one that will be examined in the remainder of this section, occurs when restrictions on both wage and employment differentials are binding. In this case there must not be any difference between the wages or employment opportunities of targeted and nontargeted employees within a given employment market; employers must pay each type of employee the same wage and must demand each type in proportion to its willingness to supply labor at that wage. In this circumstance, Jolls (2000) shows that the effects of a targeted mandate on the wages and employment of targeted employees can be captured in simple graphical form in a figure (illustrated by Figure 2) similar though not identical to Figure 1 above.

In Figure 2, S_t° and S_t' are the pre- and postmandate labor supply curves for targeted employees; D_t° is the premandate labor demand curve for targeted employees; and D_t' is a lower bound on the ultimate postmandate labor demand curve for targeted employees (meaning that the latter curve must lie above the curve D_t' in Figure 2).[14]

In analyzing the effects of a targeted mandate on the wages and employment levels of targeted employees, it is useful to separate the analysis into distinct

[14]See Jolls (2000) for an explanation of why the curve D_t' is steeper than the curve D_t°.

cases based on the relationship between the value and the cost of the mandated benefit. The straightforward case is the one in which the value of the mandated benefit equals or exceeds its cost.[15] In this case, not surprisingly, the targeted employees' wage will fall by less than the value of the mandated benefit, while their employment level will rise. This situation is depicted graphically in Figure 2. The other case is the one in which the value of the mandated benefit is less than its cost. In this case it is no longer certain that targeted employees will be better off after the mandate is imposed, but it remains reasonably likely. Indeed, as long as the fraction of nontargeted individuals in the qualified population is not too small, and the gap between the value and the cost of the mandated benefit is not too large, a targeted mandate will always make targeted employees better off, as explained in Jolls (2000). Intuitively, under these conditions the cost of the mandated benefit that is actually borne by the targeted group will be smaller than the value of the mandated benefit to this group.

Thus, targeted mandates may be justifiable on distributive grounds even when the cost of the mandated benefit exceeds its value. (Of course, distributive goals might alternatively be achieved through a tax-and-transfer regime.) In the case of general mandates, by contrast, distributive considerations cannot justify legal intervention when the cost of the mandated benefit exceeds its value because, as shown in Figure 1 (*top*), the employees' wage will fall by more than the value of the benefit to them. This effect occurs because there is no other group to whom to shift costs. But with targeted mandates, even if the value of the mandated benefit is less than its cost, the mandate may make targeted employees better off because nontargeted employees will bear some of the associated cost.

The point about potential distributive gains wholly apart from market failure is especially important because the fact that the value of a mandated benefit is less than its cost may reflect precisely the undesirable distributive situation that employment law seeks to remedy. The reason is that "value" in this framework is measured by employees' willingness to pay for the benefit by accepting lower wages, and the distributive situation of targeted employees might preclude them from accepting lower wages (see generally Dworkin 1980). If, for instance, a mandate requires employers to provide medical leave to employees with serious medical problems, the value (measured by willingness to pay) of this benefit to the targeted employees may be limited not by the utility of the leave to these employees but by their financial position. Mandated medical leave is discussed further in the next section.

---

[15] In the absence of any market failure—the assumption maintained throughout this section—a benefit whose value equals or exceeds its cost might, but conceivably would not, be provided in the absence of a mandate. Because the benefit accrues exclusively or disproportionately to targeted employees, it seems possible that the benefit would not be provided (with binding restrictions on wage and employment differentials) even if the value of the benefit exceeded its cost. This issue is not analyzed rigorously here, however.

Empirical Analysis of Targeted Mandates

As suggested above, many targeted mandates arise under employment discrimination law and, for that reason, are not analyzed further in this review.[16] The primary employment law application of the analysis of targeted mandates is workplace leave mandates, which at least in the United States arise under employment law outside of what is generally considered employment discrimination law.[17] Workplace leave mandates in the United States disproportionately target both disabled employees (through mandated entitlement to medical leave) and female employees (through mandated entitlement to leave following the birth of a child).[18] These two aspects of mandated workplace leave are considered in turn below.[19]

MANDATED MEDICAL LEAVE As noted above, the wage and employment effects of a targeted mandate depend significantly on the degree to which restrictions on wage and employment differentials between targeted and nontargeted employees are binding. Starting with restrictions on wage differentials, such restrictions are likely to be binding in the absence of significant occupational segregation between targeted and nontargeted groups. Legal restrictions on wage differentials are generally fairly easy to enforce (e.g., Posner 1987), and, moreover, employers may have incentives to adhere to norms of pay equity wholly apart from legal restrictions because of the potential morale problems that can result from inequity in wages between different groups performing the same work.

In the case of mandated entitlement to medical leave, the group of employees disproportionately (though of course not exclusively) targeted by such a mandate is employees with disabilities, some of whom will be significantly more likely to require leave than nondisabled employees. With respect to occupational segregation,

---

[16]Disability discrimination law, for instance, requires employers to make reasonable accommodations for disabling conditions—a mandate targeted to employees with disabilities (DeLeire 2000, Acemoglu & Angrist 2001). Similarly, to the extent that sex discrimination law requires health insurance coverage of maternity-related medical costs, it imposes a mandate targeted to female employees (Gruber 1994b).

[17]The Family and Medical Leave Act (FMLA), which requires employers to provide employees with leave from work under specified conditions, is not part of any of the employment discrimination statutes in the United States and is administered by the Department of Labor rather than the agency (the Equal Employment Opportunity Commission) that administers employment discrimination statutes.

[18]Mandated leave following the birth of a child is targeted to female employees even though leave is typically available to male employees because female employees who have biological children will require at least a brief period of time off from work after a birth to recover from the temporary disability associated with giving birth and, thus, will almost certainly (for purely biological reasons) be more likely than male employees to take leave.

[19]Another targeted mandate in the United States is the Mental Health Parity Act, which requires that coverage of mental and physical conditions under health insurance plans be comparable. Because this law is generally believed to be of modest practical impact, it seems unlikely to be the source of observable empirical effects.

at least in the United States employees with disabilities are not significantly segregated, so restrictions on wage differentials between employees with and without disabilities are likely to bind.

Likewise, with respect to restrictions on employment differentials, while these restrictions are unlikely to bind directly for employees with and without disabilities because of the difficulty of enforcing such restrictions (e.g., Posner 1987), the ultimate effect may be the same in analyzing mandated entitlement to medical leave because many of the conditions for which such leave will be required are unobservable to employers at the time of hiring and, thus, cannot be the basis of differential employment decisions (Jolls 2006). In this case, the analysis of targeted mandates above predicts that mandated entitlement to medical leave will increase both wages and employment levels of employees with disabilities, unless either the fraction of targeted individuals in the qualified population is too large or the cost of the leave significantly exceeds its value. In the United States, because medical leave under the FMLA is unpaid, it seems unlikely that the cost of this benefit significantly exceeds its value.

A straightforward empirical measure of the wage and employment effects of mandated entitlement to medical leave under the FMLA on employees with disabilities is a comparison of wages and employment levels of such individuals before and after the FMLA went into effect—ideally with an additional comparison between states in which mandated entitlement to medical leave under the FMLA was an innovation and those in which it was not. Both approaches suggest neutral to positive effects of mandated entitlement to medical leave on disabled employment levels (relative to nondisabled employment levels), with the most credible evidence suggesting positive effects (Jolls 2006). This evidence underlines the prospects for positive effects of targeted mandates on the employment opportunities of targeted employees, consistent with the theoretical analysis offered above.

MANDATED LEAVE FOLLOWING THE BIRTH OF A CHILD As noted above, relatively limited degrees of occupational segregation (as in the case of employees with and without disabilities in the United States) suggest that restrictions on wage differentials will be binding. But in the case of male and female employees—the groups likely to be disparately affected by mandated entitlement to leave following the birth of a child—employment markets remain quite segregated (e.g., Blau & Kahn 1999). With substantial occupational segregation, restrictions on wage differentials will tend to be of little force because the only comparisons that are drawn in the law are those between employees within the same employment market (or, more technically, those performing the same or similar work). As noted above, in the absence of binding restrictions on wage differentials, an analysis similar to that used in the previous sections remains applicable to the case of a targeted mandate.[20]

---

[20]Of course, very few employment markets are actually perfectly segregated, so that there is absolutely no opportunity to compare targeted and nontargeted employees' wage levels.

Mandated entitlement to leave from work following the birth of a child exists in a wide array of countries and has been extensively studied. Waldfogel (1999), for instance, examines female employees' wages and employment levels in the aftermath of the FMLA's enactment in the United States and finds no consistent pattern of statistically significant results. The lack of clear results may stem in part from the fact that, as Waldfogel notes, many female employees were entitled (by state legislation or firm policy) to FMLA-type benefits following the birth of a child even prior to the FMLA's enactment.

Another test of the effects of mandated entitlement to leave following the birth of a child comes from looking at the effects of European leave laws. Ruhm (1998), for instance, finds that the length of the leave period under these laws generally is negatively related to the wages of female employees and positively related to their employment levels. Note that because employees' leave is paid, in contrast to the situation under the FMLA, positive employment effects are more likely under the European laws, which are presumably valued more by employees than the FMLA because of the paid nature of the leave. (Negative labor demand effects of paid leave are blunted by government rather than employer financing of the leave.) An exception to the general pattern of Ruhm's findings is that the effect of having some mandated leave versus none—as distinguished from the effect of having a short mandated leave versus a long mandated leave—has no statistically significant effect (rather than a statistically significant negative effect) on wages of female employees. This may result from the fact that a short leave, as opposed to a long leave, imposes relatively few costs on employers, and thus provides little occasion for a wage adjustment.[21]

Overall, the empirical evidence on mandated entitlement to leave following the birth of a child suggests neutral to positive employment effects—the same broad pattern as with mandated entitlements to medical leave. Wage effects, by contrast, appear more negative with mandated leave after the birth of a child—a likely consequence of the degree of occupational segregation by sex. Note, however, that because sex (in contrast to many medical conditions) is easily observable to employers, decreasing occupational segregation by sex over time is more likely to generate job losses from mandated entitlement to leave following the birth of a child (as wage adjustments are precluded by decreased segregation) than to produce the benefits for targeted employees that may come from mandated entitlement to medical leave.

Jolls (2000) provides further discussion of the reasons that markets with significant segregation are nonetheless most naturally modeled as markets in which restrictions on wage differentials are not binding.

[21] An important subtlety in discerning the effects of mandated entitlement to leave following the birth of a child is that, as Waldfogel (1998, 1999) emphasizes, such mandates may have a sort of composition effect, moving female employees into, or keeping them in, better, higher-level jobs. If this is so, then the aggregate effects of the mandates may be more mixed and more complex than the effects suggested by the theoretical framework described above.

OVERTIME PAY REQUIREMENTS

Employers are often legally required to pay a wage premium for hours worked above a specified weekly or other threshold. In the United States, for instance, employers generally must pay one and a half times the normal wage for hours worked above 40 hours per week. This section describes both theoretical and empirical analysis of such overtime pay requirements.

Theoretical Analysis of Overtime Pay Requirements

Overtime pay requirements, like the employment law rules discussed in the preceding sections, represent a legally prescribed term in the employment relationship. However, there is an important analytic difference between overtime pay requirements and the rules considered in all of the preceding sections. In the case of overtime pay requirements, the legally prescribed term simply concerns the form within which dollars are paid to an employee, rather than some other aspect (such as the safety or privacy) of the job. In principle, then, it may be possible for employers to undo completely the effects of overtime pay requirements (Ehrenberg & Schumann 1982, pp. 36–37). To borrow Trejo's (1991) example, suppose that in the absence of overtime pay regulation, an employee works 50 hours per week and earns $11 per hour. The employer in this circumstance could satisfy the FLSA by reducing the employee's straight-time wage to $10 per hour and then paying time and a half for the 10 hours in excess of the 40-hour-per-week cutoff. The employee would be in an identical situation, working 50 hours per week for $550 in pay. By contrast, when, for instance, a particular workplace safety mandate is put into effect, employers in the new equilibrium must provide the new safety feature (possibly compensated by lower wages) and cannot directly replicate the prior equilibrium.

Of course, there are limits on the foregoing account of the undoing of overtime pay requirements. To the extent that straight-time wages are at least somewhat sticky, employers may not be able to adjust such wages continuously over time in response to the number of desired overtime hours. In addition, adjustment will be either impossible or limited for employees whose straight-time wages are at or near the legal minimum wage level prior to any requirement of overtime pay. Both of these points are emphasized by Trejo (1991). Ultimately, then, empirical evidence is necessary to determine whether the theoretical account of the irrelevance of overtime pay requirements is true in practice.

To the extent that overtime pay requirements are not completely undone—as a result of various forms of wage stickiness or other factors—is there a market failure to which overtime pay requirements might be thought to be responsive? The conventional view is that intensive use of a smaller set of employees, instead of reliance on a broader group of employees, has a negative externality effect on those individuals who are unable to obtain employment when a smaller group of employees is used intensively. To the extent that overtime pay requirements increase employment levels to some degree, it is possible that these requirements represent an effective response to the negative externality just noted.

Empirical Analysis of Overtime Pay Requirements

In an effort to determine whether overtime pay requirements are effectively undone by changes in base wages, Trejo (1991) studies differences in base wages across employees covered and not covered by the overtime pay requirements of the Fair Labor Standards Act (FLSA) in the United States. The noncovered employees used in Trejo's analyses—who are comparable to covered employees in being paid on an hourly basis—include nonsupervisory agricultural workers, many transportation employees, and certain retail and services employees. (The largest group of employees not covered by the overtime pay requirements are employees who are paid on a salary rather than an hourly basis, but these individuals would, for obvious reasons, provide a weak control group for examining the effects of overtime pay requirements on covered, hourly wage employees.) Using a sample of repeated cross sections, Trejo finds that the hourly wages of covered employees are significantly lower than the hourly wages of noncovered employees. According to Trejo, this evidence provides some suggestion that overtime pay requirements are partially, although not completely, undone by adjustments in straight-time wages. Potential limits on Trejo's empirical analysis include the fact that the results are somewhat sensitive to the measure of wages used (with weekly earnings yielding results different from those just described) and the limited degree of identification resulting from possible unobservable differences across individuals in hourly wage jobs within covered versus noncovered sectors. In contrast to Trejo, Hunt (1999), examining evidence from Germany, finds increases rather than decreases in wages in response to strengthened overtime pay requirements negotiated between unions (which are industry-wide in Germany) and employers; wages may well be less flexible in Europe than in the United States. Hunt's identification strategy has the virtue of employing both cross-sectional and time series variation.

In addition to examination of whether base wages adjust to offset overtime pay requirements, empirical work has directly studied the linked question of whether workweeks longer than 40 hours in the United States are less frequent with overtime pay requirements in place. (Only with imperfect wage adjustments should such workweeks be less frequent with overtime pay requirements in place.) Costa (2000) examines changes in the frequency of overtime hours with the passage of the FLSA and finds a significant reduction in the proportion of employees working such hours. Costa also finds much greater reduction in the South—in which more employees were at the minimum wage level and, thus, could not be subjected to wage adjustments in response to overtime pay requirements—than in the North. By contrast, Trejo (2003), using as a source of identification variation over the 1970s and 1980s in the proportion of employees within an industry who are subject to the overtime pay requirements of the FLSA, finds no effect of overtime pay requirements on the frequency of workweeks longer than 40 hours in specifications that include industry time trends. However, as Trejo notes, the coefficients on coverage changes are imprecisely estimated, making it difficult to discern whether the absence of a statistically significant effect suggests no underlying effect or simply the limited power of the empirical approach. Hamermesh & Trejo (2000) study not the FLSA but a California state law expanding the set of employees covered by a strict form of overtime pay and find significant negative effects on the level of overtime employees work. None of these studies, however, offers any evidence that, in response to a decline in long work hours, aggregate employment rises in the employment market in question—although it is obvious that a decline in workweeks longer than 40 hours is a logical predicate for such an increase. Using German data and examining the effects of industry-specific changes in overtime pay requirements, Hunt (1999) finds that, if anything, aggregate employment levels fall rather than rise in response to strengthened overtime pay requirements.

CONCLUSION

This review has offered economic analysis of workplace safety mandates, workplace privacy mandates, fringe benefits mandates, targeted mandates such as mandated medical and family leave, and overtime pay requirements. Much interesting work remains to be done on many of these topics, including the effects of some of the relatively new laws mentioned above.

As noted above, this review has focused on employment law rather than labor law. However, it bears emphasis that the two fields of law do not operate in any way independently of one another. The contours of labor law, in affecting the prevalence and power of unions, may greatly affect what sorts of employment law rules are enacted and, perhaps most importantly, the degree to which employment law rules are effectively enforced against employers. With respect to the importance of enforcement, it is difficult to disagree with Pound (1910, pp. 16, 34–35), who noted long ago that employment law in action may look quite different from employment law on the books.

ACKNOWLEDGMENTS

This review is drawn from Christine Jolls, Employment Law, in *Handbook of Law and Economics* (forthcoming in 2007). Thanks to Louis Kaplow, Daniel Klaff, Cass Sunstein, and participants at the March 13, 2004, conference for contributors to the *Handbook of Law and Economics* for helpful comments and discussions, and to Kenneth Moon for outstanding research assistance.

The *Annual Review of Law and Social Science* is online at http://lawsocsci.annualreviews.org

LITERATURE CITED

Acemoglu D, Angrist JD. 2001. Consequences of employment protection? The case of the Americans with Disabilities Act. *J. Polit. Econ.* 109(5):915–57

Akerlof GA, Dickens WT. 1982. The economic consequences of cognitive dissonance. *Am. Econ. Rev.* 72(3):307–19

Arnould RJ, Grabowski H. 1981. Auto safety

regulation: an analysis of market failure. *Bell J. Econ.* 12(1):27–48

Bartel AP, Thomas LG. 1985. Direct and indirect effects of regulation: a new look at OSHA's impact. *J. Law Econ.* 28(1):1–25

Blau FD, Kahn LM. 1999. Institutions and laws in the labor market. In *Handbook of Labor Economics*, ed. O Ashenfelter, D Card, 3A:1399–461. Amsterdam: Elsevier

Brown C. 1980. Equalizing differences in the labor market. *Q. J. Econ.* 94(1):113–34

Brown C. 1999. Minimum wages, employment, and the distribution of income. In *Handbook of Labor Economics*, ed. O Ashenfelter, D Card, 3B:2101–63. Amsterdam: Elsevier

Cain GG. 1986. The economic analysis of labor market discrimination: a survey. In *Handbook of Labor Economics*, ed. O. Ashenfelter, R Layard, 1:693–785. Amsterdam: Elsevier

Camerer CF, Kunreuther H. 1989. Decision processes for low probability events: policy implications. *J. Policy Anal. Manag.* 8(4):565–92

Costa DL. 2000. Hours of work and the Fair Labor Standards Act: a study of retail and wholesale trade, 1938–1950. *Ind. Labor Relat. Rev.* 53(4):648–64

Currie J, Madrian BC. 1999. Health, health insurance and the labor market. In *Handbook of Labor Economics*, ed. O Ashenfelter, D Card, 3C:3309–416. Amsterdam: Elsevier

Cutler DM. 2002. Health care and the public sector. In *Handbook of Public Economics*, ed. AJ Auerbach, M Feldstein, 4:2143–243. Amsterdam: Elsevier

DeJoy DM. 1989. The optimism bias and traffic accident risk perception. *Accid. Anal. Prev.* 21(4):333–40

DeLeire T. 2000. The wage and employment effects of the Americans with Disabilities Act. *J. Hum. Resour.* 35(4):693–715

Donohue JD. 2007. The law and economics of antidiscrimination law. In *Handbook of Law and Economics*, ed. AM Polinsky, S Shavell. Amsterdam: Elsevier. In press

Dworkin RM. 1980. Is wealth a value? *J. Leg. Stud.* 9(2):191–226

Ehrenberg RG, Schumann PL. 1982. *Longer Hours or More Jobs?* Ithaca, NY: Cornell Univ. Press

Gibbons R, Katz LF. 1991. Layoffs and lemons. *J. Labor Econ.* 9(4):351–80

Gray WB, Mendeloff JM. 2005. The declining effects of OSHA inspections on manufacturing injuries, 1979–1998. *Ind. Labor Relat. Rev.* 58(4):571–87

Greenwald BC. 1986. Adverse selection in the labour market. *Rev. Econ. Stud.* 53(3):325–47

Gruber J. 1994a. State-mandated benefits and employer-provided health insurance. *J. Public Econ.* 55(3):433–64

Gruber J. 1994b. The incidence of mandated maternity benefits. *Am. Econ. Rev.* 84(3):622–41

Gruber J, Madrian BC. 1994. Health insurance and job mobility: the effects of public policy on job-lock. *Ind. Labor Relat. Rev.* 48(1):86–102

Gruber J, Madrian BC. 1995. Health-insurance availability and the retirement decision. *Am. Econ. Rev.* 85(4):938–48

Gruber J, Madrian BC. 1996. Health insurance and early retirement: evidence from the availability of continuation coverage. In *Advances in the Economics of Aging*, ed. DA Wise, pp. 115–43. Chicago: Univ. Chicago Press

Gruber J, Madrian BC. 1997. Employment separation and health insurance coverage. *J. Public Econ.* 66(3):349–82

Hamermesh DS, Trejo SJ. 2000. The demand for hours of labor: direct evidence from California. *Rev. Econ. Stat.* 82(1):38–47

Hunt J. 1999. Has work-sharing worked in Germany? *Q. J. Econ.* 114(1):117–48

Ippolito RA. 1988. A study of the regulatory effect of the Employee Retirement Income Security Act. *J. Law Econ.* 31(1):85–125

Jacobson M. 2003. Drug testing in the trucking industry: the effect on highway safety. *J. Law Econ.* 46(1):131–56

Jolls C. 2000. Accommodation mandates. *Stanford Law Rev.* 53(2):223–306

Jolls C. 2004. Identifying the effects of the Americans with Disabilities Act using state-law variation: preliminary evidence on educational participation effects. *Am. Econ. Rev*. 94(2):447–53

Jolls C. 2006. *Workplace leave mandates and the employment of individuals with disabilities*. Presented at Annu. Meet. Am. Law Econ. Assoc., 16th, Berkeley, CA

Jolls C. 2007. Employment law. In *Handbook of Law and Economics*, ed. AM Polinsky, S Shavell. Amsterdam: Elsevier. In press

Jolls C, Prescott JJ. 2004. *Disaggregating employment protection: the case of disability discrimination*. Work. Pap., NBER No. 10740

Kaestner R, Simon KI. 2002. Labor market consequences of state health insurance regulation. *Ind. Labor Relat. Rev*. 56(1):136–59

Krueger AB, Meyer BD. 2002. Labor supply effects of social insurance. In *Handbook of Public Economics*, ed. AJ Auerbach, M Feldstein, 4:2327–92. Amsterdam: Elsevier

Mendeloff J. 1979. *Regulating Safety: An Economic and Political Analysis of Occupational Safety and Health Policy*. Cambridge, MA: MIT Press

Morantz AD. 2003. *Has regulatory devolution injured American workers? An empirical comparison of state and federal OSHA enforcement*. Presented at Annu. Meet. Am. Law Econ. Assoc., 13th, Toronto

Neumark D, Stock WA. 1999. Age discrimination laws and labor market efficiency. *J. Polit. Econ*. 107(5):1081–125

Posner RA. 1987. The efficiency and the efficacy of Title VII. *Univ. Penn. Law Rev*. 136(2):513–21

Pound R. 1910. Law in books and law in action. *Am. Law Rev*. 44:12–36

Rea SA. 1981. Workmen's compensation and occupational safety under imperfect information. *Am. Econ. Rev*. 71(1):80–93

Ruhm CJ. 1998. The economic consequences of parental leave mandates: lessons from Europe. *Q. J. Econ*. 113(1):285–317

Ruser JW, Smith RS. 1988. The effect of OSHA records-check inspections on reported occupational injuries in manufacturing establishments. *J. Risk Uncertain*. 1(4):415–35

Sanz-de-Galdeano A. 2006. Job-lock and public policy: Clinton's second mandate. *Ind. Labor Relat. Rev*. 59(3):430–37

Scholz JT, Gray WB. 1990. OSHA enforcement and workplace injuries: a behavioral approach to risk assessment. *J. Risk Uncertain*. 3(3):283–305

Simon KI. 2005. Adverse selection in health insurance markets? Evidence from state small-group health insurance reforms. *J. Public Econ*. 89(9–10):1865–77

Smith RS. 1976. *The Occupational Safety and Health Act*. Washington, DC: Am. Enterprise Inst. Public Policy Res.

Smith RS. 1992. Have OSHA and workers' compensation made the workplace safer? In *Research Frontiers in Industrial Relations and Human Resources*, ed. D Lewin, OS Mitchell, PD Sherer, pp. 557–86. Madison: Ind. Relat. Res. Assoc.

Summers LH. 1989. Some simple economics of mandated benefits. *Am. Econ. Rev*. 79(2):177–83

Trejo SJ. 1991. The effects of overtime pay regulation on worker compensation. *Am. Econ. Rev*. 81(4):719–40

Trejo SJ. 2003. Does the statutory overtime premium discourage long workweeks? *Ind. Labor Relat. Rev*. 56(3):530–51

Viscusi WK. 1978. Wealth effects and earnings premiums for job hazards. *Rev. Econ. Stat*. 60(3):408–16

Viscusi WK. 1979. The impact of occupational safety and health regulation. *Bell J. Econ*. 10(1):117–40

Viscusi WK. 1986. The impact of occupational safety and health regulation, 1973–1983. *RAND J. Econ*. 17(4):567–80

Viscusi WK, O'Connor CJ. 1984. Adaptive responses to chemical labeling: Are workers Bayesian decision makers? *Am. Econ. Rev*. 74(5):942–56

Waldfogel J. 1998. Understanding the 'family gap' in pay for women with children. *J. Econ. Perspect*. 12(1):137–56

Waldfogel J. 1999. The impact of the Family and Medical Leave Act. *J. Policy Anal. Manag.* 18(2):281–302
Weil D. 1996. If OSHA is so bad, why is compliance so good? *RAND J. Econ.* 27(3):618–40
Weil D. 2001. Assessing OSHA performance: new evidence from the construction industry. *J. Policy Anal. Manag.* 20(4):651–74
Weinstein ND. 1980. Unrealistic optimism about future life events. *J. Pers. Soc. Psychol.* 39(5):806–20

Annu. Rev. Law Soc. Sci. 2006. 2:387–408
doi: 10.1146/annurev.lawsocsci.2.081805.110023

First published online as a Review in Advance on August 22, 2006

TRANSNATIONAL LEGALITY AND THE IMMOBILIZATION OF LOCAL AGENCY

David Schneiderman
Faculty of Law and Department of Political Science, University of Toronto, Toronto, Ontario M5S 2C5, Canada; Visiting Sabbatical Scholar, Georgetown University Law Center, Washington, DC 20001; email: david.schneiderman@utoronto.ca

Key Words globalization, constitutionalism, foreign investment, state theory

■ **Abstract** The organizational logic of the legal rules and institutions of economic globalization treats as suspect economic regulation issuing out of the democratic processes of national and subnational communities. In this way, economic globalization can be likened to state formation: as a cultural project with the object of actively suppressing alternatives. While undermining the regulatory capacity of local publics to tame markets, transnational legality prefers to draw on the normative ideas of comparative advantage, consumer freedom, and the rule of law. These discursive strategies prove an unstable basis for legitimation without the critical supports provided by national states in gaining and maintaining the consent of local publics. As the findings of a recent international arbitration panel indicate (*CMS v. Argentina*), transnational legality prefers to view the local as a threat to the maintenance of its political-economic order, one of open borders free of rent-seeking public regulation. This will be the case even when states, like Argentina, take measures to mitigate the hardships of a severe economic downturn. Some critical theorists, like Hardt & Negri in *Empire*, similarly relegate the local to a marginal place without appreciating its contradictory but sustaining role in globalization's future. Such theoretical interventions, operating in conjunction with the disciplining effects of globalization's legal order, help to immobilize, rather than empower, resistance to the monocultures of transnational legality. The question remains whether the shaky foundations upon which the legitimacy of transnational legality are structured will prove less durable than its immobilizing effects.

In an age of economic globalization, political authority operating at the level of the national or subnational is presumed to have dried up. If, in the past, political authority was capable of checking economic power on behalf of citizens seeking to protect themselves from the deleterious effects of markets (Polanyi 1957, p. 76), politics now has some distance to go to catch up with markets. Largely immobile citizens find it difficult to countervail contemporary modes of mobile economic production that appear "as an authentically global abstraction" (Dirlik 1994, p. 350). This disenfranchisement is exacerbated by the arrival of new transnational legal rules and institutions intended to entrench constitution-like limits on the exercise of local political authority far into the future. McGinnis & Movsesian (2000, p. 515), for instance, liken the disciplinary mechanisms of the World Trade Organization (WTO) to the Madisonian checking functions of the U.S. constitution, but "on a global scale." In a similar fashion, the investment rules regime, represented by more than 2000 bilateral investment treaties (BITs) and regional trade agreements such as the North American Free Trade Agreement (NAFTA), has been characterized as performing constitution-like functions (Schneiderman 2001, Clarkson 2003). These new transnational rules and institutions, what I call transnational legality, are intended to check popular political processes and to isolate the economic from the public sphere, precisely the terms that Polanyi (1957, p. 225) used to describe functions served by the U.S. constitution.

National state authority, according to this line of analysis, not only is incapable of countervailing the power of transnational legality, but also is largely obsolete outside of the realms of security, policing, and enhancing competitiveness (Cerny 1999). If this is correct—that transnational legality has displaced many traditional functions served by national states—is this form of the global rule of law sustainable? In Foucauldian terms, we might ask, as does Fraser (2003, p. 170), "[H]ow does power operate after the decentering of the national frame, which continued to organize social regulation long after the demise of the monarch?" This review is an inquiry into the role of local agency, which I associate with the national state, in an age when powerful economic actors seek to supplant national state authority (on equating the national with the local, see Rosenau 2003, p. 85). Although transnational economic law exhibits a palpable distrust of the local, it also relies on state legal forms for the critical support structures that help maintain the legitimacy of transnational legality over time. Local lawmaking under the auspices of national states appears to be critical, then, to the ongoing success of the rules and institutions of economic globalization. Some critical theorists of economic globalization have made similar claims about the obsolescence of the local that, to the extent that ideas do matter, likely has the effect of immobilizing agency rather than enhancing it, removing from the range of potential pressure points local political actors and institutions. So if transnational law cannot be sustained without the local, versions of critical theory help to sustain transnational legality by deeming the local inconsequential.

In the first part of the review, I inquire into whether the rules and institutions of economic globalization are likely to maintain their legitimating force without the mediating role of national states. Using work in social theory and international political economy, I identify three legitimating strategies that may sustain economic globalization in the medium term, each of them unsatisfactory without the critical role played by the local. In the second part, I turn to the rules and institutions of economic globalization. A recent decision of an arbitration panel established to resolve a dispute between the Republic of Argentina and the Michigan-based multinational CMS Gas Transmission illustrates the disdain for the local in the domains of transnational legality. Constituted under the auspices of the World Bank's International Center for the Settlement of Investment Disputes (ICSID), the arbitration panel was asked to consider the consistency of measures taken in the wake of the 1999 meltdown of the Argentinian economy with a U.S-Argentine BIT. The final part of the review takes up an important theoretical intervention in the realm of economic globalization, Hardt & Negri's 2000 book, *Empire*. They similarly relegate the local to an inconsequential role in the global legal order they associate with empire. Although they show an astute understanding of globalization's constitutional architecture, they exhibit a weak appreciation of the contradictory but sustaining role states will have in globalization's future. In so doing, they theoretically close off important avenues for the counter-power of the "multitude" to resist global capitalism's legal order.

ECONOMIC GLOBALIZATION AND ITS LEGITIMACY PROBLEM

The establishment of national state forms, according to work in historical sociology, was not only a politico-economic-military and legal achievement but also a cultural one. Critical to the successful establishment of formal state apparatuses—unifying political institutions, with capitalist modes of production secured by sovereign lawmaking capacities—were cultural changes accompanying state formation. Corrigan & Sayer (1985, p. 191), for these reasons, describe English state formation as a cultural revolution. The disciplines imposed by political authority institutionalized relations of production and generated the "fictive community" associated with the English as a nation. This imagined political community (Anderson 1991) was a project of "social integration" through "moral regulation" [which Corrigan & Sayer associate primarily with Durkheim (1957) rather than with Foucault (1990)] (Ruonavaara 1997). State authority certified the validity of certain forms of memory and suppressed competing sites of allegiance and memory in the "active organization of forgetting." State formation, then, is "an ongoing cultural project," its existence in "constant jeopardy from the very facts of material difference" (Corrigan & Sayer 1985, pp. 195, 197; Gramsci 1971, p. 246). This smoothing over of difference—material, political, and cultural (Colley 1992)—results in what Corrigan & Sayer (1985) call a "violent disruption of human personality, a crippling restriction of human capacity," continuous with a "more or less violent suppression of alternatives" (p. 198):

> The ordinary procedures of state inflate to become taken-for-granted boundaries of the possible, occupying—in the same way an army does a territory—the field of social vision (p. 199).

One might want to take issue with this description of the state as a unified force field. The state is better understood as a complex ensemble of institutions with only a formal, rather than a substantive, unity (Jessop 1990, p. 256; 2002, p. 42). Bourdieu (1998, p. 2), for instance, has distinguished between the "left hand of the state"—agents of the "spending ministries" who are associated with the promotion of social welfare—and the "right hand of the state"—officials from the ministries of finance or international trade who hold inordinate sway over the direction of state policy. Insofar as these dominant branches within the state operate in a "strategically selective" manner, wherein certain social forces are privileged over others, state forms structure political possibilities along the lines that Corrigan & Sayer (1985) suggest (see Jessop 1990, p. 260).

To the extent that economic globalization has disrupted state functions, relocating its authority upwards, downwards, or nowhere at all, we might similarly consider economic globalization as being a cultural project with the normative object of actively suppressing alternatives. The integrating and homogenizing aspects of economic globalization, premised upon a single path for economic development fictitiously experienced by the developed countries of the north, is about constituting thresholds of normalcy (Coward 2005, p. 868). Deviations from the normal simply are forbidden (Tarullo 1987). This represents the constitutive and negative role law plays in the structuration of economic globalization: Legal disciplines erect barriers that cabin political possibilities and suppress alternative futures. If national states are hollowed out in the process, can this form of legality maintain its legitimacy without the mediating function served by the states and local democratic processes? Can these legal forms, in themselves, be expected to achieve the cultural transformation of the sort that Corrigan & Sayer describe in the context of English state formation?

Neoliberalism, Harvey (2005) has observed, is a theory of political economy that hypothesizes that human well-being will be advanced by the practices associated with free markets. It is the role of the state to "create and preserve an institutional framework appropriate to such practices" (Harvey 2005, p. 2). States are expected, for instance, to entrench property rights, guarantee contractual obligations, and perform security and policing functions so as to ensure the smooth operation of free markets. Economic globalization, one might say, represents the institutionalization of neoliberalism on a global scale. A variety of legal forms are critical to the achievement of these objectives (Santos 2002, p. 384). Global capital, Sassen (1996, p. 25) notes, "has made claims on national states, which have responded through the production of new forms of legality." An inquiry into these legal forms reveals much about how economic globalization is being made and the points at which it might legally be resisted or rolled back. That is, in the course of achieving security for markets—for the movement of capital, goods, and services unimpeded by national regulatory barriers—law appears everywhere.

In the pursuit of economic globalization, legal changes are occurring both without and within national legal systems, via forms of both deregulation and reregulation. If states are expected to recede in the performance of certain functions, particularly functions associated with regulating markets for the redistribution of wealth, states are also expected to adopt measures that replicate paths to successful economic development pursued by successful developed economies. Constitutionally entrenched rights to private property together with institutions for judicial review, for instance, are viewed as prerequisites to full participation in the fruits of economic globalization's benefits. As critical legal reforms at the local level appear insufficient to secure gains from trade and investment, new forms of legal regulation are proliferating in the realm of the transnational, legal forms that implicate states but yet are seemingly beyond the purview of national legal orders. The oversight functions served by the WTO, for instance, lend a public face to economic globalization's legal order, in contrast, for instance, to the less transparent oversight performed by financial markets and credit rating agencies. Investment rules, embodied in a web of over 2000 BITs and some regional agreements, represent another face of transnational legality. We can associate these developments with the idea of the "new constitutionalism," advanced by Gill (1995) in an important essay (see also Gill 2003). New constitutionalist proposals, he writes, emphasize "market efficiency, discipline and confidence; economic policy and consistency; and limitation on democratic decision making processes." The project "insulates key aspects of the economy from the influence of politicians or the mass of citizens by imposing, internally and externally, 'binding constraints' on the conduct of fiscal, monetary, and trade and investment policies" (Gill 1995, p. 412; 2003, p. 132).

There is a crack, however, in the legal forms that aim to secure the rights of global capital. Gill (2003, p. 140) notes, for instance, that the movement toward remaking the state along neoliberal lines "lacks moral credibility, legitimacy and authority." Beck (2005, p. 120) similarly asks what legitimizes these new forms of legality "*in the absence of* state democratic authority?" If political authority is the "fusion of power with legitimate social purpose" (Ruggie 1998, p. 64), then what legitimate social purposes are advanced by adhering to the regimes of transnational legality? After all, at the same time as national state functions are being hollowed out or decentered, states are not considered capable of taking measures to protect the mass of their citizens without incurring retaliation from powerful global economic actors—the stalling or withdrawal of investment, for instance—in addition to running up against the legal disciplines of the new constitutionalism. Unable to harness mobile capital for taxation purposes, states cannot be expected to deliver public goods, particularly redistributive ones (Cerny 1999, p. 127; Rodrik 1997). If there is a disjuncture between economic globalization and "the political institutionalization of new social relations" (Robinson 2001, p. 601), how can transnational legality maintain its legitimacy without the active partnership of national states? We can identify at least three powerful discursive strategies that purport to solve this legitimacy problem: (1) the pursuit of comparative advantage, (2) the advancement of consumer freedom, and (3) the promotion of the rule of law.

1. The promise of neoliberalism is that state functions become obsolete as the mass of citizens are better served by greater liberty, gains from economic efficiency, and enhanced social well-being. Comparative advantage speaks to the idea that there are structural differentiations in economic capacity around the globe, and that nations should specialize in that which they produce most

efficiently and import that which they do not. In the long run, one can expect that all—consumers and producers, workers and owners—will be better off. Contemporary international economic law is premised on this powerful idea associated with David Ricardo in the nineteenth century and modified by later developments in econometrics. Former WTO head Mike Moore (2003, p. 52) describes the "compelling logic" of comparative advantage as the "best established and the most profound observation in political economics"; *Financial Times* editor Martin Wolf (2004, p. 80) describes it as "perhaps the cleverest [idea] in economics."

It is a powerful idea not only in the world of economics and trade law but also in public culture. The U.S. news magazine *BusinessWeek* reports that 65% of polled respondents in 2000 believed globalization a "good thing," although 70% believed it drove down American wages (Steger 2005, p. 47). National states conduct themselves accordingly, opening up their economies and binding their governments to the constraints of transnational legalism, anticipating the promised gains from trade and investment. Yet these gains will be felt unevenly. As Stiglitz (2002b, p. 59) notes, economic liberalization can "wreak havoc on small emerging markets." Jobs easily can be destroyed with no corresponding economic growth, and the transition costs associated with economic globalization, including externalities and market failures, are left for markets to resolve. Despite comparative advantage's favorable press, Trebilcock & Howse (1998, p. 10) postulate that, absent a global hegemon imposing its will on weaker partners, more intensive trade policy harmonization is unlikely to unfold without "a reasonably egalitarian distribution of political influence and a common interest in overarching political objectives," conditions that seemingly will not apply in the near future. Moreover, there is some doubt that real economic benefits flow to many people in the world as a consequence of open borders in trade and investment; accompanying the growth of liberalized markets has been a growing inequality between the rich and poor states such that "global inequality remains at extraordinarily high levels" (UNDP 2005, 33). If Sen (1990, p. 37) had reason to say that *homo economicus* is "close to being a social moron," then there is equally good reason to say that a global political order premised primarily on competitive advantage is socially moronic.

2. The notion of consumer freedom—the ability to consume goods and services from any place and to travel anywhere (Lash & Urry 1994, p. 58)—best represents how economic liberty becomes individualized. It offers a space of freedom to those who face obstacles in most other areas of life (Hall 1996, p. 234). Despite this emphasis on individual agency, consumers are not so much actors as, at best, "choosers" (Appadurai 1996, p. 42). Citizens, nevertheless, appreciate the significance of this form of self-realization (Rose 1999, p. 164), choosing greater purchasing power over social welfare by reducing taxes and the size of public expenditure (Williams 1961, p. 325), while at the same time maintaining public subsidies to capital.

We might expect the legal order of economic globalization actively to constitute subjectivities—like the consumer citizen—that act reflexively, shaping and being shaped by its differential structural openings (Silbey 2005, p. 334). Forbath (1991), for instance, shows how working-class consciousness was influenced by the possibilities and limitations offered by popular understandings of U.S. constitutionalism in the *Lochner* era. The limited social visions offered by the constitutional regime silenced aspirations and elicited the consent of the labor movement "to the dominant groups' version of the natural and the good," observes Forbath (1991, p. 170). Habermasian "constitutional patriotism" might be considered in a similar light, though more enabling and operating at a regional, rather than a national, scale. The integrative effect of the European liberal legal order, Habermas (1998, p. 500) maintains, can be expected to generate an allegiance to a new nonnational constitutional order, in which case legality would beget legitimacy. Whatever the causes of the stalled European constitutional project (Walker 2005), it probably is the case that citizens, as with the labor movement in the late-nineteenth-century United States, "need to be motivated by solidarity, not merely included by law" (Calhoun 2002, p. 275; Grimm 2005, p. 199). Beck (2005, p. 60), therefore, insists that the "*masochism of economic self-interest* running amok amid the delights of the consumer society" lends only a "fragile consent" to global capitalism. The ideological backbone of neoliberalism's orthodoxy—the "culture-ideology of consumerism" (Sklair 2002)—might not be sufficient, then, to sustain globalization's systemic features over time.

3. Even if we cannot expect consumer freedom to do the necessary legitimating work, consumerism necessitates national legal orders that guarantee liberties of contract and property and the civil rights to participate equally in markets—legal principles that are associated with the idea of the rule of law. These retain an independent discursive power that cannot be lightly disregarded (Thompson 1975, p. 265). They also buttress the message that economic globalization is good for you and that, in any event, there is no alternative. Rule-of-law reforms usually are promoted within national legal institutions and structures, optimally, argue its proponents, via national constitutional change (Buchanan & Tullock 1962). Transnational variants seek to restrain state regulatory capacity that, for instance, impedes the flow of trade and investment or unreasonably upsets expected returns on investment (Schneiderman 2001). This rule-oriented approach is "preferred for its stability and predictability of governmental activity," writes Jackson (1997, pp. 109–11; 2006, pp. 88–90). This partly has been achieved, he writes, with the establishment of a world trade "constitution" under the WTO, secured above all by "an intricate set of constraints imposed by a variety of 'rules' or legal norms" (Jackson 1997, p. 339; 2006, pp. 205–6). The rule of law is deployed here to "cabin[] the tendency of governments to stray from the range of acceptable responses" (Kennedy 1994, p. 78).

> The critical supports to the rule of law, such as the heightening of protection for property rights or the guaranteeing of the obligation of contracts, call on states, as much as they do the transnational legal frame, to stand actively with economic globalization's strategy of accumulation. Democratic national states, acting as consensual intermediaries, are critical, then, to the success of the normalizing project of neoliberalism (Gill 2003, p. 141; Beck 2005, p. 148). If state authority is significantly constrained by transnational legality, "what we describe as global, including some of the most strategic functions necessary for globalization, is [also] grounded in national territories" (Sassen 1996, p. 13; 2006, pp. 231–32).

The local is implicated in the structuration of legal economic globalization in a number of ways. First, state participation is critical to erecting the scaffolding upon which the rules and structures of economic globalization operate (Panitch 1996). That is, states will have authored the legal regimes of precommitment that limit room for policy maneuverability. Second, states are expected to restructure domestic legal relations to augment the norms of transnational legality. The shift from public to private regulation and provision, in the realm of the family for instance, necessitates the reorganization of legal relations that penetrate deeply into political and social life (Harvey 2000, p. 65). The "underside of reprivatization" in these realms, Brodie (1996, p. 390) notes, "is reregulation" (see also Brenner 1999, p. 65). Accompanying judicial reforms pave the way for the "poststructural adjustment state," where the rule of law is converted "into just one more technique of regulation" (Santos 2002, pp. 339, 341). The rulings of international tribunals, relatedly, must be rendered enforceable within domestic legal structures as if they were the decisions of local courts. Lastly, states are expected to undertake legal reforms that smooth the operation of market processes, generally. The United Nations Conference on Trade and Development (UNCTAD) has annually monitored national policy measures that improve the climate for foreign direct investment. They report that, in 2004, 87% of regulatory changes within national states "implied further liberalization of investment regimes" (UNCTAD 2005, p. 22), and this is consistent with past trends.

The transnational legal rules and institutions of economic globalization enlist the powerful discourses of comparative advantage, consumer freedom, and the rule of law so as to normalize legally binding constraints. The object is to achieve a cultural transformation of the state and the subjectivity of its citizenry in much the same way that Corrigan & Sayer describe the cultural achievements of English state formation. Yet this seemingly cannot be achieved without relying on state legal forms both in structuring these legal orders and in gaining and maintaining the consent of national publics. If alternative futures that disrupt dominant understandings are to be discouraged or forestalled, then economic globalization needs the assistance of state forms to help occupy the fields of social vision.

The operative rules and structures of transnational legality, however, suggest a great deal of ambivalence, if not outright disdain, for state partners. Perhaps this should not be surprising, given the contradictory path transnational globality is expected to navigate—both decentering national states and yet relying upon state legal forms to maintain the high priority accorded to the rights of global capital. This ambivalence suggests that the legitimation strategies embraced by the proponents of transnational legality may be weak and, perhaps, unsustainable. To illustrate this difficulty, in the next section I examine a recent ruling of an arbitration panel established under the auspices of the World Bank to resolve an investment dispute between Michigan-based CMS and the Republic of Argentina. I do not attempt here to evaluate the impact of this ruling on the Argentinian legislators or its publics, nor do I determine how successfully economic globalization at present limits the horizon of expectations in Argentina. The more modest aim is to draw the outlines of the constitutionalist agenda I associate with transnational legality and the cramped residual role left for local agency in its design.

TRANSNATIONAL LEGALITY AND IMMOBILIZED STATES

If politics have not yet caught up with markets, legal forms appear to be keeping apace. In addition to a "dense network" of supranational organizations that together help to facilitate transnational economic processes, such as the International Monetary Fund (IMF), World Bank, and WTO (Robinson 2001, p. 182), there are legal constraints associated with investment disciplines that guarantee returns on investment for mobile capital. This investment rules regime is intended to keep politics at some distance from markets, entitling investors to enforce economic rights when state regulation goes too far in diminishing expected returns on investment. The combined ratcheting effect of the web of rules and institutions is perhaps best illustrated by events in the Republic of Argentina.

Described as the "poster-child of globalization, Latin style" (Bello 2005, p. 123) and an "A-plus student of the IMF" (Stiglitz 2002a), Argentina enthusiastically followed directives from Washington, DC, and the IMF to cut expenditures, pursuing the developmental path associated with the "Washington consensus" (Blustein 2005, p. 23). Large chunks of public enterprise were privatized, and currency control was surrendered by pegging the peso to the U.S. dollar (the IMF was initially skeptical of convertibility, although it came eventually to embrace it) (Blustein 2005, pp. 14, 29). The national state, in other words, performed precisely the sort of restructuring role that augments the norms of transnational legality. The Argentinian economy became unglued in 2000 as the trade deficit rose, unemployment shot up, stock prices plunged, and protestors took to the streets (30 civilians died after one day of riots in December 2001). With the collapse of the peso, thousands were thrown out of work, and foreign investors should have lost hope of reaping the high returns on their investments that had been guaranteed in the privatization heydays. Those at the bottom suffered the most: The population living in extreme poverty more than tripled between 2000 and 2003 (UNDP 2005, p. 36). In *The Economist*'s assessment, this was "an economic collapse to match the Great Depression of the 1930s" (*Economist* 2003).

There currently are approximately 30 cases worth about $16 billion pending before the dispute resolution arm of the World Bank, ICSID, against the Republic of Argentina founded on the legal disciplines of BITs (Bishop & Luzi 2005, p. 425). These are actions launched by some very large multinational corporations or their related subsidiaries based on contracts for the provision of water and sewer services, gas or oil production and transmission, information services, telecommunications, and electricity. In more than a dozen of these cases, the companies contend that the collapse in the value of their holdings in privatized Argentinian utilities were triggered by Argentina's use of fiscal emergency measures in the wake of the collapse of the peso. They mostly contend that these measures amounted either to the indirect expropriation of their investment interests or to the denial of "fair and equitable treatment" of their investment, entitling them to sunk expenses and future lost profits.

Today, international arbitration is the preferred mechanism for the resolution of these sorts of legal disputes. Tripartite arbitral panels, established under the auspices of ICSID or the United Nations Commission on International Trade Law (UNCITRAL), and other such facilities set up shop in one of a number of global venues (i.e., Washington, Vancouver, or Paris; the hearings discussed below were held in Paris), with one neutral and two side persons appointed by the parties to the dispute. Drawn from a narrow field of trade law specialists (Sornarajah 1997, Dezalay & Garth 1996), panels increasingly are moving away from discrete commercial problems traditionally resolved with reference to *lex mercatoria* to the broader public policy debates ordinarily associated with politics (Zumbansen 2002). Indeed, the capacity of state action in a wide array of policy fields is being brought into question in these disputes, precisely the aim of the investment rules regime, its supporters will say (Vandevelde 1998).

Although taking up measures for societal self-protection in the wake of a fiscal crisis that cut against the dominant grain of economic globalization, the Argentinian state was not necessarily repudiating fully globalization's legal order. The state, instead, might be seen as seeking only reform by challenging, first, the jurisdictional bases of these claims (Bishop & Luzi 2005, p. 446). In each case, the state has argued that creditors first must seek remedies under Argentinian law and in local Argentinian courts and not in global arbitration centers that rely on BIT rights. Every one of these preliminary challenges has failed. In the alternative, the state has argued that local Argentinian law applies to these commitments and not nonlocal "minimum standards of civilized justice" that are guaranteed to investors in many of these treaties. This resembles the theory articulated by Argentinian jurist Carlos Calvo in the late nineteenth century. Calvo argued that the countries of Latin America were entitled to the same degree of respect for their internal sovereignty as were the United States and the countries of Europe (Calvo 1887, p. 266). Among Calvo's precepts was the proposition that states should be free, within reason, from interference in the conduct of their domestic policy. From this, he could argue that foreign nationals could not lay claim to greater protection in their disputes with sovereign states than could the citizens of these same countries. The arbitration panel established in the CMS case rejected Argentina's arguments, and its ruling exemplifies the manner in which these disputes will be resolved (*CMS Gas Transmission Company v. República Argentina* 2005; further references are to the paragraphs in this decision). The decision also illustrates how economic globalization's legal order is intended to check local legislative action regarding markets despite the fact that national states continue to provide critical legitimating supports to the global project.

CMS initially participated in the 1995 privatization of the public company Transportada de Gas del Norte (TGN), purchasing almost 30% of the company's shares (paragraph 58). According to enabling legislation and the gas transportation license issued by the government, tariffs collected by the company were to be recouped in U.S. dollars, adjusted periodically, and converted into pesos at the time of billing (paragraphs 58, 85). The economic crisis precipitated a variety of measures for societal self-protection. The government, by emergency decree in 2001, limited the capacity of depositors to withdraw funds from bank deposits, abolished dollarization, and, because of devaluation of the peso, would no longer convert tariffs into U.S. dollars (pesification) (paragraph 66). In the case of natural gas, this also involved a temporary suspension of prices, then freezing of profits converted into dollars and the abandonment of periodic adjustments of prices. As the Republic of Argentina's pleadings explain, the redenomination of all contracts into pesos "ensured that all participants in the economy [in the wake of economic collapse] would share the necessary burden collectively" (Argentine Republic 2005, paragraph 20).

CMS, however, together with many other foreign investors, were not willing to share in this burden, and so, in July 2001, the company filed a dispute with ICSID under a U.S.-Argentinian BIT. The company claimed that it had a guaranteed rate of return on its investment, regardless of the financial hardships experienced by Argentinians or the fiscal crisis experienced by the state. On the basis of this reliance expectation, CMS had invested almost US$175 million in the purchase of shares in TGN (*CMS v. República Argentina* 2005, paragraph 68). Having reneged on its commitment, the Argentinian government's action precipitated a 92% drop in the value of CMS shares. This, the company claimed, amounted to the indirect expropriation of the company's assets without compensation, a failure to comply with the standard of fair and equitable treatment mandated under the treaty (paragraph 88), and a breach of the license's stabilization clause (covered by the BIT's "umbrella clause"). The government responded with a variety of arguments, including that the company received a reasonable rate of return in the face a bona fide emergency. Central to the Argentinian defense, however, were arguments defending the usual capacity of states and citizens to change policy direction: that governments should be "free to change such policies" to take into account "needs of social importance" (paragraphs 91–93). Argentina, in other words, should be free to revise its economic policies in order to protect citizens from the "relentlessness of the market" (Rodrik 1997, p. 36), and no public utilities license or BIT could be read as freezing the regulatory environment. This particularly should be the case when the economic harm suffered by the vast majority of Argentinian citizens was exacerbated by following IMF directives (Stiglitz 2002a).

Advancing an argument made by law professor and Justice Minister Horacio Rosatti (2003, cf. Rosatti 2005), Argentina argued that the BIT and the ICSID system of arbitration were inconsistent with Argentinian constitutional commitments to basic human rights (paragraphs 114, 119). Human rights, the state argued, were compromised by transnational commitments to guaranteed profits. The tribunal rejected the constitutional submission based upon the tribunal's own reading of the Argentinian constitution. First, provisions in the constitution assert the primacy of treaties under Argentinian law. Moreover, the constitution "carefully protects the right to property, just as the treaties on human rights do" (paragraphs 121, 239). In any event, the dispute did not affect fundamental human rights, the tribunal concluded, without further explanation (paragraphs 121, 203).

Having found constitutional harmony, the panel moved on to the company's claims. The panel found no indirect or regulatory expropriation of the company's assets (paragraphs 259–63) as CMS was still in control of its investment (paragraph 263). Argentina, however, was not only in breach of the license but also had denied the company fair and equitable treatment. The company, after all, had invested in Argentina on the basis that the state would guarantee the stability of its investment interest (paragraph 134). The panel concluded that the Argentinian program of privatization was "successful"—over $10 billion was raised—precisely because the state offered guarantees in a manner that would not "allow[] for their reversal within a few years" (paragraph 138). Because the gas transportation license was in the nature of a "guarantee," the state was obliged to honor this commitment (paragraph 161). Freezing and then declining the rate of return through pesification was not in keeping with this form of commitment through licensing. The state was ordered to pay CMS $133.2 million. Argentina has filed an application for annulment of this award under an extraordinary procedure available at the World Bank (Schreuer 2003) to set aside ICSID panel rulings (Argentine Republic 2005).

One gets a sense that the panel believed, as *Washington Post* writer Paul Blustein (2005, p. 25) argues, that Argentina gained from its aggressive embrace of the Washington consensus. Moreover, its politicians and citizens were not "wholly innocent" victims in setting the country's economy on a collision course, although, Blustein (2005, p. 6) notes, they got plenty of help from the IMF and the U.S. Treasury Board. Insofar as Argentina acted imprudently, in tying the peso to the U.S. dollar, for instance, the state should pay for the consequential economic harm suffered by foreign investors. Following the logic of the panel's ruling, investment treaties will have the effect of freezing regulatory environments when new policy initiatives have an inordinately negative impact on investment interests or, as investment lawyers Rubins & Kinsella (2005, p. 50) put it, "when local mandatory laws . . . make doing business more costly or difficult." Stable and predictable rates of return—synonymous, for the panel, with the guarantee of fair and equitable treatment (paragraphs 266–84)—mandate state immobilization in certain sectors. There would be no concomitant stability and predictability granted to the citizens of Argentina. Following many of the edicts laid down by the Washington consensus, directly benefiting companies like CMS participating in the program of denationalization, Argentinians were expected to pay for these missteps far into the future despite plausible constitutional commitments to the contrary. Although foreign investors insist on equal treatment with citizens (the principle of national treatment), this is tolerated only as long as treatment does not fall below certain minimum levels, at which point investors cannot be expected to share in the burden of a failed economic experiment—one, though, that companies like CMS actively would have endorsed.

The case illustrates how the rules and institutions of economic globalization are intended to place limits on the capacity of states to solve redistributive problems. According to the logic of *CMS*, foreign investors are to be granted priority in the wake of the financial collapse of the state; citizens cannot expect to receive similar treatment. Not only are rates of return guaranteed, citizens and their states are made fiscally responsible for these prior commitments—to the tune of $133.2 million—irrespective of fiscal capacity. It illustrates the cramped role to which states are confined when they act to protect citizens from the deleterious effects of markets, even when they act in the advancement of the collective project represented by the state's constitutional order.

If the 30 or so outstanding disputes at ICSID against the Republic of Argentina are resolved in favor of the companies, there simply is no way that Argentina could compensate all these firms for future lost profits. Despite the strict legal obligations flowing out of the investment rules regime, the system is unlikely to collapse. What is more likely is that, as in the case of foreign bond holders in the wake of the Argentine debt crisis, creditors will receive only a percentage of the money they would be owed (in that instance, roughly 70% of that debt was written off) (Helleiner 2005, p. 959).

In such a case, although transnational capital's desire for profits seems insatiable, there are limits to what can be extracted from states and their populaces. The overriding objective, perhaps, is the cultural one: to lower citizens' expectations in local state agency. Governments are expected to be accountable first and foremost to investors and not to their citizens (Gill 2003, p. 131). The investment rules regime, in this way, aims to establish thresholds of tolerable behavior promoting a culture of markets seemingly freed from the control of politics. Local policy initiatives are expected to conform to this culture of limited and constrained government, and any public that rebukes the regime's precepts can anticipate punishment of hundreds of millions of dollars in damage awards to investors. This is despite the fact that the investment rules regime is critically reliant on stable national legal orders to protect fixed and immovable investment interests. At the same time, national states are expected to take the difficult and contradictory path of both succumbing to economic globalization's legal edicts while resisting demands for nonmarket-based solutions to contemporary social problems. This seems a shaky foundation for a sustainable legal order with pretensions of universality.

EMPIRE AND IMMOBILIZED LOCAL SUBJECTS

Perhaps no book on globalization in the social sciences has generated as much heat as Hardt & Negri's 2000 book *Empire*. It has been described in *The New York Times* "Arts & Ideas" section as a "heady treatise on globalization that is sending frissons of excitement through campuses from São Paulo to Tokyo" (Eakin 2001, p. B7) and elsewhere as "academia's version of a blockbuster" (Passavant 2004, p. 2). It has precipitated several books of commentary (Balakrishnan 2003, Boron 2005, Passavant & Dean 2004) and a second, follow-up book expanding upon and modifying themes developed originally in *Empire* (Hardt & Negri 2004). *Empire* is a model in that it exhibits the tendency described above of failing to appreciate the critical role local legal orders play in sustaining the legitimacy of empire.

This is a complex book, and I focus only on a few aspects of the argument here. Simply put, Hardt & Negri's "audaciously grand" (Kalyvas 2003, p. 264) thesis is that the institutional apparatus of empire—the transnational legal order of contemporary global capitalism—will collapse under the weight of its own contradictions (not the sort under discussion so far). What precipitates its collapse is the "multitude": the mass of "immaterial" laborers that "sustains Empire and at the same time the force that calls for and makes necessary its destruction" (Hardt & Negri 2000, p. 61). What emerges in their account is a "class struggle" without limit—without the national political systems as intermediaries, that is—as "capitalist development is faced directly with the multitude, without mediation" (p. 237). Finally, as Marx predicted, "[c]apital and labor are opposed in directly antagonistic form" giving rise to a revolutionary counter-empire of the multitude.

The multitude is both a productive and deterritorializing force with mobility of labor power, in contrast to the geographically bound laborers of the old nation-state system. Hardt & Negri postulate that labor power will want to escape the limits set by empire's disciplinary effects. The multitude's penchant for mobility, they write, "indicates a real and powerful search for freedom and the formation of new, nomadic desires that cannot be contained and controlled within the disciplinary regime" (Hardt & Negri 2000, p. 253). It is a "desire for liberation" (pp. 253, 357), the "general right to control its own movement" that is the multitude's "ultimate demand" (p. 400) and the uncontainable threat to global capitalism.

Hardt & Negri theorize that empire's constitutional structure will generate new subjectivities with the ability to overtake capitalism's empire. Displacing the constitutional functions of national states is a "global constitution" premised on the idea of the "mixed constitution," associated with Polybius and Montesquieu, in which a triumvirate of power operates through the institutions of the monarchy, aristocracy, and democracy (Hardt & Negri 2000, p. 314). As in the mixed constitution, there are three tiers to the contemporary constitutional order. First, analogous to the monarch of the mixed constitution, are the powerful countries of the OECD, and at its pinnacle the United States, operating in the institutional guises of the United Nations, G8, or IMF (Hardt & Negri 2000, p. 309). Next, corresponding to the lords, are transnational corporations and, subordinate to them, the residue of nation-state authority that is confined only to a few functions: negotiating with global superpowers and transnational corporations and redistributing as little wealth as possible (p. 310). At the third and lowest tier, corresponding to the commons, are groups that represent the multitude, which may include nation states and nongovernmental organizations (NGOs) associated with global civil society (p. 311).

These three forms of power are transformed by the need to subsume labor and capital within empire, breaking down borders and destroying distance. This "mutation of spatial relationships transforms the exercise of power itself" so that each form of power merges with the other, becoming hybridized (Hardt & Negri 2000, p. 317). There also is a need to exercise authority not only over geography but over subjectivity. New forms of production, which give rise to the mobility of immaterial labor, mandate that imperial authority encounter the multitude face-to-face. Rule is now "exercised directly over the movements of productive and cooperating subjectivities," and out of this will emerge demands that will make the constitution itself, as in the past, a "site of struggle" (p. 319). Giving rise to the contradiction between political subjection and the independence of agents will be a "new social dynamic that liberates the producing and consuming subject from (or at least makes ambiguous its position within) the mechanisms of political subjection." At this point, "a real field of struggle . . . can be reopened—a true and proper situation of crisis and maybe eventually revolution" (p. 321).

This account of the immanent contradictions latent in the current global legal order is premised on the permanent demise of the national state. For Hardt & Negri (2000, p. 218), national legal orders represent "positions of resentment and nostalgia." The processes leading to the decline of the nation state in their account are "structural and irreversible" (p. 336). On this basis, Hardt & Negri can claim that national borders are no impediment to labor mobility, producing the insatiable demands of the multitude for greater freedom despite the constraints associated with empire.

There are good reasons to doubt the empirical basis for this hyperglobalist diagnosis of the contemporary scene, where states largely are obsolete in the face of global capital. This is because the purported postnational scene appears not to have given rise to greater worker mobility. Although these data are "sketchy," particularly in regard to illegal migrants, a downward trend is discernible in total migration during the 1990s (Ghose 2002, p. 16). This contrasts with the large patterns of migration characteristic of nineteenth century globalization (O'Rourke & Williamson 1999, p. c.7). Legal mobility is, at present, enhanced only for the few, such as investors, whose rights of exit and entry are guaranteed by the investment rules regime, and a class of professional entrepreneurs associated with the knowledge industry—such as lawyers, accountants, and financial advisors—whose services are considered to add value to the new economy. Laborers around the world remain mostly trapped within the confines of geographic states. Although the Mexico-U.S. border remains porous, the congressional proposal to render criminal illegal immigrants, precipitating a wave of protests by immigrants across major U.S. cities in spring 2006, surely attests to this fact.

States, moreover, continue to have some scope for policy diversity—they are not entirely disabled by the legal regime associated with empire (Hay & Marsh 2000, p. 5; Hirst & Thompson 1999). A variety of studies suggest that on matters such as welfare reform (Hay 2005) and industrial, technological, and export subsidies (Weiss 2005) there is room for policy difference despite the convergence effects of economic globalization. This is not to say that states are left intact in the face of these processes, but only that some states are in a better position to exploit the structure of the legal regime of economic globalization. Weiss (2005, p. 724) has observed, for instance, that OECD states have developed a multilateral trade legal order that "best suits their developmental trajectory." This form of "strategic activism" promotes national economic interests of powerful states over the economic well-being of more vulnerable constituencies. Their interests are advanced by the oversight provided by financial market actors, who are less keen to scrutinize the policy choices of developed countries than in policing developing ones. Financial investors, observes Mosley, "consider many dimensions of government policy when making asset allocation decisions" in the less developed and developing world, considerations that do not apply in the developed world (Mosley 2006, pp. 92, 96).

Economic globalization, from this angle, is about preferring certain local interests over others. The transnational legal order should be understood, then, as concealing, in the guise of universality, the fact that particular national projects have successfully gone global. This transference of the local to the global planes is what Santos (2002, p. 179) means by "globalized localism," in which a "given local phenomenon is successfully globalized," for example, U.S.-style intellectual property rights (Sell 2003). Complementing this process of exportation is one of importation, what Santos calls "localized globalism," in which local conditions are transformed as a result of adopting the imperatives associated with the transnational legal order (Santos 2002, p. 179). When eliding these interests—by repressing, in Bourdieu's terms, the conditions of access that give rise to the universal—theorists give cover to the most "unjustifiable of monopolies" (Bourdieu 2000, p. 70). Dezalay & Garth (1996), in an important book inspired by Bourdieu, describe a transnational struggle in the international arbitration centers of Paris and Geneva, driven by global law firms, between a flexible, case-by-case determination in accordance with the traditional law merchant (*lex mercatoria*) and a rigid, more predictable, rule-bound approach favored by Anglo-American trade lawyers. The U.S. rule-of-law side, Dezalay & Garth (1996, p. c.4) report, is in the ascendance. I have argued that a U.S.-style constitutional property right, in the form of a transnational takings rule, has been successfully globalized via the web of over 2000 BITs (Schneiderman 2000). Sassen (2004, p. 650) has fruitfully exploited the notion that specific instantiations of the local can go global by theorizing the role of nonstate actors operating in very specific, even peripheral, localities but "constituted at multiple scales" in global networks. Klug (2005,

p. 119), for instance, describes a transnational movement of HIV/AIDS activists and health, consumer, and development NGOs, working in cooperation with developing states, having some success in improving access to patented drugs despite a recalcitrant pharmaceutical industry and their allied national states. A series of rulings issued by South African courts, prodding the ANC-led government into modest action, has contributed immensely to the success of the Treatment Action Campaign movement in gaining access to drugs for black South Africans. The water wars of Cochabamba, Bolivia, a much heralded tale of local resistance led by a coalition of union activists and peasant leadership, resulted in the renationalization of the municipal water supply (Schneiderman 2004) (and spawned an investor dispute, since settled; see Vis-Dunbar & Peterson 2006). The coalition represented, according to García Linera (2004, p. 75), a "new territorial-type organization," one that built upon pre-existing solidaristic communities operating at the local level.[1] Hardt & Negri's analysis does not account well for the success of these movements, particularly their local manifestations. Hardt & Negri's account, in sum, "misrecognizes" (Buchanan & Pahjua 2004, p. 76) that the legal regimes of economic globalization are expressions of particular national interests that are intended to suppress other, alternative formulations of competing interests that take shape, and often are given expression, at local levels (Bourdieu 2005, p. 230).

In multiple ways, then, states play active roles in the structuration of economic globalization. "In their dual role as both home and host to business global actors and companies," writes Beck, "governments play a crucial, indeed an increasingly important, role in enforcing global business interests" (Beck 2005, p. 161). This is because, Beck argues, capital depends on state formations to legitimate the transnational legal forms that dominate states and citizens in the global age. Without the legitimating processes contained within existing national political systems, these forms of domination "could quite easily collapse like a house of cards in the tiny breeze created by public curiosity" (p. 148). For this reason, Beck concludes, "without the state and without politics, there can be no business activity" (p. 157). Beck unnecessarily overstates the point. If, as Hardt & Negri describe it, imperial government acts only to discipline and oppress the multitude in negative relations of repression, states play critical mediating roles in rendering transnational processes acceptable, if not desirable. By rendering invisible the role of the local in globalization's scaffolding, Hardt & Negri also negate the points at which globalization might legally be resisted or rolled back. The counter-power to empire, thereby, is disabled. If the state is immobilized by the investment rules regime, the counter-power to empire is immobilized in the very specific locales at which economic globalization takes legal shape.

Hardt & Negri (2004) refine, even reconfigure, their diagnosis in a follow-up book, *Multitude*, departing somewhat from their verdict that national states are

---

[1]García Linera describes the coalition as giving expression to the demands of the "multitude." He is referring to the concept of "multitude-form" as developed by René Zavaleta (García Linera 2004, p. 85, fn. 10) rather than to Hardt & Negri's "multitude."

irreversibly obsolete. "To avoid confusion," they write in this latest book, "we are not arguing here that in this interregnum nation-states are no longer powerful but rather that their powers and functions are being transformed in a new global framework" (p. 163). Nation states "remain important," they reiterate. "States continue to perform many of their traditional functions in the interregnum but are transformed by the emerging global power they tend increasingly to serve." Hardt & Negri (2004, p. xiii) emphasize that, in *Empire*, they were observing "a tendency" in which empire would emerge as the only "lasting" vehicle for global power. In the interregnum, however, national states continue to perform critical functions. Labor mobility, relatedly, is also dislodged from the central place it held in their analysis in *Empire*. If "mobility increasingly defines the labor market as a whole" (Hardt & Negri 2004, p. 133)—a point that does not stand up well to empirical testing—their emphasis now is on the disruptive role of "migrant" workers, who cross over and thus partially undermine "every geographical barrier" (p. 134). To the extent that Hardt & Negri have retreated from their earlier findings, they will have laid down theoretical foundations for counter-hegemonic resistance that will render local agency more material.

CONCLUSION

In the course of being transformed within and disciplined without by the rules and institutions associated with the new constitutional order of economic globalization, states help to sustain that very legal order. As discussed in the opening of this review, the legitimating strategies of transnational legality appear unconvincing without the partnership role offered by national states. Even Hardt & Negri appear to have come around to the idea that national state authority, though constrained, remains central to the structuration of transnational legality. Yet, the legal order of transnationalism is designed precisely so as to undermine state legal projects undertaken to protect the social welfare of citizens where they conflict with market-derived models. If the state's role is marginalized, if not derided—as when Argentinians were penalized for taking self-protective measures in the face of an economic meltdown—the transnational regime paradoxically threatens to undermine the means by which its legitimacy may be maintained. The structural tilt of the legal order, then, may render the contemporary project of economic globalization unsustainable. Critical theorists like Hardt & Negri, however, may help to keep it afloat. Their initial verdict, somewhat revised in later writing, is that national states have become irreversibly obsolete. In so doing, Hardt & Negri deny local agents an important pressure point by which reform, if not transformation, of empire's legal order can be pursued.

Economic globalization, as in the case of state formation, is an "ongoing cultural project" that is in "constant jeopardy" from the fact of material inequality within and across national states (Corrigan & Sayer 1985, p. 197). What is called for here is an opening up, rather than concealment, of the spaces and places through which the legal order of economic globalization can be politicized, interrogated, and rolled back.

ACKNOWLEDGMENTS

Thanks to Patrick Macklem, Kerry Rittich, and Pratima Rao for critical guidance.

LITERATURE CITED

Anderson B. 1991. *Imagined Communities: Reflections on the Origin and Spread of Nationalism*. London: Verso. Rev. ed.

Appadurai A. 1996. *Modernity at Large: Cultural Dimensions of Globalization*. Minneapolis: Univ. Minn. Press

Argentine Republic. 2005. Application for Annulment and Request for Stay of Enforcement of Arbitral Award. ICSID Case No. Arb/01/08

Balakrishnan G, ed. 2003. *Debating Empire*. London: Zed Books

Beck U. 2005. *Power in the Global Age: A New Global Political Economy*. Transl. K Cross. London: Polity

Bello W. 2005. *Dilemmas of Domination*. New York: Metropolitan Books

Bishop RD, Luzi RA. 2005. Investment claims: first lessons from Argentina. In *International Investment Law and Arbitration: Leading Cases from the ICSID, NAFTA, Bilateral Treaties and Customary International Law*, ed. T Weiler, pp. 425–69. London: Cameron May

Blustein P. 2005. *And the Money Kept Rolling In (and Out): Wall Street, the IMF, and the Bankrupting of Argentina*. New York: Public Affairs

Boron A. 2005. *Empire and Imperialism: A Critical Reading of Michael Hardt and Antonio Negri*. Transl. J Casiro. London: Zed Books

Bourdieu P. 1998. *Acts of Resistance: Against the Tyranny of the Market*. Transl. R Nice. New York: New Press

Bourdieu P. 2000. *Pascalian Meditations*. Transl. R Nice. Stanford, CA: Stanford Univ. Press

Bourdieu P. 2005. *The Social Structures of the Economy*. Transl. C Turner. Cambridge, UK: Polity

Brenner N. 1999. Beyond state-centrism: space, territoriality, and geographic scale in globalization studies. *Theory Soc*. 28:39–78

Brodie J. 1996. New state forms, new political spaces. In *States Against Markets: The Limits of Globalization*, ed. R Boyer, D Drache, pp. 383–98. London: Routledge

Buchanan JM, Tullock G. 1962. *The Calculus of Consent: Logical Foundations of Constitutional Democracy*. Ann Arbor: Univ. Mich. Press

Buchanan R, Pahuja S. 2004. Legal imperialism: empire's invisible hand? See Passavant & Dean 2004, pp. 73–93

Calhoun C. 2002. Constitutional patriotism and the public sphere: interests, identity, and solidarity in the integration of Europe. See De Greiff & Cronin 2002, pp. 275–312

Calvo C. 1887. *Le droit international theorique et pratique*, Vol. 1. Paris: Guillaumin et Cie. 4th ed.

Cerny PG. 1999. Globalization and the changing logic of collective action. In *Theory and Structure in International Political Economy*, ed. C Lipson, BJ Cohen, pp. 111–41. Cambridge, MA: MIT Press

Clarkson S. 2003. *Uncle Sam and US: Globalization, Neoconservatism and the Canadian State*. Toronto: Univ. Toronto Press

CMS Gas Transmission Company c. República Argentina, Case No. ARB/01/08, (2005)

Colley L. 1992. *Britons: Forging the Nation 1707–1837*. New Haven, CT: Yale Univ. Press

Corrigan P, Sayer D. 1985. *The Great Arch: English State Formation as Cultural Revolution*. Oxford: Basil Blackwell

Coward M. 2005. The globalisation of enclosure: interrogating the geopolitics of empire. *Third World Q*. 26:855–72

De Grieff P, Cronin C, eds. 2002. *Global Justice and Transnational Politics*. Cambridge, MA: MIT Press

Dezalay Y, Garth B. 1996. *Dealing in Virtue*. Chicago: Univ. Chicago Press

Dirlik A. 1994. The postcolonial aura: Third World criticism in the age of global capitalism. *Crit. Inq*. 20:328–56

Durkheim E. 1957. *Professional Ethics and Civic Morals*. Transl. C Brookfield. London/New York: Routledge

Eakin E. 2001. What is the next big idea? The buzz is growing. *NY Times*, July 7, p. B7

Economist. 2003. Survey: Liberty's great advance. *The Economist*, June 28, p. 4

Forbath WE. 1991. *Law and the Shaping of the American Labor Movement*. Cambridge, MA: Harvard Univ. Press

Foucault M. 1990. *The History of Sexuality*. Vol. 1: *An Introduction*. New York: Vintage Books

Fraser N. 2003. From discipline to flexibilization? Rereading Foucault in the shadow of globalization. *Constellations* 10:160–71

García Linera Á. 2004. The "multitude." In *Cochabamba! Water War in Bolivia*, ed. O Olivera, T Lewis, pp. 65–86. Cambridge, MA: South End Press

Ghose AK. 2002. *Trade and international labor mobility*. Int. Labor Off. Employ. Pap. 2002/33. Geneva: ILO

Gill S. 1995. Globalisation, market civilisation, and disciplinary neoliberalism. *Millenium: J. Int. Stud*. 24:399–423

Gill S. 2003. *Power and Resistance in the New World Order*. Hampshire: Palgrave Macmillan

Gramsci A. 1971. *Selections from the Prison Notebooks of Antonio Gramsci*. Transl. Q Hoare, GN Smith. New York: International Publishers

Grimm D. 2005. Integration by constitution. *Int. J. Const. Law* 3:193–208

Habermas J. 1998. *Between Facts and Norms: Contributions to a Discourse Theory of Law and Democracy*. Transl. W Rehg. Cambridge, MA: MIT Press

Hall S. 1996. The meaning of new times. In *Stuart Hall: Critical Dialogues in Cultural Studies*, ed. D Morley, K-H Chen, pp. 223–37. London: Routledge

Hardt M, Negri A. 2000. *Empire*. Cambridge, MA: Harvard Univ. Press

Hardt M, Negri A. 2004. *Multitude: War and Democracy in the Age of Empire*. New York: Penguin

Harvey D. 2000. *Spaces of Hope*. Berkeley: Univ. Calif. Press

Harvey D. 2005. *A Brief History of Neo-Liberalism*. Oxford: Oxford Univ. Press

Hay C. 2005. Too important to leave to the economists? The political economy of welfare entrenchment. *Soc. Policy Soc*. 4:197–205

Hay C, Marsh D. 2000. Introduction: demystifying globalization. In *Demystifying Globalization*, ed. C Hay, D Marsh, pp. 1–17. London: Macmillan

Helleiner E. 2005. The strange story of Bush and the Argentine debt crisis. *Third World Q*. 951–70

Hirst P, Thompson G. 1999. *Globalization in Question: The International Economy and the Possibilities of Governance*. Cambridge, UK: Polity. 2nd ed.

Jackson JH. 1997. *The World Trading System: Law and Policy of International Economic Relations*. Cambridge, MA: MIT Press. 2nd ed.

Jackson JH. 2006. *Sovereignty, the WTO and Changing Fundamentals of International Law*. Cambridge, UK: Cambridge Univ. Press

Jessop B. 1990. *State Theory: Putting the Capitalist State in Its Place*. University Park: Penn. State Univ. Press

Jessop B. 2002. *The Future of the Capitalist State*. Cambridge, UK: Polity

Kalyvas A. 2003. Feet of clay? Reflections on Hardt's and Negri's *Empire*. *Constellations* 10:264–79

Kennedy D. 1994. The international style in postwar law and policy. *Utah Law Rev.* 1994:7–103

Klug H. 2005. Campaigning for life: building a new transnational solidarity in the face of HIV/AIDS and TRIPS. In *Law and Globalization from Below: Towards a Cosmopolitan Legality*, ed. B de Sousa Santos, CA Rodríguez-Garavito, pp. 118–39. Cambridge, UK: Cambridge Univ. Press

Lash S, Urry J. 1994. *Economies of Signs and Space*. London: Sage

McGinnis JO, Movsesian ML. 2000. The World Trade Constitution. *Harvard Law Rev.* 114:511–605

Moore M. 2003. *A World Without Walls: Freedom, Development, Free Trade and Global Governance*. Cambridge, UK: Cambridge Univ. Press

Mosley L. 2006. Constraints, opportunities, and information: financial market-government relations around the world. In *Globalization and Egalitarian Distribution*, ed. P Bardhan, S Bowles, M Wallerstein, p. 87. New York/Princeton, NJ: Russell Sage Found./Princeton Univ. Press

O'Rourke K, Williamson JG. 1999. *Globalization and History: The Evolution of a Nineteenth Century Atlantic Economy*. Cambridge, MA: MIT Press

Panitch L. 1996. Rethinking the role of the state. In *Globalization: Critical Reflections (International Political Economy Yearbook)*, ed. J Mittelman, 9:83–113. Boulder: Lynne Reiner

Passavant PA. 2004. Postmodern republicanism. See Passavant & Dean 2004, pp. 1–20

Passavant PA, Dean J, eds. 2004. *Empire's New Clothes: Reading Hardt and Negri*. New York: Routledge

Polanyi K. 1957. *The Great Transformation: The Political and Economic Origins of Our Time*. Boston: Beacon

Robinson W. 2001. Social theory and globalization: the rise of the transnational state. *Theory Soc.* 30:157–200

Rodrik D. 1997. *Has Globalization Gone Too Far?* Washington, DC: Inst. Int. Econ.

Rosatti HD. 2003. Los tratados bilaterales de inversion, el arbitraje internacional obligatorio y el sistema constitucional Argentine. *La Ley,* Oct. 15, p. 1283

Rosatti HD. 2005. Translation of Dr. Rosatti's 'Globalization, Statism and Law (Argentina and ICSID)' article. Transl. GS Tawil, MM Bomchil. *Transnatl. Disput. Manag.* 2(3). http://www.transnational-dispute-management.com

Rose N. 1999. *The Powers of Freedom: Reframing Political Thought*. Cambridge, UK: Cambridge Univ. Press

Rosenau JN. 2003. *Distant Proximities: Dynamics Beyond Globalization*. Princeton, NJ: Princeton Univ. Press

Rubins N, Kinsella NS. 2005. *International Investment, Political Risk and Dispute Resolution: A Practitioner's Guide*. Dobbs Ferry, NY: Oceana

Ruggie JG. 1998. *Constructing the World Polity: Essays on International Institutionalization*. London: Routledge

Ruonavaara H. 1997. Moral regulation: a reformulation. *Sociol. Theory* 15:277–93

Santos B de Sousa. 2002. *Toward a New Legal Common Sense: Law, Globalization, and Emancipation*. London: Butterworths Lexis-Nexis

Sassen S. 1996. *Losing Control? Sovereignty in an Age of Globalization*. New York: Columbia Univ. Press

Sassen S. 2004. Local actors in global politics. *Curr. Sociol.* 52:649–70

Sassen S. 2006. *Territory, Authority, Rights: From Medieval to Global Assemblages*. Princeton, NJ: Princeton Univ. Press

Schneiderman D. 2000. Investment rules and the new constitutionalism. *Law Soc. Inq.* 25:757–86

Schneiderman D. 2001. Investment rules and the rule of law. *Constellations* 8:521–37

Schneiderman D. 2004. Globalisation, governance and investment rules. In *Global Governance in the Twenty-First Century*. ed. JN Clarke, GR Edwards, pp. 67–91. London: Palgrave

Schreuer C. 2003. Three generations of ICSID annulment proceedings. In *Annulment of ICSID Awards*, ed. E Gaillard, Y Banifatemi, pp. 17–42. Huntington, NY: Juris

Sell SK. 2003. *Private Power, Public Law: The Globalization of Intellectual Property Rights*. Cambridge, UK: Cambridge Univ. Press

Sen AK. 1990. Rational fools: a critique of the behavioral foundations of economic theory. In *Beyond Self-Interest*, ed. J Mansbridge, pp. 25–43. Chicago: Univ. Chicago Press

Silbey SS. 2005. After legal consciousness. *Annu. Rev. Law. Soc. Sci.* 1:323–68

Sklair L. 2002. *Globalization: Capitalism and Its Alternatives*. Oxford: Oxford Univ. Press

Sornarajah M. 1997. Power and justice in foreign investment arbitration. *J. Int. Arbitrat.* 14:103–40

Steger MB. 2005. *Globalism*. Lanham: Rowman & Littlefield. 2nd ed.

Stiglitz JE. 2002a. Argentina, shortchanged: why the nation that followed the rules fell to pieces. *Washington Post*. May 12, p. B1

Stiglitz JE. 2002b. *Globalization and Its Discontents*. New York: Norton

Tarullo DK. 1987. Beyond normalcy in the regulation of international trade. *Harvard Law Rev.* 100:546–628

Thompson EP. 1975. *Whigs and Hunters: The Origin of the Black Act*. New York: Pantheon

Trebilcock M, Howse R. 1998. Trade liberalization and regulatory diversity: reconciling competitive markets with competitive politics. *Eur. J. Law Econ.* 6:5–37

United Nations Conference on Trade and Development (UNCTAD). 2005. *World Investment Report 2005: Transnational Corporations and the Internationalization of R&D*. New York/Geneva: United Nations

United Nations Development Programme (UNDP). 2005. *Human Development Report 2005: International Cooperation at a Crossroads: Aid, Trade and Security in an Unequal World*. New York: UNDP

Vandevelde KJ. 1998. The political economy of a bilateral investment treaty. *Am. J. Int. Law* 92:621–41

Vis-Dunbar D, Peterson LE. 2006. Bolivian water dispute settled, Bechtel forgoes compensation. *Invest. Treaty News*, Jan. 20. http://www.iisd.org/pdf/2006/itn_jan20_2006.pdf (accessed July 15, 2006)

Walker N. 2005. Europe's constitutional momentum and the search for polity legitimacy. *Int. J. Const. Law* 3:211–38

Weiss L. 2005. Global governance, national strategies: how industrialized states make room to move under the WTO. *Rev. Int. Polit. Econ.* 12:723–49

Williams R. 1961. *The Long Revolution*. Harmondsworth, UK: Penguin

Wolf M. 2004. *Why Globalization Works*. New Haven, CT: Yale Univ. Press

Zumbansen P. 2002. Piercing the legal veil: commercial arbitration and transnational law. *Eur. Law J.* 8:400

Subject Index